S0-AJD-517

Novels
for Students

**Presenting Analysis, Context and Criticism on
Commonly Studied Novels**

Volume 2

Diane Telgen, Editor

Carol Jago, Santa Monica High School, Advisor
Kathleen Pasquantonio, Novi High School, Advisor

Foreword by Anne Devereaux Jordan, Teaching and Learning Literature

GALE
DETROIT • NEW YORK • TORONTO • LONDON

STAFF

Diane Telgen, *Editor*

Laura Brooks, F. Brett Cox, Scott Gillam, Enid Harlow, David Levine, Nancy C. McClure, Barbara J. Parker, Beverly Schneider, Michael Thorn, Giselle Weiss, Elizabeth A. Weston, *Sketchwriters*

Marilyn Allen, Linda R. Andres, Shelly Andrews, Joanna Brod, Sheryl Ciccarelli, Alan Hedblad, Kevin S. Hile, Melissa Hill, Motoko Fujishiro Huthwaite, Arlene M. Johnson, Paul Loeber, Thomas F. McMahon, Zoran Minderovic, Andrew Seagram, Gerard J. Senick, Crystal A. Towns, Kathleen L. Witman, *Contributing Editors*

Joyce Nakamura, *Managing Editor*

Victoria B. Cariappa, *Research Team Manager*
Michele P. LaMeau, *Research Specialist*
Laura C. Bissey, Julia C. Daniel, Tamara C. Nott, Tracie A. Richardson, Cheryl L. Warnock, *Research Associates*
Alfred A. Gardner III, *Research Assistant*

Susan M. Trosky, *Permissions Manager*
Maria L. Franklin, *Permissions Specialist*
Michele M. Lonoconus, *Permissions Associate*
Mary K. Grimes, *Image Cataloger*

Mary Beth Trimper, *Production Director*
Evi Seoud, *Assistant Production Manager*
Shanna Heilveil, *Production Assistant*

Randy Bassett, *Image Database Supervisor*
Mikal Ansari, Robert Duncan, *Imaging Specialists*
Pamela A. Reed, *Photography Coordinator*

Cover design: Michelle DiMercurio, *Art Director*
Page design: Pamela A. E. Galbreath, *Senior Art Director*

™
This book is printed on acid-free paper that meets the minimum requirements of American National Standard for Information Sciences—Permanence Paper for Printed Library Materials, ANSI Z39.48-1984.

ISBN 0-7876-1687-7
ISSN 1094-3552
Printed in the United States of America

10 9 8 7 6 5 4 3 2

Table of Contents

The Informed Dialogue: Interacting with Literature

When we pick up a book, we usually do so with the anticipation of pleasure. We hope that by entering the time and place of the novel and sharing the thoughts and actions of the characters, we will find enjoyment. Unfortunately, this is often not the case; we are disappointed. But we should ask, has the author failed us, or have we failed the author?

We establish a dialogue with the author, the book, and with ourselves when we read. Consciously and unconsciously, we ask questions: "Why did the author write this book?" "Why did the author choose that time, place, or character?" "How did the author achieve that effect?" "Why did the character act that way?" "Would I act in the same way?" The answers we receive depend upon how much information about literature in general and about that book specifically we ourselves bring to our reading.

Young children have limited life and literary experiences. Being young, children frequently do not know how to go about exploring a book, nor sometimes, even know the questions to ask of a book. The books they read help them answer questions, the author often coming right out and *telling* young readers the things they are learning or are expected to learn. The perennial classic, *The Little Engine That Could, tells* its readers that, among other things, it is good to help others and brings happiness:

> "Hurray, hurray," cried the funny little clown and all the dolls and toys. "The good little boys and girls in the city will be happy because you helped us, kind, Little Blue Engine."

In picture books, messages are often blatant and simple, the dialogue between the author and reader one-sided. Young children are concerned with the end result of a book—the enjoyment gained, the lesson learned—rather than with how that result was obtained. As we grow older and read further, however, we question more. We come to expect that the world within the book will closely mirror the concerns of our world, and that the author will *show* these through the events, descriptions, and conversations within the story, rather than *telling* of them. We are now expected to do the interpreting, carry on our share of the dialogue with the book and author, and glean not only the author's message, but comprehend how that message and the overall affect of the book were achieved. Sometimes, however, we need help to do these things. *Novels for Students* provides that help.

A novel is made up of many parts interacting to create a coherent whole. In reading a novel, the more obvious features can be easily spotted—theme, characters, plot—but we may overlook the more subtle elements that greatly influence how the novel is perceived by the reader: viewpoint, mood and tone, symbolism, or the use of humor. By focusing on both the obvious and more subtle literary elements within a novel, *Novels for Students* aids readers in both analyzing for message and in determining how and why that message is communicated. In the discussion on Harper Lee's *To*

Kill a Mockingbird (Vol. 2), for example, the mockingbird as a symbol of innocence is dealt with, among other things, as is the importance of Lee's use of humor which "enlivens a serious plot, adds depth to the characterization, and creates a sense of familiarity and universality." The reader comes to understand the internal elements of each novel discussed—as well as the external influences that help shape it.

"The desire to write greatly," Harold Bloom of Yale University says, "is the desire to be elsewhere, in a time and place of one's own, in an originality that must compound with inheritance, with an anxiety of influence." A writer seeks to create a unique world within a story, but although it is unique, it is not disconnected from our own world. It speaks to us *because* of what the writer brings to the writing from our world: how he or she was raised and educated; his or her likes and dislikes; the events occurring in the real world at the time of the writing, and while the author was growing up. When we know what an author has brought to his or her work, we gain a greater insight into both the "originality" (the world of the book), and the things that "compound" it. This insight enables us to question that created world and find answers more readily. By informing ourselves, we are able to establish a more effective dialogue with both book and author.

Novels for Students, in addition to providing a plot summary and descriptive list of characters—to remind readers of what they have read—also explores the external influences that shaped each book. Each entry includes a discussion of the author's background, and the historical context in which the novel was written. It is vital to know, for instance, that when Ray Bradbury was writing *Fahrenheit 451* (Vol. 1), the threat of Nazi domination had recently ended in Europe, and the McCarthy hearings were taking place in Washington, D.C. This information goes far in answering the question, "Why did he write a story of oppressive government control and book burning?" Similarly, it is important to know that Harper Lee, author of *To Kill a Mockingbird,* was born and raised in Mon-

roeville, Alabama, and that her father was a lawyer. Readers can now see why she chose the south as a setting for her novel—it is the place with which she was most familiar—and start to comprehend her characters and their actions.

Novels for Students helps readers find the answers they seek when they establish a dialogue with a particular novel. It also aids in the posing of questions by providing the opinions and interpretations of various critics and reviewers, broadening that dialogue. Some reviewers of *To Kill A Mockingbird,* for example, "faulted the novel's climax as melodramatic." This statement leads readers to ask, "Is it, indeed, melodramatic?" "If not, why did some reviewers see it as such?" "If it is, why did Lee choose to make it melodramatic?" "Is melodrama ever justified?" By being spurred to ask these questions, readers not only learn more about the book and its writer, but about the nature of writing itself.

The literature included for discussion in *Novels for Students* has been chosen because it has something vital to say to us. *Of Mice and Men, Catch-22, The Joy Luck Club, My Antonia, A Separate Peace* and the other novels here speak of life and modern sensibility. In addition to their individual, specific messages of prejudice, power, love or hate, living and dying, however, they and all great literature also share a common intent. They force us to *think*—about life, literature, and about others, not just about ourselves. They pry us from the narrow confines of our minds and thrust us outward to confront the world of books and the larger, real world we all share. *Novels for Students* helps us in this confrontation by providing the means of enriching our conversation with literature and the world, by creating an *informed* dialogue, one that brings true pleasure to the personal act of reading.

Sources

Harold Bloom, *The Western Canon, The Books and School of the Ages,* Riverhead Books, 1994.

Watty Piper, *The Little Engine That Could,* Platt & Munk, 1930.

Anne Devereaux Jordan
Senior Editor, *TALL*
(*Teaching and Learning Literature*)

Introduction

Purpose of the Book

The purpose of *Novels for Students* (*NfS*) is to provide readers with a guide to understanding, enjoying, and studying novels by giving them easy access to information about the work. Part of Gale's "For Students" Literature line, *NfS* is specifically designed to meet the curricular needs of high school and undergraduate college students and their teachers, as well as the interests of general readers and researchers considering specific novels. While each volume contains entries on "classic" novels frequently studied in classrooms, there are also entries containing hard-to-find information on contemporary novels, including works by multicultural, international, and women novelists.

The information covered in each entry includes an introduction to the novel and the novel's author; a plot summary, to help readers unravel and understand the events in a novel; descriptions of important characters, including explanation of a given character's role in the novel as well as discussion about that character's relationship to other characters in the novel; analysis of important themes in the novel; and an explanation of important literary techniques and movements as they are demonstrated in the novel.

In addition to this material, which helps the readers analyze the novel itself, students are also provided with important information on the literary and historical background informing each work. This includes a historical context essay, a box comparing the time or place the novel was written to modern Western culture, a critical overview essay, and excerpts from critical essays on the novel. A unique feature of *NfS* is a specially commissioned overview essay on each novel by an academic expert, targeted toward the student reader.

To further aid the student in studying and enjoying each novel, information on media adaptations is provided, as well as reading suggestions for works of fiction and nonfiction on similar themes and topics. Classroom aids include ideas for research papers and lists of critical sources that provide additional material on the novel.

Selection Criteria

The titles for each volume of *NfS* were selected by surveying numerous sources on teaching literature and analyzing course curricula for various school districts. Some of the sources surveyed included: literature anthologies; *Reading Lists for College-Bound Students: The Books Most Recommended by America's Top Colleges;* textbooks on teaching the novel; a College Board survey of novels commonly studied in high schools; a National Council of Teachers of English (NCTE) survey of novels commonly studied in high schools; the NCTE's *Teaching Literature in High School: The Novel;* and the Young Adult Library Services Association (YALSA) list of best books for young adults of the past twenty-five years.

Input was also solicited from our expert advisory board, as well as educators from various areas. From these discussions, it was determined that each volume should have a mix of "classic" novels (those works commonly taught in literature classes) and contemporary novels for which information is often hard to find. Because of the interest in expanding the canon of literature, an emphasis was also placed on including works by international, multicultural, and women authors. Our advisory board members—current high school teachers—helped pare down the list for each volume. If a work was not selected for the present volume, it was often noted as a possibility for a future volume. As always, the editor welcomes suggestions for titles to be included in future volumes.

How Each Entry Is Organized

Each entry, or chapter, in *NfS* focuses on one novel. Each entry heading lists the full name of the novel, the author's name, and the date of the novel's publication. The following elements are contained in each entry:

- **Introduction:** a brief overview of the novel which provides information about its first appearance, its literary standing, any controversies surrounding the work, and major conflicts or themes within the work.

- **Author Biography:** this section includes basic facts about the author's life, and focuses on events and times in the author's life that inspired the novel in question.

- **Plot Summary:** a description of the major events in the novel, with interpretation of how these events help articulate the novel's themes. Lengthy summaries are broken down with subheads.

- **Characters:** an alphabetical listing of major characters in the novel. Each character name is followed by a brief to an extensive description of the character's role in the novel, as well as discussion of the character's actions, relationships, and possible motivation.

  Characters are listed alphabetically by last name. If a character is unnamed—for instance, the narrator in *Invisible Man*—the character is listed as "The Narrator" and alphabetized as "Narrator." If a character's first name is the only one given, the name will appear alphabetically by the name.

  Variant names are also included for each character. Thus, the full name "Jean Louise Finch" would head the listing for the narrator of *To Kill a Mockingbird,* but listed in a separate cross-reference would be the nickname "Scout Finch."

- **Themes:** a thorough overview of how the major topics, themes, and issues are addressed within the novel. Each theme discussed appears in a separate subhead, and is easily accessed through the boldface entries in the Subject/Theme Index.

- **Style:** this section addresses important style elements of the novel, such as setting, point of view, and narration; important literary devices used, such as imagery, foreshadowing, symbolism; and, if applicable, genres to which the work might have belonged, such as Gothicism or Romanticism. Literary terms are explained within the entry, but can also be found in the Glossary.

- **Historical and Cultural Context:** This section outlines the social, political, and cultural climate *in which the author lived and the novel was created.* This section may include descriptions of related historical events, pertinent aspects of daily life in the culture, and the artistic and literary sensibilities of the time in which the work was written. If the novel is a historical work, information regarding the time in which the novel is set is also included. Each section is broken down with helpful subheads.

- **Critical Overview:** this section provides background on the critical reputation of the novel, including bannings or any other public controversies surrounding the work. For older works, this section includes a history of how novel was first received and how perceptions of it may have changed over the years; for more recent novels, direct quotes from early reviews may also be included.

- **Sources:** an alphabetical list of critical material quoted in the entry, with full bibliographical information.

- **For Further Study:** an alphabetical list of other critical sources which may prove useful for the student. Includes full bibliographical information and a brief annotation.

- **Criticism:** an essay commissioned by *NfS* which specifically deals with the novel and is written specifically for the student audience, as well as excerpts from previously published criticism on the work.

  In addition, each entry contains the following highlighted sections, set apart from the main text as sidebars:

- **Media Adaptations:** a list of important film and television adaptations of the novel, including source information. The list also includes stage adaptations, audio recordings, musical adaptations, etc.

- **Compare and Contrast Box:** an "at-a-glance" comparison of the cultural and historical differences between the author's time and culture and late twentieth-century Western culture. This box includes pertinent parallels between the major scientific, political, and cultural movements of the time or place the novel was written, the time or place the novel was set (if a historical work), and modern Western culture. Works written after the mid-1970s may not have this box.

- **What Do I Read Next?:** a list of works that might complement the featured novel or serve as a contrast to it. This includes works by the same author and others, works of fiction and nonfiction, and works from various genres, cultures, and eras.

- **Study Questions:** a list of potential study questions or research topics dealing with the novel. This section includes questions related to other disciplines the student may be studying, such as American history, world history, science, math, government, business, geography, economics, psychology, etc.

Other Features

NfS includes "The Informed Dialogue: Interacting with Literature," a foreword by Anne Devereaux Jordan, Senior Editor for *Teaching and Learning Literature (TALL)*, and a founder of the Children's Literature Association. This essay provides an enlightening look at how readers interact with literature and how *Novels for Students* can help teachers show students how to enrich their own reading experiences.

A Cumulative Author/Title Index lists the authors and titles covered in each volume of the *NfS* series.

A Cumulative Nationality/Ethnicity Index breaks down the authors and titles covered in each volume of the *NfS* series by nationality and ethnicity.

A Subject/Theme Index, specific to each volume, provides easy reference for users who may be studying a particular subject or theme rather than a single work. Significant subjects from events to broad themes are included, and the entries pointing to the specific theme discussions in each entry are indicated in **boldface.**

Each entry has several illustrations, including photos of the author, stills from film adaptations (when available), maps, and/or photos of key historical events.

Citing Novels for Students

When writing papers, students who quote directly from any volume of *Novels for Students* may use the following general forms. These examples are based on MLA style; teachers may request that students adhere to a different style, so the following examples may be adapted as needed.

When citing text from *NfS* that is not attributed to a particular author (i.e., the Themes, Style, Historical Context sections, etc.), the following format should be used in the bibliography section:

"The Adventures of Huckleberry Finn." *Novels for Students.* Ed. Diane Telgen. Vol. 1. Detroit: Gale, 1997. 8–9.

When quoting the specially commissioned essay from *NfS* (usually the first piece under the "Criticism" subhead), the following format should be used:

James, Pearl. Essay on "The Adventures of Huckleberry Finn." *Novels for Students.* Ed. Diane Telgen. Vol. 1. Detroit: Gale, 1997. 8–9.

When quoting a journal or newspaper essay that is reprinted in a volume of *NfS,* the following form may be used:

Butler, Robert J. "The Quest for Pure Motion in Richard Wright's *Black Boy.*" *MELUS* 10, No. 3 (Fall, 1983), 5–17; excerpted and reprinted in *Novels for Students,* Vol. 1, ed. Diane Telgen (Detroit: Gale, 1997), pp. 61–64.

When quoting material reprinted from a book that appears in a volume of *NfS,* the following form may be used:

Adams, Timothy Dow. "Richard Wright: 'Wearing the Mask,'" in *Telling Lies in Modern American Autobiography* (University of North Carolina Press, 1990), 69–83; excerpted and reprinted in *Novels for Students,* Vol. 1, ed. Diane Telgen (Detroit: Gale, 1997), pp. 59–61.

We Welcome Your Suggestions

The editor of *Novels for Students* welcomes your comments and ideas. Readers who wish to suggest novels to appear in future volumes, or who have other suggestions, are cordially invited to contact the editor. You may contact the editor via e-mail at: **CYA@gale.com.** Or write to the editor at:

Editor, *Novels for Students*
Gale Research
835 Penobscot Bldg.
645 Griswold St.
Detroit, MI 48226-4094

Literary Chronology

1818: Emily Jane Brontë is born on July 30, 1818, to the Reverend Patrick and Maria Branwell Brontë.

1847: Emily Brontë's *Wuthering Heights: A Novel* is published with Anne Brontë's *Agnes Grey.*

1848: Emily Brontë dies of tuberculosis on December 19, 1848.

1857: Joseph Conrad is born Józef Teodor Konrad Korzeniowski on December 3, 1857, to Apollo and Evelina Bobrowska Korzeniowski, near Berdichev in the Ukraine.

1873: Willa Cather is born December 7, 1873, in the village of Back Creek (now Gore), near Winchester, Virginia.

1884: Willa Cather's family moves to join her father's relatives among the ethnically diverse settlers of Nebraska's Great Plains, an area that would inspire several of her novels, including *My Ántonia.*

1890: Joseph Conrad, having joined the British Merchant Marines in the 1870s, makes a trip to the Belgian Congo in 1890. During this time he sails the Congo River, an event crucial to the development of his novel *Heart of Darkness.*

1896: F. Scott Fitzgerald is born September 24, 1896, in St. Paul, Minnesota.

1899: Joseph Conrad completes *Heart of Darkness* in February, 1899 when it first appears in serial form; it is published in 1902.

1911: William Golding is born September 19, 1911, to Alec and Mildred Golding, in Cornwall, England.

1914: Ralph Ellison is born March 1, 1914 in Oklahoma City, Oklahoma.

1916: Ras the Exhorter, in Ralph Ellison's *Invisible Man,* resembles the flamboyant nationalist Marcus Garvey, who founds the Universal Negro Improvement Association in 1916.

1918: Willa Cather's *My Antonia,* her novel about prairie life, is published in 1918.

1920: The 18th Amendment, outlawing the sale, manufacture, or transportation of alcohol—known as Prohibition—goes into effect. This law led to the creation of "speakeasies"—illegal bars—and an increase in organized crime, both reflected in F. Scott Fitzgerald's novel *The Great Gatsby.* Prohibition is eventually repealed in 1933.

1924: Joseph Conrad dies of a heart attack on August 3, 1924, at Oswalds, Bishopsbourne, near Canterbury. He is buried at Canterbury.

1925: Robert Edmund Cormier is born January 17, 1925, in Leominster, Massachusetts.

1925: F. Scott Fitzgerald's *The Great Gatsby* is published on April 10, 1925.

1926: Harper Lee is born on April 28, 1926, in Monroeville, Alabama, to Amasa Coleman and Frances Finch Lee. Her full name is Nelle Harper Lee.

1926: John Knowles is born to James Myron and Mary Beatrice Shea Knowles on September 16, 1926, in the coal mining town of Fairmont, West Virginia.

1927: Daniel Keyes is born August 9, 1927, to William and Betty Alicke Keyes, in Brooklyn, New York.

1928: Maya Angelou is born Marguerite Annie Johnson on April 4, 1928, to Bailey and Vivian Baxter Johnson, in St. Louis, Missouri.

1930: Chinua Achebe is born to Isaiah Okafo and Janet N. Iloegbunam Achebe on November 16, 1930, in Ogidi, Nigeria. His full name is Albert Chinualumogu Achebe.

1931: The Scottsboro Incident occurs in March, 1931. A fight breaks out between some white and black youths on a freight train in Alabama. The white youths are thrown off the train, and in retaliation, accuse the black youths of raping two white girls. The black youths are arrested and jailed. Their trials only take three days; eight youths are given the death sentence and one is given life imprisonment. The U.S. Supreme Court reverses the Scottsboro conviction in 1932, and the youths are retried. They are retried again in 1936, and in 1937 the major Alabama newspapers advocate the release of the defendants. It is not until 1950 that the last of the youths is paroled. This highly publicized and volatile case had an impact on Harper Lee, whose *To Kill a Mockingbird* involves a black man falsely accused of raping a white woman.

1935: Ken Elton Kesey is born September 17, 1935, in La Junta, California.

1940: F. Scott Fitzgerald dies of a heart attack on December 21, 1940 in Hollywood, California. He is buried in Rockville Union Cemetery in Rockville, Maryland, then is reburied near his parents in St. Mary's Cemetery in Rockville, Maryland in 1975.

1941: William Golding, captain of a British rocket-launching craft in the British Navy, is present at the sinking of the *Bismarck*—the crown ship of the German Navy. He also takes part in the D-Day landings in France in June 1944. These wartime experiences inform the background of his classic *Lord of the Flies.*

1941: Anne Tyler is born in Minneapolis, Minnesota, on October 25, 1941, to Lloyd Parry and Phyllis Mahon Tyler.

1947: Willa Cather dies of a cerebral hemorrhage in New York on April 24, 1947.

1952: Ralph Ellison's *Invisible Man* is published.

1953: Ralph Ellison's *Invisible Man* wins the National Book Award, which honors American books of the highest literary merit.

1954: Sandra Cisneros is born on December 20, 1954, to Alfredo Cisneros Del Moral and Elvira Cordero Anguiano, in Chicago, Illinois.

1954: William Golding's *Lord of the Flies* is published in England. It is published in America the following year.

1958: Chinua Achebe's *Things Fall Apart,* published in 1958, is his first novel.

1958: Chinua Achebe's *Things Fall Apart* wins the Margaret Wong Memorial Prize.

1959: John Knowles's *A Separate Peace* is published in Britain in 1959. The first American edition appears on leap year day in 1960, after being rejected by eleven publishers. It sells 7,000 copies in its first printing and receives critical acclaim.

1960: Ken Kesey becomes a paid volunteer in government-sponsored drug experiments at the Veteran's Hospital in Menlo Park, California; there he is introduced to psychoactive drugs such as mescaline and LSD. These experiences, plus those gained working in a psychiatric hospital, help form his first published novel, *One Flew Over the Cuckoo's Nest.*

1960: John Knowles's *A Separate Peace* wins the Faulkner Award and the National Book Award. This success allows Knowles to resign from his job at Holiday and become a full-time writer.

1960: Harper Lee completed the first draft of *To Kill a Mockingbird* in June, 1958. Its official publication date is July, 1960.

1961: Harper Lee receives the Pulitzer Prize for *To Kill a Mockingbird* in April, 1961. She is the first woman to win the prize since 1942, when Ellen Glasgow received it.

1962: Ken Kesey's *One Flew Over the Cuckoo's Nest* is published.

1966: Daniel Keyes wrote "Flowers for Algernon," a short story, in 1959. It was published in *The Magazine of Fantasy and Science Fiction* and won the Hugo Award. Keyes adapted it into his first novel, *Flowers for Algernon,* which is published in 1966.

1966: Daniel Keyes's *Flowers for Algernon* wins the Nebula Award, which recognizes excellence in science fiction writing.

1970: Maya Angelou's *I Know Why the Caged Bird Sings* is published.

1974: Robert Cormier's *The Chocolate War* is published.

1979: Robert Cormier's *The Chocolate War* wins the Lewis Carroll Shelf Award, which is given to those "classic" titles that contain enough of the qualities of *Alice in Wonderland* to sit on the same book shelf. The award has since been discontinued.

1982: Anne Tyler's *Dinner at the Homesick Restaurant* is published.

1982: Anne Tyler's *Dinner at the Homesick Restaurant* wins a PEN/Faulkner Award for Fiction. The PEN/Faulkner Award for Fiction honors the best work of fiction published by an American writer in a calendar year.

1983: Sandra Cisneros's *The House on Mango Street* is published.

1983: William Golding receives the Nobel Prize in Literature for his body of work.

1993: William Golding dies of a heart attack on June 19, 1993, in Perranarworthal, near Falmouth, England.

1994: Ralph Ellison dies of cancer on April 16, 1994, in New York, New York.

Acknowledgments

The editors wish to thank the copyright holders of the excerpted criticism included in this volume and the permissions managers of many book and magazine publishing companies for assisting us in securing reproduction rights. We are also grateful to the staffs of the Detroit Public Library, the Library of Congress, the University of Detroit Mercy Library, Wayne State University Purdy/ Kresge Library Complex, and the University of Michigan Libraries for making their resources available to us. Following is a list of the copyright holders who have granted us permission to reproduce material in this volume of *NfS*. Every effort has been made to trace copyright, but if omissions have been made, please let us know.

COPYRIGHTED EXCERPTS IN *NFS*, VOLUME 2, WERE REPRODUCED FROM THE FOLLOWING PERIODICALS:

The African Studies Review, v. 26, September, 1993. © 1993 African Studies Association. All rights reserved. Reproduced by permission.

The CEA Critic, v. 37, 1975. Copyright © 1975 by the College English Association, Inc. Reproduced by permission.

Critique: Studies in Modern Fiction, v. X, 1968. Copyright © 1968 Helen Dwight Reid Educational Foundation. Reproduced with permission of the Helen Dwight Reid Educational Foundation, published by Heldref Publications, 1319 18th Street, NW, Washington, DC 20036-1802.

English Journal, v. 58, September, 1969 for "Ellison's Ambitious Scope in 'Invisible Man'" by Stewart Lillard. Copyright © 1969 by the National Council of Teachers of English. Reproduced by permission of the publisher and the author. *English Journal,* v. 58, December, 1969 for "'A Separate Peace': Meaning and Myth" by Marvin E. Mengeling. Copyright © 1969 by the National Council of Teachers of English. Reproduced by permission of the publisher and the author. *English Journal,* v. 81, September, 1992 for "Coming of Age in Novels by Rudolfo Anaya and Sandra Cisneros" by Dianne Klein. Copyright © 1992 by the National Council of Teachers of English. Reproduced by permission of the publisher and the author.

The Massachusetts Review, v. VII, Autumn, 1966. © 1966. Reprinted from *The Massachusetts Review,* The Massachusetts Review, Inc. by permission. *The Massachusetts Review,* v. XVIII, Winter, 1977. © 1977. Reprinted from *The Massachusetts Review,* The Massachusetts Review, Inc. by permission.

The Midwest Quarterly, v. XXXVII, Autumn, 1995. Copyright, 1995, by The Midwest Quarterly, Pittsburg State University. Reproduced by permission.

Prairie Schooner, v. XLVIII, Summer, 1974. © 1974 by University of Nebraska Press. Reproduced from Prairie Schooner by permission of the University of Nebraska Press.

South Atlantic Bulletin, v. XLI, May, 1976. Copyright © 1976 by South Atlantic Modern Language Association. Reproduced by permission.

Southern Literary Journal, v. 16, Fall, 1983. Copyright 1983 by the Department of English, University of North Carolina at Chapel Hill. Reproduced by permission.

University Review, v. XXXIII, March, 1967 for "A Note on Fitzgerald's 'The Great Gatsby'" by David F. Trask. Copyright 1967 The Curators of the University of Missouri. Reproduced by permission of the publisher and the author.

The Victorian Newsletter, n. 68, Fall, 1985 for "The Waif at the Window: Emily Brontë's Feminine 'Bildungsroman'" by Annette R. Federico. Reproduced by permission of The Victorian Newsletter and the author.

COPYRIGHTED EXCERPTS IN *NFS*, VOLUME 2, WERE REPRODUCED FROM THE FOLLOWING BOOKS:

Campbell, Patricia J. From *Presenting Robert Cormier.* Revised edition. Twayne Publishers, 1989. Copyright 1989 by G. K. Hall & Co. All rights reserved. Reproduced with the permission of Twayne Publishers, a division of Simon & Schuster, Inc.

Holborn, David G. From "A Rationale for Reading John Knowles' 'A Separate Peace,'" in *Censored Books: Critical Viewpoints.* Nicholas J. Karolides, Lee Burress, John M. Kean, eds. The Scarecrow Press, Inc., 1993. Copyright © 1993 by Nicholas J. Karolides, Lee Burress, John M. Kean. Reproduced by permission.

Johnson, Claudia Durst. From *To Kill a Mockingbird: Threatening Boundaries.* Twayne Publishers, 1994. Copyright © 1994 by Twayne Publishers. All rights reserved. Reproduced with the permission of Twayne Publishers, a division of Simon & Schuster, Inc.

Manning, Carol S. From "Welty, Tyler, and Traveling Salesmen: The Wandering Hero Unhorsed," in *The Fiction of Anne Tyler.* Edited by C. Ralph Stephens. University Press of Mississippi, 1990. Copyright © 1990 by the University Press of Mississippi. All rights reserved. Reproduced by permission.

May, Jill. From "In Defense of 'To Kill a Mockingbird,'" in *Censored Books: Critical Viewpoints.* Nicholas J. Karolides, Lee Burress, John M. Kean, eds. The Scarecrow Press, Inc., 1993. Copyright © 1993 by Nicholas J. Karolides, Lee Burress, John M. Kean. Reproduced by permission.

Moore, Opal. From "Learning to Live: When the Bird Breaks from the Cage," in *Censored Books: Critical Viewpoints.* Nicholas J. Karolides,

Lee Burress, John M. Kean, eds. The Scarecrow Press, Inc., 1993. Copyright © 1993 by Nicholas J. Karolides, Lee Burress, John M. Kean. Reproduced by permission.

Quinn, Laura. From "Moby Dick vs. Big Nurse: A Feminist Defense of a Misogynist Text, 'One Flew over the Cuckoo's Nest,'" in *Censored Books: Critical Viewpoints.* Nicholas J. Karolides, Lee Burress, John M. Kean, eds. The Scarecrow Press, Inc., 1993. Copyright © 1993 by Nicholas J. Karolides, Lee Burress, John M. Kean. Reproduced by permission.

Sarr, Ndiawar. From "The Center Holds: The Resilience of Ibo Culture in 'Things Fall Apart,'" in *Global Perspectives on Teaching Literature: Shared Visions and Distinctive Visions.* Sandra Ward Lott, Maureen S. G. Hawkins, Norman McMillan, eds. National Council of Teachers of English, 1993. © 1993 by the National Council of Teachers of English. All rights reserved. Reproduced by permission of the publisher and the author.

Scholes, Robert. From *Structural Fabulation: An Essay on Fiction of the Future.* University of Notre Dame Press, 1975. Copyright © 1975 by University of Notre Dame Press; Notre Dame, IN 46556. Used by permission of the publisher.

Slayton, Paul. From "Teaching Rationale for William Golding's 'Lord of the Flies'," in *Censored Books: Critical Viewpoints.* Nicholas J. Karolides, Lee Burress, John M. Kean, eds. The Scarecrow Press, Inc., 1993. Copyright © 1993 by Nicholas J. Karolides, Lee Burress, John M. Kean. Reproduced by permission.

Small, Robert, Jr. From "'Flowers for Algernon' by Daniel Keyes," in *Censored Books: Critical Viewpoints.* Nicholas J. Karolides, Lee Burress, John M. Kean, eds. The Scarecrow Press, Inc., 1993. Copyright © 1993 by Nicholas J. Karolides, Lee Burress, John M. Kean. Reproduced by permission.

Wright, Walter F. From *Romance and Tragedy in Joseph Conrad.* University of Nebraska Press, 1949. Copyright University of Nebraska Press, 1949. Renewed 1976 by Walter F. Wright. Reproduced by permission.

PHOTOGRAPHS AND ILLUSTRATIONS APPEARING IN *NFS*, VOLUME 2, WERE RECEIVED FROM THE FOLLOWING SOURCES:

AP/WIDE WORLD PHOTOS: Achebe, Chinua, photograph. AP/Wide World Photos. Reproduced by permission. Angelou, Maya (suit and sweater), photograph. AP/Wide World Photos. Reproduced by permission Cisneros, Sandra (in jacket with white curly trim), photograph. AP/Wide World Photos. Reproduced by permission. Ellison, Ralph, photograph. AP/Wide World Photos. Reproduced by permission. Golding, William (cabled V-neck), photograph. AP/Wide World Photos. Reproduced by permission. Handicapped boys learning, 1962, California, photograph. AP/Wide World Photos, Inc. Reproduced by permission. Ibo girls dancing with woman, 1970, photograph. AP/Wide World Photos, Inc. Reproduced by permission. Kesey, Ken, photograph. AP/Wide World Photos. Reproduced by permission. Keyes, Daniel (holding "Unveiling Claudia"), photograph. AP/Wide World Photos. Reproduced by permission. Knowles, John, photograph. AP/Wide World Photos. Reproduced by permission. Lee, Harper, photograph. AP/Wide World Photos. Reproduced by permission. Sharecropper's house (people on porch), 1937, Memphis, Tennessee, photograph. AP/Wide World Photos, Inc. Reproduced by permission. Two customers entering "Tops" Diner, 1952, photograph. AP/Wide World Photos, Inc. Reproduced by permission. Tyler, Anne, at home (cross legged), 1965, Montreal, photograph. AP/Wide World Photos, Inc. Reproduced by permission.

ARCHIVE PHOTOS, INC.: Brando, Marlon, and Martin Sheen in the film "Apocalypse Now," photograph. Archive Photos. Reproduced by permission. Conrad, Joseph (facing right), photograph. Archive Photos. Reproduced by permission. Edwards, Hugh, and Tom Chapin in the film "Lord of the Flies," photograph. Archive Photos. Reproduced by permission. Fitzgerald, F. Scott (in coat and hat, head and shoulders), photograph. Archive Photos. Reproduced by permission. Ku Klux Klansmen kneeling in a circle, 1920s, photograph. Archive Photos. Reproduced by permission. "Top Withens" farm on foggy moors, setting for "Wuthering Heights," photograph. Archive Photos, Inc. Reproduced by permission.

THE BETTMANN ARCHIVE/NEWSPHOTOS, INC.: Four men drinking at a speakeasy during Prohibition, photograph. Corbis-Bettmann. Reproduced by permission. Freeman, Dr., performing a lobotomy, 1949, photograph. UPI/Corbis-Bettmann. Reproduced by permission. Inspecting overturned bus amidst bombing rubble, 1940, London, photograph. UPI/Corbis-Bettmann. Reproduced by permission. Men using segregated drinking fountains, photograph. Corbis-Bettmann. Reproduced by permission. Police arresting black man, 1943, Harlem Riots, New York City, photograph. UPI/Corbis-Bettmann. Reproduced by permission. Robertson, Cliff (holding a mouse), in the film "Charly," photograph. UPI/Corbis-Bettmann. Reproduced by permission. Unemployed black men talking together, 1935, Lennox Avenue, Harlem, photograph. Corbis-Bettmann. Reproduced by permission. View across quadrangle, vertical building with Gothic elements, Sterling Library, Yale University, photograph. Corbis-Bettmann. Reproduced by permission.

CORMIER, ROBERT: Cormier, Robert (in library aisle), photograph by Beth Bergman. Reproduced by permission.

GALE RESEARCH INC. (Detroit): Map of Nigeria (showing major land formations and towns), illustration. Gale Research Inc. Reproduced by permission. Map of the Democratic Republic of the Congo (Zaire), illustration. Gale Research Incorporated. Reproduced by permission.

GAMMA-LIAISON: Tyler, Anne (chambray shirt over turtleneck), photograph by D. Walker. Gamma-Liaison. Reproduced by permission.

THE KOBAL COLLECTION: Glover, John (in Franciscan robes), in the film "The Chocolate War," photograph. The Kobal Collection. Reproduced by permission. Nicholson, Jack, with Josip Elic and Will Sampson, in the basketball scene from the film "One Flew Over the Cuckoo's Nest," photograph. The Kobal Collection. Reproduced by permission. Olivier, Laurence, and Merle Oberon in the film "Wuthering Heights," photograph. The Kobal Collection. Reproduced by permission. Peck, Gregory, Phillip Alford, Mary Badham, John Megna, in the movie "To Kill A Mockingbird," photograph. The Kobal Collection. Reproduced by permission. Redford, Robert and Mia Farrow in the film "The Great Gatsby," 1974, photograph. The Kobal Collection. Reproduced by permission.

THE LIBRARY OF CONGRESS: Cather, Willa (feathered hat, fur collar), photograph by Carl Van Vechten. The Library of Congress.

PARAMOUNT PICTURES CORPORATION: Stevenson, Parker and John Heyl in a scene from the 1973 film "A Separate Peace." Paramount Pictures, 1972. Copyright © 1972 by Paramount Pictures Corporation. All rights reserved. Reproduced by permission.

SOURCE UNKNOWN: Brontë, Emily (profile), painting by Bramwell Brontë. Woman walking in wind, illustration by W. T. Benda. From "My Ántonia," by Willa Cather.

The Chocolate War

Robert Cormier
1974

The publication of *The Chocolate War* in 1974 is now seen as a ground-breaking event in the establishment of young adult literature as a separate genre. Robert Cormier's novel was originally conceived as an adult book, for all his previous fiction had been for adults. Nevertheless, it quickly became both an inspiration to other writers and publishers for teens and the standard by which much subsequent young adult literature has been judged. Shocking in its relentless and unsentimental representation of the power and control exerted by bullying adults and boys at a Catholic school, the novel was criticized by some early reviewers for its failure to include for its young readers a redeeming resolution. (Cormier had resisted pressure from a number of publishers to alter the ending.)

The plot for *The Chocolate War* was inspired by an event in Cormier's own life. When his son decided, without repercussion, not to sell chocolates in his school's annual sale, Cormier asked himself, "What if?" This question, he has declared, is the spark for all his writing. If the novel had been simply about harassment and intimidation among a group of boys, it would not have been in any way remarkable. What makes it disturbing is the collusion between the Catholic teaching staff and a group of boys known as the Vigils who exert a Mafia-like influence at the school and employ psychological tactics against other pupils and staff. One of *The Chocolate War*'s principle themes is the futility of individual protests and resistance in

Robert Cormier

the face of such power structures and, by implication, the importance of collective action.

Author Biography

Robert Cormier was born January 17, 1925, in Leominster, Massachusetts, and has lived in the town for most of his life. After attending Fitchburg State College, he began a career in journalism, first with the radio station WTAG (1946-48). He then worked at the Worcester *Telegraph & Gazette* and, for a longer period, the *Fitchburg Sentinel.* He gave up full-time journalism in 1966 to concentrate on novel-writing, but continued to work as a columnist and associate editor for the *Sentinel.* He won a number of awards for his human interest column (published under the byline John Fitch IV), and a volume of autobiographical essays, edited by his wife—*I Have Words To Spend: Reflections of A Small-Town Editor* (1991)—helps to explain the relationship between the upbeat realism of his journalistic work and the cynicism of his imaginative fiction.

His first three books were adult novels. Although none achieved any notable success, the third, *Take Me Where The Good Times Are,* is sig-

nificant because in it he established the fictional Monument City, a small New England town modeled on his native Leominster. Monument is the setting for much of Cormier's young adult fiction, including his fourth book, *The Chocolate War.* There had been a nine-year gap between his last adult novel and this, his first book published for teenagers. The delay was occasioned by considerable publisher resistance to the book and also by Cormier's own initial resistance to his agent's suggestion that the book should be submitted as a young adult novel. Although the action of the novel takes place in a closed and repressed environment at some considerable remove from the openness and permissiveness of late-sixties and early-seventies America, the imprint of the time in which it was written is present in several interludes.

Cormier did not return to the adult novel. He has been happy to develop the niche established by *The Chocolate War.* His next book, *I Am The Cheese,* is a psychological nightmare based on the U.S. Witness Relocation Program and *After the First Death* went even further in depicting hopelessness. Each of these titles from the seventies remains popular, although school boards have from time to time moved to ban them from school libraries. In 1985 Cormier published the sequel *Beyond The Chocolate War,* in which many of the same characters continue to exert their evil influence at Trinity High. The storyline makes the theme of the earlier book—a leader's power emanates from those who allow themselves to be led—even more explicit.

A more recent title, *Tenderness,* about a teenage girl's fixation with a psychopathic killer, demonstrates that even in his seventies Cormier is prepared to confront daring subject matter.

Plot Summary

Part I—Setting the Scene

In the first chapter of Robert Cormier's 1974 novel, *The Chocolate War,* the reader is introduced to Jerry Renault, a freshman at Trinity, a private all-male Catholic high school in New England. It is early fall, and Jerry is trying out for the position of quarterback on the freshman football team. He is faring poorly, however, having just received a crushing blow from a defenseman. When he is finally able to get onto his feet again, his coach, impatient with his overall performance, sends him to the showers. As Jerry walks back to the locker room, he reflects on his sense of isolation (a feeling he experiences repeatedly in the novel), yet is nonetheless encouraged by the coach's injunction that he "show up tomorrow."

The second chapter introduces two more important characters, Archie Costello and Obie. Both are members of the officially secret student organization called the Vigils. Archie is the "Assigner" of the Vigils—the one in charge of assigning to various students the pranks and other disruptive acts that constitute the Vigils' main contribution to the school. It is a position that carries a great deal of influence with it; at least Obie, the group's secretary, terms Archie's power "awesome." The two are in the bleachers while Jerry's football practice is going on. The scene opens with an important exchange between the two characters, one in which the pessimistic outlook that seems to pervade the novel's core is first articulated:

> "You're a real bastard," Obie said finally, his frustration erupting, like a coke exploding from a bottle after you shake it. "You know that?"
>
> Archie turned and smiled at him benevolently, like a goddam king passing out favors.
>
> "Jesus," Obie said, exasperated.
>
> "Don't swear, Obie," Archie chided. "You'll have to tell it in confession."
>
> "Look who's talking. I don't know how you had the nerve to receive communion at chapel this morning."
>
> "It doesn't take nerve, Obie. When you march down to the rail, you're receiving The Body, man. Me, I'm just chewing a wafer they buy by the pound in Worcester."
>
> Obie looked away in disgust.
>
> "And when you say 'Jesus,' you're talking about your leader. But when I say 'Jesus,' I'm talking about a guy who walked the earth for thirty-three years like any other guy but caught the imagination of some PR cats. PR for Public Relations, in case you don't know, Obie."
>
> Obie didn't bother to answer. You couldn't ever win an argument with Archie. He was too quick with the words.

Archie then makes some "assignments"; Jerry, over Obie's objection, is chosen for the final task recorded.

Archie is later called into the office of the school's acting headmaster, Brother Leon, to discuss the chocolate sale. Leon informs Archie that this year's sale will differ from previous years' sales in some significant ways, and he takes the unprecedented step of soliciting the help of the Vigils (though without naming them).

Roland Goubert, called The Goober, is perhaps Jerry's only friend at the school. He receives an assignment from the Vigils, which he carries out with a little last-minute help. The results of the stunt, presented in Chapter 11, cause one teacher to have a breakdown. In Chapter 6, Brother Leon, under the guise of teaching a lesson about political connivance, humiliates a student in the classroom—he is, by reputation, a feared teacher. In Chapter 7 Cormier introduces Emile Janza, the brutish upperclassman who subsequently figures so centrally in the tormenting of Jerry. It is revealed in Chapter 9 that the death of Jerry's mother affected him deeply and created a wall between Jerry and his father, a well-meaning but emotionally broken man; the force of Jerry's loneliness is brought home.

Part II—Jerry's Assignment

Chapter 13 marks a major turning point in the novel, for it is here that the chocolate sale begins in earnest, although a kickoff pep rally is described a few chapters before. Brother Leon is calling out the names of the students in his class and having them indicate whether or not they will participate in the sale; participation is supposedly voluntary. When he reaches the name "Renault," Jerry tells him that he will not sell the chocolates. His obstinacy continues through the next couple of chapters, causing a bit of a stir among the members of the student body. In Chapter 16, Leon blackmails a student into revealing that Jerry is refusing participation in order to fulfill a Vigils' assignment, which at this point is scheduled to be completed shortly. It is thus with a light heart that Brother Leon goes through the list in the following chapter—according to his information, Jerry's assignment has at this point been completed, and he anticipates Jerry's joining the sale. He receives a second surprise, then, when Jerry announces that he is "not going to sell the chocolates."

Jerry spends the rest of that day and night second guessing his action, even trying to figure out why he did what he did. He wakes up the next morning exhausted, deciding that he now knows what a hangover feels like. On his way to school, he unexpectedly receives congratulations on his action from several students, though when he gets to school, he is confronted by the Goober, who urges him to stop holding out. Jerry assures him that the Vigils are no longer involved, but claims that he "just can't" back down: "I'm committed now."

Archie, apparently for his own enjoyment, sabotages a Vigils' stunt, after which Obie vows to get even. Enthusiasm for the sale is low, in part because of Jerry's stance, and it is reported that sales are below last years' figures—a potentially disastrous situation, given that the school has committed to selling twice as much as in previous years. Several boys even discuss the merits of Jerry's stance, though none have enough courage to stop selling chocolates themselves.

The Goober then informs Jerry that he is quitting the football team and has decided not to go out for track in the spring. "There's something rotten in that school," he tells Jerry by way of explanation, then goes further still and uses the word "evil." Still he urges Jerry, unsuccessfully, to sell chocolates, while Jerry is equally unsuccessful in his attempt to recruit him back onto the team.

In Chapter 24, Brian Cochran, appointed by Brother Leon to be treasurer of the chocolate sale, tells Archie that Leon has "overextended the school's finances," and thus that if the chocolate sale is not a success, both he and the school are in trouble. That night, Archie receives a phone call from Leon, threatening him and the Vigils with serious repercussions if the sale does not succeed, and in particular if something is not done about Jerry. Thus the next day Jerry is called before the Vigils, and Archie attempts to coerce him into giving up his crusade. Jerry, though, holds his ground, and in the end Archie can only "ask" him to quit his holdout, much to the surprise, and chagrin, of Obie and John Carter, the Vigils' president.

Soon after at another Vigils' meeting, another student, an upperclassman named Frankie Rollo, acts quite defiantly to Archie and the others, until Carter loses his patience and beats up Rollo. The group attributes Rollo's cavalier attitude to the influence of Jerry's crusade and decides something must be done. Archie, having been silenced momentarily by Carter's act, proposes that they make selling the chocolates "the thing to do," and thus isolate Jerry from the rest of the student body, a plan to which the rest of the group gives provisional assent.

III. Jerry's Exile

At this point, two significant things happen: the sale of chocolates increases dramatically, and Jerry increasingly becomes an object of hostility. Concerning the chocolate sale, it becomes clear that the Vigils are orchestrating large-scale distributions of chocolates all across town. They attribute the sales to each member of the student body, so that everyone except Jerry reaches or exceeds their quota. The Goober, who has stopped selling at a

certain point in solidarity with his friend, is passing by the school gym when he sees himself fraudulently awarded his fiftieth sale; the experience crushes him.

For his part, Jerry is subject to some anonymous rough treatment on the football field and constant harassing phone calls. One day he is taunted by Emile Janza for being "queer" (which he is not). Then, when he starts to show signs, despite himself, that he is ready for a fight, several other boys converge on him and he is badly beaten. After the beating, he becomes "invisible" at school—ignored by everyone, so that when he walks down the halls, the other students part before him "like the Red Sea."

IV. Jerry's Martyrdom

Around this time, the chocolate sale ends. All but fifty boxes—Jerry's boxes—have been sold, and Brother Leon is ecstatic. Archie, meanwhile, has come up with a plan for the remaining chocolates: a boxing "match," to be held on the football field one night, between Jerry and Emile Janza. Rather than a traditional free-for-all, however, the "match" will be combined with a raffle, in which the spectators (the members of the student body) can buy tickets and write down blows that they want one or the other to give to his opponent. The recipient of the punch is not allowed to avoid being hit. Archie manages through various means to convince both Jerry and Emile to participate.

The "match" begins according to plan: Carter reads out the directions on each ticket drawn, and both Jerry and Emile follow them, Emile unsurprisingly getting the better of things. Soon, though, Carter draws a ticket on which the buyer has called for an illegal below-the-belt hit, and without thinking he reads it out. He and the other Vigils immediately recognize the mistake, but it's too late: Emile, acting immediately as he has throughout, goes for Jerry's groin; Jerry understandably tries to block the blow. Emile, thinking Jerry has cheated, decides his action negates the rules altogether. He attacks Jerry with a flurry of blows, eventually knocking him out.

Chaos ensues, until the stadium lights mysteriously go out. Archie goes back to the school building to investigate and is met by Brother Jacques. Having an inkling of what has gone on with Brother Leon, the Vigils, and the chocolates, Brother Jacques chastizes Archie for this latest Vigils stunt. Leon soon shows up, though, and demonstrates to Archie's satisfaction that he is "still in command," thus putting to rest any possibility that

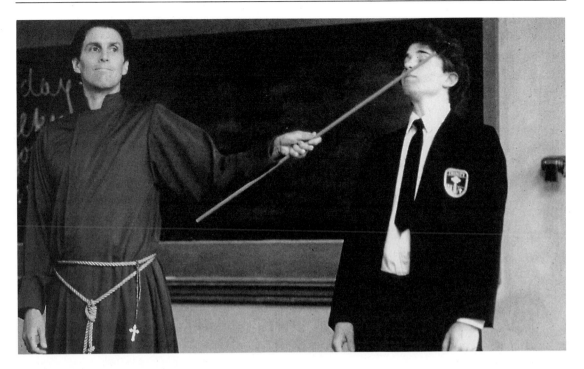

Scene from the film The Chocolate War, *1988.*

Archie and the other Vigils will suffer any serious consequences for their stunt. Meanwhile, The Goober comforts Jerry alone in the boxing ring, waiting for an ambulance to arrive. The novel ends with Archie and Obie sitting in the bleachers talking, just as they did when they first saw Jerry.

Characters

Howie Anderson

President of the junior class, Anderson is notable for almost knocking out Carter in an intramural boxing match. Described as an 'intellectual roughneck', he plays only a tiny part in the novel, yet his appearance in Chapter 21 is significant for his refusal to agree to Richy Rondell's suggestion of a class boycott in support of Jerry. Howie says, "No, Richy. This is the age of do your own thing. Let everybody do his thing. If a kid wants to sell, let him. If he doesn't, the same thing applies."

Brother Andrew

Jerry's art teacher. In Chapter 28 Brother Andrew asks for an art assignment which Jerry has already completed and handed in.

Danny Arcangelo

One of the characters in Chapter 21 who, in private, expresses sympathy for Jerry's stand. (Danny is in conversation with Kevin Chartier.) By extension he is being criticized for their failure to translate this into public support.

Gregory Bailey

An A-grade pupil, made to bear the brunt of Brother Leon's object lesson in political connivance (Chapter 6). "You turned this classroom into Nazi Germany for a few moments," Leon says, after the class has failed to defend Bailey against the accusation of cheating.

Ellen Barrett

A girl Jerry looks forward to seeing at the bus stop. Jerry's hopes of dating her are ruined after she mistakes him for another boy and talks rudely to him over the phone.

Carlson

A senior, Carlson is described as thin and mild. Emile Janza siphons gas from Carlson's car, confident that there will not be any repercussions.

Media Adaptations

- The film version of *The Chocolate War,* produced by Jonathan D. Krane and Simon R. Lewis, and directed by Keith Gordon, was released in 1988, starring John Glover as Brother Leon, Ilan Mitchell-Smith as Jerry, and Wally Ward as Archie. Available from Management Company Entertainment Group.

- A sound recording of an edited version of the novel was narrated by Andrew Jarkowsky and published by Westminster on a single audio cassette in 1977.

- A complete, unabridged sound recording of the novel, read by Frank Muller, recorded on four audio cassettes, was released by Old Greenwich Listening Library in 1988.

David Caroni

The recipient of a Trinity scholarship, "sweet-faced" David Caroni is blackmailed by Brother Leon in Chapter 16 into trading information about Jerry Renault's Vigils assignment (a ten-day embargo on chocolate selling) in return for having a wrongly-marked F-grade paper reconsidered. Caroni finds the episode deeply dispiriting: "If teachers did this kind of thing, what kind of world could it be?"

John Carter

John Carter, all-star guard on the football team and president of the Boxing Club, is also president of the Vigils. Cormier emphasizes Carter's physical prowess. In Chapter 12 he is described as a "big beefy varsity guard who looked as if he could chew freshmen up and spit them out." Although elsewhere referred to as "almost as big a bastard" as Archie, Carter is a more straightforward bully. He is distrustful of the other's tactics, and more than ready to get physical to prove that force is more effective than cleverness. In Chapter 27 Archie disapproves of Carter's readiness to beat up an insolent junior, Frankie Rollo. In a key moment Carter flattens him with a single punch and effectively puts Archie on probation. Carter disagrees with Archie's decision to associate the Vigils with the chocolate sale.

Tubs Casper

Casper, forty pounds overweight, is seen in Chapter 14 cycling around the neighborhood selling chocolates, intending to spend the returns on his girlfriend, Rita.

Kevin Chartier

Experiencing difficulty selling the chocolates, Kevin Chartier phones his friend Danny Arcangelo and the two of them discuss, inconclusively, joining the boycott.

Coach

The football coach, never mentioned by name, is nevertheless an important presence in the book. Encountered in the opening chapter, we see him pressing Jerry hard and accidentally spitting on him. His bullying coaching style is initially unsympathetic, but is viewed as an increasingly healthy counterpoint to the murky machinations of Archie and Leon.

Brian Cochran

A senior, not "exactly a hotshot in the psychology department," who is volunteered by Brother Leon to be treasurer of the chocolate sale, a job which he performs with clerical efficiency. In the course of the sale he becomes aware that sales are being falsely attributed to certain individuals in order to encourage others. He keeps his disapproval to himself. Ultimately, when the sale is pronounced over, he is worried by the tidiness of the figures, but again keeps quiet.

Archie Costello

Fiendishly concocting assignments for the Vigils and eventually directing his devilish ingenuity against the hero, Jerry, Archie is introduced to the reader in Chapter 2 as "the bastard" with an uncanny ability to manipulate people. He annoys his stooge, Obie, with his "phony hip moods." It is Archie who delivers the first major assignment of the novel to Roland Goubert—loosening the screws in all the furniture in Brother Eugene's classroom. His crucial role is established in Chapter 4, when Brother Leon invokes, through Archie, the Vigils' support for the upgraded annual chocolate sale. Archie blackmails another pupil, Emile Janza, by pretending to hold a photo of him masturbating in the toilet, but the real point of their chilling confrontation in Chapter 15 is to establish Janza as a crude and guileless demon in contrast to Archie's cerebral and wickedly playful malevolence.

Archie provides an unwholesome line of communication between the adults and the students. He is not above taking advantage of this position to gain personal amusement at his fellow-Vigils' expense, as in Chapter 20, when a collective assignment against Brother Jacques (Obie and the rest of the class get up and do a jig whenever Jaques utters the word "environment") backfires. Jacques, clearly tipped off in advance by Archie, goes out of his way to used the word as often as possible, with exhausting results. This episode further exacerbates Obie's antagonism towards Archie.

Archie is eventually persuaded by Brother Leon that pressure must be brought to bear on Jerry to force him to sell chocolates. He begins, in conjunction with Emile Janza, by arranging to have Jerry accused of being a "queer," and then beaten up. He then stage-manages the climactic final encounter of the novel, a boxing match between Jerry and Emile. At the end we see Archie unrepentantly admitting to Obie that he tipped Brother Leon off about the boxing match, so that he could stand at a distance and watch.

Harold Darcy

After the general mood has turned against Jerry, Darcy self-righteously speaks up in class to demand an explanation: "Everybody else is doing his part, why isn't Renault?"

Tommy Desjardins

Desjardins is cited as coming from one of the school's top families. His father is a dentist.

Brother Eugene

It is Brother Eugene's classroom, Room Nineteen, which is the subject of the first major Vigil assignment undertaken in the book. All the screws are loosened so that every item of furniture will collapse at the merest touch. Brother Eugene is destroyed by this experience and is absent from the school in the second half of the novel, presumed to be on sick leave.

Fontaine

A minor character notable for being one of the pupils committed to the chocolate sale. He sells ten boxes in the first week and is among the first to reach his quota.

The Goober

See Roland Goubert

Roland Goubert

Roland Goubert, nicknamed The Goober, is tall and skinny and good at running. He has bad acne. From the moment he is made the subject of the first assignment—he spends over six hours loosening the screws in Brother Eugene's room and eventually has to have Vigil assistance to complete the task—the reader is made to sympathize with him, and to feel that he is a potential ally for Jerry. In Chapter 12 he makes the most of a pass from Jerry and scores for the freshman football team. We sometimes see things from his point of view, particularly in Chapters 13 and 14 when the drama of the chocolate sale is developed in terms of Goubert's apprehension of Brother Leon's state of mind. Towards the climax of the book he is amongst those who have their sales falsely reported. It is claimed that he has reached his quota when he has, in fact, sold only twenty-seven boxes. This is a turning point. He does not speak up and rushes to his locker in tears, knowing that he has betrayed Jerry. After this he is absent from school for a number of days, before returning in time to witness Jerry's destruction in the boxing ring.

Mrs. Hunter

Housekeeper to Mr. Renault.

Brother Jacques

Brother Jacques is a new teacher who appears halfway through the novel and is untainted by the regime. He is quickly made to bear the brunt of a Vigil stunt, but he has been forewarned by Archie and is able to turn the tables on the boys. It is Jacques who has his hand on the light switch towards the end of Chapter 37—and who then admonishes Archie in tones of cold contempt. In the following chapter, however, Jacques' protest is undermined by the arrival of Brother Leon.

Emile Janza

Described as "a brute" with "small eyes," Janza is the type of pupil who likes to sit at the front of the class, infuriating the teacher with a soft whistling or a tapping of the foot. He was once caught by Archie with his trousers down, masturbating in the toilet. For a long time he believes that Archie has an incriminating photograph, referred to in Chapter 7 as the "picture that haunted his life." Emile is a straightforwardly ruthless bully, intimidating younger pupils into buying him cigarettes. Sheer malice and enjoyment of the game motivate his participation in Chapter 31, when he accosts Jerry, accuses him (at Archie's bidding) of being a closet homosexual, and then (on his own initiative) roughs him up with a group of accomplices. Archie is then able to use this incident to set up the final, bizarre boxing match between Emile and Jerry.

Brother Leon

Brother Leon is the pale, ingratiating, and slyly venomous Assistant Headmaster. When the Headmaster becomes sick, Leon takes over management of the school. In his teaching he controls his pupils by being intellectually unpredictable and with his ability to make examples of them, as in the cruel game he plays on Bailey in Chapter 6. It has been his decision to double the quota and the price in the annual chocolate sale and the financial foolhardiness of this project leads him to seek a commitment of support from the Vigils. He speaks in a whisper but there is always a barely controlled violence beneath the surface, as evidenced in Chapter 16 when he snaps a piece of chalk in two while talking to a pupil called Caroni. Once he has identified Jerry as the primary cause for the poor general progress of the sale, he becomes obsessed with revenge. The treasurer of the sale, Brian Cochran, compares his demeanor to that of a "mad scientist … in an underground laboratory." The practicalities of revenge are handed over to Archie, but Leon comes forward at the horrible denouement to the boxing match, to stand in triumph beside Archie. In most respects Leon has won. The chocolate sale has achieved its objectives. Jerry has been beaten. And an overt partnership has been forged with the Vigils.

Obie

Obie is Archie's stooge and general errand-boy for the Vigils. He has a thin, sharp face, is constantly yawning, and is presented as intellectually inferior to Archie, whom he alternately admires and detests. He is manipulated by Archie and often made to take an active part in one of the Vigil assignments, such as the stunt perpetrated on Brother Jacques. This is a festering cause of resentment. At the end of the book Obie attempts to outwit Archie by unexpectedly presenting him with the Vigils' box of marbles (which serves as a check on Archie's power) at the start of the boxing match and challenging him to pick two. In the final chapter we find Obie in low-key conversation with Archie. "Maybe the black box will work the next time, Archie," he says. Archie treats this comment with scorn and asks Obie for a Hershey bar.

Mr. James R. Renault

Jerry's father is a pharmacist. He works irregular hours and is often asleep when at home. His favorite word is "fine" and he has a resigned outlook on life, but Jerry considers his father's existence to be dull and meaningless.

Jerry Renault

Jerome E. Renault is the son of James R. Renault, a pharmacist. His mother has recently died. The reader's introduction to Jerry, in Chapters 1 and 3, is crucial. Together these chapters establish Jerry as a sportsman and a teenager with all the normal masculine urges, but one who goes out of his way to avoid confrontation. When his football coach is shouting at him and some saliva hits his face, he wants to protest, "Hey, coach, you spit on me." Instead, he is polite. And after looking at a *Playboy* in Chapter 3, he has a confrontation with a hippy who taunts him as a "Square boy. Middle-aged at fourteen, fifteen. Already caught in a routine." Jerry does not respond. "He hated confrontations."

He misses his mother and, sensing the drabness in his father's working life, develops a desire to do something with his own life. His refusal to participate in the chocolate sale is initially part of a Vigil assignment lasting ten days. But some inner volition leads him to extend his boycott beyond this period. This individual defiance is presented in earth-shattering terms. "Cities fell. Earth opened. Planets tilted. Stars plummeted. And the awful silence." Jerry's lone protest is partly inspired by a poster displayed in the back of his locker. It shows a man walking alone on the beach, with a captioned quote from poet T. S. Eliot: "Do I dare disturb the universe?" Beyond answering this challenge Jerry has no satisfactory explanation for his friend The Goober, or for himself, as to why he is still refusing to sell the chocolates.

Jerry becomes the target of a Vigil campaign to force him to join the chocolate sale. There are anonymous phone calls to his home. His locker, including the important poster, is ransacked. An art assignment is stolen. He is beaten up by Emile Janza and some of his cronies, and then systematically ostracized. Presented with the opportunity of getting back at Janza, he agrees to Archie's plans for a boxing match on the athletics field. The outcome of this final Vigil antic is that Jerry is badly beaten and seriously hurt. When The Goober leans over him, Jerry wants to tell him to play ball, to play by the rules, and not to go out on a limb, not to try and disturb the universe. But Jerry cannot speak. He is taken away in an ambulance and the reader is left to wonder how serious his injuries might be.

Although the action in the novel is not always seen from Jerry's point of view, he is clearly the pivotal character, and the one with whom the reader sympathizes. The novel was shocking in its time because of the manner in which its main character was so clearly and unequivocally defeated.

Frankie Rollo

An insolent junior who is beaten up by Carter for insulting Archie at a Vigils meeting. His taunting, particularly his statement, "Hell, you guys can't even scare a punk freshman into selling a few lousy chocolates...," forces Archie to take action against Jerry to maintain his position of authority.

John Sulkey

"Lousy at sports and a squeaker at studies," Sulkey is one of the first to reach his quota in the chocolate sale.

Themes

Courage and Cowardice

"I've got guts," Jerry murmurs to himself in the opening chapter, after hitting the ground following a heavy tackle on the sports field. Tackled three times in succession, Jerry is insulted by the coach, but he leaves the field determined to make the team. This opening scene establishes Jerry as a character who has the courage to withstand physical pain. He can get up again after being knocked down and come back for more. But there is another pain afflicting him. In the same opening chapter we discover that his mother is dead. It is the painful memory of her death, rather than the bruising he has received on the football field, which induces the nausea that ends Chapter 1. The straightforward physicality and competitiveness of football—in Chapter 28 it is called, from Jerry's point of view, the "honest contact of football"—is throughout contrasted with the psychological and emotional leverage exerted by both the Vigils and Brother Leon.

Archie is not without courage. Though he has never picked a black marble from the box (which would require him to carry out an assignment himself), the possibility is always there. He has the courage of his own convictions, especially in Chapter 27 when he resists Carter's insistence that the time for psychological tactics is over and the way should be cleared for straightforward physical bul-

Topics for Further Study

- Pretend that you are Brian Cochran, treasurer for the chocolate sale. Design an accounts sheet on which you would be able to record the progress of the sale. Complete it according to the information given in the novel.

- Make a list of all the scenes that take place outside the school, and analyze the importance of each one.

- Illustrate the varying types of physical and psychological bullying explored in the novel, with specific reference to Archie Costello, John Carter, Emile Janza, and Brother Leon.

- You are a film director preparing to shoot the scene in which Bailey is accused of cheating. Plan very carefully how you intend to use the camera at each stage of the scene, and what you intend each shot to convey to the audience.

- Cormier worked for many years as a newspaper journalist. Imagine that, following complaints from Jerry's father, you have been sent to investigate recent events at the school. Who will you interview? What do you imagine will be their responses to your questions?

lying. Cowardice is found in the general student body of Trinity, among those who would like to join Jerry in the boycott but are too scared to do so. Some boys, John Sulkey, for example, are committed to the chocolate sale, either because they see it as a personal challenge or because they have been convinced by Brother Leon's sermons. The vast majority, however, would drop out if they could. Ultimately, they carry on not out of respect for the school, or fear of Brother Leon, but because they do not have the courage to stand up to Archie and the Vigils.

Peer Pressure

Peer pressure is an important theme in the novel, particularly the pressure to remain silent and toe the line. When Brother Leon gives his lesson in political connivance (the encouragement of evil by the failure to condemn) in Chapter 6, Cormier manages to convey several things at the same time. The irony of Leon being the agent of the message— "You turned this classroom into Nazi Germany for a few moments"—is not lost on the reader. As the book develops one can see fascist techniques being applied by both Leon and the Vigils to control behavior. In the later stages of the chocolate sale, misinformation is a key factor in maintaining peer pressure. False figures regarding individual progress towards quotas are announced. Those directly affected are flattered to have their sales figures inflated and therefore keep quiet. Others feel under increased pressure to persevere with the selling. The most poignant individual response to this particular pressure is that of Roland Goubert "The Goober" who, as a silent and secret act of solidarity with Jerry, has stopped selling chocolates after twenty-seven boxes. When he is falsely announced as having reached his quota he shrinks away without saying anything: "He willed himself to feel nothing. He didn't feel rotten. He didn't feel like a traitor. He didn't feel small and cowardly." Cormier, however, does intend the reader to see cowardice and treachery in both the individual and group behavior.

Victim and Victimization

The conversation between Archie and Emile Janza (two of a kind in some respects) in Chapter 15 is seen from Archie's point of view. Archie is victimizing Janza, pretending that he holds an incriminating photograph. Janza is observed victimizing a young freshman, forcing him to run off and obtain some cigarettes. "The world was made up of two kinds of people—those who were victims and those who victimized." This is Archie's observation. His self-awareness and lack of self-deception are key characteristics. Brother Leon is far less straightforward, but Cormier juxtaposes the chapters in the novel very carefully. It is significant that in Chapter 16 we see Leon smoothly victimizing David Caroni into releasing information about Jerry's Vigil assignment. Leon, outwardly the respectable Assistant Head of a boy's school, is just as corrupt as Archie and Emile, and Caroni is left to wonder, "Were teachers as corrupt as the villains you read about in books or saw in movies and television?"

Individualism

In Chapter 6 Leon hypocritically praises Bailey for being "true to himself." When Jerry exhibits just this quality, Leon does all that he can to break him down. It is important to understand that Jerry's boycott of the chocolate sale is at no stage based on a point of principle relating to the sale itself. To begin with he is simply acting in accordance with a Vigil assignment. Continuing the boycott beyond the ten-day assignment is an act of individual defiance which Jerry is unable fully to explain to himself. His individual stand arises out of the circumstances of his personal life—the recent loss of his mother, the apparent tedium of his father's existence as a pharmacist—and from his fascination with the poster hanging in his locker (with its quote from T. S. Eliot, "Do I dare disturb the universe?"). It has little to do with any specific opposition to Leon's fund-raising appeal. In conversation with Goober, Jerry says, "It's not the Vigils, Goob. They're not in it anymore. It's me." At the end of the book, after the sale has succeeded and Jerry has been seriously damaged by Janza in the boxing ring, Jerry is anxious to pass on some newly-acquired knowledge to Goubert but cannot speak. However, the reader is allowed to share Jerry's point of view. For all of authority's inducements to develop individualism and to "be true to yourself," and the exhortations of hippies not to be "square," Jerry has discovered, "They don't want you to do your thing, not unless it happens to be their thing too." And more importantly he has discovered what happens if you try: "They murder you."

Good and Evil

Brother Leon's manipulative, sadistic nature is demonstrated in Chapter 16, when he deceives Caroni to get information about Jerry; in Chapter 24, when it is revealed he misused the school's finances to purchase the chocolates; and in Chapter 38, when he dismisses the brutal beating of Jerry by declaring, "Boys will be boys...." Archie exerts a malevolent control over Trinity through his role as The Vigils' Assigner. Manipulation, fear, and intimidation force the other students to carry out his orders, which often prove destructive to those involved. By even allowing The Vigils to exist, the brothers allow corruption to flourish at Trinity. Brother Leon's willingness to share power with The Vigils, as when he asks for help with the chocolate sale, further erodes moral authority. Cormier also makes it clear that by acquiescing to Archie and Leon, the students at Trinity in essence cooperate with forces of evil, as in Chapter 6 when Leon torments Gregory Bailey while the other students remain silent.

Jerry functions as a traditional hero. He is a typical high school student with ordinary skills and talents who must overcome tremendous pressure with little to rely on except his own will. By refusing to help with the chocolate sale, Jerry stands in opposition to the corrupt, established order. That he is ultimately defeated is perhaps less important than the idea that he stood firm in his convictions, although some critics have argued that the book ends on a despairing note, as evil triumphs over good.

God and Religion

There are several biblical references in the opening two chapters. Jerry's habit of thinking one thing but saying another is compared to Peter, who denied Christ before the Crucifixion: "he had been Peter a thousand times and a thousand cocks had crowed in his lifetime." In Chapter 2 it is quickly established that the story takes place at a Catholic school, where the boys regularly participate in confession and receive communion. Obie, looking out at the football field, compares the shadows formed by the goalposts to empty crucifixes. Obie thinks to himself, "That's enough symbolism for one day," and Cormier does not press the religious theme in the rest of the novel.

Style

Point of View

The shifting narrative point of view is one of the most distinctive features of *The Chocolate War*. Its chapters are mostly short, and it is unusual for one character's point of view to be pursued in the following chapter. Despite this, there is no doubt as to the "hero" or main character of the novel. The opening chapter encourages the reader to identify with Jerry Renault, the young quarterback who bravely gets to his feet after a number of heavy tackles and who dreams of making the football team. Those early incidents on the football field, and Jerry's handling of them, suggest that we are to encounter a conventional hero who, through determination and courage, will overcome obstacles and achieve his objectives.

The novel has a very large cast—most of Jerry's class group is mentioned by name. The other boys from whose point of view we regularly see parts of the action are Archie Costello, Obie, Emile Janza, and Roland Goubert. However, there are still more points of view used for single and precise purposes. Two examples of these are David Caroni, who in Chapter 16 is used by Cormier as the agent for revealing Brother Leon's inherent corruption, and Brian Cochran, who in Chapter 22 and

elsewhere, as treasurer for the sale, discovers and mulls over the accounting irregularities. Occasionally the narrative point of view further fragments so that one chapter will present a composite viewpoint. Cormier uses this technique to convey the ongoing chocolate sale, as in Chapter 14. The result is a book with a much more complex narrative structure than the majority of adult novels, let alone young adult novels. The deployment of multiple points of view has since become Cormier's trademark as a novelist. In *The Chocolate War* his use of this technique is so skillful and finely judged that the reader never becomes confused and, more importantly, never loses the underlying identification with Jerry.

Structure

The reader's sympathy with Jerry, in a book told from multiple points of view, is sustained by key interludes which occur at regular intervals throughout the novel. These interludes are different in kind from the circumstances in which other characters are put. Jerry is the only character who is observed having a life outside of school and the chocolate sale. A number of minor characters are depicted in scenes removed from school life, but they are either having telephone conversations about the sale or are out on their bikes trying to find buyers for the chocolates. Jerry has a personal life (he is grieving for his dead mother, he looks on the petty life of his pharmacist father with disdain, he fancies a girl at the bus stop, he looks at adult magazines) and, most importantly, he is the one character with conventionally noble aspirations. He aspires to be on the football team, and he is inspired by the poster hanging in his locker to stand alone and make an individual protest against the prevailing order. The structure of the novel is such that we increasingly see the story as a battle between the individual versus authority. The undercurrent of physical bullying in the school, represented by Emile Janza, encourages our expectation that the larger battle will end in a key confrontation.

Climax

Robert Cormier is on record as saying that he loves detective stories because "they always deliver a beginning, middle and end, a satisfying climax or epiphany." The ending of *The Chocolate War* is certainly climactic. But it is also unconventional. Our expectations of a classic confrontation, in which the hero will perhaps get bloodied but will emerge victorious, are mocked by the surreally absurd terms on which Jerry and Emile are made to fight one another in the closing scene. They have to take turns throwing punches, as directed by the crowd. Animal instincts are kept at bay by these balletic rules for only so long, and once they are let loose Jerry is brutally destroyed. The sudden eclipse of the hero and the collapse of his motivating belief in doing his own thing and daring to disturb the universe, combined with the equivocal exit of Jerry from the book (the reader is left guessing as to the seriousness of his injuries), make for a downbeat conclusion. The novel's denouement has been criticized by some commentators on children's literature for purveying the message that evil prevails. Taken at face value, the climax to *The Chocolate War,* and indeed the endings of many of Cormier's other novels, can be used to support this criticism.

Symbols and Imagery

Cormier's use of imagery in this novel emphasizes the fact that these events take place at a Catholic school, and religious symbolism underwrites much of the action in the novel. We do see Jerry's defeat as a kind of crucifixion, but there is certainly no simplistic allegory or correlation intended. Rather, the gently insinuated biblical references encourage us to view the events of the novel in global or even metaphysical terms.

Setting

Most of the action in *The Chocolate War* takes place at Trinity, a Catholic boys' school. Other than knowing that it has an athletic and football field, the reader is given very little visual description of the school. Cormier concentrates on character rather than place. But it is important for a general understanding of Cormier's work to know that he has chosen to set nearly all of his young adult fiction in and around the small town of Monument, a fictional equivalent of his own Massachusetts hometown. Trinity is not in Monument, although one of the pupils has recently transferred from Monument High. But the surrounding district is conceived as typical of suburban America, and the closed, claustrophobic environment of the school is a microcosm for the world at large.

Historical Context

The 1960s/1970s Counterculture

The Chocolate War was written in the early seventies and published in 1974. Its story is told almost without reference to the world at large. Chap-

ter 3 is therefore highly significant. In this chapter Jerry, after taking a copy of *Playboy* down from the top shelf of a magazine rack and surreptitiously browsing, has an exchange at a bus-stop with a confrontational drop-out. Cormier's description of the group from which the confrontational young man emerges is both specific and various. "They were now part of the scenery like the Civil War Cannon and the World War Monuments, the flagpole. Hippies. Flower Children. Street People. Drifters. Drop-Outs. Everybody had a different name for them." In other words, they are exemplars of the counterculture that thrived in America in the late 1960s and was still a strong cultural and social presence in 1974. Jerry is mocked by their spokesman as a "square," as someone hidebound by his smart uniform, his obedience to rules, and his sense of guilt (which has just been exhibited in his recollection of having to quickly get rid of the only pornographic magazine he had ever dared take home).

Cormier, it must be noted, refrains from using the words "protesters" or "draft-dodgers" in connection with this group. They are specifically not political protesters, but social drop-outs. Fred Inglis, in his book *The Promise of Happiness: Value and Meaning in Children's Fiction,* writes that Cormier "sounds like another dispirited radical of the 1968 generation, of Miami and the siege of Chicago. The radical moral taken to heart after a term and a half on the steps of Nixon's Pentagon was that all structures of authority and institutions were deadly, and all would, in their super-ruthless and efficient way, break the spirit of the individual." However, cautious criticism of the book and its cultural context makes a distinction between the chord it struck with its audience in the resonances remarked upon by Inglis, and the deeper intentions of the author. Brother Leon's reprehensibly hypocritical classroom simulation of Nazi Germany is used by Cormier to incriminate both Leon himself and the other boys. Jerry, although he hates Leon from then onwards, is unaffected by the leaden political message of the lesson. His impulse has not been to protest, but to escape: "He wished he wasn't here in the classroom. He wanted to be out on the football field, fading back, looking for a receiver."

Fund-Raising and Private Education

Fund-raising fulfilled, and still fulfills, a substantial role in the annual budget of a private school such as Trinity. It also plays a part in public schools, where parent and student groups work to fund extracurricular activities from sports to music to clubs. Participation by pupils in annual raffles, sales, or other revenue-producing activities is normally non-controversial. What makes the Trinity sale different is the application of quotas to students, the sudden doubling of the quotas (together with a doubling in the price of the chocolates), the compulsion to meet those quotas, and the corrupt duplicity of Leon's secret agreement with the Vigils.

Critical Overview

The Chocolate War can justifiably claim to be the novel which persuaded commentators to take young adult literature seriously as a new genre. The novel caused controversy on its publication and has continued to do so since. Several attempts have been made to ban it from school and college libraries and from recommended reading lists. Objections range from a general distaste for the book's portrayal of triumphant evil to specific criticism of the language used by the boys and the depiction of sexual activity. Chapter 15 recounts how Archie discovered Emile Janza masturbating in the toilet and pretended to take a photo. "Stepping into the men's room to grab a quick smoke, Archie had pulled open the door to one of the stalls and confronted Janza sitting there, pants dropping on the floor, one hand furiously at work between his legs." It was unusual to find such frank description of adolescent sexual activity in a book published for children.

It was even more unusual, outside of fantasy literature, to encounter truly evil characters in children's books. As Nancy Veglahn commented in *The Lion and the Unicorn: A Critical Journal of Children's Literature:* "Robert Cormier is one of the few writers of realistic fiction for young adults who creates genuinely evil characters. Unlike fantasy and science fiction books, which abound with embodiments of cosmic malevolence, realistic novels seem to shy away from villains…. [This] is not true of Robert Cormier. There is no moral blandness in his books, no picture of a world in which all will be well if everyone just tries a little harder."

It is exactly Cormier's refusal to end his books on a note of hope or uplift which his critics complain about. Six years after *The Chocolate War*'s first publication, Norma Bagnall, writing in *Top of the News*, challenged the notion that Cormier was a writer of realistic fiction. Was it realistic to depict a world in which there were no decent char-acters capable of standing up to evil? In the case of this particular novel, she especially objected to the fact that there is no adult character in the novel ready and able to give Jerry support. "It is as inaccurate to present only the sordid and call it realistic as it has been in the past to present only the idealistic." According to the critic, the fact that the book is "brilliantly structured and skilfully written" made its distorted view of reality all the more dangerous.

This viewpoint was echoed soon afterwards by Fred Inglis, in his *The Promise of Happiness: Value and Meaning in Children's Fiction.* Taking Bagnall's objections one stage further, Inglis argued that there was a group of new writers for older children who were systematically destroying innocence by breeding a mood of cynicism. He chose Cormier and *The Chocolate War* as an exemplar of this. "What is deeply wrong with *The Chocolate War* … is its grossness and indelicacy in telling its child-readers that heroism is, strictly, such a dead end." He later added, "The *intention* of *The Chocolate War* seems to be to force the child directly up against the pain of pain, the facts of cruelty and oppression, by way of showing him that the adults have always told lies about the world's being a fine and benign place."

Although the book still finds its critics, it is noticeable that earlier detractors such as Bagnall and Inglis seemed to fail to grasp that the book was addressed to a new audience. It was not a book for children, but for young adults. The book's intended audience made it an immediate commercial success. It has been continually available since first publication and along with subsequent novels has helped to establish Cormier's position as America's leading young adult novelist. Sylvia Patterson Iskander, writing in the *Concise Dictionary of American Literary Biography,* included the following summary: "[Cormier] has brought controversy and, simultaneously, a new dimension to the field of young-adult literature. He has earned the respect of his readers, regardless of their age, because of his refusal to compromise the truth as he sees it."

Criticism

Stan Walker

In the following essay, Walker, a doctoral candidate at the University of Texas, analyzes how The Chocolate War *can be interpreted within the con-*

What Do I Read Next?

- *I Am the Cheese,* Cormier's second young adult novel, published in 1977, is an effective psychological thriller based on the U.S. Witness Relocation Program.

- In 1985 Cormier published a sequel to *The Chocolate War. Beyond The Chocolate War* includes most of the original characters. An important new character is Ray Bannister, a magician who uses a guillotine as part of his act.

- *Fade* (1988), one of Cormier's bleakest and most graphic novels, is a supernatural story about a New England family's ability to become physically invisible.

- *Tenderness* (1997) is a novel which demonstrates that Cormier, in his seventies, has lost none of his power to shock. The novel describes a teenage girl's fixation with a young psychopathic killer.

- *The End of the Affair* (1951) by Graham Greene is Cormier's favorite book, by his favorite author.

- *Calling Home* (1991) by Michael Cadnum, about how a teen's guilt over causing the death of his friend leads him into alcoholism. A reviewer in *The Horn Book Magazine* has said of Cadnum's work: "Not since Robert Cormier has such a major talent emerged in adolescent literature."

---

text of Christian beliefs. He also notes that while the pessimism of the novel can be seen as a product of its times, its power to disturb readers makes it timeless.

Robert Cormier's *The Chocolate War* begins with a seemingly serious remark: "They murdered him." We quickly realize that this is the author's way of telling us, with humorous exaggeration, that a character, who we learn is named Jerry Renault, has just received a heavy hit during football practice. As the novel progresses, though, other details emerge, and our reading of this remark changes. We come to see in it a reference to Christ's "murder," and thus to see Jerry's rebellion against the chocolate sale and everything it stands for as being patterned in part on Christ's "rebellion." Other details complicate this association, however, so that by the end of the novel we are left not with a portrait of Christian triumph, but rather with a set of anguished questions: Is there any purity or "sincerity" (or in Christian terms, redemption) in the world, a world that seems to be so thoroughly corrupt? If there is, can one (like Christ) attain it by refusing to compromise one's beliefs—by refusing to "bend"—and thus risking everything, even being "murdered," for those beliefs? And can that refusal be an example by which others profit: can others be redeemed by such a self-sacrifice?

That these questions are "anguished" suggests that the novel's outlook is a bleak one; and indeed, there is a pervasive pessimism at the core of *The Chocolate War*. None of the "adult" power structures in the novel—family, church, school—seem to offer any haven to the adolescent boys who are the novel's focus. Parents, who play at best a peripheral role, are ineffectual or absent. The "brothers" at Trinity, the Catholic prep school where *The Chocolate War* is set, are by and large no better, either weak, like Brother Eugene, or cruel and hypocritical, like the novel's central authority figure, Brother Leon. Not only is Leon cruel and hypocritical, he is also more concerned for the school's material well-being, represented by the chocolate sale, than he is for the boys' spiritual nurturing. Indeed, his concern for the "spiritual" seems to be limited to the boys' "school spirit," his euphemism for their enthusiasm for the sale. The further disclosure that he has made some illegal transactions in setting up the sales drive, while it makes some of his actions understandable, and thus to some extent, perhaps, sympathetic, has the primary effect of sealing our verdict that he is one of the novel's arch-villains.

The other arch-villain in the novel is Archie Costello. Like Brother Leon, Archie is not a wholly unsympathetic character. We see him at points alone and vulnerable, though we probably feel that because of his hubris (excessive pride), he is more deserving of the discomfort he experiences than are the other characters in the novel (including, perhaps, Brother Leon). At the same time, it is Archie who is the guiding spirit of the Vigils, the officially secret student group that controls so many aspects of the boys' lives at Trinity. It is he who articulates the cynical outlook that so troubles the novel. In the novel's second chapter, for example, when we first meet him, he has an exchange with Obie, the Vigils' secretary, in which he claims that to him, the communion ceremony means nothing more than "chewing a wafer," while Jesus is not his "leader," but rather "a guy who walked the earth for thirty-three years like any other guy but caught the imagination of some PR cats."

The effect of these remarks is to suggest that nothing one might do has the potential for any larger/higher significance, in a "spiritual" sense—that if Jesus, the supposed Son of God, was in reality just a "guy," then we too can be nothing more than just "guys." And if we are all just "guys," then we can hope for nothing better than some form of worldly success (to have good "PR" people behind us), or failing that, survival. All action, then, is reduced to power "games," and all people, as Archie says to Carter at the boxing "match" near the end of the novel, are "bastards," "greedy and cruel." Carter, like Obie, reacts with "disgust" to Archie's statements—it is "as if there was no goodness at all in the world," he subsequently reflects—yet he, like Obie, has no answer to them. Indeed, no answer is readily forthcoming from any character in the novel, for such a response, Cormier seems to be saying, cannot be made in words, but must come in the form of action: you cannot argue the cynic out of his cynicism, in other words; you must show him that he is "wrong."

The main attempt to "respond" to Archie is of course made by Jerry Renault. As noted earlier, it is intimated from the beginning of the novel that Jerry will in some respects "imitate" Christ in his role in the novel. At the same time, it is also intimated that Jerry will be unable to fulfill this daunting task. Having gotten up after the crushing hit in the first chapter, he is accidently spat upon by his coach, and his response to this ill-treatment, to affirm that he is fine, is not what he feels it should have been: "he was a coward about stuff like that, thinking one thing and doing another—he had been Peter a thousand times and a thousand cocks had crowed in his lifetime." In comparing himself to Peter, Jerry is alluding to the Christian Last Supper and to Christ's prediction that he would be betrayed by one of his disciples and that the rest would abandon him. When Peter hears this, he says that he would never abandon Jesus, to which Jesus responds, "Verily I say unto thee, That this night, before the cock crow, thou shalt deny me thrice" (Matthew 26:34). Ironically, in responding as he does to his coach, Jerry has literally "turned the other cheek" (recall that the coach spits on his cheek), and so not denied but followed Christ, by

following his teachings. That Jerry views this as cowardice indicates that he is unable to see the full implications of Christ's example—that if he has "imitated" Christ, he has done so without knowing it.

In the subsequent events of *The Chocolate War,* neither Jerry nor any of the other characters in the novel ever realize the significance of his actions in Christian terms (ironically, given that the novel's setting is a Catholic school). Even the climactic boxing "match," reminiscent as it is of a Roman gladiatorial show, in which Jerry the "martyr" is thrown in to face the beast-like Emile Janza, produces no such realization in anyone. For Jerry at least, the more real model for his actions is T. S. Eliot's J. Alfred Prufrock, whose timid query, "Do I dare disturb the universe?", is the caption of a poster hung in his locker. Here too, Jerry is at first "[not] sure of the poster's meaning," nor does he seem to know that it is Prufrock in whose mouth Eliot puts the famous question. After a while, though, he feels he understands the poster's significance, and Prufrock's question, answered cautiously in the affirmative—"Yes, I do, I do. I think"—becomes his battle cry.

By the end of his trials, though, a far darker picture of things has emerged in the novel. After the boxing "match," Jerry does feel he has had an epiphany or deep insight into things, but it is not one that affirms his decision to "disturb the universe." On the contrary, he has decided that one should stay in line, that "doing your own thing" is useless, when that "thing" does not happen to coincide with the interests of those in power—that rebellion is "a laugh, … a fake." What Jerry has discovered, Cormier suggests, is the modern world's "heart of darkness," for in referring to Jerry's discovery as "the knowledge, the knowledge," he is assumably echoing the famous last words of Mr. Kurtz in Joseph Conrad's novella, *Heart of Darkness :* "The horror! The horror!" As Zibby Oneal puts it in an essay in *Censored Books: Critical Viewpoints,* "Within himself, [Jerry] discovers, are the very things he has fought—the hatred and the violence."

With this discovery, Jerry's insistence that ignoring what he has learned will only lead to one's "murder" recalls the Christian example from the beginning of the novel, only to deny it at last. Christianity in the modern world, Cormier appears to be saying, is at best a sort of shadowy absolute against which our relative failings can be measured; at worst, it is an outdated myth with no bearing on the "real world." If there is to be any sort of "second coming," moreover, it will not be in the form of a Jerry Renault, trying to "imitate" Christ. Instead, he suggests by echoing a line from W. B. Yeats' poem, "The Second Coming" (1921), it will take the form of a general spread of coldness, hardness, and cruelty among people—the qualities that characterize figures like Archie and Brother Leon. (Yeats embodies this "coming" as a "rough beast" "with lion body and the head of a man, [and] / A gaze blank and pitiless as the sun," and says that just after he has this vision of the "beast," "The darkness drops again." Cormier alludes to this final line at the end of Chapter 37 when Obie catches a glimpse of Brother Leon at the top of a hill, watching the "match" below: "The face vanished as the darkness fell.")

In coming to terms with the novel's pessimistic core, we should consider it in the context of the United States of the early 1970s, when *The Chocolate War* was published. The country was then still emerging from a very tumultuous and largely unprecedented part of its history, marked by widespread unrest, much of it violent. Widespread, too, was the belief among the protesters that all leaders and all systems of control should be distrusted, and eventually done away with, if possible. "Do your own thing" was a byword of the times, and for a while many felt that if everyone truly and honestly did so, the bad "things" (war, racial hatred) would somehow come out right. By the end of the 1960s, however, the fact that the war in Vietnam was still raging, combined with some ugly outbreaks of civil violence and a more general breakdown of the drug-based "counterculture," produced in many people feelings of fatigue, bitterness and disillusion, even paranoia—feelings that only became sharper with the emergence of the Watergate scandal in 1973. These widespread feelings are reflected not only in some of the literature of the period (e.g., Robert Stone's *Dog Soldiers*), but also in movies (*The Parallax View, Serpico*) and other media. This soured idealism is in evidence as well in *The Chocolate War,* not only in Jerry's conclusion about the uselessness of "doing your own thing," but also for example in Cormier's use of the word "beautiful" (another byword of 1960s idealism), which is pervasive and ironic.

If this pessimism was widespread in American culture generally, though, it was, Zibby Oneal reminds us, still very new to young people's fiction: "*The Chocolate War* was immediately—and understandably—controversial. It broke new ground … toppling dearly-held taboos, upsetting any number of conventions." In its willingness in particular to tell young adults that sometimes "failure happens" and "despair ensues," Oneal notes that the book still has the power to disturb readers. It is this continuing challenge to readers as much as anything else, perhaps, that makes *The Chocolate War* still timely—still more than a period piece.

Source: Stan Walker, in an essay for Novels for Students, Gale, 1997.

Patricia J. Campbell

In the following excerpt, Campbell discusses Cormier's writing style, use of imagery, and literary and biblical allusions in The Chocolate War.

"They murdered him." The opening line of *The Chocolate War*. Three words that describe the whole movement of the plot. The process of "murdering" Jerry Renault is the subject; it remains only to tell who and why and how they felt about it. And what it meant.

On the surface the story is straightforward enough, moving along quickly in brief, intense scenes. We first see Jerry slamming through a football practice. He is a freshman at Trinity High School in Monument, and making the team is important to him, a small compensation for the recent death of his mother and the gray drabness of his life with his defeated father. The camera shifts to the stands; there we meet Archie, the villainous brains of the secret society called the Vigils. He is plotting "assignments" with his henchman Obie, cruel practical jokes to be carried out by selected victims. On the way home, Jerry is confronted at the bus stop by a hippie vagrant who challenges his passive conformity. Meanwhile, the malevolent Brother Leon, acting headmaster of Trinity, has called Archie into his office to break the traditional conspiracy of silence about the Vigils by asking for their help in the school chocolate sale. As Archie later discovers, Leon, in a bid for power while the headmaster is in the hospital, has overextended the school's funds to take advantage of a bargain in twenty thousand boxes of chocolates. Archie is delighted to have the vicious brother capitulate to him. Now we see Archie in action, as an inoffensive kid called The Goober is assigned to loosen every screw in a classroom so that it falls into debris the next morning at the first touch. But no assignment is complete until Archie has drawn from a box containing six marbles—five white and one black. If the black turns up—as it never has yet—Archie himself must carry out the assignment. But again the marble is white. Next we see Leon in action, tormenting a shy student with false accusations of cheating while the class watches tensely, then turning on the group to accuse them of condoning the cruelty by their silence. An even more vicious character is the bestial Emile Janza, who is in bondage to Archie over an obscene snapshot. Now the cast is complete and the action begins.

To show Leon where the power lies, Archie secretly assigns Jerry to refuse to sell the chocolates for ten days. Brother Leon is enraged but impotent as every day at roll call Jerry continues to answer "No." Suspecting a plot, Leon calls honor student David Caroni into his office and threatens to spoil the boy's perfect academic record with an undeserved F unless he reveals the secret. Terrified, Caroni tells him about the assignment. Finally the ten days are up, but Jerry, for reasons he only dimly understands, still continues stubbornly to refuse to sell the chocolates. Surreptitious approval for Jerry's stand begins among the other students, and for the first time he begins to understand the words on a poster he has taped in his locker: "Do I dare disturb the universe?" The sales begin to drop off. Leon, panicked, pressures Archie; Archie pressures Jerry before the Vigils, but Jerry clings to his resolve. Soon it becomes apparent that the power of both Leon and the Vigils will be destroyed by the failure of the chocolate sale. When Carter, the jock president of the Vigils, in frustration resorts to his fists to subdue a contemptuous assignee at a Vigils' meeting, Archie realizes Jerry's resistance must be destroyed utterly. The Vigils take charge of the chocolates, and under their secret management sales mount dramatically. With this turn of the tide, the school is caught up in the enthusiasm. Jerry is ostracized and tormented, first secretly by the Vigils and then openly by the whole student body. Finally Archie prods Emile Janza to taunt Jerry into a fistfight, but characteristically Emile hires some children to do the actual beating. The Goober, in a belated show of support, decides to stop selling, but his gesture is futile. Soon the sale is over, and only Jerry's fifty boxes of chocolates remain. Archie conceives a diabolical scheme for final vengeance. Under cover of a supposed night football rally, he stages a "raffle" for the last boxes of chocolates. He offers Jerry "a clean fight" with Emile Janza, and Jerry, wanting desperately to hit back at everything, accepts. Only when he and Emile are already in the boxing ring are the rules explained. The raffle tickets are instructions for blows and the recipient is forbidden to defend himself. But now Carter and Obie come forward with the black box. Archie's luck holds; the marble is white. The fight begins as

planned, but Emile's animal rage is quickly out of control, and the mob goes wild as he beats Jerry savagely. The carnage is stopped when one of the brothers arrives and turns out the lights, but it is too late for Jerry. Terribly injured and lying in The Goober's arms, he begs him not to disturb the universe, but to conform, to give in. An ambulance takes him away, and Archie, who has seen Brother Leon watching with approval in the shadows, is left triumphant.

The novel works superbly as a tragic yarn, an exciting piece of storytelling. Many young adults, especially younger readers, will simply want to enjoy it at this level, and Cormier himself would be the first to say that there is nothing wrong with that. A work of literature should be first of all a good story. But a work of literature also has resonance, richness, a broader intent than just the fate of the characters. For the reader who wants to dig a bit beneath the surface, there is a wealth of hidden meaning and emotion in *The Chocolate War*. How does Cormier achieve this atmosphere of dark, brooding inevitability? What are the overarching themes from which the events of the plot are hung? And, most of all, just what is the crucial thing that he is trying to tell us?

A look at Cormier's style in this book will show first of all the driving, staccato rhythms. The sentences are short and punchy, and the chapters are often no more than two pages. He uses dialogue to move the action quickly forward and to establish character and situation in brief, broad strokes. His technique is essentially cinematic; if he wants to make a psychological or philosophical point he does so visually with a symbolic event or an interchange between characters, rather than reflecting in a verbal aside. Tension is built by an escalating chain of events, each a little drama of its own. "Rather than waiting for one big climax, I try to create a lot of little conflicts," he explains [in "An Interview with Robert Cormier" in *Lion and the Unicorn*]. "A series of explosions as I go along."

The point of view snaps back and forth from boy to boy in succeeding chapters, a more focused use of the technique called "omniscient observer." First we see Archie through Obie's eyes, then we are inside Jerry's head, then we watch Leon and The Goober squirm under Archie's gaze, then we are looking up at him from Emile's dwarfish mind, then we watch Brother Leon's classroom performance through Jerry's quiet presence, and so on. The variety of perspectives develops our understanding of the characters and reveals the complex interweaving of motivations and dependencies. The shift is unobtrusive but can be easily detected by a close look at the text. Less subtly, there are occasional tags that clue the reader to a change in voice: Brian Cochran and Obie, for instance, are inclined to think, "For crying out loud!," while Archie, among others, is addicted to the ironic use of the word *beautiful.* Cormier is too fine a writer, of course, to descend to imitation slang in order to indicate that this is a teenager speaking. Nothing dates a book more quickly than trendiness, as he learned from "The Rumple Country," and his understanding of the quality of adolescence goes far deeper than picking up the latest expression.

Much has been made of Cormier's imagery, and many essays and articles have been written on his metaphors and similes, his allusions and personifications. Sometimes it seems that Cormier is merely exercising his virtuosity for the reader: "his voice curled into a question mark," or "he poured himself liquid through the sunrise streets." But most of the time his metaphors are precisely calculated to carry the weight of the emotion he is projecting. Carter, about to tackle Jerry, looks "like some monstrous reptile in his helmet." Leon, thwarted, has "a smile like the kind an undertaker fixes on the face of a corpse." Jerry, happy, scuffles through "crazy cornflake leaves" but, sad, sees autumn leaves flutter down "like doomed and crippled birds." Jerry's father, preparing their loveless dinner, slides a casserole "into the oven like a letter into a mailbox." Sometimes the imagery is vividly unpleasant, as some reviewers have complained, but it is always appropriate to the intensity of the thing that Cormier is trying to say. There is a whole bouquet of bad smells in *The Chocolate War,* starting with Brother Leon's rancid bacon breath. The evening comes on as "the sun bleeding low in the sky and spurting its veins." Sweat moves like small moist bugs on Jerry's forehead. The vanquished Rollo's vomiting sounds like a toilet flushing.

Literary and biblical allusions, too, enrich the alert reader's experience of the novel. Shakespeare, the Bible, and the poetry of T.S. Eliot are the most obvious sources. "Cut me, do I not bleed?" thinks Emile, like Shylock. For Jerry, like Saint Peter, a thousand cocks have crowed. The quotation on the poster in his locker is from Eliot's "The Love Song of J. Alfred Prufrock." [Bruce Clements in *Horn Book*] has gone so far as to write an essay drawing parallels between Jerry and Hamlet, Archie and Iago. Cormier denies building in this particular analogy, but admits that such references may come

from his subconscious. The sophisticated reader, too, can absorb them subliminally, without conscious analysis.

Many of these allusions are not isolated flourishes, but fit together into larger structures of meaning. As one example, the Christian symbolism in *The Chocolate War* is an indication of the importance of the book's theme to Cormier. Before tracing that imagery, however, it is essential to clarify that the school itself is not part of this symbolism. It is a gross misunderstanding of the theme of the book to interpret it as an attack on parochial schools or the Catholic Church. If that had been Cormier's intention, it should be quite clear from his biography that he would have drawn on his childhood memories to picture a school where nuns, not brothers, presided. No, the fact that Trinity is a Catholic school is as irrelevant to the meaning of the story as that fact is irrelevant to the characters. But Cormier does use Christian symbolism to show the cosmic implications of the events he is relating. When Jerry refuses to sell the chocolates, the language suggests the Book of Revelation [as Betty Carter and Karen Harris state in "Realism in Adolescent Fiction" in *Top of the News*]: "Cities fell. Earth opened. Planets tilted. Stars plummeted." In the first chapter, the goal posts remind Obie of empty crucifixes, and in the last chapter, after Jerry's martyrdom, they again remind him of— what? In his graceless state, he can't remember. When Jerry is challenged to action by the hippie, the man looks at him from across a Volkswagen so that Jerry sees only the disembodied head. The image is John the Baptist, he who was beheaded by Herod after he cried in the wilderness to announce the coming of Christ. Archie's name has myriad meanings from its root of "arch": "principal or chief," "cleverly sly and alert," "most fully embodying the qualities of its kind"; but most significantly, the reference is to the Archangel, he who fell from Heaven to be the Fallen Angel, or Lucifer himself. The Vigils, although Cormier admits only to a connotation of "vigilantes," resonate with religious meaning. The candles placed before the altar in supplication are vigil candles, and a vigil is a watch on the night preceding a religious holiday. The members of the gang stand before Archie, who basks in their admiration like a religious statue before a bank of candles [according to Kenneth L. Donelson and Alleen Pace Nilsen in *Literature for Today's Young Adults*]. But most important, the understanding of the ultimate opposing forces of good and evil in *The Chocolate War* is a deeply Christian, or perhaps even a deeply Catholic, vision.

Source: Patricia J. Campbell, "The Chocolate War," in *Presenting Robert Cormier,* revised edition, Twayne Publishers, 1989, pp. 40–51.

Patricia J. Campbell

In the following excerpt, Campbell describes the ways Leon, Archie, and Emile personify evil.

How does the theme of this book fit into Cormier's fascination for the nature of human confrontation with the Implacable? All of the three villians are vulnerable, and if they cannot quite be placated, they can at least be manipulated. They are quick to see each other's weaknesses and quick to take advantage of them for more secure positions of power. Leon has put himself in a shaky place by his overreaching ambition, and Archie sees him "riddled with cracks and crevices—running scared—open to invasion." Archie fears Leon's power over him as his teacher, and his domination of the Vigils is dependent on thinking up ever more imaginative assignments. And then there is the black box—a nemesis over which he has no control. Emile's weakness is his stupidity; he is easily conned by Archie into believing in the imaginary photograph. So none of the three is an implacable, unconquerable force; all are subject to fears and weaknesses.

Why then does Jerry's lone refusal seem so very doomed from the beginning? Why does the contest seem so unequal; why does the action move so inevitably toward tragedy? The answer lies in the nature of what it is he is saying "no" to. What he is opposing is not Brother Leon, not Archie, not Emile, but the monstrous force that moves them, of which they are but imperfect human agents. The Goober gives it a name: " 'There's something rotten in that school. More than rotten.' He groped for the word and found it but didn't want to use it. The word didn't fit the surroundings, the sun and the bright October afternoon. It was a midnight word, a howling wind word." The word is *evil.*

The unholy trinity of Trinity are studies in the human forms of evil. Brother Leon, who as a priest is supposedly an agent of the Divine, has sold his soul for power, even down to his exultation in the small nasty tyrannies of the classroom. Cormier has said [in Alleen Pace Nilsen's article "The Poetry of Naming in Young Adult Books" in *ALAN Review*] that he chose the name Leon, a bland, soft name, to match the brother's superficial blandness. "And so is evil bland in its many disguises," he adds. Leon's appearance is deceptive: "On the surface, he was one of those pale, ingratiating kind of men who tiptoed through life on small, quick feet." "In the classroom Leon was another person altogether. Smirking, sarcastic. His thin, high voice venomous. He could hold your attention like a cobra. Instead of fangs, he used his teacher's pointer, flicking out here, there, everywhere." Leon's skin is pale, damp, and his moist eyes are like boiled onions or specimens in laboratory test tubes. When he blackmails Caroni into revealing Jerry's motivation, his fingers holding the chalk are like "the legs of pale spiders with a victim in their clutch." After he has demolished the boy, the chalk lies broken, "abandoned on the desk, like white bones, dead men's bones." The image that gradually accumulates around Leon is that of a hideous, colorless insect, a poisonous insect, crawling damp from its hiding place under a rock. Or perhaps he has emerged from even deeper underground, as Jerry suspects when he sees "a glimpse into the hell that was burning inside the teacher."

Archie is far subtler and will utimately, when he is an adult, be more dangerous, because he is not in bondage to ambition. True, he revels in the captive audience of the Vigils, but he is not really part of that or any political structure. "I am Archie" he gloats, Archie alone. For him, the pleasure is in building intricate evil structures for their own sake. "Beautiful!" he cries as Brother Eugene falls apart like the furniture in his room, as Leon squirms under the pressure of Jerry's refusal, as Jerry struggles ever deeper into the exitless trap Archie has made for him. Yet, Archie, too, is in hell, the hell of understanding only the dark side of human nature. "People are two things," he tells Carter. "Greedy and cruel." From this knowledge comes his strength, his ability to make anybody do anything. But it is bottomless emptiness. "Life is shit," he says without emotion.

Emile is the purest embodiment of evil. In him we see the horror of evil's essential quality: silliness. Emile loves to "reach" people. He giggles when he leaves a mess in the public toilet, when he secretly gives an already-tackled football player an extra jab, when he loudly accuses a shy kid of farting on a crowded bus. Essentially evil is pointless. Purpose and structure belong to goodness; evil can only turn back on itself in chaos. Archie and Leon have clothed their evil with intelligence and worldly power, but Emile's surrender to darkness is revealed in all its terrible nakedness. The others recognize his nonhumanity quite clearly. "An animal," they call him.

Archie is amused by Emile's simplicity but also chilled by the recognition of a kinship he is not willing to acknowledge. Emile, however, in his perverse innocence, easily sees that he and Archie are "birds of a feather," and that their differences are only a matter of intelligence. An even more terrible innocence is that of the children whom Emile recruits to ambush Jerry. "Animals," he calls them in turn, and they emerge crouching from the bushes to do his bidding like the twittering hordes of little devils in a painting by Hieronymus Bosch.

Both Archie and Emile have cross-wired their sexual energies into sadism. Emile wishes he could tell Archie how he sometimes feels "horny" when he does a particularly vicious thing. The sources of Archie's most maliciously creative ideas are found in his sexual energy, as Cormier made clear in a chapter that was never printed. In these deleted pages Archie, backed into a corner by thinking of Jerry's recalcitrance, attempts to masturbate, but his powerlessness against the situation renders him impotent. Finally he gets the glimmering of an idea—and an erection—and conceives the scheme for the boxing match that will destroy Jerry at the same moment that he achieves his climax. The chapter is stunning in its sensuality, but Cormier [as he admits in "The Cheerful Side of Controversy,"], on the advice of his editor and because he found he was reluctant to allow his own daughter to read it, removed it from the final manuscript.

All three villains are completely devoid of any sense of guilt. Indeed, Archie often congratulates himself on his compassion. Brother Leon is all surface; his soul is hollow, and he is the one character whose interior monologue we never hear. Repentance is totally foreign to him. Emile is even a bit defensive at being defined as a bad guy. "All right, so he liked to screw around a little, get under people's skin. That was human nature, wasn't it? A guy had to protect himself at all times. Get them before they get you. Keep people guessing—and afraid."

In chapter 4 Brother Leon mentions that Archie's father "operates an insurance business." This one shred of information is all we know about Archie's background. What could the home life of such a monster be? For that matter, what parent could live with Emile? Does Brother Leon have an aged mother somewhere? What were they all like as children? The questions are intriguing but pointless. [In "Interview with Robert Cormier" in *Lion and the Unicorn*] Cormier deliberately gives us no hint of the origins of their devotion to darkness. "People can't say Archie did this because he was

a deprived child or he was a victim of child abuse. I wanted him judged solely on his actions." To understand is to forgive, and to forgive real evil is to make alliance with it. To render these characters psychologically understandable would be to humanize them, to undermine their stature as instruments of darkness, and therefore to erase the theme of opposition to the Implacable.

For those who would turn their eyes away from the ultimate and prefer a smaller and more comfortable theme, Cormier has thoughtfully provided an alternative. It is possible to view the book as an examination of tyranny. The pattern overlaps but is not identical. Seen this way, the trinity has a different cast. There are three structures of misused power: the school, as headed by Brother Leon; the athletic department, as headed by the coach; and the mob, as headed by Archie. Each has a passive assistant to tyranny, characters who have decent impulses but are ineffectual because they lack the courage to act. Obie is Archie's reluctant stooge; Carter agrees with the coach's approval of violence; and Brother Jacques despises Leon but condones his actions by not opposing. Shadowy outlines of the government, the military, and the Church might appear in this interpretation.

The question ultimately turns back, no matter whether tyranny or absolute evil is the enemy, to "How can we resist?" If evil had inherent power, there would be no answer. But Leon, Archie, and Emile all find their power source in their victim's own weaknesses. Leon even plays contemptuously with it in the classroom, when he tells the boys that they have become Nazi Germany by their fearful silence. Emile has very early discovered that most people want peace at any price and will accept almost any embarrassment or harassment rather than take a stand or make a fuss. "Nobody wanted trouble, nobody wanted to make trouble, nobody wanted a showdown." Archie, too, has realized that "the world was made up of two kinds of people—those who were victims and those who victimized." But the moment Jerry, of his own volition, refuses to sell the chocolates, he steps outside this cynical definition. In that is the source of hope.

Jerry at first has no idea why he has said no. "He'd wanted to end the ordeal—and then that terrible *No* had issued out of his mouth." But Jerry's life has been "like a yawning cavity in his chest" since his mother's death. His father is sleepwalking through his days, a man for whom everything and nothing is "Fine!," a pharmacist who once wanted to be a doctor and now denies even that such an ambition ever existed. Like Prufrock, he is too numb to live and too afraid to act. When Jerry looks into the mirror he is appalled to see his father's face reflected in his own features. The hippie and the poster dare him to disturb the universe, and when he finally says no he is taking a stand against far more than a chocolate sale. And it is Brother Leon himself who has taught Jerry that not to resist is to assist.

Jerry is the *only one* who has learned that lesson, and this is what makes his destruction inevitable. Evil is implacable and merciless to a lone hero, in spite of the folk myth to the contrary. But could it have turned out differently? What if the marble had been black? Or Jerry's first blow had knocked Emile out? But these would have been arbitrary tamperings by the author. Ironically, the key to the real triumph of good comes again from Brother Leon. If others had joined Jerry.... There are a number of places in the story where this might have happened. The Goober, of course, is often on the verge of acting on his friendship for Jerry, but in the end, like Hamlet, he only thinks, and doesn't act until too late. For a moment he even hopes that it will all end in a stalemate. The Goober speaks for all the others in wanting to avoid confrontation at any cost. Obie might have acted on his disgust for Archie: "I owe you one for that!" he thinks when pushed too far. In the end he settles only for hoping that fate will punish Archie with a black marble. Carter, too, might have used his simple strength to end it.

Any of these isolated actions might have started the group movement that would have saved Jerry and defeated Leon and the Vigils. Even without such a spur the school comes close to following Jerry's example at the midpoint in the sale. But the motivation is negative—they are tired of selling and selfishly individual—"let each one do his own thing." Without a conscious joining together for the good of all, they can easily be maneuvered separately back into doing the Vigils' will.

So here at last is Cormier's meaning. As [Renee Hoxie] has written [in a letter in *Wilson Library Bulletin*], "Jerry's defeat is unimportant. What is important is that he made the choice and that he stood firm for his convictions." Only by making that gesture can we hold on to our humanity, even when defeat is inevitable. But there is more—when the agents of evil are other human beings, perhaps good can win if enough people have the courage to take a stand together. Evil alliances are built with uneasy mutual distrust, but

only goodness can join humans with the self-transcending strength of sympathy and love.

Source: Patricia J. Campbell, "The Chocolate War," in *Presenting Robert Cormier,* revised edition, Twayne Publishers, 1989, pp. 40–51.

Sources

Norma Bagnall, "Realism: How Realistic Is It? A Look at *The Chocolate War,*" in *Top of the News,* Vol. 36, no. 2, Winter, 1980, pp. 214-17.

Fred Inglis, "Love And Death In Children's Novels," in his *The Promise Of Happiness: Value And Meaning in Children's Fiction,* Cambridge University Press, 1981, pp. 271-291.

Sylvia Patterson Iskander, "Robert Cormier," in *Concise Dictionary of American Literary Biography: Broadening Views 1968-1988,* Gale, 1989, pp. 34-51.

Nancy Veglahn, article in *The Lion And The Unicorn: A Critical Journal of Children's Literature,* June, 1988, pp. 12-18.

For Further Study

Authors and Artists for Young Adults, Vol. 19, Gale, 1996, pp. 65-76.
> A full-length sketch which includes useful summaries of Cormier's other books and ample reference to contemporary reviews.

Betty Carter and Karen Harris, "Realism in Adolescent Fiction: In Defense of *The Chocolate War,*" in *Top of the News,* Vol. 36, No. 3, Spring, 1980, pp. 283-85.
> A direct response to Norma Bagnall's essay in the previous edition of the journal.

Paul Heins, review of *I Am the Cheese,* in *The Horn Book Magazine,* Vol. LIII, No. 4, August, 1977, pp. 427-28.
> Heins, reviewing Cormier's next book after *The Chocolate War,* calls it "a novel in the tragic mode, cunningly wrought, shattering in its emotional implications."

Anne Scott MacLeod, "Robert Cormier and the Adolescent Novel," in *Children's Literature in Education,* Vol. 12, No. 2, Summer, 1981, pp. 74-81.
> An attempt to portray Cormier as a political novelist.

Anita Silvey, in an interview with Robert Cormier, Part I, in *The Horn Book Magazine,* Vol. LXI, No. 2, March-April, 1985, pp. 145-55.
> In this interview Cormier discusses his initial resistance to writing a sequel to *The Chocolate War.*

Joe Stines, "Robert Cormier," in *Dictionary of Literary Biography, Volume 52: American Writers for Children since 1960,* Gale, 1986, pp. 107-14.
> The entry covers all Cormier's work up to 1985, including his three early adult novels, and includes a page from the penultimate draft of *Beyond The Chocolate War,* showing the author's corrections.

Dinner at the Homesick Restaurant

Anne Tyler

1982

Critics generally consider *Dinner at the Homesick Restaurant,* Anne Tyler's ninth novel, to be among her best work. It won the PEN/Faulkner Award for fiction and was nominated for a National Book Critics Circle award and the 1983 Pulitzer Prize. Also a commercial success, it has to date sold more than 60,000 copies in hardcover and more than 655,000 in paperback. Published in 1982, the medium-length fiction spans several decades in the history of the Tull family of Baltimore, Maryland. Often compared to William Faulkner's novel *As I Lay Dying,* the narrative begins with 85-year-old Pearl Tull, blind and on her deathbed, attempting to reconcile with her role as a deserted wife and single parent. Will her three grown children— Cody, Jenny, and Ezra—forgive her for sometimes being a physically and verbally abusive mother? Told from alternating points of view, *Dinner at the Homesick Restaurant* is ultimately about how growing up in an unconventional, turbulent family affected three children in very different ways.

Although many critics considered the novel less optimistic than her other work, it drew much praise for its psychological insight, rich characterization, well-developed plot structure, and impressive handling of multiple points of view. Like many of her other novels—including *Earthly Possessions, Searching for Caleb,* and *The Accidental Tourist*—*Dinner at the Homesick Restaurant* is about the burden of a person's past, be it personal, familial, or historical.

Author Biography

Anne Tyler was born on October 25, 1941, in Minneapolis, Minnesota, to chemist Lloyd Parry Tyler and social worker Phyllis Mahon Tyler. The daughter of Quakers, hers was a somewhat nomadic childhood, living in such places as Chicago; Duluth, Minnesota; and Cleo, North Carolina (in which her family lived in an experimental collective community in the mountains). When Anne was eleven, her family settled in Raleigh, North Carolina. Adapting to this relatively cosmopolitan environment did not come easily, since up until that time, the young girl was unfamiliar with such conveniences as the telephone. Tyler ultimately adjusted, sometimes doing field work on tobacco plantations and observing the quirks and dialects of her coworkers. In high school, she planned to become a book illustrator. Phyllis Peacock, one of her English teachers, also instructed Reynolds Price, who became a successful novelist and a friend of Tyler's.

Attending Duke University on full scholarship, Tyler took a writing course taught by Reynolds Price and majored in Russian. In 1961, she graduated Phi Beta Kappa with a B.A. and briefly pursued graduate work at Columbia University. From 1962 to 1963, Tyler worked as a Russian bibliographer at Duke University; in May, 1963, she married the Iranian medical student and novelist Taghi Mohammed Modaressi. While her husband completed his residency at McGill University in Montreal, Tyler took a job as the assistant to the librarian of McGill's Law Library.

In Montreal, Tyler wrote her first two novels, *If Morning Ever Comes* (1964) and *The Tin Can Tree* (1965), neither of which received much critical attention. However, the critics who took notice praised the author's maturity and anticipated her future success. By the time Tyler had published her fifth novel, *Celestial Navigation* (1974), critics such as Gail Godwin and John Updike agreed she was a literary force to be reckoned with. With the publication of *Dinner at the Homesick Restaurant* (1982), her place as one of the best and most significant American novelists of her generation seemed secure. In addition to several novels, more than fifty of Anne Tyler's short stories have been published to date.

Along the way, Tyler has received countless literary awards, including the *Mademoiselle* award for writing (1966); Award for Literature, American Academy and Institute of Arts and Letters, (1977);

Anne Tyler

Janet Heidinger Kafka prize (1981), PEN/Faulkner Award for Fiction (1983), and the Pulitzer Prize for Fiction (1989). With the latter award and the 1990 motion picture *The Accidental Tourist*—based on Tyler's novel of the same name—some of the writer's popularity has spread into the American mainstream.

While not an easy author to categorize, Tyler has often been described as a Southern writer, setting her early novels in the South, and is frequently compared to William Faulkner and Eudora Welty. In spite of her great productivity, she remains something of an enigma: an extremely private person who grants few interviews and shuns most public appearances.

Plot Summary

Part I: Pearl

Dinner at the Homesick Restaurant is the story of the Tull family of Baltimore, Maryland, told first from the perspective of Pearl Tull, and then from the perspective of each of her children, Cody, Ezra, and Jennifer. Because the novel is told from differing points of view, readers often witness the same event several times, with different emphasis.

Chapter One, "Something You Should Know," opens as Pearl Tull lies dying in her Baltimore home. Her son Ezra sits next to her. She recalls her life, not in chronological order, but in the way memory works, one memory sparking the next. She begins by recalling how she had almost lost her oldest son Cody as a baby and that near loss was the catalyst for her having more children. From this memory, she moves farther back in time and recollects meeting and marrying Beck Tull, a traveling salesman. Pearl was thirty at the time, nearing spinsterhood. Her marriage did not turn out as she had planned. Beck moved the family from place to place and neither Pearl nor her children were able to form connections with other people. Finally, Beck tells Pearl that he does not want to be married any longer, and he leaves the family, now settled in Baltimore. Pearl finds herself a single mother with children aged fourteen, eleven, and nine. In order to keep up the appearance of a normal marriage, Pearl lies to her children, family, and friends, saying Beck is away on business. Pearl recalls a time when the family was together in the country and Beck was teaching Cody how to use his new bow and arrow. Cody accidentally shoots his mother in shoulder. The wound festers; when Pearl has it treated, she nearly dies from an allergy to penicillin.

Amidst the memories of her younger days and of her children's childhoods, Pearl surfaces into the present periodically. At these times, she thinks about her own impending death, her funeral (and how surprised Beck will be when he is invited), and her adult children. She wonders if her children blame her for something and she thinks that there must be something wrong with each of her children. As the chapter closes, Pearl drifts off. Whether she drifts to sleep, or to death, we cannot tell at this moment.

Part II: The Family

Each of the next chapters of *Dinner at the Homesick Restaurant* is a self-contained unit, told from the point of view of one of the children. Taken together, they allow the reader to follow each of the children through adulthood. Cody's story opens before his father has left, on the day that Cody accidentally shoots his mother with an arrow when Ezra interferes with his aim. From here the competition Cody feels with Ezra grows. Over the years, Cody engages in an unending series of sneaky tricks to get Ezra in trouble. Ezra remains largely unconscious of the practical jokes played on him by his brother. Nevertheless, when Pearl goes on one of

her periodic "rampages," it is Cody who attempts to protect the younger children from Pearl's violence.

As an adult, Cody continues to feel jealousy toward Ezra. Eventually, he meets, woos, and marries Ruth Spivey, the woman engaged to Ezra. Even after marrying Ruth, Cody is jealous of Ezra and so he moves Ruth and their son Luke away from Baltimore, rarely writing and even more rarely visiting.

Jenny's story begins at the time when she is about to find herself as the only child at home. Cody is off to college, and Ezra has been drafted. She is uneasy; although her mother seems to treat her more kindly now, Jenny still fears her mother's abuse.

Jenny eventually leaves home for college. While there, she meets Harley Baines, a genius geneticist. They marry just as Jenny begins medical school. The marriage soon fails and Jenny finds herself back in Baltimore. Jenny remarries an artist who leaves her several months before their daughter Becky is born. Finally, Jenny, now a pediatrician, marries a man with six children whose wife has abandoned him.

Ezra's story centers around his work at Scarlatti's Restaurant. When Mrs. Scarlatti dies, she leaves the restaurant to Ezra, who renames it The Homesick Restaurant. Here he prepares the kind of food that people are homesick for, the kind of food that they had at home. Ezra always tries to arrange dinners for his family at the restaurant; however, someone in the family always ruins his best plans by exploding with anger and walking out.

After losing his fiancee to his brother Cody, Ezra never marries and becomes the chief caretaker for his mother, Pearl, whose eyesight and health are failing. Often, Ezra reads his mother's diary entries and describes old photographs to Pearl, who seems to be searching for something. Pearl finally seems to be satisfied when Ezra reads her a particular diary entry:

> "Early this morning … I went out behind the house to weed. Was kneeling in the dirt by the stable with my pinafore a mess and the perspiration rolling down my back, wiped my face on my sleeve, reached for the trowel and all at once thought, Why, I believe that at just this moment I am absolutely happy."

> His mother stopped rocking and grew very still.

> "The Bedloe girls' piano scales were floating out her window," he read, "and a bottle fly was buzzing in the grass, and I saw that I was kneeling on such a beautiful green little planet. I don't care what else

might come about. I have had this moment. It belongs to me."

That was the end of the entry. He fell silent.

"Thank you, Ezra," his mother said. "There's no need to read anymore."

Part III: Dinner at the Homesick Restaurant

The concluding chapter of the book opens with the news of Pearl's death, told from Cody's point of view. All the members of Pearl's family gather for her funeral, and Cody discovers that Ezra has invited their father to attend. After the funeral ends, an old man approaches Cody, who suddenly recognizes him as their father. All of the Tulls, including the long-absent Beck, head to The Homesick Restaurant for the funeral dinner. This time it is Cody who loses his temper. "You think we're a family," Cody says to his father. "You think we're some jolly, situation-comedy family when we're in particles, torn apart, torn all over the place, and our mother was a witch." Beck disappears when everyone's attention is suddenly drawn to Jenny's husband's baby, who is choking. After Jenny saves the baby, they realize Beck is gone. All but Cody rush out into the street to try to find Beck. Ironically, it is Cody who finds his father when he finally goes to look. In the moments they spend together before the rest of the family finds them, Beck tells Cody the story of his marriage and why he left them. As Cody looks down the street, he sees the members of his family rushing toward him. He finds himself "surprised and touched. He felt that they were pulling him toward them—that it wasn't they who were traveling, but Cody himself." For the first time, Cody is drawn to his family; the book closes with his memory of his mother and with his memory of the archery trip.

Characters

Harley Baines

Harley is the first of Jenny Tull's three husbands. Intellectual Harley shares at least one similarity with his mother-in-law, Pearl: They are both obsessively organized. For example, Harley arranges his textbooks "by height and blocks of color." A minor, comical character.

Becky

Unable to properly handle the pressures of medical school, Jenny vents her frustrations by

Media Adaptations

- A 1985 audio recording of *Dinner at the Homesick Restaurant* is available on two cassettes from Random House Audio.

- Another of Tyler's novels, *The Accidental Tourist,* was filmed in 1988 with William Hurt, Kathleen Turner, and Geena Davis (who won an Oscar for her role). The film also was cited by the New York Film Critics as best film, and is available from Warner Home Video.

physically and emotionally abusing her only biological child, Becky. Fortunately, Jenny realizes the damage she is inflicting and enlists the aid of Pearl to temporarily care for her young daughter. Becky grows up to develop some eating disorders (like her mother once had), but whether this is due to heredity or environment is left unexplained in the novel.

Emmaline

One of Pearl Tull's few close friends, Emmaline is the only woman with whom Pearl almost shares her secret that Beck has abandoned her and the children.

Mrs. Parkins

The fortune teller who convinces Jenny to marry her first husband.

Josiah Payson

Ezra's slow-witted but sweet friend from childhood, Josiah becomes a cook at The Homesick Restaurant. Jenny befriends him while Ezra is away from home, but when Pearl catches them in a potentially romantic situation, she slaps Jenny and cruelly calls Josiah, "A crazy! A dummy! A retarded person."

Mrs. Scarlatti

Something of a surrogate mother to Ezra Tull, Mrs. Scarlatti is the owner of Scarlatti's Restaurant. Originally, she is Ezra's boss; ultimately he becomes her business partner. She leaves the entire restaurant property to him after she dies. (He then changes its name to The Homesick Restaurant.) Unlike Pearl, Ezra's biological mother, Mrs. Scarlatti is a relaxed, flexible woman. When she is dying and Ezra changes the restaurant's atmosphere, she initially takes offense, but ultimately reconciles to his vision.

Joe St. Ambrose

Jenny Tull's third husband, a man whose former wife abandoned him and their large family. Despite this tragedy, Joe remains a pleasant, friendly person. The novel implies that Jenny marries him mostly because she loves nurturing his needy children.

Slevin St. Ambrose

One of Jenny Tull's stepchildren, an intelligent but troubled teenager. Emotionally withdrawn, Slevin has difficulty accepting Jenny as his new mother until he learns that Jenny's father abandoned her just as Slevin's mother abandoned him.

Beck Tull

A salesman by profession, Beck Tull is the handsome, psychologically fragile man who rescues the thirty-year-old Pearl from probable spinsterhood. The novel implies her family is of a higher socioeconomic status than his. After more than fifteen years of marriage and three children (Cody, Jenny, and Ezra), he abandons his wife and family, prompting Pearl to insightfully refer to him as "the invisible presence. The absent presence." A family outing, in which Cody and Ezra quarrel over an archery set and Pearl is almost killed by a wayward arrow, precipitates Beck's leaving—a cause and effect relationship that Beck only acknowledges at the end of the novel. With the terse announcement that he doesn't "want to stay married" and that he "won't be visiting the children," Beck walks out. Understandably, Beck's departure had an enormous, lasting effect on Pearl and their children, although they all reacted in very different ways.

At the conclusion of *Dinner at the Homesick Restaurant,* Beck explains his departure as a reaction to his incapacity to deal with "the grayness, grayness of things; half-right-and-half-wrongness of things." Although he is not really a malevolent character, his behavior is probably the cruelest unconscious event in the novel.

Cody Tull

Elder son of Pearl and Beck Tull and brother to Ezra and Jenny, Cody is probably the least sympathetic character in the novel. He also dominates the novel in that Tyler dedicates more chapters to his point of view than to any other character. A troubled childhood (a father who deserted the family, a physically and verbally abusive mother) contributed to some of his worst character traits—meanness, greed, and jealousy (particularly in regard to Ezra, their mother's favorite child).

But it would be simplistic to blame all of his character faults to victimization; after all, Ezra and Jenny turned into nice people. Part of Cody's problems result from his unspoken guilt over his father's departure. Fourteen at the time, he wonders "Was it something I said? Was it something I did? Was it something I didn't do, that made you go away?" He is not to blame here, but since he does not articulate his feelings, nobody in the family understands the extent of his guilt.

Another explanation for Cody's emotional development lies in a need to dominate others; in doing so, he is as domineering as his father was unreliable. He becomes a very successful efficiency expert, an ideal profession for a control-oriented person who doesn't enjoy the present moment. He buys his mother the Baltimore row house which she formerly rented, not out of love, but rather as one more way of competing with Ezra for her affection. The teenaged Cody engineers a variety of schemes to make his tranquil, non-competitive brother look foolish, but by far his cruelest action as an adult is marrying Ruth, his brother's fiancee. That he does not even really like Ruth is more evidence of Cody's obsessive competition to win the love of a mother whom he once called "a raving, shrieking, unpredictable witch." By the conclusion of the novel, Cody, in a face-to-face conversation with the father he hasn't seen in over three decades, learns the truth about his father's abandonment and somewhat reconciles with his bad behavior and history of hurt and anger.

Ezra Tull

Many critics and readers consider Ezra Tull—the younger son of Pearl and Beck Tull and brother to Cody and Jenny—to be the novel's most sympathetic character. Clearly his mother's pet, Ezra as an adult minimizes the abusive side of Pearl's nature. After Cody, at the final family dinner, describes the recently deceased Pearl as "a raving, shrieking, unpredictable witch," Ezra defends her: " ... she wasn't always angry. Really, she was angry very seldom, only a few times widely spaced ...." Many instances of his warmth and generosity exist: he is the only family member to care for the dying Pearl; he tends to Mrs. Scarlatti, his business partner, when she is dying; he befriends the oddball Josiah; he arranges the reunion between Beck and the Tull family; he even refuses to bear a grudge when Cody steals Ruth, the woman whom Ezra loved and intended to marry.

However, Ezra's tendency to see only the sunny side of life often renders him passive. When he as a middle-aged man discovers a possibly malignant lump on his right thigh, his first reaction is "All right. Let it happen. I'll go ahead and die." Unlike his siblings, he never attended college, never married, in fact never really left home, having always shared a house with his mother. Yet ironically, when Ezra witnesses the feeble side of Pearl, he is less affectionate than usual: "He trusted his mother to be everything for him. When she cut her finger with a paring knife, he had felt defeated by her incompetence."

Throughout the novel Ezra strives to have one uninterrupted family dinner at his restaurant—The Homesick Restaurant—but someone, often Pearl, always destroys the continuity by departing early. Unable to achieve this feat until the novel's conclusion, Ezra extends his affection to his neighbors and co-workers.

Jenny Tull

Jenny Tull is the only daughter of Pearl and Beck Tull and sister to Cody and Ezra. Like her brothers, she suffered the desertion of her father as a child and occasional rages of physical and psychological abuse from her mother. Like Cody and to a lesser extent Ezra, she recalls the painful events of childhood, most of which revolve around her mother. At one point, she recalls her mother as a shrieking witch whose "pale hair could crackle electrically from its bun" and whose "eyes could get small as hatpins." She remembered her mother slamming her against a wall more than once and denigrating her as "cockroach" and "hideous little sniveling guttersnipe." Some of her memories manifest themselves in her dreams, particularly one in which Pearl says in an "informative and considerate tone of voice," that "she was raising Jenny to eat her."

Jenny, however, is far from a self-pitying victim. She goes to college and becomes a competent pediatrician. While none of her three marriages are particularly happy, Jenny is able to raise her stepchildren (who have been deserted by their natural mother) with warmth and efficiency. As a pediatrician, she is sort of surrogate parent to many of her clients.

Having witnessed the worst of her mother as a child, Jenny realizes they have some things in common. Like Pearl, Jenny entered into her first marriage out of recklessness, a sense of adventure. Both are intelligent, intense women with some proclivities toward child abuse under stressful situations. Unlike Pearl, Jenny realizes these tendencies early on and turns her only child over to Pearl— ironically enough—when Jenny cannot take care of her. Determined to be a happier person, Jenny decides to "make it through on a slant. She was trying to lose her intensity." Although she is a generally sympathetic character, Jenny has some flaws. She often jokes her way out of real problems, for example, when her stepson Slevin is having difficulty in school. When her third husband, Joe, suggests they have more children, she intentionally refuses to believe he is serious. Despite such shortcomings, Jenny is a good example of a character who has overcome a difficult childhood and does not reduce herself to a victim.

Luke Tull

The son of Cody and Ruth Tull, Luke is smart enough to understand some of his father's ulterior motives. For example, Luke realizes that the bus ticket which teenaged Cody bought for Pearl was less a gift to her than a means to keep her away during Ezra's birthday. Understanding that Cody obsesses over bitter memories, he comments, "What are you, crazy? How come you go on hanging on to these things, year after year after year?" Physically, he is a combination of Beck, Cody, and Ezra Tull, but temperamentally, he is more rational than any of them. Some critics have written that Luke represents the hope that future generations may break cycles of ill will or bad habits.

Pearl Tull

The matriarch of the Tull clan, Pearl is a rather complex character, not simply "a witch" as two of her children have occasionally described her. Born into a good family, Pearl married fairly late in life to Beck Tull, a handsome farm equipment salesman. Although the union spared her from spinsterhood, she resented having to move every time her husband was transferred at work. Wherever she and her husband settled, Pearl kept herself isolated from the community, a pattern that continued throughout her life. Early in *Dinner at the Homesick*

Anne Tyler, at home in Montreal, 1965.

Restaurant, Beck abandons her and their children, with little more explanation than that he doesn't "want to be married" any longer and that he "won't be visiting the children."

There is actually as much to admire in Pearl as there to detest. First, she is extremely independent and resourceful, sometimes to the detriment of herself. For example, as a young woman, she spurns a college education, because that would be "an admission of defeat." When she suffers a broken arm, Pearl waits almost 48 hours to get medical assistance because she doesn't want to leave the children with the neighbors. When Beck de-

parts, Pearl doesn't succumb to self-pity; she finds an uninteresting job as a cashier at a grocery store and determines to raise the children single-handedly. A fastidious housekeeper and a perfectionist, she is ultimately as tough on herself as on her children. Yet with her children, she is sometimes too tough, physically and psychologically abusing them in uncontrollable fits of anger. As she is dying, she categorizes Cody, Jenny, and Ezra as "duckers and drafters," and remembers herself as "an angry sort of mother" who was "continually on edge ... too burdened ... too alone." She wonders if her children will forgive her for being a less than satisfactory parent. In short, Pearl has set impossibly high standards for herself that nobody could satisfy without some assistance, and she is usually too proud to request help.

Ironically, in middle age, Pearl partly redeems herself as a parent by caring for Jenny's daughter when Jenny simply cannot. She also loses some of her anger as she makes the transition from middle age to old age. She possesses much insight into her family. For example, on one occasion, Pearl likens her children's growing up with the "gradual dimming of light at her bedroom door, as if they took some radiance with them as they moved away from her." Her description of her favorite child, Ezra, ("so sweet and clumsy it could break your heart") captures his disposition perfectly.

Ruth Tull

Originally a cook in The Homesick Restaurant and fiancee to Ezra Tull, she ultimately marries his brother Cody after he pursues her relentlessly. A homely woman with a poor self-image, Ruth is initially suspicious of Cody's attention. Pearl, however, is the only one who grasps Cody's real motivation: to steal away his brother's bride-to-be simply for the sport, the competition. Despite her lack of self-confidence, Ruth is in some ways smarter than her husband, Cody. For instance, while he is attracted to the glamour of owning a farm, she knows what hard work it really requires.

Sam Wiley

Sam Wiley is Jenny Tull's second husband. Jenny describes him as "the one she loved best." A handsome painter, he abandons Jenny when she is pregnant with Becky. It is implied the marriage failed because it required too much passion.

Themes

Alienation and Loneliness

The related themes of alienation and loneliness permeate this novel about the impact of a father's desertion on his wife and family. In the pivotal character of Pearl Tull, Tyler gives us an extremely alienated individual, at least in the sense of being alienated from her community. After Beck deserts her (after more than fifteen years of marriage), she determines to raise her three children single-handedly, without the slightest assistance from anyone in the neighborhood. Since she can't even confide in her close friend Emmaline that her husband

Topics for Further Study

- Discuss the changes that have occurred in the American family's structure from 1930 to the present. Compare and contrast the Tull family against different American families today.

- Explore the ways in which individuals can prevent child abuse and how to deal with it if it occurs.

- Discuss the heredity versus environment question. How much of who we are is determined by genes, and how much is determined by our home environment? Give some examples of specific scientific studies to support your position.

abandoned her, Pearl obviously won't let on to the neighbors. Further, she refuses to discuss the desertion with her children; hence, they are left with the temporary impression that their salesman-father is away on a trip. While Pearl takes pride in her psychology ("They never asked about him. Didn't that show how little importance a father has?... Apparently, she had carried this off—made the transition so smoothly that not a single person guessed. It was the greatest triumph of her life."), the damage of not drawing out her children's true feelings is evident throughout the novel. While today a single-parent family is no longer unusual, it was rather atypical in suburban America in the 1940s and 1950s when the Tull children were growing up.

Pearl's standoffishness has this effect on her eldest son, Cody: "What he wouldn't give to have a mother who acted like other mothers! He longed to see her gossiping with a gang of women in the kitchen.... He wished he had some outside connection, something beyond this suffocating house." Despite being brought up in such an isolated home, Jenny and Ezra as adults are responsible, caring members of their communities. Ezra, in particular, conveys sincere affection for his neighbors and his business associates, never angling for personal gain in the manner of his older brother.

Growth and Development

To what extent do the three Tull children reconcile with their troubled childhood? To what extent do they transcend it? Tyler addresses these rather complex questions in her novel but does not arrive at firm answers. First, Jenny, through the distance of time, realizes she has acquired some of her mother's good and bad character traits (e.g., her orderliness, intelligence, intensity, yet also her tendencies toward child abuse during stressful situations). She gradually but deliberately develops a more relaxed, humorous disposition, becoming a generally happier person in the process but also sacrificing some passion for members of her immediate family.

Ezra, on the other hand, remains something of a child well into middle age: Unmarried, childless, still living with his mother, and never having known real sexual passion (he courts his fiancee, Ruth, in a nearly platonic manner before Cody steals her away), he discerns something missing in his life. "Let it be" is the theme that dominates his existence. He sees himself as being "ruled by a dreamy mood of acceptance that was partly the source of all his happiness and partly his undoing." As Mary Ellis Gibson has written in *Southern Literary Journal*, "Ezra is the most thorough fatalist in *Dinner at the Homesick Restaurant*." Even so, he develops some coping skills. Mrs. Scarlatti, a woman much more traditionally maternal than Pearl, comes to see Ezra as a surrogate son; Ezra also gives and reciprocates strong affection to many non-family members, including his nephew Luke and his misfit friend Josiah Payson. Perhaps most important, he channels a great deal of his energy and love into making his restaurant a friendly, homey environment—if not necessarily a financial success.

Finally, Cody, the most aggressive of the Tull children, remains as competitive in adulthood as in childhood; stealing his brother's girlfriend, working diligently to be financially successful, maneuvering to win the maternal warmth that he has already had for many years (Pearl feels affection toward him but does not show it often or well.) None of the above brings much happiness to Cody, who remains guilt-ridden, angry, and confused about his motivations until the conclusion of the novel when he confronts the father who left him more than thirty years ago. In that scene, Cody achieves a sort of epiphany, at least partly understanding his actions and reactions in a troubled past.

Even Pearl, perhaps the least likely family candidate for transformation, undergoes some change. She redeems herself somewhat by becoming a much better grandparent than she was a mother and allowing her children as adults to make their own decisions and mistakes. She may not approve of Jenny making three less-than-satisfactory marriages, but she does not interfere to the extent she once did. Toward the end of her long life, she reminisces calmly—not consumed by her former rage—about her life and three children. While she still believes that "something was wrong with all of her children," and "wondered if her children blamed her for something," Pearl does not have the real desire to pursue the matter and quietly dies.

Style

Point of View

One of the principal strengths of *Dinner at the Homesick Restaurant* is that it is told from so many different points of views so effectively. Of the novel's ten chapters, two belong to Pearl, two to Jenny, two to Ezra, three to Cody, and one to Cody's son, Luke. Each of the chapters reveals something unique or unusual about the character from whose point of view dominates. As a result of alternating the narration, the reader understands the main characters better than they understand themselves.

Setting

The setting for *Dinner at the Homesick Restaurant* is mostly Baltimore, Maryland, a city that figures prominently in many Tyler novels. Pearl has spent most of her adult life there; Ezra has lived almost all of his life in this city; Jenny, with the exception of her college and medical school years, is a Baltimorean; only the nomadic Cody, whose jobs and upward mobility require much travel and moving, spends considerably less time in Baltimore. The time frame of the novel covers roughly fifty-five years, from the middle 1920s—the time of Pearl's marriage—to 1979, the year of her death. This period of more than half a century allows Tyler to richly develop the motivations, complexities, contradictions, and nuances of her main characters.

Symbolism

The title of the novel refers to Ezra's restaurant, an eating place he inherited from his business partner, Mrs. Scarlatti. As many critics have stressed, "homesick" has many different meanings. It can mean "sick for home" (this best applies to Jenny), "sick at home" (Ezra), and "sick from home" (Cody). The concept of time is symbolic for time management consultant Cody, who often desires to escape from unpleasant moments in the present by stepping into pleasant past moments. "If only Einstein were right and time were a kind of river you could choose to step into at any place along the shore," he tells his son Luke.

Irony

Although darker than many of Anne Tyler's novels, *Dinner at the Homesick Restaurant* contains many humorously ironic moments. For example, after Pearl's death the minister delivers a respectfully generic eulogy in which he calls her "a devoted wife and a loving mother and a pillar of the community." But Cody is aware "that she hadn't been anyone's wife for over a third of a century; that she'd been a frantic, angry, sometimes terrifying mother; and that she'd never shown the faintest interest in her community." Another example of irony is how hard-driven Cody is particularly competitive with Ezra, probably the least competitive major character in the novel. Sometimes, Ezra does not even realize when Cody is in competition with him, for example, when Cody is desperately wooing Ruth before Ezra marries her. When Cody perceives Ezra as "his oldest enemy," he is actually referring to a person incapable of hating anyone. Also ironic is Jenny's tendency to lavish more affection on her stepchildren than on her husband or members of her immediate family.

Comic Relief

Some of the minor characters in the novel provide this quality. Harley Baines, Jenny's first husband, is so controlling (e.g., telling Jenny how many times to chew her food) and methodical (e.g., arranging his textbooks by height and blocks of color) that his brief appearance is comic. Ruth's inability to accept compliments (e.g., when Cody buys her copper-colored roses to match her hair, she thinks he is mocking her) is both amusing and touching. Some of Tyler's matter-of-fact observations (e.g., when Ezra's best cook quits because a horoscope recommends it) also lend occasional comic relief to this novel.

Epiphany

At least two moments in *Dinner at the Homesick Restaurant* qualify as epiphanies, or sudden realizations of the meaning of things. First, in the novel's conclusion, Cody has a private conversation with Beck, the father who abandoned him as a teenager. In the course of their talk, Cody at least partly reconciles with some of his unhappiness and cruelty. Second, Jenny has her own spiritual awakening after she physically abuses her young daughter Becky: "All of her childhood returned to her: her mother's blows and slaps and curses, her mother's pointed fingernails digging into Jenny's arm...." Subsequently, she suffers a nervous breakdown but recovers (with Pearl's help) and goes on to develop a less driven, happier personality.

Historical Context

Child Abuse in America

Although *Dinner at the Homesick Restaurant* traces the evolution of the fictional Tull family from roughly 1925 to 1979, its theme of child abuse is particularly relevant to the 1980s, the decade in which the novel was published. The first national studies to determine the prevalence of child abuse were conducted in 1974; five years later, the federal Child abuse Prevention and Treatment Act mandated periodic National Incidence Reports. By 1984—two years after *Dinner at the Homesick Restaurant* was released—the American Humane Association (AHA) claimed that there were roughly 1.7 million abused or neglected children in the United States. The 1988 Study of National Incidence and Prevalence of Child abuse and Neglect arrived at a total of 1.5 million abused or neglected children, and their report broke down the statistics into three categories of abuse—physical, sexual, and emotional. The report also found that more than one thousand children died as a direct result of maltreatment in the year 1986.

In *Dinner at the Homesick Restaurant* Pearl Tull periodically abuses her three children physically and emotionally, although never sexually. Jenny Tull, to a lesser extent, abuses her daughter in stressful situations, although Jenny is sensitive enough to realize it and seek help. Most of Pearl's abusive behavior is related to the stress of raising a family alone at a time when single parenting was uncommon and single parents had few services to which they could turn to for help. Compounding this situations are Pearl's perfectionist tendencies

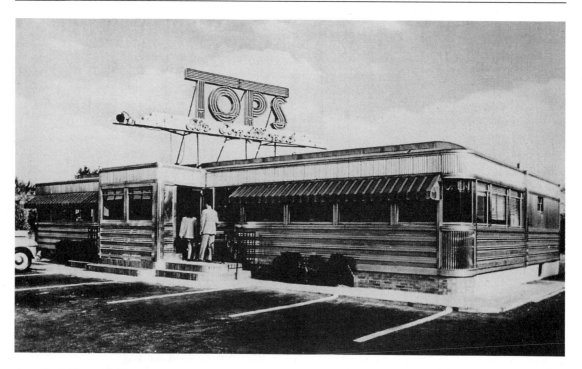

A typical diner, 1952.

and her intense refusal to accept that her marriage was a failure. The extent of her mistreatment of the children is uncertain, since the memories of each child differ sharply. While they all experience or observe some degree of Pearl's rage, none of the children consider the possibility of reporting it to the authorities, an omission in keeping with the spirit of the American times and the lack of social service agencies at that time in history.

Today a greater effort is placed on fighting many of the contributing factors that often lead to child abuse or neglect—poor parenting skills, mental health problems, and substance abuse, to name a few. There are also more social agencies focused on dealing with real or suspected instances of abuse, along with federal and state efforts targeted at its prevention.

Critical Overview

Dinner at the Homesick Restaurant, originally published in the United States by Knopf in 1982, qualified as a critical and commercial success for its somewhat reclusive author, Anne Tyler. In one of her few interviews, Tyler said as quoted in *Dictionary of Literary Biography Yearbook,* "I think what I was doing was saying 'Well, all right, I've joked around about families long enough; let me tell you now what I really believe about them.'"

Although her opinion produced a book less optimistic than some of her previous novels, critics (many of whom had ignored Tyler's previous novels) responded positively for the most part. Although Elizabeth Evans in her book *Anne Tyler* and some other critics thought that using Pearl's deathbed was not a particularly original structural device, the consensus was that Tyler's perception of an unconventional, emotionally scarred family rang fascinating, poignant, and true.

Many commended Tyler's control over multiple points of view, as well as her rich characterizations, and a complex plot structure. In a *Yale Review* interview with Barbara Lazear Ascher, the writer Eudora Welty lavished more general praise on Tyler: "She is the best.... I told her once if I could have written the last sentence of *Dinner at the Homesick Restaurant,* I'd have been happy for the rest of my life." John Updike, in his *New Yorker* review of the author's ninth novel, was no less complimentary: "She has arrived, I think, at a new level of power, and gives us a lucid and delightful yet complex and sombre improvisation on her favorite theme, family life." Kathleen Woodward in her chapter "Forgetting and Remembering" from the book *Anne Tyler as Novelist* wrote, "With Pearl

Tull, Tyler gives us an indelible compelling portrait of a woman in her last years."

Benjamin DeMott, in *The New York Times Book Review,* praised Tyler because she "edges deeper into a truth that's simultaneously (and interdependently) psychological, moral and formal—deeper than many living novelists of serious reputations have penetrated, deeper than Miss Tyler has gone before." He also observed that "there's a touch of Dostoyevsky's 'Idiot' in Ezra, a hint of the unposturing selflessness." Donna Gerstenberger, in the "Everybody Speaks" chapter from *Anne Tyler as Novelist,* wrote, "The meaning, the triumph of *Dinner at the Homesick Restaurant* resides, I think, in the family members' ability to learn to reread the text of self of family relationships that have been previously constructed under immense pressure."

Other critics pointed out that part of Tyler's success was that she did not look for easy answers or convenient scapegoats in her work. For example, Paula Gallant Eckard noted in *Southern Literary Journal,* "Tyler resists the temptation to indict parents, particularly mothers, for the transgressions of the past and the ultimate shaping of offspring."

A minority of reviewers panned Tyler's novel. For example, James Wolcott, in his highly negative review printed in *Esquire,* said *Dinner at the Homesick Restaurant* "is hobbled from page one by its rickety plot structure…. Deathbed retrospectives have been worked to the nub in fiction, and Tyler doesn't come up with any spiffy ways to soup up and customize her time machine."

With its immediate popular critical reception, *Dinner at the Homesick Restaurant* won the PEN/Faulkner award for Fiction and was nominated for both a National Book Critics Circle award and the 1983 Pulitzer Prize. In 1986, Tyler actually won the National Book Critics Circle award, and by 1989, the Pulitzer Prize for her novel *Breathing Lessons.* As prolific in the 1990s as she was from the beginning of her career, Tyler continues to publish an average of one novel every few years, but seldom talks publicly about her work. Most of her novels concern, to some extent, the joys, ambiguities, and pain in the typical American family. Her more recent books include *Saint Maybe* (1991), and *Ladder of Years* (1995).

Criticism

Diane Henningfeld

Henningfeld is a professor of English at Adrian College. In the following essay, she traces the critical history of Tyler's Dinner at the Homesick Restaurant *and explores the various psychological interpretations of the novel.*

Anne Tyler published her ninth novel, *Dinner at the Homesick Restaurant* in 1982. Set in Baltimore, the novel tells the story of Pearl Tull and her children, Cody, Ezra and Jenny, as they attempt to come to terms with a pivotal event, their abandonment by Beck Tull, husband to Pearl and father to the children.

Dinner at the Homesick Restaurant received excellent reviews on its publication. In the *New York Times Book Review,* Benjamin DeMott called it "a border crossing" for Tyler, a book which pushes her "deep into truth." Likewise, John Updike wrote that Tyler had reached "a new level of power, and gives us a lucid and delightful yet complex and somber improvisation on her favorite theme, family life."

Not all reviewers, however, described *Dinner at the Homesick Restaurant* so positively. Vivian Gornick in *The Village Voice* accused Tyler of "arrested development" because of the lack of sexual energy in her novel. She called Tyler's prose "sexually anesthetized." James Wolcott, in a review for *Esquire,* suggested that the novel "is hobbled from page one on by its rickety plot structure."

Anne Tyler provides for us the way she thinks about *Dinner at the Homesick Restaurant* in an interview with Sarah English: "I think what I was doing was saying, 'Well, all right, I've joked about families long enough; let me tell you what I really believe about them.'" A number of critics write extensively on just what it is that Tyler believes about families, using *Dinner at the Homesick Restaurant* as their evidence. For example, Anne Hall Petry argues in *Understanding Anne Tyler* that what Tyler "really believes" can be uncovered by a close examination of the word homesick. The word operates on three levels, according to Petry: homesick, as caused by a longing for home when one is away from home; homesick, as in sick of home, a condition often felt by children eager to be on their own; and homesick, as in sick from home, a psychological or emotional illness caused by the home environment.

Certainly, *Dinner at the Homesick Restaurant* can be read from a number of different critical ap-

What Do I Read Next?

- *The Ballad of the Sad Cafe and other Stories,* Carson McCullers's 1951 novel. Considered by many critics to be the author's finest work, this story is about a twisted love triangle in a small southern town during the 1940s.

- *As I Lay Dying.* In William Faulkner's 1930 novel, the dying matriarch Addie Bundren bears many similarities to Pearl Tull in *Dinner at the Homesick Restaurant.* The two novels are also somewhat alike structurally.

- Anne Tyler's Pulitzer Prize-nominated 1985 novel *The Accidental Tourist* is about a travel writer coping with the loss of his only son.

- *The Portable Chekhov.* Published in 1947, this volume includes twenty-eight short stories, two plays, and a vivid selection of letters by Anton Chekhov, generally considered one of the greatest and most prolific Russian writers.

proaches. For example, it is possible to read the novel as a sociological study of abuse and isolation. Because Pearl is so concerned with keeping up the appearances of a happy family, she hides the fact of Beck's desertion from her children, her neighbors, her family, and even her closest friend. Elizabeth Evans argues that the "most poignant example" of Pearl's isolation occurs when she "refuses to allow herself to confide in her old friend Emmaline." Further, the isolation and responsibility of being a single parent cause such strain for Pearl that she often attacks her own children in verbal and physical abuse, as Jenny recalls: "Which of her children had not felt her stinging slap, with the claw-encased pearl in her engagement ring that could bloody a lip at one flick?.... She herself, more than once had been slammed against a wall, been called 'serpent,' 'cockroach,' 'hideous little sniveling guttersnipe.'" Tellingly, just as sociological studies demonstrate, the pattern of abuse repeats itself. When Jenny is a single parent herself, trying to care for her infant daughter Becky while coping with medical school, she finds herself abusing her own daughter: "She slammed Becky's face into her Peter Rabbit dinner plate and gave her a bloody nose. She yanked a handful of hair. All her childhood returned to her...."

Other critics choose to read *Dinner at the Homesick Restaurant* from a psychological perspective. In such a reading, the critic often concentrates on the effect of Beck's absence on each of the children, noting the way that their development and maturity have been damaged by their father's desertion. Joseph B. Wagner goes so far as to suggest that Beck's departure is the "single most powerful factor in the development of the central characters.... The rest of their lives are so molded by that departure that their personalities correspond to psychoanalytic profiles of children who, at similar ages, are also abandoned by their fathers."

In another psychological study, Joseph C. Voelker sees in each of the children the idealization process. Each child longs for and attempts to recreate the ideal family for himself or herself. Cody, for example, longs for a mother who stays at home and visits with other housewives. Later, he buys a farmhouse and imagines himself settling in with his family, something he never does in reality. Ezra idealizes the notion of the family dinner at his business, The Homesick Restaurant. Although someone (usually Pearl) always explodes into anger each time he tries to arrange the perfect family dinner, he nonetheless repeats the scene throughout the book. Rather than starting a family himself, he nurtures strangers by providing them with food. Jenny goes through three marriages trying to find the perfect family. In her third marriage, to a man who has six children and who has been abandoned by his wife, she finds her ideal: the sheer activity of raising so many children protects her from emotional investment in them.

Finally, it is possible to examine *Dinner at the Homesick Restaurant* from a formal approach. That is, by examining the literary tools Tyler uses to construct her novel, we can begin to understand not only *what* the novel means but also *how* it means. One critic who takes a formal approach to the novel is Donna Gerstenberger. In her essay, "Everybody Speaks," she examines the narrative voice Tyler constructs for her novel. Gerstenberger writes that this voice is one of "calm reasonableness," and that she "democratically parcels out reason and unreason so evenly, individual voices in her novels seem to have an equal claim on the reader...." In other words, each of the points of view Tyler uses in *Din-*

ner at the Homesick Restaurant helps to establish that none of the characters is all good, or all bad, all sane or all insane. This evenness in voice allows us to read all of the characters sympathetically.

Similarly, a formal approach often takes into account images and metaphors. By comparing an abstract idea to something concrete, the writer is able to reveal her meaning subtly. Robert W. Croft argues that food is the central metaphor of *Dinner at the Homesick Restaurant.* Food represents physical and emotional nurturing. Thus, in the early part of the book, Pearl's refusal to feed her children adequately becomes symbolic of her inability to emotionally nurture the children. After a particularly violent episode of abuse, for example, "Cody had such a loaded feeling in his throat, he never wanted to eat again." Jenny's abuse of her daughter Becky occurs as she tries to feed her.

Tyler often uses food in moments of healing in the book, as well. When Jenny suffers a nervous breakdown, her mother feeds her and helps her to regain her health. Ezra repeatedly tries to heal his family by planning and hosting family dinners at the Homesick Restaurant. By the end of the book, it seems at least possible that the family will be able to complete one dinner together, although even here Tyler leaves us in doubt. The long-absent Beck agrees to come to the dinner, but says, " ... I warn you, I plan to leave before that dessert wine's poured."

Just as food is a paradox in that it represents both moments of violence and of healing, there are other telling paradoxes and contradictions in the story. As Gerstenberger argues, each of the characters shares in the telling of the story of the Tull family, and thus each seems to wield equal authority in the telling. Nonetheless, each character's story is self-contradictory. For example, Cody, the child who feels the most anger at his father's departure, manages to recreate his father's life in his own family. As a successful efficiency engineer, he moves his family from town to town, never letting them put down roots or establish themselves. Ironically, it is Cody who seems to make peace with his father by the end of the book and it is Cody who reintegrates his father back into the family: "Cody held on to his elbow and led him toward the others." Jenny, too, provides us with a model of self-contradiction. Throughout the book, she seems to be the child most affected by Pearl's abuse. When she is at home with her mother after Cody has left for college and Ezra has left for the army, she is uneasy and has nightmares that her mother

is a witch. Nonetheless, after she leaves home and her first marriage begins to fail, she returns home. In the place where she was least safe as a child, she feels most safe as an adult: "She loosened; she was safe at last, in the only place where people knew exactly who she was and loved her anyway."

And perhaps this is what Tyler "really believes" about families: that they are themselves paradoxical and self-contradictory. Families are havens as well as prisons, the place of much joy and the place of much sorrow. By the end of the book, we see that each Tull child has created and recreated his or her life and family through the act of memory. In *Dinner at the Homesick Restaurant,* memory is like nothing so much as one of Ezra's recipes. Each character, through the act of memory, experiments with what to leave in and what to take out, adjusting here and there, like adding salt to stew. Beck's arrival in the closing pages of the book provides the missing ingredient that each has struggled to find throughout the book. There are still troubling and contradictory messages on the closing pages. During his mother's funeral, for example, Cody reflects "That her life had been very long indeed, but never full; *stunted* was more like it." Nevertheless, Cody's final memories of his mother are of her "upright form along the grasses, her hair lit gold, her small hands smoothing her bouquet while the arrow journeyed on." These peaceful, positive memories suggest, at least, that the family story can always be revised.

Source: Diane Henningfeld, in an essay for *Novels for Students,* Gale, 1997.

Carol S. Manning

In the following excerpt, Manning argues that Dinner at the Homesick Restaurant *takes the familiar figure of the wandering adventurer and portrays him as "irresponsible, vain, and self-centered" by showing the effects of his absence on his family. She compares his role in Tyler's novel to that of King McLain in Eudora Welty's* The Golden Apples.

A familiar and appealing figure of the hero in narrative is that of the adventurer who wanders either alone or with male comrades in quest of some goal or in simple harmony with nature. He encounters heroic adventures along the way. The image has come down to us from Odysseus, is seen in American fiction in a character such as James Fenimore Cooper's Natty Bumppo, and has received wide circulation through western movie heroes such as Shane and the Lone Ranger. This hero is almost always unmarried and hence does not have the encumbrance of a wife or family to handicap his freedom. But even if, like Odysseus, the hero *is* married and with child, his family rarely enters his mind, and the author largely ignores the day-by-day circumstances of those left at home. Thus the family is seldom a concern of the reader. The story or novel is *about* the free-roaming hero and his adventures....

With her short stories "The Hitch-Hikers" and "Death of a Traveling Salesman," [Eudora] Welty separates herself from this romantic tradition by focusing on wanderers who learn that such freedom is not necessarily something to relish. In a subsequent work, *The Golden Apples,* she counters this romantic tradition more sharply. So does the younger author Anne Tyler in her novel *Dinner at the Homesick Restaurant.* Both writers undermine the male fantasy of the free-spirited hero by focusing on what the fantasy ignores. As viewed by these clear-eyed realists, the wandering hero is not single but married, and it is the home world he in effect deserts that the authors take as their focus. Exhibiting similar visions, Welty and Tyler portray the roaming hero—in the guise of a traveling salesman—as irresponsible, vain, and self-centered. They thus unmask and unhorse the romantic quester.

Though distinctly different works, *The Golden Apples* and *Dinner at the Homesick Restaurant* have striking similarities. Both traveling salesmen in these narratives are conceited, flamboyant men.... Tyler's Beck Tull lacks the exalted status that [Welty's King MacLain] has inherited—in fact, Beck seems to have no family history—and therefore depends chiefly on his charm and good looks to get ahead. Like King, he is, as a young man, handsome, vain, and courtly. "Lean and rangy," he waves his black hair extravagantly; his eyes are such a brilliant blue that they seem unreal; and he woos women with gifts of chocolates and flowers, many compliments, and perfect manners ("he was respectful to a fault and never grabbed at her the way some other men might").

The women these handsome, flamboyant heroes court and marry are themselves similar yet are opposites of their husbands. Both cavaliers surprisingly undertake fast and fierce courtships of women the neighbors consider unlikely candidates for marriage. King woos Snowdie Hudson, who, being an albino, had seemed destined to remain a wallflower and a school teacher all her life. Beck woos Pearl Cody, who, at age 30, is already con-

sidered an old maid—and is six years older than Beck. The like-named Snowdie and Pearl are swept off their feet by the dashing King and Beck. Married, Snowdie and Pearl turn to meticulous housekeeping and homemaking. As one character says of Snowdie, "At her house it was like Sunday even in the mornings, every day, in that cleaned up way." Similarly, Pearl concentrates on making each house she and her husband move into "airtight and rustproof and waterproof." At first, it looks as though neither woman will have any children. But finally, Snowdie has twin sons and Pearl has two sons and a daughter.

Meanwhile, their husbands are off selling their wares—King peddles tea and spices; Beck's line is farm and garden equipment. After a few years, King comes home less and less often and then seems to have disappeared for good, leaving his hat on the banks of the Big Black River to hint that he has drowned. In contrast, Beck's departure is sudden. After twenty years of coming home more or less regularly on weekends, he announces one Sunday in 1944 that he doesn't want to stay married any longer. He packs and leaves that very night.

In running away, both men are, like the conventional roaming hero, seeking adventure and glamor but also escape from the responsibilities, confinement, and expectations of home. Despite his law degree, King had become a traveling salesman in the first place so he could come and go as he pleases—could, as he says, "make considerable trips off and only [have] my glimpses of the people back here." He allegedly returns one afternoon a few years after disappearing but beats a hasty retreat when confronted with a vision of home responsibilities in the forms of his young, rambunctious twin sons on roller skates. Beck also returns after two or three years, but rather than announcing himself, he spies on his family from across the street, as King had spied on his through a porch window. When Beck sees his oldest son come out, pick up the evening newspaper and casually flip it in the air, he conveniently concludes that his family is getting along well enough without him, so he too hastily beats a retreat. Beck doesn't want to get close to anyone: "Oh, it's closeness that does you in," he says. Near the end of the novel, Beck tells his son that he had deserted his family because of the "grayness of things; half-right-and-half-wrongness of things. Everything tangled, mingled, not perfect any more. I couldn't take that," he says. "Your mother could, but not me." So Beck—like King and the other wandering heroes—pursues his own whims and leaves his wife to cope with the tangled, imperfect home world.

But whereas King and Beck avoid the grayness of home, the authors of these works do not. For in contrast to the male fantasy that focuses on the adventures of the wanderer, *The Golden Apples* and *Dinner at the Homesick Restaurant* focus on the home world that the hero flees. By thus showing us the consequences of his desertion of his family, Welty and Tyler unhorse the hero. They further deflate his romantic image by revealing him to be an ordinary—not glamorous—man when he does briefly pop up in the narrative.

Throughout most of Tyler's long novel and Welty's complex, interrelated cycle of stories, the runaway husband is absent both from home and from the fictional scene, yet he is never forgotten by those he has left behind. In fact, Beck's and King's desertions of their families are *the* crucial events in the lives of their wives and children.... Whereas King leaves his family in a small town where he and the family are well known, Beck leaves his family in a Baltimore neighborhood, where he is virtually unknown and goes unmissed. In fact, part of Beck's problem, in contrast to King's, is that Beck fears he is a nobody. But whereas Beck's absence makes no ripple in the community, it causes his wife Pearl as much pain as King's causes Snowdie. Though she has come to see him as a slangy, incompetent, unreliable man, Pearl nonetheless dreams about him, longs for his return, and plans how nice she will act if he does: "He would come with presents for them and she'd be the one to open the door—perfumed, in her Sunday dress, maybe wearing a bit of rouge."

Both wives also feel humiliated by their husbands' desertions. Initially, Snowdie tries to cover King's absence by telling the neighbors that her husband has to be away because of fragile health; he needs "the waters." Similarly, for years Pearl pretends to her children and the neighbors that Beck is only on an extended business trip. Fearing the gossip and charity of the neighbors, both Snowdie and Pearl in their pride keep close counsel with themselves. Pearl shuts all the neighbors out, allows herself no friends. Snowdie continues to contribute to community life but maintains a personal distance.

Still another cost of the husbands' wanderlust is financial hardship for their families. The abandoned wives have to find some means to support their families, and this in a time when work opportunities for women are few. Snowdie takes in

boarders, and Pearl gets a job as a cashier in a local grocery store. Once her children begin to leave home and their rooms become available, Pearl takes in boarders as well.

Just as Snowdie and Pearl suffer as a consequence of their husbands' wanderlust, so do their children.... Pearl Tull's children, who are 14, 11, and 9 when their father runs away, are all emotionally stunted by his desertion. The middle child Ezra is the stay-at-home and nurturer in this case, while Cody and Jenny feel driven to get away. Beck's desertion affects Cody, the oldest, most noticeably and directly. He ever after wonders if he is to blame for his father's leaving. Addressing his father in one of his interior monologues, as Welty's Ran MacLain does at the beginning of his story, Cody wonders, "Was it something I said? Was it something I did? Was it something I didn't do, that made you go away?" Because he senses that his brother is his mother's favorite, Cody especially desires his father's love and attention. He becomes absorbed with climbing the business ladder of success, to prove himself, unlike his father, a good provider for his family, but also in hopes of winning his father's appreciation and approval, should Beck ever return. Cody even enters his father's profession—he is a traveling salesman, of sorts. But what he sells is efficiency and ideas, and he is expert in his field. In leaving home, Cody is not, like Beck, seeking adventure and escape from home responsibilities. Indeed, in his determination to avoid repeating his father's life, he takes his wife and son with him wherever he goes, and he consistently aids his mother financially.

Cody and his siblings suffer doubly from their father's desertion, first simply from their father's absence and second from the consequences of that absence on their mother. Pearl's behavior toward her children is erratic. After a long day on her feet at the grocery store, she frequently comes home feeling tired, overworked, put upon, lonely, and frustrated by her limited ability to provide. Turning abusive, she takes her frustration and resentment out on her children, attacking them both physically and verbally.

Near the ends of their works, both Eudora Welty and Anne Tyler bring the missing husband back on the scene. Though distinctly different in detail, these endings are strikingly similar in scene, purpose, and effect. The occasion in each case is a funeral—Katie Rainey's funeral in *The Golden Apples,* at which the whole Morgana community gathers; and Pearl Tull's funeral in *Dinner,* at which

Pearl's whole family gathers. These endings humanize the runaway husbands and further undermine the familiar fantasy of the admirable, free-spirited adventurer....

In the last chapter of *Dinner at the Homesick Restaurant,* Beck Tull comes back home to attend his wife's funeral. Though he has not seen his family for 35 years, Pearl has made sure he is there at the end. Having him invited to the funeral may be her means of triumphing over him: she causes him, after 35 years of absence, to fulfill at least one of his obligations as husband and father. Or getting him to the funeral may be her revenge on him, for she anticipates that he will expose himself to his children as still the vain, weak man she knew him to be decades before.

And she is right. Now 79 years old, Beck still wears his hair in "a fan-shaped pompadour, still thick and sharply crimped," and he comes dressed nattily, in a pinstriped but "ill-fitting navy blue suit" with a "gangsterish air." Despite his long desertion of his family, he seems to expect to be welcomed home with open arms and to be made a great to-do over—as though he had been away on some noble quest or is returning a hero of war. When his oldest son Cody recognizes him, Beck responds, Tyler tells us, "with a triumphant nod" and the words, "'Yes, ... it's your father speaking, Cody.'" But in one of the funniest scenes in contemporary literature, Beck's children rob their father of his expected welcome as returning hero. Proving themselves the children of their mother, who had gone on for years pretending her absentee husband was only away on a prolonged business trip, they seem hardly fazed by Beck's presence now. Sweet Ezra politely treats him as just one of the family rather than as honored guest; Cody mockingly pretends that Beck has never been away; and Jenny seems about as interested in her father as she would be in any stranger off the street.

Just as Beck's children have never understood why their father left, neither has the reader known what exactly precipitated his departure. So at the end of the novel, through a conversation between Cody and Beck, Tyler makes sure both Cody and the reader realize that Beck's wandering has in no way been noble, glamorous, or even purposeful. It is in this conversation that Beck refers to not having been able to stand the imperfectability, the grayness, of family life. He indicates that, after one more example of that grayness, he had impulsively left his wife:

> "I was sitting over a beer in the kitchen that Sunday evening and all at once, not even knowing I'd do it, I said, 'Pearl, I'm leaving.'"

His actions in the years that followed were just as unplanned, just as reflective of his wishy-washy character. He "[h]ad a few pals, a lady friend from time to time," accepted whatever transfers the company gave him. In his infrequent notes home to his wife, he bragged about the opportunities opening up before him when there were no such opportunities (and Beck was not the man to make opportunities happen). In his old age, he, like King (and like Odysseus), fears that he has ended up on the wrong end of his travels: he sorrowfully anticipates that, now that his wife has died, his current "lady friend" will expect him to marry her at last.

In focusing on the day-to-day lives of those left at home, then, Welty and Tyler have uncovered the realism ignored by male fantasies about wandering adventurers. They expose the emotional pain and hardships faced by those left at home. But this focus on the home reveals something else as well: the strength of the wives left to cope as best they can. Neither Snowdie nor Pearl is faultless, despite their suggestive names, yet both display a competence and a valor that deserve to be sung. As conventional and as faithful as Penelope, both wives wait longingly for 30-odd years for the return of their wandering husbands, yet both survive and succeed quite well without those husbands. Indeed, when her husband does ultimately return to her in his sixties, Snowdie MacLain discovers that this fulfillment of her wish isn't such a blessing after all. "I don't know what to do with him," Miss Snowdie says, and Welty adds:

> When her flyaway husband had come home a few years ago, at the age of sixty-odd, and stayed, they said she had never gotten over it—first his running away, then his coming back to her.

Had Pearl Tull been so unfortunate as to get *her* "flyaway husband" back, no doubt she would have experienced the same rude awakening. Moreover, had a clear-eyed realist—or a female Homer—told the Odysseus story, Penelope would, I suspect, have had the final line in that epic. Having lived, like Snowdie and Pearl, more of her life *without* her husband than *with* him, surely she would have been more jolted by than overjoyed by his return. Penelope might say, with Snowdie and Pearl, "I don't know what to do with him."

Source: Carol S. Manning, "Welty, Tyler, and Traveling Salesmen: The Wandering Hero Unhorsed," in *The Fiction of Anne Tyler,* edited by C. Ralph Stephens, University Press of Mississippi, 1990, pp. 110–18.

Mary Ellis Gibson

In the following excerpt, Gibson suggests that Dinner at the Homesick Restaurant *contains Tyler's most complex treatment of the idea that one's fate may be determined by one's family situation.*

A careful reading of Tyler's recent work suggests a philosophical coherence and depth residing in aptly chosen domestic details. Like many writers, southern and otherwise, Tyler is obsessed with family, but this obsession does not fall into the familiar pattern of nature versus nurture, of maturity forged out of or against familial influences. Instead, for Tyler the familial becomes the metaphysical. Family is seen in the light of cosmic necessity, as the inevitable precondition of human choice. As Updike perceptively says of *Dinner at the Homesick Restaurant,* "genetic comedy ... deepens into the tragedy of closeness, of familial limitations that work upon us like Greek fates and condemn us to lives of surrender and secret fury." Updike is surely right to suggest that fatedness is at the center of Tyler's family fictions.

Yet fate in these novels is not precisely the fate of Greek tragedy. Tyler's fates lie somewhere between the classical Greek fates, or *moira,* who work our destinies in accordance with some cosmic order—those fates who preside over Sophoclean irony—and the more oppressive fate or *heimarmene* of the gnostic dualists and their anti-metaphysical descendents the existentialists. In Tyler's fiction, tragedy and comedy, or the mix of them, grow not from the conjunction of a hero's *hybris* and his fate but from the contest between human caring and nihilism. Again and again we see Tyler's characters, with their rootedness, their entanglements, and their inherited predispositions, come up against the possibility of change. Tyler's families live through a repeating pattern of desertion and reunion. Those who desert—or escape—inevitably carry their pasts with them; those who remain are in danger of becoming too passive, of awakening to find themselves in situations not of their making, of becoming dissociated from their own bodies and the physical world around them. In narrative structure, in characterization, and in the emblems through which she describes the human plight, Tyler works an intricate commentary on the nature of fate and on the importance of family to individual understandings of fate and responsibility.

These fundamental concerns come together with the greatest complexity in Tyler's most recent and, I think, her best novel, *Dinner at the Homesick Restaurant.* The novel opens at the bedside of

Pearl Cody Tull, eighty-five years old, blind, and dying in a row house in urban Baltimore. Pearl's memories of the half-century since she married Beck Tull and left her genteel home in Raleigh, N.C., are interwoven with her three children's attempts to understand their father's desertion, their mother's love and anger, and their own responsibility for themselves. Cody, the eldest, has become a travelling man like his father, but a successful and driven efficiency expert rather than a two-bit salesman. Ezra, the middle child, watches faithfully at his mother's bedside, while she reflects that he "hadn't really lived up to his potential." Never having gone to college, Ezra runs a restaurant on St. Paul Street, the Homesick Restaurant, where his greatest pleasure is cooking for others and his continually frustrated hope is for his own family to finish a celebratory meal together. The youngest child, Jenny, has become a pediatrician. She has left her first husband whom she married in order not to be "defenceless," and she has been deserted by her second. Almost by accident she stumbles into a third marriage to a man with a half-dozen children who feel as wounded by their own mother's desertion as Jenny does by Beck Tull's. Pearl Tull reflects that each of her children has an important flaw. In their turn, her children have inherited much of their mother's temperament, and their lives have been formed in response to her abuse. Like her mother, Jenny fears closeness with her own family; like his mother, Cody is prone to violent rages.

All these strands of the Tulls' story are developed through a complex narrative structure. The careful weaving of past, present, and future is an advance on Tyler's earlier novels, and narrative structure here focuses more clearly then before on the present as a moment of crisis between past and future. While the Tulls' story suggests no overarching cosmic pattern or design, no future rewards or punishment, no justice on earth or hereafter, it focuses our attention on moments of transition when the family comes together to celebrate or to mourn a change. For the Tulls, almost any moment can be a moment of crisis, almost any conversation can be revealing. So it is not surprising when Pearl thinks to herself on her deathbed, "You could pluck this single moment out of all time ... and still discover so much about her children.."...

The narrative structure of the novel as a whole is designed to bring past and future together more subtly than in any of Tyler's earlier novels, except perhaps *Searching for Caleb.* Tyler no longer relies on dated chapter headings to peg down chronology as she did in *Celestial Navigation* and in *Mor-*

gan's Passing. The third person narration of *Dinner at the Homesick Restaurant* allows her to move easily from one character's thoughts to another's and to move back and forth in time. Thus she avoids the sometimes jolting and mechanical transitions from past to present that characterize her first-person novel *Earthly Possessions.*

The "Beaches on the Moon" episode of *Dinner at the Homesick Restaurant* best illustrates the new subtlety of Tyler's narrative structure and the thematic coherence it makes possible. The novel begins in 1979, the year of Pearl's death, moves backward in time to Pearl's childhood, to Beck's desertion in 1944, and to various events of the children's growing up and their adult lives. Each episode brings us close to one of the central characters and shows us the family largely through his or her eyes. "Beaches on the Moon," a chapter at the center of the novel, shows us Ezra's "tragedy" through his mother's recollections. Cody has "stolen" his brother Ezra's fiancee, Ruth Spivey, a "country cook" from the West Virginia hills. Years later (in the early 1970's) Pearl with Ezra's help keeps up her habit of spring cleaning Cody's farmhouse—the place near Baltimore where he had once meant for Ruth to live. The chapter is an intricate weaving together of past and present. It carries us through the narrative of Cody's marriage and Ezra's grief, but more importantly it brings us face to face with Pearl's most direct meditation on the familial fate. This moment is made possible by the pattern of Pearl's recollections; the present of Pearl's sweeping and cleaning becomes the fulcrum between past and future.

The chapter begins several years before Pearl's death, before her encroaching blindness, but the image of Pearl at the beginning of the novel, blind and ill, presides over the view of her here. From present tense narration the chapter shifts to past perfect and then to past tense, as Pearl recalls Ezra's grief. Past and present alternate rapidly as the chapter follows both Pearl's cleaning and her relationship with Cody and Ruth after their marriage. At the very end of the chapter Pearl is reminded of an incident still farther back in the past—back in the pre-World War I days when her school friend Linda Lou eloped with the history teacher. As the chapter returns to its predominant present, Pearl reflects that even Linda Lou's scandalous baby is an old man by now. Like Pearl herself and like Cody's farmhouse, he is greying toward death.

These complex recollections make possible and understandable Pearl's most direct confronta-

tion with what she considers to be the family fate. As Pearl remembers Cody's marriage and his deliberate distance, she confronts the failure of her family. The narrative shifts to the present tense:

> Pearl believes now that her family has failed. Neither of her sons is happy, and her daughter can't seem to stay married. There is no one to accept the blame for this but Pearl herself, who raised these children single-handed and did make mistakes, oh, a bushel of mistakes. Still, she sometimes has the feeling that it's simply fate, and not a matter for blame at all. She feels that everything has been assigned, has been pre-ordained; everyone must play his role. Certainly she never intended to foster one of those good son/bad son arrangements, but what can you do when one son is consistently good and the other consistently bad? What can the sons do, even?

Pearl ends these reflections by encountering the force of time directly in the shape of her own aging face:

> In the smallest bedroom, a nursery, a little old lady in a hat approaches. It's Pearl, in the speckled mirror above a bureau. She leans closer and traces the lines around her eyes. Her age does not surprise her. She's grown used to it by now. You're old for so much longer than you're young, she thinks. Really it hardly seems fair.

Finally Pearl draws comfort from her futile spring cleaning, a present and future testament of her concern. Together, she thinks, she and Ezra will go on cleaning season after season, "the two of them bumping down the driveway, loyal and responsible, together forever." This view of Pearl, like the other episodes in *Dinner at the Homesick Restaurant,* implicitly shows us the importance of the past for shaping the present and the future, and vice versa; we know that even as Pearl herself is aging toward death her children, aging too, are devising ways of going on with their lives....

Virtually all of the major characters in *Dinner at the Homesick Restuarant* think of themselves as fated, though they may be equally mistaken in passively accepting or in willfully seeking to change their fates. At the first family dinner in Ezra's restaurant, when he announces his partnership in the business, Ezra reflects optimistically on the family gathering: "It's just like fate." (But the dinner is fated as always to end in a family quarrel.) Ezra's passivity is the consequence of his fatalism and of his misjudgment about the nature of his family's fates. Approaching forty at the end of the no el, Ezra thinks to himself, "He had never married, never fathered children, and lost the one girl he had loved out of sheer fatalism, lack of force, a willing assumption of defeat. (*Let it be* was the theme that ran through his life. He was ruled by a dreamy mood of acceptance that was partly the source of all his happiness and partly his undoing.)" Ezra is the most thorough fatalist in *Dinner at the Homesick Restaurant,* and in this he is somewhat like Jeremy Pauling in Tyler's earlier novel *Celestial Navigation.* Interestingly, Ezra is also Pearl Tull's favorite child—mother and son share a certain fatalism, but Pearl lacks Ezra's dreamy acceptance. She is all sharp edges, and while she is passive in important matters of concern to her children, she rebels at the one thing no one can alter, her encroaching blindness.

In contrast to Ezra's dreamy fatalism and Pearl's angry, self-justifying fatalism is Cody's relentless activity. Early in their acquaintance Cody catches Ruth reading her horoscope. *"Powerful ally will come to your rescue. Accent today on high finance,"* Ruth reads with a sneer. "I mean who do they reckon they're dealing with?" Cody determines to become himself Ruth's "powerful ally." Out of sheer desire to have whatever Ezra has, he will make Ruth's horoscope prove true. Yet for all his relentless will, Cody can't make himself accept what he has or who he is. After he is injured in an industrial accident and quarrels with his family, Cody thinks his life is like "some kind of plot where someone decided, long before I was born, I would live out my days surrounded by people who were … nicer than I am, just naturally nicer without even having to try.…" Cody tries with all his energies to have the world for himself; as an efficiency expert he is obsessed with the control of time. Yet even he feels, especially when presented with his family, that his life is plotted in a pattern he did not design. His very relentlessness seems fated, and it makes him less sympathetic than the more passive Ezra.

Jenny, in contrast, is the only character in the novel who comes to deny the family fate, though at one time she too has asked herself, "Was this what it came to—that you never could escape? That certain things were doomed to continue, generation after generation?" In her youth Jenny has tried to protect herself from fate. She marries partly in response to a fortune teller's advice that otherwise she will be "destroyed by love." Approaching middle age, she has learned to "make it through life on a slant," and she reflects ironically that the fortune teller was wrong—love cannot destroy her. She is alternately disengaged and engaged with life, ironically distant and yet taking responsibility for herself and her children. And she refuses to believe family determines future. As she tells one of her

step-children, "I don't see the need to blame adjustment, broken homes, bad parents, that sort of thing. We make our own luck, right?"

Jenny could easily be taken to speak for Anne Tyler, who has herself said she tends to see life through a "sort of mist of irony." But the novel suggests that even Jenny can't altogether make her own luck. As if to point to the problem clearly, Jenny's daughter repeats and enlarges her mother's flaws. Jenny, who is always eating lettuce and lemon juice, has a daughter who is anorexic. Analogously, Tyler's novel doesn't make its own luck either. In spite of comic moments, things are never resolvable into an unequivocally happy ending.

This interplay of fatalism and will is even more complex in Anne Tyler's novels than I have so far suggested. Fate is never reducible to a series of statements about it; and Tyler's work has the power to engage us seriously because she uses in her own quirky way the oldest emblems of the plight of humans who feel fated in destinies without meaningful cause.

The sense of having been thrown into an alien world may be expressed in nausea, in homesickness, or in what Annette Kolodny calls [in *Feminist Criticism,* edited by Cheryl L. Brown and Karen Olson] reflexive perception—the sense of finding oneself in a situation, of being dissociated from one's body or the world around one. In Tyler's novels the problem of homesickness is presented concretely through minor characters; her novels are filled with hitchhikers and other waifs. More importantly, nausea, homesickness, and dissociation are the stuff of the lives of Tyler's central characters. These motifs permeate *Dinner at the Homesick Restaurant,* though their expression is less extreme here than in Tyler's earlier novels *Celestial Navigation* and *Earthly Possessions*.…

Dinner at the Homesick Restaurant, I believe, goes beyond these earlier novels both in subtlety and humanity. While it retains the philosophical dimension of Tyler's earlier novels, it makes the situations of aloneness and homesickness meaningful through conditions which are, at least superficially, less unusual than those in the two earlier novels. But despite ordinary domestic appearancs, the characters' situations in *Dinner at the Homesick Restaurant* are extreme. (By implication, all of our situations are extreme.) All of the Tull family experience dissociation from themselves and their actions. Pearl, for example, says, "Sometimes I stand outside my body and just watch it all, totally separately." All the Tulls, too, live with loneliness and fear. None of this is glossed over, none of it is finally mitigated by the happenings of plot. Beck Tull at last arrives for a family dinner—but only on the occasion of Pearl's funeral.

And yet, Tyler manages to suggest that people do go on attempting to nourish each other. At the funeral dinner Beck looks down the table and exclaims in surprise, "It looks like this is one of those big, jolly, noisy, rambling ... why, *families!*" Cody retorts, "You think we're a family.... You think we're some jolly, situation-comedy family when we're in particles, torn apart, torn all over the place, and our mother was a witch." In many ways Cody is right. Yet the Tulls *are* a family. The narrator of Tyler's novel never consigns them to total fragmentation and alienation, and the Tulls never quite give up on themselves. As the narrator observes, "In fact, they probably saw more of each other than happy families did. It was almost as if what they couldn't get right, they had to keep returning to."

Tyler never quite becomes either a fatalist or a nihilist, though both attitudes seem possible given the human situation as she sees it. The question of fate—of necessity without meaningful design—as it is developed in Tyler's narrative suggests that Tyler's fictional world is kin to those of gnostic dualism and of twentieth-century existentialism. Yet there is no superior wisdom to which Tyler's characters might awaken, and their choices are not so bleak as they are in the existentialist novel. Forlornness and ironies there are in plenty, but Tyler's irony is not mordant. Instead, it can be tinged with humor, as if to imply that ironic distance is as authentic as and more survivable than despair. As her latest title suggests, fatalism and despair are balanced by attempted human sympathy and nourishment; homesickness may make possible human efforts to connect. Tyler's world is in fact something like Pascal's, but without a god toward whom to make a leap of faith. In the *Pensées,* Pascal writes, "I am frightened and amazed at finding myself here rather than there; for there is no reason whatever why here rather than there, why now rather than then." For Tyler's characters such fear and amazement are mingled, with fear often overpowering amazement. For the novelist herself, amazement predominates in the "setting-apart situation" she believes is necessary to art. "I am still surprised, to this day," she writes, "to find myself where I am. My life is so streamlined and full of modern conveniences. How did I get here? I have given up

hope, by now, of ever losing my sense of distance; in fact, I seem to have come to cherish it."

Tyler's recent novels, particularly *Celestial Navigation, Earthly Possessions,* and *Dinner at the Homesick Restaurant,* are structured by her investigation of what such a "sense of distance" means. She insists on asking directly questions of metaphysical dimension: Why are we here? How do we happen to be who we are? Tyler's characters long for a comprehensible design, a celestial pattern by which or toward which they might navigate. In their gropings toward explanations for their own motives and choices, the question of fate recurs with a singular urgency. It is the measure against which we see Tyler's ordinary families struggle toward a modicum of sympathy and grace.

Source: Mary Ellis Gibson, "Family as Fate: The Novels of Anne Tyler," in *Southern Literary Journal,* Vol. 16, Fall, 1983, pp. 47–58.

Sources

Barbara Lazear Ascher, "A Visit with Eudora Welty," in *Yale Review,* Vol. 74, No. 1, autumn, 1984, p. 149.

Benjamin DeMott, "Funny, Wise and True," in *New York Times Book Review,* March 14, 1982, p. 14.

Paula Gallant Eckard, "Family and Community in Anne Tyler's *Dinner at the Homesick Restaurant,*" in *Southern Literary Journal,* Vol. 22, No. 2, Spring 1990, pp. 33-44.

Sarah English, "Anne Tyler," in *Dictionary of Literary Biography Yearbook: 1982,* Gale, 1983, p. 194.

Elizabeth Evans, *Anne Tyler,* Twayne Publishers, 1993.

Donna Gerstenberger, "Everybody Speaks," in *Anne Tyler as Novelist,* edited by Dale Salwak, University of Iowa Press, 1994, pp. 138-46.

Mary Ellis Gibson, "Family as Fate: The Novels of Anne Tyler," in *Southern Literary Journal,* Vol. 15, No. 3, fall, 1983, pp. 47-58.

John Updike, "On Such a Beautiful Green Little Planet," in *The New Yorker,* April 5, 1982, pp. 193-97.

James Wolcott, "Strange New World," in *Esquire,* April 1982, p. 123-4.

Kathleen Woodward, "Forgetting and Remembering," in *Anne Tyler as Novelist,* edited by Dale Salwak, University of Iowa Press, 1944.

For Further Study

Robert W. Croft, *Anne Tyler: A Bio-Bibliography,* Greenwood Press, 1995.

A useful volume that opens with a short biography of Tyler, includes a listing of primary sources, and concludes with an extensive annotated bibliography of secondary sources.

Mary J. Elkins, "*Dinner at the Homesick Restaurant :* Anne Tyler and the Faulkner Connection," in *Atlantis,* Vol. 10, No. 2, Spring 1985, pp. 93-105.

Compares and contrasts Tyler's *Dinner at the Homesick Restaurant* to William Faulkner's *As I Lay Dying.*

Susan Gilbert, "Anne Tyler," in *Southern Women Writers: The New Generation,* edited by Tonette Bond Inge, University of Alabama Press, 1990, pp. 251-78.

Feminist reading of Tyler's novels through *Accidental Tourist.*

Vivian Gornick, "Anne Tyler's Arrested Development," in *Village Voice,* March 30, 1982, pp. 40-1.

Review faults Tyler for lack of sexual energy in the novel.

Karen L. Levenback, "Functions of (Picturing) Memory," in *Anne Tyler as Novelist,* edited by Dale Salwak, University of Iowa Press, 1994, pp. 77-85.

Short essay on the act of remembering in Tyler's novels.

Alice Hall Petry, "Dinner at the Homesick Restaurant," in her *Understanding Anne Tyler,* University of South Carolina Press, 1990, pp. 186-209.

Author discusses the different connotations of the term "homesick," as it relates to major characters in Tyler's novel.

Alice Hall Petry, editor, *Critical Essays on Anne Tyler,* G.K. Hall, 1992.

Excellent all-around source on Tyler; contains reprints of important reviews of *Dinner at the Home-*

sick Restaurant by John Updike and Benjamin De-Mott as well as critical essays by noted Tyler scholars.

Dale Salwak, *Anne Tyler as Novelist,* University of Iowa Press, 1994.

Collection of seventeen essays focusing on distinctive features of Tyler's novels, including her concern with family life. Includes interviews with Tyler's mother and former teachers.

Caren J. Town, "Rewriting the Family During Dinner at the Homesick Restaurant," in *Southern Quarterly,* Vol. 31, No. 1, fall, 1992, pp. 14–23.

The critic discusses how in *Dinner at the Homesick Restaurant* each major character attempts to construct an ideal fictional family for himself or herself.

Joseph C. Voelker, "Dinner at the Homesick Restaurant," in his *Art and the Accidental in Anne Tyler,* University of Missouri Press, 1989, pp. 125-46.

A psychological study of the characters of *Dinner at the Homesick Restaurant.*

Joseph B. Wagner, "Beck Tull: The Absent Presence in *Dinner at the Homesick Restaurant,*" in *The Fiction of Anne Tyler,* edited by Ralph C. Stephens, University Press of Mississippi, 1990, pp. 73-83.

The critic discusses the impact of Beck Tull's desertion on his wife and three children.

Anne R. Zahlan, "Anne Tyler," in *Fifty Southern Writers after 1900: A Bio-Bibliographical Source Book,* edited by Joseph M. Flora and Robert Baines, Greenwood Press, pp. 491–504.

An excellent overview of Tyler biography, themes, and criticism.

Flowers for Algernon

Daniel Keyes

1966

Originally published as a short story in 1958, *Flowers for Algernon* appeared as a full-length novel in 1966 and has remained a critical and popular success. The novel is told as a series of "Progress Reports" written by Charlie Gordon, a thirty-two-year-old man whose Intelligence Quotient (IQ) of 68 is tripled by an experimental surgical procedure. Unfortunately, the effects of the operation wear off after several months, and at the end of the novel Charlie is once more of subnormal intelligence. Although originally published as a work of science fiction—the short story won the World Science Fiction Convention's Hugo Award and the novel won the Nebula Award of the Science Fiction Writers of America—Daniel Keyes's story has achieved wide popularity outside the science fiction field. Much of the novel's power comes from Keyes's remarkable use of first-person point of view, as Charlie's entries move from semi-literacy to complex sophistication and back to semi-literacy. And the character of Charlie Gordon is a memorable portrait of alienation, of an individual who is at odds with his society and who struggles to have satisfactory relationships with others. The novel gained additional fame when its 1968 film version, *Charly,* earned Cliff Robertson an Academy Award as Best Actor for his portrayal of Charlie Gordon. Although some critics have found portions of the novel overly predictable or sentimental, Keyes's most famous work has continued to enjoy great popularity. Over thirty years after publication, *Flowers for Algernon* is still regarded with both respect and affection by

readers within both the science fiction community and the public at large.

Author Biography

Daniel Keyes was born in Brooklyn, New York, on August 9, 1927. He was educated at Brooklyn College, where he received an A.B. degree in 1950. After graduation, Keyes worked briefly as an associate editor for the magazine *Marvel Science Fiction* while pursuing his own writing career; he later taught high school English in Brooklyn. In 1952 he married Aurea Georgina Vazquez, with whom he had three children. Keyes returned to Brooklyn College, received an A.M. degree in 1961, and went on to teach English on the university level, first at Wayne State University in Detroit, Michigan, and then at Ohio University, where in the 1970s he became Professor of English and director of the university's creative writing center.

Keyes was still teaching high school English when he first published the work that would make his reputation. The original short story version of "Flowers for Algernon" appeared in *The Magazine of Fantasy and Science Fiction* in 1959. After the story won the Hugo Award for best science fiction story of the year and was adapted as a television drama, Keyes expanded the story into a novel, published in 1966. The novel won the Nebula Award of the Science Fiction Writers of America (tying with Samuel R. Delany's *Babel-17*) and was filmed in 1968 as *Charly*. The film was a notable success, earning Cliff Robertson an Academy Award as Best Actor for his portrayal of Charlie Gordon.

Although none of Keyes' other work has achieved the popular and critical success of *Flowers for Algernon,* he has continued to write while pursuing a full-time career in English academics. He published two other novels, *The Touch* (1968) and *The Fifth Sally* (1980), and the nonfiction works *The Minds of Billy Milligan* (1981) and *Unveiling Claudia: A True Story of a Serial Murder* (1986). Both *The Minds of Billy Milligan* and *The Fifth Sally* share with *Flowers for Algernon* a concern with extraordinary psychological states, as both books examine the phenomenon of multiple personalities. Indeed, Keyes was able to write his book on Billy Milligan—the first person in the United States ever acquitted of a major felony on the grounds of multiple personalities—only after

Daniel Keyes

several of Milligan's selves read *Flowers for Algernon* and agreed to work with the author.

Now retired from Ohio University and living in Boca Raton, Florida, Keyes has recently completed a new novel and seen his work attain tremendous popularity in Japan. *Daniel Keyes Collected Stories* (1993) and *The Daniel Keyes Reader* (1994), and the sequel to *The Minds of Billy Milligan, The Milligan Wars* (1993), have all been published in Japan, with *The Milligan Wars* appearing in a U.S. edition in 1996.

Plot Summary

Part I—Charlie Becomes a Genius

Flowers for Algernon is told as a series of "Progress Reports" written by Charlie Gordon, a thirty-two-year-old man with an IQ of 68. As Keyes's novel opens, Charlie has volunteered to be the subject of an experimental surgical procedure which would more than triple his IQ. Although Charlie is of subnormal intelligence, he is unusually motivated, taking night school classes at the Beekman University Center for Retarded Adults. At first, he is afraid he won't be chosen for the project. He doesn't understand what to do when he is asked to tell what he sees in inkblots, and when he traces through a diagram of a maze in competition with Algernon, a mouse who is running an actual maze, Algernon always wins. Nonetheless, Charlie is chosen by the scientists in charge of the project— Professor Nemur, the psychologist who developed the technique, and Dr. Strauss, the neurosurgeon who performs the actual operation.

After the surgery, Charlie returns to his job as a janitor at Donner's Bakery, where nobody is aware of his operation. The sad state of Charlie's life prior to the surgery is made clear when Joe Carp and Frank Reilly, whom Charlie regards as his friends, take him out to a bar, get him drunk, make fun of him, and leave him to find his way home.

As time passes, however, it becomes obvious that Charlie is getting smarter. At the bakery, he successfully operates a complicated machine that mixes baking dough. His performances on the psychological tests improve, and he finally beats Algernon at running the maze—a significant development, as the mouse has had its intelligence raised by the same surgical procedure that Charlie underwent. And his Progress Reports are more sophisticated and articulate than before.

As Charlie's IQ increases, so does his awareness of himself and others. Now, when his "friends" make fun of him, he understands their true motivations. He steadily advances at work, but takes no satisfaction from it because the other employees resent him. Eventually, his coworkers at the bakery are so unnerved by his unexplained changes that they sign a petition demanding that he be fired. The only one who doesn't, an old woman named Fanny Birden, nonetheless thinks Charlie's condition "ain't right" and wishes he could return to "the good simple man" he had been.

Charlie also realizes that he has fallen in love with Alice Kinnian, the night school teacher who originally recommended him for the operation. Despite the gentleness of her rejection, Charlie is terribly upset, as he is when he catches Gimpy, the one person at the bakery who had been kind to him, stealing. Charlie is becoming aware that factual knowledge and intellectual ability may not prepare a person to deal with all of life's problems.

Part II—Charlie as a Genius

As Charlie tries to cram a lifetime of intellectual and emotional development into a period of months, he also increases his self-awareness by recovering lost memories, a process triggered by

sleep-learning devices and continued through his ongoing psychotherapy sessions with Dr. Strauss. Through a series of flashbacks, we learn the agonizing details of Charlie's early life. Charlie's father, Matt, tried to do the best he could for his son. But Charlie's mother, Rose, denied that there was anything "wrong" with him and beat him when he was unable to learn like other children. However, when Charlie's sister Norma was born with normal intelligence, Rose turned against Charlie and sought to "protect" Norma from him, reacting with particular violence to anything he did that showed his developing sexuality. Finally, after an hysterical outburst in which Rose threatened to kill Charlie, Matt took Charlie to live with his uncle Herman. When Herman died several years later, Rose tried to have Charlie committed to the Warren State Home and Training School, an institution for the mentally handicapped, but Charlie avoided this when the owner of Donner's Bakery, a lifelong friend of his uncle Herman, offered him a job. The "new" Charlie now realizes that both his extraordinary motivation to learn and his confused responses to women are rooted in how he was treated by his mother.

As Charlie's IQ surges to nearly triple its original level, his relationship with Alice deepens, but when she is finally able to return his feelings, his childhood traumas leave him unable to make love to her. More importantly, the gap between their respective IQs makes it harder and harder for them to communicate, a problem the genius Charlie now has with almost everyone. In particular, he has come to regard Nemur and Strauss, who previously seemed unapproachable geniuses, as narrowly-focused specialists more interested in acquiring fame and power than they are in increasing knowledge and helping others. When Nemur and Strauss take Charlie and Algernon to a psychologists' conference in Chicago to announce the success of their procedure, Charlie is outraged by their treating him like an object on display rather than as a human being. He is also disturbed by what appears to be an error in Nemur's analysis of the "waiting period" after the operation. Disgusted, Charlie deliberately lets Algernon loose in the conference room. While the others are frantically trying to recover the mouse, Charlie slips Algernon in his pocket, leaves the conference, and returns to New York, where he rents an apartment and drops out of sight.

Now completely on his own, Charlie devotes himself to reading, thinking, and recovering his memories. During this time he forms a relationship with Fay Lillman, a painter who lives down the hall. Charlie is attracted to Fay's free spirit and lack of inhibitions, but, as with Alice, he is unable to have a sexual relationship with her. His sense of isolation increases. Yearning for meaningful contact with others, he walks the streets of New York feeling an "unbearable hunger" for human contact. He even goes to visit his father, who left his mother several years earlier. His father fails to recognize him, and Charlie cannot bring himself to reveal his identity. A few days later, while dining alone in a restaurant, Charlie witnesses a young man drop a stack of dishes:

> When the owner came to see what the excitement was about, the boy cowered—threw up his arms as if to ward off a blow.
>
> "All right! All right, you dope," shouted the man, "don't just stand there! Get the broom and sweep up that mess. A broom ... a broom! you idiot! It's in the kitchen. Sweep up all the pieces."
>
> When the boy saw that he was not going to be punished, his frightened expression disappeared, and he smiled and hummed as he came back with the broom. A few of the rowdier customers kept up the remarks, amusing themselves at his expense.
>
> "Here, sonny, over here. There's a nice piece behind you ... "
>
> "C'mon, do it again ..."
>
> "He's not so dumb. It's easier to break 'em than to wash 'em...."
>
> As the boy's vacant eyes moved across the crowd of amused onlookers, he slowly mirrored their smiles and finally broke into an uncertain grin at the joke which he did not understand.
>
> I felt sick inside as I looked at his dull, vacuous smile—the wide, bright eyes of a child, uncertain but eager to please, and I realized what I had recognized in him. They were laughing at him because he was retarded.
>
> And at first I had been amused along with the rest.
>
> Suddenly, I was furious at myself and all those who were smirking at him. I wanted to pick up the dishes and throw them. I wanted to smash their laughing faces. I jumped up and shouted: "Shut up! Leave him alone! He can't understand. He can't help what he is ... but for God's sake, have some respect! *He's a human being!*"

The incident makes Charlie decide to return to Beekman University and work on his own to perfect Nemur and Strauss's procedure so that it might help others like himself.

After returning to the University, Charlie renews his relationship with Alice but is still unable to make love to her. He turns back to Fay, whom he does not truly love but with whom he is able, finally, to have a sexual relationship. Eventually,

though, Charlie becomes so immersed in his research that he moves into the lab and breaks off with Fay, who resents the time he devotes to his work—and who also has never known the truth about Charlie. Time is of the essence, as Algernon is beginning to show signs of instability and decline. Charlie works feverishly to determine if the effects of his operation will last, driven both by his fear of reverting to his former self and his desire to find any information at all that might help other mentally handicapped people. He also begins to achieve a more mature insight into his own nature and that of other people. In a confrontation with Nemur, Charlie declares that "intelligence and education that hasn't been tempered by human affection isn't worth a damn."

Part III—Charlie Loses His Genius

Finally, Charlie's completes his research. In a letter to Nemur, he announces his discovery of the "Algernon-Gordon Effect": "artificially-induced intelligence deteriorates at a rate of time directly proportional to the quantity of the increase." Charlie will revert to his former IQ within a matter of months. Shortly after this discovery, Algernon dies.

Faced with the prospect of losing all he has gained, Charlie seeks to come to terms with himself and his memories. He visits his mother and sister, who still live in Brooklyn. Rose has sunk into senility and only momentarily recognizes her son. Norma, far from being the hateful rival Charlie remembers, is a kind and intelligent woman who sincerely regrets both Charlie's hardships and her own inability to help him through them.

Charlie also comes to terms with Alice Kinnian, who is determined to stick by him as long as possible. Having put the ghosts of his past to rest, he is finally able to make love to her, and they are fully together for a brief time. But Charlie's decline is rapid, and he pushes Alice away before he completely reverts to his former self.

Charlie's final Progress Reports reflect his rapid deterioration as his writing reverts to its earlier semi-literacy. However, he has retained some memory of his experiences, and perhaps some insight as well. When he goes back to his old job at the bakery, he notes, "if they make fun of you dont get sore because you remember their not so smart like you once thot they were." The bakery workers accept him back; Carp and Reilly, who formerly had tormented Charlie, defend him when a new worker makes fun of him. However, Charlie finally decides to leave New York for good and check him-

From the film Charly, *an adaptation of* Flowers for Algernon, *starring Cliff Robertson, 1968.*

self into the Warren State Home and Training School. His final Progress Report, dated only eight months after the first, asks that someone "put some flowrs on Algernons grave in the bak yard."

Characters

Algernon

The mouse who was the first subject of the surgery which raised Charlie's intelligence. Charlie forms a close emotional bond with the mouse, who is the only other creature to have had its intelligence artificially raised. Its experiences, and fate, parallel Charlie's.

Fanny Birden

An older woman who works at the bakery with Charlie and who is the only employee who does not sign a petition demanding Charlie's resignation after his IQ is raised. She compares the change in Charlie's intelligence to Adam and Eve eating of the fruit of the Tree of Knowledge and wishes that Charlie "could go back to being the good simple man you was before."

Joe Carp

One of Charlie's coworkers at the bakery, and, with Frank Reilly, one of his chief tormentors.

Mr. Arthur Donner

The owner of the bakery where Charlie works, Mr. Donner is a friend of Charlie's Uncle Herman and gave Charlie his job there. Unlike many others at the bakery, he treats Charlie decently, if condescendingly.

Gimpy

A worker at Donner's bakery who treats Charlie better than many of the other workers do. However, Gimpy is the cause of one of the post-operative Charlie's first major crises when Charlie sees him stealing from the cash register. When Charlie confronts him about stealing, Gimpy says, "I always stood up for you. I should of had my head examined."

Charlie Gordon

The narrator and central character of *Flowers for Algernon,* Charlie Gordon is a 32-year-old man with an IQ of 68. As a child, Charlie had a father who loved him and tried to take care of him, but he was abused by his mother, an emotionally unstable woman. His mother at first refused to admit that there was anything "wrong" with Charlie and beat him when he did not perform up to the standards of other children. When Charlie's sister was born with normal intelligence, his mother admitted his handicap but became obsessed with the fear that Charlie would harm his sister—especially, that he would sexually molest her. This unreasoning fear led Charlie's mother to violently repress any display of sexuality on Charlie's part and, eventually, to threaten to kill him if he was not removed from their home.

This pattern of childhood abuse marked the adult Charlie in two significant ways: with repressed sexuality and with a strong desire to learn. It was the latter that led him to take night classes at the Beekman School and which led to his being accepted as a subject for an operation that would raise his intelligence. Before the operation, Charlie is perceived as a "good, simple man" and a "likeable, retarded young man." His main goal in undergoing the operation is "to be smart like other pepul so I can have lots of friends who like me."

However, once Charlie attains normal intelligence, he sees that many people he thought were his friends were actually ridiculing and abusing him, and once he attains a genius IQ, he finds himself as remote and alienated from other people as he had been previously. He struggles to deal with the emotions he now has the intellect to recognize, but which his intellect alone cannot control. He also works to recover and come to terms with memories of his childhood. Through it all, Charlie's main desire is what it always has been: to be treated as a human being and to be able to establish satisfactory relationships with other human beings.

Although Charlie demonstrates some character flaws after his intelligence peaks, such as arrogance and self-absorption, he is basically a good man. When he realizes that the surgical procedure is flawed, he throws himself into research to discover the flaw, feeling that if his efforts contribute at all to "the possibility of helping others like myself, I will be satisfied." When he finally determines that nothing can be done to prevent his return to his pre-operative state, he does what he can to come to terms with his family and those around him, and they in turn recognize his worth as a human being. Even after Charlie returns to his previous subnormal level of intelligence, he has learned to be understanding of the failings of others because they are "not so smart like you once thot they were." Although the experiment has failed, Charlie Gordon has not.

Matt Gordon

Charlie's father, a salesman of barbershop supplies. He is basically a kind man who loves his son and tries to protect him but who is consistently overpowered by his wife: first, by her hysterical denial that Charlie is handicapped, and then by her equally hysterical conviction that Charlie is a danger to their daughter. When Rose threatens to kill Charlie, Matt takes Charlie to his Uncle Herman, who offers Charlie a refuge. Years later, Matt finally leaves Rose and opens his own barbershop. When the adult Charlie seeks him out, he does not recognize his son.

Norma Gordon

Charlie's sister. Charlie's memory of her is of a "spoiled brat" who hated him and treated him badly. However, when the adult Charlie visits the adult Norma, who now has full-time care of their senile mother, he finds a grown woman who is "warm and sympathetic and affectionate." She genuinely regrets her youthful hostility towards her brother, and wants to reestablish contact with him.

Media Adaptations

- The original short story version of *Flowers for Algernon* was adapted for television as *The Two Worlds of Charlie Gordon* for CBS Playhouse in 1961.

- The novel *Flowers for Algernon* was made into the feature film *Charly* in 1968. Cliff Robertson won the Academy Award as Best Actor for his portrayal of Charlie Gordon. Available from CBS/Fox Home Video.

- The novel has also been presented on the stage. David Rogers adapted the novel as a two-act play, *Flowers for Algernon,* in 1969; a dramatic musical, *Charlie and Algernon,* was first produced in Canada in 1978 and played on Broadway in 1980. Stage plays based on the novel have also been produced in France, Australia, Poland, and Japan.

- *Flowers for Algernon* has also been adapted for radio: as a monodrama for Irish radio in 1983, and as a radio play in Czechoslovakia in 1988.

Rose Gordon

Charlie's mother. She is an emotionally unstable woman who was largely unable to cope with having a mentally handicapped child. During Charlie's early childhood, she refused to admit that he was anything other than "normal" and beat him when he was unable to perform at the same level as other children. After Charlie's sister Norma was born without mental handicaps, Rose quit trying to make Charlie "normal" and became obsessed with "protecting" Norma from him. Eventually, Rose breaks down completely, declares that Norma is in danger of being sexually molested by Charlie, and threatens to kill him if he is not removed from their home. When Charlie reestablishes contact with his mother many years later, he discovers an old woman far gone into senility who barely recognizes her son.

Hilda

A nurse who attends Charlie immediately after the operation and who tells him that the scientists should not have altered his intelligence. She compares their action to Adam and Eve eating the fruit of the Tree of Knowledge and being cast out of Eden.

Miss Alice Kinnian

Charlie Gordon's teacher at the Beekman University Center for Retarded Adults, the person who recommends Charlie for the procedure which raises his intelligence, and the woman Charlie loves. Alice is an intelligent and dedicated woman who takes a strong personal interest in Charlie and consistently treats him in a responsible and respectful manner. As Charlie's intelligence increases, she guides him as best she can; when he falls in love with her, she gently declines. However, they maintain a close friendship, and Alice eventually finds herself returning Charlie's feelings, only to discover that the traumas of his past prevent him from making love to her. She remains his friend, despite the increasing distance his towering intelligence places between them. When the operation finally fails and Charlie enters his decline, they are finally able to have a romantic relationship. Alice tries her best to stick by Charlie, even when he pushes her away, but when he is finally back where he began, with an IQ of 68, she is forced to admit that he is lost to her and that she has to go on with her life.

Fay Lillman

A free-spirited artist who lives across the hall from Charlie when he "disappears" in New York. When Charlie first sees her painting in her underwear, she thinks nothing of it, and she does not hesitate to crawl along a window ledge to get to Charlie's apartment. Charlie eventually enters into a sexual relationship with her, although he does not love her, and she provides Charlie with a whirlwind social life of drinking, dancing, and having a good time. Although she evidently feels genuine affection for Charlie, she is uninterested in his research, perhaps in part because she does not know that Charlie has had his intelligence artificially raised. When Charlie moves into the lab because Fay is interfering with his work, she loses interest in him and drifts away.

Bertha Nemur

Professor Harold Nemur's wife. An ambitious woman who used her father's influence to get Professor Nemur the grant that funded his research and who is constantly pressuring her husband to excel and produce great results. According to Burt Selden, she is why Nemur is "under tension all the time, even when things are going well...."

Professor Harold Nemur

The psychologist who developed the theories behind the operation which raised Charlie's intelligence. Nemur is a brilliant scientist but egotistical and ambitious, the latter stemming partially from pressures from his wife. He is eager to establish his reputation as the discoverer of the process that made Charlie a genius and rushes to make the results of the experiment public, against the advice of the other scientists working on the project. He does not initially want Charlie to be the subject of the experiment, and after Charlie's IQ is raised, relations between the two are often strained, as Charlie's intelligence eventually exceeds Nemur's. This hostility culminates in a shouting match between the two during which Charlie accuses Nemur of treating him as less than a human being and Nemur accuses Charlie of having become "arrogant, self-centered," and "antisocial."

Frank Reilly

One of Charlie's coworkers at the bakery, and, with Joe Carp, one of his chief tormentors.

Burt Seldon

A graduate student who assists Professor Nemur and Dr. Strauss. He is in charge of Charlie's psychological testing, and he treats Charlie in a more relaxed and friendly fashion than either of the senior scientists. It is through Burt that Charlie gets much of his information about Nemur and Strauss, and it is Burt who suggests that the post-operative Charlie needs to develop "understanding" and "tolerance."

Dr. Strauss

Dr. Strauss, Professor Nemur's partner, is the neurosurgeon who performs the surgery that raises Charlie's IQ. He is more sympathetic to and concerned for Charlie than is Nemur. He advocates that Charlie be chosen for the experiment, intervenes when Charlie has a potentially violent confrontation with Nemur, and tries to look after Charlie when the effects of the experiment have finally worn off.

Thelma

A nurse at the Warren State Home who impresses Charlie by her devotion to her patients. Because he already knows he is regressing and could end up as a resident of Warren, Charlie wonders what it would be like to have her care for him.

Themes

Science and Technology

Relating the story of a mentally impaired man whose intelligence is increased through surgery and then lost, *Flowers for Algernon* touches on a number of literary themes. The most obvious of the novel's themes is the use and abuse of science and technology. The critic Mark R. Hillegas has identified *Flowers for Algernon* as the type of science fiction which deals with "problems imagined as resulting from inventions, discoveries, or scientific hypotheses"—in this case, a surgical procedure that can turn a person of subnormal intelligence into a genius. While the novel does not specifically take an anti-technology stance, it does make clear the limitations of technology as a "quick fix" to human problems—Charlie's operation is, ultimately, a failure in that he does not remain a genius. In a reversal of the classic notion of tragedy, the "flaw" which causes Charlie's downfall is not within him, but in the technology which sought to change him.

Knowledge and Ignorance

The idea that "there are some things humanity was not meant to know" may be traced in modern literature to Mary Shelley's novel *Frankenstein* (1818), and in some ways *Flowers for Algernon* contains echoes of Shelley's tale. The critic Thomas D. Clareson has directly connected Keyes's novel to *Frankenstein* in that Keyes combines the figures of the mad scientist and the "inhuman" creation into "the single figure of Charlie Gordon." This theme is further emphasized by the comments of Hilda, a nurse, and Fanny Birden, one of Charlie's coworkers, which compare his operation to the acquisition of forbidden knowledge in the Garden of Eden, which resulted in Adam and Eve being thrown out of Paradise.

However, *Flowers for Algernon* does not argue that humans should not try to attain knowledge, but rather that they should be conscious of the limitations of a purely intellectual approach to life. When Charlie buries himself in research to try to find the solution to the flaw in the operation, he declares, "I'm living at a peak of clarity and beauty I never knew existed." But later, dur-

Topics for Further Study

- Research the history of public attitudes towards mental retardation in the United States and discuss the problems Charlie Gordon faces in the novel in the context of this history.

- Research Sigmund Freud's theories of psychology and discuss how Charlie Gordon's emotional problems (*not* his low IQ) can be explained in terms of Freudian analysis.

- Read the original short story version of *Flowers for Algernon* and compare it with the novel. What changes have been made, and how do those changes affect the reader's response to the story?

ing an argument with Professor Nemur, Charlie acknowledges that intelligence alone isn't enough: "intelligence and education isn't worth a damn … all too often a search for knowledge drives out the search for love."

Alienation and Loneliness

In an early "progress report," Charlie writes that he wants to be smart "so I can have lots of friends who like me." Unfortunately, once he becomes a genius, he discovers that there are a whole new set of problems that prevent him from establishing satisfactory relationships with other people. He has substituted one sort of alienation for another, as the condescension and cruelty he once faced from humanity has been replaced by misunderstanding, insensitivity, and fear. He falls in love with Alice Kinnian, the teacher who recommended him for the operation, but he realizes, "I am just as far away from Alice with an I.Q. of 185 as I was when I had an I.Q. of 70." Almost everything Charlie does in the novel is motivated by his desire to understand himself and establish functional relationships with others, perhaps most dramatically expressed when he wanders the streets of New York City by himself: "for a moment I brush against someone and sense the connection."

Atonement and Forgiveness

A major aspect of the novel is Charlie's efforts to understand and come to terms with the various people who have hurt him throughout his life: his mother, who physically and emotionally abused him; his father, who failed to defend him; his coworkers at the bakery, who brutalized him; the scientists who raised his intelligence but treated him like a laboratory animal. It is significant that when Charlie realizes the effects of the operation will not last, his major goal is to locate his family and establish some sort of peace with them. When he finally locates his mother, he tells himself, "I must understand the way she saw it. Unless I forgive her, I will have nothing." The tragedy of Charlie's fall from genius is relieved somewhat by the knowledge that he has come to terms with the people who mistreated him. In his last progress report, he writes, "if they make fun of you dont get sore because you remember their not so smart like you once thot they were."

Prejudice and Tolerance

Written during the height of the civil rights movement in the United States, *Flowers for Algernon* shows a profound concern with the rights of individuals to be treated as individuals, no matter what their condition in life. The early pages of the novel paint a grim portrait of how the mentally handicapped are treated, as Charlie is continually abused, verbally and physically, by his coworkers at the bakery. And when he becomes a genius, he is subject to a different sort of dehumanization, as the scientists in charge of the experiment regard him "as if I were some kind of newly created thing.... No one ... considered me an individual— a human being." This is perhaps most dramatically expressed when, witnessing a slow-witted boy being ridiculed for breaking dishes in a restaurant, Charlie lashes out at the customers: "Leave him alone! He can't understand. He can't help what he is ... but for God's sake, have some respect! *He's a human being!*"

Sex

Although the novel is not primarily focused on sexual issues, a good deal of attention is paid to the fact that Charlie is sexually repressed as a result of an abused childhood. His mother, terrified that her "retarded" son would sexually assault his "normal" sister, violently repressed all normal displays of adolescent sexuality. The adult Charlie, once his intelligence has been raised to where he can understand the issues involved, initially has difficulty establishing a sexual relationship with Fay Lillman, a neighbor who seeks out his company, and is unable to have a physical relationship with Alice Kinnian, the woman he is in love with. Charlie's ability to have sex with Fay and, eventually, with Alice, is seen as an important step in overcoming past traumas and becoming a fully functional adult.

Style

Point of View

Keyes's remarkable use of first-person ("I") point of view is perhaps the most important source of *Flowers for Algernon*'s narrative power. Charlie's journey from an IQ of 68 to one almost three times as high, and his fall back into subnormal intelligence, is told in the form of "Progress Reports" written by Charlie for the scientists conducting the experiment that raised his IQ. The reports before and soon after the operation are written in nonstandard English, full of the kind of mistakes one would expect from writing by a mentally handicapped adult:

> Dr Strauss says I shoud rite down what I think and remembir and evrey thing that happins to me from now on. I dont no why but he says its importint so they will see if they can use me.

As Charlie's intelligence grows, his reports become more and more literate and sophisticated:

> I've got to realize that when they continually admonish me to speak and write simply so that people who read these reports will be able to understand me, they are talking about themselves as well.

The striking contrasts between the earlier and later entries, both in style and content, dramatize both the changes Charlie undergoes and the obstacles he must overcome. Even more dramatic is the contrast between the high-IQ entries and the final entries, when Charlie loses his intelligence and falls back into the semi-literacy of the earlier entries. Keyes's use of Charlie as the narrator makes the reader's experience of Charlie's inevitable fate more immediate and more moving, and shows that, as a reviewer in the *Times Literary Supplement* put it, Keyes "has the technical equipment to keep us from shrugging off the pain."

Foreshadowing

Another source of the novel's power is the inevitability of Charlie's fate, once we learn that the results of the experiment will not be permanent.

But even before we learn that the experiment has failed, Keyes offers several moments of foreshadowing, events which hint at what is to come. The most obvious of these center around Algernon the mouse, who has had the same operation as Charlie and whose progress and deterioration both mirrors and forecasts Charlie's own. When Algernon begins to grow restive, has trouble running the maze, and starts biting people, it does not bode well for Charlie. In addition, two minor characters—Hilda, a nurse, and Fanny Birden, one of Charlie's coworkers at the bakery—both invoke the story of Adam and Eve's expulsion from the Garden of Eden, which foreshadows Charlie's own "fall" from genius. Charlie's trip to the Warren State Home while he still possesses heightened intelligence foreshadows what is in store when he finally loses that intelligence. And, in a more subtle moment early in the novel, as Charlie is on the operating table before the surgery, he tells Dr. Strauss that he's scared. When Dr. Strauss reassures him that he will "just go to sleep," Charlie replies, "thats what I'm skared about"—a foreshadowing, perhaps, of Charlie's later descent into darkness.

Setting

The setting of *Flowers for Algernon* is New York City, with a brief episode in Chicago, in the present or near future. Although the physical landscape and cultural background is not a major part of the novel, critic Robert Scholes has noted that the very normality and non-distinctiveness of the setting makes the one "different" element of the novel—the surgical procedure that raises Charlie's IQ—all the more distinctive. And at one point in the novel, when Charlie has taken Algernon and is hiding out from the scientists, the crowded urban landscape of New York City becomes an important part of Charlie's attempts to come to terms with his situation: "on a hot night when everyone is out walking, or sitting in a theater, there is a rustling, and for a moment I brush against someone and sense the connection between the branch and trunk and the deep root."

Irony

Irony—the difference between the way things appear to be and the way they really are—plays an important part in *Flowers for Algernon*. Early in the novel, we see that Charlie's coworkers at the bakery, especially Joe Carp and Frank Reilly, are condescending and abusive towards him, insulting him to his face and playing cruel tricks on him. Charlie, however, writes that "Lots of people laff at me and their my friends and we have fun…. I cant wait to be smart like my best friends Joe Carp and Frank Reilly." Once Charlie becomes smart, he realizes that these people are not his friends, but he is then faced with another irony. Before the operation, he wanted "to be smart like other pepul so I can have lots of frends who like me." But his increased IQ causes the bakery workers to be afraid of him, the scientists who had been kindly and wise figures turn out to be limited human beings who see Charlie more as a laboratory experiment than a human being, and heightened intelligence is no help when he falls in love with Alice Kinnian. As Charlie the genius notes, "Ironic that all my intelligence doesn't help me solve a problem like this." And in a final irony, when Charlie returns to his IQ of 68 and seeks his old job back, Joe and Frank, the men who had persecuted him before, defend him against an attack from a new worker.

Tragedy

In literature, tragedy refers to works where a person, often of great achievement, is destroyed through a character flaw that he or she possesses. In classic tragedy, this "fall" is often from a great height (Oedipus and Hamlet were both royalty, for example) and is inevitable, given the character's character flaw. *Flowers for Algernon* is certainly about a fall from a height, and Charlie's descent from genius to subnormal intelligence is inevitable. Charlie does have character flaws—an arrogance and impatience which appear when he becomes a genius—but these do not lead to his fall. Instead, the "flaw" is outside of Charlie, in the technology which raises him to a great height and then allows him to fall back down. In this way, Keyes is able to use the devices of tragedy to make a very modern point: that our technology is as imperfect as we are.

Historical Context

Civil Rights in the 1960s

The issue which lies at the heart of *Flowers for Algernon* is Charlie Gordon's struggle to be recognized and treated as a human being. Prior to his operation, he was regarded as somehow less than fully human because of his subnormal intelligence. After the operation, he is discriminated against in a different way, as ordinary people shun him and the scientists who raised his IQ treat him as little more than another laboratory specimen. It should come as no surprise that this story of a person who

Compare & Contrast

- **1960s:** The civil rights movement was in full force, with passage of legislation addressing discrimination against African Americans and increasing awareness of the rights of other oppressed groups, including the mentally handicapped. However, prejudice was still widespread, and there was as yet little to no legal protection for mentally handicapped persons.

  Today: Legislative and legal protection for the mentally handicapped is extensive, while public sensitivity to the rights of the handicapped has increased markedly. Terms such as "retarded" and "feeble-minded" have been replaced with less negatively-charged terms such as "mentally challenged" and "developmentally disabled." However, civil rights as a whole is in a volatile period, as the public at large seems increasingly resistant to the demands of minority groups.

- **1960s:** Psychoanalysis is increasingly accepted as a means of dealing with mental illness, while the theories of Sigmund Freud enjoy widespread public awareness and acceptance.

  Today: The treatment of emotional disorders is increasingly diverse, with traditional psychoanalysis complemented by various holistic, Eastern, and "New Age" approaches, as well as by the development of increasingly effective antidepressants and other psychoactive drugs. However, the theories of Sigmund Freud are not as widely accepted as in the past, and the public at large appears impatient with what it sees as abnormal or dangerous behavior "excused" because of past trauma.

- **1960s:** The pressures of the Cold War lead to an unprecedented amount of spending on scientific research by both the U.S. government and private foundations and corporations.

  Today: With the Cold War over and budgets shrinking, competition for research funding is more intense than ever, and funding agencies are increasingly reluctant to support research that does not have immediate, practical results.

---

manages to be a member of two different minorities—the mentally handicapped and the mentally superior—should have appeared during a time of growing awareness of the problems and the rights of minority groups.

The period from the first publication of *Flowers for Algernon* as a short story to its publication as a novel, the period from 1959 to 1966, saw the rise of the civil rights movement in the United States. Although most immediately and dramatically focused on the task of securing equal rights for African Americans, the civil rights movement was accompanied by increasing attention to the issue of fair and equal treatment for all. The 1964 Civil Rights Bill prohibited racial discrimination; 1966, the year *Flowers for Algernon* was published, saw the founding of the National Organization for Women. The rights of the mentally handicapped were also addressed during this time: in 1962 the President's Panel on Mental Retardation was organized, leading in 1968 to the Declaration of the General and Specific Rights of the Mentally Retarded. By the 1970s, the term "retardation" was replaced with "developmental disability," and specific provisions for the protection of the mentally handicapped from violence and discrimination became law. *Flowers for Algernon*'s message of tolerance and understanding for the mentally handicapped reflects the social and political struggles of its day, and the years following the novel's publication saw many of these issues regarding developmental disability finally addressed in the legislature and the courts.

Psychology and the Rise of Scientific Research

In addition to the Civil Rights movement, the 1950s and 1960s also saw the rise of psychoanaly-

Mentally handicapped children in school, Sonoma, California, 1962.

sis as a generally accepted method of dealing with emotional disorders. The theories of Sigmund Freud, which saw human motivation as stemming largely from unconscious desires which are often traceable to childhood experiences and which frequently center on sex, were particularly influential during this time. Freud's theories were so widely discussed that most people, even if they were not trained in psychoanalysis, probably had some familiarity with concepts such as repression, neurosis, and the unconscious. Accordingly, the novel's focus on psychological themes, especially Charlie's emotional problems stemming from the abuse he suffered from his mother, was immediately familiar to the readers of the 1960s.

Also on the rise in the 1950s and 1960s was funding for scientific research. Locked in a Cold War with the Soviet Union and still remembering Nazi Germany's V-2 rockets and the terrifying success of the atomic bomb, the United States during this era spent an unprecedented amount of money on scientific research. Government organizations such as the National Science Foundation, as well as private foundations and corporations, poured millions of dollars into scientific research. This included "basic" research that would not necessarily yield immediate practical applications. With so much money available, competition for funding in-

tensified and universities became increasingly focused on obtaining and keeping research funding. In *Flowers for Algernon,* Professor Nemur and Dr. Strauss's funding from the "Welburg Foundation," as well as the pressure Nemur feels to publish his results and secure his professional reputation, directly reflect this trend.

Critical Overview

There is not as much critical commentary on *Flowers for Algernon* as there is on some other contemporary novels. What criticism does exist has occasionally found fault with the novel on the grounds of sentimentality or predictability, but on the whole the critical response has been favorable. Critics have also noted the novel's status as a work of science fiction.

Typical of the critical response to Keyes's novel is Mark R. Hillegas' 1966 *Saturday Review* essay, which ranks *Flowers for Algernon* with Kurt Vonnegut's *Player Piano* and Walter M. Miller, Jr.'s *A Canticle for Leibowitz* as a "work of quality science fiction," although Hillegas finds the novel "considerably less powerful" than Vonnegut's or Miller's novels. Hillegas also notes that Keyes's novel is occasionally "marred by a cliched dialogue or a too predictable description." Nonetheless, he finds that the novel "offers compassionate insight into the situation of the mentally retarded" and is "profoundly moving."

Other contemporary reviews sounded much the same note. Eliot Fremont-Smith, writing in the *New York Times* in 1966, states that Keyes "has taken the obvious, treated it in a most obvious fashion, and succeeded in creating a tale that is convincing, suspenseful, and touching—all in modest degree, but it is enough." Despite the many potential problems, such as how to convincingly show Charlie as a genius, "the skill shown here is awesome," and "affecting, too—how otherwise explain the tears that come to one's eyes at the novel's end?" Similarly, a reviewer in the *Times Literary Supplement* finds some of the minor characters "less successfully created" but praises the novel as "a far more intelligent book than the vast majority of 'straight' novels."

What critical attention *Flowers from Algernon* has received since its original publication has come mostly from scholars discussing the novel as a work of science fiction. In his 1975 book *Structural Fabulation: An Essay on Fiction of the Future*, Robert Scholes discusses the novel as "minimal SF" that, unlike some works of science fiction, "establishes only one discontinuity between its world and our own"—in other words, the experiment which raises Charlie's intelligence. Scholes finds the novel "beautifully problematic" and asserts that its power derives largely from the fact that the results of the operation are impermanent. While "Keyes has fleshed out his idea with great skill," Scholes also sees the novel as "deficient in artistic integrity" because of its existence as both a short story and a novel.

More recently, the noted British SF writer and critic Brian W. Aldiss, in his 1986 book *Trillion Year Spree: The History of Science Fiction*, compares Charlie to the character of Lenny in John Steinbeck's *Of Mice and Men*. Unlike other critics, Aldiss prefers the original short story to the novel: "This moving story lost something of its power when expanded to novel length." And in his 1990 study *Understanding Contemporary American Science Fiction*, Thomas D. Clareson claims that Keyes "revitalized the myth of Frankenstein by introducing a fresh narrative perspective" and combining "Mary Shelley's nameless creature and the crazed scientist into the single figure of Charlie." Clareson further notes that the novel's "narrative perspective" makes it "unique in the science fiction pantheon."

Criticism

F. Brett Cox

F. Brett Cox is an assistant professor of English at Gordon College in Barnesville, Georgia. In the following essay, he explores how Flowers for Algernon *both works as and transcends science fiction, particularly in its exploration of themes of alienation and humanity.*

Like Harper Lee and J. D. Salinger, Daniel Keyes is an author whose reputation rests on a single remarkable novel. Keyes' *Flowers for Algernon,* like Lee's *To Kill a Mockingbird* and Salinger's *The Catcher in the Rye,* is a powerful story of alienation, of an individual who is at odds with his society and who struggles to have satisfactory relationships with others. Unlike Lee's and Salinger's novels, however, *Flowers for Algernon* is also a work of science fiction: the type of science fiction, according to *Saturday Review* critic Mark R. Hillegas, that "deals with moral, social, psychological, theological, or philosophical problems imagined as resulting from inventions, discoveries, or scientific hypotheses." While firmly within the "literary" tradition of Lee and Salinger, therefore, *Flowers for Algernon* also stands in the tradition of such classic science fiction novels as Kurt Vonnegut, Jr.'s *Player Piano*, Ray Bradbury's *Fahrenheit 451,* and Walter M. Miller, Jr.'s *A Canticle for Leibowitz.*

Keyes' story is also noteworthy for its success in many different forms. It was originally published as a short story, which was adapted in 1961 as a television play entitled *The Two Worlds of Charlie Gordon.* The full-length novel version was adapted in 1968 as the feature film *Charly.* The short story won the World Science Fiction Convention Hugo Award for best story of 1959, the novel won the Science Fiction Writers of America Nebula Award as best novel of 1966, and Cliff Robertson, the actor who portrayed Charlie Gordon in the feature film, won the Academy Award for Best Actor.

The science fiction idea of *Flowers for Algernon* is simple: what if people could undergo a surgical procedure that would raise their IQ's? The first person to undergo such an operation is Charlie Gordon, a 32-year-old man with an IQ of 68. Unlike many other mentally handicapped adults, Charlie is highly motivated to learn. He goes to night school at the Beekman University Center for Retarded Adults and repeatedly states his desire to be smarter than he is. It is this level of motivation, finally, that convinces the scientists in charge of the project to accept him as the second subject for the procedure, the first having been a mouse named Algernon.

Much of the novel's power comes from Keyes' remarkable use of first-person point of view. *Flowers for Algernon* is told in the form of "Progress Reports" written by Charlie for the scientists conducting the project. The reports before and soon after the operation are written in nonstandard English, full of the kind of mistakes one would expect from writing by a mentally handicapped adult:

> Dr Strauss says I should rite down what I think and remembir and evrey thing that happins to me from now on. I dont no why but he says its importint so they will see if they can use me. I hope they use me becaus Miss Kinnian says mabye they can make me smart. I want to be smart. My name is Charlie Gordon I werk in Donners bakery where Mr Donner gives me 11 dollers a week and bred or cake if I want. I am 32 yeres old and next month is my birthday.

As Charlie's intelligence grows, his Progress Reports become more and more literate and sophisticated. Three months after the operation, he writes:

> I've got to realize that when they continually admonish me to speak and write simply so that people who read these reports will be able to understand me, they are talking about themselves as well. But still it's frightening to realize that my fate is in the hands of men who are not the giants I once thought them to be, men who don't know all the answers.

The striking contrasts between the earlier and later entries, both in style and content, dramatize both the changes Charlie undergoes and the obstacles he must overcome. Keyes' deft handling of point of view helps to ensure that, unlike in many science fiction novels, the ideas in *Flowers for Algernon* are expressed through the novel's characters, and not the other way around.

The two quotes above also represent the central conflict of the novel: the difference between Charlie's, and the scientists', expectations of what can be accomplished through increased intelligence, and the reality of what intelligence alone can and cannot do. Before the operation, Charlie wants to be smart, not to gain power or advancement, but to improve his relationships with other people: "I dont care so much about beeing famus. I just want to be smart like other pepul so I can have lots of friends who like me." However, as Charlie's IQ increases, so does his disillusionment. When his "friends" make fun of him, he understands their true motivations: "Now I know what they mean when they say 'to pull a Charlie Gordon.'" He

What Do I Read Next?

- *The Minds of Billy Milligan* is Daniel Keyes's 1981 nonfiction study of the case of Billy Milligan. When Milligan was arrested and charged with rape in 1977, he was found to have at least twenty-four distinct personalities. Milligan became the first person in U.S. history to be acquitted of a major felony by reason of multiple personality.

- *The Science Fiction Hall of Fame, Vol. I,* edited by Robert Silverberg, is a 1970 anthology of classic science fiction stories which contains Keyes's original short story version of "Flowers for Algernon."

- Theodore Sturgeon's *More Than Human,* published in 1953, is a classic science fiction novel which, like *Flowers for Algernon,* is based on psychology and deals with the alienation of unusual individuals.

- The character of Boo Radley in *To Kill a Mockingbird* by Harper Lee, published in 1960, is another example of an emotionally disabled victim of childhood abuse who is shunned by society.

- Novelist and critic Brian W. Aldiss has compared Charlie Gordon to Lenny, one of the main characters in John Steinbeck's classic American novel *Of Mice and Men* (1940).

- *Flowers for Algernon* has been compared to *A Canticle for Leibowitz,* Walter M. Miller, Jr.'s 1959 novel of the world after a nuclear holocaust, as an example of "quality" science fiction.

steadily advances at work, but "all of the pleasure is gone because the others resent me." He falls in love with Alice Kinnian, the night school teacher who originally recommended him for the operation, and is devastated by her rejection. Charlie is becoming aware that factual knowledge and intellectual ability alone do not prepare a person to deal with all of life's problems: "Ironic that all my intelligence doesn't help me solve a problem like this."

As Charlie learns more about the people in his life, he also learns more about himself. The postoperative sleep learning he undergoes to increase his store of factual knowledge also triggers his recovery of long-suppressed memories. These memories, recorded in the Progress Reports as they occur, reveal the harrowing details of Charlie's early life, especially concerning his abusive mother, Rose. At first, she denied there was anything "wrong" with Charlie and beat him when he was unable to learn like other children. However, after Charlie's sister Norma was born with normal intelligence, Rose turned against Charlie. Obsessively (and needlessly) fearful of Charlie molesting Norma, Rose reacted with particular violence to any behavior that showed evidence of his normally developing sexuality. Charlie's extraordinary motivation to learn, therefore, as well as his difficulty in expressing his sexual desires for women, are rooted in how he was treated by his mother. Keyes thus places the novel's emphasis on psychology firmly within the tradition of Freudian analysis, which sees human motivation as stemming largely from unconscious desires which are often traceable to childhood experiences and which frequently center on sex.

By the time Charlie's IQ peaks at nearly triple its original level, he realizes he was mistaken to think, as he did before the operation, that with increased intelligence "you can have lots of friends to talk to and you never get lonely." His relationship with Alice has deepened, but when she is finally able to return his feelings, he is unable to make love to her. More importantly, the gap between their respective IQs makes it harder and harder for them to communicate, a problem Charlie now has with almost everyone. As Burt, the graduate student who administers Charlie's psychological tests, points out to him, "You've got a superb mind now.... But you're lopsided. You know things. You see things. But you haven't developed understanding or—I have to use the word—tolerance." In particular, Charlie has come to regard Nemur and Strauss, the scientists in charge of the project, as narrowly-focused specialists more interested in acquiring fame and power than they are in increasing knowledge and helping others. His disappointment with them turns into fear when he discovers that there is a flaw in Professor Nemur's analysis of the "waiting period" following the operation, a flaw which may indicate that the results of the operation are not permanent.

By this point in the novel, Keyes has firmly established what critic Thomas D. Clareson has called *Flowers for Algernon's* "double-edged theme: the unthinking brutality with which society treats the mentally retarded and the terrible isolation of soaring intellect."

After walking out on a psychology conference where the scientists "talk[ed] about me as if I were some kind of newly-created thing," Charlie turns his back on both Alice and the project scientists. But despite his genius-level IQ and newfound personal freedom, his sense of isolation increases. He forms a relationship with Fay Lillman, an artist who knows nothing of Charlie's "former" life and whose uninhibited, free-spirited lifestyle is a sharp contrast to both the earnest and responsible Alice and the demanding, controlling project scientists. But, as with Alice, he is unable to have a sexual relationship with her. Yearning for meaningful contact with others, he walks the streets of New York feeling an "unbearable hunger" for contact with others. He even goes to visit his father, who left his mother several years earlier. His father fails to recognize him, and Charlie, sensing himself about to be disappointed yet again, does not reveal his identity: "I wasn't his son. That was another Charlie. Intelligence and knowledge had changed me, and he would resent me—as the others from the bakery resented me—because my growth diminished him."

There follows one of the key moments in the novel when, while dining alone in a restaurant, Charlie witnesses an obviously slow-witted young man drop a stack of dishes. Seeing his earlier self in this young man, Charlie is outraged by the abusive response of the young man's boss and the condescension of the customers, doubly so because "at first I had been amused along with the rest." After this incident, Charlie decides to return to Beekman University and begin his own research to try and perfect the procedure that raised his IQ.

The Progress Reports Charlie writes while engaged in his own research reveal a Charlie Gordon who is, for the first time, a fully functional adult. He works feverishly, driven by his fear of reverting back to his former self—Algernon is beginning to show signs of instability and decline. However, Charlie is also driven by his desire to help others like himself: "if [my research] adds even one jot of information to whatever else has been discovered about mental retardation and the possibility of helping others like myself, I will be satisfied," and by the sheer joy of discovery: "I'm living at a peak of clarity and beauty I never knew existed." He is finally able to distance himself from his childhood traumas and make love to Fay. Most importantly, he begins to achieve a more mature insight into his own nature and that of other people. In a violent argument with Nemur, Charlie declares that "intelligence and education that hasn't been tempered by human affection isn't worth a damn…. But all too often a search for knowledge drives out the search for love."

Eventually, Charlie discovers the flaw in the experiment, and his worst fear is realized. His raised intelligence is not permanent; within a few months, he will return to his former mental state. How Charlie faces this devastating news shows that, beyond his increased IQ, he has learned far more important lessons of tolerance, understanding, and acceptance. "No one is in any way to blame for what has happened," he writes shortly before he enters his final decline. "I don't want anyone to suffer because of what happens to me." After visiting his mother, who has fallen into senility and only sporadically recognizes her son, Charlie realizes that she is no longer a target for hatred: "I must understand the way she saw it. Unless I forgive her, I will have nothing." He finally is able to make love to Alice, the only person he has truly loved, and for a brief period they have a complete and fulfilling relationship.

But Charlie's decline is even more rapid than his ascent. He leaves Alice and the others of the project rather than have them witness his return to subnormal intelligence, a process depicted in agonizing detail as his Progress Reports return to the broken English and lack of awareness they exhibited before the operation. Charlie's return to his former state is all the more poignant because, although he has lost his intelligence, he has not lost all of the insights he gained: "if they make fun of you dont get sore because you remember their not so smart like you once thot they were." At the end of the novel, Charlie prepares to go voluntarily to the Warren State Home for the mentally handicapped, leaving a final request regarding Algernon, who had died two months earlier: "please if you get a chanse put some flowrs on Algernons grave in the bak yard."

Keyes has published two other novels and three nonfiction books, all of which also deal with themes of psychology and the structure of the human personality, but *Flowers for Algernon* remains his most famous work. Although critics have been largely positive about the novel, their praise has

sometimes been accompanied by negative comments, usually along the lines of Mark R. Hillegas' suggestion that the novel is occasionally "marred by a cliched dialogue or a too predictable description." These reservations, however, have not kept critics from acknowledging *Flowers for Algernon* as an unusually powerful and moving work of literature, or kept two generations of readers from keeping it in print. In the words of a *Times Literary Supplement* critic, although the novel is "painful," it is also "important and moving…. Mr. Keyes has the technical equipment to prevent us from shrugging off the pain."

Source: F. Brett Cox, in an essay for *Novels for Students*, Gale, 1997.

Robert Small, Jr.

In the following excerpt, Small traces Flowers for Algernon *through several incarnations, and praises it as a successful example of fiction that answers the question "what if?"*

Daniel Keyes' *Flowers for Algernon* appeared first in the form of a long short story in 1959 in *The Magazine of Fantasy and Science Fiction,* and in 1960 received from the World Science Fiction Society the Hugo Award for the Best Novelette of that year. It seems to have been immediately recognized as a piece of literature well above the routine, for it was anthologized in the next two years in *Fifth Annual of the Year's Best Science Fiction, Best Articles and Stories,* and *Literary Cavalcade.* In the years that followed, it re-appeared as a television play by the Theater Guild under the title, *The Two Worlds of Charlie Gordon,* in 1966 in an expanded version as a novel, and later still in 1968 as a film with the title *Charly.* The film's star, Cliff Robertson, received an Oscar for his performance. The novel version received the Nebula Award for the Best Novel of 1966 from the Science Fiction Writers of America.

Reviews of the novel on its first appearance were generally very favorable and tended to praise its treatment of mental retardation. For example, the *Times Literary Supplement* said the following:

> a good example of that kind of science fiction which uses a persuasive hypothesis to explore emotional and moral issues. By doing more justice than is common to the complexity of the central character's responses it gives body to its speculations. In its ideas, especially in its speculations about the relationship between I.Q. and maturity, this is a far more intelligent book than the vast majority of "straight" novels. Moreover, the intelligence is displayed in a treat-

ment of subject-matter which is bound to affect us as both important and moving.

It has, then, achieved literary success in an unusual variety of forms, and may well be the best known work of science fiction to the general public, that is, to non-science fiction fans. This success has come about because, as Robert Scholes puts it, "it was based on a powerful concept which worked well in all those forms."

Although it originally appeared in a magazine devoted to science fiction, fictional science is used sparingly, allowing the author, with one exception to the ordinary and real, to answer the "What if?" that is the trade mark of this literary genre. Keyes raises the question, What if an operation could be discovered that allowed a retarded person to develop not only average intelligence but to become the world's most brilliant man? The author answers that question by inventing such a procedure and then allowing the reader to follow that development stage by stage as the subject of the experiment, Charlie Gordon, a slow-witted but pleasant and kind man, becomes [as Robert Scholes describes him in *Structural Tabulation*] increasingly "an impatient, aggressive, arrogant, and unlovable man as his powers increase, inspiring envy, jealousy, and even fear in others." Aware of what is happening to him, Charlie fights the negative change in his personality, but fails to overcome his contempt for the ordinary individuals around him. Here is a quotation from his journal when he is at his most arrogant:

> But there were other kinds of papers too—P. T. Zellerman's study on the difference in the length of time it took white rats to learn a maze when the corners were curved rather than angular, or Worfel's paper on the effect of intelligence level on the reaction-time of rhesus monkeys. Papers like these made me angry. Money, time, and energy squandered on the detailed analysis of the trivial.

Keyes "what if" question is one that might occur to any reader, for who would not wish to become a genius? But the story is not merely a pleasant fantasy. Rather, Keyes returns the reader to reality by having the effects of the operation gradually reverse themselves. Charlie, who has been the butt of jokes by the "normal" people he works with, gradually regains their friendship as his mind returns to its retarded state and he returns mostly but not fully to his more pleasant personality, "affection grounded in pity" Scholes calls it. Charlie is retarded at the beginning of the story, and he is not aware that the friends he has are not real friends, that they treat him with disrespect, look down upon

him, and enjoy a sense of superiority because they are not like him:

> Gimpy hollered at me because I droppd a tray full of rolles I was carrying over to the oven. They got derty and he had to wipe them off before he put them in to bake. Gimpy hollers at me all the time when I do something rong, but he reely likes me because hes my frend. Boy if I get smart wont he be serprised.

At the end, when these former friends begin to treat him as they formerly had, he accepts them but with more understanding of who they are and why they act as they do. He comments:

> Evrybody looked at me when I came downstairs and started working in the toilet sweeping it out like I use to do. I said to myself Charlie if they make fun of you dont get sore because you remember their not so smart like you once thot they were.

Writing in *Library Journal* [February 1, 1966] shortly after the story appeared in its novel form, Keyes described his story this way:

> *Flowers for Algernon* is the story of a man's inner journey from a world of retardation to a world of high intelligence. Charlie Gordon lives through comic, sad, and ironic experiences as he emerges from his mental darkness, through the various stages of perceiving and understanding levels of knowledge, into the light of complex awareness of the world, of people, and of himself.

A major contributor to the success of the work in novelette and novel form is the fact that the author tells the story by means of a notebook that Charlie begins to keep at the behest of the doctor involved. Thus we see both the low level of literacy and thought that marks Charlie at the start of the adventure, as well as the sweetness of his character, by means of those journal entries. And we like him and yet feel the contempt that Scholes tells us is the basis for pity. At the same time, the story as told through Charlie's own journal, effectively carries out one of the main qualities that proponents of literature claim for it, immediacy of experience, that is, empathetic power. In Scholes' words, "It conveys to us the deprivation involved in mental retardation as no amount of reports or exhortations could possibly do." For example, Charlie writes, "If your smart you can have lots of friends to talk to and you never get lonely by yourself all the time." And later, reflecting on his former state when he encounters a retarded boy, he writes,

> It infuriated me to remember that not too long ago I—like this boy—had foolishly played the clown.
>
> And I had almost forgotten.
>
> Only a short time ago, I learned that people laughed at me. Now I can see that unknowingly I joined them in laughing at myself. That hurts most of all.

As the effects of the operation appear, the entries in the notebook parallel those changes. Charlie's style evolves from short, awkward sentences and partial sentences cluttered with misspellings and marked by a limited vocabulary into, first, what Scholes calls "a rich, vigorous syntax." Then, as Charlie's mind begins its retreat to its former state, his style gradually reflects that change, though it can be argued at the end of the novel he has retained perhaps a bit of the grasp of language that he had at the height of his mental powers.

At first, Charlie is not aware that he is losing the intelligence that he has gained. Soon, however, his still superior mind realizes what is happening, and he struggles to keep what he has gained. As he goes over what he still knows, as he practices and practices what he has learned, each entry in the notebook showing yet further loss, Charlie takes on an heroic stature as someone who has seen the marvelous, lost it, but remains determined at least to keep its memory alive. And Charlie is not bitter. Rather, after a first bout with anger and frustration, as he works to retain what he is losing, he regains the sweetness of his temper, his kindness, tolerance, and generosity. Here he is in the midst of his struggle to keep what he is gradually losing:

> I dont no why Im dumb agen or what I did rong. Mabye its because I dint try hard enuf or just some body put the evel eye on me. But if I try and practis very hard mabye Ill get a littel smarter and no what all the words are. I remembir a littel bit how nice I had a feeling with the blue book that I red with the toren cover. And when I close my eyes I think about the man who tored the book [the smart Charlie] and he looks like me only he looks different and he talks different but I dont think its me because its like I see him from the window.
>
> Anyway thats why Im gone to keep trying to get smart so I can have that feeling agen. Its good to no things and be smart and I wish I new evrything in the hole world. I wish I could be smart agen rite now. If I could I would sit down and reed all the time.

The story, then, has much to offer a reader, and it seems especially well suited to a young reader. The premise is easy to understand and one that most of us, including children, can identify with—the desirability of becoming smarter. Keyes's "what if" question is, in fact, probably one that most students have wished for in the competitive world of the school. At the same time, young readers can be helped through Charlie's entries at the beginning and close of the story to see into the world of someone like Charlie and understand that it is he, not the false friends around him, who is worthy of respect. As the story progresses, they can identify

with his exultation over his growing intellect; but they can also see that the arrogance and cruelty resulting from his superior intellect make him less than he could be, less in some ways than the earlier Charlie was. As the process reverses itself and Charlie becomes less smart, young readers can surely feel the terrible sense of loss that Charlie feels and realize that he faces that loss far better than they might. They can admire the determination that he displays to the very end of the story to hold on to what he can of his new found understanding.

Many teachers have recognized the fact that *Flowers for Algernon* would make an effective focus for reading and discussing in an English class, and so it has been used extensively with middle and high school classes. It appears on many recommended reading lists for these grades, including the National Council of Teachers of English *Books for You,* the American Library Association's *Outstanding Books for the College Bound,* and the H. W. Wilson company's *Senior High School Library Catalog.* The Perfection Form company has prepared a set of work sheets to accompany its study, and versions of it have appeared in school literature anthologies.

But its use has not been without censorship problems. Two of the most common points of objection to literature by would-be censors have been aimed at it: sex and religion. Charlie is, of course, a young man. As such, he would realistically have an interest in sex; and Keyes does devote a few passages to rather tame sexual encounters. As a result it has been called pornographic and sexually explicit, although it surely is neither. In addition, because the operation changes Charlie from the man that some readers feel their God meant Charlie to be, it has been accused of tampering with the will of God, of turning men—the doctors, that is—into gods, and of supernaturalism, although the story clearly dwells in the world of science fiction rather than fantasy. It is, these critics argue, only for God to give mankind intellect. It was Satan who aspired to such power; and so if a work of literature shows a human possessing such powers, that work is clearly irreligious and perhaps Satanic. The Office for Intellectual Freedom of the American Library Association and People for the American Way have documented numerous recent cases; it is listed in ALA's *Hit List* as one of the most frequent targets of censorship.

The power of *Flowers for Algernon* lies partly in the original concept, the "what if" that Keyes asks and then answers. More important, the novel gives its readers profound insights into people, retarded, average, brilliant, kind and cruel, and it does so with stylistic brilliance and control. Perhaps most important, it creates one of those rare truly round fictional characters, to use Forester's term, who surprise convincingly, who have lives before and after the story is told, who seem to possess free will. Keyes' accomplishment is all the more impressive because his character changes so drastically during the course of the novel, yet remains for the reader one human, and one we continue to care about past the end of the novel. Toward that end, Charlie writes in his last entry,

> If you ever reed this Miss Kinnian [his former teacher] dont be sorry for me. Im glad I got a second chanse in life like you said to be smart because I lerned alot of things that I never even new were in this werld and Im grateful I saw it all even for a littel bit. And Im glad I found out about my family and me. It was like I never had a family til I remembird about them and saw them and now I know I had a family and I was a person just like evryone.

Source: Robert Small, Jr., "*Flowers for Algernon* by Daniel Keyes," in *Censored Books: Critical Viewpoints,* edited by Nicholas J. Karolides, Lee Burress, and John M. Kean, Scarecrow Press, 1993, pp. 249–255.

Robert Scholes

Scholes is an American scholar and critic who has written widely on postmodern realistic fiction. In the following excerpt, he discusses Flowers for Algernon *as a work of science fiction, dividing its main idea into two halves: the operation to develop Charlie's intelligence—a familiar motif in science fiction—and the impermanence of the operation, which distinguishes the novel as an original and powerful work. Additionally Scholes observes that the book's packaging circumvents questions about its genre.*

Daniel Keyes's *Flowers for Algernon* might be called minimal SF. It establishes only one discontinuity between its world and our own, and this discontinuity requires no appreciable reorientation of our assumptions about man, nature, or society. Yet this break with the normal lifts the whole story out of our familiar experiential situation. It is the thing which enables everything else in the novel, and it is thus crucial to the generation of this narrative and to its affect on readers. How crucial this idea is can be seen in the story's history, which, as it happens, makes an interesting fable in itself. It first appeared as a long story in *The Magazine of Fantasy and Science Fiction* in April 1959. It received a Hugo award in 1960 for the best science fiction novelette of the year. It was then reprinted in *The Best from Fantasy and Science Fiction* and in the *Fifth Annual of the Year's Best Science Fiction,* both published in 1960, and in *Best Articles and Stories* and *Literary Cavalcade* in 1961. It was made into a television drama and then rewritten to appear as a full-length novel in 1966. Then it was made into a movie and given, of course, a new title: *CHARLY* (with the *R* childishly reversed). In 1967 it appeared in paperback and has now been through more than thirty printings. My paperback copy, which is from the thirty-second printing (1972), has a scene from the film on the cover, with the word *CHARLY* prominently displayed, and a bundle of "rave" quotations from reviewers on the back cover. Nowhere on the cover of this book does the expression "science fiction" appear. Even the Hugo award (which is at least as reliable an indicator of quality as, say, the Pulitzer Prize for Fiction) goes unmentioned. Inside, in very fine print, the ultra-snoopy purchaser may find in the back pages some words about the author, which indicate that this work first appeared as a "magazine story" (but the name of the magazine is suppressed) and that it won a Hugo award as the "best science novelette" in 1960. Even there, the cautious editors have managed to avoid the stigmatizing expression. *Flowers for Algernon* has gone straight, folks; it has passed the line around the SF ghetto, and to remind us of its sordid history would be downright impolite. And it might chase away a lot of potential customers who "hate science fiction."

An interesting fable, is it not, from which a number of conclusions may be drawn. It certainly reveals something about attitudes toward SF in various quarters, and this is instructive as well as amusing. But it also reveals something about the genre itself. *Flowers for Algernon* could succeed in four distinct forms (novelette, TV drama, full-length film, and full-length novel) because it was based on a powerful concept which worked well in all those forms. Daniel Keyes had an exceptionally good idea for a work of fiction, and the idea is what made it originally and still makes it a work of SF. The idea is simply that an operation might be performed on a severely retarded adult male, which would enable his mind not merely to catch up with those of his peers but actually to surpass theirs. That is half of the idea. The other half, which completes and justifies this idea, is that the effects of the operation would prove impermanent, so that the story involves our watching the protagonist grow into a genius unconsciously, and then consciously but helplessly slip back toward a state of semi-literacy. When this mental voyage has come full circle, the story is over.

For many people, I suspect, the first half of this idea constitutes the domain of SF, a land of inconsequential wish-fulfillment in which the natural laws that constitute the boundaries of human life are playfully suspended. But the best writers of structural fabulation do not settle for mere imaginative play. Daniel Keyes completed the circuit of his idea, and the beauty and power of the resulting story were acknowledged by his readers at the eighteenth World Science Fiction Convention, where he was awarded the Hugo. It should be added that Keyes's execution of his idea was fully adequate to the original conception. He undertook to present the story through a journal kept by the protagonist himself, at the request of his doctor. Thus, we see the growth of Charlie Gordon's mind through the evolution of his prose style as well as in the events narrated. (Mr. Keyes, we might note, happens to be an English teacher.) Charlie acquires a competence in grammar, an extensive lexicon, and a rich, vigorous syntax—and then gradually loses all these, as his mental powers fade. He also becomes an impatient, aggressive, arrogant, and unlovable man as his powers increase, inspiring envy, jealousy, and even fear in others. But as he loses his mental competence he regains the affection of those around him—an affection grounded in pity, which is, as Joseph Conrad knew, a form of contempt.

This tale is beautifully problematic. It conveys to us the deprivation involved in mental retardation as no amount of reports or exhortations could possibly do it. And it does this by the fabulative device of an apparently miraculous scientific discovery. It is fabulation that promotes speculation, and speculation that is embodied in an emotionally powerful fable. The intensity of our emotional commitment to the events of any fiction, of course, is a function of countless esthetic choices made by the author—at the level of the word, the sentence, the episode, the character, the ordering of events, and the manner of the presentation. These aspects of *Flowers for Algernon* cannot be dismissed without devoting much more space-time to this story than is available here. I must assert, merely, that Keyes has fleshed out his idea with great skill, and I invite those interested to investigate the text for themselves....

I should like to use this occasion to examine an aspect of this story which is typical of the genre as a whole, and of the special qualities which seem to differentiate it from other kinds of fiction. Like many works of SF, *Flowers for Algernon* appeared first as a story and then was "expanded" into a novel. Now all of our training in esthetics and all of our background in the critical thought of Flaubert and James, for instance, must lead us to believe that a work of verbal art consists of one set of words in one particular order. Thus, this idea of expansion seems to have more to do with packaging and merchandising than it can do with art. To some extent this must be admitted. The shapes of genres have always had something to do with the means of their communication and the needs of their audiences. But if the "same" story can appear in two different versions just to suit the exigencies of commercial publication as a magazine story and a book, then we may rightfully feel that the work must be deficient in artistic integrity.

Source: Robert Scholes, "Structural Fabulation," in *Structural Fabulation: An Essay on Fiction of the Future,* University of Notre Dame Press, 1975, pp. 45-76.

Sources

Brian W. Aldiss, with David Wingrove, in *Trillion Year Spree: The History of Science Fiction,* Gollancz, 1986.

Thomas D. Clareson, *Understanding Contemporary American Science Fiction: The Formative Period, 1926-1970,* University of South Carolina Press, 1990, pp. 231-33.

Eliot Fremont-Smith, "The Message and the Maze," in *New York Times,* March 7, 1966, p. 25.

Mark R. Hillegas, "Other Worlds to Conquer," in *Saturday Review,* Vol. 49, March 26, 1966, pp. 33-4.

"Making up a Mind" (review of *Flowers for Algernon*), in *Times Literary Supplement*, No. 3360, July 21, 1966, p. 629.

Robert Scholes, "Structural Fabulation," in his *Structural Fabulation: An Essay on Fiction of the Future,* University of Notre Dame Press, 1975, pp. 45-76.

For Further Study

DISCovering Most-Studied Authors, Gale, 1996.
    Offers biographical and critical information about Keyes.

The Great Gatsby

F. Scott Fitzgerald
1925

In 1925, *The Great Gatsby* was published and hailed as an artistic and material success for its young author, F. Scott Fitzgerald. It is considered a vastly more mature and artistically masterful treatment of Fitzgerald's themes than his earlier fiction. These works examine the results of the Jazz Age generation's adherence to false material values. In nine chapters, Fitzgerald presents the rise and fall of Jay Gatsby, as related in a first-person narrative by Nick Carraway. Carraway reveals the story of a farmer's son-turned racketeer, named Jay Gatz. His ill-gotten wealth is acquired solely to gain acceptance into the sophisticated, moneyed world of the woman he loves, Daisy Fay Buchanan. His romantic illusions about the power of money to buy respectability and the love of Daisy—the "golden girl" of his dreams—are skillfully and ironically interwoven with episodes that depict what Fitzgerald viewed as the callousness and moral irresponsibility of the affluent American society of the 1920s. America at this time experienced a cultural and lifestyle revolution. In the economic arena, the stock market boomed, the rich spent money on fabulous parties and expensive acquisitions, the automobile became a symbol of glamour and wealth, and profits were made, both legally and illegally. The whirlwind pace of this post-World War I era is captured in Fitzgerald's Gatsby, whose tragic quest and violent death foretell the collapse of that era and the onset of disillusionment with the American dream. By the end of the novel, the reader slowly realizes that Carraway is transformed as he

recognizes Gatsby's moral superiority to the Buchanans. In fact, the triumph of Gatsby's legacy is reached by Nick Carraway's ruminations at the end of the book about Gatsby's valiant, however futile, attempts to regain his past love. The discrepancy between Gatsby's dream vision and reality is a prominent theme in this book. Other motifs in the book include Gatsby's quest for the American Dream; class conflict (the Wilsons vs. the Buchanans and the underworld lowbrows vs. Gatsby); the cultural rift between East and West; and the contrast between innocence and experience in the narrator's life. A rich aesthetic experience with many subtleties in tone and content, this novel can be read over and over again for new revelations and continued pleasure.

Author Biography

F. Scott Fitzgerald was an American novelist and short-story writer of the Roaring Twenties. Since his early work shows a romantic feeling for "the promises of life" at college and in "The East," he acquired the epithet "the spokesman of the Jazz Age." His first novel, *This Side of Paradise,* was the first American novel to deal with college undergraduate life in the World War I era. A handsome and charming man, Fitzgerald was quickly adopted by the young generation of his time. His second novel, *The Beautiful and the Damned,* is a lively but shallow book, but his third, *The Great Gatsby,* is one of the most penetrating descriptions of American life in the 1920s.

Born in St. Paul, Minnesota, on Sept. 24, 1896, Scott Fitzgerald was the son of Edward Fitzgerald, who worked for Proctor and Gamble and brought his family to Buffalo and Syracuse, New York for most of his son's first decade. Edward Fitzgerald's great-great-grandfather was the brother of the grandfather of Francis Scott Key, who wrote the poem "The Star-Spangled Banner." This fact was of great significance to Mrs. Fitzgerald, Mollie McQuillan, and later to Scott. Mollie Fitzgerald's own family could offer no pretensions to aristocracy but her father, an Irish immigrant who came to America in 1843, was a self-made businessman. Equally important was Fitzgerald's sense of having come from two widely different Celtic strains. He had early on developed an inferiority complex in a family where the "black Irish half … had the money and looked down on the Maryland side of the family who had, and really had … 'breeding,' " ac-

F. Scott Fitzgerald

cording to Scott Donaldson in the *Dictionary of Literary Biography.* Out of this divergence of classes in his family background arose what critics called F. Scott's "double vision." He had the ability to experience the lifestyle of the wealthy from an insider's perspective, yet never felt a part of this clique and always felt the outsider.

As a youth Fitzgerald revealed a flair for dramatics, first in St. Paul, where he wrote original plays for amateur production, and later at the Newman Academy in Hackensack, New Jersey. At Princeton, he composed lyrics for the university's famous Triangle Club productions. Fitzgerald was also a writer and actor with the Triangle Club at college. Before he could graduate, he volunteered for the army during World War I. He spent the weekends writing the earliest drafts of his first novel. The work was accepted for publication in 1919 by Charles Scribner's Sons. The popular and financial success that accompanied this event enabled Fitzgerald to marry Zelda Sayre, whom he met at training camp in Alabama. Zelda played a pivotal role in the writer's life, both in a tempestuous way and an inspirational one. Mostly, she shared his extravagant lifestyle and artistic interests. In the 1930s she was diagnosed as a schizophrenic and was hospitalized in Switzerland and then Maryland, where she died in a fire.

For some time, Fitzgerald lived with his wife in Long Island. There, the setting for *The Great Gatsby,* he entertained in a manner similar to his characters, with expensive liquors and entertainment. He revelled in demonstrating the antics of the crazy, irresponsible rich, and carried this attitude wherever he went. Especially on the Riviera in France, the Fitzgeralds befriended the elite of the cultural world and wealthy classes, only to offend most of them in some way by their outrageous behavior. Self-absorbed, drunk, and eccentric, they sought and received attention of all kinds. The party ended with the hospitalization of Zelda for schizophrenia in Prangins, a Swiss clinic, and, coincidentally, with the Great Depression of 1929, which tolled the start of Scott's personal depression.

In the decade before his death, Fitzgerald's troubles and the debilitating effects of his alcoholism limited the quality and amount of his writing. Nonetheless, it was also during this period that he attempted his most psychologically complex and aesthetically ambitious novel, *Tender Is the Night* (1934). After Zelda's breakdown, Fitzgerald became romantically involved with Sheila Graham, a gossip columnist in Hollywood, during the last years of his life. He also wrote but did not finish the novel *The Last Tycoon,* now considered to be one of his best works, about the Hollywood motion picture industry. Fitzgerald died suddenly of a heart attack, most likely induced by a long addiction to alcohol, on December 21, 1940. At the time of his death, he was virtually forgotten and unread. A growing Fitzgerald revival, begun in the 1950s, led to the publication of numerous volumes of stories, letters, and notebooks. One of his literary critics, Stephen Vincent Benet, concluded in his review of *The Last Tycoon,* "you can take off your hats now, gentlemen, and I think perhaps you had better. This is not a legend, this is a reputation— and, seen in perspective, it may well be one of the most secure reputations of our time."

Plot Summary

A dinner party

Nick Carraway, the narrator, announces that he is writing his account two years after the events described. Aged twenty-nine, in the spring of 1922, he travels East from his midwestern home to work as a bond salesman in New York. He has rented a house on West Egg, sandwiched between the man-

sions along the shore of Long Island Sound. He knows nobody except his distant cousin Daisy Buchanan, who lives with her wealthy husband Tom on East Egg, across the bay. Nick drives over to dinner with the couple, whom he has not seen in years, and their guest Jordan Baker. Tom, an athletic polo player, betrays his boorish arrogance as he expounds a racist theory he has read. Daisy's magical voice compels Nick forward to listen to her, but he suspects her sincerity when she says she is unhappy. In contrast, dark-haired Jordan strikes Nick with her jaunty self-assurance. At one point, Nick's neighbour "Gatsby" is mentioned and Daisy catches the name in surprise. Dinner is tense; Jordan reveals that it is Tom's mistress telephoning him, and Daisy appears to know. Returning to West Egg, Nick first sees Gatsby. As Nick is about to call to him, Gatsby stretches out both arms towards the water or the green dock light opposite; Nick is mystified.

Myrtle's party

Commuting across the "valley of ashes" to the city, Tom suddenly pulls Nick from their train to meet his mistress, Myrtle. She is a blowsy, vital woman, the wife of servile garage-owner George Wilson. Myrtle catches the next train with them, and impulsively buys a puppy while she and Tom insist that Nick accompany them to their city apartment. Nick reads discreetly while the couple are in the bedroom. Myrtle decides to throw a party, and the apartment fills with people and social chatter. The puppy blinks in the smoky air, the party gets progressively drunker, and Nick wonders what the scene would look like to an observer outside. Myrtle starts chanting Daisy's name, and Tom brutally breaks her nose: the sound of wailing accompanies Nick as he leaves.

Gatsby's party

Nick describes the lavish parties that nightly transform Gatsby's garden. One afternoon a butler brings Nick a formal invitation, and at the party Nick is relieved to spot Jordan in the swirling crowd. Nick hears many extravagant and contradictory rumors from the guests. He and Jordan come across comical "Owl Eyes," a bespectacled man trying to sober up in the library. Later, an elegant young man invites Nick for a hydroplane excursion next morning, and as Nick confesses he has never met their host, the man reveals himself to be Gatsby. Later still, Jordan is called to speak with Gatsby in the house, and then hints at his amazing story but won't tell more. Leaving the party, Nick sees a car in a ditch with its wheel off; the drunken culprit cannot understand the car's predicament. Nick interrupts the story here to reflect that he was actually very busy in the weeks between these three parties described, enjoying the adventure of New York. He catches up with Jordan again and learns more of her character: unlike Nick, she is incurably dishonest, and a careless driver.

Lunch in New York

Gatsby drives Nick to lunch in the city and tells him more about his past. Nick is unsure whether to believe it all but decides to trust Gatsby when he produces an authentic-looking medal as proof. Gatsby then hints of a favor he will ask Nick that day. They have lunch with a sinister friend of Gatsby's, Meyer Wolfsheim, who was apparently responsible for fixing the 1919 World Series. When Tom Buchanan appears, Gatsby looks embarrassed and disappears before Nick can introduce the men.

Tea with Jordan

That afternoon, Jordan tells Nick the story and makes Gatsby's request. Jordan met Daisy in 1917 and in the company of a young soldier. For a time after, Jordan heard only rumors of her before Daisy became engaged to Tom. As bridesmaid, Jordan witnessed Daisy's distress the eve of the wedding, as she held a mysterious letter until it dissolved. Yet the couple married and travelled, although Tom got in the papers after a car accident with another girl, and Daisy had a little girl. When "Gatsby" was mentioned at their recent dinner party, Jordan realized that this is Daisy's young soldier. Gatsby bought his house to be opposite Daisy, hoping she would appear at a party. As she hasn't, he now wants Nick to ask Daisy to tea so that he might meet her again. This afternoon, Nick first kisses Jordan, whose real presence contrasts to Gatsby's ghostly devotion to Daisy.

Reunion

Nick invites Daisy to tea and the day arrives, pouring rain. Despite Gatsby's nervousness, Daisy does arrive. The reunion is difficult, but after Nick leaves the couple alone they are "radiant" together on his return. They take Nick over to Gatsby's house so that Gatsby can show it off, and Gatsby is clearly overwrought by the significance of the occasion after such a long wait.

> Almost five years! There must have been moments even that afternoon when Daisy tumbled short of his dreams—not through her own fault, but because of the colossal vitality of his illusion. It had gone be-

yond her, beyond everything. He had thrown himself into it with a creative passion, adding to it all the time, decking it out with every bright feather that drifted his way. No amount of fire or freshness can challenge what a man will store up in his ghostly heart.

Another party

Nick reflects on Gatsby's "notoriety," and to clear up misconceptions he provides a brief biography of "James Gatz" who, at seventeen, invented and transformed himself into Jay Gatsby. Nick is over at his neighbour's one afternoon as Tom Buchanan drops by with another couple. The three are rude guests, and leave before Gatsby can join them, as he had planned to. The following Saturday, Tom escorts Daisy there, dismissing the extravagance as a "menagerie." Gatsby and Daisy dance, then sit on Nick's porch together as Nick keeps a lookout for Tom. Afterwards, Gatsby says that Daisy doesn't understand. Gatsby obviously expects to repeat the past: when Daisy renounces Tom, she and Gatsby can begin where they left off five years before.

Confrontation

Nick is invited to the Buchanans' with Gatsby and Jordan on a sweltering day at the end of the summer, during which Daisy has spent much time with Gatsby. Daisy's daughter Pammy says hello, then the group casts about for something to do. Daisy suggests the city. When an innocent comment betrays her feelings for Gatsby in front of Tom, the tension worsens. Daisy gets into Tom's car with Gatsby, and Jordan and Nick ride with Tom. Tom stops at Wilson's garage, and is dismayed to hear that Wilson plans to get away with Myrtle. Nick sees Myrtle intent at the window, plainly thinking that Jordan is Daisy. They take a suite at the Plaza Hotel for mint juleps. Finally, Gatsby tells Tom that Daisy doesn't love her husband and they confront one another, as Daisy falters.

> "Oh, you want too much!" she cried to Gatsby. "I love you now—isn't that enough? I can't help what's past." She began to sob helplessly. "I did love him once—but I loved you too."
>
> Gatsby's eyes opened and closed.
>
> "You loved me *too?*" he repeated.

Aftermath

The two men drive their own cars away, and Gatsby and Daisy go on ahead while Nick remembers that it is his thirtieth birthday. The story abruptly mentions a "witness" at the "inquest."

Wilson, acting suspiciously, revealed to the coffee-store proprietor Michaelis that he had locked his wife up. Later, Myrtle runs in front of a car from the city, and is killed. Nick resumes his perspective as Tom's car pulls up to the commotion at the garage. It becomes clear that the "death car" was Gatsby's. Arriving back at the Buchanans', Nick finds Gatsby keeping a watch for Daisy, worried about Tom. Nick gathers that Daisy was driving the car that Myrtle ran in front of because she probably believed that Tom was in it.

Nick warns Gatsby his car will be traced, but he will not leave Daisy, his "grail." Nick describes Gatsby's version of their courtship and Daisy's marriage. Gatsby plans to swim, and Nick leaves with a compliment of friendship and thanks for hospitality. Nick then pieces together the times and events that lead Wilson to find Gatsby in the pool, and shoot him and then himself.

Conclusion

Nick arranges the funeral at which only one former guest, Owl Eyes, appears, and meets with Gatsby's pathetically proud father. Nick reflects that the East is haunted for him, and he decides to go home. Nick has chance meetings with both Jordan and Tom, and is already distant from them. He looks at Gatsby's house before leaving, imagining past wonder at the sight of this new world, relating this with Gatsby's own belief and wonder.

Characters

Jordan Baker

Jordan Baker is an attractive, impulsive, childhood friend of Daisy Buchanan. She is the first person to bring up the subject of Gatsby to Nick Carraway. She also relates the sad story of his relationship with Daisy and Daisy's doomed marriage to the philandering Tom Buchanan. While intrigued by her good looks, Nick recalls that he saw her picture in photos of the sporting life at Asheville, Hot Springs, and Palm Beach in connection with a "critical, unpleasant story." The reader later discovers this concerns a time she cheated in a major golf tournament. Her insincerity with Nick in their love affair is another example of her detached personality. When she first appears in the novel, she is lounging on a sofa with Daisy "as cool as their white dresses and their impersonal eyes in the absence of all desire," like two princesses in an unreal world. Both women use and dispose of people, as Gatsby and Nick experience

firsthand. In Fitzgerald's long line of sensual, modern flapper characters, Jordan is one of the most well-known. There is an amoral aura about her, and her world revolves around herself and false material values. Jordan is distinguished from Daisy in her hard, unsentimental view of romance.

Daisy Buchanan

Daisy Buchanan is one of the true "Golden Girls" of Fitzgerald's stories, the wealthy, hard-to-get debutante. In this book, she is the love interest of Jay Gatsby, who builds his mansion for her, and views her East Egg home from the point of its green light. She is the cousin of Nick Carraway, and was brought up in Louisville society. She was the young love of Gatsby when he was a soldier. He does not see her after he is called to battle overseas. During the interim, she meets Tom Buchanan and marries him. At first happy in this marriage, she later discovers that Tom is having affairs. She withdraws into a dream world, yet never loses interest in the illusion of her love with Gatsby. Daisy flirts with him and entertaining his obsessive interest until she commits murder and he takes the rap. Then, she hides behind the protection of her husband, a cruel brute, who uses and abuses people. Moreover, Daisy's voice is the voice of money, as Nick discovers. Her whole careless world revolves around this illusion: that money makes everything beautiful, even if it is not. The danger is, like Gatsby, she carries the "well-forgotten dreams from age to age." Her spiritual lightness parallels her material wealth, and she hides behind Tom when Gatsby is in danger.

Tom Buchanan

Tom Buchanan is the villain of this novel and has Nazi-like theories of race. Nick knew him from Yale and describes him as "one of the most powerful ends that ever played football" there. From an "enormously wealthy" family, he brings a string of polo ponies from Lake Forest, Illinois, to the East. He and Daisy spend a year in France and "drifted here and there unrestfully wherever people played polo and were rich together," before ending up in East Egg. After college, Tom changes and becomes, the writer notes, a blond thirty-year-old with a "rather hard mouth and a supercilious manner." He tells Nick that, based on a book Tom has read and obviously reveres, "The Rise of the Colored Empires," civilization is "going to pieces" and that the white race will be "submerged." Nick observes that Tom and Daisy belonged to a "secret society" that ruined, through their insensitivity and carelessness,

From the film The Great Gatsby, *starring Robert Redford and Mia Farrow, Paramount, 1974.*

other peoples' lives. Tom is demeaning to George Wilson, his mistress's husband, who owns a garage in the wasteland between New York and East Egg. He also mistreats Myrtle herself, whom he violently hits in front of her sister and Nick when she mentions Daisy's name. The overall impression the reader has of this character is his physical power and brute strength. He is a fairly one-dimensional figure in this sense. Tom is indirectly responsible for Gatsby's death because he uses Wilson's hatred and jealousy against Gatsby in making Wilson believe that Myrtle was Gatsby's mistress.

Nick Carraway

The character of Nick Carraway functions prominently in this novel. He is a transplanted Midwesterner who buys a house in West Egg and sells bonds on Wall Street in New York City. Young and attractive, Nick becomes friends with Jordan Baker at a dinner party, where he is reunited with his cousin, Daisy. Nick, who claims to be the only honest person he knows, succumbs to the lavish recklessness of his neighbors and the knowledge of the secret moral entanglements that comprise their essentially hollow lives. While he is physically attracted to Jordan, he recognizes her basic dishonesty and inability to commit to a relationship. He muses on the loss of his innocence and youth when

he is with her on his thirtieth birthday and sees himself driving on a road "toward death through the cooling twilight." Lacking the romantic vision of Gatsby, Nick sees life now as it is. Nick deduces that Gatsby is both a racketeer and an incurable romantic, whose ill-gotten wealth has been acquired solely to gain prominence in the sophisticated, moneyed world of Daisy's circle.

Nick is the moral center of the book. From his perspective, we see the characters misbehave or behave admirably. In keeping with Nick's code of conduct, inherited from his father, we learn from the very beginning of the novel that he is "inclined to reserve all judgments" about people because whenever he feels compelled to criticize someone he remembers "that all the people in this world haven't had the advantages that you've had." His father also told him, prophetically, that "a sense of the fundamental decencies is parcelled out unequally at birth." At the novel's end, most readers find that Nick is more akin to Gatsby than to any other character in the book. Insofar as Gatsby represents the simplicity of heart Fitzgerald associated with the Midwest, he is really a great man. His ignorance of his real greatness and misunderstanding of his notoriety endear him to Nick, who tells him he is better than the "whole rotten bunch put together."

Media Adaptations

- *The Great Gatsby* was first adapted as a film by Richard Maibaum as producer and Elliott Nugent as director. It stars Alan Ladd, Betty Field, Macdonald Carey, Barry Sullivan, and Shelley Winters, Paramount, 1949.

- The second film was produced by David Merrick, directed by Jack Clayton, and written for the screen by Francis Ford Coppola. The cast features Robert Redford, Mia Farrow, Bruce Dern, Sam Waterston, and Karen Black, Paramount, 1974; available from Paramount Home Video.

- The novel has been recorded twice, once by The Audio Partners, Listening Library. Three sound cassettes, unabridged, read by Alexander Scourby, 1985.

- The other sound recording is by Recorded books, Audiobooks. Three sound cassettes, unabridged, read by Frank Muller, 1984.

Ewing

See Mr. Klipspringer

Jay Gatsby

One of the most fascinating figures in American literary history, Jay Gatsby is a self-created personage, the embodiment of the American Dream. As Nick discovers, Gatsby's parents were poor farmers, whom he had never accepted as his parents. "The truth was that Gatsby of West Egg, Long Island, sprang from his Platonic conception of himself." He developed out of an idealization of the American Dream, and the Golden Girl who personified that. One day, while attending a small Lutheran college in southern Minnesota and feeling dismayed by having to work as a janitor to put himself through school, Gatsby spots the moored yacht of Dan Cody. In an action that changes the young boy's life, Cody welcomes him aboard his yacht and introduces him to fine living. Gatsby becomes the protege of the wealthy goldminer and lives with him until Cody dies. With some wealth of his own and dreams of more, he goes into the army.

His fate is truly sealed when he meets the most popular girl in the Alabama town near his army post. She becomes the embodiment of the American Dream for him instantly, and from that moment they fall in love and he is determined to have the girl named Daisy. He becomes impressed with her beautiful home and many boyfriends. Perhaps attracted to her material value, she becomes his sole reason for being. When he considers his penniless state, he vows never to lose her in that way again, for while he is called to fight and is away at war, she marries a wealthy Midwesterner named Tom Buchanan. Gatsby commits himself to "the following of a grail" in his pursuit of her and what she represents. This obsession is characteristic of a dreamer like Gatsby, who loses a sense of reality but rather believes in "a promise that the rock of the world was founded securely on a fairy's wing."

Jay Gatsby successfully completes his military obligation and attends Oxford afterwards. He then returns to America and becomes involved in a drug ring. In his criminal affairs, he quickly gains wealth. The next time he sees Daisy, however, she is married to Tom Buchanan and lives on Long Island. To be close to her, Gatsby buys a mansion across the bay and gives extravagant parties in the hopes that Daisy will come to one. He discovers that Nick is a distant cousin of Daisy and gets Nick to take him to see her.

Gatsby's parties are vulgar, in spite of his polite manners, and he lacks a sense of security despite the outward manifestation of his ego. Nevertheless, his loyalty to his dream and idealism mark him as one of the tragic heroes in American literature.

Mr. Klipspringer

Mr. Klipspringer is a hanger-on, who lives off Gatsby by boarding at his mansion. He does liver exercises on the floor when Nick tours with Daisy and Gatsby. A "dishevelled man in pajamas," he gives nothing back to Gatsby. Gatsby compliments Klipspringer, or Ewing, as he calls him, for his piano playing of popular songs. One of these features the lines: "One thing's sure and nothing's surer/The rich get richer and the poor get children/Ain't we got fun?" As most of the characters' names in Fitzgerald's stories, Klipspringer resonates as the name of someone who jumps around and "clips" or robs people of something.

Michaelis

A coffee-store owner who lives next to the Wilsons. He is the chief witness at the inquest about Myrtle's death.

Owl Eyes

This minor character illuminates the character of Jay Gatsby. He finds that the books in Gatsby's library are real, even though the pages are uncut. Like the books, Gatsby is the real thing, but unformed, unlettered, and for all his financial cunning, ignorant.

Furthermore, the ocular imagery in the book is enhanced by this character's role since various acquaintances of the mysterious Gatsby lend their truth to his real story.

George Wilson

George Wilson feels henpecked by his wife Myrtle. A victim of circumstance, he has a poor life and can only work to make a living and must ask the man who is having an affair with his wife, Tom Buchanan, for a car with which to move away. Full of anger and frustration about his wife's disloyalty, Wilson acts on his impulses and kills someone who is just as much a victim of the Buchanans as he. According to Nick, "he was a blonde, spiritless man, anemic, and faintly handsome. When he saw us … hope sprang into his light blue eyes." He is a true product of the wasteland between the suburban world of wealth and New York City.

Myrtle Wilson

Myrtle Wilson is the mistress of Tom Buchanan and wife of George Wilson, men representing distinctly separate classes on the social spectrum. Myrtle clearly aspires to a life of wealth with Tom, who humors her with gifts: a puppy, clothes, and various personal items. Nick describes her as a stout woman in her mid-30s, who carries "her surplus flesh sensuously as some women can." She has a vitality and ignores her husband "as if he were a ghost" when Tom appears. She is another one of Tom's victims since he physically hits her in the face at her mention of Daisy's name, and is murdered by a speeding car she thinks belongs to Tom, as she rushes out to greet it.

Meyer Wolfsheim

Meyer Wolfsheim is one of Jay Gatsby's underworld contacts in bootlegging and racketeering. Fitzgerald based this character on a real gangster who fixed the 1919 World Series, Arnold Rothstein. We see Wolfsheim at the Metropole and in dark settings. One of Wolfsheim's notable characteristics is his wearing of cufflinks made of human molars. He is so selfish and insecure that he refuses to attend Gatsby's funeral. Nick sees the gangster part of Gatsby's life as one of the ways he made his money, but he separates Gatsby's character from true insensitive, subhuman criminals like Wolfsheim. Gatsby stands by Daisy when she commits a crime, but Wolfsheim will not honor his relationships.

Themes

Culture Clash

By juxtaposing characters from the West and East in America in *The Great Gatsby,* Fitzgerald was making some moral observations about the people who live there. Those in the Midwest—the newly arrived Nick Carraway—were fair, relatively innocent, unsophisticated, while those who lived in the East for some time—Tom and Daisy Buchanan—were unfair, corrupt, and materialistic. The Westerners who moved East, furthermore, brought the violence of the Old West days to their new lives. Fitzgerald romanticizes the Midwest, since it is where the idealistic Jay Gatz was born and to where the morally enlightened Nick returns. It serves metaphorically as a condition of the heart, of going home to a moral existence rooted in basic, conservative values. Further, the houses of East Egg and West Egg represent similar moral differences. The East is where Daisy and Tom live, and the West is where Gatsby and Nick live. Fitzgerald refers to the West as the green breast of a new world, a reflection of a man's dream, an America subsumed in this image. The materialism of the East creates the tragedy of destruction, dishonesty, and fear. No values exist in such an environment.

American Dream

Gatsby represents the American dream of self-made wealth and happiness, the spirit of youth and resourcefulness, and the ability to make something of one's self despite one's origins. He achieved more than his parents had and felt he was pursuing a perfect dream, Daisy, who for him embodied the elements of success. Gatsby's mentor, Dan Cody, was the ultimate self-made man who influenced Gatsby in his tender, impressionable youth. When Gatsby found he could not win Daisy's love, he pursued the American Dream in the guise of Cody. Inherent in this dream, however, was the possibil-

Topics For Further Study

- Read three of Fitzgerald's short stories dealing with the Jazz Age and compare and contrast these to *The Great Gatsby*. Suggested stories are: "The Rich Boy," "The Diamond as Big as the Ritz," and "Absolution." Investigate the role of religion and material well being in Fitzgerald's fiction, based on his life.

- It is said that Fitzgerald's life mirrored the life of America during the decades of the 1920s and 1930s. Chart the decline and growth of America's economy during this time and draw parallels between them and Fitzgerald's life during those particular periods.

- Much has been written of the American expatriate writers in Paris. Read a book by or about these authors, such as *A Charmed Circle* or *The Sun Also Rises* and define the characteristics of these expatriates, their attitudes to events in the U.S. and Europe, and their choice of lifestyle. Include Fitzgerald's trips to Paris and the Riviera in your observations.

- Conservative v. liberal elements in society create specific legislation designed to protect the interests of all citizens. Prohibition was one example of the U.S. goverment's attempts to appease those who opposed the overabundance of liquor in the society. What are other examples of this in the field of education in the 1920s? Demonstrate how the conservative/liberal elements operated in other countries at that time.

- Examine the Dadaist art movement in Europe— as demonstrated in the works of Marcel Duchamps—and compare its tenets and manifestations to the New York adaptation of this popular art form. Note the philosophy behind this movement and relate it to the Wasteland motif in *The Great Gatsby*.

- Relate the tales of Bonnie and Clyde's shooting spree, Al Capone's underworld activities, and other major scandals of the times. Examine why gangsterism and crime were romanticized in the Twenties, and why they are romanticized today as well.

---

ity of giving in to temptation and to corrupt get-rich-quick schemes like bootlegging and gambling. Fitzgerald's book mirrors the headiness, ambition, despair, and disillusionment of America in the 1920s: its ideals lost behind the trappings of class and material success.

Examples of the American Dream gone awry are plentiful in *The Great Gatsby:* Meyer Wolfsheim's enterprising ways to make money are criminal; Jordan Baker's attempts at sporting fame lead her to cheating; and the Buchanans' thirst for the good life victimizes others to the point of murder. Only Gatsby, who was relatively unselfish in his life, and whose primary flaw was a naive idealism, could be construed as fulfilling the author's vision of the American Dream. Throughout the novel are many references to his tendency to dream, but in fact, his world rests insecurely on a fairy's wing.

On the flip side of the American Dream, then, is a naivete and a susceptibility to evil and poor-intentioned people.

Appearances and Reality

Since there is no real love between Gatsby and Daisy, in *The Great Gatsby,* there is no real truth to Gatsby's vision. Hand in hand with this idea is the appearances and reality theme. Fitzgerald displays what critics have termed an ability to see the face behind the mask. Thus, behind the expensive parties, Gatsby is a lonely man. Though hundreds had come to his mansion, hardly anyone came to his funeral. Owl Eyes, Mr. Klipspringer, and the long list of partygoers simply use Gatsby for their pleasures. Gatsby himself is a put-on, with his "Oggsford" accent, fine clothes, and "old boy" routine; behind this facade is a man who is involved in racketeering. Gatsby's greatness lies in his capacity for illusion. Had he seen Daisy for what she was, he could not have loved her with such singleminded devotion. He tries to recapture Daisy, and for a time it looks as though he will succeed. But he must fail, because of his inability to separate the ideal from the real. The famous verbal exchange between Nick and Gatsby typifies this: concerning his behavior with Daisy, Nick tells him he can't repeat the past. "Can't repeat the past," Gatsby replies, "Why of course you can!"

Moral Corruption

The wealthy class is morally corrupt in *The Great Gatsby,* and the objective correlative (a term coined by poet and critic T. S. Eliot that refers to an object that takes on greater significance and comes to symbolize the mood and world of a literary work) in this case is the eyes of Dr. Eckleburg, which preside over the valley of ashheaps near Wilson's garage. There are no spiritual values in a place where money reigns: the traditional ideas of God and Religion are dead here, and the American dream is direly corrupted. This is no place for Nick, who is honest. He is the kind of person who says he is one of the few honest people he's ever met, and one who is let down by the world of excess and indulgence. His mark of sanity is to leave the wasteland environment to return home in the West. In a similar manner, T. S. Eliot's renowned poem "The Wasteland" describes the decline of Western civilization and its lack of spirituality through the objective correlative (defining image) of the wasteland.

Style

Point of View

The Great Gatsby is told from the point of view of Nick Carraway, one of the main characters. The technique is similar to that used by British novelist Joseph Conrad, one of Fitzgerald's literary influences, and shows how Nick feels about the characters. Superbly chosen by the author, Nick is a romantic, moralist, and judge who gives the reader retrospective flashbacks that fill us in on the life of Gatsby and then flash forward to foreshadow his tragedy. Nick must be the kind of person whom others trust. Nick undergoes a transformation himself because of his observations about experiences surrounding the mysterious figure of Jay Gatsby. Through this first-person ("I") narrative technique,

we also gain insight into the author's perspective. Nick is voicing much of Fitzgerald's own sentiments about life. One is quite simply that "you can never judge a book by its cover" and often times a person's worth is difficult to find at first. Out of the various impressions we have of these characters, we can agree with Nick's final estimation that Gatsby is worth the whole "rotten bunch of them put together."

Setting

As in all of Fitzgerald's stories, the setting is a crucial part of *The Great Gatsby.* West and East are two opposing poles of values: one is pure and idealistic, and the other is corrupt and materialistic. The Western states, including the Midwest, represent decency and the basic ethical principles of honesty, while the East is full of deceit. The difference between East and West Egg is a similar contrast in cultures. The way the characters line up morally correlates with their geographical choice of lifestyle. The Buchanans began life in the West but gravitated to the East and stayed there. Gatsby did as well, though only to follow Daisy and to watch her house across the bay. His utter simplicity and naivete indicates an idealism that has not been lost. Nick remains the moral center of the book and returns home to the Midwest. To him, the land is "not the wheat or the prairies or the lost Swede towns, but the thrilling returning trains of my youth, and the street lamps and sleigh bells in the frosty dark and the shadows of holly wreaths thrown by lighted windows on the snow. I am part of that." He finds that he is unadaptable to life in the East. The memory of the East haunts him once he returns home. Another setting of importance is the wasteland of ash heaps, between New York City and Long Island, where the mechanization of modern life destroys all the past values. Nick's view of the modern world is that God is dead, and man makes a valley of ashes; he corrupts ecology, corrupts the American Dream and desecrates it. The only Godlike image in this deathlike existence are the eyes of Dr. J. L. Eckleburg on a billboard advertising glasses.

Satire

Fitzgerald wrote *The Great Gatsby* in the form of a satire, a criticism of society's foibles through humor. The elements of satire in the book include the depiction of the *nouveau riche* ("newly rich"), the sense of vulgarity of the people, the parties intended to draw Daisy over, the grotesque quality of the name "Great" Gatsby in the title. Satire originated in the Roman times, and similarly criticized the rich thugs with no values, tapped into cultural pessimism, and gave readers a glimpse into chaos. *The Great Gatsby* is the tale of the irresponsible rich. Originally, the title of the book was "Trimalchio," based on an ancient satire of a man called Trimalchio who dresses up to be rich.

Light/Dark Imagery

In *The Great Gatsby,* the author uses light imagery to point out idealism and illusion. The green light that shines off Daisy's dock is one example. Gatsby sees it as his dream, away from his humble beginnings, towards a successful future with the girl of his desire. Daisy and Jordan are in an aura of whiteness like angels—which they are not, of course, yet everything in Gatsby's vision that is associated with Daisy is bright. Her chatter with Jordan is described as "cool as their white dresses and their impersonal eyes" by Nick. The lamp light in the house is "bright on [Tom's] boots and dull on the autumn-leaf yellow of her hair." Gatsby comments to Daisy and Nick how the light catches the front of his house and makes it look splendid, and Nick notes how Daisy's brass buttons on her dress "gleamed in the sunlight." Between the frequent mention of moonlight, twilight, and the women's white gowns, Fitzgerald alludes to the dreamlike qualities of Gatsby's world, and indirectly, to Nick's romantic vision. On the other hand, Meyer Wolfsheim, the gambler, is seen in a restaurant hidden in a dark cellar when Gatsby first introduces him to Nick. "Blinking away the brightness of the street, my eyes picked him out obscurely in the anteroom," says Nick.

Historical Context

The Jazz Age and the Roaring Twenties

The Jazz Age began soon after World War I and ended with the 1929 stock market crash. Victorious, America experienced an economic boom and expansion. Politically, the country made major advances in the area of women's independence. During the war, women had enjoyed economic independence by taking over jobs for the men who fought overseas. After the war, they pursued financial independence and a freer lifestyle. This was the time of the "flappers," young women who dressed up in jewelry and feather boas, wore bobbed hairdos, and danced the Charleston. Zelda Fitzgerald and her cronies, including Sara Murphy, exemplified the ultimate flapper look. In *The Great Gatsby,* Jordan Baker is an athletic, independent woman, who maintains a hardened, amoral view of life. Her character represents the new breed of woman in America with a sense of power during this time.

As a reaction against the fads and liberalism that emerged in the big cities after the war, the U.S. Government and conservative elements in the country advocated and imposed legislation restricting the manufacture and distribution of liquor. Its organizers, the Women's Christian Temperance Movement, National Prohibition Party, and others, viewed alcohol as a dangerous drug that disrupted lives and families. They felt it the duty of the government to relieve the temptation of alcohol by banning it altogether. In January, 1919, the U.S. Congress ratified the 18th Amendment to the Constitution that outlawed the "manufacture, sale, or transportation of intoxicating liquors" on a national level. Nine months later, the Volstead Act passed, proving the enforcement means for such measures. Prohibition, however, had little effect on the hedonism of the liquor-loving public, and speakeasies, a type of illegal bar, cropped up everywhere. One Fitzgerald critic, Andre Le Vot, wrote: "The bootlegger entered American folklore with as much public complicity as the outlaws of the Old West had enjoyed."

New York City and the Urban Corruption

Prohibition fostered a large underworld industry in many big cities, including Chicago and New York. For years, New York was under the control of the Irish politicians of Tammany Hall, which assured that corruption persisted. Bootlegging, prostitution, and gambling thrived, while police took money from shady operators engaged in these activities and overlooked the illegalities. A key player in the era of Tammany Hall was Arnold Rothstein (Meyer Wolfsheim in the novel). Through his campaign contributions to the politicians, he was entitled to a monopoly of prostitution and gambling in New York until he was murdered in 1928.

A close friend of Rothstein, Herman "Rosy" Rosenthal, is alluded to in Fitzgerald's book when Gatsby and Nick meet for lunch. Wolfsheim says that "The old Metropole…. I can't forget so long as I live the night they shot Rosy Rosenthal there." This mobster also made campaign contributions, or paid off, his political boss. When the head of police, Charles Becker, tried to receive some of Rosenthal's payouts, Rosenthal complained to a reporter. This act exposed the entire corruption of

Compare & Contrast

- **1920s:** The Ku Klux Klan stages a parade in Washington D.C. with 40,000 marchers in white hoods.

  Today: The neo-Nazi and white "skinhead" supremist movements have taken hold in parts of the U.S. A bombing suspect in the Oklahoma City federal building explosion, which killed over 160 people, expresses his anger at the FBI's mishandling of a standoff with a separatist group at Waco, Texas, in which the compound burned and many people were killed.

- **1920s:** Prohibition is passed, prohibiting the manufacture and sale of liquor. Al Capone takes over as boss of Chicago bootlegging from racketeer Johnny Torrio, who retires after sustaining gunshot wounds.

  Today: The use and abuse of alcohol grows in the U.S., as does participation in the twelve-step program called Alcoholics Anonymous, drug rehabilitation centers, and other support mechanisms designed to stem the fallout from drug abuse. Though still powerful in the drug and prostitution business, several Mafia dons, including John Gotti, are imprisoned for life.

- **1920s:** Political machines like New York's Tammany Hall openly and directly influence the outcome of elections by paying lawmakers and police to make or enforce policies in their favor.

  Today: While direct bribery of politicians and police is neither open nor widespread, there are still political scandals regarding funding of political campaigns. Members of both Democratic and Republican parties have been accused of taking illegal contributions, and campaign finance reform is a hot political issue.

Tammany Hall and the New York police force. Two days later, Becker's men murdered Rosenthal on the steps of the Metropole. Becker and four of his men went to the electric chair for their part in the crime.

The Black Sox Fix of 1919

The 1919 World Series was the focus of a scandal that sent shock waves around the sports world. The Chicago White Sox were heavily favored to win the World Series against the Cincinnati Reds. Due to low game attendance during World War I, players' salaries were cut back. In defiance, the White Sox threatened to strike against their owner, Charles Comiskey, who had refused to pay them a higher salary. The team's first baseman, Arnold "Chick" Gandil, approached a bookmaker and gambler, Joseph Sullivan, with an offer to intentionally lose the series. Eight players, including left fielder Shoeless Joe Jackson, participated in the scam. With the help of Arnold Rothstein, Sullivan raised the money to pay the players, and began placing bets that the White Sox would lose. The Sox proceeded to suffer one of the greatest sports upsets in history, and lost three games to five. When the scandal was exposed, due to a number of civil cases involving financial losses on the part of those who betted for the Sox, the eight players were banned from baseball for life and branded the "Black Sox." In the novel, Gatsby tells Nick that Wolfsheim was "the man who fixed the World Series back in 1919." Shocked, Nick thinks to himself, "It never occurred to me that one man could start to play with the faith of fifty million people—with the single-mindedness of a burglar blowing a safe." Gatsby himself is tied to possibly shady dealings throughout the course of the book. He takes mysterious phone calls and steps aside for private, undisclosed conversations. It was said that "one time he killed a man who found out that he was nephew to von Hindenburg and second cousin to the devil."

The Cover Artwork

Fitzgerald's editor, Maxwell Perkins, commissioned a full-color, illustrated jacket design from

A speakeasy, where people could illegally purchase alcohol during Prohibition in the 1920s.

the Spanish artist Francis Cugat. Cugat had worked previously on movie poster and sets and was employed as a designer in Hollywood. The Art Deco piece that he produced for the novel shows the outlined eyes of a woman looking out of a midnight blue sky above the carnival lights of Coney Island in Manhattan. The piece was completed seven months before the novel, and Fitzgerald may have used it to inspire his own imagery. He calls Daisy the "girl whose disembodied face floated along the ark cornices and blinding signs" of New York.

Critical Overview

Just before *The Great Gatsby* was to appear—with a publication date of April 10, 1925—the Fitzgeralds were in the south of France. Fitzgerald was waiting for news from Max Perkins, his publisher, and cabled him to request "Any News." The 29-year-old author had won critical acclaim for his first novel, *This Side of Paradise* but had faltered with the less-than-perfect *The Beautiful and the Damned.* He was earnest about being considered one of the top American writers of his time, and needed the boost that his third novel might give him to achieve that status.

During his lifetime, Fitzgerald was generally praised for *The Great Gatsby;* it is usually considered to be his finest accomplishment and the one most analyzed by literary critics. The established opinion, according to biographer Arthur Mizener in *The Far Side of Paradise,* is best represented by renowned critic Lionel Trilling: "Except once, Fitzgerald did not fully realize his powers.... But [his] quality was a great one and on one occasion, in *The Great Gatsby,* it was as finely crystallized in art as it deserved to be." *Saturday Review* critic William Rose Benét said that the book "revealed matured craftsmanship." Even harsh critics like Ernest Hemingway and H. L. Mencken praised the writer, as quoted by Mizener. Said the notoriously abrasive Mencken in a letter to the author: "I think it is incomparably the best piece of work you have done." Nevertheless, he qualified this compliment with a complaint that the basic story was "somewhat trivial, that it reduces itself, in the end, to a sort of anecdote." Ring Lardner liked it "enormously" but his praise was too thin, for Fitzgerald's tastes: "The plot held my interest ... and I found no tedious moments. Altogether I think it's the best thing you've done since *Paradise.*" Some of the initial reviews in newspapers called the book unsubstantial, since Fitzgerald dealt with unattractive characters in a superficially glittery setting. His friend, Edmund Wilson, called it "the best thing you have done—the best planned, the best sustained, the best written." All reviews, good and bad, affected Fitzgerald deeply.

From an artistic perspective, Fitzgerald's third novel was as close to a triumph as he would ever get. Financially, however, the book was a failure since he was over $6200 in debt to Scribners, his publisher, and sales of the book did not cover this by October of 1925. By February, a few more books were sold and then sales leveled out. The summer of 1925 for Fitzgerald was one of "1000 parties and no work." His drinking continued to affect his work. For the rest of his life, nothing he wrote quite measured up to *Gatsby.* In fact, when he walked into a book shop in Los Angeles and requested one of his books, he discovered they were out of print.

In the early 1950s, Fitzgerald's works began to enjoy a revival; in addition to *Gatsby, Tender Is the Night,* with its psychological bent, appealed to readers. Critics found similarities between Fitzgerald and English poet John Keats and novelist Joseph Conrad. Joseph N. Riddel and James Tuttleton analyzed American-born novelist Henry James's impact on Fitzgerald, since both men wrote about the manners of a particular culture. *Gatsby* was compared to T. S. Eliot's poem "The Waste Land" and to Ernest Hemingway's novel *The Sun Also Rises*. The mythic elements of the novel have been studied by Douglas Taylor, Robert Stallman, and briefly by Richard Chase in *The American Novel and Its Tradition*

Symbolism in *Gatsby* focuses on Dr. T. J. Eckleburg's eyes, the Wasteland motif, and the color symbolism. Gatsby has ironically been likened to Christ, and Nick Carraway, the storyteller, to Nicodemus, in a Christian interpretation of the novel. Relatively speaking, most of Fitzgerald's short stories have been sorely neglected by critics, though a steady stream of critical comment appears every year. It has been difficult for critics to detach Fitzgerald the writer from Fitzgerald the legend. Sociological, historical, and biographical approaches to teaching literature have predominated in past decades. Now, more attention is being given to a close reading of *Gatsby* for its artistry.

Criticism

Casie E. Hermanson

In the following essay, Hermanson, a doctoral candidate at the University of Toronto, examines the roles of the major characters in The Great Gatsby *and how the novel both depicts its own time and deals with timeless issues of ambiguity and tragedy.*

Published in 1925, *The Great Gatsby* became an immediate classic and propelled its young author to a fame he never again equalled. The novel captured the spirit of the "Jazz Age," a post-World War I era in upper-class America that Fitzgerald himself gave this name to, and the flamboyance of the author and his wife Zelda as they moved about Europe with other American expatriate writers (such as Ernest Hemingway). However, *Gatsby* expresses more than the exuberance of the times. It depicts the restlessness of what Gertrude Stein (another expatriate modernist writer) called a "lost generation." Recalling T. S. Eliot's landmark poem "The Wasteland" (1922), then, *Gatsby* also has its own "valley of ashes" or wasteland where men move about obscurely in the dust, and this imagery of decay, death, and corruption pervades the novel and "infects" the story and its hero too. Because the novel is not just about one man, James Gatz or Jay Gatsby, but about aspects of the human condition of an era, and themes that transcend time al-

together, it is the stuff of myth. Gatsby's attempts to attain an ideal of himself and then to put this ideal to the service of another ideal, romantic love, are attempts to rise above corruption in all its forms. It is this quality in him that Nick Carraway, the novel's narrator, attempts to portray, and in so doing the novel, like its hero, attains a form of enduring greatness.

The novel is narrated in retrospect; Nick is writing the account two years after the events of the summer he describes, and this introduces a critical distance and perspective which is conveyed through occasional comments about the story he is telling and how it must appear to a reader. The time scheme of the novel is further complicated as "the history of that summer" of 1922 contains within it the story of another summer, five years before this one, when Gatsby and Daisy first courted. This is the story that Jordan tells Nick. As that earlier summer ended with Gatsby's departure for the war in the fall, so the summer of Nick's experience of the East ends with the crisis on the last hot day (the day of mint juleps in the hotel and Myrtle Wilson's death) and is followed by Gatsby's murder by George Wilson on the first day of fall. This seasonal calendar is more than just a parallel, however. It is a metaphor for the blooming and blasting of love and of hope, like the flowers so often mentioned. Similarly, the novel's elaborate use of light and dark imagery (light, darkness, sunshine, and shadow, and the in-between changes of twilight) symbolizes emotional states as well.

In-between time (like the popular song Klipspringer plays on Gatsby's piano: *In the meantime / In between time / Ain't we got fun?*) is described by Nick as the time of profound human change. While this can describe Daisy's change between her affair with Gatsby and the couples' reunion, it may also characterize the general sense of restlessness and profound changes happening in these first years after World War One. Daisy (the days-eye, or the sun) is dressed in white and is associated with light and sunshine throughout the novel, and she is very much a seasonal creature. It is impossible, then, for Gatsby to catch this light and fix it in one place or one time. Daisy's constant quality is like the light in the novel, she is always changing. Gatsby's own devotion to her has a permanence that Daisy cannot live up to, yet Gatsby seems committed to an idea of Daisy that he has created rather than to the real woman she is. Daisy's changeability is not at fault in Gatsby's failure. Although she is careless in the way that people like Tom are careless in their wealth and treatment of

What Do I Read Next?

- *The Twenties* by Edmund Wilson, one of Fitzgerald's friends at Princeton University and his entire life, is an interesting introduction to the decade and to the many cultural figures in America at that time. Another book by Wilson that chronicles the Twenties and Thirties is *The Shores of Light,* 1952. Personal impressions, sketches, letters, satires, and pieces on the classics of American literature are included in this book.

- *Heart of Darkness* (1899) by Joseph Conrad, was a literary favorite of Fitzgerald, who used the Polish author's narrative technique in *The Great Gatsby.* The short novel is the story of the civilized Mr. Kurtz, who travels to the savage heart of Africa, only to find his evil soul.

- *Citizen Kane,* Orson Welles's legendary 1941 film, is about a mogul who acquires tremendous financial success but finds that the true source of his happiness is a childhood memory of "Rosebud." Once again, the true values of gains and losses are examined in this well-known classic.

- *Six Tales of the Jazz Age and Other Stories,* F. Scott Fitzgerald, 1922. This is the author's second collection of short stories, the most notable of which is "The Diamond as Big as the Ritz." The recurrent theme of fantasy and winning the top girl and financial success is central to this and other stories.

- *Great Expectations* (1861) by Charles Dickens tells of a grim childhood and an orphan's encounter with wealth and lost love in England during the Victorian era. In its realistic mode, one can find a number of differences between this story and Fitzgerald's, yet striking similarities as well, in regard to dreams and human relationships.

---

other people, Daisy is naturally not able to renounce time itself in the way Gatsby does in order to meet him again in the past.

Gatsby is gorgeous and creates a sense of wonder in Nick for the daring nature of his impossible but incorruptible dream. It is the attempt itself and the firm belief that he can achieve the impossible that makes Gatsby more than the sum of his (somewhat shabby) reality. As a seventeen-year-old he transformed himself from plain James Gatz, to Jay Gatsby for whom anything is possible. As he rowed out to Dan Cody's sumptuous yacht off the shore of Lake Superior, he was crossing towards opportunity, and a Platonic conception of himself (based on the Greek philosopher Platos' theory of perfect forms, which interprets everything on earth as a better or worse copy of these forms, as well as the conception of a new self-identity). Gatsby conforms to an ideal of himself that transforms reality into possibility. This audacity and disregard for ties binding him to his own past is his apprenticeship

for loving Daisy. In defiance of the class difference separating them, he aspires high to this girl in a golden tower, the "king's" daughter, whose voice is full of money. Gatsby does not seem to realize that his idea of Daisy, whom he weds with a kiss one summer night has as little bearing on reality as Jay Gatsby does.

Gatsby is a romantic, but he is also made up of romantic stories by other people who speculate and rumor about his unknown past. Nick takes it upon himself to tell the story and thus to tell Gatsby's story as he pieced it together from different sources, and Nick characterizes himself as someone who understands Gatsby better, who wants to set the record straight, and who sides with Gatsby against the world that made him up and then deserted him. It is Nick alone who arranges Gatsby's funeral and meets with his father, and the bitterness of the lesson about humanity that Nick learns from this experience affects the way he tells the story. Certainly, Nick is also romanticizing

Gatsby. He contrasts the wondrous hope which Gatsby embodied against the corruptness of his bootlegging business (Gatsby's fortune in fact came from illegal alcohol sales) and against the more corrupt society which preyed on Gatsby. Against the background of the times and of upper-class society like that represented at his parties, Gatsby's extraordinary gift for hope and his romantic readiness stand out as transcendent.

Nick's own role in the novel shares much of the nature of paradox and ambiguity which characterizes the whole. The novel is as much about Nick as it is about Gatsby and his colossal dream of Daisy. Nick is an involved outsider, privileged or burdened with the role of witness and recorder of events. While he protests often of his unwillingness to participate in other's embroilments and is frequently irritated or exasperated by them, he participates nevertheless. He is implicated in Tom's relationship with Myrtle by virtue of his presence with them (and the uncomfortable period he spends in the living room of the lovers' apartment while they are in the bedroom together implicates him further as a passive accomplice) while he retains his sense of distance through moral superiority. Similarly, Nick performs the service of go-between (or pander) for Gatsby and Daisy; the couple reunite in his house, and he invites Daisy there for this purpose. At Gatsby's party he acts as lookout, keeping a watchful eye for Tom while the couple slip over to sit on Nick's own porch. This ambivalence in his character undermines his statements about himself as being one of the few honest people that he has ever known, and has led to many critics considering him a kind of smug voyeur. However, Nick's own sense of being both enchanted and repelled by his experiences is at the source of the novel's larger depiction of a meretricious society both enchanting and repelling, and it is this quality which enables Nick to find Gatsby both the representative of everything for which he has an unaffected scorn, and at the same time the embodiment of gorgeous hope. In this way, a story often marked by sordid dealings and dismissed by Nick in one breath (writing two years later) as the abortive sorrows and short-winded elations of men can also be a holocaust or fully developed tragedy.

In considering the novel as tragedy, the role of fate (or fortune in its other sense) figures large. The novel is conspicuous in its lack of a religious belief system; God is absent from the skies over East and West Egg. Part of the restlessness of a postwar generation may describe the quest for a belief that can fill the void created by this loss, or the results of a hedonistic lifestyle that will distract people from it altogether. Nick clings to his declared preference for honesty and being a careful driver in a world of metaphorically careless drivers. Daisy is one who lives for the moment, and for whom glimpses of tomorrow and the day after that and the day after that are terrifying lapses of a willful blindness to such matters (and blindness is one of the novel's themes). Gatsby has his own willful blindness in the form of his enduring ideals and the dreams these ideals have created. In classical mythology, which the novel draws on heavily, the goddess Fortune is also blind in that she favors no one (she is often figured with one eye open and one eye closed, winking like Daisy herself) as she turns her wheel about, thereby deciding the fates of human beings. One question of the novel, then, is who (or what) is at the wheel? The blind eyes that watch over the world of the novel are those of Dr. T. J. Eckleburg on an old billboard in the valley of ashes. After Myrtle's death, her husband George is looking at these when he says God sees everything. Nothing seems able to intervene in Gatsby's own inexorable fate, as Wilson tracks him down to murder him in the mistaken belief that Gatsby was driving the death car that killed Myrtle. This sense of predetermined destiny contributes to the novel as tragedy.

For all characters, the relationship between the past and the future is at issue, as well as personal responsibility for the choices they make in navigating the present between these. Nick appears to believe that being careful will keep him out of harm, but he is more of a careless driver than he realizes, as Jordan comments to him after Gatsby's death and after their affair is over. Gatsby himself recalls another careless driver. In Greek mythology Phaeton tried to harness his chariot to the sun and suffered for his presumption. Similarly, Gatsby tries with his yellow car (and all that it symbolizes) to catch Daisy, and fails just as surely. The many echoes of classical mythology recall to the novel a much more distant past (and a mythical kind of narrative) in order to make sense of the New World of America. The novel ends by uniting Gatsby's dream born from his past with the American dream from another past, a dream that is as incorruptible and unreal, indicating the way in which the future of this story may be found in the past: So we beat on, boats against the current, borne back ceaselessly into the past.

Source: Casie E. Hermanson, in an essay for *Novels for Students,* Gale, 1997.

Charles Thomas Samuels

In the following excerpt, Samuels describes Fitzgerald's two great achievements in The Great Gatsby: *the "triumph of language" and his creation of the book's narrator, Nick Carraway.*

[*The Great Gatsby's*] fundamental achievement is a triumph of language.

I do not speak merely of the "flowers," the famous passages: Nick's description of Gatsby yearning toward the green light on Daisy's dock, Gatsby's remark that the Buchanans' love is "only personal," the book's last page. Throughout, *The Great Gatsby* has the precision and splendor of a lyric poem, yet well-wrought prose is merely one of its triumphs. Fitzgerald's distinction in this novel is to have made language celebrate itself. Among other things, *The Great Gatsby* is about the power of art.

This celebration of literary art is inseparable from the novel's second great achievement—its management of point of view, the creation of Nick. With his persona, Fitzgerald obtained more than objectivity and concentration of effect. Nick describes more than the experience which he witnesses; he describes the act and consequences of telling about it. The persona is—as critics have been seeing—a character, but he is more than that: he is a character engaged in a significant action.

Nick is writing a book. He is recording Gatsby's experience; in the act of recording Gatsby's experience he discovers himself.

Though his prose has all along been creating for us Gatsby's "romantic readiness," almost until the very end Nick insists that he deplores Gatsby's "appalling sentimentality." This is not a reasoned judgment. Nick disapproves because he cannot yet affirm. He is a Jamesian spectator, a fastidious intelligence ill-suited to profound engagement of life. But writing does profoundly engage life. In writing about Gatsby, Nick alters his attitude toward his subject and ultimately toward his own life. As his book nears completion his identification with Gatsby grows. His final affirmation is his sympathetic understanding of Gatsby and the book which gives his sympathy form: both are a celebration of life; each is a gift of language. This refinement on James's use of the persona might be the cause of Eliot's assertion that *The Great Gatsby* represented the first advance which the American novel had made since James.

In Nick's opening words we find an uncompleted personality. There are contradictions and perplexities which (when we first read the passage) are easily ignored, because of the characteristic suavity of his prose. He begins the chronicle, whose purpose is an act of judgment and whose title is an evaluation, by declaring an inclination "to reserve all judgments." The words are scarcely digested when we find him judging:

> The abnormal mind is quick to detect and attach itself to this quality [tolerance] when it appears in a normal person, and so it came about that in college I was unjustly accused of being a politician, because I was privy to the secret griefs of wild, unknown men.

The tone is unmistakable—a combination of moral censure, self-protectiveness, and final saving sympathy that marks Nick as an outsider who is nonetheless drawn to the life he is afraid to enter. So when he tells us a little later in the passage that "Reserving judgments is a matter of infinite hope," we know that this and not the *noblesse oblige* he earlier advanced explains his fear of judging. Nick cannot help judging, but he fears a world in which he is constantly beset by objects worthy of rejection. He is "a little afraid of missing something"; that is why he hears the promise in Daisy's voice, half-heartedly entertains the idea of loving Jordan Baker, and becomes involved with the infinite hope of Jay Gatsby—"Gatsby, who represented everything for which [Nick had] an unaffected scorn."

When Nick begins the book he feels the same ambivalence toward Gatsby that characterizes his attitude toward life: a simultaneous enchantment and revulsion which places him "within and without." When he has finished, he has become united with Gatsby, and he judges Gatsby great. Finally he has something to admire; contemplating Gatsby redeems him from the "foul dust [which had] temporarily closed out [his] interest in the abortive sorrows and short-winded elations of men."

The economy with which Fitzgerald presents those sorrows and short-winded elations is another of the book's major achievements. In *The Great Gatsby* Fitzgerald contrived to develop a story by means of symbols while at the same time investing those symbols with vivid actuality. Everything in the book is symbolic, from Gatsby's ersatz mansion to the wild and aimless parties which he gives there, yet everything seems so "true to life" that some critics continue to see that novel primarily as a recreation of the 20's. *The Great Gatsby* is about the 20's only in the sense that *Moby Dick* is about whaling or that *The Scarlet Letter* is about Puritan Boston. Comparing the liveliness of Fitzgerald's book with Melville's or, better still, with Hawthorne's (which resembles its tight dramatic structure and concentration), you have a good indication of the peculiar distinction in Fitzgerald's work.

Of the novel's symbols, only the setting exists without regard to verisimilitude, purely to project meaning. *The Great Gatsby* has four locales: East Egg, home of the rich Buchanans and their ultra-traditional Georgian Colonial mansion; West Egg where the once-rich and the parvenus live and where Gatsby apes the splendor of the Old World; the wasteland of the average man; and New York, where Nick labors, ironically, at the "Probity Trust." East and West Egg are "crushed flat at the contact end"; they represent the collision of dream and dreamer which is dramatized when Gatsby tries to establish his "universe of ineffable gaudiness" through the crass materials of the real world. The wasteland is a valley of ashes in which George Wilson dispenses gasoline to the irresponsible drivers from East and West Egg, eventually yielding his wife to their casual lust and cowardly violence.

Fitzgerald's world represents iconographically a sterile, immoral society. Over this world brood the blind eyes of Dr. T. J. Eckleburg: the sign for an oculist's business which was never opened, the symbol of a blindness which can never be corrected. Like other objects in the book to which value might be attached, the eyes of Dr. Eckleburg are a cheat. They are not a sign of God, as Wilson thinks, but only an advertisement—like the false promise of Daisy's moneyed voice, or the green light on her dock, which is invisible in the mist.

These monstrous eyes are the novel's major symbol. The book's chief characters are blind, and they behave blindly. Gatsby does not see Daisy's vicious emptiness, and Daisy, deluded, thinks she will reward her gold-hatted lover until he tries to force from her an affirmation she is too weak to make. Tom is blind to his hypocrisy; with "a short deft movement" he breaks Myrtle's nose for daring to mention the name of the wife she is helping him to deceive. Before her death, Myrtle mistakes Jordan for Daisy. Just as she had always mistaken Tom for salvation from the ash-heap, she blindly rushes for his car in her need to escape her lately informed husband, and is struck down. Moreover, Daisy is driving the car; and the man with her is Gatsby, not Tom. The final act of blindness is specifically associated with Dr. Eckleburg's eyes. Wilson sees them as a sign of righteous judgment and righteously proceeds to work God's judgment on earth. He kills Gatsby, but Gatsby is the wrong man. In the whole novel, only Nick sees.

And his vision comes slowly, in the act of writing the book.

The act of writing the book is, as I have said, an act of judgment. Nick wants to know why Gatsby "turned out all right in the end," despite all the phoniness and crime which fill his story, and why Gatsby was the only one who turned out all right. For, in writing about the others, Nick discovers the near ubiquity of folly and despair.

The novel's people are exemplary types of the debasement of life which is Fitzgerald's subject. Daisy, Tom, and Jordan lack the inner resources to enjoy what their wealth can give them. They show the peculiar folly of the American dream. At the pinnacle, life palls. Daisy is almost unreal. When Nick first sees her she seems to be floating in midair. Her famous protestation of grief ("I'm sophisticated. God, I'm sophisticated") is accompanied by an "absolute smirk." Her extravagant love for Gatsby is a sham, less real than the unhappy but fleshly bond with Tom which finally turns them into "conspirators." Her beauty is a snare. Like Tom's physical prowess, it neither pleases her nor insures her pleasure in others. Tom forsakes Daisy for Myrtle and both for "stale ideas." Jordan's balancing act is a trick; like her sporting reputation, a precarious lie. They are all rich and beautiful—and unhappy.

Yearning toward them are Myrtle and Gatsby. Like Gatsby, Myrtle desires "the youth and mystery that wealth imprisons and preserves … gleaming … above the hot struggles of the poor." Unlike him, her "panting vitality" is wholly physical, merely pathetic; whereas Gatsby's quest is spiritual and tragic. Myrtle is maimed and victimized by Daisy's selfish fear of injury (Daisy could have crashed into another car but, at the last minute, loses heart and runs Myrtle down); Gatsby's death is but the final stage of disillusionment, and he suffers voluntarily.

Gatsby is, of course, one of the major achievements I have been noting. Although we see little of him and scarcely ever hear him speak, his presence is continually with us; and he exists, as characters in fiction seldom do, as a life force. He recalls the everlasting yea of Carlyle, as well as the metaphysical rebellion of Camus. His "heightened sensitivity to the promise of life" is but one half of his energy; the other being a passionate denial of life's limitations. Gatsby's devotion to Daisy is an implicit assault on the human condition. His passion would defy time and decay to make the glorious first moment of wonder, which is past, eternally present. His passion is supra-sexual, even super-personal. In his famous remark to Nick about Daisy's love for Tom, he is making two assertions: that the "things between Daisy and Tom [which Tom insists] he'll never know" are merely mundane and that the Daisy which he loves is not the Daisy which Tom had carried down from the Punch Bowl but the Daisy who "blossomed for him like a flower," incarnating his dream, the moment he kissed her. Gatsby's love for life is finally an indictment of the life he loves. Life does not reward such devotion, nor, for that reason, does it deserve it. Gatsby is great for having paid life the compliment of believing its promise.

When Hamlet dies amidst the carnage of his bloody quest for justice, he takes with him the promise that seeming will coincide with being and the hope that man can strike a blow for truth and save a remnant of the universe. When Ahab dies a victim to his own harpoon, he kills the promise that man may know his life and the hope that knowledge will absolve him. When Gatsby dies, more innocently than they (since, though a "criminal," he lacks utterly their taste for destruction), he kills a promise more poignant and perhaps more precious, certainly more inclusive than theirs: Gatsby kills the promise that desire can ever be gratified.

Source: Charles Thomas Samuels, "The Greatness of 'Gatsby,'" in *The Massachusetts Review,* Vol. VII, No. 4, Autumn, 1966, pp. 783–94.

David F. Trask

In the following excerpt, Trask asserts that The Great Gatsby *is Fitzgerald's critique of the American dream and the outmoded values of traditional America.*

F. Scott Fitzgerald's *The Great Gatsby* is certainly more than an impression of the Jazz Age, more than a novel of manners. Serious critics have by no means settled upon what that "more" might be, but one hypothesis recurs quite regularly. It is the view that Fitzgerald was writing about the superannuation of traditional American belief, the obsolescence of accepted folklore. *The Great Gatsby* is about many things, but it is inescapably a general critique of the "American dream" and also of the "agrarian myth"—a powerful demonstration of their invalidity for Americans of Fitzgerald's generation and after.

The American dream consisted of the belief (sometimes thought of as a promise) that people of talent in this land of opportunity and plenty could reasonably aspire to material success if they ad-

hered to a fairly well-defined set of behavioral rules–rules set forth in a relatively comprehensive form as long ago as the eighteenth century by Benjamin Franklin. In addition, Americans easily assumed that spiritual satisfaction would automatically accompany material success. The dream was to be realized in an agrarian civilization, a way of life presumed better—far better—than the urban alternative. Thomas Jefferson firmly established the myth of the garden—the concept of agrarian virtue and the urban vice—in American minds. During the turbulent era of westward expansion the myth gained increasing stature.

James Gatz of North Dakota had dreamed a special version of the American dream. Fitzgerald tells us that it constituted "a promise that the rock of the world was founded securely on a fairy's wing." When Gatz lay dead, his father told Nick Carraway that "Jimmy was bound to get ahead." As a child, Gatz set about preparing to realize his dream. He early decided that he could contemplate future glory so long as he scheduled his life properly and adhered to a set of general resolves—resolves quite obviously derivative from *Poor Richard.* "No smokeing [*sic*] or chewing." "Bath every other day." "Be better to parents." Yes, James Gatz was *bound* to get ahead, bound as securely to his goal as was Captain Ahab to the pursuit of the white whale. *The Great Gatsby* is the chronicle of what happened when James Gatz attempted to realize the promise of his dream.

Gatz thought himself different—very different—from the common run of mankind. We learn that his parents were "shiftless and unsuccessful"—and that "his imagination had never really accepted them as his parents at all." He possessed a "Platonic conception of himself. He was a son of God." As a son of God—*God's boy*—he "must be about His Father's business." What was that business? It was "the service of a vast, vulgar, and meretricious beauty." Gatz plainly imagined himself a Christ—one of the anointed—born of earthly parents but actually a son of God. This is what Fitzgerald sought to convey in establishing that "Jay Gatsby of West Egg, Long Island, sprang from his Platonic conception of himself." That conception moved him to seek out goodness and beauty—certainly a prostituted goodness and beauty, but goodness and beauty nevertheless.

When his moment came—at seventeen—James Gatz changed his name. The question of the name change has not received the attention it deserves. Some believe that Fitzgerald derived

"Gatsby" from the slang term for pistol current during the Jazz Age—gat. Others see in the act of changing names an intimation of "Jewishness" in the hero, a view supported by the frequency of the name "Jay" among the Jews. Jay Gould comes immediately to mind as do Jay Cooke and J.P. Morgan. Also, it is known that the inspiration for the novel came from Fitzgerald's chance encounter with a Jewish bootlegger.

It is, of course, conceivable that Fitzgerald had some or even all of these things in mind, and it is also possible that he had still another thought. Could it be, however unlikely, that he was rendering the literal "Jesus, God's boy" in the name of Jay Gatsby? (In ordinary pronunciation, the 't' easily changes to "d" as in "Gad.") This conjecture might appear hopelessly far-fetched, were it not for Fitzgerald's discussion of Gatz's "Platonic conception of himself," and his direct use of the phrase "son of God." In any case, Gatsby began his pursuit of goodness and beauty when he changed his name, and that pursuit ultimately ended in tragedy.

Fitzgerald develops the tragedy of Jay Gatsby as the consequence of his quixotic quest for Daisy Buchanan. Daisy represents that "vast, vulgar, and meretricious beauty" to which Gatsby aspired. When Jay met Daisy, he realized that he had "forever wed his unutterable visions to her perishable breath." He knew that "his mind would never romp again like the mind of God." When he kissed her, "she blossomed for him like a flower and the incarnation was complete." What was the incarnation? In Daisy, Gatsby's meretricious dream was made flesh. He sought ever after to realize his dream in union with her.

The trouble with Gatsby's quest was that Daisy was completely incapable of playing the role assigned to her. She was as shallow as the other hollow people who inhabited Fitzgerald's Long Island. She could never become a legitimate actualization of Gatsby's illegitimate dream. Gatsby was himself culpable. He was not truly God's boy perhaps, but he possessed a certain grandeur, an incredible ability to live in terms of his misguided dream. Nick Carraway understood this, telling Gatsby at one point that he was "worth the whole damned crowd put together."

Both Gatsby and Tom Buchanan, Daisy's husband, possessed wealth. Gatsby at least used his wealth to seek out beauty and claim it for himself. Buchanan the lecher lacked any larger goals. In the end, Daisy chooses to remain with Buchanan, and

Gatsby is murdered by the deranged husband of Myrtle Wilson, Buchanan's mistress, who had been accidentally run down and killed by Daisy. Buchanan serves as Gatsby's executioner; he allows George Wilson to believe that Gatsby had killed Myrtle.

Gatsby was as alone in death as he had been in life. Of all the hordes who had accepted his largesse when alive, only one—an unnamed "owl-eyed man" who had admired Gatsby's books—appeared at the funeral. He delivered a pathetic epitaph: "The poor son-of-a-bitch."

The tragedy is over; Fitzgerald speculates on its meaning through the narrator, Nick Carraway. Carraway notes that Jay and the others—Nick himself, his sometime girl friend Jordan Baker, Daisy, and Tom—all were from the Middle West. It was not the Middle West of popular imagination, of the lost agrarian past, but rather the cities of the middle border. "That's my Middle West," muses Carraway, "not the wheat or the prairies or the lost Swede towns, but the thrilling returning trains of my youth, and the street lamps and sleigh bells in the frosty dark and the shadows of holly wreaths thrown by lighted windows on the snow." Carraway continues: Gatsby and his friends "were all Westerners, and perhaps we possessed some deficiency in common which made us subtly unadaptable to Eastern life." The East held many attractions, but the expatriate Westerner lived there at his peril. So Carraway went home. He could at least survive, though he might not prosper, in prairie cities.

Why had Gatsby failed? It was because the time for dreaming as Gatsby dreamed had passed. In what must be, in its implications, one of the most moving passages in American literature, Fitzgerald completes his commentary on Jay Gatsby: "His dream must have seemed so close that he could hardly fail to grasp it. He did not know it was already behind him, somewhere back in that vast obscurity behind the city, where the dark fields of the republic rolled on under the night."

The future to which Gatsby aspired is indeed in the past. His dream—the American dream—had been nurtured in the agrarian past that was no more. Fitzgerald's symbolism is never more ingenious than in his depiction of the bankruptcy of the old agrarian myth. This task he accomplishes through the most haunting and mysterious of the symbols which appear in the book—the eyes of Dr. T. J. Eckleburg. Here is one of the cruelest caricatures in the American novel. For Dr. T. J. Eckleburg is none other than a devitalized Thomas Jefferson, the pre-eminent purveyor of the agrarian myth.

What is it that Dr. Eckleburg's eyes survey? It is the valley of democracy turned to ashes—the garden defiled: "This is a valley of ashes—a fantastic farm where ashes grow like wheat into ridges and hills and grotesque gardens; where ashes take the forms of houses and chimneys and rising smoke and, finally, with a transcendent effort, of men who move dimly and already crumbling through the powdery air. Occasionally a line of gray cars crawls along an invisible track, gives out a ghastly creak, and comes to rest, and immediately the ash-gray men swarm up with leaden spades and stir up an impenetrable cloud, which screens their obscure operations from your sight … [Dr. Eckleburg's] eyes, dimmed a little by many paintless days under sun and rain, brood on over the solemn dumping ground." Fitzgerald thus presents a remarkably evocative description of the corruption that had befallen Jefferson's garden.

At the very end of the novel, Fitzgerald betrays his affection for the myth of the garden, despite his awareness that it could no longer serve Americans. His narrator Carraway once again serves as the vehicle for his thoughts: "And as the moon rose higher the inessential houses began to melt away until gradually I became aware of the old island here that flowered once for Dutch sailor's eyes—a fresh, green breast of the new world. Its vanished trees, the trees that had made way for Gatsby's house, had once pandered in whispers to the last and greatest of all human dreams; for a transitory enchanted moment man must have held his breath in the presence of this continent, compelled into an aesthetic contemplation he neither understood nor desired, face to face for the last time in history with something commensurate to his capacity for wonder."

Alas, poor Jay Gatsby! "Gatsby believed in the green light, the orgiastic future that year by year recedes before us. It eluded us then, but that's no matter—tomorrow we will run faster, stretch out our arms further … And one fine morning—" Alas, all of us! The novel ends on a desperately somber note: "So we beat on, boats against the current, borne back ceaselessly into the past."

American writers in the Twenties were an entirely new breed—divorced from the literary tradition which had matured between the Civil War and World War I. That tradition culminated in the literary Establishment presided over by William Dean Howells in the last years before the outbreak of the

Great War. Henry F. May has summarized the basic tenets of Howells and his minions in *The End of American Innocence:* Howells "had always insisted that real truth and moral goodness were identical, and he had always held that politics and literature were both amenable to moral judgment. He had always believed that American civilization was treading a sure path, whatever the momentary failures, toward moral and material improvement."

What had outmoded Howells? It was the realization, anticipated before the Great War but complete only in the Twenties, that America had been transformed—transformed by the onset of an overwhelming process of industrialization and urbanization which had superannuated traditional American beliefs—beliefs nurtured in the bosom of the agrarian past.

In these circumstances, a revolution in manners and morals was inevitable. World War I augmented rather than inaugurated the trend. Postwar writers undertook a comprehensive critique of traditional faith. Some abhorred the change; others welcomed it. In any case, almost all of the great writers of the Twenties accepted the fact of the intellectual and emotional revolution deriving from the obsolescence of prewar standards. They launched a comprehensive critique of traditional faiths, and for their efforts they received much public notice and approbation.

What accounts for the success of these literary revolutionists? The answer resides in the fact that America was generally "new" in the Twenties. George Mowry and other recent historians have effectively documented the distinctive "modernity" of America in the wake of World War I—a modernity discernible in the mass culture as well as among the elite. The transitional years had passed; the change from the rural-agricultural past to the urban-industrial future was relatively complete, and readers as well as writers responded to this reality. To be sure, the defenders of the old America ensconced behind crumbling barricades in the Old South and the farther Middle West fought extensive rearguard actions—fundamentalist assaults on evolution, prohibitionist bans on spiritous liquors, and racist campaigns for the preservation of white Anglo-Saxon Protestant America—but these were last desperate attempts to postpone the inevitable. The most important fact about reaction in the Twenties was that it failed. In each instance "modernity" ultimately triumphed over tradition.

Significant writers in the Twenties were above all dedicated to the imposing task of pointing out the error of living in terms of obsolete values—however useful those values might have been in the past. This effort is perhaps most obvious in the novels of Ernest Hemingway. In *The Sun Also Rises* Hemingway wastes little time investigating the reasons why Jake Barnes, Lady Brett, Robert Cohn, and other characters in the novel must live differently than before. Hemingway's emphasis is on method—on how to live in the revolutionized context. Scott Fitzgerald dealt with the other side of the coin—the bankruptcy of the old way. Jay Gatsby's dream was patently absurd—however noble, however "American." Benjamin Franklin and Thomas Jefferson were unsound guides to life in the modernity of the vast eastern Urbana, the East of West Egg, Long Island—and also for life in the new Midwest to which the chastened Carraway returned. The final irony of the novel is that Fitzgerald could discern no beauty in the city to compare with the beauty, however meretricious, inherent in Gatsby's Platonic conception of himself.

Source: David F. Trask, "A Note on Fitzgerald's *The Great Gatsby*," in *University Review,* Vol. XXXIII, No. 3, March, 1967, pp. 197–202.

Sources

William Rose Benét, "An Admirable Novel," in *Saturday Review of Literature* May 9, 1925.

Scott Donaldson, "F. Scott Fitzgerald," in *Dictionary of Literary Biography,* Volume 9: American Novelists, 1910–1945, edited by James J. Martine, Gale, 1981, pp. 3–18.

Arthur Mizener, *The Far Side of Paradise* (biography; includes several letters to Fitzgerald), Avon, 1965.

Andre Le Vot, *F. Scott Fitzgerald: A Biography,* translation by William Byron, Doubleday, 1983.

Edmund Wilson, in a letter to F. Scott Fitzgerald on April 11, 1925, in his *Letters on Literature and Politics: 1912–1972,* edited by Elena Wilson, Farrar, Straus, 1977, pp. 121–22.

For Further Study

Harold Bloom, editor, *F. Scott Fitzgerald's 'The Great Gatsby': Modern Critical Interpretations,* Chelsea House, 1986.
> This book contains eight articles with an introduction, on the novel's structure, *Gatsby* as an "American" novel, and the wasteland, and includes the article by David Parker, "Two Versions of the Hero."

Harold Bloom, editor, *Gatsby,* Major Literary Characters Series, Chelsea House, 1991.
> This comprehensive collection of articles focusing on the novel's "hero," Gatsby, begins with 25 critical

extracts on the character and the author from letters, reviews, and articles. Of particular interest is the article by Arnold Weinstein, "Fiction as Greatness: The Case of Gatsby" (1985) which reads the novel as being about making meaning, or creating belief. This includes both Gatsby's fiction of himself and Nick's story of this. The collection also includes an important early article on the time theme by R. W. Stallman, "Gatsby and the Hole in Time" (1955).

M. J. Bruce, editor, *New Essays on 'The Great Gatsby',* Cambridge University Press, 1985.
> This shorter work (five articles with an introduction) also includes an interesting overview of the novel's impact on fiction and criticism over the decades: "*Gatsby*'s Long Shadow: Influence and Endurance," by Richard Anderson.

Colin S. Cass, " 'Pandered in Whispers': Narrative Reliability in *The Great Gatsby*," in *College Literature,* Vol. 7, 1980, pp. 113-24.
> Investigates the role of narrator Nick Carraway in the novel and his reliability as the narrator of events.

A. T. Crosland, *A Concordance to F. Scott Fitzgerald's 'The Great Gatsby',* Gale, 1975.
> The concordance provides cross-referenced lists of every word in the novel, assisting in consideration of the use and frequency of certain words or word-groups (such as "eye," "blind," "see," "blink," "wink," and the famous accidental use of "irises," for example).

Scott Donaldson, editor, *Critical Essays on F. Scott Fitzgerald's 'The Great Gatsby',* G. K. Hall, 1984.
> This balanced survey of critical issues (21 essays with an introduction, and excerpts from letters to and from Fitzgerald about the novel) contains some of the now-classic articles or chapters from other books. It features treatments of sources for the novel, the novel's complicated revisions in its composition, and the historical aspect of the work.

F. Scott Fitzgerald, *The Great Gatsby,* edited by Matthew J. Bruccoli, Cambridge University Press, 1991.
> Bruccoli's critical edition of the novel contains the useful "apparatus" (notes keyed to page numbers in the novel) which had been published separately in 1974, when the novel was still under copyright protection. This edition now explains many of the novel's more obscure references, and points to some of its infamous inconsistencies (the age of Daisy Fay's daughter, for instance). Bruccoli himself is perhaps the most prolific of Fitzgerald's biographers and critics, and has also edited numerous editions of Fitzgerald's correspondence, manuscript facsimiles, notebooks, and even accounts ledgers.

Fitzgerald-Hemingway Annual, various years.
> This yearly periodical devotes itself to the works of F. Scott Fitzgerald and Ernest Hemingway.

Alfred Kazin, *F. Scott Fitzgerald: The Man and His Work,* Twayne, 1951.
> This collection of essays on the author's literature is considered to be one of the best single volumes of criticism on Fitzgerald. Arranged chronologically,

the material ranges from early reviews of the first novel through other critical reactions to Fitzgerald.

Ernest Lockridge, editor, *Twentieth-Century Interpretations of 'The Great Gatsby': A Collection of Critical Essays,* Prentice Hall, 1968.
An earlier collection of seven articles and nine brief "View Points" on the novel, briefly encapsulating a range of different approaches to the novel.

Irving Malin, "'Absolution': Absolving Lies," in*The Short Stories of F. Scott Fitzgerald: New Approaches in Criticism,* edited by Jackson Bryer, University of Wisconsin Press, 1982.
This article links the ideas of the short story with the *The Great Gatsby.* The author demonstrates how Fitzgerald is, to some extent, a religious writer.

James R. Mellow, *Invented Lives,* Houghton Mifflin, 1984.
This is a full portrait of Fitzgerald, his hunger for fame, his destructive marriage, and a backward look to an era that continues to dazzle us with its variety and intrigue.

James E. Miller, Jr., *The Fictional Technique of F. Scott Fitzgerald,* New York University, 1964.
This book discusses the literary influences on Fitzgerald's career, most significantly, Edmund Wilson, H. L. Mencken, Ring Lardner, and Ernest Hemingway.

James Tuttleton, *The Novel of Manners,* Norton, 1972.
The book offers a revealing perspective on Fitzgerald's ability to identify social and cultural manners in the 1920s American society. Reference is made to Henry James and other writers' works.

Heart of Darkness

Joseph Conrad

1899

Joseph Conrad's *Heart of Darkness*, now his most famous work, was first published in 1899 in serial form in London's *Blackwood's Magazine*, a popular journal of its day. The work was well received by a somewhat perplexed Victorian audience. It has since been called by many the best short novel written in English. At the time of its writing (1890), the Polish-born Conrad had become a naturalized British citizen, mastered the English language, served for ten years in the British merchant marines, achieved the rank of captain, and traveled to Asia, Australia, India, and Africa. *Heart of Darkness* is based on Conrad's firsthand experience of the Congo region of West Africa. Conrad was actually sent up the Congo River to an inner station to rescue a company agent—not named Kurtz but Georges-Antoine Klein—who died a few days later aboard ship. The story is told in the words of Charlie Marlow, a seaman, and filtered through the thoughts of an unidentified listening narrator. It is on one level about a voyage into the heart of the Belgian Congo, and on another about the journey into the soul of man. In 1902, *Heart of Darkness* was published in a separate volume along with two other stories by Conrad. Many critics consider the book a literary bridge between the nineteenth and twentieth centuries and a forerunner both of modern literary techniques and approaches to the theme of the ambiguous nature of truth, evil, and morality. By presenting the reader with a clearly unreliable narrator whose interpretation of events is often open to question, Conrad forces the reader to

take an active part in the story's construction and to see and feel its events for him- or herself.

Author Biography

Joseph Conrad was born Josef Teodor Konrad Walecz Korzeniowski in a Russian-ruled province of Poland (now part of the Ukraine) on December 3, 1857. His father was a poet, a writer, and a political activist. His mother was also politically involved. As a result of his parents' participation in the Polish independence movement, young Conrad and his mother and father were forced into exile in Northern Russia in 1863. In the next five years, by the time Conrad was eleven, both his parents had died and the boy had been sent to live with various relatives. Conrad dropped out of school when he was sixteen and took up life on the sea, first joining the French merchant marines and sailing as apprentice and then steward to Martinique and the West Indies. At the age of twenty-one, Conrad joined a British ship, and served with the British merchant marines for ten years. During this time he achieved the rank of captain, became a naturalized British citizen, and travelled to Asia, Africa, Australia, and India. A trip to the Belgian Congo in 1890, during which Conrad sailed the Congo River, was crucial to the development of the 1899 work *Heart of Darkness.*

Poor health, from which Conrad had suffered all his life, forced his retirement from the British merchant marines in 1894. Conrad had begun writing while still in the service, basing much of his work on his life at sea. His first novel, *Almayer's Folly,* was published in 1895 and began Conrad's difficult and often financially unrewarding career as a writer. Not until 1913, with the publication of the novel *Chance,* did he achieve true critical and financial success. Nevertheless, Conrad managed to earn his living by his pen, writing all his novels in his acquired language, English, and always returning to the sea and the outskirts of civilization for his most enduring themes.

In addition to *Heart of Darkness,* Conrad's most notable early works include *The Nigger of the "Narcissus"* (1897), *Lord Jim* (1900), *Youth* (1902), and *Typhoon* (1902). The novels which are widely regarded as Conrad's greatest works are *Nostromo* (1904), *The Secret Agent* (1907), *Under Western Eyes* (1911), and *Chance.* The novel *Victory,* which appeared in 1915, may be the best known of these later works. Conrad collaborated

Joseph Conrad

on two novels with his friend and fellow novelist Ford Madox Ford, *The Inheritors* (1901) and *Romance* (1903).

Joseph Conrad married in 1896, had two sons, and died of a heart attack in England on August 3, 1924. He was buried in Canterbury Cathedral, where many of England's greatest writers lie. Although he often struggled to write in his adopted language, Conrad is now considered one of the greatest prose stylists in English literature.

Plot Summary

Chapter I

Literally speaking, the action of *Heart of Darkness* is simply the act of storytelling aboard a ship on the river Thames around the turn of the twentieth century. An unnamed narrator, along with four other men, is aboard the anchored *Nellie* waiting for the tide to turn. They trade sea stories to pass the time. One of these men is Charlie Marlow, whose story will itself be the primary narrative of *Heart of D...kness.* Before Marlow begins his tale, however, the unnamed narrator muses to himself on a history of exploration and conquest which also originated on the Thames, the waterway connecting London to the sea. The narrator mentions Sir Francis Drake and his ship the *Golden Hind,* which travelled around the globe at the end of the sixteenth century, as well as Sir John Franklin, whose expedition to North America disappeared in the Arctic Ocean in the middle of the nineteenth century.

As the sun is setting on the *Nellie,* Marlow also begins to speak of London's history and of naval expeditions. He, however, imagines an earlier point in history: he sketches the story of a hypothetical Roman seaman sent north from the Mediterranean to the then barely known British Isles. This is Marlow's prelude to his narration of his own journey up the Congo river, and he then begins an account of how he himself once secured a job as the captain of a river steamer in the Belgian colony in Africa. From here on the bulk of the novella is Marlow's narration of his journey into the Congo.

Through an aunt in Brussels, Belgium's capital, Marlow manages to get an interview with a trading company which operates a system of ivory trading posts in the Belgian Congo (formerly Zaire, now the Democratic Republic of the Congo). After a very brief discussion with a Company official in Brussels and a very strange physical examination by a Company doctor, Marlow is hired to sail a steamer between trading posts on the Congo River. He is then sent on a French ship down the African coast to the mouth of the Congo.

From the mouth of the Congo Marlow takes a short trip upriver on a steamer. This ship leaves him at the Company's Lower Station. Marlow finds the station to be a vision of hell—it is a "wanton smash-up" with loads of rusting ancient wreckage everywhere, a cliff nearby being demolished with dynamite for no apparent reason, and many starving and dying Africans enslaved and laboring under the armed guard of the Company's white employees. Marlow meets the Company's chief accountant, who mentions a Mr. Kurtz—manager of the Inner Station—for the first time and describes him as a "very remarkable person" who sends an enormous amount of ivory out of the interior. Marlow must wait at the Lower Station for ten days before setting out two hundred miles overland in a caravan to where his steamer is waiting up the river at the Central Station.

After fifteen days the caravan arrives at the Central Station, where Marlow first sees the ship which he is to command. It is sunk in the river. Marlow meets the manager of the Central Station, with whom he discusses the sunken ship. It will, they anticipate, take several months to repair. Over the course of the

next several weeks Marlow notices that the rivets he keeps requesting for the repair never arrive from the Lower Station, and when he overhears the manager speaking with several other Company officials he begins to suspect that his requests are being intercepted; that is, that the manager does not want the ship to get repaired for some reason.

Chapter II

Overhearing a conversation between the manager and his uncle, Marlow learns some information which begins to make some sense of the delays in his travel. Kurtz, chief of the Inner Station, has been in the interior alone for more than a year. He has sent no communication other than a steady and tremendous flow of ivory down to the Central Station. The manager fears that Kurtz is too strong competition for him professionally, and is not particularly interested in seeing him return.

Marlow's steamer, however, finally gets fixed and he and his party start heading up river to retrieve Kurtz and whatever ivory is at the Inner Station. On board are Marlow, the manager, several employees of the Company, and a crew of approximately twenty cannibals. The river is treacherous and the vegetation thick and almost impenetrable throughout the journey. At a place nearly fifty miles downstream from the Inner Station they come across an abandoned hut with a sign telling them to approach cautiously. Inside the hut Marlow discovers a tattered copy of a navigation manual in which undecipherable notes are written in the margins.

Nearing the Station in a heavy fog, the ship is attacked from the shore by arrows, and the passengers—"pilgrims," Marlow calls them—fire into the jungle with their rifles. Marlow ends the attack by blowing the steam whistle and scaring off the unseen attackers, but not before his helmsman is killed by a spear. Marlow imagines that he will not get to meet the mysterious Kurtz, that perhaps he has been killed, and suddenly realizes something:

> "I made the strange discovery that I had never imagined him as doing, you know, but as discoursing. I didn't say to myself, 'Now I will never see him,' or, 'Now I will never shake him by the hand,' but, 'now I will never hear him.' The man presented himself as a voice. Not of course that I did not connect him with some sort of action. Hadn't I been told in all the tones of jealousy and admiration that he had collected, bartered, swindled, or stolen more ivory than all the other agents together? That was not the point. The point was in his being a gifted creature, and that of all his gifts the one that stood out preeminently, that carried with it a sense of real presence, was his abil-

ity to talk, his words—the gift of expression, the bewildering, the illuminating, the most exalted and the most contemptible, the pulsating stream of light, or the deceitful flow from the heart of an impenetrable darkness."

When they finally reach the Inner Station they are beckoned by a odd Russian man who is a sort of disciple of Kurtz's. He turns out also to have been the owner of the hut and navigation manual Marlow found downstream. He speaks feverishly to Marlow about Kurtz's greatness.

Chapter III

The Russian explains to Marlow that the Africans attacked the ship because they were afraid it was coming to take Kurtz away from them. It appears that they worship Kurtz, and the Inner Station is a terrifying monument to Kurtz's power. The full extent of Kurtz's authority at the Inner Station is now revealed to Marlow. There are heads of "rebels" on stakes surrounding Kurtz's hut and Marlow speaks of Kurtz presiding over "unspeakable" rituals. When Kurtz is carried out to meet the ship—by this time he is very frail with illness—he commands the crowd to allow him to be taken aboard without incident. As they wait out the night on board the steamer the people of the Inner Station build fires and pound drums in vigil.

Late that night Marlow wakes up to find Kurtz gone, so he goes ashore to find him. When he tracks him down, Kurtz is crawling through the brush, trying to return to the Station, to the fires, to "his people," and to his "immense plans." Marlow persuades him to return to the ship. When the ship leaves the next day with the ailing Kurtz on board the crowd gathers at the shore and wails in desperate sadness at his disappearance. Marlow blows the steam whistle and disperses the crowd.

On the return trip to the Central Station Kurtz's health worsens. He half coherently reflects on his "soul's adventure," as Marlow describes it, and his famous final words are: "The horror! The horror!" He dies and is buried somewhere downriver on the muddy shore.

When Marlow returns to Belgium he goes to see Kurtz's fiancée, his "Intended." She speaks with him about Kurtz's greatness, his genius, his ability to speak eloquently, and of his great plans for civilizing Africa. Rather than explain the truth of Kurtz's life in Africa, Marlow decides not to disillusion her. He returns some of Kurtz's things to her—some letters and a pamphlet he had written—and tells her that Kurtz's last word was her name. Marlow's story ends and the scene returns to the anchored *Nellie*

where the unnamed narrator and the other sailors are sitting silently as the tide is turning.

Characters

The Aunt

The Aunt uses her influence to help Charlie Marlow secure an appointment as skipper of the steamboat that will take him up the Congo River. Echoing the prevailing sentiments of the Victorian day, the Aunt speaks of missions to Africa as "weaning the ignorant millions from their horrid ways."

The Chief Accountant

The Chief Accountant, sometimes referred to as the Clerk, is a white man who has been in the Congo for three years. He appears in such an unexpectedly elegant outfit when Marlow first encounters him that Marlow thinks he is a vision. Both the Chief Accountant's clothes and his books are in excellent order. He keeps up appearances, despite the sight of people dying all around him and the great demoralization of the land. For this, he earns Marlow's respect. "That's backbone," says Marlow.

The Clerk
See The Chief Accountant

The Company Manager
See The Manager

The Doctor

The Doctor measures Marlow's head before he sets out on his journey. He say he does that for everyone who goes "out there," meaning Africa, but that he never sees them when they return. The Doctor asks Marlow if there's any madness in his family and warns him above all else to keep calm and avoid irritation in the tropics.

The Fireman

The Fireman is an African referred to as "an improved specimen." He has three ornamental scars on each cheek and teeth filed to points. He is very good at firing the boiler, for he believes evil spirits reside within and it is his job to keep the boiler from getting thirsty.

The Foreman

The Foreman is a boilermaker by trade and a good worker. He is a bony, yellow-faced, bald wid-

Still from the 1979 film Apocalypse Now, *starring Marlon Brando and Martin Sheen, which was a modern-day interpretation of* Heart of Darkness *set during the Vietnam War.*

ower with a waist-length beard and six children. His passion is pigeon flying. By performing a jig and getting Marlow to dance it with him, he shows that the lonely, brutalizing life of the interior of Africa can make people behave in bizarre ways.

Captain Fresleven

Fresleven, a Danish captain, was Marlow's predecessor. He had been killed in Africa when he got into a quarrel over some black hens with a village chief. He battered the chief over the head with a stick and was in turn killed by the chief's son. Fresleven had always been considered a very quiet and gentle man. His final actions show how drastically a two-year stay in Africa can alter a European's personality.

The Helmsman

A native, the Helmsman is responsible for steering Marlow's boat. Marlow has little respect for the man, whom he calls "the most unstable kind of fool," because he swaggers in front of others but becomes passive when left alone. He becomes frightened when the natives shoot arrows at the boat and drops his pole to pick up a rifle and fire back. The Helmsman is hit in the side by a spear. His blood fills Marlow's shoes. His eyes gleam brightly as he stares intently at Marlow and then dies without speaking.

The Intended

The Intended is the woman to whom Kurtz is engaged and whom he had left behind in Belgium. One year after his death, she is still dressed in mourning. She is depicted as naive, romantic, and, in the opinion of Victorian men of the day, in need of protection. She says she knew Kurtz better than anyone in the world and that she had his full confidence. This is an obviously ironic statement, as Marlow's account of Kurtz makes clear. Her chief wish is to go on believing that Kurtz died with her name on his lips, and in this, Marlow obliges her.

The Journalist

The Journalist comes to visit Marlow after Marlow has returned from Africa. He says Kurtz was a politician and an extremist. He says Kurtz could have led a party, any party. Marlow agrees and gives the journalist a portion of Kurtz's papers to publish.

Mr. Kurtz

Kurtz, born of a mother who was half-English and a father who was half-French, was educated in England. He is an ivory trader who has been alone

Media Adaptations

- Directed by Nicolas Roeg, *Heart of Darkness* was adapted for television and broadcast on TNT in 1994. The film features Tim Roth as Marlow and John Malkovich as Kurtz, and is available on cassette from Turner Home Entertainment.

- The structure of *Heart of Darkness* was incorporated into Francis Ford Coppola's award-winning 1979 film *Apocalypse Now,* starring Marlon Brando and Martin Sheen. The insanities presented in the book as stemming from isolation in the African jungle are in the film transposed to the jungles of Vietnam. Available from Paramount Home Video.

- Two sound recordings of *Heart of Darkness* exist. Both are abridged and produced on two cassettes each. One was recorded by HarperCollins in 1969, is narrated by Anthony Quayle, and runs 91 minutes. The other is a 180-minute recording, published by Penguin-High Bridge audio in 1994, with narration by David Threlfall.

in the jungles of Africa for a long time. No one has heard from him in nine months. The Company Manager says Kurtz is the best ivory trader he has ever had, although he suspects him of hoarding vast amounts of ivory. Marlow is sent to rescue him, although he has not asked for help. The word "kurtz" means "short" in German, but when Marlow first sees the man, seated on a stretcher with his arms extended toward the natives and his mouth opened wide as if to swallow everything before him, he appears to be about seven feet tall. Though gravely ill, Kurtz has an amazingly loud and strong voice. He commands attention. Kurtz, previously known to Marlow by reputation and through his writings on "civilizing" the African continent, is revealed upon acquaintance to be a dying, deranged, and power-mad subjugator of the African natives. Human sacrifices have been made to him. Rows of impaled human heads line the path to the door of his cabin. Kurtz is both childish and fiendish. He talks to the very end. His brain is haunted by shadowy images. Love and hate fight for possession of his soul. He speaks of the necessity of protecting his "intended" and says she is "out of it," a sentiment Marlow will later echo. Kurtz's final words, uttered as he lies in the dark waiting for death, are: "The horror! The horror!" With this utterance, Kurtz presumably realizes the depth to which his unbridled greed and brutality have brought him. That realization is transferred to Marlow, who feels bound to Kurtz both through the common heritage of their European background and the infinite corruptibility of their natures as men.

Kurtz's Cousin

Kurtz's Cousin is an organist. He tells Marlow Kurtz was a great musician. Marlow doesn't really believe him but can't say exactly what Kurtz's profession was. Marlow and the Cousin agree Kurtz was a "universal genius."

The Manager

The Manager, a man of average size and build with cold blue eyes, inspires uneasiness in Marlow, but not outright mistrust. He is an enigma. He is smart, but cannot keep order. His men obey him but do not love or respect him. The Manager has been in the heart of Africa for nine years, yet is never ill. Marlow considers the Manager's greatness to lie in that he never gives away the secret of what controls him. Marlow speculates that perhaps there is nothing inside him, and maybe that is why he is never ill. The Manager says Kurtz is the best agent he ever had; yet he also says Kurtz's method is unsound and that he has done more harm than good to the Company. When Marlow discovers his ship is in need of repair, the Manager tells him the repairs will take three months to complete. Marlow considers the man "a chattering idiot," but his three-month estimate turns out to be exactly right.

The Manager's boy

The Manager's "boy," an African servant, delivers the book's famous line, "Mistah Kurtz—he dead."

The Manager's Uncle

The Manager's Uncle, a short, paunchy man whose eyes have a look of "sleepy cunning," is the leader of the group of white men who arrive at the Central Station wearing new clothes and tan shoes. The group calls itself the "Eldorado Exploring Expedition," and uses the station as a base from which to travel into the jungle and plunder from its inhabitants. Marlow observes that they steal from the land "with no more moral purpose at the back of it than there is in burglars breaking into a safe." The Manager's Uncle and the Manager refer to Kurtz as "that man."

Charlie Marlow

Marlow, a seaman and a wanderer who follows the sea, relates the tale that makes up the bulk of the book. He is an Englishman who speaks passable French. He sits in the pose of a preaching Buddha as he tells a group of men aboard the *Nellie,* a cruising yawl in the River Thames, the story of his journey into the interior of the Congo. Marlow had previously returned from sailing voyages in Asia and after six years in England decided to look for another post. He speaks of his boyhood passion for maps and of his long fascination with Africa, that "place of darkness." Through the influence of his aunt, Marlow is appointed captain of a steamer and charged with going up river to find Kurtz, a missing ivory trader, and bring him back. Marlow says he is acquainted with Kurtz through his writing and admires him. His trip upriver is beset with difficulties. Marlow encounters several acts of madness, including a French man-of-war relentlessly shelling the bush while there appears to be not a single human being or even a shed to fire upon. Later, he comes upon a group of Africans who are blasting away at the land, presumably in order to build a railway, but Marlow sees no reason for it, there being nothing in the way to blast. Everywhere about him, he sees naked black men dying of disease and starvation.

Revulsion grows within him over the white man's dehumanizing colonization of the Congo. It reaches a peak when Marlow finally meets Kurtz and sees the depths of degradation to which the man has sunk. Nevertheless, Marlow feels an affinity toward Kurtz. He sees in him both a reflection of his own corruptible European soul and a premonition of his destiny. Although Kurtz is already dying when Marlow meets him, Marlow experiences him as a powerful force. When Kurtz says, "I had immense plans," Marlow believes the man's mind is still clear but that his soul is mad. Marlow takes the dying Kurtz aboard his steamer for the return trip down river. He feels a bond has been established between himself and Kurtz and that Kurtz has become his "choice of nightmares." When Marlow hears Kurtz's last words, "The horror! The horror!", he takes them to be Kurtz's final judgment on his life on earth. Seeing a kind of victory in that final summing up, Marlow remains loyal to Kurtz.

One year after Kurtz's death, Marlow visits Kurtz's fiancée, who has been left behind in Brussels. He finds her trusting and capable of immense faith. Marlow believes he must protect her from all the horrors he witnessed in Africa in order to save her soul. When the girl asks to hear Kurtz's final words, Marlow lies and says he died with her name on his lips. Marlow then ceases his tale and sits silently aboard ship in his meditative pose.

The Narrator

The Narrator remains unidentified throughout the book. He tells the reader the story Charlie Marlow told to him and three other men (the captain or Director of the Companies, the accountant, and the lawyer) as they sat aboard the becalmed *Nellie* on London's River Thames, waiting for the tide to turn. The Narrator is an attentive listener who does not comment on or try to interpret the tale. He is, instead, a vessel through which Marlow's story is transmitted, much as Conrad is a vessel through whom the entire book is transmitted. When Marlow finishes speaking, the Narrator looks out at the tranquil river and reflects that it "seemed to lead into the heart of an immense darkness."

The Official

The Official demands that Marlow turn over Kurtz's papers to him, saying the Company has the right to all information about its territories. Marlow gives him the report on "Suppression of Savage Customs," minus Kurtz's final comment recommending extermination, and says the rest is private. The Official looks at the document and says it's not what they "had a right to expect."

The Pilgrim in Pink Pajamas
See The Pilgrim

The Pilgrim

The Pilgrim is a fat white man with sandy hair and red whiskers. He wears his pink pajamas tucked into his socks. He cannot steer the boat. He assumes Kurtz is dead and hopes many Africans, whom he and all the other white people refer to as "savages," have been killed to avenge Kurtz's death. Marlow tells the Pilgrim he must learn to fire a rifle from the shoulder. The pilgrims fire from the hip with their eyes closed.

The Pilgrims

The Pilgrims are the European traders who accompany Marlow into the jungle. They fire their rifles from the hip into the air and indiscriminately into the bush. They eventually come to look with disfavor upon Marlow, who does not share their opinions or interests. When they bury Kurtz, Marlow believes the Pilgrims would like to bury him as well.

The Poleman

See The Helmsman

The Russian

The Russian is a twenty-five-year-old fair-skinned, beardless man with a boyish face and tiny blue eyes. He wears brown clothes with bright blue, red, and yellow patches covering them. He looks like a harlequin—a clown in patched clothes—to Marlow. As he boards Marlow's boat, he assures everyone that the "savages" are "simple people" who "meant no harm" before he corrects himself: "Not exactly." The Russian dropped out of school to go to sea. He has been alone on the river for two years, heading for the interior, and chatters constantly to make up for the silence he has endured. The Towson's Book on seamanship, which Marlow had discovered previously, belongs to the Russian. Marlow finds the Russian an insoluble problem. He admires and envies him. The Russian is surrounded by the "glamour" of youth and appears unscathed to Marlow. He wants nothing from the wilderness but to continue to exist. The Russian describes Kurtz as a great orator. He says one doesn't talk with him, one listens to him. He says Kurtz once talked to him all night about everything, including love. "This man has enlarged my mind," he tells Marlow. The Russian presents Marlow with a great deal of information about Kurtz, chiefly that Kurtz is adored by the African tribe that follows him, that he once nearly killed the Russian for his small supply of ivory, and that it was Kurtz who ordered the attack on the steamer to scare them away.

The Savages

"Savages" is the blanket term the white traders use to refer to all African natives, despite their differing origins. The savages range from the workers dying of starvation and disease at the Outer Station to the cannibals who man Marlow's boat to the tribe who worships Kurtz. For the most part Marlow comes to consider all the natives savages, although he expresses some admiration for the cannibals, who must be very hungry but have refrained from attacking the few white men on the boat because of "a piece of paper written over in accordance with some farcical law or other." When Marlow first arrives in Africa, he is appalled by the whites' brutal treatment of the natives, and never expresses agreement with the pilgrims who eagerly anticipate taking revenge on the savages. He also seems to be shocked by the addendum to Kurtz's report that says, "Exterminate all the brutes!" Nevertheless, Marlow never sees beyond the surface of any of the natives. He compares watching the boat's fireman work to "seeing a dog in a parody of breeches and a feather hat, walking on his hind-legs," and shocks the pilgrims when he dumps the body of the helmsman overboard instead of saving it for burial. For Marlow, the native "savages" serve only as another illustration of the mystery Africa holds for Europeans, and it is because of this dehumanization that several critics consider *Heart of Darkness* a racist work.

The Swedish Captain

The Swedish Captain is the captain of the ship that takes Marlow toward the mouth of the Congo. He tells Marlow that another Swede has just hanged himself by the side of the road. When Marlow asks why, the Swedish Captain replies, "Who knows? The sun too much for him, or the country perhaps."

The Woman

The Woman is the proud, "wild-eyed and magnificent" African woman with whom Kurtz has been living while in the interior. She is the queen of a native tribe. When she sees Marlow's steamer about to pull away and realizes she will never see Kurtz again, she stands by the river's edge with her hands raised high to the sky. She alone among the natives does not flinch at the sound of the ship's whistle. Marlow considers her a tragic figure.

The Young Agent

The Young Agent has been stationed at the Central Station for one year. He affects an aristocratic manner and is considered the Manager's spy by the other agents at the station. His job is to make bricks, but Marlow sees no bricks anywhere about the station. The Young Agent presses Marlow for information about Europe, then believes his answers are lies and grows bored. The Young Agent tells Marlow Kurtz is Chief of the Inner Station. He refers to Kurtz as "a prodigy … an emissary of pity and of science and progress." The Young Agent establishes a connection between Kurtz and Marlow by saying that the same group of people who sent Kurtz into Africa also recommended Marlow to come and get him out.

Themes

Alienation and Loneliness

Throughout *Heart of Darkness,* which tells of a journey into the heart of the Belgian Congo and out again, the themes of alienation, loneliness, silence and solitude predominate. The book begins and ends in silence, with men first waiting for a tale to begin and then left to their own thoughts after it has concluded. The question of what the alienation and loneliness of extended periods of time in a remote and hostile environment can do to men's minds is a central theme of the book. The doctor who measures Marlow's head prior to his departure for Africa warns him of changes to his personality that may be produced by a long stay in-country. Prolonged silence and solitude are seen to have damaging effects on many characters in the book. Among these are the late Captain Fresleven, Marlow's predecessor, who was transformed from a gentle soul into a man of violence, and the Russian, who has been alone on the River for two years and dresses bizarrely and chatters constantly. But loneliness and alienation have taken their greatest toll on Kurtz, who, cut off from all humanizing influence, has forfeited the restraints of reason and conscience and given free rein to his most base and brutal instincts.

Deception

Deception, or hypocrisy, is a central theme of the novel and is explored on many levels. In the disguise of a "noble cause," the Belgians have exploited the Congo. Actions taken in the name of philanthropy are merely covers for greed. Claiming to educate the natives, to bring them religion and a better way of life, European colonizers remained to starve, mutilate, and murder the indigenous population for profit. Marlow has even obtained his captaincy through deception, for his aunt misrepresented him as "an exceptional and gifted creature." She also presented him as "one of the Workers, with a capital [W].... Something like an emissary of light, something like a lower sort of apostle," and Conrad notes the deception in elevating working people to some mystical status they can not realistically obtain. At the end of the book, Marlow engages in his own deception when he tells Kurtz's fiancée the lie that Kurtz died with her name on his lips.

Order and Disorder

Conrad sounds the themes of order and disorder in showing, primarily through the example of the Company's chief clerk, how people can carry

Topics for Further Study

- Research the Belgian atrocities, committed in the Belgian Congo between 1889 and 1899, and compare them to the evidence of same presented in *Heart of Darkness.*

- Research Henry Stanley's three-year journey (1874-1877) up the Congo River and compare the stations Stanley founded along the river to those mentioned in *Heart of Darkness.*

- Compare the view of women, as presented in *Heart of Darkness,* to today's view. Argue whether Conrad should or should not be considered a sexist by today's standards.

- Compare the view of Africans, as presented in *Heart of Darkness,* to today's view. Argue whether Conrad should or should not be considered a racist by today's standards.

- Research a contemporary psychological study of the effects on an individual of isolation, solitude, or a wild jungle environment and compare it to Kurtz's situation.

on with the most mundane details of their lives while all around them chaos reigns. In the larger context, the Company attends to the details of sending agents into the interior to trade with the natives and collect ivory while remaining oblivious to the devastation such acts have caused. Yet on a closer look, the Company's Manager has no talent for order or organization. His station is in a deplorable state and Marlow can see no reason for the Manager to have his position other than the fact that he is never ill. On the other hand, the chief clerk is so impeccably dressed that when Marlow first meets him he thinks he is a vision. This man, who has been in-country three years and witnessed all its attendant horrors, manages to keep his clothes and books in excellent order. He even speaks with confidence of a Council of Europe which intended Kurtz to go far in "the administration," as if there is some overall rational principle guiding their lives.

Sanity and Insanity

Closely linked to the themes of order and disorder are those of sanity and insanity. Madness, given prolonged exposure to the isolation of the wilderness, seems an inevitable extension of chaos. The atmospheric influences at the heart of the African continent—the stifling heat, the incessant drums, the whispering bush, the mysterious light—play havoc with the unadapted European mind and reduce it either to the insanity of thinking anything is allowable in such an atmosphere or, as in Kurtz's case, to literal madness. Kurtz, after many years in the jungle, is presented as a man who has gone mad with power and greed. No restraints were placed on him—either from above, from a rule of law, or from within, from his own conscience. In the wilderness, he came to believe he was free to do whatever he liked, and the freedom drove him mad. Small acts of madness line Marlow's path to Kurtz: the Man-of-War that fires into the bush for no apparent reason, the urgently needed rivets that never arrive, the bricks that will never be built, the jig that is suddenly danced, the immense hole dug for no discernible purpose. All these events ultimately lead to a row of impaled severed human heads and Kurtz, a man who, in his insanity, has conferred a godlike status on himself and has ritual human sacrifices performed for him. The previously mentioned themes of solitude and silence have here achieved their most powerful effect: they have driven Kurtz mad. He is presented as a voice, a disembodied head, a mouth that opens as if to devour everything before him. Kurtz speaks of "my ivory … my intended … my river … my station," as if everything in the Congo belonged to him. This is the final arrogant insanity of the white man who comes supposedly to improve a land, but stays to exploit, ravage, and destroy it.

Duty and Responsibility

As is true of all other themes in the book, those of duty and responsibility are glimpsed on many levels. On a national level, we are told of the British devotion to duty and efficiency which led to systematic colonization of large parts of the globe and has its counterpart in Belgian colonization of the Congo, the book's focus. On an individual level, Conrad weaves the themes of duty and responsibility through Marlow's job as captain, a position which make him responsible for his crew and bound to his duties as the boat's commander. There are also the jobs of those with whom Marlow comes into contact on his journey. In *Heart of Darkness,* duty and responsibility revolve most often about

how one does one's work. A job well done is respected; simply doing the work one is responsible for is an honorable act. Yet Conrad does not believe in romanticizing the worker. Workers can often be engaged in meaningless tasks, as illustrated in the scene where the Africans blast away at the rock face in order to build a railway, but the rock is not altered by the blasts and the cliff is not at all in the way. The Company's Manager would seem to have a duty to run his business efficiently, but he cannot keep order and although he is obeyed, he is not respected. The Foreman, however, earns Marlow's respect for being a good worker. Marlow admires the way the Foreman ties up his waist-length beard when he has to crawl in the mud beneath the steamboat to do his job. (Having a waist-length beard in a jungle environment can be seen as another act of madness, even from an efficient worker.) Chapter I of the novel ends with Marlow speculating on how Kurtz would do his work. But there is a larger sense in which the themes of work and responsibility figure. Marlow says, "I don't like work—no man does—but I like what is in the work—the chance to find yourself." It is through the work (or what passes for it) that Kurtz does in Africa that his moral bankruptcy is revealed. For himself, Marlow emerges with a self-imposed duty to remain loyal to Kurtz, and it is this responsibility which finally forces him to lie to Kurtz's fiancee.

Doubt and Ambiguity

As reason loses hold, doubt and ambiguity take over. As Marlow travels deeper inland, the reality of everything he encounters becomes suspect. The perceptions, motivations, and reliability of those he meets, as well as his own, are all open to doubt. Conrad repeatedly tells us that the heat and light of the wilderness cast a spell and put those who would dare venture further into a kind of trancelike state. Nothing is to be taken at face value. After the Russian leaves, Marlow wonders if he ever actually saw him.

The central ambiguity of *Heart of Darkness* is Kurtz himself. Who is he? What does he do? What does he actually say? Those who know him speak again and again of his superb powers of rhetoric, but the reader hears little of it. The Russian says he is devoted to Kurtz, and yet we are left to wonder why. Kurtz has written a report that supposedly shows his interest in educating the African natives, but it ends with his advice, "Exterminate all the brutes!" Marlow has heard that Kurtz is a great man, yet he suspects he is "hollow to the core." In

Marlow's estimation, if Kurtz was remarkable it was because he had something to say at the end of his life. But what he found to say was "the horror!" After Kurtz's death, when various people come to Marlow representing themselves as having known Kurtz, it seems none of them really knew him. Was he a painter, a writer, a great musician, a politician, as he is variously described? Marlow settles for the ambiguous term, "universal genius," which would imply Kurtz was whatever one wanted to make of him.

Race and Racism

The subject of racism is not really treated by Conrad as a theme in *Heart of Darkness* as much as it is simply shown to be the prevailing attitude of the day. The African natives are referred to as "niggers," "cannibals," "criminals," and "savages." European colonizers see them as a subordinate species and chain, starve, rob, mutilate, and murder them without fear of punishment. The book presents a damning account of imperialism as it illustrates the white man's belief in his innate right to come into a country inhabited by people of a different race and pillage to his heart's content.

Kurtz is writing a treatise for something called the "International Society for the Suppression of Savage Customs." This implies the existence of a worldwide movement to subjugate all nonwhite races. Kurtz bestows a kind of childlike quality upon the Africans by saying that white people appear to them as supernatural beings. The natives do, indeed, seem to have worshipped Kurtz as a god and to have offered up human sacrifices to him. This innocence proceeds, in Kurtz's view, from an inferior intelligence and does not prevent him from concluding that the way to deal with the natives is to exterminate them all.

Early in his journey, Marlow sees a group of black men paddling boats. He admires their naturalness, strength, and vitality, and senses that they want nothing from the land but to coexist with it. This notion prompts him to believe that he still belongs to a world of reason. The feeling is short-lived, however, for it is not long before Marlow, too, comes to see the Africans as some subhuman form of life and to use the language of his day in referring to them as "creatures," "niggers," "cannibals," and "savages." He does not protest or try to interfere when he sees six Africans forced to work with chains about their necks. He calls what he sees in their eyes the "deathlike indifference of unhappy savages."

Marlow exhibits some humanity in offering a dying young African one of the ship's biscuits, and although he regrets the death of his helmsman, he says he was "a savage who was no more account than a grain of sand in a black Sahara." It is not the man he misses so much as his function as steersman. Marlow refers to the "savage who was fireman" as "an improved specimen." He compares him, standing before his vertical boiler, to "a dog in a parody of breeches and a feather hat, walking on his hind legs."

Violence and Cruelty

The violence and cruelty depicted in *Heart of Darkness* escalate from acts of inhumanity committed against the natives of the Belgian Congo to "unspeakable" and undescribed horrors. Kurtz (representing European imperialists) has systematically engaged in human plunder. The natives are seen chained by iron collars abut their necks, starved, beaten, subsisting on rotten hippo meat, forced into soul-crushing and meaningless labor, and finally ruthlessly murdered. Beyond this, it is implied that Kurtz has had human sacrifices performed for him, and the reader is presented with the sight of a row of severed human heads impaled on posts leading to Kurtz's cabin. Conrad suggests that violence and cruelty result when law is absent and man allows himself to be ruled by whatever brutal passions lie within him. Consumed by greed, conferring upon himself the status of a god, Kurtz runs amok in a land without law. Under such circumstances, anything is possible, and what Conrad sees emerging from the situation is the profound cruelty and limitless violence that lies at the heart of the human soul.

Moral Corruption

The book's theme of moral corruption is the one to which, like streams to a river, all others lead. Racism, madness, loneliness, deception and disorder, doubt and ambiguity, violence and cruelty—culminate in the moral corruption revealed by Kurtz's acts in the Congo. Kurtz has cast off reason and allowed his most base and brutal instincts to rule unrestrained. He has permitted the evil within him to gain the upper hand. Kurtz's appalling moral corruption is the result not only of external forces such as the isolation and loneliness imposed by the jungle, but also, Conrad suggests, of forces that lie within all men and await the chance to emerge. Kurtz perhaps realizes the depth of his own moral corruption when, as he lays dying, he utters "The horror! The horror!" Marlow feels this realization transferred to himself and understands that he too, living in a lawless state, is capable of sinking into the depths of moral corruption. The savage nature of man is thus reached at the end of the journey, not upriver, but into his own soul.

Style

Point of View

Heart of Darkness is framed as a story within a story. The point of view belongs primarily to Charlie Marlow, who delivers the bulk of the narrative, but Marlow's point of view is in turn framed by that of an unnamed narrator who provides a first-person description of Marlow telling his story. The point of view can also be seen in a third consciousness in the book, that of Conrad himself, who tells the entire tale to the reader, deciding as author which details to put in and which to leave out. Beyond these three dominant points of view are the individual viewpoints of the book's major characters. Each has a different perspective on Kurtz. These perspectives are often conflicting and are always open to a variety of interpretations. Whose point of view is to be trusted? Which narrator and which character is reliable? Conrad leaves these questions to the reader to answer, accounting for the book's complexity and multilayered meanings.

Setting

The novel takes place in the 1890s and begins on a boat sitting in the River Thames, which leads from London to the sea, waiting for the tide to turn. Marlow's story takes the reader briefly onto the European continent (Belgium) and then deep into Africa by means of a trip up the Congo River to what was then called the Belgian Congo, and back to Europe again. The Congo is described as a place of intense mystery whose stifling heat, whispering sounds, and strange shifts of light and darkness place the foreigner in a kind of trance which produces fundamental changes in the brain, causing acts that range from the merely bizarre to the most extreme and irrational violence.

Structure

The book's structure is cyclical, both in geography and chronology. It begins in the 1890s, goes back several years, and returns to the present. The voyage describes almost a perfect cir-

cle, beginning in Europe, traveling into the heart of the African continent, coming out again, and returning almost to the exact spot at which it began. The novel was originally published in serial form, breaking off its segments at moments of high drama to make the reader eager to pick up the next installment. When the full text was published in 1902, it was divided into three parts. Part I takes the story from the present-day life of the unidentified narrator to Marlow's tale, which began many years before and unfolds over a period of several months. This section leads from London into Belgium and from there to the Congo's Central Station. It ends with Marlow expressing a limited curiosity about where Kurtz's supposed moral ideas will lead him. Part II takes the journey through a series of difficulties as it proceeds deeper into the African interior and finally arrives, some two months later, at the Inner Station. It is here that Marlow meets the Russian and is told that Kurtz has "enlarged" his mind. Part III covers the period from Marlow's eventual meeting with Kurtz to his return to Europe.

Symbolism

The title of the book itself, *Heart of Darkness,* alerts the reader to the book's symbols, or items that suggest deeper interpretations beyond their literal meanings. The "heart of darkness" serves both as an image of the interior of a dark and foreign continent as well as the interior workings of the mind of man, which are dark and foreign to all observers. The literal journey into the jungle is a metaphor, or symbol, for the journey into the uncharted human soul. On another level, the voyage into the wilderness can be read as a voyage back to Eden, or to the very beginning of the world. On still another level, the actual trip into and then out of the African continent can be seen as metaphor for sin and redemption. It parallels the descent into the depths of human degradation and death (in Kurtz's case; near-death in Marlow's) and the return to the light, or life. As the book begins, the *Nellie* is waiting for the tide to turn. This can also be taken as a metaphor for the brewing revolution in the Congo at the time, for the tide of history was about to turn. The dying Kurtz himself, who is half-French and half-English and of whom Marlow says, "All Europe contributed to the making of Kurtz," can be seen as a symbol for a decaying western civilization. Other symbols in the book include the river, whose flow, sometimes fast and sometimes stagnant, mirrors the stream of life; the knitting

Map of the Democratic Republic of the Congo.

women waiting outside Marlow's interview room, who recall the Fates of Greek mythology and thus can be seen as potential judges; and the cross-legged pose in which Marlow sits during his narration, suggesting the figure of the enlightened Buddha and thus a kind of supreme wisdom. The presentation of Kurtz as a talker, a voice who enlarges the mind of his listeners, can also be taken as a symbol for Conrad himself. As a writer, Conrad talks to his listening readers and enlarges their view of the world. Marlow's function, too, is a metaphor for the author's: they both tell stories; they both make people see and feel.

Historical Context

European Presence in Africa

In 1890, Joseph Conrad secured employment in the Congo as the captain of a river steamboat; this was also the approximate year in which the main action of *Heart of Darkness* takes place. Illness forced Conrad's return home after only six months in Africa, but that was long enough for intense impressions to have been formed in the novelist's mind. Today, the river at the center of *Heart of Darkness* is called the Zaire and the

Compare
&
Contrast

- **1890s:** The iron steamship has supplanted the sailing ship. The British, French, and Dutch Merchant Marines are associated with colonization and the development of manufacturing. With the introduction of the steel steamship in the mid-nineteenth century, Great Britain takes first place in ship building and shipping.

  Today: The turbine and diesel engine bring new power and speed to shipping, and a new age of nuclear-powered shipping is launched. Ocean-going vessels are still the dominant means for world transport of commercial goods.

- **1890s:** The African slave trade has begun to die out in the Belgian Congo. The Brussels Act of 1890 is signed by eighteen nations and greatly limits the slave trade. But forced labor continues in the Congo with appalling brutality as the lucrative trade in rubber and ivory takes up where trade in human beings left off.

  Today: Slavery is all but abolished throughout the world, although it is reported to still exist in parts of Africa and Asia.

- **1890s:** Because of the ivory trade, the collection of ivory (present only in the tusks of elephants) thrives in Africa, where elephant tusks are larger than they are in Asia. Antwerp (Belgium) and London are major centers of ivory commerce, with Europe and the U.S. being major importers.

  Today: The diminishing number of elephants, due largely to their wholesale slaughter for tusks, leads to a complete ban on ivory trading. A new method of determining the origin of a tusk through DNA testing enables zoologists to fight poaching and determine where the elephant population is large enough to safely permit a limited trade.

- **1890s:** The Congo Free State is established by King Leopold II of Belgium and is to be headed by the King himself. Leopold II never visits the Congo in person and when reports of atrocities committed there by his agents reach him, he order that all abuses cease at once. His orders are ignored. Belgium annexes the Congo in 1908.

  Today: The Belgian Congo is the Democratic Republic of the Congo, and the Congo River is the Zaire. The Congolese army mutinied in 1960 and the Congo was declared independent. In 1989, the country defaults on a loan from Belgium, resulting in the cancellation of development programs. Since 1990, a trend of political turmoil and economic collapse continues, even after a relatively bloodless revolution in 1997.

- **1890s:** Christian Missionaries are very active in the Belgian Congo. They are mostly Roman Catholic and pursue what is known as the "white man's burden" to bring western religion, culture, and technology to the nations of Africa.

  Today: More than three-fourths of the inhabitants of the Democratic Republic of the Congo are Christian. Many also follow traditional religious beliefs and a substantial number belong to African Protestant groups. The population of the Congo comprises about two hundred ethnic groups, the majority of whom speak one of the Bantu languages, although the country's official language is French.

country is the Democratic Republic of the Congo, but at the time Conrad wrote of them the country was the Belgian Congo and the river the Congo.

European explorers first discovered the Congo River in 1482 and maintained a presence on it for hundreds of years thereafter, never traveling more than two hundred miles upstream. It was not until 1877, after the English-born American explorer Henry Morton Stanley had completed a three-year journey across central Africa, that the exact length and course of the mighty Congo River were known.

Stanley discovered that the Congo extends some 1,600 miles into Africa from its eastern coast to its western edge, where the river empties into the Atlantic Ocean, and that only one stretch of it is impassable. That section lies between Matadi, two hundred miles in from the mouth of the Congo, and Kinshasa, yet another two hundred miles further inland. In *Heart of Darkness,* Conrad calls Matadi the Company Station and Kinshasa the Central Station. Between those two places, one is forced to proceed by land, which is exactly what Marlow does on his "two hundred-mile tramp" between the two Stations, described in the book.

In 1878, King Leopold II (reigned 1865-1909) of Belgium asked Stanley to found a Belgian colony in the Congo. The King charged Stanley with setting up outposts along the Congo River, particularly at Matadi. Leopold II described his motives to the rest of Europe as springing from a desire to end slavery in the Congo and civilize the natives, but his actual desires were for material gain. In 1885, at the Congress of Berlin, an international committee agreed to the formation of a new country to be known as the Congo Free State. In *Heart of Darkness,* Conrad refers to this committee as the International Society for the Suppression of Savage Customs. Leopold II, who was to be sole ruler of this land, never set foot in the Congo Free State. Instead, he formed a company, called simply the Company in *Heart of Darkness,* that ran the country for him.

The Ivory Trade

A prevalent feeling among Europeans of the 1890s was that the African peoples required introduction to European culture and technology in order to become more evolved. The responsibility for that introduction, known as the "white man's burden," gave rise to a fervor to bring Christianity and commerce to Africa. What the Europeans took out of Africa in return were huge quantities of ivory. During the 1890s, at the time *Heart of Darkness* takes place, ivory was in enormous demand in Europe, where it was used to make jewelry, piano keys, and billiard balls, among other items. From 1888 to 1892, the amount of ivory exported from the Congo Free State rose from just under 13,000 pounds to over a quarter of a million pounds. Conrad tells us that Kurtz was the best agent of his time, collecting as much ivory as all the other agents combined.

In 1892, Leopold II declared all natural resources in the Congo Free State to be his property. This meant the Belgians could stop dealing with African traders and simply take what they wanted themselves. As a consequence, Belgian traders pushed deeper into Africa in search of new sources of ivory, setting up stations all along the Congo River. One of the furthermost stations, located at Stanley Falls, was the likely inspiration for Kurtz's Inner Station.

Belgian Atrocities in the Congo

The Belgian traders committed many well-documented acts of atrocity against the African natives, including the severing of hands and heads. Reports of these atrocities reached the European public, leading to an international movement protesting the Belgian presence in Africa. These acts, reflected in *Heart of Darkness,* continued, despite an order by Leopold II that they cease. In 1908, after the Belgian parliament finally sent its own review board into the Congo to investigate, the king was forced to give up his personal stake in the area and control of the Congo reverted to the Belgian government. The country was granted its independence from Belgium in 1960, and changed its name from the Democratic Republic of Congo to Zaire in 1971. A relatively bloodless revolution in 1997 returned the country's name to the Democratic Republic of the Congo.

Critical Overview

When published in 1902 in a volume with two other stories (*Youth* and *The End of the Tether*), *Heart of Darkness* was praised for its portrayal of the demoralizing effect life in the African wilderness supposedly had on European men. One respected critic of the time, Hugh Clifford, said in the *Spectator* that others before Conrad had written of the European's decline in a "barbaric" wilderness, but never "has any writer till now succeeded in bringing … it all home to sheltered folk as does Mr. Conrad in this wonderful, this magnificent, this terrible study." Another early reviewer, as quoted in Leonard Dean's *Joseph Conrad's 'Heart of Darkness': Backgrounds and Criticisms,* called the prose "brilliant" but the story "unconvincing."

In his review published in *Academy and Literature* in 1902, Edward Garnett called the volume's publication "one of the events of the literary year." Garnett said when he first read *Heart of Darkness* in serial form, he thought Conrad had "here and there, lost his way." but upon publication of the novel in book form, he retracted that opinion and now held it "to be the high-water mark of the author's talent." Garnett went on to call *Heart of Darkness* a book that "enriches English literature" and a "psychological masterpiece." Garnett was particularly taken with Conrad's keen observations of the collapse of the white man's morality when he is released from the restraints of European law and order and set down in the heart of Africa, given free reign to trade for profit with the natives. For sheer excitement, Garnett compared *Heart of Darkness* favorably to *Crime and Punishment,* published by the great Russian novelist Dostoyevsky in 1866. Garnett calls *Heart of Darkness* "simply a piece of art, fascinating and remorseless."

Kingsley Widmer noted in *Concise Dictionary of British Literary Biography* that Conrad's literary reputation declined sharply in the mid-1920s, after the publication of *Victory,* which Widmer flatly called a "bad novel." But the following generation gave rise to a revival of interest in Conrad's work, centering largely on a few works written between 1898 and 1910 and including *Heart of Darkness, The Secret Agent,* and *Lord Jim,* which were given the status of modern classics.

Widmer concluded that although "much of Conrad's fiction is patently poor," his sea stories contain a "documentary fascination in their reports of dying nineteenth-century merchant marine sailing experience." Widmer faults Conrad for gross sentimentality, shoddy melodrama, and chauvinism. But he acknowledges that Conrad's best fiction, among which he counts *Heart of Darkness, Nostromo, The Secret Sharer,* and *The Secret Agent,* which he says may be "Conrad's most powerful novel," achieves a modernism that undercuts those heavyhanded Victorian characteristics and provides the basis on which Conrad's reputation justifiably rests.

In more recent years, *Heart of Darkness* has come under fire for the blatantly racist attitudes it portrays. Some critics have taken issue with the matter-of-fact tone in which Marlow describes Africans as "savages" and "niggers" and portrays African life as mysterious and inhuman. Noted Nigerian author Chinua Achebe, for instance, argued in a *Massachusetts Review* article that "the question is whether a novel which celebrates this dehumanization, which depersonalizes a portion of the human race, can be called a great work of art. My answer is: No, it cannot." Other critics, however, have reasoned that Conrad was merely portraying the views and attitudes of his time, and others have even suggested that by presenting racist attitudes the author was ironically holding them up for ridicule and criticism.

Despite such controversy, *Heart of Darkness* has withstood the test of time and has come to be seen as one of Conrad's finest works. The way in which Conrad presents themes of moral ambiguity in this novel, never taking a side but forcing the reader to decide the issues for him- or herself is considered a forerunner of modern literary technique. Frederick Karl, in *Joseph Conrad: The Three Lives,* calls *Heart of Darkness* the work in which "the nineteenth century becomes the twentieth." Others have called it the best short novel in the English language. "*The Secret Sharer* and *Heart of Darkness,*" said Albert J. Guerard in his introduction to the novel, "are among the finest of Conrad's short novels, and among the half-dozen greatest short novels in the English language." The book continues to this day to be taught in high schools, colleges, and universities and to be held up as an example of great literature.

Criticism

Kevin Attell

In the following essay, Attell, a doctoral candidate at the University of California—Berkeley, explores how Heart of Darkness *has been viewed as both a commentary on the evils of colonialism and a philosophical exploration of the human psyche. Attell argues that critics who argue that the novel is either historical or philosophical "misses Conrad's insight that the two are in fact inseparable."*

The original publication of Joseph Conrad's *Heart of Darkness* was a three-part serialization in London's *Blackwood's Magazine* in 1899. It was subsequently published in a collection of three stories by Conrad in 1902. The date of *Heart of Darkness* should be noted, for it provides a historical context which illuminates the story's relation to both the contemporary turn-of-the-century world to which Conrad responds in the tale, and also the influential role Conrad plays in the subsequent progress of twentieth-century literary history.

Traditionally there have been two main ways of approaching the interpretation of *Heart of Darkness.* Critics and readers have tended to focus on either the implications of Conrad's intense fascination with European colonialism in Africa and around the world, or they have centered on his exploration of seemingly more abstract philosophical issues regarding, among other things, the human condition, the nature of Good and Evil, and the power of language. The former interpretive choice

What Do I Read Next?

- In *Lord Jim,* published in 1900, another maritime tale, Conrad deals with issues of honor in the face of grave personal danger and colonial imposition of will upon a native people. Marlow again becomes a narrator. Here he tells the story of Jim, a simple sailor who tried and failed to adhere to an honorable code of conduct.

- *Nostromo* (1904), Conrad's largest and most ambitious novel, has multiple heroes and flashes forward and back over a wide time frame. The familiar Conradian preoccupation with colonial interests in remote lands is here transposed to a fictional South American country seething with political unrest.

- Conrad's novel of political terrorism, *The Secret Agent* (1907), illustrates the author's fascination with a hero who, unlike Kurtz, seeks to remain neutral and avoid commitment in a world of conflict. Against his own will, Adolf Verloc, the book's double agent, is forced into actions

which result in more than one murder and a suicide.

- Set in the author's native Nigeria, Chinua Achebe's *Things Fall Apart* (1958) shows the tragic effects of European colonialism on one man.

- Winner of the 1991 National Book Award for fiction, *Middle Passage* by Charles Johnson relates the story of a free black man living in New Orleans who stows away on a ship only to discover it is a slave trader bound for Africa.

- In *Travellers in Africa: British Travelogues, 1850–1900,* Volume 1, Tim Youngs collects actual nineteenth-century British accounts of African voyages, and includes discussion of social, cultural, and racial attitudes. The volume includes an analysis of *Heart of Darkness* as a travel account, and compares Marlow's version of the Congo with that of British-American explorer Sir Henry Morton Stanley.

---

would concentrate on the ways Conrad presents European colonialism (of which he had much firsthand experience, being a sailor himself), while the latter would primarily investigate Conrad's exposition of philosophical questions. Even a cursory reading of the tale makes it clear that there is ample evidence for both of these interpretive concerns. What is perhaps less obvious, but equally important, is the way the historical reality which Conrad takes as his subject matter and the philosophical meditation to which Kurtz's story gives rise are intrinsically connected to one another.

The turn of the twentieth century was a period of intense colonial activity for most of the countries of Europe. Conrad refers to European colonialism countless times in *Heart of Darkness,* but perhaps the most vivid instance is when Marlow, while waiting in the office of the Belgian Company, sees "a large shining map [of colonial Africa], marked with all the colours of the rainbow. There was," he says, "a vast amount of red—

good to see at any time, because one knows that some real work is done there, a deuce of a lot of blue, a little green, smears of orange, and, on the East Coast, a purple patch.... However, I wasn't going into any of these. I was going into the yellow." These colors, of course, correspond to the territorial claims made on African land by the various nations of Europe: red is British, blue French, green Italian, orange Portuguese, purple German, and yellow Belgian. The map bears noting. On the one hand it establishes the massive geographical scale of Europe's colonial presence in Africa, but it also symbolically sets this presence up in relation to another central thematic concern of the novella: the popular conception of colonialism in Europe.

Conrad links the colored maps to the childlike ignorance and apathy of the European public as to what really goes on in the colonies. Just a few moments before describing the map in the office in Brussels Marlow had recalled his childhood, saying: "Now when I was a little chap I had a passion for maps. I would look for hours at South America, or Africa, or Australia, and lose myself in the glories of exploration. At that time there were many blank spaces on the earth, and when I saw one that looked particularly inviting (but they all look that) I would put my finger on it and say, When I grow up I will go there." Much of *Heart of Darkness* is then a grim and detailed exposition of the real "glories of exploration" which Marlow observes firsthand, but in these opening moments before Marlow has left for Africa Conrad has given his assessment of the perspective on the colonies from the point of view of the common European: on public display in the waiting-room of the Company office in Brussels, and in the imagination of the European public, the representation of European activity in Africa is as abstract and pleasant as a multicolored map.

Another example of the distance between the popular conception of the colonies and their reality can be found in the frequent reference made to the purportedly civilizing aspect of colonial conquest. Marlow's aunt speaks of "weaning those ignorant millions from their horrid ways" and Kurtz's early pamphlet ominously claims that "by the simple exercise of [the colonists'] will [they] can exert a power for good practically unbounded." Marlow's direct experience of the trading stations in the Congo, and Kurtz's scrawled note "Exterminate all the brutes" at the end of the pamphlet put the lie to these European pretensions to civilizing charity. And to Conrad's British readers of 1900 these revelations may have been shocking. There was, it should be noted, a growing anticolonial campaign being waged by dissidents throughout Europe at the time, and Conrad's novella can be considered a part of that campaign.

But in addition to the aggressive presentation of the grim conditions which existed in Europe's colonies—which Conrad succeeds in making very vivid—*Heart of Darkness* also creates a theme from certain philosophical problems which become central to the dawning literary movement called Modernism. Conrad shows the way the European public is profoundly ignorant (perhaps willfully) of what goes on in their colonies, but he also suggests that that very separation reveals a problematic relation between belief and reality, between representation and truth, which can also be investigated as a philosophical question. Keeping in mind the way this problem has been introduced in the novella (ie. the specific relation between Europe and its colonies), let us briefly sketch out the philosophi-

cal and literary attempts to address the problem of representation in Modernism.

Roughly speaking, Modernism had its peak in the years between World War I and World War II. The great canonical Modernists include such writers as James Joyce, Ezra Pound, Gertrude Stein, Virginia Woolf, William Faulkner, and others. In most accounts of the period what links the Modernist writers loosely together is their intensive formal experimentation with literary and linguistic techniques; that is to say, their experimentation with the actual *modes* of literary representation. Stein's experiments with syntax, Joyce's melding of languages and myths, Faulkner's endless sentences, can all be seen as various ways of working through difficult questions raised about the very nature of language and how it works. Language in Modernist literature is no longer seen as a stable vehicle for the communication of meaning, but rather it is put up for radical questioning in itself. Modernist experimentation, one might say, arises out of the doubt that language (at least language as it has been used in the past) is able to communicate or sufficient to represent meaning or truth. And the seeds of this very doubt, to bring us back to Conrad, can be seen in *Heart of Darkness*. Some of the most illustrative examples of how Conrad introduces these Modernistic concerns can be seen at the points of Marlow's narration where the actual question of *meaning* explicitly arises.

Clearly Marlow has no trouble narrating events; he is indeed quite a storyteller. Yet, at various times in the narration the flow of his speech is interrupted and he seems at a loss for words. If we pick one of these moments we can see the way Conrad is creating a theme from the very instability and inadequacy of language itself ("words," "names," the "story") to contain and convey what one might call "truth," "meaning," or "essence" (Marlow calls it all three). At a point well into his tale Marlow says:

> "At the time I did not see [Kurtz]—you understand. He was just a word for me. I did not see the man in the name any more than you do. Do you see him? Do you see the story? Do you see anything? It seems to me I am trying to tell you a dream—making a vain attempt, because no relation of a dream can convey the dream-sensation, that commingling of absurdity, surprise, and bewilderment in a tremor of struggling revolt, that notion of being captured by the incredible which is the very essence of dreams...."

He sat silent for a while.

" ... No, it is impossible; it is impossible to convey the life-sensation of any given epoch of one's existence—that which makes its truth, its meaning—its subtle and penetrating essence. It is impossible. We live, as we dream—alone...."

Conrad has set up a clear opposition in Marlow's speech here: the opposition is between language on the one hand and truth or meaning on the other. In the quoted passage Marlow is exasperated because when faced with the task of communicating something deeper than just the narrative of events he is at a loss for words—or more precisely, the words themselves fail him. His pronouncement that it is "impossible" for language to do certain things—for language to hold the *essence* of things as they exist—foreshadows the dilemma at the center of Modernist and indeed much of twentieth-century philosophical thought. But what he is trying to tell is not just "the Truth" in the abstract, but rather the truth about Kurtz, the *truth of his experience of the European colonies.* This suggests the way that the philosophical themes of the tale are intertwined with if not identical to the colonial themes. Conrad has the two coexisting in such close proximity that they in fact appear to be two sides of the same coin.

The debate, then, over whether *Heart of Darkness* should be interpreted in terms of *either* colonial and historical *or* philosophical questions misses Conrad's insight that the two are in fact inseparable. As the complex textual fusion of the two in *Heart of Darkness* implies, the seemingly abstract philosophical problems concerning language and truth arise only out of concrete problems (such as colonialism) which exist in the social world, while at the same time the concrete problems of colonial domination at the turn of the twentieth century have extensive philosophical implications.

Source: Kevin Attell, in an essay for *Novels for Students,* Gale, 1997.

Chinua Achebe

Achebe is a noted Nigerian novelist whose works include Things Fall Apart *and* Anthills of the Savannah; *he has frequently lectured in the United States and served as a professor at the University of Massachusetts—Amherst in 1987–88. In the following excerpt, Achebe argues that the racist attitudes inherent in Conrad's novel make it "totally inconceivable" that it could be considered "great art."*

Heart of Darkness projects the image of Africa as "the other world," the antithesis of Europe and therefore of civilization, a place where a man's vaunted intelligence and refinement are finally mocked by triumphant bestiality. The book opens on the River Thames, tranquil, resting peacefully "at the decline of day after ages of good service done to the race that peopled its banks." But the actual story takes place on the River Congo, the very antithesis of the Thames. The River Congo is quite decidedly not a River Emeritus. It has rendered no service and enjoys no old-age pension. We are told that "going up that river was like travelling back to the earliest beginning of the world."

Is Conrad saying then that these two rivers are very different, one good, the other bad? Yes, but that is not the real point. What actually worries Conrad is the lurking hint of kinship, of common ancestry. For the Thames, too, "has been one of the dark places of the earth." It conquered its darkness, of course, and is now at peace. But if it were to visit its primordial relative, the Congo, it would run the terrible risk of hearing grotesque, suggestive echoes of its own forgotten darkness, and of falling victim to an avenging recrudescence of the mindless frenzy of the first beginnings.

I am not going to waste your time with examples of Conrad's famed evocation of the African atmosphere. In the final consideration it amounts to no more than a steady, ponderous, fake-ritualistic repetition of two sentences, one about silence and the other about frenzy. An example of the former is "It was the stillness of an implacable force brooding over an inscrutable intention" and of the latter, "The steamer toiled along slowly on the edge of a black and incomprehensible frenzy." Of course, there is a judicious change of adjective from time to time so that instead of "inscrutable," for example, you might have "unspeakable," etc., etc.

The eagle-eyed English critic, F. R. Leavis, drew attention nearly thirty years ago to Conrad's "adjectival insistence upon inexpressible and incomprehensible mystery." That insistence must not be dismissed lightly, as many Conrad critics have tended to do, as a mere stylistic flaw. For it raises serious questions of artistic good faith. When a writer, while pretending to record scenes, incidents and their impact, is in reality engaged in inducing hypnotic stupor in his readers through a bombardment of emotive words and other forms of trickery much more has to be at stake than stylistic felicity. Generally, normal readers are well armed to detect and resist such underhand activity. But Conrad chose his subject well—one which was guaranteed not to put him in conflict with the psychological predisposition of his readers or raise the need for him to contend with their resistance. He chose the role of purveyor of comforting myths.

The most interesting and revealing passages in *Heart of Darkness* are, however, about people. I must quote a long passage from the middle of the story in which representatives of Europe in a steamer going down the Congo encounter the denizens of Africa:

> We were wanderers on a prehistoric earth, on an earth that wore the aspect of an unknown planet. We could have fancied ourselves the first of men taking possession of an accursed inheritance, to be subdued at the cost of profound anguish and of excessive toil. But suddenly, as we struggled round a bend, there would be a glimpse of rush walls, of peaked grass-roofs, a burst of yells, a whirl of black limbs, a mass of hands clapping, of feet stamping, of bodies swaying, of eyes rolling, under the droop of heavy and motionless foliage. The steamer toiled along slowly on the edge of a black and incomprehensible frenzy. The prehistoric man was cursing us, praying to us, welcoming us—who could tell? We were cut off from the comprehension of our surroundings; we glided past like phantoms, wondering and secretly appalled, as sane men would be before an enthusiastic outbreak in a madhouse. We could not remember because we were travelling in the night of first ages, of those ages that are gone, leaving hardly a sign—and no memories.
>
> The earth seemed unearthly. We are accustomed to look upon the shackled form of a conquered monster, but there—there you could look at a thing monstrous and free. It was unearthly, and the men were—No, they were not inhuman. Well, you know, that was the worst of it—this suspicion of their not being inhuman. It would come slowly to one. They howled and leaped, and spun, and made horrid faces; but what thrilled you was just the thought of your remote kinship with this wild and passionate uproar. Ugly. Yes, it was ugly enough; but if you were man enough you would admit to yourself that there was in you just the faintest trace of a response to the terrible frankness of that noise, a dim suspicion of there being a meaning in it which you—you so remote from the night of first ages—could comprehend.

Herein lies the meaning of *Heart of Darkness* and the fascination it holds over the Western mind: "What thrilled you was just the thought of their humanity—like yours.... Ugly."

Having shown us Africa in the mass, Conrad then zeros in on a specific example, giving us one of his rare descriptions of an African who is not just limbs or rolling eyes:

> And between whiles I had to look after the savage who was fireman. He was an improved specimen; he could fire up a vertical boiler. He was there below me, and, upon my word, to look at him was as edifying as seeing a dog in a parody of breeches and a feather hat, walking on his hind legs. A few months

of training had done for that really fine chap. He squinted at the steam gauge and at the water gauge with an evident effort of intrepidity—and he had filed his teeth, too, the poor devil, and the wool of his pate shaved into queer patterns, and three ornamental scars on each of his cheeks. He ought to have been clapping his hands and stamping his feet on the bank, instead of which he was hard at work, a thrall to strange witchcraft, full of improving knowledge.

As everybody knows, Conrad is a romantic on the side. He might not exactly admire savages clapping their hands and stamping their feet but they have at least the merit of being in their place, unlike this dog in a parody of breeches. For Conrad, things (and persons) being in their place is of the utmost importance.

Towards the end of the story, Conrad lavishes great attention quite unexpectedly on an African woman who has obviously been some kind of mistress to Mr. Kurtz and now presides (if I may be permitted a little imitation of Conrad) like a formidable mystery over the inexorable imminence of his departure:

> She was savage and superb, wild-eyed and magnificent.... She stood looking at us without a stir and like the wilderness itself, with an air of brooding over an inscrutable purpose.

This Amazon is drawn in considerable detail, albeit of a predictable nature, for two reasons. First, she is in her place and so can win Conrad's special brand of approval; and second, she fulfills a structural requirement of the story; she is a savage counterpart to the refined, European woman with whom the story will end:

> She came forward, all in black with a pale head, floating towards me in the dusk. She was in mourning.... She took both my hands in hers and murmured, "I had heard you were coming."... She had a mature capacity for fidelity, for belief, for suffering.

The difference in the attitude of the novelist to these two women is conveyed in too many direct and subtle ways to need elaboration. But perhaps the most significant difference is the one implied in the author's bestowal of human expression to the one and the withholding of it from the other. It is clearly not part of Conrad's purpose to confer language on the "rudimentary souls" of Africa. They only "exchanged short grunting phrases" even among themselves but mostly they were too busy with their frenzy. There are two occasions in the book, however, when Conrad departs somewhat from his practice and confers speech, even English speech, on the savages. The first occurs when cannibalism gets the better of them:

"Catch 'im," he snapped, with a bloodshot widening of his eyes and a flash of sharp white teeth—"catch 'im. Give 'im to us." "To you, eh?" I asked; "what would you do with them?" "Eat 'im!" he said curtly ...

The other occasion is the famous announcement:

Mistah Kurtz—he dead.

At first sight, these instances might be mistaken for unexpected acts of generosity from Conrad. In reality, they constitute some of his best assaults. In the case of the cannibals, the incomprehensible grunts that had thus far served them for speech suddenly proved inadequate for Conrad's purpose of letting the European glimpse the unspeakable craving in their hearts. Weighing the necessity for consistency in the portrayal of the dumb brutes against the sensational advantages of securing their conviction by clear, unambiguous evidence issuing out of their own mouth, Conrad chose the latter. As for the announcement of Mr. Kurtz's death by the "insolent black head of the doorway," what better or more appropriate *finis* could be written to the horror story of that wayward child of civilization who willfully had given his soul to the powers of darkness and "taken a high seat amongst the devils of the land" than the proclamation of his physical death by the forces he had joined?

It might be contended, of course, that the attitude to the African in *Heart of Darkness* is not Conrad's but that of his fictional narrator, Marlow, and that far from endorsing it Conrad might indeed be holding it up to irony and criticism. Certainly, Conrad appears to go to considerable pains to set up layers of insulation between himself and the moral universe of his story. He has, for example, a narrator behind a narrator. The primary narrator is Marlow but his account is given to us through the filter of a second, shadowy person. But if Conrad's intention is to draw a *cordon sanitaire* between himself and the moral and psychological malaise of his narrator, his care seems to me totally wasted because he neglects to hint however subtly or tentatively at an alternative frame of reference by which we may judge the actions and opinions of his characters. It would not have been beyond Conrad's power to make that provision if he had thought it necessary. Marlow seems to me to enjoy Conrad's complete confidence—a feeling reinforced by the close similarities between their careers.

Marlow comes through to us not only as a witness of truth, but one holding those advanced and humane views appropriate to the English liberal tradition which required all Englishmen of decency to be deeply shocked by atrocities in Bulgaria or the Congo of King Leopold of the Belgians or wherever. Thus Marlow is able to toss out such bleeding-heart sentiments as these:

They were all dying slowly—it was very clear. They were not enemies, they were not criminals, they were nothing earthly now—nothing but black shadows of disease and starvation, lying confusedly in the greenish gloom. Brought from all the recesses of the coast in all the legality of time contracts, lost in uncongenial surroundings, fed on unfamiliar food, they sickened, became inefficient, and were then allowed to crawl away and rest.

The kind of liberalism espoused here by Marlow/Conrad touched all the best minds of the age in England, Europe, and America. It took different forms in the minds of different people but almost always managed to sidestep the ultimate question of equality between white people and black people. That extraordinary missionary, Albert Schweitzer, who sacrificed brilliant careers in music and theology in Europe for a life of service to Africans in much the same area as Conrad writes about, epitomizes the ambivalence. In a comment which I have often quoted but must quote one last time Schweitzer says: "The African is indeed my brother but my junior brother." And so he proceeded to build a hospital appropriate to the needs of junior brothers with standards of hygiene reminiscent of medical practice in the days before the germ theory of disease came into being. Naturally, he became a sensation in Europe and America. Pilgrims flocked, and I believe still flock even after he has passed on, to witness the prodigious miracle in Lamberene, on the edge of the primeval forest.

Conrad's liberalism would not take him quite as far as Schweitzer's, though. He would not use the word "brother" however qualified; the farthest he would go was "kinship." When Marlow's African helmsman falls down with a spear in his heart he gives his white master one final disquieting look.

And the intimate profundity of that look he gave me when he received his hurt remains to this day in my memory—like a claim of distant kinship affirmed in a supreme moment.

It is important to note that Conrad, careful as ever with his words, is not talking so much about *distant kinship* as about someone *laying a claim* on it. The black man lays a claim on the white man which is well-nigh intolerable. It is the laying of this claim which frightens and at the same time fascinates Conrad, "... the thought of their humanity—like yours ... Ugly."

The point of my observations should be quite clear by now, namely, that Conrad was a bloody racist. That this simple truth is glossed over in criticism of his work is due to the fact that white racism against Africa is such a normal way of thinking that its manifestations go completely undetected. Students of *Heart of Darkness* will often tell you that Conrad is concerned not so much with Africa as with the deterioration of one European mind caused by solitude and sickness. They will point out to you that Conrad is, if anything, less charitable to the Europeans in the story than he is to the natives. A Conrad student told me in Scotland last year that Africa is merely a setting for the disintegration of the mind of Mr. Kurtz.

Which is partly the point: Africa as setting and backdrop which eliminates the African as human factor. Africa as a metaphysical battlefield devoid of all recognizable humanity, into which the wandering European enters at his peril. Of course, there is a preposterous and perverse kind of arrogance in thus reducing Africa to the role of props for the breakup of one petty European mind. But that is not even the point. The real question is the dehumanization of Africa and Africans which this age-long attitude has fostered and continues to foster in the world. And the question is whether a novel which celebrates this dehumanization, which depersonalizes a portion of the human race, can be called a great work of art. My answer is: No, it cannot. I would not call that man an artist, for example, who composes an eloquent instigation to one people to fall upon another and destroy them. No matter how striking his imagery or how beautiful his cadences fall such a man is no more a great artist than another may be called a priest who reads the mass backwards or a physician who poisons his patients. All those men in Nazi Germany who lent their talent to the service of virulent racism whether in science, philosophy or the arts have generally and rightly been condemned for their perversions. The time is long overdue for taking a hard look at the work of creative artists who apply their talents, alas often considerable as in the case of Conrad, to set people against people. This, I take it, is what Yevtushenko is after when he tells us that a poet cannot be a slave trader at the same time, and gives the striking example of Arthur Rimbaud who was fortunately honest enough to give up any pretenses

to poetry when he opted for slave trading. For poetry surely can only be on the side of man's deliverance and not his enslavement; for the brotherhood and unity of all mankind and against the doctrines of Hitler's master races or Conrad's "rudimentary souls."...

[Conrad] was born in 1857, the very year in which the first Anglican missionaries were arriving among my own people in Nigeria. It was certainly not his fault that he lived his life at a time when the reputation of the black man was at a particularly low level. But even after due allowances have been made for all the influences of contemporary prejudice on his sensibility, there remains still in Conrad's attitude a residue of antipathy to black people which his peculiar psychology alone can explain. His own account of his first encounter with a black man is very revealing:

> A certain enormous buck nigger encountered in Haiti fixed my conception of blind, furious, unreasoning rage, as manifested in the human animal to the end of my days. Of the nigger I used to dream for years afterwards.

Certainly, Conrad had a problem with niggers. His inordinate love of that word itself should be of interest to psychoanalysts. Sometimes his fixation on blackness is equally interesting as when he gives us this brief description:

> A black figure stood up, strode on long black legs, waving long black arms.

As though we might expect a black figure striding along on black legs to have *white* arms! But so unrelenting is Conrad's obsession.

As a matter of interest Conrad gives us in *A Personal Record* what amounts to a companion piece to the buck nigger of Haiti. At the age of sixteen Conrad encountered his first Englishman in Europe. He calls him "my unforgettable Englishman" and describes him in the following manner:

> [his] calves exposed to the public gaze ... dazzled the beholder by the splendor of their marble-like condition and their rich tone of young ivory ... The light of a headlong, exalted satisfaction with the world of men ... illumined his face ... and triumphant eyes. In passing he cast a glance of kindly curiosity and a friendly gleam of big, sound, shiny teeth ... his white calves twinkled sturdily.

Irrational love and irrational hate jostling together in the heart of that tormented man. But whereas irrational love may at worst engender foolish acts of indiscretion, irrational hate can endanger the life of the community....

Whatever Conrad's problems were, you might say he is now safely dead. Quite true. Unfortunately, his heart of darkness plagues us still. Which is why an offensive and totally deplorable book can be described by a serious scholar as "among the half dozen greatest short novels in the English language," and why it is today perhaps the most commonly prescribed novel in the twentieth-century literature courses in our own English Department here. Indeed the time is long overdue for a hard look at things.

There are two probable grounds on which what I have said so far may be contested. The first is that it is no concern of fiction to please people about whom it is written. I will go along with that. But I am not talking about pleasing people. I am talking about a book which parades in the most vulgar fashion prejudices and insults from which a section of mankind has suffered untold agonies and atrocities in the past and continues to do so in many ways and many places today. I am talking about a story in which the very humanity of black people is called in question. It seems to me totally inconceivable that great art or even good art could possibly reside in such unwholesome surroundings.

Secondly, I may be challenged on the grounds of actuality. Conrad, after all, sailed down the Congo in 1890 when my own father was still a babe in arms, and recorded what he saw. How could I stand up in 1975, fifty years after his death and purport to contradict him? My answer is that as a sensible man I will not accept just any traveller's tales solely on the grounds that I have not made the journey myself. I will not trust the evidence even of a man's very eyes when I suspect them to be as jaundiced as Conrad's....

But more important by far is the abundant testimony about Conrad's savages which we could gather if we were so inclined from other sources and which might lead us to think that these people must have had other occupations besides merging into the evil forest or materializing out of it simply to plague Marlow and his dispirited band. For as it happened, soon after Conrad had written his book an event of far greater consequence was taking place in the art world of Europe. This is how Frank Willett, a British art historian, describes it [in *African Art,* 1971]:

> Gaugin had gone to Tahiti, the most extravagant individual act of turning to a non-European culture in the decades immediately before and after 1900, when European artists were avid for new artistic experiences, but it was only about 1904-5 that African art began to make its distinctive impact. One piece is still identifiable; it is a mask that had been given

to Maurice Vlaminck in 1905. He records that Derain was "speechless" and "stunned" when he saw it, bought it from Vlaminck and in turn showed it to Picasso and Matisse, who were also greatly affected by it. Ambroise Vollard then borrowed it and had it cast in bronze ... The revolution of twentieth century art was under way!

The mask in question was made by other savages living just north of Conrad's River Congo. They have a name, the Fang people, and are without a doubt among the world's greatest masters of the sculptured form. As you might have guessed, the event to which Frank Willett refers marked the beginning of cubism and the infusion of new life into European art that had run completely out of strength.

The point of all this is to suggest that Conrad's picture of the people of the Congo seems grossly inadequate even at the height of their subjection to the ravages of King Leopold's International Association for the Civilization of Central Africa. Travellers with closed minds can tell us little except about themselves. But even those not blinkered, like Conrad, with xenophobia, can be astonishingly blind....

As I said earlier, Conrad did not originate the image of Africa which we find in his book. It was and is the dominant image of Africa in the Western imagination and Conrad merely brought the peculiar gifts of his own mind to bear on it. For reasons which can certainly use close psychological inquiry, the West seems to suffer deep anxieties about the precariousness of its civilization and to have a need for constant reassurance by comparing it with Africa. If Europe, advancing in civilization, could cast a backward glance periodically at Africa trapped in primordial barbarity, it could say with faith and feeling: There go I but for the grace of God. Africa is to Europe as the picture is to Dorian Gray—a carrier onto whom the master unloads his physical and moral deformities so that he may go forward, erect and immaculate. Consequently, Africa is something to be avoided just as the picture has to be hidden away to safeguard the man's jeopardous integrity. Keep away from Africa, or else! Mr. Kurtz of *Heart of Darkness* should have heeded that warning and the prowling horror in his heart would have kept its place, chained to its lair. But he foolishly exposed himself to the wild irresistible allure of the jungle and lo! the darkness found him out.

In my original conception of this talk I had thought to conclude it nicely on an appropriately positive note in which I would suggest from my privileged position in African and Western culture some advantages the West might derive from Africa once it rid its mind of old prejudices and began to look at Africa not through a haze of distortions and cheap mystification but quite simply as a continent of people—not angels, but not rudimentary souls either—just people, often highly gifted people and often strikingly successful in their enterprise with life and society. But as I thought more about the stereotype image, about its grip and pervasiveness, about the willful tenacity with which the West holds it to its heart; when I thought of your television and the cinema and newspapers, about books read in schools and out of school, of churches preaching to empty pews about the need to send help to the heathen in Africa, I realized that no easy optimism was possible. And there is something totally wrong in offering bribes to the West in return for its good opinion of Africa. Ultimately, the abandonment of unwholesome thoughts must be its own and only reward. Although I have used the word *willful* a few times in this talk to characterize the West's view of Africa it may well be that what is happening at this stage is more akin to reflex action than calculated malice. Which does not make the situation more, but less, hopeful.

Source: Chinua Achebe, "An Image of Africa," in *The Massachusetts Review,* Vol. XVIII, No. 4, Winter, 1977, pp. 782–94.

Walter F. Wright

In the following excerpt, Wright suggests that the scene in which Marlow conceals the nature of Kurtz's death "is really a study of the nature of truth."

The tragedy of Kurtz and the education of Marlow fuse into one story, since for Marlow that tragedy represents his furthest penetration into the heart of darkness. As Marlow enters the forest to intercept Kurtz on the way toward the ceremonial blaze he senses the fascination which the savage ritual possesses. In the light of Conrad's other tales we know that it is because he is guided by well-established habits that he is able to complete his mission and carry Kurtz back to his cot, though not before he himself has apprehended the lure of the primitive. He has duplicated in his own experience enough of Kurtz's sensations to have good reason to wonder what is real and what is a false trick of the imagination. It was this fascination and bewilderment that Conrad aimed to suggest, and the presenting of Kurtz at the most intense moment of his yielding to it was to transcend time and bring a unity of impression.

When Marlow, soon after, hears the dying pronouncement, "the horror, the horror!" he has more than a mere intellectual awareness of what the words mean; and as we have vicariously shared Marlow's quasi-hysterical emotion on the trip toward the camp fire, we feel likewise the completeness with which Kurtz has savored degradation. He is a universal genius because he has had both the dream of sweetness and sacrifice in a cause shared by others and the disillusionment of being, in the very midst of the savage adoration, irretrievably alone, devoid of all standards, all hopes that can give him a sense of kinship with anything in the universe. Now, as he faces the last darkness of all, he cannot even know that Marlow understands and that he feels no right to condemn....

Conscious will was, in the novelist's opinion, not merely fallible, but often dangerous. Reliance upon it could lead one completely away from human sentiments. In *Heart of Darkness* itself Kurtz twice replies to Marlow that he is "perfectly" conscious of what he is doing; his sinister actions are deliberate. This fact does not in the least, however, mean that Conrad wished for a condition devoid of will. He believed that man had the power to pursue the interpretation of experience with deliberate intent and by conscious endeavor to reduce it to proportions. The imagination would bring up the images and incidents, but the reason could help select and arrange them until they became the essence of art. In his trip up the Congo and in his rapid descent Marlow is protected by habits which tend to preserve sanity, but the experience is of the imagination and emotions. Were he to stop short with the mere sensations, he would have no power to distinguish reality from the unreal, to speculate, with touchstones for reference, about life. What we are coming to is the obvious question, If Kurtz's dictum represents the deepest penetration into one aspect of the mind, why did Conrad not stop there; why did he have Marlow tell the girl that Kurtz died pronouncing her name? Is the ending tacked on merely to relieve the horror, or has it a function in the conscious interpretation of life in the proportions of art? ...

The fact is that Conrad, fully capable of building to a traditional climax and stopping, wanted to put Kurtz's life in the perspective which it must have for Marlow *sub specie aeternitatis.* Marlow does not have a final answer to life, but after we have shared with him the steady penetration to the brink of degradation we have almost forgotten what life otherwise is like. It is now that Conrad's method of chronological reversal is invaluable. We are quickly returned to Europe, where the marvel of Kurtz's genius still remains, as if he had left but yesterday.

The scene in which Marlow conceals from the girl the nature of Kurtz's death is really a study of the nature of truth. If he had told the girl the simple facts, he would have acknowledged that the pilgrims in their cynicism had the truth, that goodness and faith were the unrealities. Marlow appreciates this temptation, and we are hardly to suppose that sentimental weakness makes him resist it. He does not preach to us about the wisdom he has achieved; in fact he deprecates it, and now he says merely that to tell her would be "too dark altogether." He is still perplexed as to the ethics of his deception and wishes that fate had permitted him to remain a simple reporter of incidents instead of making him struggle in the realm of human values. Yet in leaving in juxtaposition the fiancée's ideal, a matter within her own heart, and the fact of Kurtz's death, Marlow succeeds in putting before us in his inconclusive way the two extremes that can exist within the human mind, and we realize that not one, but both of these are reality.

When Marlow ends his monologue, his audience [is] aware that the universe around them, which, when we began the story, seemed an ordinary, familiar thing, with suns rising and setting according to rule and tides flowing and ebbing systematically for man's convenience, is, after all, a thing of mystery. It is a vast darkness in that its heart is inscrutable. What, then, has Marlow gained, since he has ended with this conclusion which we might, *a priori*, accept as a platitude? He has certainly helped us eliminate the false assumptions by which day to day we act as if the universe were a very simple contrivance, even while, perhaps, we give lip service to the contrary. Moreover, instead of letting one faculty of the mind dominate and deny the pertinence of the others, he has achieved a reconciliation in which physical sensation, imagination, and that conscious logic which selects and arranges have lost their apparent qualities of contradiction. He has achieved an orderly explanation, conscious and methodical, of the strange purlieus of the imagination. Because those recesses harbor shadows, the exploration must not be labeled conclusive; but the greatness of the darkness, instead of leaving a sense of the futility of efforts to dispel it, has drawn the artist to use his utmost conscious skill. Life itself, if we agree with Conrad, may tend to seem to us as meaningless and chaotic as were many of Marlow's sensations at the moment of his undergoing them, and the will may often appear to play no part at all, or a false part,

in guiding us. But the genius of art was for Conrad that it accepted the most intense and seemingly reason-defying creations of the imagination and then discovered within them, rather than superimposed upon them, a symmetry coherent and logical.

Through Marlow's orderly narrative, with its perfect identity of fact and symbol, with its transformation of time and space into emotional and imaginative intensity, the shadows have contracted, and we are better able than before to speculate on the presences which seem to inhabit the very heart of darkness. Time is telescoped and we have as if in the same moment the exalted enthusiast and the man who denied all except horror; and we realize that they are and always have been the same man. We perceive that Africa itself, with its forests, its heat, and its mysteries, is only a symbol of the larger darkness, which is in the heart of man.

Source: Walter F. Wright, "Ingress to the *Heart of Darkness*," from his *Romance and Tragedy in Joseph Conrad*, University of Nebraska Press, 1949, reprinted in *Conrad's Heart of Darkness and the Critics*, edited by Bruce Harkness, Wadsworth Publishing Company, Inc., 1960, pp. 153–55.

Sources

Hugh Clifford, a review in *The Spectator*, November 29, 1902.

Leonard F. Dean, editor, *Joseph Conrad's 'Heart of Darkness': Backgrounds and Criticisms*, Prentice-Hall, 1960.

Edward Garnett, *Conrad: The Critical Heritage*, edited by Norman Sherry, Routledge & Kegan Paul, 1973, pp. 131-33.

Albert J. Guerard, an introduction to *Heart of Darkness* and *The Secret Sharer*, Signet Books/New American Library, 1950.

Frederick R. Karl, *Joseph Conrad: The Three Lives*, Farrar, Straus, 1979.

Kingsley Widmer, "Joseph Conrad," in *Concise Dictionary of British Literary Biography*, Volume 5: *Late Victorian and Edwardian Writers, 1890-1914*, Gale Research, 1992, pp. 84-122.

For Further Study

Peter J. Glassman, *Language and Being: Joseph Conrad and the Literature of Personality*, Colombia University Press, 1976.

   Chapter 6 develops a philosophically tinged argument about the relation between language and death in *Heart of Darkness*.

Eloise Knapp Hay, *The Political Novels of Joseph Conrad,* Chicago University Press, 1963, pp. 107-161.

    The author relates the political component of *Heart of Darkness* to its stylistic techniques.

Douglas Hewitt, *Conrad: A Reassessment,* Bowes, 1952.

    Chapter 2 treats *Heart of Darkness* together with the other early tales which also have Marlow as their narrator.

Stephen K. Land, *Paradox and Polarity in the Fiction of Joseph Conrad,* St. Martin's Press, 1984.

    A 311-page book in which Stephen Land takes a critical look at several of Conrad's works, including *Heart of Darkness* and *Nostromo.* Land pays particular attention to an examination of the Conradian hero.

Bernard Meyer, *Joseph Conrad: A Psychoanalytic Biography,* Princeton University Press, 1967, pp. 168-184.

    Chapter 9 deals with *Heart of Darkness* within the book's broader project of a psychoanalytic reading of the relation between Conrad's life and his fiction.

Benita Parry, *Conrad and Imperialism,* Macmillan, 1983, pp. 20-39.

    The author develops an argument about Conrad's ambiguous relation to European colonialism. Chapter 2 treats *Heart of Darkness* directly.

Norman Sherry, *Conrad: The Critical Heritage,* Routledge & Kegan Paul, 1973.

    A collection of contemporary reviews of Conrad's work. Contains ten reviews of *Heart of Darkness.*

Bruce E. Teets and Helmut E. Gerber, *Joseph Conrad, An Annotated Bibliography of Writings About Him,* Northern Illinois University Press, 1971.

    An extremely useful bibliography of Conrad criticism, from contemporary reviews to later critical studies and articles.

Cedric Watts, *A Preface to Conrad,* Longman, 1982.

    Explains the themes that recur in Conrad's work. More generally about Conrad's ideas than a reading of *Heart of Darkness* or any single work of his.

The House on Mango Street

The House on Mango Street, which appeared in 1983, is a linked collection of forty-four short tales that evoke the circumstances and conditions of a Hispanic American ghetto in Chicago. The narrative is seen through the eyes of Esperanza Cordero, an adolescent girl coming of age. These concise and poetic tales also offer snapshots of the roles of women in this society. They uncover the dual forces that pull Esperanza to stay rooted in her cultural traditions on the one hand, and those that compel her to pursue a better way of life outside the *barrio* on the other. Throughout the book Sandra Cisneros explores themes of cultural tradition, gender roles, and coming of age in a binary society that struggles to hang onto its collective past while integrating itself into the American cultural landscape. Cisneros wrote the vignettes while struggling with her identity as an author at the University of Iowa's Writers Workshop in the 1970s. She was influenced by Russian-born novelist and poet Vladimir Nabokov's memoirs and by her own experiences as a child in the Chicago *barrio.* This engaging book has brought the author critical acclaim and a 1985 Before Columbus American Book Award. Specifically, it has been highly lauded for its impressionistic, poetic style and powerful imagery. Though Cisneros is a young writer and her work is not plentiful, *The House on Mango Street* establishes her as a major figure in American literature. Her work has already been the subject of numerous scholarly studies and is often at the fore-

Sandra Cisneros

1983

front of works that explore the role of Latinas in American society.

Author Biography

The experiences of Esperanza, the adolescent protagonist of *The House on Mango Street,* closely resemble those of Sandra Cisneros's childhood. The author was born to a Mexican father and a Mexican American mother in 1954 in Chicago, Illinois, the only daughter of seven children. The family, for whom money was always in short supply, frequently moved between the ghetto neighborhoods of Chicago and the areas of Mexico where her father's family lived. Cisneros remembers that as a child she often felt a sense of displacement. By 1966 her parents had saved enough money for a down payment on a run-down, two-story house in a decrepit Puerto Rican neighborhood on Chicago's north side. There Cisneros spent much of her childhood. This house, as well as the colorful group of characters Cisneros observed around her in the *barrio,* served as inspiration for some of the stories in *The House on Mango Street.*

The author once remarked, "Because we moved so much, and always in neighborhoods that appeared like France after World War II—empty lots and burned-out buildings—I retreated inside myself." Cisneros was an introspective child with few friends; her mother encouraged her to read and write at a young age, and made sure her daughter had her own library card. The author wrote poems and stories as a schoolgirl, but the impetus for her career as a creative writer came during her college years, when she was introduced to the works of Donald Justice, James Wright, and other writers who made Cisneros more aware of her cultural roots.

Cisneros graduated from Loyola University in 1976 with a B.A. in English. She began to pursue graduate studies in writing at the University of Iowa, and earned a Master of Fine Arts degree in creative writing in 1978. Cisneros says that through high school and college, she did not perceive herself as being different from her fellow English majors. She spoke Spanish only at home with her father, but otherwise wrote and studied within the mainstream of American literature. At the University of Iowa Writers' Workshop, Cisneros found her true voice as an author. Compared with her more privileged, wealthier classmates from more stable environments, Cisneros's cultural difference

Sandra Cisneros

as a Chicana became clear. Though at first she imitated the style and tone of acclaimed American authors, Cisneros came to realize that her experience as a Hispanic woman differed from that of her classmates and offered an opportunity to develop her own voice. Cisneros once remarked, "Everyone seemed to have some communal knowledge which I did not have—My classmates were from the best schools in the country. They had been bred as fine hothouse flowers. I was a yellow weed among the city's cracks." The author began to explore her past experiences, which served as the inspiration of many of her stories and distinguished her from her peers. Her master's thesis, *My Wicked Wicked Ways* (Iowa, 1978, published as a book in 1987) is a collection of poems that begins to explore daily experiences, encounters, and observations in this new-found voice.

Cisneros has held several fellowships that have allowed her to focus on her writing full-time. These awards have enabled her to travel to Europe and to other parts of the United States, including a stint in Austin, Texas, where she experienced another thriving community of Latin American culture. She has also taught creative writing and worked with students at the Latino Youth Alternative High School in Chicago.

Plot Summary

The House on Mango Street is the coming of age story of Esperanza Cordero, a preadolescent Mexican American girl (Chicana) living in the contemporary United States. A marked departure from the traditional novel form, *The House on Mango Street* is a slim book consisting of forty-four vignettes, or literary sketches, narrated by Esperanza and ranging in length from two paragraphs to four pages. In deceptively simple language, the novel recounts the complex experience of being young, poor, female, and Chicana in America. The novel opens with a description of the Cordero family's house on Mango Street, the most recent in a long line of houses they have occupied. Esperanza is dissatisfied with the house, which is small and cramped, and doesn't want to stay there. But Mango Street is her home now, and she sets out to try to understand it.

Mango Street is populated by people with many different life stories, stories of hope and despair. First there is Esperanza's own family: her kind father who works two jobs and is absent most of the time; her mother, who can speak two languages and sing opera but never finished high school; her two brothers Carlos and Kiki; and her little sister Nenny. Of the neighborhood children Esperanza meets, there is Cathy, who shows her around Mango Street but moves out shortly thereafter because the neighborhood is "getting bad." Then there are Rachel and Lucy, sisters from Texas, who become Esperanza and Nenny's best friends. There is Meme, who has a dog with two names, one in Spanish and one in English, and Louie the boy from Puerto Rico whose cousin steals a Cadillac one day and gives all the children a ride.

Then there are the teenage girls of Mango Street, whom Esperanza studies carefully for clues about becoming a woman. There is Marin from Puerto Rico, who sells Avon cosmetics and takes care of her younger cousins, but is waiting for a boyfriend to change her life. There is Alicia, who must take care of her father and siblings because her mother is dead, but is determined to keep going to college. And there is Esperanza's beautiful friend Sally, who marries in the eighth grade in order to get away from her father but is now forbidden by her husband to see her friends. Esperanza, Nenny, Lucy, and Rachel discover that acting sexy is more dangerous than liberating when a neighbor gives them four pairs of hand-me-down

high heels. They strut around the neighborhood acting like the older girls until a homeless man accosts them. After fleeing, the girls quickly take off the shoes with the intention of never wearing them again.

The grown women Esperanza comes across on Mango Street are less daring and hopeful than the teenage girls, but they have acquired the wisdom that comes with experience. They advise Esperanza not to give up her independence in order to become a girlfriend or wife. Her Aunt Lupe, who was once pretty and strong but is now dying, encourages Esperanza to write poetry. Her mother, who was once a good student, a "smart cookie," regrets having dropped out of school. There are other women in the neighborhood who don't fit into either category, like Edna's Ruthie, a grown-up who "likes to play." While the text implies that Ruthie is developmentally disabled, Esperanza perceives her as somebody who "sees lovely things everywhere."

Through observing and interacting with her neighbors, Esperanza forms a connection to Mango Street which conflicts with her desire to leave. At the funeral for Rachel and Lucy's baby sister she meets their three old aunts who read her palm and her mind:

> Esperanza. The one with marble hands called me aside. Esperanza. She held my face with her blue-veined hands and looked and looked at me. A long silence. When you leave you must remember always to come back, she said.
>
> What?
>
> When you leave you must remember to come back for the others. A circle, understand? You will always be Esperanza. You will always be Mango Street. You can't erase what you know. You can't forget who you are.
>
> Then I didn't know what to say. It was as if she could read my mind, as if she knew what I had wished for, and I felt ashamed for having made such a selfish wish.
>
> You must remember to come back. For the ones who cannot leave as easily as you. You will remember? She asked as if she was telling me. Yes, yes, I said a little confused.

The three sisters tell Esperanza that while she will go far in life she must remember to come back to Mango Street for the others who do not get as far. By the novel's end Esperanza has realized that her writing is one way to maintain the connection to Mango Street without having to give up her own independence. She will tell the stories of the "ones who cannot out."

Characters

Alicia

"Alicia Who Sees Mice" is a young woman burdened by taking care of her family while attending college in order to escape her way of life in the *barrio*. She is only afraid of mice, which serve as a metaphor for her poverty.

Cathy

Cathy, "Queen of Cats," as Esperanza calls her because of her motley collection of felines, is one of Esperanza's neighborhood playmates. Cathy tells Esperanza that she and her family are leaving because the neighborhood into which Esperanza has just moved is going downhill.

Carlos Cordero

Carlos is Esperanza's younger brother. The brothers have little interaction with Esperanza and Nenny outside of the structure of the household.

Esperanza Cordero

"In English my name means hope. In Spanish it means too many letters," says Esperanza Cordero. In a child-like voice, Esperanza records impressions of the world around her. Her perceptions range from humorous anecdotes pulled from life in the *barrio* to more dark references to crime and sexual provocation. Through Esperanza's eyes, the reader catches short yet vivid glimpses of the other characters, particularly the females in Esperanza's neighborhood. In part, Esperanza finds her sense of self-identity among these women. With a sense of awe and mystery, for example, she looks to older girls who wear black clothes and makeup. She experiments with womanhood herself in "The Family of Little Feet," a story in which Esperanza and her friends cavort about the neighborhood in high heel shoes, but are forced to flee when they attract unwanted male attention. Esperanza's sense of self-identity is also interwoven with her family's house, which emerges throughout the book as an important metaphor for her circumstances. She longs for her own house, which serves as a symbol of the stability, financial means, and sense of belonging that she lacks in her environment: "a house all my own—Only a house quiet as snow, a space for myself to go, clean as paper before the poem."

As the stories develop, Esperanza matures. She turns from looking outward at her world to a more introspective viewpoint that reveals several sides of her character. Esperanza is a courageous girl who recognizes the existence of a bigger world beyond her constraining neighborhood, and who, toward the end of the book, is compelled by her own inner strength to leave the *barrio*. Nonetheless, Esperanza demonstrates empathy for those around her, particularly those who do not see beyond the confines of their situations: "One day I will say goodbye to Mango. I am too strong for her to keep me here forever. One day I will go away. Friends and neighbors will say, What happened to that Esperanza? Where did she go with all these books and paper? Why did she march so far away? They will not know I have gone away to come back. For the ones I left behind. For the ones who cannot out." In "Bums in the Attic," Esperanza says, "One day I'll own my own house, but I won't forget who or where I came from." The tension between Esperanza's emotional ties to this community and her desire to transcend it establish a sense of attraction and repulsion that characterize the work.

Kiki Cordero

Kiki, "with hair like fur," is Esperanza's younger brother.

Magdalena Cordero

"Nenny" is Esperanza's younger sister. Esperanza sees her little sister as childish and unable to understand the world as she does: "Nenny is too young to be my friend. She's just my sister and that was not my fault. You don't pick your sisters, you just get them and sometimes they come like Nenny." However, because the two girls have brothers, Esperanza understands that Nenny is her own responsibility to guide and protect. Esperanza and Nenny share common bonds both as sisters and as Chicana females. In the story "Laughter," a certain neighborhood house reminds both sisters of Mexico, a connection possible only because of their shared experience: "Nenny says: Yes, that's Mexico all right. That's what I was thinking exactly."

Mama Cordero

Esperanza's mother is typical of the women in Latin American communities whose life is defined by marriage, family, children, and traditionally female activities. Mama reveals herself as a superstitious figure who tells Esperanza that she was born on an evil day and that she will pray for her. Mama operates as a caretaker and has authority over her household, and she is portrayed as a martyr, sacrificing her own needs for those of her family. "I could've been somebody, you know?" Mama proclaims to Esperanza, explaining that she left school because she was ashamed that she didn't have nice clothes. Mama wishes for her daughters a better life outside the cycle of subjugation that characterizes her own, and she views education as the ticket out of that way of life.

Nenny Cordero

See Magdalena Cordero

Papa Cordero

Esperanza's father is portrayed as a man burdened with the obligation of providing for his family. Papa holds up a lottery ticket hopefully as he describes to the family the house they will buy one day. In the story "Papa Who Wakes Up Tired in the Dark," Papa reveals his vulnerability to Esperanza, his eldest child, when he learns of his own father's death and asks her to convey the news to her siblings while he returns to Mexico for the funeral.

Earl

This man with a southern accent, a jukebox repairman according to Esperanza, appears in the story "The Earl of Tennessee." He occupies a dark basement apartment and brings home women of ill repute whom Esperanza and her friends naively take to be his wife.

Elenita

Elenita, "witch woman" who tells fortunes with the help of Christian icons, tarot cards, and other accouterments, tells Esperanza after reading her cards that she sees a "home in the heart. This leaves Esperanza disappointed that a "real house" does not appear in her future.

Louie

The oldest in a family of girls, Louie and his family rent a basement apartment from Meme Ortiz's mother. His cousin Marin lives with the family and helps take care of his younger sisters. Although Louie is really her brother's friend, Esperanza notices that he "has two cousins and that his t-shirts never stay tucked in his pants."

Lucy

Lucy is a neighborhood girl whom Esperanza befriends even though her clothes "are crooked and old." Lucy and her sister Rachel are among the first friends Esperanza makes when she moves onto Mango Street.

Mamacita

In "No Speak English," Mamacita is the plump mother of a man across the street, a comic and

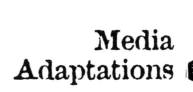

Media Adaptations

- *The House on Mango Street* was adapted as a sound recording entitled *House on Mango Street; Woman Hollering Creek,* published by Random House in 1992. It is read by Sandra Cisneros.

tragic figure who stays indoors all the time because of her fear of speaking English.

Marin

Marin is a Puerto Rican neighbor, an older girl with whom Esperanza and her friends are fascinated. Marin wears makeup, sells Avon, and has a boyfriend in Puerto Rico whom she secretly intends to marry, but meanwhile, she is responsible for the care of her younger cousins.

Minerva

Minerva is a young woman not much older than Esperanza who "already has two kids and a husband who left."

Juan Ortiz

"Meme" is a neighbor of Esperanza's who has a large sheepdog. "The dog is big, like a man dressed in a dog suit, and runs the same way its owner does, clumsy and wild and with the limbs flopping all over the place like untied shoes."

Meme Ortiz

See Juan Ortiz

Rachel

Rachel is Lucy's sister, a sassy girl according to Esperanza. Esperanza and Lucy parade around the neighborhood in high heel shoes with her in the story "The Family of Little Feet."

Rafaela

Rafaela stays indoors and observes the world from her windowsill, "because her husband is afraid Rafaela will run away since she is too beautiful to look at." Rafaela stands as a symbol for the interior world of women on Mango Street, whose lives are circumscribed and bound by the structure of home and family.

Ruthie

Ruthie, "the only grown-up we know who likes to play," is a troubled, childlike woman whose husband left her and was forced to move from her own house in the suburbs back to Mango Street with her mother.

Sally

Sally wears black clothes, short skirts, nylons, and makeup. Esperanza looks upon her with fascination and wonder, and wants to emulate her, but the dark side of Sally's life is revealed in her relationship with her abusive father. She trades one type of ensnarement for another by marrying a marshmallow salesman before the eighth grade.

Sire

Sire is a young man who leers at Esperanza as she walks down the street, provoking in her inextricable feelings of desire, foreboding, and fear. Esperanza says that "it made your blood freeze to have somebody look at you like that."

The Three Sisters

"The Three Sisters" are Rachel and Lucy's elderly aunts who come to visit when Rachel and Lucy's baby sister dies. The three ladies recognize Esperanza's strong-willed nature, and plead with her not to forget the ones she leaves behind on Mango Street when she flees from there one day.

Rosa Vargas

In the story, "There Was an Old Woman She Had So Many Children She Didn't Know What to Do," Rosa is portrayed as a woman left in the lurch by a husband who abandoned her and their unruly kids. "They are bad those Vargas, and how can they help it with only one mother who is tired all the time from buttoning and bottling and babying, and who cries every day for the man who left without even leaving a dollar for bologna or a note explaining how come."

Themes

Coming of Age

Through various themes in *The House on Mango Street* Esperanza reveals herself as both a product of the community in which she lives and one of the only figures courageous enough to transcend her circumstances. Like all adolescents, Esperanza struggles to forge her own identity. In many respects, Esperanza's own keen observations and musings about the women in her neighborhood are her way of processing what will happen to her in the future and what is within her power to change. On the one hand, she is surrounded by adolescent myths and superstitions about sexuality. In the story "Hips," the adolescent Esperanza contemplates why women have hips: "The bones just one day open. One day you might decide to have kids, and then where are you going to put them?" Esperanza boldly experiments with the trappings of womanhood by wearing high heels in "The Family of Little Feet," and in "Sally," she looks enviously to the girl as an image of maturity: "My mother says to wear black so young is dangerous, but I want to buy shoes just like yours." However, Esperanza's brushes with sexuality are dangerous and negative in "The First Job" and "Red Clowns," and she feels betrayed by the way love is portrayed by her friends, the movies, and magazines. Esperanza observes characters such as Sally, Minerva, and Rafaela, who, through early and abusive marriages, are trapped in the neighborhood and into identifying themselves through their male connections. After witnessing this, Esperanza says in "Beautiful & Cruel," "I have decided not to grow up tame like the others who lay their necks on the threshold waiting for the ball and chain." Esperanza also forges her identity through the metaphor of the house. Her longing for a house of her own underscores her need for something uplifting and stable with which she can identify. Throughout the book there is a tension between Esperanza's ties to the *barrio* and her impressions of another kind of life outside of it. Ultimately, Esperanza's ability to see beyond her immediate surroundings allows her to transcend her circumstances and immaturity.

Culture and Heritage
Difference

Esperanza keenly observes the struggles of Hispanic Americans who wish to preserve the essence of their heritage while striving to forge productive lives within American culture. It is through the sordid details of the lives of Esperanza's neighbors that we glimpse the humorous, moving, and tragic sides of these struggles. Esperanza's community serves as a microcosm of Latinos in America, and her own identity is interwoven with the identity of the neighborhood. People in the *barrio* relate to one another because of a shared past and current experience. In "Those Who Don't," Esperanza considers the stereotypes and fears that whites have of Latinos and vice versa. Cisneros weaves together popular beliefs, traditions, and other vestiges of the countries from which she and her neighbors trace their ancestry. In "No Speak English," for example, an old woman paints her walls pink to recall the colorful appearance of the houses in Mexico, a seemingly hopeless gesture in the drab underbelly of Chicago. She wails when her grandson sings the lyrics to an American television commercial but cannot speak Spanish. The tragic Mamacita risks losing her identity if she assimilates, like her little grandson, into American culture. In "Elenita, Cards, Palm, Water," the so-called "witch woman" of the neighborhood preserves the old wives' tales, superstitions, and traditional remedies for curing headaches, forgetting an old flame, and curing insomnia.

Despite these ties to the past, Esperanza leaves no doubt that she is destined to leave this neighborhood for a bigger world outside the *barrio,* an allusion to her dual cultural loyalties. Esperanza believes that one day she will own her own house outside the neighborhood. However, she also leaves no doubt that she will return one day for those unable to leave the environment on their own. In "Bums in the Attic," for example, she describes how she will let bums sleep in the attic of her house one day, "because I know how it is to be without a house." In "The Three Sisters," Esperanza gives further foreshadowing that she will one day leave Mango Street, but will return to help others. "You will always be Mango Street," three ladies tell her. "You can't erase what you know. You can't forget who you are." Esperanza leaves the reader with the notion that she will leave but will not forget her roots. Though she does not always want to belong to this environment, she realizes that her roots are too strong to resist. The books and papers Esperanza takes with her at the end of the book are her means of freedom from the ugly house and the social constraints on the neighborhood.

Gender Roles

The House on Mango Street is dedicated "a las Mujeres"—to the women. As the narrator, Esperanza offers the reader the greatest insights into the lives of female characters. One of the most enduring themes of the book is the socialization of females within Chicano society based on the fixed roles of the family. Cisneros explores the dynam-

Topics for Further Study

- Characterize the social constraints of the women in Esperanza's neighborhood, and describe how Esperanza both responds to and transcends the social forces in her environment.

- Discuss the metaphor of the house in *The House on Mango Street.*

- Discuss *The House on Mango Street* in relationship to the history of Mexican Americans in large cities of the United States.

ics of women's lives within this precarious and male-dominated society, where the conditions of females are predetermined by economic and social constraints. For most women in the neighborhood, these constraints are too powerful to overcome. However, Esperanza possesses the power to see beyond her circumstances and the world of the ghetto, while those around her fall prey to it and perpetuate its cycle. Esperanza's mother is typical of a Hispanic woman grounded in this way of life.

Throughout the book, Esperanza deals with themes of womanhood, especially the role of single mothers. The interior world of females whose lives are tied to activities inside the house is contrasted with the external world of males, who go to work and operate in society at large. In "Boys & Girls," for example, Esperanza notes the difference between herself and her brothers: "The boys and the girls live in separate worlds. The boys in their universe and we in ours. My brothers for example. They've got plenty to say to me and Nenny inside the house. But outside they can't be seen talking to girls."

Esperanza offers a feminine view of growing up in a Chicano neighborhood in the face of a socialization process that keeps women married, at home, and immobile within the society. The women in this book face domineering fathers and husbands, and raise children, often as single parents, under difficult circumstances. Many tales have tragic sides, such as those that paint the constrained existence of some of the women and girls in the neighborhood under the strong arm of husbands or fathers. The story "There Was an Old Woman She Had So Many Children She Didn't Know What to Do," tells of an abandoned young wife and her unruly children. In "Linoleum Roses," Sally is not allowed to talk on the phone or look out the window because of a jealous, domineering husband. Girls marry young in this society: "Minerva is only a little bit older than me but already she has two kids and a husband who left." But Esperanza is a courageous character who defies the stereotypes of Chicanas. She laments the attitudes that prevail in her community. Of her name, Esperanza says, "It was my great-grandmother's name and now it is mine. She was a horse woman too, born like me in the Chinese year of the horse—which is supposed to be bad luck if you're born female—but I think this is a Chinese lie because the Chinese, like the Mexicans, don't like their women strong." It is Esperanza's power to see beyond the barriers of her neighborhood, fueled by her education gained through reading and writing, that keep her from being trapped in the same roles as the women who surround her.

Style

Point of View

The House on Mango Street is narrated by the adolescent Esperanza, who tells her story in the form of short, vivid tales. The stories are narrated in the first person ("I"), giving the reader an intimate glimpse of the girl's outlook on the world. Although critics often describe Esperanza as a childlike narrator, Cisneros said in a 1992 interview in *Interviews with Writers of the Post-Colonial World:* "If you take Mango Street and translate it, it's Spanish. The syntax, the sensibility, the diminutives, the way of looking at inanimate objects—that's not a child's voice as is sometimes said. That's Spanish! I didn't notice that when I was writing it." Incorporating and translating Spanish expressions literally into English, often without quotation marks, adds a singular narrative flavor that distinguishes Cisneros's work from that of her peers.

Setting

The House on Mango Street is set in a Latino neighborhood in Chicago. Esperanza briefly describes some of the rickety houses in her neighborhood, beginning with her own, which she says is "small and red with tight steps in front." Of Meme Ortiz's house, Esperanza says that "Inside the floors slant—And there are no closets. Out front there are

twenty-one steps, all lopsided and jutting like crooked teeth." Mamacita's son paints the inside walls of her house pink, a reminder of the Mexican home she left to come to America. The furniture in Elena's house is covered in red fur and plastic. Esperanza gives the impression of a crowded neighborhood where people live in close quarters and lean out of windows, and where one can hear fighting, talking, and music coming from other houses on the street. Esperanza describes the types of shops in the concrete landscape of Mango Street: a laundromat, a junk store, the corner grocery. Cats, dogs, mice, and cockroaches make appearances at various times. However, while Esperanza gives fleeting glimpses of specific places, the images that the girl paints of her neighborhood are mostly understood through the people that inhabit it.

Structure

Just like Esperanza, whose identity isn't easy to define, critics have had difficulty classifying *The House on Mango Street.* Is it a collection of short stories? A novel? Essays? Autobiography? Poetry? Prose poems? The book is composed of very short, loosely organized vignettes. Each stands as a whole in and of itself, but collectively the stories cumulate in a mounting progression that creates an underlying coherence; the setting remains constant, and the same characters reappear throughout the tales. Cisneros once explained: "I wanted to write stories that were a cross between poetry and fiction—[I] wanted to write a collection which could be read at any random point without having any knowledge of what came before or after." Despite the disjunctive nature of the stories, as they evolve, Esperanza undergoes a maturation process, and she emerges at the end showing a more courageous and forthright facade.

Imagery

Despite certain underlying threads that link the tales in *The House on Mango Street,* the stories nonetheless remain disembodied from the kind of master narrative that typifies much of American fiction. The stories have a surreal and fragmented quality consistent with short, impressionistic glimpses into the mind of Esperanza. Rather than relying on long descriptive and narrative sequences that characterize many novels in English, Cisneros reveals dialogue and evokes powerful imagery with few words. With a minimum number of words, Cisneros includes humorous elements like the nicknames of her playmates, family, and neighbors—Nenny, Meme, and Kiki, for example. But she also, with few descriptive elements, evokes the ugliness of violence and sexual aggression swirling around her in the *barrio*. The author's carefully crafted, compact sentences convey poignant meanings that can be read on different levels. Seemingly simple dialogue reveals deeper, underlying concerns of the narrator. A straightforward dialogue between Esperanza and Nenny about a house that reminded the girls of Mexico in the story "Laughter," for example, evokes the connection of the girls to one another and to the country of their heritage. The bizarre yet moving experiences of Esperanza evoke a social commentary but do not explicitly state it. Cisneros strikes a tenuous balance between humor and pathos, between tragic and comic elements.

Symbols

Several important symbolic elements characterize *The House on Mango Street*. First, the image of the house is a powerful one. The house that Esperanza lives in—small, crooked, drab—contrasts with the image of the house that Esperanza imagines for herself in "Bums in the Attic": "I want a house on a hill like the ones with the gardens where Papa works." But the metaphor of the house is more than pure materialism. The house represents everything that Esperanza does not have—financial means and pleasant surroundings—but more importantly, it represents stability, triumph, and transcendence over the pressures of the neighborhood. Throughout the book, especially in stories such as "The House on Mango Street," and "A Rice Sandwich," Esperanza struggles with the embarrassment of poverty: "You live *there?* The way she [aunt] said it made me feel like nothing. *There.* I lived *there.*" Another important symbol in the book are the trappings of womanhood—shoes, makeup, black clothes—that fascinate and intimidate the adolescent Esperanza, who carefully observes the other women in her community. Although at times these signs of womanhood leave Esperanza feeling betrayed, in "Beautiful & Cruel," she sees them as potential for power: "In the movies there is always one with red red lips who is beautiful and cruel. She is the one who drives the men crazy and laughs them all away. Her power is her own. She will not give it away."

Tone

Cisneros's writing is often compared to music for its poetic, lyrical quality. *The House on Mango Street* has a strong aural character, and the author clearly has an interest in sound that comes through in much of her poetry. Esperanza speaks in a singsong voice, with the repetitive quality of a nursery rhyme. Cisneros's tone is at once youthful and lighthearted, but displays a tragic or menacing tone at times. Cisneros once commented, "I wanted stories like poems, compact and lyrical and ending with reverberation." In her more recent works, Cisneros has outgrown the girlish voice of Esperanza and takes on more mature themes while retaining this distinctive lyrical quality in her writing.

Historical Context

Mexican Immigration to the United States

Cisneros plays on her dual Mexican American heritage throughout her work, and *The House on Mango Street* in particular reflects the experience of Mexicans in the United States. In the mid-nineteenth century, Mexico ceded its northern territories (present-day California, Arizona, and New Mexico) to the United States at the end of the Mexican War, and Mexican landowners lost many of their rights under the Treaty of Guadalupe Hidalgo. From about 1900 to 1920, immigrants from Mexico were actively recruited into the United States as low-cost labor for railroad, mining, and other industries, especially throughout the southwestern United States. Mexican immigration was widespread and unregulated through the 1920s, when immigration from Mexico and some other countries hit its peak. Between World War I and World War II, however, Mexican immigration came to a halt due in part to the pressures of the Great Depression, and Mexican Americans faced repatriation, poverty, and rampant discrimination.

Despite their contribution and service to the U.S. Army during World War II, Mexican Americans continued to face discrimination upon returning home after World War II. For example, many Mexican Americans were treated like second-class citizens. And throughout the fifties and sixties, despite their eagerness to integrate more fully into American society, Mexican Americans were still treated as "outsiders" by mainstream American culture. Despite their push for civil rights throughout the 1960s and the 1970s, many Chicanos still faced discrimination that limited opportunities for advancement. By 1983, when *The House on Mango Street* was published, stringent U.S. immigration laws had long limited the number of Mexicans who were allowed to immigrate to the United States. Those who had immigrated legally or been born in America still experienced stereotyping and biases in American culture at large. In "Those Who Don't," Cisneros evokes the stereotyping of Mexican Americans: "Those who don't know any better come into our neighborhood scared. They think we're dangerous. They think we will attack them with shiny knives."

Because of the discrimination often leveled at Spanish-speaking populations by English-speaking Americans, many Mexican Americans choose to resist speaking Spanish except among family within the privacy of their homes. Cisneros, for example, remembers that she only spoke Spanish with her father at home, while otherwise being fully integrated within the mainstream American educational system. On the other hand, other Mexican Americans, particularly those of the older generations who retained a nostalgia for their mother country, never relinquished the use of Spanish as their primary tongue. In *The House on Mango Street,* for example, Mamacita consciously refused to speak English because for her it represented a blatant rejection of her past and her identity, and she limited her English vocabulary to "He not here," "No speak English," and "Holy smokes." Esperanza's father remembers eating nothing but "hamandeggs" when he first arrived in the United States because it was the only English phrase he knew. In the United States today, there is a renewed interest among the younger generation of Mexican Americans to learn and more fully appreciate the Spanish language.

Hispanic American Population and Culture

The largest number of Mexican Americans in the United States are concentrated in southern California and Texas, with another sizable population in New York City. As one of the largest cities in the United States, Chicago historically has also attracted immigrants from around the world, including those from Mexico. Cisneros and her mother were born in the United States, as are many of the characters in *The House on Mango Street.* Nevertheless, they retain strong ties with their Mexican heritage and are integrated into the Mexican American communities throughout the country. In different parts of the country, these groups are referred to as "Mexican American," "Mexicanos," "Chicanos," and sometimes by the more general terms "Hispanics" or "Latinos," which collectively describes people from those cultures colonized by Spain from the fifteenth century to the present, including Cuba, Puerto Rico, Mexico, and many

other countries. The population of Hispanics in the United States continues to swell, and by some estimates, they will make up about thirteen percent of the nation's population by the early years of the twenty-first century.

Historically, Mexican American men and women have suffered negative stereotyping and prejudices that prevented them from securing desirable jobs and being upwardly mobile within the society. Therefore, many remain concentrated in low-income neighborhoods like the one portrayed in *The House on Mango Street.* Poverty is a reality faced by many Mexican American populations living in the United States. In *The House on Mango Street,* the theme of poverty pervades the stories. In "Alicia Who Sees Mice," for example, the mice are a symbol of poverty. Alicia, who stays up late studying because she "doesn't want to spend her whole life in a factory or behind a rolling pin," sees the mice scurrying around after dark, a symbol of her circumstances in the neighborhood. In *The House on Mango Street,* the source of Esperanza's embarrassment about her house and her circumstances derives from the poverty that many Mexican Americans face. In "Bums in the Attic," the economic disparity between "people who live on hills" and those who live in the *barrio* is clear.

The role of women within the history of the Hispanic community is significant. Although in *The House on Mango Street* and other works by Cisneros, some Mexican American women are portrayed as trapped within a cycle of socialization, Cisneros noted in a 1992 interview in *Interviews with Writers of the Post-Colonial World,* "I have to say that the traditional role is kind of a myth. The traditional Mexican woman is a fierce woman. There's a lot of victimization but we are also fierce. We are very fierce."

Cisneros says she was influenced by American and British writers throughout high school, and she remembers reading works such as Lewis Carroll's *Alice's Adventures in Wonderland.* But only when she was introduced to the Chicago writing scene in college and graduate school did Cisneros come in contact with Chicano writers. Later, Chicano writers like Gary Soto, Lorna Dee Cervantes, and Alberto Ríos were also among her circle of colleagues. Today, Sandra Cisneros stands foremost among Chicana writers who emerged in the 1980s, including Ana Castillo, Denise Chávez, and Gloria Anzaldúa.

Critical Overview

Although *The House on Mango Street* is Cisneros's first novel and appeared without high expectations, over time it has become well known and lauded by critics. Bebe Moore Campbell, writing in *New York Times Book Review,* called *The House on Mango Street* a "radiant first collection." The book, published in 1983, has provided Cisneros broad exposure as a writer. Her works are not numerous, but this book established the author as a major figure in contemporary American literature. Her work has already been the subject of scholarly works by historians of Chicana and women's studies. In 1985, it was awarded the Before Columbus American Book Award. Today many high schools and university departments, including Women's Studies, Ethnic Studies, English, and Creative Writing, use the book in college courses. Cisneros has read her poetry at several conferences and has won several grants and awards in the United States and abroad.

Critics usually discuss the importance of *The House on Mango Street* in terms of its incisive portrayal of the race-class-gender paradigm that characterizes the Hispanic experience in the United States. The book eloquently expresses the tensions of growing up a minority in a white-dominated society and growing up a woman in a male-dominated society, accompanied by feelings of alienation and loneliness, change and transformation. Like many Chicano writers, Cisneros touches on themes of overcoming the burden of race, gender, and class, with which all the women in the book are strapped to a greater or lesser extent. Her vivid and powerful descriptions combined with her funny and compelling dialogue persuasively capture the essence of women's lives within this precarious society.

Critics also comment on the particularly feminine viewpoint of the socialization process that Cisneros offers as an important element of the work. In this regard, Cisneros parallels the work of other Chicana writers, forging a viewpoint heretofore only offered by male Hispanic American authors. Cisneros notes that it has taken longer for female Chicana writers to get educated and make contributions parallel to those of the male Chicano writers who have been publishing works a few decades longer. Esperanza is portrayed as a bold girl who experiments with nontraditional roles of females within her society: "I have begun my own kind of war. Simple. Sure. I am one who leaves the table like a man, without putting back the chair or picking up the plate." Cisneros says that she writes about the things that haunt her from her past. "In my writing as well as in that of other Chicanas and other women, there is the necessary phase of dealing with those ghosts and voices most urgently haunting us, day by day."

Throughout her education Cisneros was exposed to mainstream English writing, and thus she began her own writing by imitating these authors. Her first poems were published in the journals *Nuestro* and *Revista Chicano-Riqueña,* which gave Cisneros the confidence to turn to major book publishers thereafter. Although *The House on Mango Street* took five years to complete, she found her own voice and her own literary direction. Most critics comment on Cisneros's ability to convey powerful images through short, compact statements, and to vividly portray an experience or feeling in just a few words. Eduardo F. Elias noted that, "Hers is the work of a poet, a painter with words, who relies on sounds, plural meanings, and resonances to produce rich and varied images in each reader's mind."

Cisneros has won numerous prestigious awards, most notably the 1985 Before Columbus American Book Award, and has read her poetry in public both in the United States and abroad. In the late 1980s, Cisneros spent time in Austin, Texas under a Paisano Dobie Fellowship, and won first and third prizes in the Segundo Concurso Nacional del Cuento Chicano from the University of Arizona for some of her short stories. In 1992 she received a National Endowment for the Arts grant, which permitted her to travel in Europe and develop new themes for her work. In the spring of 1993 she was in residence at the Fondation Michael Karolyi in Vence, France. Prior to winning these awards, she taught at Latino Youth Alternative High School in Chicago from 1978 to 1980. Her work is widely studied in the university and high school settings, and it fits well into different disciplines, including Women's Studies, American literature, and Mexican American history.

Criticism

Janet Sarbanes

In the following essay, Sarbanes, a doctoral candidate at the University of California—Los Angeles, assesses The House on Mango Street *as an unusual example of both the novel form and the bil-*

What Do I Read Next?

- *My Wicked Wicked Ways,* published as a book in 1987 by Sandra Cisneros, is an adaptation of her master's thesis from the University of Iowa. This collection of poems expresses various themes of the writer's early career.

- *Woman Hollering Creek and Other Stories* is Cisneros's 1991 collection of stories characterizing Mexican Americans living in San Antonio, Texas. The book explores the process of socialization and cultural assimilation of Mexicans and Mexican Americans into American society.

- *Bad Boys* is a short collection of poems by Sandra Cisneros published in 1980. Like *The House on Mango Street,* the poems in *Bad Boys* revolve around stories from Hispanic neighborhoods and are characterized by short, vivid phrases that evoke impressionistic images of her characters.

- *The Rodrigo Poems,* another collection of poetry by Sandra Cisneros published in 1985, re-flects a more mature voice that characterizes Cisneros's work after *The House on Mango Street.* These poems are inspired by the author's travels in Europe, and evoke her encounters with men, all of whom are anonymously referred to as "Rodrigo."

- *Baseball in April: And Other Stories* by Gary Soto (1990) realistically captures the daily lives of young Hispanics in this collection of eleven short stories.

- Nicholasa Mohr's *Nilda,* published in 1973, features a Puerto Rican girl living in the barrio of New York City during World War II, where she meets discrimination every day.

- 1995's *The Air Down Here: True Tales from a South Bronx Boyhood,* is a collection of reminiscences from Gil C. Alicea and Carmen Desena, who talk of real life for a teen in a Hispanic neighborhood of New York City.

---

dungsroman *("coming of age" story) as previously explored from the Chicano perspective.*

Sandra Cisneros is a Chicago-born Chicana activist, poet, and fiction writer. She has published two collections of poems, *Bad Boys* (1980) and *My Wicked Wicked Ways* (1987), and a collection of short stories entitled *Woman Hollering Creek* (1991). Her novel, *The House on Mango Street,* (1983) was awarded the Before Columbus American Book Award.

The House on Mango Street is the fictional autobiography of Esperanza Cordera, an adolescent Mexican American girl who wants to be a writer. Unlike the chapters in a conventional novel, the forty-four vignettes, or literary sketches, which make up the novel could each stand on its own as a short story. Read together, they paint a striking portrait of a young Chicana struggling to find a place in her community without relinquishing her sense of self.

Critics have identified the novel as an example of the growing up story, or *bildungsroman,* which forms a general theme of Chicano and Chicana literature. But Cisneros's text differs from the traditional Chicano bildungsroman, in which the boy becomes a man by first acquiring self-sufficiency and then assuming his rightful place as a leader in the community. It also differs from the traditional Chicana bildungsroman, in which the girl must give up her freedom and sense of individuality in order to join the community as a wife and mother. The goal of Esperanza, this novel's protagonist and narrator, is to fashion an identity for herself which allows her to control her own destiny and at the same time maintain a strong connection to her community.

The novel's central image is the image of the *house.* The book begins with a description of the Corderos' new house on Mango Street, a far cry from the dream house with "a great big yard and grass growing without a fence" they'd always wanted, the house that would give them space and freedom. Instead, the house on Mango Street is "small and red with tight steps in front and windows so small you'd think they were holding their breath." Though her parents insist they are only there temporarily, Esperanza knows the move is probably permanent. This is the house, the street, the identity she must now come to terms with one way or another.

As evidenced by her reaction to the new house, Esperanza has a very strong sense of place: both of where she is and of where others are in relation to her. In the opening vignette she tells of when a nun from her school passed by the ramshackle apartment the Cordero family lived in before Mango Street and asked Esperanza in surprise if she lived there. Esperanza confesses "The way she said it made me feel like nothing." Esperanza also struggles with being "placed" by her race and class in houses that are not hers, as in "Rice Sandwich," when another nun assumes she lives in "a row of three-flats, the ones even the raggedy men are ashamed to go into."

Mango Street is populated by people who feel out of place, caught between two countries—like Mamacita in "No Speak English," who wants to return to Mexico. When her husband insists that the United States is her home and she must learn to speak English, Mamacita "lets out a cry, hysterical, high, as if he had torn the only skinny thread that kept her alive, the only road out." Esperanza herself feels caught between two cultures because of her name: "At school they say my name funny as if the syllables were made out of tin and hurt the roof of your mouth. But in Spanish my name is made out of a softer something, like silver." Rather than be defined by either pronunciation, however, Esperanza asserts: "I would like to baptize myself under a new name, a name more like the real me, the one nobody sees. Esperanza as Lisandra or Maritza or Zeze the X."

As a girl on the cusp of adulthood, Esperanza is particularly concerned with the place of women in Latino culture. In "My Name," she describes how her great-grandmother, also named Esperanza, was forced to marry her great-grandfather and then placed in his house like a "fancy chandelier." The house became for her, as it is for many of the women Esperanza observes, a site of confinement: "she looked out the window her whole life, the way so many women sit their sadness on an elbow." This image of the *ventanera* or woman by the window, recurs throughout the novel. As Esperanza

looks around Mango Street, she sees other women trapped in their houses, women like Rafaela, who gets locked indoors when her husband goes out to play poker because she is too beautiful. Rafaela, who has traded in her own sexuality and independence for security and respectability, wishes she could go to "the dance hall down the street where women much older than her throw green eyes easily like dice and open homes with keys."

Another *ventanera* is Esperanza's friend Sally, who marries before she has finished eight grade in order to escape her father's house. Rather than freedom, however, a house of her own merely means more restrictions for Sally: her husband does not allow her to talk on the telephone or have friends visit or even look out of the window. Instead, Sally looks at "all the things they own: the towels and the toaster, the alarm clock and the drapes." But she, too, must give over control of her life to her husband. Cisneros employs conventional romantic imagery to describe her new home: "the linoleum roses on the floor, the ceiling smooth as wedding cake," but in Sally's case the romance is a trap, the roses and the wedding cake are the floor and ceiling of her cage.

By making the narrator of her novel a preadolescent girl, Cisneros represents Mango Street from the point of view of someone who is not yet placed, not yet put into position. Esperanza's is a voice that can question, a voice of hope (Esperanza), a voice of transition. She is not inside the house looking out, like many of the other girls and women, nor is she outside the community looking in with strange eyes, like the nuns. Often she is out in the street, looking in at the other women—observing, analyzing, evaluating their situation.

In an interview with Pilar Rodriguez-Aranda in the *America's Review*, Cisneros discusses what she perceives to be the two predominant and contradictory images of women in Mexican culture: La Malinche and la Virgen de Guadalupe. The La Malinche myth figures women as sexual, evil, and traitorous. The way history tells it, Malinche was an Aztec noblewoman who was presented to Cortes, the Spanish conqueror of Mexico, and served as his lover, translator, and strategist. This is the historical Malinche, but she has come to stand in Mexican culture for the prostitute, the bearer of illegitimate children, responsible for the foreign Spanish invasion which put an end to the Aztec empire. The Malinche myth is the reason the pretty young women of Mango Street are locked in their houses when their husbands go out. The other image Cisneros mentions in her interview, that of the Virgen de Guadalupe, or Mexican Madonna, encourages women to be self-sacrificing wives and mothers. As demonstrated above, however, it hardly works better for the women in her novel.

There are women in the community, however, who encourage Esperanza to resist both images. There is Alicia, who takes two trains and a bus to her classes at the university because "she doesn't want to spend her whole life in a factory or behind a rolling pin." There is her mother, who in "Smart Cookie" warns Esperanza against letting the shame of being poor keep her from living up to her potential: "Shame is a bad thing, you know. It keeps you down. You know why I quit school? Because I didn't have nice clothes. No clothes, but I had brains." There is her Aunt Lupe, who encourages her to write poems, telling her "it will keep you free." There are also the "three sisters," three old aunts of Esperanza's friends Lucy and Rachel who come to Mango Street to attend the funeral of their baby sister. Like supernatural beings, the three sisters appear out of nowhere, possessed of mind reading and fortune telling powers. With the image of three sisters Cisneros makes reference to the Fates of Greek mythology, three old crones who know the fate of all human beings. The sisters look at Esperanza's palms and tell her she will go far, but they also tell her that wherever she goes, she will take Mango Street with her. They remind her, too: "You must remember to come back. For the ones who cannot leave as easily as you."

While Esperanza may not accept the house on Mango Street as her home—that is to say, while she may refuse to accept the self that is handed to her—she *does* ultimately accept Mango Street as a part of herself. She comes to identify with the street itself, that border space which is within the community (within Chicano culture), but outside of the house (outside of the traditional feminine gender role). As the novel draws to a close, Esperanza begins to realize that storytelling, or writing, is one way to create this relationship between self and community, to carve out her own place in the world: "I put it down on paper and then the ghost does not ache so much. I write it down and Mango says goodbye sometimes. She does not hold me with both arms. She sets me free." But, Esperanza reminds us and herself," I have gone away to come back. For the ones I left behind. For the ones who cannot out." Like Cisneros, Esperanza will free them with her stories.

Source: Janet Sarbanes, in an essay for *Novels for Students*, Gale, 1997.

Thomas Matchie

In this excerpt, Matchie presents The House on Mango Street *as a contemporary parallel to the classic* Adventures of Huckleberry Finn *and* The Catcher in the Rye, *describing the three young protagonists as similarly innocent and vulnerable, and noting that each character develops his or her own identity in reaction to a specific environment.*

In 1963 in a collection of articles entitled *Salinger,* Edgar Branch has a piece in which he explores the "literary continuity" between Mark Twain's *The Adventures of Huckleberry Finn* and J. D. Salinger's *Catcher in the Rye.* Branch claims that, though these two books represent different times in American history, the characters, the narrative patterns and styles, and the language are strikingly similar, so that what Salinger picks up, according to Branch, is an archetypal continuity which is cultural as well as literary. I would like to suggest a third link in this chain that belongs to our own time, and that is Sandra Cisneros's *The House on Mango Street.* Published in 1989, this novella is about an adolescent, though this time a girl who uses, not the Mississippi or Manhattan Island, but a house in Chicago, to examine her society and the cultural shibboleths that weigh on her as a young Chicana woman.

Though not commonly accepted by critics as "canonical," *The House on Mango Street* belongs to the entire tradition of the bildungsroman (novel of growth) or the kunstlerroman (novel inimical to growth), especially as these patterns apply to women. One can go back to 19th-century novels like Harriet Wilson's *Our Nig* (1859), where a black woman working in the house of a white family in Boston is treated as though she were a slave. Later, Charlotte Gilman's *The Yellow Wallpaper* (1889) depicts a woman who goes crazy when she is confined to a room in a country house by her husband, a doctor who knows little about feminine psychology. Finally, in Kate Chopin's *The Awakening* (1899), the protagonist literally moves out of the house to escape her Creole husband, but cannot find a male with whom to relate in this patriarchal culture.

In *Mango Street,* a hundred years later, Esperanza is actually part of a six-member family of her own race, but that does not prevent an enslavement parallel to Nig's. Though not limited to a single room as in *Yellow Wallpaper,* Esperanza's house is a symbol of sexual as well as cultural harassment, and she, like the narrator in Gilman's story, is a writer whose colorful images help her create a path to freedom. And as in *The Awakening,* Esperanza dreams of leaving her house, an action that like Edna's is related to all kinds of men who make up the power structure in her Chicana world.

So in a general way Cisneros's novel belongs to a female tradition in which culture and literary quality are important. But for her, far more significant as literary models are Huck Finn and Holden Caufield, primarily because they are adolescents growing up in culturally oppressive worlds. Cisneros's protagonist, like them, is innocent, sensitive, considerate of others, but extremely vulnerable. Like them, Esperanza speaks a child's language, though hers is peculiar to a girl and young budding poet. And like her predecessors, she grows mentally as time goes on; she knows how she feels, and learns from the inside out what in Holden's terms is "phony," and what with Huck she is willing to "go to hell" for. There are, of course, other Chicano novels that are bildungsromans, such as Tomás Rivera's ... *y no se lo tragó la tierra,* but none presents a better parallel to Huck and Holden than Cisneros's Esperanza.

It may seem that the two boy's books are really journeys, while *Mango Street* is limited to a house, and therefore set—the opposite of a geographical quest. But when one looks at the patterns of the novels, what the boys go out to see simply comes past Esperanza, so that the effect is the same. She is simply a girl, and does not have the cultural opportunity to leave as they do. What is more important is that *Mango Street* continues a paradigm of growth where a young person encounters an outside world, evaluates it in relationship to herself, and then forges an identity, something that includes her sexuality and the prominence of writing in her life....

Esperanza actually loves her father, though as with Holden's he is virtually absent from the narrative. As Marcienne Rocard points out [in "The Remembering Voice in Chicana Literature (*Americas Review*)] Chicanas concentrate intensely on "human relationships between generations"— something not stressed in Twain and Salinger. Esperanza thinks her father is brave; he cries after the death of a grandmother, and his daughter wants to "hold and hold and hold him." But this same father perpetuates a structure that traps women. The girl's mother, for instance, has talent and brains, but lacks practical knowledge about society because, says Esperanza, Mexican men "don't like their women strong." Her insight into an abusive father comes through her best friend Sally, whose father "just

forgot he was her father between the buckle and the belt." So Sally leaves home for an early unhappy marriage. Another friend, Alicia, goes to the university to break the pattern of her dead mother's "rolling pin and sleepiness," but in studying all night and cooking, too, she begins to imagine that she sees mice, whereupon her father belittles her. Esperanza says Alicia is afraid of nothing, "except four-legged fur. And fathers." Gradually, Esperanza comes to see that the pressure on women in Chicana families comes from a system she simply, though painfully, has to leave....

Truly, all three books are wrought with violence, which the protagonists seem to forgive....

Esperanza also feels for the victims of violence. What is interesting is that she sometimes interprets violence in a broad sense as injustice, or something in society that keeps people homeless, or in shabby housing. In the attic of her new house she'll have, not "Rats," but "Bums" because they need shelter. She has visions of the violence done to Geraldo, "another wetback," who rented "two-room flats and sleeping rooms" while he sent money back to Mexico; killed one night by a hit-and-run driver, he (in the minds of his people) simply disappeared. That violence becomes worse when individuals are confined to their homes. Mamacita, the big woman across the street, is beautiful but cannot get out because she "No speak English"—a phenomenon doubly tragic because her baby sings Pepsi commercials. But mostly Esperanza identifies with wives mistreated by men who confine them to their homes. Raphaela is locked in because she is too beautiful for her jealous husband. Earl, a jukebox repairman, and Sire, who drinks beer, hold their wives tight lest they relate to anybody else. Things like this make Esperanza's "blood freeze." She dreams of being held too hard. Once, after letting a man kiss her because he was "so old," she says he "grabs me by the face with both hands and kisses me on the mouth and doesn't let go." So, like Holden and Huck, this girl cares for others because of the violence done to them (and herself) in all kinds of contexts....

Ironically, Esperanza already has a family whom she loves, but that does not free her, for her father is gone and her mother stuck. She ... longs for friends, talking first about a temporary friend Cathy who then moves away. Later, she takes some of her sister's money to buy a share in a bike with her neighbors Rachel and Lucy so she can play with them, but that is fleeting. As she matures and sees what is happening to people, she picks four trees, which like her have "skinny necks and pointy elbows." Others, like Nenny, do not appreciate those trees, but for Esperanza, they "teach," helping her to realize that like them she is here and yet does not belong. And like the trees Esperanza, who thinks in images, must continue to reach. Her goal, like that of Huck and Holden, is not to forget her "reason for being" and to grow "despite concrete" so as to achieve a freedom that's not separate from togetherness.

All three protagonists have friends who fail them, usually in some kind of romantic context....

Esperanza's best friend Sally is ... a kind of romantic. She paints her eyes like Cleopatra and likes to dream.... Tragically, it is Sally who betrays her friend and admirer in the monkey garden (an animal pen turned old car lot) where she trades the boys' kisses for her lost keys, while all concerned laugh at Esperanza for trying to defend her friend with a brick. Later, Sally leaves Esperanza alone at the fair next to the "red clowns" (at once comical and tragic figures) where she is molested because her romantic friend "lied." Actually, the whole experience is a lie, given what she had been led to expect.

Still, all three have a moral center, a person they can count on, or should be able to....

[Esperanza] has a little sister, Nenny, for whom she feels responsible. Nenny, however, is ... too little. Esperanza often refers to her as "stupid" and in the chapter on "Hips," where Esperanza is becoming more aware of the sexual role of a woman's body, she says Nenny just "doesn't get it." Her real hope comes in Aunt Lupe who is dying—"diseases have no eyes," says the young poet. In a game the girls invent, they make fun of Lupe, and for this Esperanza, like Huck, feels she will "go to hell." Actually, it is Lupe who listens to the girl's poems and tells her to "keep writing." That counsel becomes the basis of Esperanza's future apart from Mango Street.

It is important to recognize that the three novels contain religious language that at once seems to undercut traditional religion, and in the mouths of the young seems to say more than they realize....

For Esperanza, religion is a cultural thing; in her Catholic world, God the father and Virgin Mother are household terms. But for this young poet, religion takes on mythic or poetic dimensions. She sees herself, for instance, as a red "balloon tied to an anchor," as if to say she needs to transcend present conditions where mothers are trapped and fathers abusive. She even sees herself molested in

a monkey garden (a modern Eden) among red clowns (bloodthirsty males). She appeals to Aunt Lupe (Guadalupe, after the Mexican Virgin Mother), who tells her to write, to create. In the end, when Esperanza meets three aunts, or sisters (her trinity), she in effect has a spiritual vision, one which she describes in concrete language. One is cat-eyed, another's hands are like marble, a third smells like Kleenex. The girl uses these sights, smells, and touches to envision poetically her future house. As with Huck and Holden, there is something she does not fully understand. What she knows is that through these *comadres* (co-mothers) she will give birth to something very new. Like the two male protagonists, she longs for a respect and compassion absent in her experiences on Mango Street, and these women are her spiritual inspiration.

The ending of *Mango Street* is also very significant in terms of literary continuity. Just prior to the end Esperanza meets the three aunts at the funeral of a sister of her friends Lucy and Rachel; they tell her she cannot forget who she is and that if she leaves she must come back. In the end the girl recognizes that she both belongs and does not belong to Mango street. Then she vows to return to the house because of the "ones who cannot" leave. One reason for this is her writing, which has made her strong. She plans to "put it down on paper and then the ghost does not ache so much." What this means relative to other women's novels is that she reverses a trend. In *Our Nig,* Nig is dissipated in the end. The protagonist of *Yellow Wallpaper* goes crazy before literally crawling over her dominating husband's body. Edna in *The Awakening* swims to her death rather than face a culture that will not recognize her identity. Not so with Esperanza. She is strong (something Mexican women should not be), perfectly aware of the problems with a patriarchal culture, and because of her love for her people, albeit abused and dehumanized, vows to return, and it is the writing which gives her the strength....

There is one other way in which Cisneros seems to look to her predecessors for literary and cultural continuity, and that is the way she as an author comes into the text....

In *Mango Street* Cisneros has created the voice of a child, who is also a poet, a writer. For the most part that voice is consistent, but sometimes not. Once when Esperanza is playing an outside voice puts her friends and herself in perspective:

Who's stupid?

Rachel, Lucy, Esperanza and Nenny.

In this case it is the author who seems to be speaking. And when Lupe is dying, and Esperanza helps lift her head, suddenly we are inside Lupe: "The water was warm and tasted like metal." Here the author's presence is unmistakable. Perhaps Cisneros's most significant intrusion comes when Esperanza says that Mexican men do not "like their women strong"—a comment that belongs more to an adult than a child, and it seems to underpin the whole novel....

So Cisneros, like Twain and Salinger, seems to enter the narrative to help define its ultimate meaning. Unlike the boys' quests, however, this novel is a collection of genres—essays, short stories, poems—put together in one way to show Esperanza's growth, but in another to imitate the part-by-part building of an edifice. Indeed, the house on Mango Street does not just refer to the place Esperanza is trying to leave, but to the novel itself as "a house" which Esperanza as character and Cisneros as author have built together. Huck may go out to the territory, rejecting civilization, and Holden may tell his story to gain the strength to return, but Esperanza through her writing has in fact redesigned society itself through a mythical house of her own.

In this regard, Lupe once told Esperanza to "keep writing," it will "keep you free." At that time the girl did not know what she meant, but in the end Esperanza says "she sets me free," so in a sense the house is already built—a monument to her people and her sex.... Indeed, Esperanza is very different from the other women in the text. She has learned from them and not made their mistakes. So she is not trapped like her mother, Alicia, or Sally, or the others. Like Huck and Holden, she is the example for other Chicana women whom Cisneros would have us take to heart. Indeed, as the witch woman Elenita predicted earlier, Esperanza elects to build a "new house, a house made of heart." And in the tradition of, but distinct from Huck and Holden, that is just what she has accomplished.

Source: Thomas Matchie, "Literary Continuity in Sandra Cisneros's *The House on Mango Street*," in *The Midwest Quarterly,* Vol. XXXVII, No. 1, Autumn, 1995, pp. 67–79.

Dianne Klein

In this excerpt, Klein describes the character Esperanza's coming of age as a woman, a Chicana, and, at least for now, a resident of Mango Street.

At birth, each person begins a search to know the world and others, to answer the age-old ques-tion, "Who am I?" This search for knowledge, for truth, and for personal identity is written about in autobiographies and in bildungsroman fiction. For years, though, the canon of United States literature has included predominantly the coming-of-age stories of white, heterosexual males. Where are the stories of the others—the women, the African Americans, the Asian Americans, the Hispanics, the gay males and lesbians? What differences and similarities would we find in their bildungsromans? Many writers, silenced before, are now finding the strengths, the voices, and the market for publica-tion to tell their stories.

Chicano/a writers, like African Americans, Asian Americans, and others, are being heard; in autobiography and in fiction, they are telling their coming-of-age stories.... *The House on Mango Street* by Sandra Cisneros (1989) [is one] such Chicano/a [work] of fiction. [In this text,] Cisneros show[s] the forces—social and cultural—that shape and define [her] characters.... [The novel shows] the struggle of the Chicano/a people to find identities that are true to themselves as individuals and artists but that do not betray their culture and their people.

This is no mean feat, considering that Anglos did not teach them to value their cultural heritage and experiences, that they were shown no Chicano/a role models, that, in fact, they were often discouraged from writing. Cisneros says [in her book, *From a Writer's Notebook*] that as a writer growing up without models of Chicano/a literature, she felt impoverished with nothing of personal merit to say.

> As a poor person growing up in a society where the class norm was superimposed on a tv screen, I couldn't understand why our home wasn't all green lawn and white wood.... I rejected what was at hand and emulated the voices of the poets ... big, male voices ... all wrong for me ... it seems crazy, but ... I had never felt my home, family, and neighborhood unique or worthy of writing about....

Cisneros, being an only daughter in a family of six sons, was often lonely. She read, in part, to escape her loneliness. Cisneros reflects that her aloneness "was good for a would-be writer—it al-lowed ... time to think ... to imagine ... to read and prepare." Cisneros in "Notes to a Young(er) Writer" [*The Americas Review*] explains that her reading was an important "first step." She says she left chores undone as she was "reading and read-ing, nurturing myself with books like vitamins."...

Cisneros' *House on Mango Street* is ... nar-rated by a child protagonist. Esperanza, the protagonist, tells about her life on Mango Street; we see her family, friends, and community, their daily troubles and concerns. By the end of the story, she has gained understanding about both herself and her community/culture.... *The House on Mango Street* is the story of growing awareness which comes in fits and starts, a series of almost epiphanic narrations mirrored in a structure that is neither linear nor traditional, a hybrid of fictive and poetic form, more like an impressionistic painting where the subject isn't clear until the viewer moves back a bit and views the whole. Esperanza tells her story in a series of forty-four, individually titled vignettes. Ellen McCracken [*in Breaking Boundaries*] believes that this bildungsroman, which she prefers to label a "collection" rather than a novel, "roots the individual self in the broader ... sociopolitical reality of the Chicano/a community."

For Esperanza in *The House on Mango Street,* the notion of "house"—or a space of her own—is critical to her coming of age as a mature person and artist. Ramón Saldívar says [in *Chicano Narrative*] that this novel "emphasizes the crucial roles of racial and material as well as ideological conditions of oppression." At the beginning of the novel, Esperanza explains how her parents talk about moving into a "real" house that "would have running water and pipes that worked." Instead she lives in a run-down flat and is made to feel embarrassed and humiliated because of it. One day while she is playing outside, a nun from her school walks by and stops to talk to her.

Where do you live? she asked.

There, I said pointing to the third floor.

You live *there?*

There. I had to look where she pointed–the third floor, the paint peeling, wooden bars Papa had nailed in the windows so we wouldn't fall out. You live there? The way she said it made me feel like nothing.

Later in the novel, in a similar occurrence, a nun assumes that Esperanza lives in an even worse poverty-stricken area than, in fact, is the case. Julián Olivares says [in *Chicana Creativity and Criticism*] thus the "house and narrator become identified as one, thereby revealing an ideological perspective of poverty and shame." Esperanza desires a space of her own, a real home with warmth and comfort and security, a home she wouldn't be ashamed of. For Esperanza, the house is also a necessity; echoing Virginia Woolf, she needs "A House of My Own" in order to create, a "house quiet as snow ... clean as paper before the poem."

Other houses on Mango Street do not live up to Esperanza's desires either, for they are houses that "imprison" women. Many vignettes illustrate this. There is the story of Marin who always has to baby-sit for her aunt; when her aunt returns from work, she may stay out front but not go anywhere else. There is also the story of Rafaela whose husband locks her indoors when he goes off to play dominoes. He wishes to protect his woman, his "possession," since Rafaela is "too beautiful to look at." And there is Sally whose father "says to be this beautiful is trouble.... [H]e remembers his sisters and is sad. Then she can't go out." Sally marries, even before eighth grade, in order to escape the confinement and abuse of her father's house, but in the vignette, "Linoleum Roses," we see her dominated as well in the house of her husband.

She is happy.... except he won't let her talk on the telephone. And he doesn't let her look out the window....

She sits home because she is afraid to go outside without his permission.

Esperanza sees, as Olivares notes, that "the woman's place is one of domestic confinement, not one of liberation and choice." And so, slowly, cumulatively, stroke by stroke, and story by story, Esperanza comes to realize that she must leave Mango Street so that she will not be entrapped by poverty and shame or imprisoned by patriarchy.

Another element of the bildungsroman is the appearance of a mentor who helps guide the protagonist....

In *The House on Mango Street* there is an ironic twist to the guidance of mentors, for often Esperanza is guided by examples of women she does *not* want to emulate, such as Sally and Rafaela. [There] are several role models who sometimes give her advice. They nurture her writing talent, show her ways to escape the bonds of patriarchy, and remind her of her cultural and communal responsibilities. Minerva is a young woman who, despite being married to an abusive husband, writes poems and lets Esperanza read them. She also reads Esperanza's writing. Aunt Lupe, dying of a wasting illness, urges Esperanza to keep writing and counsels her that this will be her freedom. Alicia, who appears in two stories, is, perhaps, the best role model. While she must keep house for her father, she still studies at the university so she won't be trapped. Alicia also reminds Esperanza that Esperanza *is* Mango Street and will one day return. McCracken says that Alicia fights "what patriarchy expects of her" and at the same time represents a clear-sighted, non-mystified vision of the barrio.... [S]he embodies both the antipatriarchal themes and the social obligation to return to one's ethnic community.

The story, "Three Sisters," is a kind of subversive fairytale. Esperanza attends the wake of her friends' baby sister and is suddenly confronted by three mysterious old women. These women examine Esperanza's hands, tell her to make a wish, and advise, "When you leave, you must remember always to come back.... [Y]ou can't forget who you are... [C]ome back for the ones who cannot leave as easily as you." They direct her to remember her responsibilities to her community. In this bildungsroman, Esperanza is reminded consistently that the search for self involves more than mere personal satisfaction. All of these women offer guidance to help Esperanza in her coming of age.

[The protagonist] must endure other rites of passage to reach full personhood and understanding....

Esperanza's rites of passage ... speak through the political realities of Mango Street.... Her major loss of innocence has to do with gender and with being sexually appropriated by men. In the vignette, "The Family of Little Feet," Esperanza and her friends don high heels and strut confidently down the street. They are pleased at first with their long legs and grown-up demeanors, then frightened as they are leered at, yelled to, threatened, and solicited. McCracken says, "Cisneros proscribes a romantic or exotic reading of the dress-up episode, focusing instead on the girls' discovery of the threatening nature of male sexual power."

Perhaps Esperanza's "descent into darkness" occurs in the story "Red Clowns." Unlike the traditional bildungsroman, the knowledge with which she emerges is not that of regeneration, but of painful knowledge, the knowledge of betrayal and physical violation. In this story, she is waiting for Sally, who is off on a romantic liaison. Esperanza, all alone, is grabbed and raped. Afterward, she says, "Sally, make him stop. I couldn't make them go away. I couldn't do anything but cry. I don't remember. It was dark.... [P]lease don't make me tell it all." In this story, Esperanza is also angry and calls Sally "a liar" because through books and magazines and the talk of women she has been led to believe the myth of romantic love. [In "The Politics of Rape," (*The Americas Review*)] María Herrera-Sobek calls this story a "diatribe" that is directed not only at Sally,

but at the community of women in a conspiracy of silence ... silence in not denouncing the "real" facts of life about sex and its negative aspects in violent sexual encounters, and *complicity* in romanticizing and idealizing unrealistic sexual relations.

Esperanza, triply marginalized by race, class, and gender, has lost her innocence. Yet, despite this pain and violation, she manages to tell her story. She has come of age, and she understands that in the future she must serve *both* herself and her community.

I will say goodbye to Mango.... Friends and neighbors will say, what happened to that Esperanza? ... They will not know I have gone away to come back. For the ones I left behind. For the ones who cannot out.

Source: Dianne Klein, "Coming of Age in Novels by Rudolfo Anaya and Sandra Cisneros," in *English Journal,* Vol. 81, No. 5, September, 1992, pp. 21–6.

Sources

Bebe Moore Campbell, "Crossing Borders," *New York Times Book Review,* May 26, 1991, p. 6.

Sandra Cisneros, "Interview with Sandra Cisneros," in Reed Dasenbrock and Feroza Jussawalla, *Interviews with Writers of the Post-Colonial World,* University Press of Mississippi, 1992.

Eduardo F. Elias, "Sandra Cisneros," *Dictionary of Literary Biography, Volume 122: Chicano Writers, Second Series* edited by Francisco A. Lomeli and Carl Shirley, Gale Research, 1992, pp. 77-81.

Eduardo F. Elias, "The House on Mango Street," *Reference Guide to American Literature,* 3rd edition, edited by Jim Kamp, Gale Research, 1994, p. 992.

Eduardo F. Elias, "Sandra Cisneros," *Reference Guide to American Literature,* 3rd edition, edited by Jim Kamp, Gale Research, 1994, pp. 200-02.

For Further Study

Pilar E. Rodriguez Aranda, interview in *The Americas Review,* Spring, 1990, pp. 64-80.

An interview with Cisneros which focuses on the writing of *The House on Mango Street* as well as on the general trend of Latinas "reinventing themselves" in relation to their culture.

Maria Elena de Valdes, "In Search of Identity in Cisneros's *The House on Mango Street,*" in *The Canadian Review of American Studies,* Volume 23:1 (Fall), 1992, pp. 55-72.

Emphasizes the importance of Esperanza's "highly lyrical" narrative voice.

Erlinda Gonzalez-Berry and Tey Diana Rebolledo, "Growing Up Chicano: Tomas Rivera and Sandra Cisneros," in *Revista Chicano-Riquena,* Volume 13:34, 1985, pp. 109-19.

Considers Cisneros' novel as an example of the growing up story which forms a general theme in Chicano literature.

Ellen McCracken, "Sandra Cisneros' *The House on Mango Street:* Community-Oriented Introspection and the Demystification of Patriarchal Violence," in *Breaking Boundaries: Latina Writing and Critical Readings,* edited by Anuncion Horno-Delgado, Eliana Ortega, Nina M. Scott, Nancy Saporta Steinbach, University of Massachusetts Press, 1989, pp. 62-71.

Discusses *The House on Mango Street* as a "marginalized text" which contradicts the individualistic values of the male-dominated literary canon.

Julián Olivares, "Sandra Cisneros' The House on Mango Street, and the Poetics of Space," in *Chicana Creativity and Criticism: Charting New Frontiers in American Literature,* Arte Público, 1988, pp. 160-69.

Claims that Cisneros "employs her imagery as a poetics of space," but reverses the conventional emphasis on the home as a site of comfort and the outside world as a source of anxiety.

Renato Rosaldo, "Fables of the Fallen Guy," in *Criticism in the Borderlands: Studies in Chicano Literature, Culture and Ideology,* edited by Hector Calderon and Jose David Saldivar, Duke University Press, 1991, pp. 84-93.

Situates *The House on Mango Street* and Cisneros in the context of earlier narratives of cultural authenticity written by Latino writers featuring male warrior-heroes.

Ramón Saldívar, "The Dialectics of Subjectivity: Gender and Difference in Isabella Rios, Sandra Cisneros, and Cherrie Moraga," in *Chicano Narrative: The Dialectics of Difference,* University of Wisconsin Press, 1990, pp. 171-99.

Discusses the intersection of race, gender, and class in *The House on Mango Street.*

I Know Why the Caged Bird Sings

Maya Angelou
1970

I Know Why the Caged Bird Sings is the first—and many say the best—of five autobiographical volumes the gifted African American author, Maya Angelou, wrote. It is a remarkably vivid retelling of the turbulent events of her childhood, during which she shuttled back and forth between dramatically different environments in rural Stamps, Arkansas, slightly raunchy St. Louis, Missouri, and glitzy San Francisco, California. It is also the annals of her relationships with a rich and diverse cast of characters. Chief among these are her determined, strict, and wise grandmother Annie Henderson; her crippled and bitter uncle Willie Johnson; her bright and imaginative brother Bailey Johnson Jr.; her playboy father Bailey Johnson; and her beautiful, brilliant, and worldly mother, Vivian Baxter Johnson. A host of other unforgettable characters fill out the cast for this earnest, sometimes sardonic retelling of the drama of Maya Angelou's growing-up years. During these years, she struggled against the odds of being black at a time when prejudice, especially in the South, was at its height. But most of all her story is the story of discovering who she is—of working her way through a multifaceted identity crisis. The source of the title of the book is a poem by Paul Laurence Dunbar entitled "Sympathy." "I know why the caged bird sings," writes the poet. "When he beats his bars and he would be free. It is a plea, that upward to Heaven he flings. I know why the caged bird sings!"

Author Biography

When Maya Angelou was three and her brother, Bailey, was four, her parents divorced and shipped the two young children to live with their paternal grandmother, Annie Henderson, in the stark, dusty black section of Stamps, Arkansas. Annie had status in the black community: She owned and ran a successful general store that supplied the black community with food and sundries. She also owned an extra house that she rented to a family of poor white people who occasionally came to the store to taunt her and her family.

During the Depression, Mrs. Johnson (also known as Sister Johnson) was able to lend money to both blacks and whites in need of cash. Later, she was able to use this as a kind of clout when she confronted offensive former borrowers. Stolid, confident, strong and wise, she was Maya and Bailey's first role model—a strict one who taught them cleanliness, godliness, and respect for others. Their lives revolved around the store and its customers and the church, which Maya viewed with a certain amount of skepticism.

A bright child, as was her brother, she learned quickly and did well in the black school she attended. An elegant neighbor, Mrs. Flowers, took Maya under her wing and taught her to love books. The children adjusted well to life in Stamps, in spite of the prejudice they experienced from and toward whites. Their lives were rich with people, including grumpy Uncle Willie, their crippled uncle who hung out in the store most of the time, unable to do any meaningful work. They were part of a close, caring community that extended to the bridge that transversed the gap that sharply divided the black and white sections of town.

Suddenly one day, the children's father, Bailey Johnson Sr., arrived in a car to swoop them up and take them to live with their mother, Vivian Baxter Johnson, in St. Louis. Through good looks, wits and guts, their mother was able to provide them with a better standard of living. But disaster struck when their mother's live-in boyfriend, Mr. Freeman, seduced and violently raped Maya. After a brief court trial, Freeman was sentenced to jail. He never made it: their mother's brothers beat him to death behind a slaughter house. Hospitalized for her injuries and traumatized, Maya returned home a changed child. She would not talk or smile. To others, she was thoroughly disagreeable. Finally, her mother was unable to tolerate this behavior any longer. She returned the children to their grand-

Maya Angelou

mother in Stamps, where Maya gradually came out of her shell and resumed the familiar patterns of her pre-St. Louis life.

After graduating from grade school, she and her brother returned to live with their mother, who had moved to San Francisco. With her mother's support, Maya became a confident teenager who managed to force her way into a job as a streetcar conductor at the age of fifteen. She was the first black to achieve this status. Confused about her sexuality, she decided to prove she was a normal woman by demanding and having sex with a young neighbor. The one-time liaison ended up with the birth of Maya's son, Guy Johnson.

As she continued her journey toward adulthood and ultimate multiple successes, she experienced life at its best and at its worst. At one point, she brushed against prostitution and drugs. Her several marriages ended in divorce, in part because she had so many agendas for her life. She kept her first husband's name as her surname. After completing high school in San Francisco and attending an art school there, she studied music and dance, tutored in the latter art with dancers Martha Graham, Pearl Primus and Ann Halprin. She also studied drama with Frank Silvera and Gene Frankel. She became a dancer, playwright, actress, director, singer, poet, composer and politician. She spent four years in Ghana pursuing a knowledge of her heritage—and discovered that essentially she was an American. Tapped by Martin Luther King, she served as Northern coordinator of the Southern Christian Leadership Converence in 1959 and 1960, and published the first of her series of autobiographical novels, *I Know Why the Caged Bird Sings,* in 1970. She has been a writer in residence and a professor at numerous universities around the world, won numerous awards for both acting and writing and received honorary degrees from leading universities and served on the boards of several prestigious arts and civic organizations. She was honored at President Clinton's first inauguration in 1993, where she recited one of her celebrated poems.

Plot Summary

Part I

The first of five autobiographical works, *I Know Why the Caged Bird Sings,* focuses on the recollections and adult understanding of Maya Angelou's growing up female and black in the America of the 1930s and 1940s. The author begins this volume with a description of her young self standing in front of the church to deliver a short poem on Easter. Although she describes herself as very dark and ugly with "steel wool" for hair, here she imagines that someday her true self will emerge. She'll be blonde, blue-eyed, and white.

The first chapter proper, however, shows us three-year-old Marguerite (Maya) and her four-year-old brother Bailey arriving by train to live with their father's mother, Mrs. Annie Henderson, in Stamps, Arkansas. The children's parents have ended their marriage and sent the young children off by train with notes instructing "To Whom It May Concern" of their names, origin, and destination. Once in Stamps, the children's lives revolve around the church, the school, and helping "Momma" and their lame Uncle Willie with the Wm. Johnson General Merchandise Store, referred to by all in the community as "The Store." Their grandmother had built the business up from a simple lunch wagon for field workers.

Since the Store acts as a focus of the community, Marguerite and Bailey become acquainted with the daily lives of everyone in the black section of town. They wait on the field hands before they load up in wagons reminiscent of the plantations and serve them in the evenings when they re-

turn worn and beaten from the fields. They know Mr. McElroy as an independent black man. They watch the Reverend H. Thomas get the best of the Sunday chicken. And they survive the Depression and keep the Store going by exchanging commodities given out by the government for items from the shelves. The children do their lessons under Uncle Willie's stern hand and fall in love with books, especially Shakespeare, around the fire in the back of the store at night.

Part II—St. Louis

Quite suddenly, though, their father shows up in Stamps with no prior contact but Christmas presents the year before. Their father drives Marguerite and Bailey to their mother and her family in St. Louis. Here, Grandmother Baxter presides as a Precinct Captain, and their loud, tough uncles have city jobs. Their mother, Vivian Baxter, whom Bailey names "Mother Dear," has been trained as a pediatric nurse but lives with Mr. Freeman and supplements her income by dealing cards. Marguerite and Bailey adjust quickly to city life and do well in school.

One morning when Mother hasn't come home yet and Bailey is out, Mr. Freeman approaches Marguerite sexually. She had sat on his lap and hugged him before, mistaking his attentions as ordinary and "fatherly." Today, however, he turns up the volume on the radio to drown out her cries and brutally rapes the eight-year-old girl. When he is finished, he warns her that if she tells, he'll kill Bailey.

> "We were just playing before." He released me enough to snatch down my bloomers, and then he dragged me closer to him. Turning the radio up loud, too loud, he said, 'if you scream, I'm gonna kill you. And if you tell, I'm gonna kill Bailey.' I could tell he meant what he said. I couldn't understand why he wanted to kill my brother. Neither of us had done anything to him. And then.
>
> Then there was the pain. A breaking and entering when even the senses are torn apart. The act of rape on an eight-year-old body is a matter of the needle giving because the camel can't. The child gives, because the body can, and the mind of the violator cannot.

Unable to hide the injury from Maya's mother, Mr. Freeman is discovered, and he is put on trial for the crime. When his lawyer gets him freed on a technicality, his body is later found. Presumably, the uncles have kicked him to death. At this point Marguerite feels responsible for his death and stops talking. Without explanation, the children soon find themselves on a train going back to Stamps. Their lives resume as before they left, with the community accepting them completely.

A segregated drinking fountain.

Part III—Return to Stamps

Back in the rural South, Marguerite witnesses her grandmother's triumph when some young white girls try to shame her. Joe Louis keeps the World's Heavy-Weight Championship title while they listen on the store's radio. After years of silence, Marguerite is befriended by Mrs. Bertha Flowers, a "gentlewoman" who gently persuades her to begin talking again by loaning her books to be read aloud and together. At a picnic Marguerite sneaks off to read and then makes her first friend of her own age. She graduates with honors from grammar school in 1940. She works for a short while as domestic help.

Momma abruptly decides to take them to their parents, who now live in California, when Bailey comes to the Store in shock. He had been made to handle a dead black man's body and witness the brutality of whites to blacks. Bailey cannot understand the hatred, and his grandmother fears for his safety.

Part IV—California

World War II has just started, and San Francisco booms with wartime activities. Their mother is now married to "Daddy Clidell," the first father Marguerite knows. She attends a nearly all-white school and does well, but is bored except for social studies and night classes she takes at the California Labor School. Marguerite has many glamorous daydreams when her father invites her "to vacation" with him in southern California. Once there, however, she becomes quickly disillusioned with her father's girlfriend, the trailer park, and her father.

On a day trip to Mexico with her father, she gets a glimpse of the exotic life she had imagined. But her father gets too drunk, and Marguerite drives them all the way to the border, nearly without mishap. Back at the trailer, her father's girlfriend Dolores cuts Marguerite during a fight. Her father takes Marguerite to friends, but she leaves and finds herself part of a racially mixed community of young people living on their own in a junkyard. After a month, she calls her mother and returns to San Francisco.

In San Francisco she finds her brother and mother constantly at odds until Bailey finally moves out, eventually joining the Merchant Marines. Dissatisfied and restless, Marguerite decides to get a job. She ends up battling bureaucracy to become the first black conductorette on the street cars. Still young, but more mature than her peers, Marguerite becomes confused by her newly awakening sexual feelings and seduces a young man.

Three weeks later she realizes she's pregnant, but on Bailey's advice keeps the pregnancy a secret so that she can finish high school. Once she has graduated two days after V-Day, she leaves a note on Daddy Clidell's bed informing her parents of her pregnancy. Soon after, her son is born, and her mother takes care of him. Maya loves her son, but is afraid to touch him because she's always been "awkward." Finally, however, her mother puts the three-week old baby to sleep with Marguerite. At first Marguerite protests, then struggles to say awake so she won't crush the baby. Later on, though, her mother wakes her to demonstrate how she has protected her son even in her sleep.

Characters

Vivian Baxter Bailey

Maya's mother is a beautiful, sexy, vibrant, smart woman with more than a little common sense. She loves her children, and she listens to them uncritically—with the exception of her final blow-up with Bailey Jr. Energetic, she pursues several careers. She rents out rooms in her large home in San Francisco and manages casinos. She is also a one-time nurse. She gradually weans Maya from the restricted environment of Stamps and brings her into the freer environment of a city without lynchings. She's not afraid to confront people who have displeased her. For example, when she learns that Mr. Freeman has raped Maya, he's out the door immediately. She carries a gun and uses it strategically when she is threatened by a traitorous business partner. A strong and appealing individual, she is unforgettable.

Grandmother Baxter

Grandmother Baxter, Maya's maternal grandmother, was an octoroon—a person with one-eighth African American blood—which meant that her skin was white. She plays a very minor role in Maya's life, but she's interesting because she has infiltrated St. Louis politics to the point where she has considerable influence.

Daddy Clidell

Daddy Clidell, Mother's second husband, is "the first father I would know." A successful businessman, he adds stability to Maya's life.

Daddy

See Bailey Johnson Sr.

Media Adaptations

- *I Know Why the Caged Bird Sings* was made into a TV movie in 1979 starring Diahann Carroll, Ruby Dee, Esther Rolle, Roger E. Mosely, Paul Benjamin, and Constance Good, directed by Fielder Cook. Available from Knowledge Unlimited, Inc.

Mrs. Flowers

Mrs. Flowers is an elegant black lady who lives in Stamps. She makes Maya proud to be an African American. Knowing that Maya is an outstanding student, she provides her with the best of literature and introduces her to formal customs such as afternoon tea.

Mrs. Annie Henderson

Maya's grandmother, whom Maya calls Momma, is a strong, independent, righteous woman. Her family, her store, and her church are the focal points of her life. She rules Maya and Bailey with an iron hand and a velvet glove, teaching them cleanliness, godliness, respect, and courtesy. Successful and prosperous, she is never stingy. During the Depression, she lends money to blacks and whites alike. Later she takes her chances by taking a dangerously ill Maya to a white dentist. When he refuses to treat a Negro, she tells him to get out of town that very day. He is rightfully intimidated by her. She is a strong, determined, and unafraid woman. Nevertheless, she knows the boundaries of the prejudiced society in which the black people of Stamps dwell. The threat of a lynching is never far away. Says Maya of her grandmother, "I don't think she ever knew that a deep-brooding love hung over everything she touched."

Bailey Johnson Jr.

Maya's brother, Bailey, is her best friend. A bright and imaginative companion, he shares her love of books and of drama. Bailey is somewhat more likely than Maya to get into trouble (but nothing major), especially when he reaches his adolescent years. He has a brief sexual affair with a rather loose girl. He loves St. Louis and his mother and resents it when he has to return to Stamps because of Maya's withdrawal after the rape. When he is sixteen, he moves out of his mother's San Francisco house after he and his mother have a fight. Basically, they can't live with each other and they can't live without each other, Maya explains. Eventually, Bailey joins the Merchant Marine.

Bailey Johnson Sr.

Maya's unpredictable father, Bailey Johnson Sr., cares about his children but only in a casual way. Well spoken and impeccably dressed, he earns his living as a doorman in a hotel. Before that, he was a dietician in the U.S. Navy. But at heart he's a boastful, self-important, hard-drinking playboy who sleeps around and deceives women about his marital intentions.

Marguerite Johnson

See Maya Johnson

Maya Johnson

Maya Johnson is a brilliant, sensitive young black woman with keen insight into her environment and the people in it. Her observations and her expressed feelings are so real that the reader begins to absorb her vivid if tragic universe. Early on in the book, she describes herself as "a too-big Negro girl, with nappy black hair, broad feet and a space between her teeth that would hold a number-two pencil." Her childhood dream is to wake up some day with light-blue eyes and long, straight blond hair.

Life in Stamps is timeless but not tedious. The days and seasons follow one another in orderly sequence as Maya helps in the store, attends school, play-acts with her brother Bailey Jr., listens to grown-up talk as neighbors gather in the store and attends church services and church picnics (the latter usually with a sense of skeptical irony). Maya's mentor, the elegant Mrs. Flowers, introduces her to the world of literature and afternoon tea.

Mischief as well as irony is very much part of Maya's nature. When she takes a job as a maid in a white person's house, her employer's friends urge them to call her Mary, not Marguerite, deeming the latter too long a name for a little black girl. She manages to extricate herself from the unpleasant situation by plotting with Bailey to break her employer's favorite piece of bric-a-brac. Solitary and

within herself, teased by schoolmates, Maya has few friends her own age, although she finally links up with another school pariah, Louise Kendricks.

The sudden departure from Stamps to St. Louis is traumatic at first. But when Maya meets her beautiful, lively, smart mother, she likes her immediately. It is a different world in St. Louis—one where her mother prospers by pursuing several careers—as a realtor, an entertainer, and a casino hostess. All would have been fine if Mr. Freeman, her mother's boyfriend, had not raped her. But after the hospitalization, the trial, and the trauma, Maya becomes a gloomy and silent child. Soon, her mother sends both Maya and Bailey back to Stamps and their grandmother. Maya seems to shift from one environment to the other automatically. Her adaptability and acceptance of change is amazing— as is her growing independence, which may be the inevitable result of never knowing where she'll be next.

Back in San Francisco with her mother, after an abortive Mexican vacation with her father and a one-month stay with homeless kids in Los Angeles, she begins to acquire self-confidence. At the age of fifteen, she lies her way into a job as a streetcar conductor—the first black conductor ever hired. Confused by her emerging sexuality, she decides to prove that she is a woman by inviting a teenage neighbor to have sex with her. This one-time encounter results in pregnancy. With a teenager's characteristic avoidance of unpleasant confrontations, she keeps the pending birth to herself until three weeks before the baby is born. Finally, she takes the baby boy into her bed and heart—with the encouragement of her mother.

Miss Kirwin

Miss Kirwin is Maya's favorite teacher at San Francisco's George Washington High School, which Maya describes as "the first real school I attended." Miss Kirwin is one of those rare teachers who respect their students. She is also able to stimulate their minds by getting them involved in the *San Francisco Chronicle* and other news media.

Momma

See Annie Henderson

Mother

See Vivian Baxter Bailey

Ritie

See Maya Johnson

Sister

See Annie Henderson

George Taylor

A self-pitying Stamps widower who uses his grief as a way to win the sympathy of others. Ignorant and superstitious, he frightens the young Maya by saying that he saw a blue-eyed baby angel hovering over him.

The Reverend Howard Thomas

A pompous preacher who makes the circuit of the Arkansas area that includes Stamps. He visits every three months and stays with the Johnsons. A colossal eater, he is fat and slovenly. Maya and Bailey hate him.

Uncle Willie

Maya's Uncle Willie is a proud but shattered man. Rendered a cripple by some childhood accident, he desperately seeks a way to be needed and appreciated. When some strangers come to buy something, he pulls himself up erect behind the counter and pretends to be normal—probably enduring great pain in the process. While gruff and often disagreeable, he loves the children. His main activity is helping in the store.

Themes

American Dream

For Maya Angelou, in *I Know Why the Caged Bird Sings,* the American dream was somewhere over the bridge in the white part of town. Through her keen perception and her probing insight into her character Marguerite Johnson, she sees reality in all its beauty and ugliness. Eventually, Marguerite comes to terms with the fact that she is forever black and that she can succeed in a world filled with prejudice. The best example of this is her persistence in becoming the first black streetcar conductor in San Francisco. She has learned to outwit her tormentors, who include snobby whites, pretentious blacks, and most of the men she encounters along the difficult path of growing up.

Coming of Age

Along the way, Marguerite has many mentors to guide her in *I Know Why the Caged Bird Sings*— her grandmother Annie Henderson, Mrs. Flowers, her mother Vivian Baxter Johnson, and her high-school teacher, Miss Kirwin. All her guides are

Topics for Further Study

- Research the history of the Ku Klux Klan in the 1930s and 1940s and today. Note any changes in the activities of this organization over the years and debate whether or not it is still a danger to U.S. society.

- Compare employment practices and laws in the 1930s and the 1940s with those of today. Emphasize the status of women and minorities.

- Argue whether or not affirmative-action programs have outlived their usefulness. Support your argument with specific examples and current statistics.

strong women who have preceded her and have survived the similar trials of youth that she is going through. Angelou's portrayal of black males is quite negative; most of the male characters in the book are the weak links in the chain toward her success. It thus becomes a feminist manifesto as well as the story of a shy and awkward black child who blossoms into an assured and self-confident young woman. Writes Angelou, "The fact that the adult American Negro female emerges a formidable character is often met with amazement, distaste and even belligerence. It is seldom accepted as an inevitable outcome of the struggle won by survivors and deserves respect if not enthusiastic acceptance."

Prejudice and Tolerance

Prejudice in I Know Why the Caged Bird Sings takes different forms in the three places where the Johnson children spend their young years. In deep-South Arkansas, lynchings are the ultimate threat to black freedom. In St. Louis, their white-seeming octoroon (one-eighth black) grandmother Baxter has special influence in the political arena of a seamy city. And their mother creates a buoyant and independent life through wit, talent, beauty, and determination. In San Francisco, Marguerite fights the establishment to go where no black has gone before.

Education

Although *I Know Why the Caged Bird Sings* is often referred to as an autobiography, Angelou's use of novelistic techniques make literary study of the work a valuable endeavor.

Throughout *I Know Why the Caged Bird Sings*, Maya Angelou's strong belief in the power of education is evident. It is education, through reading, which brings Marguerite out of her silence after her rape, and education that allows her to create a better life for herself. In the author's own life, it was her love of knowledge and her intelligence that propelled her into multiple and exciting careers.

Style

Point of View

Although *I Know Why the Caged Bird Sings* is often referred to as an autobiography, Angelou's use of novelistic techniques makes literary study of the work a valuable endeavor.

Throughout *I Know Why the Caged Bird Sings*, we see people, places, and events through the imagination of Marguerite. While she often keeps her own counsel, she carries on a private dialogue with herself that is in turn poetic, humorous, sardonic, and tragic. Gifted with the ability to see through shams and affectations, she cuts through to the quick of her observations. She knows intuitively what is real and what is phony, and she processes all this information intellectually over her growing-up years and gradually forms a positive self-image. The shy, awkward child becomes the determined, talented young adult.

Narration

Key to communicating Marguerite's point of view is the narration of the novel. Angelou uses the first person "I" to tell events, giving the reader direct access to Marguerite's thoughts and concerns. Since the narration is limited to what Marguerite chooses to tell, the reader only gets to see events through her perceptions, and can only learn about other characters from Marguerite's descriptions and assumptions. This technique is common in autobiographical works, however, whose intention is to communicate the experiences of one individual.

Setting

The multiple settings in *I Know Why the Caged Bird Sings* in which Marguerite acquires her diversified knowledge of people and culture also highlight the difficulties she has in integrating her experiences into a single philosophy and identity. But by the end of the book the reader feels that she knows who she is and what she wants in life. What the reader can't know is how far she may stray from this identity before she discovers her true self.

Allusion

Throughout the novel Marguerite alludes, or makes reference to, several songs and poems that come to have significance for her. When a group of white children torment Marguerite's grandmother, "Momma" begins singing a series of hymns as a way to turn aside their attempts to humiliate her. These songs, such as "Bread of Heaven," recall the spirituals sung by slaves as a means of dealing with the cruelties of slavery. During Marguerite's eighth-grade graduation, after a white speaker only speaks of limited roles for her and her fellow graduates, she feels bitterness and shame until the valedictorian leads the audience in "Life Ev'ry Voice and Sing," a poem by James Weldon Johnson. Made into a song and considered the "Negro national anthem," this poem helps Marguerite recall the difficult but triumphant struggle her ancestors have been through: "I was no longer simply a member of the proud graduating class of 1940; I was a proud member of the wonderful, beautiful Negro race." And of course, the title of the book makes reference to an inspirational poem by Paul Laurence Dunbar entitled "Sympathy," which recalls themes of freedom and self-discovery.

Historical Context

Conflicts over Civil Rights

Although the action in *I Know Why the Caged Bird Sings* takes place in the early 1930s through the late 1940s, just after World War II had finally ended, the book was published in 1970, at a time of civil unrest and protest in the nation's black communities. The civil rights movement had splintered with the assassination of its chief architect, Dr. Martin Luther King Jr., in April 1968, and protest riots followed. African Americans wavered between following the pacifism that had characterized his leadership and a more outspoken form of protest that had arisen during the last years of King's life. For a time, the latter won out, driven by a climbing black population in many of the nation's major cities. Fueled by outrage over the prejudice, poverty, crime, and unemployment that kept black Americans living in the inner cities—in ar-

Compare
&
Contrast

- **1930s:** Blacks are barred from voting in the South; although this discrimination by race is illegal, states use poll taxes and other laws to restrict voting rights.

  1970: After the Voting Rights Act of 1965 and Civil Rights Act of 1968, racial discrimination is banned from housing, public places, and the voting booth. African Americans begin to successfully run for political office in greater numbers.

  Today: Blacks are entitled to vote all over the United States, many cities in both North and South have black mayors, and many black men and women serve in both the U.S. House and Senate.

- **1930s:** Schools are segregated and unequal, and blacks are blocked from living in white neighborhoods all over the U.S.

  1970: School segregation is illegal, and some courts have even ordered busing to enforce desegregation of schools.

  Today: Enforced desegregation has been successfully challenged in the courts. School segregation and housing discrimination is illegal but persists anyway, as economic factors often split populations into racially divided neighborhoods.

- **1930s:** During the Depression, there are limited job opportunities for African Americans, who face overt prejudice in both the South and North.

  1970: Affirmative Action programs begin to be enacted to offer minorities, including women and blacks, greater access to jobs and education.

  Today: Civil Rights Laws protect the employment rights of blacks and other minorities, although affirmative action programs are themselves being challenged as discriminatory.

- **1930s:** Lynching—a form of vigilante "justice" in which white mobs torture and murder blacks—often goes unpunished.

  1970: Lynching is prosecuted as murder, and is seen less and less, even in the South.

  Today: Racial attacks by mobs on individuals are very rare, although individual crimes are often motivated by racial hatred. Race-related violence is often prosecuted as a separate crime.

---

eas no whites would live—major race riots broke out in Los Angeles, Detroit, Chicago, and New York, among many other cities, resulting in death, injury, and destruction of property. In part, such violence stemmed from a consciousness raised by the Black Power movement, which had gained prominence beginning in 1966. Its tenets overtly pitted blacks against whites. Oakland, California, was home to the Black Panther movement, a group of militant, armed urban youth who advocated the arming of ghetto residents against predatory and racially intolerant police officers. Predictably, these two groups of gun-bearers met head-to-head in a number of violent episodes in California cities. Meanwhile, the Vietnam War preoccupied civil rights workers in King's nonviolence camp. The conflict in southeast Asia was draining valuable financial resources away from the war on poverty within America and also drawing an inordinate number of inner-city youth to their deaths in its faraway jungles.

Black Arts Movement

The written word was a powerful tool in the struggle for African American rights and the creation of a black voice in national affairs. Primarily associated with writer-poet Amiri Baraka (formerly known, when he was a Beat poet, as LeRoi Jones), the black arts movement included members who espoused the philosophy that for black artists to indulge in empty avant-gardism or to create art that was grounded in the personal rather than the political was folly. These members of the black arts movement held that black artists, unlike their mid-

Members of the Ku Klux Klan, a white supremacist group, kneeling around the flag in the 1920s.

dle-class white counterparts, did not have the luxury of refusing to politicize their work. Some young mavericks of the movement openly criticized forerunners like Paul Laurence Dunbar, Jean Toomer, and Langston Hughes, as well as the Harlem Renaissance as a whole, for a presumed lack of social consciousness. Angelou's book came out in striking contrast to the black arts movement since her own personal experience never takes a back seat to the problems of society. However, *I Know Why the Caged Bird Sings* is directed at other blacks, even though Angelou was well aware that a white audience would read it too. This idea of the black arts movement—that black writers must stop protesting to whites and start educating blacks—is one with which Angelou's autobiography is in accord.

The not-so-new South

In the late 1960s, civil rights activists were still struggling to achieve equality in many arenas, just as they had throughout the years Angelou depicts in *Caged Bird*. After the Civil War, hopes ran high among black Americans that their social, political, and economic lot in life would markedly improve. However, white Southerners employed strategies that dashed these hopes and halted the strides made toward civil rights following the war. In response to the Fifteenth Amendment to the U.S. Constitu-

tion, which guaranteed that the right of citizens to vote would not be denied by any state on account of race, Southern states quickly moved to exclude black voters on other, nonracial grounds—for example, an inability to read or to pay a poll tax. Similarly, they passed laws to establish a policy of segregation in society at large.

States could legally force black citizens to live in separate neighborhoods and to use separate telephone booths, restrooms, drinking fountains, cemeteries—and even different Bibles on which to swear in the courtroom. This social situation prevails in Stamps, Arkansas, where Angelou grows up and where a strict color line, marked by the railroad tracks, divides the black from the white parts of town.

Elsewhere in the United States the situation began to change by the mid-1940s, the period in which the autobiography ends. In *Hansberry v. Lee* (1940) the Supreme Court ruled that blacks could not be restricted from purchasing homes in white neighborhoods. And in *Morgan v. Commonwealth of Virginia* (1946) the Court ruled that segregation in interstate bus travel was unconstitutional. Yet there was also violent resistance to such change. A riot broke out, for example, after black welders were assigned to work along with white welders in an Alabama shipyard, and white supremacist groups such as the Ku Klux Klan dedicated themselves to "punishing" blacks for standing up for their rights. They were responsible for many mob killings, known as lynchings; in the 1940s the number of blacks lynched in Arkansas alone since the 1880s had exceeded 200. The practice would not die out completely until the late 1960s and remained a very real threat during the period that Angelou recounts in her autobiography.

Ongoing migration

In the early part of the century, many blacks in the South had to scratch out a living by hiring themselves out to the white landowners as cotton-pickers. As agriculture became more mechanized, this meager source of income dried up. Many black families migrated to northern cities, in hopes of finding jobs in the North's booming industries. The passing of nativist immigration laws in the 1920s provided added impetus to Southern blacks in their northward migration. These new restrictions meant the virtual closing of U.S. borders to the working-class southern and eastern Europeans who had previously made up a large portion of the factory labor force in cities such as New York and Detroit. The void soon became filled by black Americans willing to relocate hundreds of miles for the chance to become industrial workers outside the South. The decades in which *Caged Bird* takes place saw 458,000 blacks leaving the South in the 1930s and 1,345,400 in the 1940s. However, many were also disappointed to find that the North was no cure for racism against blacks. Prejudice just wore a different face.

Prohibition-Era St. Louis

The young characters in *I Know Why the Caged Bird Sings* are in St. Louis during the era of Prohibition (1920-33), when the manufacture and sale of alcohol was outlawed in the United States. During the time of Prohibition, speakeasies and gambling dens became the gathering places of drinkers, gamblers, and pleasure-seekers. Maya's mother undoubtedly was involved in illegal activities in the casinos where she worked. But Prohibition badly damaged U.S. society when the mob moved in and took over the liquor industry. Therefore, it is hard to criticize Maya's mother for breaking a bad law, especially since she was trying to support a family. Prohibition was repealed in 1933, although every Southern state continued to place certain restrictions on liquor—perhaps because of the influence of conservative Christian churches, which traditionally disdained alcohol. In contrast, Northern states abandoned most legislative controls.

Critical Overview

Published in 1970, *I Know Why the Caged Bird Sings* won critical acclaim and was nominated for the National Book Award. Wrote critic Sidonie Ann Smith in *Southern Humanities Review,* "Angelou's genius as a writer is her ability to recapture the texture of the way of life in the texture of its idioms, its idiosyncratic vocabulary and especially in its process of image-making." This book, the first of five in a series describing her life and her continuing search for self-realization, was the best received of the collection. Some posit that the reason is that in her subsequent autobiographical novels, Angelou—who went through many ups and downs in her life—was a less appealing character, though her lifelong achievements thus far seem to belie such criticism.

Critical analysis of Angelou's autobiographical prose has mainly focused on *Caged Bird* and its portrayal of a black woman's coming of age. Assessing the work within the tradition of African American memoirs, George Kent notes in *African American Autobiography: A Collection of Critical Essays* that the work stands out in its use of the imagination: "*I Know Why* creates a unique place within black autobiographical tradition ... by its special stance toward the self, the community, and the universe, and by a form exploiting the full measure of imagination necessary to acknowledge both beauty and absurdity." Other critics have examined the manner in which Angelou's characters survive in a hostile world. Myra K. McMurry, for instance, observes in *South Atlantic Bulletin* how Momma serves as a role model for Marguerite, and indeed for all people fighting racism: "She triumphs not only in spite of her restrictions, but because of them. It is because, as a Black woman, she must maintain the role of respect toward the white children that she discovers another vehicle for her true emotions. She has used her cage creatively to transcend it." Suzette A. Henke suggests in *Traditions, Voices, and Dreams* that this autobiographical work, in presenting a voice that is not often heard, "has the potential to be ... a revolutionary form of writing." In the "comic and triumphant" end of the novel, writes Henke, Marguerite's "victory suggests an implicit triumph over the white bourgeoisie [middle class], whose values have flagrantly been subverted."

While the work has been praised, analyzed, and taught in classrooms, it has also met with censorship. The graphic portrayal of Marguerite's rape as well as the acceptance of her teenage, out-of-wedlock pregnancy have inspired the most challenges. However, Opal Moore suggests that these events offer students a chance to examine important issues. As she writes in *Censored Books: Critical Viewpoints:* "With the appropriate effort, this literary experience can assist readers of any racial or economic group in meeting their own, often unarticulated doubts, questions, fears, and perhaps assist in their own search for dignity."

Criticism

Edward E. Eller

Eller is an assistant professor of English at Northeast Louisiana University. In the following essay, he examines how the autobiographical story of Marguerite Johnson can stand in for the larger experience of African Americans fighting racism.

Encouraged by her editor and family to remember and write about her childhood, Maya Angelou produced the first of five autobiographies and the literary work for which she is probably best known, *I Know Why the Caged Bird Sings.* She acknowledges them by writing, "I thank my mother, Vivian Baxter, and my bother, Bailey Johnson, who encouraged me to remember. And a final thanks to my editor at Random House, Robert Loomis, who gently prodded me back into the lost years." Perhaps those memories have assisted her in her diverse and incredibly productive career. In addition to the autobiographies generally recognized as a sort of "never-finished canvas," Angelou has published volumes of poetry, composed musical scores, and worked as a freelance writer and editor in America and abroad. She has also written, directed, and acted on stage and screen, and recited for the world her poem *On the Pulse of the Morning* for President Bill Clinton's 1993 inauguration.

Whatever the medium or type of artistic endeavor, Angelou most often celebrates the endurance and triumph of the individual over adversity. As Angelou says, "I speak to the black experience but I am always talking about the human condition—about what we can endure, dream, fail at, and still survive." When we read *I Know Why the Caged Bird Sings,* we may at first wonder

how anyone could survive that childhood, but we come to realize the answers to that survival.

Of course, there are many ways to interpret this book. Some critics look for its formal literary devices such as imagery or symbols. Most recognize it as a type of *bildungsroman* or a "coming of age" book that traces individual, social, and intellectual development. Others take the book's organization and link that to a more personal, coming to political-social awareness on Angelou's part. One critic, Pierre A. Walker, maintains that the structure "reveals a sequence that leads Maya progressively from helpless rage and indignation to forms of subtle resistance, and finally to outright and active protest." In other words, Maya starts out helpless and angry about social injustices, then learns how to resist without confrontation, and finally actively and vocally protests racism and oppression.

All these interpretations make valid points, as do many others. However, Angelou herself points us to one of the most important aspects of the book. In an interview, she relates how many people come up to her and say, "I just wrote, I mean, I just *read* your book." Angelou understands these slips of the tongue to mean that the readers identity with her in the book, as if it were their own autobiography. In fact, if we focus on the contrasts in *Caged Bird,* then we see a young, black girl's coming-of-age in the America of the 1930s and 1940s that shows us what it means, or can mean, to be human.

Contrasts and opposites fill the book, and many are quite obvious. Over and over again, the girl Marguerite (Maya) compares herself to her brother Bailey. While he is handsome, quick, and glib, she refers to herself as ugly, awkward, and tongue-tied. In Stamps, Arkansas, where the children spend much of their childhood, nothing much happens except the same rounds of chores, schoolwork, church, and helping Momma and Uncle Willie in the Store. Maya says of this sameness, "The country had been in the throes of the Depression two years before the Negroes in Stamps knew it." The town was so segregated that the children can hardly believe that whites are real.

On the other hand, St. Louis and San Francisco teem with activities and peoples. There are bars and restaurants and music and dancing with their mother in St. Louis and the boom of wartime later in San Francisco where the streets are crowded with soldiers and workers of all nationalities. Momma may be strong and smart, but her darkness and countrified speech sometimes make Maya cringe. Grandmother Baxter, though, is "nearly white," a trained professional nurse, with a German accent. Other contrasts, however, come upon us more subtly, in part because of the *episodic* structure of the book. Almost every chapter reads as a complete short story or episode that doesn't need all the other details of the book to be understood. Every episode contains its contrasts as well.

How many of us have not imagined ourselves different than the way we are, especially when we're young? This sort of imagining on the part of young Maya opens *Caged Bird* and shows us the first of many contrasts. The young girl stands before the Colored Methodist Episcopal Church congregation in Stamps, Arkansas. She wears a cut-down, redone white woman's dress. It is made of taffeta, however, and the girl feels that this material makes up for its "awful" lavender color. She just knew that when people saw her in that dress that her grandmother, Momma, had done over by hand, that they would recognize her real self. Her "real hair, which was long and blonde, would take the place of that kinky mass, and her light blue eyes would hypnotize them." They would come to understand why she didn't pick up a Southern accent or the common slang, and why she had to be "forced to eat pigs tails and snouts." She "was really white" and self-assured as a movie star, just now under "a cruel fairy stepmother's spell" that had turned her into "a too-big Negro girl with nappy black hair, broad feet and a space between her teeth that would hold a number two pencil." But here on Easter morning she ends up mumbling her lines and running out. Angelou ends this episode, "If growing up is painful for the Southern Black girl, being aware of her own displacement is the rust on the razor that threatens the throat. It is an unnecessary insult." It is painful to be aware. It is painful to be separate.

The reality of herself, the imagined self, and this sense of displacement must eventually be reconciled. As she matures, she sheds the notion of becoming white and comes to be proud of her race and her heritage. After her period of silence and under the tutelage of the gentlewoman, Miss Bertha Flowers, "our side's answer to the richest white woman in town," she learned she must "always be intolerant of ignorance, but understanding of illiteracy." She learned from Miss Flowers that mute words on a page take life when "infused" with the human voice. She takes extreme pride in Momma's standing up and speaking out to the white dentist (the only dentist in Stamps) who wouldn't treat Maya's toothache because he'd "sooner stick his hand in a dog's mouth." Although her imaginings

What Do I Read Next?

- Other autobiographical volumes by Maya Angelou include *Gather Together in My Name* (1974), *Singin' and Swingin' and Gettin' Merry Like Christmas* (1976), *The Heart of a Woman* (1981), and *All God's Children Need Traveling Shoes* (1986).

- Alice Walker's *The Color Purple* (1982) tells of the spiritual and personal awakening of a young black woman oppressed by racism and sexual abuse.

- *The Bluest Eye* (1969) by Nobel Prize-winner Toni Morrison relates a similar story of a young black girl trying to grow up in a racist world, but with a different ending.

- Harper Lee's *To Kill a Mockingbird* (1960), in which a country lawyer in a deep-South town in the 1930s represents a black man falsely accused of raping a white woman.

- *Light in August* (1932) by William Faulkner tells of the pursuit and eventual torture and murder of a black man suspected of sleeping with a white woman.

of that "showdown" are quite different than the reality, Maya knows the difference this time, liking her own version better.

Maya wrestles to come to terms with other contradictions that do not make sense. Joe Louis successfully defends the heavyweight championship title, yet the people listening to the fight on the Store's radio must stay with friends close by. "It wouldn't do for a Black man and his family to be caught on a lonely country road on a night when Joe Louis had proved we were the strongest people in the world." She feels anger at her grammar school graduation when the white school official, Donleavy, speaks of the future for the white and black schools. The white school will get "new microscopes and chemistry equipment" while the black students would get a playing field. "The white kids were going to have the chance to become Galileos and Madame Curries" while we would be athletes, "maids and farmers, handymen and washerwomen." The man with his "dead words" had killed the promise and hope of the occasion. But she then revels in the triumph as the valedictorian Henry Reed gives his address, "To Be or Not to Be," and turns to the class, leading them in "Lift Ev'ry Voice and Sing" so that the time was theirs again, or as Maya says, "We were on top again. As always, again. We survived. The depths had been icy and dark, but now a bright sun spoke to our souls. I was no longer simply a member of the proud graduating class of 1940; I was a proud member of the wonderful, beautiful Negro race." She has resolved the conflict of white perceptions and actions with the reality and the triumphant spirit of her community's endurance. However, the hardest to reconcile surely comes with the brutal rape of her as a child.

When Angelou writes about the rape she suffered from her mother's boyfriend in St. Louis, she describes this horrible violation with a reference to a biblical passage. "The act of rape on an eight-year-old body is a matter of the needle giving because the camel can't. The child gives, because the body can, and the mind of the violator can't." The biblical language and reference connects this horrifying episode to a spiritual tent revival she later attends in Stamps. She relates, "Hadn't He Himself said it would be easier for a camel to go through the eye of a needle than for a rich man to enter heaven?" This connection seems impossibly contradictory. One act is of violation and oppression that results in Mr. Freeman's death and five years of fearful silence for Maya. The other act involves redemption and affirmation of life everlasting. How does one reconcile brutality here and the promise of milk and honey?

Just as the child had to give in to her rapist because she had no choice but to endure and survive, the blacks had no choice. The songs at the revival and songs heard from the honky-tonk as people walked home "asked the same questions. How long, oh God? How long?" How many times would black men have to hide in the cellars because some crowd is out for blood? How long would Momma bear with stoic composure white girls' insults? How long must any of us try to reconcile the contradictions of bigotry or sexism? Or any of the injustices people seem so intent on inflicting on another? Surely, Angelou's answer would be, as long a necessary for survival and not a moment longer. When we resolve those contradictions in our own lives, those opposites that exist simultaneously, we

find the courage to be human. As we overcome those conflicts, we learn to survive because we must. Because we are human. Because Angelou shows us we can do more than endure. We can triumph. "Can't do is like Don't Care. Neither of them have a home."

Source: Edward E. Eller, in an essay for *Novels for Students,* Gale, 1997.

Opal Moore

In this excerpt, Moore enumerates the challenges that have been brought forth against I Know Why the Caged Bird Sings *and explains why she believes it to be a positive reading experience for young people.*

I Know Why the Caged Bird Sings, the autobiography of Maya Angelou, is the story of one girl's growing up. But, like any literary masterpiece, the story of this one black girl declaring "I can" to a color-coded society that in innumerable ways had told her "you can't, you won't" transcends its author. It is an affirmation; it promises that life, if we have the courage to live it, will be worth the struggle. A book of this description might seem good reading for junior high and high school students. According to People for the American Way, however, *Caged Bird* was the ninth "most frequently challenged book" in American school. *Caged Bird* elicits criticism for its honest depiction of rape, its exploration of the ugly spectre of racism in America, its recounting of the circumstances of Angelou's own out-of-wedlock teen pregnancy, and its humorous poking at the foibles of the institutional church. Arguments advocating that *Caged Bird* be banned from school reading lists reveal that the complainants, often parents, tend to regard any treatment of these kinds of subject matter in school as inappropriate—despite the fact that the realities and issues of sexuality and violence, in particular, are commonplace in contemporary teenage intercourse and discourse. The children, they imply, are too innocent for such depictions; they might be harmed by the truth.

This is a curious notion—that seriousness should be banned from the classroom while beyond the classroom, the irresponsible and sensational exploitation of sexual, violent, and profane materials is as routine as the daily dose of soap opera. The degradation of feeling caused by slurs directed against persons for their race/class/sex/sexual preference is one of the more difficult hurdles of youthful rites of passage. But it's not just bad TV or the meanness of children. More and more, society is serving an unappetizing fare on a child-sized plate—television screens, t-shirt sloganeers, and weak politicians admonish children to "say 'no' to drugs and drugpushers"; to be wary of strangers; to have safe sex; to report their own or other abusing parents, relatives or neighbors; to be wary of friends; to recognize the signs of alcoholism; to exercise self control in the absence of parental or societal controls; even to take their Halloween candy to the hospital to be x-rayed before consumption. In response to these complications in the landscape of childhood, parent groups, religious groups, and media have called for educators to "bring morality back into the classroom" while we "get back to basics" in a pristine atmosphere of moral non-complexity, outside of the context of the very real world that is squeezing in on that highly touted childhood innocence every single day.

Our teenagers are inundated with the discouragements of life. Ensconced in a literal world, they are shaping their life choices within the dichotomies of TV ads: Bud Light vs. "A mind is a terrible thing to waste." Life becomes a set of skewed and cynical oppositions: "good" vs. easy; yes vs. "catch me"; "right" vs. expediency.

In truth, what young readers seem most innocent of these days is not sex, murder, or profanity, but concepts of self empowerment, faith, struggle as quest, the nobility of intellectual inquiry, survival, and the nature and complexity of moral choice. *Caged Bird* offers these seemingly abstract (adult) concepts to a younger audience that needs to know that their lives are not inherited or predestined, that they can be participants in an exuberant struggle to subjugate traditions of ignorance and fear. Critics of this book might tend to overlook or devalue the necessity of such insights for the young.

Caged Bird's critics imply an immorality in the work based on the book's images. However, it is through Angelou's vivid depictions of human spiritual triumph *set against a backdrop* of human weakness and failing that the autobiography speaks dramatically about moral choice. Angelou paints a picture of some of the negative choices: white America choosing to oppress groups of people; choosing lynch law over justice; choosing intimidation over honor. She offers, however, "deep talk" on the possibility of positive choices: choosing life over death (despite the difficulty of that life); choosing courage over safety; choosing discipline over chaos; choosing voice over silence; choosing compassion over pity, over hatred, over habit;

choosing work and planning and hope over useless recrimination and slovenly despair. The book's detractors seem unwilling to admit that morality is not edict (or an innate property of innocence), but the learned capacity for judgement, and that the necessity of moral choice arises only in the presence of the soul's imperfection.

Self empowerment, faith, struggle as quest, survival, intellectual curiosity, complexity of choice—these ideas are the underpinning of Maya Angelou's story. To explore these themes, the autobiography poses its own set of oppositions: Traditional society and values vs. contemporary society and its values; silence vs. self expression; literacy vs. the forces of oppression; the nature of generosity vs. the nature of cruelty; spirituality vs. ritual. Every episode of *Caged Bird,* engages these and other ideas in Maya Angelou's portrait of a young girl's struggle against adversity—a struggle against rape: rape of the body, the soul, the mind, the future, of expectation, of tenderness—towards identity and self affirmation. If we cannot delete rape from our lives, should we delete it from a book about life?

Caged Bird opens with the poignant, halting voice of Marguerite Johnson, the young Maya Angelou, struggling for her own voice beneath the vapid doggerel of the yearly Easter pageant:

"What you lookin at me for?"

"I didn't come to stay...."

These two lines prefigure the entire work. "What you lookin at me for..." is the painful question of every black girl made selfconscious and self doubting by a white world critical of her very existence. The claim that she "didn't come to stay" increases in irony as the entire work ultimately affirms the determination of Marguerite Johnson and, symbolically, all of the unsung survivors of the Middle Passage, to do that very thing—to stay. To stay is to affirm life and the possibility of redemption. To stay—despite the circumstance of our coming (slavery), despite the efforts to remove us (lynching) or make us invisible (segregation).

Angelou, in disarmingly picturesque and humorous scenes like this opening glimpse of her girl-self forgetting her lines and wetting her pants in her earliest effort at public speech, continually reminds us that we survive the painfulness of life by the tender stabilities of family and community. As she hurries from the church trying to beat the wetness coursing down her thighs, she hears the benedictory murmurs of the old church ladies saying, "Lord bless the child," and "Praise God."

This opening recitation lays a metaphorical foundation for the autobiography, and for our understanding of the trauma of rape that causes Marguerite to stifle her voice for seven years. In some ways, the rape of Marguerite provides the center and the bottom of this autobiographical statement.

Critics of the work charge that the scenes of seduction and rape are too graphically rendered:

> He [Mr. Freeman] took my hand and said, "Feel it." It was mushy and squirmy like the inside of a freshly killed chicken. Then he dragged me on top of his chest with his left arm, and his right hand was moving so fast and his heart was beating so hard that I was afraid that he would die.... Finally he was quiet, and then came the nice part. He held me so softly that I wished he wouldn't ever let me go.

The seeming ambivalence of this portrait of the dynamics of interfamilial rape elicits distaste among those who prefer, if rape must be portrayed at all, for it to be painted with the hard edges of guilt and innocence. Yet, this portrait reflects the sensibilities of eight-year-old Marguerite Johnson—full of her barely understood longings and the vulnerability of ignorance:

> ... Mama had drilled into my head: "Keep your legs closed, and don't let nobody see your pocketbook."

Mrs. Baxter has given her daughter that oblique homespun wisdom designed to delay the inevitable. Such advice may forewarn, but does not forearm and, characteristic of the period, does not even entertain the unthinkable improbability of the rape of a child. Aside from this vague caution, and the knowledge that "lots of people did 'it' and they used their 'things' to accomplish the deed...," Marguerite does not know how to understand or respond to the gentle, seemingly harmless Mr. Freeman because he is "family," he is an adult (not to be questioned), and he offers her what appears to be the tenderness she craves that had not been characteristic of her strict southern upbringing.

When asked why she included the rape in her autobiography, Angelou has said [in *Conversations with Maya Angelou,* edited by Jeffrey M. Elliot], "I wanted people to see that the man was not totally an ogre." And it is this fact that poses one of the difficulties of rape and the inability of children, intellectually unprepared, to protect themselves. If the rapists were all terrible ogres and strangers in dark alleys, it would be easier to know when to run, when to scream, when to "say no." But the devastation of rape is subtle in its horror and betrayal which creates in Marguerite feelings of complicity in her own assault. When queried by Mr. Freeman's defense attorney about whether Mr. Freeman had

ever touched her on occasions before the rape, Marguerite, recalling that first encounter, realizes immediately something about the nature of language, its inflexibility, its inability to render the whole truth, and the palpable danger of being misunderstood:

> I couldn't ... tell them how he had loved me once for a few minutes and how he had held me close before he thought I had peed in my bed. My uncles would kill me and Grandmother Baxter would stop speaking, as she often did when she was angry. And all those people in the court would stone me as they had stoned the harlot in the Bible. And Mother, who thought I was such a good girl, would be so disappointed. But most important, there was Bailey. I had kept a big secret from him.

To protect herself, Marguerite lies: "Everyone in the court knew that the answer had to be No. Everyone except Mr. Freeman and me."

Some schools that have chosen not to ban *Caged Bird* completely have compromised by deleting "those rape chapters." It should be clear, however, that this portrayal of rape is hardly titillating or "pornographic." It raises issues of trust, truth and lie, love, the naturalness of a child's craving for human contact, language and understanding, and the confusion engendered by the power disparities that necessarily exist between children and adults. High school students should be given the opportunity to gain insight into these subtleties of human relationships and entertain the "moral" questions raised by the work....

Caged Bird, in this scene so often deleted from classroom study, opens the door for discussion about the prevalent confusion between a young person's desire for affection and sexual invitation. Certainly, this is a valuable distinction to make, and one that young men and women are often unable to perceive or articulate. Angelou also reveals the manner by which an adult manipulates a child's desire for love as a thin camouflage for his own crude motives. A further complication to the neat assignment of blame is that Marguerite's lie is not prompted by a desire to harm Mr. Freeman, but out of her feelings of helplessness and dread. Yet, she perceives that the effect of that lie is profound—so profound that she decides to stop her own voice, both as penance for the death of Mr. Freeman and out of fear of the power of her words: "... a man was dead because I had lied."

This dramatization of the ambiguity of truth and the fearfulness of an Old Testament justice raises questions of justice and the desirability of truth in a world strapped in fear, misunderstanding, and the inadequacy of language. The story reveals how violence can emerge out of the innocent routines of life; how betrayal can be camouflaged with blame; that adults are individual and multidimensional and flawed; but readers also see how Marguerite overcomes this difficult and alienating episode of her life.

However, the work's complexity is a gradual revelation. The rape must be read within the context of the entire work from the stammer of the opening scene, to the elegant Mrs. Flowers who restores Marguerite's confidence in her own voice to the book's closing affirmation of the forgiving power of love and faith. Conversely, all of these moments should be understood against the ravaging of rape.

Marguerite's story is emblematic of the historic struggle of an entire people and, by extension, any person or group of people. The autobiography moves from survival to celebration of life and students who are permitted to witness Marguerite's suffering and ascendancy might gain in the nurturing of their own potential for compassion, optimism and courage....

If parents are concerned about anything, it should be the paucity of assigned readings in the junior high and high school classrooms, and the quality of the classroom teaching approach for this (and any other) worthwhile book.... *Caged Bird* establishes oppositions of place and time: Stamps, Arkansas vs. St. Louis and San Francisco; the 1930s of the book's opening vs. the slave origins of Jim Crow, which complicate images related to certain cultural aspects of African-American life including oral story traditions, traditional religious beliefs and practices, ideas regarding discipline and displays of affection, and other materials which bring richness and complexity to the book, but that, without clarification, can invite misapprehension. For example, when Marguerite smashes Mrs. Cullinan's best pieces of "china from Virginia" by "accident," the scene is informative when supported by its parallels in traditional African-American folklore, by information regarding the significance of naming in traditional society, and the cultural significance of the slave state practice of depriving Africans of their true names and cultural past. The scene, though funny, should not be treated as mere comic relief, or as a meaningless act of revenge. Mrs. Cullinan, in insisting upon "re-naming" Marguerite Mary, is carrying forward that enslaving technique designed to subvert identity; she is testing what she believes is her prerogative as a white

person—to establish *who* a black person will be, to call a black person by any name she chooses. She is "shock[ed] into recognition of [Marguerite's] personhood" ([as Angelou writes in] *Black Women Writers*). She learns that her name game is a very dangerous power play that carries with it a serious risk.

With sufficient grounding, *I Know Why the Caged Bird Sings* can provide the kinds of insights into American history and culture, its values, practices, beliefs, lifestyles, and its seeming contradictions that inspired James Baldwin to describe the work, on its cover, as one that "liberates the reader into life simply because Maya Angelou confronts her own life with such a moving wonder, such a luminous dignity," and as "... a Biblical study of life in the midst of death." A book that has the potential to liberate the reader into life is one that deserves our intelligent consideration, not rash judgements made from narrow fearfulness. Such a work will not "teach students a lesson." It will demand an energetic, participatory reading. It will demand their seriousness. With the appropriate effort, this literary experience can assist readers of any racial or economic group in meeting their own, often unarticulated doubts, questions, fears, and perhaps assist in their own search for dignity.

Source: Opal Moore, "Learning to Live: When the Bird Breaks from the Cage," in *Censored Books: Critical Viewpoints,* Nicholas J. Karolides, Lee Burress, John M. Kean, eds., 1993, pp. 306–16.

Myra K. McMurry

In this excerpt, McMurry explores the image of the caged bird as a symbol of Angelou's struggle for self-realization in spite of the rigid roles that threatened her individuality.

As a songwriter, journalist, playwright, poet, fiction and screenwriter, Maya Angelou is often asked how she escaped her past. How does one grow up, Black and female, in the rural South of the thirties and forties without being crippled or hardened? Her immediate response [in an interview by Sheila Weller for Intellectual Digest,] "How the hell do you know I did escape?" is subtly deceptive. The evidence of Angelou's creative accomplishments would indicate that she did escape; but a closer look reveals the human and artistic complexity of her awareness. For the first volume of her autobiography, *I Know Why the Caged Bird Sings,* is not an exorcism of or escape from the past, but a transmutation of that past. The almost novelistic clarity of *Caged Bird* results from the artistic tension between Angelou's recollected self and her authorial consciousness. Implicit in this dual awareness is the knowledge that events are significant not merely in themselves, but also because they have been transcended.

Angelou takes her title from Paul Laurence Dunbar's poem, "Sympathy." Dunbar's caged bird sings from the frustration of imprisonment; its song is a prayer. Angelou's caged bird sings also from frustration, but in doing so, discovers that the song transforms the cage from a prison that denies selfhood to a vehicle for self-realization. The cage is a metaphor for roles which, because they have become institutionalized and static, do not facilitate interrelationship, but impose patterns of behavior which deny true identity.

In *Caged Bird* Angelou describes her efforts to adapt to the role of a young Black girl, the painfully humorous failures, and the gradual realization of how to transcend the restrictions. At a very early age, the child Angelou, Marguerite Johnson, is an intensely self-conscious child; she feels that her true self is obscured. The autobiography opens with an episode in which Marguerite must recite a poem beginning, "What you looking at me for?" As she struggles for her lines in the Easter morning church service, she is conscious of her dual self, which is the constant subject of her fantasies. Beneath the ugly disguise—the lavender dress cut-down from a white woman's throwaway, the skinny legs, broad feet, nappy hair, and teeth with a space between—was the real Marguerite Johnson, a sweet little white girl with long blond hair, "everybody's dream of what was right with the world." She mixes elements of fairy tale and Easter story to imagine that a cruel fairy stepmother had changed her from her true self to her present condition. And she relishes the recognition scene in which people will say, " 'Marguerite (sometimes it was "dear Marguerite"), forgive us, please, we didn't know who you were,' and [she] would answer generously, 'No, you couldn't have known. Of course I forgive you.' " This introductory episode is emblematic of the child's perspective. She is in a cage which conceals and denies her true nature, and she is aware of her displacement. Someone whispers the forgotten lines and she completes the poem, which suggests transcendence:

What you looking at me for?

I didn't come to stay.

I just come to tell you it's Easter Day.

But for Marguerite there is no transcendence. After painful confinement in the humiliating situation, the pressure of her true self to escape takes on a physical urgency. She signals request to go to the toilet and starts up the aisle. But one of the children trips her and her utmost control is then effective only as far as the front porch. In her view the choice was between wetting her pants or dying of a "busted head," for what was denied proper vent would surely back up to her head and cause an explosion and "the brains and spit and tongue and eyes would roll all over the place." The physical violence of the destruction imagined is the child's equivalent for the emotional violence of self-repression.

In Marguerite's world, rigid laws govern every aspect of a child's life: there are laws for addressing adults by proper title, laws for speaking and more for not speaking, laws about cleanliness and obedience, and about performance in school and behavior in church. Although she respects her brother Bailey for his ability to evade some laws, Marguerite is an obedient child. Her transgressions come, not of willful disobedience, but from loss of control in confrontations in which she is physically overpowered by a larger force.

Much of the story of growing up as Marguerite Johnson is the story of learning to control natural responses. Not to laugh at funny incidents in church, not to express impatience when the guest preacher says too long a blessing and ruins the dinner, not to show felt fear, are part of preparation for life in a repressive society.

Although much of Marguerite's repression is related to her being a child, the caged condition affects almost everyone in her world. The customers in her grandmother's store were trapped in the cotton fields; no amount of hope and work could get them out. Bailey, for all his clever manipulations, was "locked in the enigma ... of inequality and hate." Her Uncle Willie's own body is his cage. Marguerite observes with the sensitivity of the adult Angelou looking back that he "must have tired of being crippled, as prisoners tire of penitentiary bars and the guilty tire of blame." When Marguerite catches Uncle Willie pretending not to be crippled before some out-of-town visitors, she finds the common condition of being caged and the desire to escape ground for sympathy. "I understood and felt closer to him in that moment than ever before or since."

Even the indomitable grandmother, Anne Henderson, rises each morning with the consciousness of a caged animal. She prays, "Guide my feet this day along the straight and narrow, and help me to put a bridle on my tongue." But it is from her that Marguerite begins to learn how to survive in the cage. Angelou recalls a particular incident that happened when she was about ten years old in which she began to realize her grandmother's triumph. Momma, as Marguerite calls her, has come onto the porch to admire a design that Marguerite had raked in the yard. At the approach of some troublesome "powhitetrash" children, Momma sends Marguerite inside where she cowers behind the screen door. Momma stands solidly on the porch humming a hymn. The impudent children tease, mimic, and insult the older, respectable woman who, by any measure that Marguerite can think of, is their superior. As Marguerite watches and suffers humiliation for her grandmother, she wants to scream at the girls and throw lye on them, but she realizes that she is "as clearly imprisoned behind the scene as the actors outside are confined to their roles." Throughout the performance, Momma stands humming so softly that Marguerite knows she is humming only because her apron strings vibrate. After the children leave, Momma comes inside and Marguerite sees that she is beautiful; her face is radiant. As Momma hums "Glory, glory, hallelujah, when I lay my burden down," Marguerite realizes that whatever the contest had been, Momma had won. Marguerite goes back to her raking and makes a huge heart design with little hearts inside growing smaller toward the center, and draws an arrow piercing through all the hearts to the smallest one. Then she brings Momma to see. In essence she is using the design to organize feelings she could not otherwise order or express, just as Momma has used the song to organize her thoughts and feelings beyond the range of the children's taunts. She triumphs not only in spite of her restrictions, but because of them. It is because, as a Black woman, she must maintain the role of respect toward the white children that she discovers another vehicle for her true emotions. She has used her cage creatively to transcend it.

The same principle works for a group as well as for an individual. What Maya Angelou had understood intuitively or subconsciously as a ten-year-old comes to the level of conscious realization after her eighth-grade graduation. Marguerite's graduation ceremony begins in an aura of magic, but just after the national anthem and the pledge of allegiance, the point at which they normally would have sung the song they considered to be the Negro national anthem, the principal nervously signals the students to be seated. Then he introduces as commencement speaker a white politician who is on his way to another engagement and must speak out of order so that he can leave. His speech and the suppression of feeling his mere presence entails are humiliating reminders to the students of the restrictive white world in which they live. He talks of plans for an artist to teach at Central High, the white school, and of new microscopes and equipment for the Chemistry labs at Central. For Lafayette County Training School he promises the "only colored paved playing field in that part of Arkansas" and some equipment for the home economics building and the workshop. The implications of his talk are crushing to the graduates. For Marguerite the occasion is ruined; she remembers that

> Graduation, the hush-hush magic time of frills and gifts and congratulations and diplomas, was finished for me before my name was called. The accomplishment was nothing. The meticulous maps, drawn in three colors of ink, learning and spelling decasyllabic words, memorizing the whole of The Rape of Lucrece—it was for nothing. Donleavy had exposed us.

> We were maids and farmers, handymen and washerwomen, and anything higher that we aspired to was farcical and presumptuous.

The white politician rushes off to his next engagement, leaving a gloom over the ceremony. One student recites "Invictus"—"I am the master of my fate, I am the captain of my soul"—but now it is a farce. As Henry Reed, the valedictorian, gives his address, Marguerite wonders that he could go on. But at the end, Henry turns to the graduates and begins to sing the song omitted earlier, the Negro national anthem. The students, parents and visitors respond to the familiar song—their own song, and as they sing, "We have come over a way that with tears has been watered, / We have come, treading our path through the blood of the slaughtered," the separate, isolated individuals become a community with a common soul:

> We were on top again. As always again. We survived. The depths had been icy and dark, but now a bright sun spoke to our souls. I was no longer simply a member of the proud graduating class of 1940; I was a proud member of the wonderful, beautiful Negro race.

Source: Myra K. McMurry, "Role-Playing as Art in Maya Angelou's *Caged Bird*," in *South Atlantic Bulletin,* No. 2, May, 1976, pp. 106–11.

Sources

Suzette A. Henke, "Women's Life-Writing and the Minority Voice: Maya Angelou, Maxine Hong Kingston, and Alice Walker," in *Traditions, Voices, and Dreams: The American Novel since the 1960s,* edited by Melvin J. Friedman and Ben Siegel, University of Delaware Press, 1995, pp. 210-33.

George Kent, "Maya Angelou's 'I Know Why the Caged Bird Sings' and Black Autobiographical Tradition," in *African American Autobiography: A Collection of Critical Essays,* Prentice-Hall, 1993, pp. 162-70.

Myra K. McMurry, "Role-Playing as Art in Maya Angelou's *Caged Bird,"* in *South Atlantic Bulletin,* No. 2, May, 1976, pp. 106–11.

Opal Moore, "Learning to Live: When the Bird Breaks from the Cage," in *Censored Books: Critical Viewpoints,* Nicholas J. Karolides, Lee Burress, John M. Kean, eds., 1993, pp. 306–16.

Sidonie Ann Smith, "The Song of a Caged Bird: Maya Angelou's Quest after Self-Acceptance," in *The Southern Humanities Review,* Fall, 1973, pp. 365–75.

For Further Study

James Bertolino, "Maya Angelou Is Three Writers: I Know Why the Caged Bird Sings," in *Censored Books: Critical Viewpoints,* edited by N. J. Karolides, L. Burgess, and J. M. Kean, The Scarecrow Press, 1993, pp. 299-305.

Bertolino views Angelou as a gifted shaper of words and literary devices, an intensely honest person, and an important social commentator.

Jeffrey M. Elliot, editor, *Conversations with Maya Angelou,* University of Mississippi Press, 1989.

An insightful collection of reprinted interviews with Angelou.

Onita Estes-Hicks, "The Way We Were: Precious Memories of the Black Segregated South," in *African American Review,* Vol. 27, No. 1, pp. 9-18.

Estes-Hicks places Angelou's autobiography within the tradition of Black Southern autobiographies by comparing and contrasting with other writers.

Mary Jane Lupton, "Singing the Black Mother: Maya Angelou and Autobiographical Continuity," in *Black American Literature Forum,* Vol. 24, No. 2, Summer 1990, pp. 257-76.

Discusses the unifying theme of motherhood in Angelou's autobiographies.

Carol E. Neubauer, "Maya Angelou: Self and a Song of Freedom in the Southern Tradition," in *Southern Women Writers: The New Generation,* edited by T. Bond Inge, The University of Alabama Press, 1990, pp. 114-42.

Summarizes Angelou's career and discusses recurring themes in her poetry, including "Caged Bird."

Sondra O'Neale, "Reconstruction of the Composite Self: New Images of Black Women in Maya Angelou's Continuing Autobiography," in *Black Women Writers (1950-1980): A Critical Evaluation,* edited by M. Evans, Anchor Press/Doubleday, 1984, pp. 25–37.

O'Neale discusses Angelou's racial identification and how she subverts stereotypical ideas of the Black Woman.

Mary Vermillion, "Reembodying the Self: Representations of Rape in 'Incidents in the Life of a Slave Girl' and 'I Know Why the Caged Bird Sings',", in *Biography,* Vol. 15, No. 3, Summer, 1992, pp. 243-60.

Vermillion gives a sensitive and perceptive discussion of the rape and its connection to a larger theme of oppression in the autobiography.

Pierre A. Walker, "Racial Protest, Identity, Words, and Form in Maya Angelou's 'I Know Why the Caged Bird Sings', " in *College Literature,* Vol. 222, Oct. 1995, pp. 91-108.

Walker focuses on the literary qualities to assert the autobiography traces the steps of the author's political self from racial helplessness to active protest.

Invisible Man

Ralph Ellison
1952

At its appearance in 1952, *Invisible Man* was immediately hailed as a masterpiece. A work both epic and richly comic, it won the National Book Award for its author, Ralph Ellison. *Invisible Man* has been translated into fourteen languages and has never been out of print. A 1965 Book Week poll of two hundred writers and critics selected it as the most distinguished novel of the previous twenty years. Written in the style of a *bildungsroman,* or novel of education, the book chronicles the sometimes absurd adventures of a young black man whose successful search for identity ends with the realization that he is invisible to the white world. *Invisible Man* is structurally complex and densely symbolic; some critics, in fact, faulted it for what they saw as literary excess. A major controversy centered on the book's intended audience: some black critics argued that it was or should have been a "race" novel, while white critics were relieved that it was not. It also aroused the ire of black nationalists for sacrificing the broader concerns of black nationhood in the defense of a narrow individualism. This contentiousness dissipated over time, however, and the novel's enduring qualities are now undisputed. *Invisible Man* deals with themes of individuality, identity, history, and responsibility. The protagonist is repeatedly exhorted to look beneath the surface of things. Although Ellison freely acknowledged his debt to both European and African American literary traditions, he used an astonishing range of African American folk forms in constructing his protagonist's universe.

Critics agree that the influence of *Invisible Man* on American literature in general, and its role in bringing the blues and folklore into the mainstream of black experience in particular, is incalculable.

Author Biography

As a boy, Ralph Waldo Ellison announced that his ambition was to become a Renaissance man. "I was taken very early," he would write, "with a passion to link together all I loved within the Negro community and all those things I felt in the world which lay beyond." Ellison was born on March 1, 1914, in Oklahoma City, Oklahoma, to Ida Millsap and Lewis Ellison, who died when Ralph was three. Ellison's mother worked tirelessly to provide a stimulating environment for Ralph and his brother, and her influence on the writer was profound.

In 1933, at the age of nineteen, Ellison hopped a freight train to Tuskegee Institute in Macon County, Alabama, where he majored in music. In the summer of 1935 he traveled north to New York City to earn money for his last year in college; he never returned to Tuskegee. Instead, he stayed in New York and worked for a year as a freelance photographer, file clerk, and builder and seller of hi-fi systems, still intending a career in music. But then Richard Wright, the noted author of *Black Boy* and *Native Son,* invited him to write a book review for the 1937 issue of *New Challenge,* and Ellison's career was decided.

In 1938 Ellison joined the Federal Writers Project, which gave him opportunities to do research and to write, and helped to build his appreciation of folklore. Like other black intellectuals in the 1930s, he found the Communist party's active anti-racist stance appealing, but Ellison was also a fervent individualist, and he never became a party member. During 1942 Ellison was managing editor of the *Negro Quarterly,* but thereafter he turned to writing stories. Two of his most acclaimed stories before the publication of *Invisible Man* were "Flying Home" (1944) and "King of the Bingo Game" (1944); both dealt with questions of identity. Ellison met Fanny McConnell in 1944, and the couple married in 1946.

During World War II Ellison served as a cook in the merchant marines. He returned to the United States in 1945 and began *Invisible Man.* The novel appeared in 1952 and was a commercial and critical success, winning the National Book Award in

Ralph Ellison

1953, although some black nationalists felt the novel was not political enough. Ellison continued to write short stories, and in 1964 he published *Shadow and Act,* a collection of essays and interviews about the meaning of experience. Many awards and lecture and teaching engagements followed, both at home and abroad, and Ellison became regarded as an expert on African American culture and folklore, American studies, and creative writing.

The major question of Ellison's later life was whether and when he would publish another novel. He had reportedly been working on a book since 1955, but his progress was slow, and in 1967 a fire at Ellison's home destroyed about 350 pages of the manuscript. The novel was left unfinished at his death, although eight excerpts from it have been published in literary journals. In 1986 Ellison published *Going to the Territory,* a collection of previously published speeches, reviews, and essays. He died of pancreatic cancer on April 16, 1994.

Plot Summary

Prologue

Ralph Ellison's *Invisible Man* chronicles the life of an unnamed, first-person narrator from his youth in the segregated American South of the 1920s to a temporary "hibernation," twenty years later, in a "border area" of Harlem. From his "hole in the ground," this "invisible man" responds to his "compulsion to put invisibility down in black and white" by telling his story. He begins by attempting to explain his own invisibility: "I am invisible, understand, simply because people refuse to see me." The tendency of others to distort what they see or to see "everything and anything" except him leads the narrator to question his own existence. As a result, he feels resentment toward those who refuse to acknowledge his reality. When he bumps into one such person on the street, the narrator responds to the man's slurs with swift violence. He is kept from killing him only by the unnerving realization that his victim did not, in fact, *see* him as another human being but rather as a "phantom" or a mirage. The narrator notes one curious advantage of invisibility, a "slightly different sense of time" that allows one to "see around corners." After accidentally smoking a "reefer" and experiencing a hallucinogenic journey back through history to slave times, the narrator recognizes that his awareness of invisibility alone gives him a more useful sense of sight. He has, as he puts it, "illuminated the blackness of my invisibility," and it remains for him to explain, in the rest of the novel, what has brought him to this newfound understanding of his own identity and of his role in American society.

Chapters 1-6

The narrator begins his story with his memories of youth and adolescence in a small southern town. He recalls first, as the most baffling but powerful memory of his childhood, the final instructions of his dying grandfather that he must live as a "traitor" and "a spy in the enemy's territory." These words become "like a curse" to the narrator as he grows older, for he finds reward in living a life of outward humility and he doesn't understand how such a life might be called "treachery." Asked by the leading white citizens of the town to repeat his graduation speech extolling submissiveness, the narrator finds himself required to participate in a battle royal, a blindfolded boxing match with nine of his schoolmates. Bloodied from the fight and humiliated by the racist jeers of the white men, the narrator still delivers his speech about "social responsibility" and receives, as a "badge of office," a brief case and a college scholarship.

The narrator's education at the "state college for Negroes" comes to an abrupt end during his ju-

nior year, when he shows a wealthy white benefactor of the college, Mr. Norton, parts of the South that the college wishes to hide from its Northern visitors. Mr. Norton is horrified by what he hears from Jim Trueblood (a black sharecropper who has impregnated his own daughter) and by what he sees in the Golden Day (a "slave-quarter" brothel). Because he has thus embarrassed the school and threatened its reputation, the narrator is temporarily expelled by the president of the college, Dr. Bledsoe. After listening to an impassioned speech about the school's mission by Homer A. Barbee, the narrator is advised by Bledsoe to go to New York to earn his fees for the following year. Provided with sealed letters to several of the school's "friends" in the North, the narrator boards a bus, optimistic that he will soon return to complete his education.

Chapters 7-14

The narrator's confidence soon wavers, when a veteran from the Golden Day heading North on the same bus urges him to "come out of the fog" and "learn to look beneath the surface" of his life. Once in New York the narrator feels alternately confident and frightened, more free than in the South but more confused. His doubts increase after his first six letters yield no job opportunities. With his seventh letter the narrator meets Young Emerson, the disillusioned son of one of the college's wealthy benefactors, from whom he learns that Bledsoe's letters of introduction in fact bar him from ever returning to the school. Stunned by this discovery, the narrator abandons his loyalty and submission to the college and knows that he will "never be the same."

Finding work at the Liberty Paint factory, the narrator is branded a "fink" by the unionized workers, then moments later is accused of being a unionizer by Lucius Brockway. Before the end of the day he contributes to a boiler-room explosion that leaves him seriously injured and unconscious. He awakes in the factory hospital, where, in order to assure that "society will suffer no traumata on his account," doctors attempt to "cure" him with an electric-shock lobotomy. After his release from the hospital, the narrator is unsure of who he is, feeling disconnected from both his mind and his body. Drifting back to Harlem, he is taken in by Mary Rambo, an elderly black woman he meets coming out of the Lenox Avenue subway. Here his search for identity becomes an "obsession," and he roams the city without purpose until he comes across an eviction in progress. Speaking to the angry crowd

Unemployed men in a Harlem neighborhood, Lenox Avenue, 1935.

in defense of the elderly black couple, the narrator comes to the attention of a member of the politically radical Brotherhood. Recruited as a spokesperson for their cause, the narrator accepts a new name and a "new identity" and resolves once again to "leave the old behind."

Chapters 15-25

After parting from Mary and moving into an apartment provided by the Brotherhood, the narrator delivers his first speech at a political rally. Encouraged by his own performance and the emotional reaction of the crowd, he resolves to find a meaningful identity in the Brotherhood that is "not limited by black and white." After the narrator meets Tod Clifton, another young black man active in the Brotherhood, the two are involved in a street fight with the black nationalist Ras the Exhorter. Although denounced by Ras for working side by side with white men, the narrator is "dominated by the all-embracing idea of Brotherhood" and convinced that he plays a "vital role" in the work of the organization. His confidence is momentarily shaken by an anonymous warning that he not "get too big," but he is reminded of what he is working for by Brother Tarp's gift of a leg link that he had filed open to escape from a southern chain gang.

The narrator begins to question the aims of the Brotherhood after he is denounced by Brother Wrestrum and is transferred out of Harlem to lecture downtown on "the Woman Question." When he returns to Harlem after Tod Clifton's disappearance, he finds the movement weakened and disorganized and discovers Clifton on the street hawking paper Sambo dolls. Moments later, the narrator watches as Clifton is gunned down by a police officer. With his eyes opened to aspects of Harlem and of the Brotherhood that he had never seen before, the narrator leads a funeral march for Clifton at which he abandons "scientific" political arguments for honest emotional expression. Roaming the streets of Harlem after again being denounced by the Brotherhood, the narrator discovers a world of contradiction and "possibility" that causes him to see his past experiences in a new light:

> … leaning against that stone wall in the sweltering night, I began to accept my past and, as I accepted it, I felt memories welling up within me. It was as though I'd learned suddenly to look around corners; images of past humiliations flickered through my head and I saw that they were more than separate experiences. They were me; they defined me. I was my experiences and my experiences were me, and no blind men, no matter how powerful they became, even if they conquered the world, could take that, or change one single itch, taunt, laugh, cry, scar, ache,

rage or pain of it. They were blind, bat blind, moving only by the echoed sounds of their own voices.... They were very much the same, each attempting to force his picture of reality upon me and neither giving a hoot in hell for how things looked to me. I was simply a material, a natural resource to be used. I had switched from the arrogant absurdity of Norton and Emerson to that of Jack and the Brotherhood, and it all came out the same—except I now recognized my invisibility.

After this powerful recognition, the narrator resolves to undermine the Brotherhood. But before he can discover their plans for him and for Harlem, he is swept up in a riot initiated by Ras, now called "the Destroyer." Narrowly escaping death at the hands of Ras and his henchmen, the narrator falls into an open manhole where he sleeps, dreams, and eventually decides to "take up residence."

Epilogue

From his "hole in the ground," the narrator ends his story by reflecting on his painful past, his present uncertainty and anger, and the possibility that he may yet emerge from his "hibernation" and—though still an invisible man in American society—find "a socially responsible role to play."

Characters

The Reverend Homer A. Barbee

A blind preacher from Chicago of substantial rhetorical skill who gives the Founder's Day speech at the college.

Dr. A. Herbert Bledsoe

Dr. Bledsoe is the president of the college attended by the invisible man. Called "Old Buckethead" by the students, he is a shrewd survivor who has spent his career humoring the white trustees in the hopes of retaining his position. A person of considerable affectation, he can manage even in striped trousers and a swallow-tail coat topped by an ascot tie to make himself look humble. He is aghast when the invisible man tells him that he took Mr. Norton to see Jim Trueblood because that's what the trustee wanted to do: "My God, boy! You're black and living in the South—did you forget how to lie?" His recipe for success is to attain power and influence by making the right contacts and "then stay in the dark and use it!" His self-interest makes him capable of betrayal, as when he lets the invisible man head off for New York City think-

Media Adaptations

- *Invisible Man* was recorded by Dr. Marion J. Smith for Golden Voice Production, 1993.

ing that the letters he is carrying addressed to various trustees are letters of recommendation.

Lucius Brockway

The invisible man's irascible second supervisor at Liberty Paints. "Lucius Brockway not only intends to protect hisself, he *knows how* to do it! Everybody knows I been here ever since there's been a here." His one worry is that the union will do him out of a job.

Brother Tod Clifton

Young and handsome, Clifton is the leader of the Brotherhood youth: "a hipster, a zoot suiter, a sharpie." He has run-ins with Ras the Exhorter over their philosophical differences. He is friendly and helpful to the invisible man, despite the hero's being made his superior. "I saw no signs of resentment," says the invisible man in admiration, "but a complete absorption in the strategy of the meeting.... I had no doubt that he knew his business." Brother Clifton has put his full faith in the brotherhood, and when he is abandoned by it, his despair is total. He plunges "outside of history," becoming a street peddler selling paper black sambo dolls, and is murdered by the police. His death is a defining moment for the invisible man.

Emma

One of the first members of the Brotherhood the invisible man meets. The hero is skeptical of the Brotherhood's motives when he hears Emma ask, "But don't you think he should be a little blacker?"

Grandfather

The invisible man's grandfather, whom the protagonist had always thought of as a model of desirable conduct. He is dead when the novel begins, but his influence on the invisible man is powerful. His dying words were, "Son, … I never told you, but our life is a war and I have been a traitor all my born days, a spy in the enemy's country ever since I give up my gun back in the Reconstruction. Live with your head in the lion's mouth. I want you to overcome 'em with yeses, undermine 'em with grins, agree 'em to death and destruction, let 'em swoller you till they vomit or bust wide open.… Learn it to the younguns." These words prick the invisible man's complacency, and he remembers them as a curse that haunts him throughout his journey, a reminder that all is not right in the world.

Halley

The spirited manager at The Golden Day.

Brother Hambro

Hambro takes the invisible man through a four-month period of intense study and indoctrination after his arena speech to the Brotherhood to correct his "unscientific" tendencies. "A tall, friendly man, a lawyer, and the Brotherhood's chief theoretician." he tells the invisible man that "it's impossible *not* to take advantage of the people.…The trick is to take advantage of them in their own best interest."

Invisible Man

The unnamed protagonist of the novel. In explaining to the reader what he has done to be so "black and blue," the hero says, "I was looking for myself and asking everyone except myself questions which I, and only I, could answer." By the end of his adventures, he will conclude "that I am nobody but myself. But first I had to discover that I am an invisible man!" The invisible man starts his tale as an innocent, one who believes that "humility was the secret, indeed, the very essence of progress." His greatest aspiration is to be an assistant to Dr. Bledsoe, the president of his college, who kowtows to whites in an attempt to hold on to his position. The invisible man believes, consciously or unconsciously, "the great false wisdom … that white is right" and that it is "advantageous to flatter rich white folks." He grudgingly admires other blacks who do not share his scruples; for instance, he is both humiliated and fascinated by the sharecropper Jim Trueblood's self-confessed tale of incest, and he is similarly impressed by the vet at The Golden Day: "I wanted to tell Mr. Norton that the man was crazy and yet I received a fearful satisfaction from hearing him talk as he had to a white man."

Although he has the "queer feeling that I was playing a part in some scheme which I did not understand," he ignores his instincts, as when, for instance, he personally delivers to prospective employers in New York City what he foolishly believes to be positive letters of recommendation from Dr. Bledsoe "like a hand of high trump cards." For every two steps forward, he takes one back. His experience in the factory hospital, for example, is a kind of awakening, and he develops an "obsession with my identity" that causes him to "put into words feelings which I had hitherto suppressed." But though he is skeptical of the Brotherhood's motives in recruiting him—"What am I, a man or a natural resource?"—and their obvious emphasis on the "we," the invisible man sets aside his misgivings and embraces the organization; "it was a different, bigger 'we,'" he tells himself. He is kind, joining the Brotherhood partly out of desire to pay Mary Rambo the rent money he owes her, and loyal to people like Brother Tarp and Brother Clifton in whom he senses a fundamental goodness. But he is forever second-guessing himself, and it takes the raw injustice of Brother Clifton's murder to spark the invisible man into consciousness: "Outside the Brotherhood we were outside history; but inside of it they didn't see us.… Now I recognized my invisibility." At first defiant—"But to whom can I be responsible, and why should I be, when you refuse to see me?"—by the end of the novel the invisible man is ready to come out, "since there's a possibility that even an invisible man has a socially responsible role to play."

Brother Jack

The Brotherhood's district leader for Harlem, he befriends the invisible man after hearing him address a crowd gathered to witness the eviction of an elderly black couple, and sets about recruiting him to the Brotherhood. That his motives might be suspect is evident from the beginning, when he asks the invisible man, "How would you like to be the new Booker T. Washington?" (Washington was viewed negatively as an accommodationist by many blacks) and warns him, "You mustn't waste your emotions on individuals, they don't count." Brother Jack turns out to be the author of an anonymous threat mailed to the invisible man.

Mr. Kimbro

The invisible man's first supervisor at Liberty Paints.

Mr. Norton

A white philanthropist and trustee of the college attended by the invisible man, Mr. Norton describes himself as "a trustee of consciousness" and believes that the students of the college are his "fate." He calls his "real life's work ... my first-hand organizing of human life." A romantic about race, he insists on being taken to the old slave quarters, where he expects to hear a lively folktale but instead is treated to a matter-of-fact account of incest by Jim Trueblood. Norton is the cause of the invisible man's expulsion from the school.

Old Bucket-head

See Dr. A. Herbert Bledsoe

Mary Rambo

Mary Rambo runs a rooming house and takes the invisible man in after finding him ill in the street following his stay in the factory hospital. The only person to treat him with genuine affection, Mary is cynical about the big city, and puts her faith in the newcomers from the south: "I'm in New York, but New York ain't in me." The invisible man does not think of Mary as a "'friend'; she was something more—a force, a stable, familiar force like something out of my past which kept me from whirling off into some unknown which I dared not face."

Ras the Exhorter

Modeled on Marcus Garvey, though not a caricature of him. Ras is a flamboyant West African nationalist who preaches black pride, a return to Mother Africa, and a willingness to die for one's principles. Ras and the Brotherhood are engaged in a perpetual turf war, and Ras repeatedly exhorts the black members of the Brotherhood to remember their history. He says to Brother Tod Clifton: "You *my* brother, mahn. Brothers are the same color; how the hell you call these white men *brother?*... Brothers the same color. We sons of Mama Africa, you done forgot? You black, BLACK! ... You African. AFRICAN!"

Rinehart

A mysterious figure who signs himself a "Spiritual Technologist." The reader never meets Rinehart, but the invisible man is mistaken for him by so many different people that he ends up putting together a fascinating though confusing composite: "Still, could he be all of them: Rine the runner and Rine the gambler and Rine the briber and Rine the lover and Rinehart the Reverend? Could he himself be both rind and heart? What is real anyway? ... Perhaps the truth was always a lie." It is in trying to figure out Rinehart that the invisible man begins to see both how complex reality is and that it is possible to live with contradictions.

Sybil

Wife of a member of the Brotherhood with whom the invisible man has a brief liaison in the hope of gaining inside information on the organization.

Brother Tarp

An old but ideologically vigorous member of the Brotherhood. "He can be depended upon in the most precarious circumstance," Brother Jack tells the invisible man. Brother Tarp hangs on the invisible man's office wall a picture of Frederick Douglass, which reminds him of his grandfather. Unlike the invisible man, who left the south more or less voluntarily, Brother Tarp was forced to escape to the north after spending nineteen years on a chain gang because "I said no to a man who wanted to take something from me." He gives the invisible man a link from his ankle iron as a keepsake.

Jim Trueblood

Once respected as a hard worker and a lively storyteller, Jim Trueblood is a black sharecropper who has since shamed the black community and who shocks Mr. Norton with his matter-of-fact account of incest with his daughter. Despite the awfulness of his crime, Trueblood's refusal to stint on the details or to make excuses for himself reveals a basic integrity that is reflected in his name, and the invisible man listens to him with a mixture of horror and admiration.

Veteran at the Golden Day

A skilled doctor who served in France and on his return to the States is run out of town and ends up in the local mental hospital. He attends to Mr. Norton after his heart attack at the Golden Day. The invisible man is impressed with the bold way the vet talks to the white trustee. The vet is the first person to grasp the invisible man's dilemma: "You cannot see or hear or smell the truth of what you see."

Peter Wheatstraw

A kindly rubbish man the invisible man meets in the streets of Harlem singing the blues and who makes him think nostalgically of home.

Brother Wrestrum

A troublemaker, jealous of the invisible man. He makes a false accusation that indirectly results in the protagonist's being taken out of Harlem and sent downtown.

Themes

Identity

In *Invisible Man,* an unnamed protagonist sets out on a journey of self-discovery that takes him from the rural south to Harlem. Learning who he is means realizing that he is invisible to the white world, but by the end of his journey the hero has the moral fiber to live with such contradictions. The overwhelming theme of the novel is that of identity. While the novel has to do with questions of race and prejudice, most critics agree that these ideas are subsumed under the broader questions of who we think we are, and the relationship between identity and personal responsibility. The invisible man's moment of self-recognition occurs almost simultaneously with his realization that the white world does not see him, but Ellison seems to be saying, "Well, don't worry about that." Until the invisible man can see himself, he can only be passive, "outside of history." At the beginning of the novel, even Jim Trueblood has a stronger sense of himself than does the hero: "and while I'm singen' them blues I makes up my mind that I ain't nobody but myself and ain't nothin' I can do but let whatever is gonna happen, happen." In fact, everybody but the invisible man seems to be aware of his problem. The vet at The Golden Day sees it, remarking to Mr. Norton: "Already he is—well, bless my soul! Behold! a walking zombie! Already he's learned to repress not only his emotions but his humanity. He's invisible, a walking personification of the Negative, the most perfect achievement of your dreams, sir! The mechanical man!" And Mr. Bledsoe, the college president, tells the hero, "You're nobody, son. You don't exist—can't you see that?" Ironically, when the invisible man offers to prove his identity to the son of Mr. Emerson, a white trustee, the son answers him in the careless manner of someone for whom identity has never been a question, "Identity! My God! Who has any identity any more anyway?" When the invisible man joins the Brotherhood, Brother Jack gives him a "new identity."

Though he constantly stumbles, every misstep seems to bring the hero a little closer to solving the puzzle of who he is. For example, after the operation at the hospital, when a doctor holds up a sign that reads "WHO WAS BUCKEYE THE RABBIT?", the invisible man begins thinking about his identity. And in the wake of Brother Clifton's murder, he remembers past humiliations and sees that they have defined him.

Individualism

Another theme that pervades the novel is that of individuality. Although he may be uncertain of his identity, the invisible man has never quite lost the sense that he is an individual. One of the superficial arguments he uses for leaving Mary Rambo without saying goodbye to her is that people like her "usually think in terms of 'we' while I have always tended to think in terms of 'me'—and that has caused some friction, even with my own family." He rationalizes the Brotherhood's emphasis on the group by deluding himself into thinking that it is a "bigger 'we.'" But though he tries, the invisible man cannot fully suppress his individuality, which continues to intrude on his consciousness. After his first official speech to the Brotherhood, he remembers unaccountably the words of Woodridge, a lecturer at the college, who told his students that their task was "that of making ourselves individuals.... We create the race by creating ourselves." At the funeral for Brother Tod Clifton, whose murder is one of several epiphanies, or moments of illumination, in the novel, the invisible man looks out over the people present and sees "not a crowd but the set faces of individual men and women."

Duty and Responsibility

The theme of responsibility has to do with making choices and accepting the consequences of our actions. The invisible man uses the term at several reprises, but it is only toward the end of his adventures that he is able to match the word with its true meaning. In the course of the "battle royal," he uses the words "social responsibility" to impress the Board of Education, because "whenever I uttered a word of three or more syllables a group of voices would yell for me to repeat it." When he cannot get Dr. Bledsoe to see that what has happened to Dr. Norton is not his fault, the hero believes that by taking "responsibility" for the mishap he will be able to get on with his career. But what he means by taking responsibility is smoothing things over, and he cannot control the result. As he moves from one troubling experience to another, however, a growing maturity is evident, and people come to depend on him. When Brother Jack asks him by what authority he organized the rally for the people following Brother Tod Clifton's funeral, the invisible man tells him it was on his "personal responsibility," and offers a coolly reasoned defense. At the end of the novel, when he is about to leave his hole, he talks about the "possibility of action" and explains that even an "invisible man has a socially responsible role to play," echoing with mild irony the phrase he once used without thinking.

Blindness

Blindness as a kind of moral and personal failing is a recurring motif, or theme, in the novel. Whether inflicted by others, as in the "battle royal," where the young men are forcibly blindfolded, or as evidence of confusion, as when the invisible man describes stumbling "in a game of blindman's buff," the idea of blindness is used to multiple effect. The Reverend Homer A. Barbee is literally blind, Brother Jack has a glass eye, white people cannot see the invisible man, and the hero cannot see himself. A variation on the theme is the idea of looking but not seeing, of not *trying* to see, which comes back to the theme of responsibility. Various characters impress on the invisible man the importance of not accepting things as they are. "For God's sake," the vet from The Golden Day tells him, "learn to look beneath the surface. Come out of the fog, young man." And the son of the white trustee Emerson asks him, "Aren't you curious about what lies behind the face of things?"

History and Folklore

In *Invisible Man* history and identity are inextricably bound: we are the sum of our history and our experience. This message is brought home in the novel both overtly—"What is your past and where are you going?" Ras the Exhorter asks an uncomfortable Brother Tod Clifton—and indirectly, as in Mary Rambo's advice to the invisible man that it is the young who will make changes but "something's else, it's the ones from the South that's got to do it, them what knows the fire and ain't forgot how it burns. Up here too many forgits." That is, you are your history, but only if you remember it. An inventory of the sad belongings of the couple the hero finds on the Harlem sidewalk reads like a synopsis of the story of blacks in America, and the power of the associations the objects evoke inspires the invisible man to address a crowd for the first time. Closely related to the theme of history is the motif of folklore as a link

Topics for Further Study

- Research some of the major demographic shifts occurring in the world today, and compare the reasons for them with those that motivated the Great Migration North of 1910–1970 in the United States.

- Explore current policies in medical ethics and informed consent and explain how these would affect the circumstances of the kind of operation performed on the invisible man in Ellison's novel.

- Investigate current housing laws regarding the elderly, and explain how the couple who are evicted from their apartment in winter in the novel would be affected by them, and what their options for alternative living arrangements might be.

to the past, particularly folktales, jazz, and the blues. The simple folk who appear in the book all seem rooted in a way the invisible man and others are not, and have a sureness about them that is reflected in their names: Jim Trueblood, Mary Rambo, Peter Wheatstraw, even Ras the Exhorter. Likewise, the hero's grandfather has a "stolid black peasant's face." The vet at The Golden Day, who is a mental patient but does not appear to be completely insane, tells Mr. Norton that he had made a mistake in forgetting certain "fundamentals.... Things about life. Such things as most peasants and folk peoples almost always know through experience, though seldom through conscious thought."

Style

Point of View

At the outset of *Invisible Man,* the unnamed hero is in transition. He has discovered that he is invisible and has retreated from the world in defiance; but the reader senses that all is not resolved.

In the adventure that the invisible man proceeds to relate in the first person ("I"), his voice changes over time from that of a naive young man, to someone who is clearly more responsible though still confused, to a person willing to deal with the world whatever the risks. The novel is framed by a Prologue and Epilogue. The story opens in the present, switches to flashback, and then returns to the present, but a step forward from the Prologue. Writing down the story has helped the hero to make up his mind about things. Leonard J. Deutsch attributes the complexity of the novel in part to this juxtaposition of perspectives of the "I" of the naive boy and the "I" of the older, wiser narrator. Anthony West, on the other hand, writing in *The New Yorker,* called the Prologue and the Epilogue "intolerably arty … the two worst pieces of writing in the work."

Setting

Invisible Man is set in an indeterminate time frame sometime between the 1930s and 1950s. The protagonist's adventures take him from an unnamed southern town to New York City, mirroring the migration during the period of the novel of over a quarter of a million African Americans from the rural south to the urban north in search of jobs. The novel opens on the campus of a southern black college whose buildings and environs are repeatedly described in honeyed terms. Nevertheless, in retrospect the hero remembers it also as a flower-studded wasteland maintained by the money of white philanthropists blind to the surrounding poverty. The action then moves to Harlem, a part of New York City associated with several political and cultural elements of importance in the novel: the active recruiting of black intellectuals by the Communist party in the United States, the rise of black nationalism, and the golden age of jazz.

Symbol

Invisible Man is rich with symbols that have given critics fertile ground for interpretation. For example, the "battle royal" that opens the book represents the novel in a nutshell and serves as a microcosmic portrayal of race relations in a socially segregated society. The narrator will clutch to him the briefcase the Board of Education awards him throughout his adventures, though he will burn its contents—which symbolize his middle-class aspirations—at the end. Ellison gives his characters names that often suggest something about their personalities, for example, Dr. Bledsoe, Jim Trueblood, Brother Wrestrum, or equally significant, as in the case of the protagonist, he does not name

them at all. Songs figure significantly in the novel. In the prologue, for instance, the hero remembers the words to a Louis Armstrong song, "What did I do / To be so black / And blue?" and at the end of the catastrophic visit to the slave quarters, which will result in the hero's expulsion from college, the children are singing "London Bridge Is Falling Down." The lobotomy-like operation undertaken to make the hero more amiable backfires and instead brings him somewhat to himself, constituting a symbolic rebirth.

Literary Styles

The many stylistic elements used in *Invisible Man* are part of what make it such a literary tour de force. Warren French, for example, has described the formal organization of the narrative as "a series of nested boxes that an individual, trapped in the constricting center, seeks to escape." Several critics cite the use of varied literary styles, from the naturalism of the events at the college campus, to the expressionism, or subjective emotions, of the hero's time with the Brotherhood, to the surrealism that characterizes the riot at the end of the novel. *Invisible Man* can be classed as a *bildungsroman,* or novel of education, similar to Voltaire's *Candide,* in which the hero moves from innocence to experience. It has also been called picaresque because of the episodic nature of the hero's adventures, but this term implies a shallowness that the invisible man is finally able to overcome. Comedy and irony are used to good effect in both the episode with Jim Trueblood and the scene at The Golden Day. But most important, Ellison drew on the knowledge of African American folklore he acquired in his days with the Federal Writers Project, and the influence of that tradition, particularly jazz and the blues, is inextricably woven into the thought and speech of the characters. The Reverend Homer A. Barbee's address, for example, is alive with gospel rhythms: " 'But she knew, she knew! She knew the fire! She knew the fire! She knew the fire that burned without consuming! My God, yes!' "

Historical Context

The Great Migration

The civil rights movement of the 1950s and 1960s had its genesis in the Great Migration, the move north of 6.5 million black Americans from

Compare
&
Contrast

- **1930s:** Following an active policy of inclusion, the Communist party recruits many black leaders and thinkers.

  1952: A "witch-hunt" for communists begun by U.S. Senator Joseph McCarthy continues through the early 1950s and ruins many careers.

  Today: The 1980s see the collapse of communism in Eastern Europe. In America, politics is increasingly middle-of-the-road. American communists are a small fringe group.

- **1930s:** The U.S. labor movement gains support under the New Deal, but prejudice against African Americans is widespread.

  1952: Union membership peaks in 1945 at 35.5% of the non-agricultural workforce and is still strong in the 1950s.

  Today: Unions are fully integrated. But membership is at an all-time low, and unions are forced to compromise on wages and benefits to preserve jobs.

- **1930s:** Brain surgery to correct the behavior of mentally ill patients, or lobotomy, is widely practiced between 1936 and 1956.

  1952: Lobotomy is largely abandoned in favor of alternative treatments including tranquilizers and psychotherapy.

  Today: Psychoactive drugs have become the first line of treatment for mental illness, and a de-emphasis of institutional care and the closing of mental hospitals have produced increased homelessness.

- **1930s:** Big bands in the swing era give way to bebop, the basis for modern jazz, which arises in Kansas City and Harlem. Major influences are Charlie Parker, Dizzy Gillespie, and Thelonius Monk.

  1952: Progressive, or cool, jazz, with less convoluted melodic lines, begins in New York City in the late 1940s and early 1950s. Lester Young and Miles Davis are major figures in the movement, which is better received critically than bebop.

  Today: After a period of several decades of experimentation, including a style called fusion, jazz settles into a revivalist phase. Popular artists include Wynton and Branford Marsalis, David Murray, and John Carter.

---

the rural South. This created large black communities like New York's Harlem and Chicago's South Side. In the early 1900s, black migration increased dramatically with the beginning of World War I in 1914, in response to the demand for factory workers in the north. While the move did not bring social justice to blacks, it did provide some social, financial, and political benefits, and it established the issue of race in the national consciousness. Both Ralph Ellison and his protagonist, like so many before them, made the journey north. When the invisible man tells the vet from The Golden Day that he's going to New York, the vet answers, "New York! That's not a place, it's a dream. When I was your age it was Chicago. Now all the little black boys run away to New York."

Northern black factory workers could expect to make two to ten times as much as their southern counterparts, and thus newly arrived blacks from the south had an uneasy relationship with organized white labor. Their reluctance to jeopardize their access to the industrial job market by taking part in labor agitation was exploited by their employers to frustrate unions who hired black laborers to replace strikers. It was already clear by the 1930s that America's labor movement could only survive through integration, and between 1935 and the end of World War II, 500,000 blacks joined the Congress of Industrial Organizations (CIO). But white opposition to bringing blacks into the unions persisted up to the time Ellison wrote *Invisible Man.* At Liberty Paints an office boy tells the invisible man, "The wise guys firing the regular guys and putting on you colored college boys. Pretty smart. That way they don't have to pay union wages." And when Lucius Brockway mistakenly

Police arresting a man during the 1943 Harlem riots.

thinks the invisible man has gone to a labor meeting, he fairly explodes. "'That damn union,' he cried, almost in tears. 'That damn union! They after my job! For one of us to join one of them damn unions is like we was to bite the hand of the man who taught us to bathe in the bathtub!'"

American communists strongly advocated racial tolerance, thereby winning the support of black leaders and intellectuals, particularly during the Depression. Like Richard Wright, Ellison leaned on the party for financial support and because it offered him a way of getting published. Nevertheless, Ellison objected to what he considered to be a kind of thought control, and he never became a party member. During World War II, when the party advised against pushing issues of racial segregation in the U.S. armed forces, Ellison became disillusioned. In *Invisible Man,* the hero returns from an absence only to discover that "there had been, to my surprise, a switch in emphasis from local issues to those more national and international in scope, and it was felt for the moment the interests of Harlem were not of first importance."

Nationhood and Civil Rights

In 1916, Marcus Garvey came to the United States from Jamaica and founded the Universal Negro Improvement Association (UNIA). Like Ras the Exhorter in *Invisible Man,* Garvey was an ardent and flamboyant nationalist, and he electrified Harlem with his message of black pride and self-determination through the recolonization of Africa. But Garvey's arguments for racial separation were at odds with the integrationist efforts of communists, and the schism between the two groups would outlast Garvey's political demise in 1921. Another significant black nationalist figure of the 1930s was Sufi Abdul Mohammed; elements of his colorful personality turn up in *Invisible Man* in both Ras the Exhorter and Rinehart, the mysterious numbers runner and preacher.

Some 400,000 black soldiers served in World War I, but they found that their devotion did not translate into respect abroad during the war or at home after it. Once overseas, blacks were relegated to menial tasks, were passed over for combat duty, and were subjected to continual harassment by whites. The society to which they returned was even more conservative on issues of race than the one they had left. The black press, particular W. E. B. Du Bois's influential magazine *The Crisis,* was loud in its condemnation of reports of discriminatory treatment made by returning black soldiers. The outrage felt by black veterans is described in an incident in *Invisible Man,* where a group of black World War I veterans cause a disturbance at a whorehouse and bar called The Golden Day. One veteran describes how he had served as a surgeon in France under the Army Medical Corps but was chased out of town on his return to America.

The prospect of a new draft in the wake of the eruption of conflict in Europe again in 1939 led to civil rights protests in the early 1940s and violent racial incidents between white southerners and black northerners at military bases across the United States. The issue was responsible for the Harlem riot of 1943. The climax of *Invisible Man* is a riot in Harlem allegedly instigated by the Brotherhood; the event is based in part on a riot that occurred there in 1935, which some commentators blamed on communist agitators.

Critical Overview

Invisible Man was published to instant acclaim, though its complexity did not necessarily make it an easy read. Writing in *Commentary* in 1952, Saul Bellow called it "a book of the very first order, a superb book," praising in particular the episode in which Jim Trueblood tells his tale of incest to Mr. Norton. "One is accustomed to expect excellent novels about boys, but a modern novel about men is exceedingly rare." Anthony West wrote in *The New Yorker* that *Invisible Man* was "an exceptionally good book and in parts an extremely funny one" and praised its "robust courage," though he recommended skipping the Prologue and Epilogue and "certain expressionist passages conveniently printed in italics." Like Bellow, West congratulated Ellison on having written a book "about being colored in a white society [that] yet manages not to be a grievance book" and noted Ellison's "real satirical gift for handling ideas at the level of low comedy." In his study *Native Sons,* Edward Margolies noted the importance of jazz and the blues to the narrative and commented that what Ellison "seems to be saying [is] that if men recognize first that existence is purposeless, they may then be able to perceive the possibility of shaping their existence in some kind of viable form—in much the same manner as the blues artist gives form to his senseless pain and suffering." However, Margolies bemoaned the thematic weakness of the novel, which is that "Ellison's hero simply has nowhere to go once he tells us he is invisible." In a 1963 article in *Dissent,* Irving Howe called the novel a brilliant though flawed achievement. "No white man could have written it, since no white man could know with such intimacy the life of the Negroes from the inside; yet Ellison writes with an ease and humor which are now and again simply miraculous."

The style of the novel has occasionally been criticized as excessive—Howe found Ellison "literary to a fault"—but even the novel's critics found much to praise in the symbolism, style, and narrative structure. Opinion was divided over the section dealing with the Brotherhood. West called it "perhaps the best description of rank-and-file Communist Party activity that has yet appeared in an American novel," but Bellow found it less than convincing, and Howe wrote that "Ellison makes his Stalinist figures so vicious and stupid that one cannot understand how they could ever have attracted him or any other Negro."

The biggest controversy over the book has always had to do with whether or not it was intended for a universal audience. Bellow praised Ellison for not having "adopted a minority tone. If he had done so, he would have failed to establish a true middle-of-consciousness for everyone." Howe felt rather that "even Ellison cannot help being caught up with the idea of the Negro, ... for plight and protest are inseparable from that experience," though he did

not say whether this was good or bad. Warren French asserts in *Reference Guide to American Fiction* that the book has frequently been misread: it is neither unique to the black experience nor "picaresque," but both broader and more sophisticated. David Littlejohn straddled the debate, called *Invisible Man* "essentially a Negro's novel ... written entirely out of a Negro's experience, ... [b]ut it is not a 'Negro novel.'... It is his story, really, not the race's, not the war's, except insofar as he is of the race and in the war." Black nationalists argued that Ellison was not stringent enough, and John Oliver Killens and Amiri Baraka were particularly vocal critics. Ellison's defense was that he had never been a propagandist.

In 1953 *Invisible Man* was awarded the National Book Award for fiction. But controversy over what it meant and to whom continued. In his preface to the 1981 commemorative edition of the novel, Charles Johnson, whose *Middle Passage* won the National Book Award in 1990, remembers a time in the 1960s when "both Ellison and poet Robert Hayden were snubbed by those under the spell of black cultural nationalism, and when so many black critics denied the idea of 'universality' in literature and life." This attitude was largely reversed during the 1970s when white critics tired of waiting for Ellison's hypothetical second novel and black readers began to be more appreciative of the book's portrayal of black experience. Whatever the nature of the critical debate, *Invisible Man* has proved its staying power. Leonard Deutsch wrote that for all its brutal realism and cynicism, *Invisible Man* "is basically a comic and celebratory work, for the hero is ultimately better off at the end: he has become the shaping artist of his tale."

Criticism

Anthony M. Dykema-VanderArk

In the following essay, Dykema-VanderArk, a doctoral candidate at Michigan State University, examines how the individual journey of the "Invisible Man" can represent the larger American experience. He asserts that Ellison's novel concludes that "living as a true American requires faith—faith in equality and democracy when they are most out of reach, in the possibility of coming together when segregation predominates, in human complexity when society is obsessed with stereotypes."

What Do I Read Next?

- *Notes of a Native Son* (1955) is the first volume of James Baldwin's eloquent and influential essays about being black in America and abroad.

- *Middle Passage* (1990) is Charles Johnson's National Book Award-winning tale of freedman Rutherford Calhoun's voyage to Africa as a stowaway aboard the slave ship *Republic.*

- Nobel prize-winner Toni Morrison's novel *Jazz* (1992) captures the rhythms and mood of African American life in Harlem in the 1920s.

- *Native Son* (1940) by Richard Wright tells the story of Bigger Thomas's losing battle to escape the traps of race and class in Chicago in the 1930s after the job he takes working for a wealthy white family goes tragically awry.

- Ellison's *Shadow and Act* (1964) is a collection of essays and interviews in which the author explores the meaning of existence and experience.

From his earliest published writings in the late 1930s until his death in 1994, Ralph Ellison remained an outspoken commentator on American literature, culture, race, and identity, but his reputation has always rested most solidly on his one published novel, *Invisible Man.* Since its publication in 1952, *Invisible Man* has consistently been singled out as one of the most compelling and important novels of this century. Praised for both its artistic originality and its thematic richness, the novel continues to find new readers not least because of the reading experience it provides—at once inspiring and unsettling, lucid and complex, approachable and profoundly challenging. From the powerful first line of the novel ("I am an invisible man"), readers are engaged in the life of the narrator, this "invisible man," as he tries to tell his story and "put invisibility down in black and white." Moreover, the novel urges its readers to undertake a similar quest along with the narrator: to

examine the painful realities of American history and culture and, in the end, to seek the ways in which they, too, may have "a socially responsible role to play."

Like the familiar opening of *Moby-Dick* ("Call me Ishmael"), *Invisible Man* begins with a prologue by the novel's first-person narrator, but in this case the introduction comes without a name: "I am an invisible man." The narrator's name remains hidden to the reader throughout the novel, but the importance of names and the act of naming becomes clear as his story unfolds. The narrator is "named" by nearly every person he encounters in the novel: He is, for example, a "boy" and a "nigger" to the "leading white citizens" of his town; just the same (to his surprise) to Dr. Bledsoe; a "cog" in the machine of Mr. Norton's "fate"; little more than a laboratory animal to the doctors in the factory hospital; a race-traitor to Ras the Exhorter; and a "natural resource" to the Brotherhood. Each person or group that the narrator encounters tries to identify him, to impose an identity upon him, while ignoring or denying his own emotional and psychological sense of self. As he reflects on his experiences from his "hole in the ground," he understands that this misnaming is the real source of his identity crisis. He is "invisible" not from any lack of physicality or intelligence but because of a willed action of those around him, "simply because people refuse to see me." But this blindness, this desire to call him by any name but his own, initially affects even the narrator himself. It takes him, as he acknowledges, "a long time and much painful boomeranging of my expectations to achieve a realization everyone else appears to have been born with: That I am nobody but myself."

Achieving that "realization" requires the narrator to come to terms with his personal history and with his place in the larger history of America. The first words of the narrator's story in the first chapter of the book—"It goes a long way back ..."—establish immediately the importance of history and memory to his quest, and his narrative itself constitutes both memory and history "in black and white." Much of the tension of the story, however, results from the narrator's conflicted understanding of history and his desire to stifle his memories, to disconnect himself from his past. As he recollects his experiences at the college, for example, the narrator struggles to determine "what was real, what solid, what more than a pleasant, time-killing dream?" After rejecting the identity that he possessed at the college, the narrator is left with "the problem of forgetting it," of quieting "all the contradictory voices shouting" inside his head. The narrator's difficulty in leaving his past behind resonates throughout his story, from the recurring voice and image of his grandfather to the physical reminders of his past that he carries with him throughout the novel.

Two physical objects in particular—Primus Provo's "FREE PAPERS" and Brother Tarp's chain link—act as vivid emblems of the painful realities of America's past. The narrator wants to believe that the legacy of slavery and southern chain-gangs belong to the distant past: When he reads the "fragile paper" that once released a man from slavery, he tells himself, *It has been longer than that, further removed in time ....*" But, as he begins to perceive in the factory hospital, the narrator's quest for his own "freedom" and identity can only be fulfilled when he recovers that history, when he understands its continuing relevance as part of his own past. He recognizes this connection fully only after rejecting the Brotherhood's "scientific" language in favor of a more personal sense of history: "I began to accept my past and, as I accepted it, I felt memories welling up within me.... Images of past humiliations flickered through my head and I saw that they were more than separate experiences. They were me; they defined me." Only after seeing this composite picture of his past does the narrator recognize not only his invisibility but also the "great potentialities" and "possibilities" that exist in spite of that invisibility.

Of course, "potentialities" and "possibilities" are just what the narrator finds—for a time—in the grand missions of the Founder's college and the Brotherhood. At the college, the narrator identifies himself with Mr. Norton and with Dr. Bledsoe and feels that he is "sharing in a great work"; likewise, in the Brotherhood, he believes that he has found "a way to have a part in making the big decisions, of seeing through the mystery of how the country, the world, really operated." What attracts the narrator to both groups is, in part, versions of history and visions of the future that are full of meaning, purpose, and direction. But both groups, he eventually learns, maintain a strict control over all "possibilities," conceal all "contradictions," and, as the vet at the Golden Day prophesied, finally see the narrator as "a thing and not a man." These groups give him a "role" to play, but only as an "automaton," a "child," a "black amorphous thing."

When the narrator ends his story, then, by wondering if "even an invisible man has a socially responsible role to play," it is clear that the answer to his question rests on the entirety of his narrative and has no simple solution. "Social responsibility," first of all, is precisely what the racist "leading white citizens" of his southern town desired from him, the responsibility of keeping himself in a submissive and segregated "place." In contrast, the responsible role that the narrator seeks for the future will go hand in hand with a belief—even if it is his alone—in the "social equality" that he inadvertently pronounced to the horror of the white men. Such a role will also rest on "personal responsibility" and emotional integrity of the sort that Jack and the Brotherhood denied to him. The narrator desires a role that neither engulfs his identity, his humanity, and his memory, nor requires, in his words, "Rinehartism-cynicism." For his "mind," his self, to be satisfied, he can neither "take advantage of the people" nor take no responsibility at all: He "must come out" to play a meaningful part in society, whether or not he remains invisible to the people he encounters there. In the end, the narrator finds the key to his identity in a healthy contradiction, both "denouncing" and "defending" his society, saying "yes" and saying "no," affirming a world whose "definition is possibility" at the same time he refuses to be blind to negations of that promise.

A sense of "contradiction" and "possibility" may also, finally, be the key to the artistic power and continuing relevance of Ellison's *Invisible Man.* Just as his narrator offers "no phony forgiveness," no unambiguous moral to his story, so Ellison leaves many of the tensions and competing elements unresolved. Ellison implies that the truth of American society cannot be encompassed in absolutes such as hope or despair, idealism or cynicism, even love or hate, but rather requires a willingness on the part of each citizen to see both extremes and hold them in balance. As Ellison envisions it, living as a true American requires faith—faith in equality and democracy when they are most out of reach, in the possibility of coming together when segregation predominates, in human complexity when society is obsessed with stereotypes. That the novel continues to move readers almost half a century after it was written testifies not only to the power of Ellison's storytelling but also to the continuing relevance of these themes. Ellison's success in reaching new readers each year affirms, it seems, the narrator's final, unanswered question: "Who knows but that, on the lower frequencies, I speak for you?"

Source: Anthony M. Dykema-VanderArk, in an essay for *Novels for Students,* Gale, 1997.

Stewart Lillard

In the following excerpt, Lillard places Invisible Man *within the epic tradition and calls the novel "a most successful attempt ... to produce the great American Negro epic."*

[In *Invisible Man*], Ellison attempted to portray the theme of Negro endurance and cultural continuity by devising a plot which would include a maximum of experiences common to the American Negroes, but which could be employed by a wandering hero in an episodic manner. For this plot he relied heavily on the social migration theme that promised equality to the Southern Negro but shattered his hopes in an economic jungle which ended with a dispossession in Harlem....

In the novel one unnamed youth progresses from a high school setting in Greenwood to the Southern college for Negroes and from there to Harlem. He does not remain in Harlem but seeks employment in the white neighborhoods of New York City and expresses interest in a scientific Brotherhood before returning to Harlem. In the final riot scene he flees from Harlem and discovers an underground cellar near Harlem situated in a white community bordering the Negro ghetto. His motivation for leaving Greenwood was the scholarship presented him by the white community of the town. At the college, the hero again felt an external motivating force which this time catapulted him from the Southern college to New York supposedly under the same expectations that faced Eddie, Harry, and Marvin (of earning his college expenses for the next school year); but he soon felt the true motivating impulse of expulsion.... [Although] the hero in *Invisible Man* has achieved no recognition of his identity, he has developed a workable solution and method of continued searching.

Within the episodic migration theme, Ellison developed a central character ... [who] is nameless and achieves an enlarged symbolic position. As he confronts the idiosyncrasies and overt violence of his environment and the white man's world that closes its doors to him, he is able to portray the frustrations and victories common to every man ("Who knows but that, on the lower frequencies, I speak for you?"); thereby, he achieves universal magnitude equivalent to the requirements for an epic hero.

Robert Bone, in his attempt [in "Ralph Ellison and the Use of Imagination," *Anger and Beyond* 1966], to classify *Invisible Man* as a picaresque novel, recognizes the heroic qualities in the un-named character's confrontations with reality: "His [Ellison's] heroes are not victims but adventurers. They journey toward the possible in all ignorance of accepted limits. In the course of their travels, they shed their illusions and come to terms with reality." The internal evidence from the novel further substantiates the heroic qualities of the hero, who alone must contend frequently with the machinations of the white mind.

During the high school address before the drunken audience at the smoker in Chapter 1, the speaker illustrates his speech with the account of "a ship lost at sea" whose sailors ask for fresh water from the first friendly vessel they meet. The reply stresses self-reliance: "Cast down your bucket where you are." Like the captain of the distressed vessel, the Negro youth has been taught to seek help where it can be obtained. He must seek and strive for his own identity within society.

The encounter with Mr. Norton following the ill-fated Golden Day episode again resounds with an emphasis on self-reliance, for Mr. Norton explains that "'Self-reliance is a most worthy virtue. I shall look forward with the greatest of interest to learning your contribution to my fate.'" Do not Dr. Bledsoe's letters manipulate the hero into a position of being rejected by Mr. Emerson in New York City, a rejection that forces the hero to rely on his own skills rather than the reputation of his Southern alma mater ("... that though the wide universe if full of good, no kernel of nourishing corn can come to him but through his toil bestowed on that plot of ground which is given to him to till")?

Following the youth's symbolic second birth from the prefrontal lobotomy machine, he collides with the street crowds of New York without a protective shield (his college ties that opened doors for him, or a strong body that enabled him to work in non-union plants and remain temporarily outside his Harlem environment); and he soon struggles for a new identity, although his "tail feathers" have been "picked clean" like Poor Robin's. It is his encounter with a "yam" seller in Harlem that reverses his bewilderment and enables him to regain an identity:

> This is all very wild and childish, I thought, but to hell with being ashamed of what you liked. No more of that for me. I am what I am! I wolfed down the yam and ran back to the old man....

Although this discovery and the search for identity has begun, it remains a disheveled stream of arabesqueness at the conclusion of the novel. Ellison's hero apparently has yet a host of worlds to vanquish.

In his struggle the hero cannot act independently of all external forces. Ellison's central hero is governed by his paternal grandfather's deathbed command to act the part of an intelligencer toward the white society and "overcome 'em with yeses." The hero, moreover, is also controlled by a naturalistic fate that is almost as important as the classical Olympian interference. Beneath this fate, the hero is allowed some degree of independence whereby he may become self-reliant. But this self-reliance is restricted to the Negro world; regardless of his solutions for establishing his identity, the society in which the hero lives and must find work is a segregated society that limits his opportunities. Unlike the racial injustice portrayed in Ellison's vignette, "The Birthmark" (*New Masses,* July 2, 1940), when Matt and Clara are repulsed by the brutality and barbarism of a lynching, the segregated social conditions in *Invisible Man* manipulate the hero as though they were an amoral fate in which the hero finds himself. Within his limitations, the hero refuses to retreat from his heroic search for his identity. In the *Epilogue* he realizes his need to return to the streets of Harlem rather than live continually in complacent seclusion. (The only men worthy of praise of the gods during the heroic age were those who accomplished noble deeds.) And so the hero reasons, "Life is to be lived, not controlled; and humanity is won by continuing to play in face of certain defeat"—a restatement of the conflict that plagued men for centuries.

Along with his grandfather's deathbed command, which haunts the hero throughout the novel as Anchises' predictions in the underworld influenced Aeneas' struggle in Italy or as Achilles' potential return to his father would have eliminated his chances for universal fame, a limited number of additional epic similarities appear in Ellison's novel: the hero's Dantesque descent in the *Prologue,* Sybil's Circean attempts to detain the hero from his mission, examples of gory combat, and one mock epic battle.

In the *Prologue* the Negro youth's descent into a cave that appears in a "reefer" dream is similar to Dante's progress into *Inferno* following his night of wandering in a lonely woods. During the Brotherhood portion of the novel the hero has been denounced by the party leaders, but before he can effect his separation from the organization he is transferred to the downtown section of New York and assigned to lecture on the position of women in the United States. The women of the Brotherhood and Sybil in Chapter 24 are unable to seduce the hero. Their attempt to sap his stoic will has failed, and they are unable to preclude his search for identity.

The battle scenes and physical flights from death echo of primitive combat. Near the end of the Harlem Riot, the hero "ran expecting death between the shoulder blades or through the back of my head, and as I ran I was trying to get to Mary's." In the *Epilogue* his description of his personal feelings upon recognition of his fated position in society reeks of gory details:

> *That* is the real soul-sickness, the spear in the side, the drag by the neck through the mob-angry town, the Grand Inquisition, the embrace of the Maiden, the rip in the belly with the guts spilling out, the trip to the chamber with the deadly gas that ends in the oven so hygienically clean—only it's worse because you continue stupidly to live.

But Ellison, the Ellison of subtle humor, does not neglect at least one mock epic battle as Ras the Exhorter fights the uniformed New York policemen: "'Hell, yes, man, he had him a big black hoss and a fur cap and some kind of old lion skin or something over his shoulders and he was raising hell. Goddam if he wasn't a *sight,* riding up and down on this ole hoss, you know, one of the kind that pulls vegetable wagons, and he got him a cowboy saddle and some big spurs.'" The unnamed hero from a nebulously defined town of Greenwood and the college for Negroes in the South has migrated to Harlem where he witnesses mock-chivalry and chaos but has yet failed to achieve his own identity.

Although the central character in *Invisible Man* is fictitious and nameless, the chaos that swirls about him in the final chapters presents a scene similar to the Harlem Riot of 1943. Ellison's clever meshing of fiction with historical fact and his structural development in the novel tend to produce a surface adventure with historical significance.

Intertwining through the episodes is Ellison's use of lyrics, which often are effective digressions and possess ironic overtones that suggest an atmosphere of defeat or of victory. Moreover, the spirituals and hymns, blues and jazz, recall slavery work songs and catastrophes that weld the centuries of the American Negroes' experiences into a collective event of suffering and expectation....

As a novelist, Ellison seems to have engaged his literary talents in a conscious effort of recording a century of Negro culture in *Invisible Man.* He records speech habits and musical lyrics of an oral tradition before they are lost to future ages. But his greater achievement is that he couches the lyrics and sermons within a framework of Negro expressions and history. His novel becomes no mere anthology of unrelated selections, but a unified presentation of the American Negroes' culture and heritage. The lyrics, moreover, reflect glimpses of the white culture that dominated the slavery and reconstruction eras of the South and was modified by Negro choirs. Spirituals and anthems left behind by the hero on the Southern college campus reappear in a pejorative form of insult ("Go Down Moses") voiced by the intoxicated members of the scientifically oriented Brotherhood. Conversely, the spiritual theme of "Swing Low Sweet Chariot" resounded throughout sections of Dvořák's *New World Symphony.*

In the hospital scene following the paint factory explosion, the hero is reminded of a work song as he struggles to free himself from the machine and as he attempts to recall his past identity. Mary Rambo's use of the "Backwater Blues" and Trueblood's singing of primitive blues laments are two characteristic examples of Ellison's heavy reliance on the blues form. Trueblood's children and those of Brother Hambro, in New York, sing nursery and game songs, but the songs are those borrowed from the Anglo-Scottish community. Ellison's use of animal lyrics ("Poor Robin"), the jazz of the musical bars in New York, and the Harlem jive of Peter Wheatstraw ("She's got feet like a monkey / Legs like a frog—Lawd, Lawd!") together form a composite, along with his other musical types, of the American Negroes' culture and the experiences to which the invisible hero was subjected.

The musical references and lyrics parallel the geographic settings used in the structure of the novel and provide evidence of a cultural heritage that existed long before the events in the hovel occurred. They are the remains of a primitive oral tradition among the American Negroes that Ellison sought to record in their authentic context before they were lost or obscured in fragmented passages in printed anthologies. The scope of the novelist was ambitious enough, and the once oral musical tradition has become literature.

Ralph Ellison's "love" for the American scene somehow inspired him to capture the American Negroes' culture in an artistic form, and his *Invisible Man* is Ellison's attempt—a most successful attempt—to produce the great American Negro epic. For the reader aware of the American Negroes' culture, it is an Odyssey in disguise.

Source: Stewart Lillard, "Ellison's Ambitious Scope in Invisible Man," in *English Journal,* Vol. 58, No. 6, September, 1969, pp. 833–39.

William J. Schafer

In the following excerpt, Schafer explores how Ellison's "invisible man" can be seen as an anti-hero in search of an identity.

The anti-hero of *Invisible Man,* though we come to know him intimately, remains nameless. He is no-man and everyman on a modern epic quest, driven by the message his grandfather reveals in a dream: "To Whom It May Concern … Keep This Nigger-Boy Running." His primary search is for a name—or for the self it symbolizes. During his search he is given another name by the Brotherhood, but it is no help. When he becomes a "brother," he finds that brotherhood does not clarify his inner mysteries.

In creating his anti-hero, Ellison builds on epic and mythic conventions. The nameless voyager passes through a series of ordeals or trials to demonstrate his stature. First, he passes through the initiation-rites of our society—the battle royal (exposing the sadistic sexuality of the white southern world) and speechmaking that sends him to college are parts of this rite of passage, and he is tormented into the adult world. He passes this test by demonstrating his servility and naively interpreting his grandfather's dictum: "Live with your head in the lion's mouth. I want you to overcome 'em with yeses, undermine 'em with grins, agree 'em to death and destruction, let 'em swoller you till they vomit or bust wide open." This is the first outlook of the invisible man—the paranoia fostered by "them," the white oppressors; the boy here is Buckeye the Rabbit, the swift clever animal living by its wits beneath the jaws of the killer.

When he arrives at college, he is confronted by the deceit and duplicity of Negroes who have capitulated to a white world; he is broken by the powerful coalition of Bledsoe the Negro president and Norton the white trustee. His second trial shows him that the struggle is not a simple one of black against white, that "they" are more complex than his first experiences showed. He finds that both black and white can be turned against him.

The second phase of his career commences in the trip to New York, an exile from "paradise"; in the city, he finds Bledsoe's seven magic passports to success in the white world, the letters of recommendation, are actually betrayals, variations of the dream-letter: "Keep This Nigger-Boy Running." Thus, his primary illusions are shattered, but there are many more layers to the cocoon in which he sleeps.

For he is first of all a dreamer, a somnambulist, and sleep and dreams figure significantly in his image of himself. As he reassesses himself, his metaphor for new discoveries is the same: "…it was as though I had been suddenly awakened from a deep sleep." Yet each sleep and each awakening (little deaths and births) prove to be interlocked layers of his existence, a set of never-ending Chinese boxes. One climactic section of the novel details his second crucial awakening—the "descent into the underworld" which occurs in chapters 10 and 11.

Like the hero of myth and ritual, Ellison's invisible man finally descends from life on the mortal plane into an underworld of death. This is the substance of the entire New York section of the novel. On arriving in the city, he recalls the plucked robin of the old song and imagines himself the victim of a fantasy-letter: "My dear Mr. Emerson … The Robin bearing this letter is a former student. Please hope him to death, and keep him running." Then he takes the job at Liberty Paints, keeping white paint white by adding drops of pure black, under the ironic slogan, "If It's Optic White, It's The Right White", which (like "If you're white, all right, if you're black, stay back") has been invented by a Negro, the ancient and malevolent Lucius Brockway. The anti-hero becomes a machine within the machines, and he finds that Brockway, an illiterate "janitor" is the heart of the whole industry. In the boiler room, an inferno, he is betrayed again by a Negro and "killed" through his treachery. But the death is the ritual death of the hero's career—a death which leads to resurrection and a new identity.

After the explosion, the anti-hero awakens in a hospital, where he is resurrected by white doctors using an electroshock machine. Chapter 11 opens with a monstrous image of the demons of this underworld: "I was sitting in a cold, white rigid chair and a man was looking at me out of a bright third eye that glowed from the center of his forehead." The doctors revive him ("We're trying to get you started again. Now shut up!" to the accompaniment of fantastic effects—Beethoven motifs and a trumpet playing "The Holy City" and dreamlike dialogue from the surgeons:

> "I think I prefer surgery. And in this case especially, with this, uh … background. I'm not so sure that I don't believe in the effectiveness of simple prayer."

> "The machine will produce the results of a prefrontal lobotomy without the negative effects of the knife."
> "Why not a castration, doctor?"

Then, as he is revived, the doctors construct an heroic identity for him, recapitulating his existence as a Negro, starting with the first folkmyth guises of the clever Negro–Buckeye the Rabbit and Brer Rabbit: "… they were one and the same: 'Buckeye' when you were very young and hid yourself behind wide innocent eyes; 'Brer' when you were older." The electrotherapy machine is an emblem of the mechnical society imprisoning the anti-hero: "I could no more escape than I could think of my identity. Perhaps, I thought, the two things are involved with each other. When I discover who I am, I'll be free." This lesson of the resurrection is carried through the rest of the anti-hero's journey.

The apparatus which resurrects the invisible man is a mechanical womb, complete with umbilical cord attached to his stomach which is finally cut by the doctors; he is delivered of the machine, and the doctors pronounce his new name—yet he remains nameless. The doctors, who follow a "policy of enlightened humanitarianism" declare that this New Adam will remain a social and economic victim of the machine: "You just aren't prepared for work under our industrial conditions. Later, perhaps, but not now."

The anti-hero sallies forth after his revival in the underworld "overcome by a sense of alienation and hostility" when he revisits the scene of the middleclass Negro arrivals in New York. He is now painfully aware of the hostility of his world, and he reacts not passively ("in the lion's mouth") but aggressively. In a symbolic gesture, he dumps a spittoon on a stranger whom he mistakes for his first nemesis, Bledsoe. The act is that of a crazed messiah: "You really baptized ole Rev!" Then he goes forth for a harrowing of hell.

He joins the Brotherhood, an infernal organization which meets at the Chthonian club. In the Brotherhood, he rises to authority, becomes a respected leader and demagogue and is finally again betrayed by the wielders of power, whites who manipulate Negro stooges for their own ends. But at the end of this episode, the penultimate phase of the hero's career, he meets two important emblematic figures: Ras the Destroyer and Rinehart the fox. Ras, the black nationalist leader, is his crazed counterpart, and he harasses the invisible man until the night of the riots, when he attempts to hang and spear the anti-hero as a scapegoat for the mob—a dying god to appease the violence Ras releases. A contrast is Rinehart, who like Renyard is a master of deception and multiple identities:

"Rine the runner and Rine the gambler and Rine the briber and Rine the lover and Rine the reverend." He is a tempter, and the invisible man nearly succumbs to his temptation to freedom without responsibility; he strolls through Harlem disguised as Rinehart, the visible-invisible man who passes undetected through many identities. Ras offers the assurance of one undivided black identity and Rinehart the assurance of many shifting amoral identities—the faces of stability and flux. But the anti-hero avoids both traps, turning Ras's spear on him and shucking the dark glasses and wide hat of Rinehart, then finally dropping literally out of sight underground at the climax of the riot. Ellison has said [in *Writers at Work,* 1965] that he took Rinehart's name from the "suggestion of inner and outer," seeming and being, and that he is an emblem of chaos—"He has lived so long with chaos that he knows how to manipulate it." So Rinehart and Ras both represent chaos, two versions of disorder.

Loss of identity, sleeping and blindness are the figures that express the invisible man's confusion and despair as his world disintegrates. Then, after the cultural malaise climaxes in the riot, the final phase of the anti-hero's progress begins, a descent into the tomb—the netherworld across the Styx where heroes rest: "It's a kind of death without hanging, I thought, a death alive.... I moved off over the black water, floating, sighing... sleeping invisibly." So he remains immortal and waiting, like the heroes of myth who disappear and are believed to wait should the world require them—like King Arthur and Finn MacCool, sleeping giants blended into the landscape. The invisible man, now grown into Jack-the-Bear, turns to New York's sewer system, a black and labyrinthine underground—a fitting anti-hero's mausoleum.

In this black crypt he destroys his old selves one by one as he searches for light, erasing his past—burning his high school diploma, a doll which is a bitter totem of Tod Clifton's demise, the name given him by the Brotherhood, a poison-pen note, all the tokens of his identity. Then he dreams of castration and sees that the retreat has been his crucifixion—he has been cut off from the world of possibility: "Until some gang succeeds in putting the world in a strait jacket, its definition is possibility. Step outside the narrow borders of what men call reality and you step into chaos—ask Rinehart, he's a master of it—or imagination." Imagination in the end redeems the anti-hero and makes his flight from battle a victory, for it gives us his story. In his tomb he is not dead but hibernating, preparing for a spring of the heart, a return which may be either death or resurrection:

> There's a stench in the air, which, from this distance underground, might be the smell either of death or of spring—I hope of spring. But don't let me trick you, there *is* a death in the smell of spring and in the smell of thee as in the smell of me.

The Easter of the spirit may be the emergence of the new man—no longer an anti-hero, invisible, nameless and dispossessed, but a true hero—or it may be the death of our culture.

The resurrection motif ties the story in the frame of prologue and epilogue, in the voice from underground:

> ... don't jump to the conclusion that because I call my home a "hole" it is damp and cold like a grave; there are cold holes and warm holes. Mine is a warm hole. And remember, a bear retires to his hole for the winter and lives until spring; then he comes strolling out like the Easter chick breaking from its shell. I say all this to assure you that it is incorrect to assume that, because I'm invisible and live in a hole, I am dead. I am neither dead nor in a state of suspended animation. Call me Jack-the-Bear, for I am in a state of hibernation.

Buckeye the Rabbit has grown into the formidable Jack-the-Bear (recalling the Bear's Son of the sagas) as the anti-hero has passed his trials and journeyed on his downward path, reliving the recent history of the Negro. He lies in wait beneath the inferno, under the underworld, listening for the hero's call.

Source: William J. Schafer, "Ralph Ellison and the Birth of the Anti-Hero", in *Critique: Studies in Modern Fiction,* Vol. 10, No. 2, 1968, pp. 81–93.

Sources

Saul Bellow, "Man Underground," in *Commentary,* June, 1952, pp. 608–10.

Leonard J. Deutsch, "Ralph Ellison," in *Dictionary of Literary Biography, Volume 2: American Novelists since World War II,* edited by Jeffrey Helterman and Richard Layman, Gale Research, 1978, pp. 136–40.

Warren French, "Invisible Man," in *Reference Guide to American Literature,* 3rd edition, St. James Press, 1994, pp. 993–94.

Irving Howe, "Black Boys and Native Sons," in *Dissent,* Autumn, 1963.

Charles Johnson, "The Singular Vision of Ralph Ellison," preface to *Invisible Man,* Modern Library, 1994, pp. vii-xii.

David Littlejohn, in *Black on White: A Critical Survey of Writing by American Negroes,* Viking, pp. 110–119.

Edward Margolies, "History as Blues: Ralph Ellison's 'Invisible Man,' " in his *Native Sons: A Critical Study of Twentieth-Century Negro American Authors,* Lippincott, 1968, pp. 127–48.

Anthony West, "Black Man's Burden," in *The New Yorker,* Volume 28, No. 15, May 31, 1952, pp. 93–96.

For Further Study

Kimberly W. Benston, editor, *Speaking for You: The Vision of Ralph Ellison,* Howard University Press, 1987.

A wide-ranging collection of essays on Ellison's fiction and nonfiction as well as interviews with Ellison and poems written in his honor.

Ralph Ellison, *The Collected Essays of Ralph Ellison,* edited by John F. Callahan, Modern Library, 1995.

A recent collection of all of Ellison's essays, reviews, and interviews, some previously unpublished. Includes the complete text of Ellison's two published collections, *Shadow and Act* and *Going to the Territory,* as well as his introduction to the Thirtieth Anniversary Edition of *Invisible Man.*

Ralph Ellison, *Conversations with Ralph Ellison,* edited by Maryemma Graham and Amritjit Singh, University Press of Mississippi, 1995.

A collection of interviews with Ellison including considerable commentary on *Invisible Man.*

John Hersey, editor, *Ralph Ellison: A Collection of Critical Essays,* Prentice-Hall, 1974.

A collection of early reviews, an interview with Ellison, and several important essays on *Invisible Man.*

Alan Nadel, *Invisible Criticism: Ralph Ellison and the American Canon,* University of Iowa Press, 1988.

Nadel reads Ellison's novel as a commentary on the formation of the American literary canon through its allusions to canonical figures such as Emerson, Melville, and Twain.

Robert G. O'Meally, *The Craft of Ralph Ellison,* Harvard University Press, 1980.

An important critical study of Ellison's life and his writing, with particular attention to Ellison's characters and the "fictional world" they inhabit.

Robert G. O'Meally, editor, *New Essays on Invisible Man,* Cambridge University Press, 1988.

A collection of five recent essays on *Invisible Man* with an historical overview in O'Meally's Introduction.

Susan Resneck Parr and Pancho Savery, *Approaches to Teaching Ellison's Invisible Man,* Modern Language Association, 1980.

Though intended primarily for teachers, this collection of brief essays also offers the first-time reader several productive avenues into Ellison's novel.

David Remnick, "Visible Man," in *The New Yorker,* March 14, 1994, pp. 34-38.

Published just one month before Ellison's death, this essay discusses the importance of his writings to discussions of race in America since the 1960s.

Eric J. Sundquist, editor, *Cultural Contexts for Ralph Ellison's Invisible Man,* Bedford, 1995.

This useful collection "illuminates and contextualizes" Ellison's novel by gathering various historical and cultural documents, including speeches, essays, songs, and folktales.

Joseph F. Trimmer, editor, *A Casebook on Ralph Ellison's Invisible Man,* Thomas Y. Crowell, 1972.

A collection of essays that places Ellison in the context of both a "racial heritage" and an "artistic heritage" and concludes with a listing of "possible discussion questions or research topics."

Lord of the Flies

William Golding

1954

Despite its later popularity, William Golding's *Lord of the Flies* was only a modest success when it was first published in England in 1954, and it sold only 2,383 copies in the United States in 1955 before going out of print. Critical reviews and British word of mouth were positive enough, however, that by the time a paperback edition was published in 1959, *Lord of the Flies* began to challenge *The Catcher in the Rye* as the most popular book on American college campuses. By mid-1962 it had sold more than 65,000 copies and was required reading on more than one hundred campuses.

The book seemed to appeal to adolescents' natural skepticism about the allegedly humane values of adult society. It also captured the keen interest of their instructors in debating the merits and defects of different characters and the hunting down of literary sources and deeper symbolic or allegorical meanings in the story—all of which were in no short supply. Did the ending of the story—a modern retelling of a Victorian story of children stranded on a deserted island—represent the victory of civilization over savagery, or vice versa? Was the tragic hero of the tale Piggy, Simon, or Ralph? Was Golding's biggest literary debt owed to R. M. Ballantyne's children's adventure story *The Coral Island* or to Euripides's classic Greek tragedy *The Bacchae*?

Though the popularity of Golding's works as a whole has ebbed and grown through the years, *Lord of the Flies* has remained his most read book. The questions raised above, and many more like

them, have continued to fascinate readers. It is for this reason, more than any other, that many critics consider *Lord of the Flies* a classic of our times.

Author Biography

From an unknown schoolmaster in 1954, when *Lord of the Flies* was first published, William Golding became a major novelist over the next ten years, only to fall again into relative obscurity after the publication of the generally well-received *The Spire* in 1964. This second period of obscurity lasted until the end of the 1970s. The years 1979 to 1982 were suddenly fruitful for Golding, and in 1983 he was awarded the Nobel Prize in Literature. How does one account for a life filled with such ups and downs? There can be no one answer to that question, except perhaps to note that Golding's motto, "Nothing Twice," suggests a man with an inquiring mind who was not afraid to try many different approaches to his craft. He knew that while some of his efforts might fail, others would be all the stronger for the attempt.

Born in 1911, Golding was the son of an English schoolmaster, a many-talented man who believed strongly in science and rational thought. Golding often described his father's overwhelming influence on his life. The author graduated from Oxford University in 1935 and spent four years (later described by Golding as having been "wasted") writing, acting, and producing for a small London theater. Golding himself became a schoolmaster for a year, after marrying Ann Brookfield in 1939 and before entering the British Royal Navy in 1940.

Golding had switched his major from science to English literature after two years in college—a crucial change that marked the beginning of Golding's disillusion with the rationalism of his father. The single event in Golding's life that most affected his writing of *Lord of the Flies,* however, was probably his service in World War II. Raised in the sheltered environment of a private English school, Golding was unprepared for the violence unleashed by the war. Joining the Navy, he was injured in an accident involving detonators early in the war, but later was given command of a small rocket-launching craft. Golding was present at the sinking of the *Bismarck*—the crown ship of the German Navy—and also took part in the D-Day landings in

William Golding

France in June 1944. He later described his experience in the war as one in which "one had one's nose rubbed in the human condition."

After the war, Golding returned to teaching English and philosophy at the same school where he had begun his teaching career. During the next nine years, from 1945 until 1954, he wrote three novels rejected for their derivative nature before finally getting the idea for *Lord of the Flies.* After reading a bedtime boys adventure story to his small children, Golding wondered out loud to his wife whether it would be a good idea to write such a story but to let the characters "behave as they really would." His wife thought that would be a "first class idea." With that encouragement, Golding found that writing the story, the ideas for which had been germinating in his mind for some time, was simply a matter of getting it down on paper.

Golding went on to write ten other novels plus shorter fiction, plays, essays, and a travel book. Yet it is his first novel, *Lord of the Flies,* that made him famous, and for which he will probably remain best known. Golding died of a heart attack in 1993.

Plot Summary

On the Island: Chapters 1–2

William Golding sets his novel *Lord of the Flies* at a time when Europe is in the midst of nuclear destruction. A group of boys, being evacuated from England to Australia, crash lands on a tropical island. No adults survive the crash, and the novel is the story of the boys' descent into chaos, disorder, and evil.

As the story opens, two boys emerge from the wreckage of a plane. The boys, Ralph and Piggy, begin exploring the island in hopes of finding other survivors. They find a conch shell, and Piggy instructs Ralph how to blow on it. When the other boys hear the conch, they gather. The last boys to appear are the choirboys, led by Jack Merridew. Once assembled, the boys decide they need a chief and elect Ralph. Ralph decides that the choir will remain intact under the leadership of Jack, who says they will be hunters.

Jack, Ralph, and Simon go to explore the island and find a pig trapped in vines. Jack draws his knife, but is unable to actually kill the pig. They vow, however, to kill the pig the next time. When the three return, they hold a meeting. The conch becomes a symbol of authority: whoever has the conch has the right to speak. Jack and Ralph explain to the others what they have found. Jack continues his preoccupation with his knife. The boy with the clearest understanding of their situation is Piggy. He tells them they are on an island, that no one knows where they are, and that they are likely to be on the island for a very long time without adults. Ralph replies, "This is our island. It's a good island. Until the grownups come to fetch us we'll have fun." One of the "littluns," the group of youngest boys, says that he is afraid of the "beastie." The "biguns" try to dissuade him, saying there are no beasties on the island. However, it is at this moment that Jack asserts himself against Ralph, saying that if there were a beastie, he would kill it.

Discussion returns to the possibility of rescue. Ralph says that rescue depends on making a fire so that ships at sea could see the smoke. The boys get overly excited, with Jack as the ringleader, and all but Piggy and Ralph rush off to the top of the mountain to build a fire. They forget about the conch and the system of rules they have just made. At the top of the mountain, Ralph uses Piggy's glasses to light the fire. They are careless and set fire to the mountain. Piggy accuses them of "acting like kids." He

reminds the older boys of their responsibility to the younger boys. At this moment they realize that one of the littluns is missing.

The Beast: Chapters 3–11

The story resumes days later with Simon and Ralph trying to build shelters on the shore. Jack is away hunting. When he returns, there is antagonism between Ralph and Jack. Jack is beginning to forget about rescue and is growing tired of the responsibility of keeping the fire going, a task for which he has volunteered his choir. The growing separation between the boys is marked by Ralph's insistence on the importance of shelter and Jack's on the hunting of meat.

In the next chapter, Golding describes the rhythm of life on the island. By this point, Jack has begun to paint his face with mud and charcoal when he hunts. At a crucial moment, the fire goes out, just as Ralph spots a ship in the distance. In the midst of Ralph's distress, the hunters return with a dead pig. In the ensuing melee, one of the lenses in Piggy's glasses gets broken.

Ralph calls an assembly in order to reassert the rules. The littluns bring up their fear of the beastie yet again, saying that it comes from the sea. Simon tries to suggest that the only beast on the island is in themselves; however, no one listens. Ralph once again calls for the rules. Jack, however, plays to the fear of the boys, and says, "Bollocks to the rules! We're strong—we hunt! If there's a beast, we'll hunt it down! We close in and beat and beat and beat—!" The meeting ends in chaos. Ralph, discouraged, talks with Piggy and Simon about their need for adults. "If only they could get a message to us…. If only they could send us something grownup … a sign or something."

The sign that appears, however, comes when all the boys are asleep. High overhead rages an air battle and a dead parachutist falls to the island. When the boys hear the sound of the parachute, they are sure it is the beast. Jack, Ralph, and Simon go in search. Climbing to the top of the mountain, they see "a creature that bulged." They do not recognize the figure as a dead parachutist, tangled in his ropes, and swaying in the wind.

When the boys return to the littluns and Piggy at the shelters, Jack calls an assembly. He calls Ralph a coward and urges the boys to vote against Ralph. They will not, and Jack leaves. Ralph tries to reorganize the group, but notices that gradually most of the biguns sneak off after Jack. The scene shifts to Jack, talking to his hunters. They go off on a hunt in which they kill a sow, gruesomely and cruelly. They cut off the pig's head and mount it on a stick in sacrifice to the beast. Meanwhile, Simon wanders into the woods in search of the beast. He finds the head, now called in the text "The Lord of the Flies." Simon feels a seizure coming on as he hallucinates a conversation with the head:

> Simon's head was tilted slightly up. His eyes could not break away and the Lord of the Flies hung in space before him.
>
> "What are you doing out here all alone? Aren't you afraid of me?"
>
> Simon shook.
>
> "There isn't anyone to help you. Only me. And I'm the Beast."
>
> Simon's mouth labored, brought forth audible words.
>
> "Pig's head on a stick."
>
> "Fancy thinking the Beast was something you could hunt and kill!" said the head. For a moment or two the forest and all the other dimly appreciated places echoed with the parody of laughter. "You knew didn't you? I'm part of you? Close, close, close! I'm the reason why it's no go? Why things are what they are?"

Simon falls into unconsciousness. When he awakens, he finds the decomposed body of the parachutist, and realizes that this is what the boys think is the beast. He gently frees the dead man from his ropes.

Back at the shelters, Ralph and Piggy are the only ones left. The two go to see Jack and the hunters, and they find a big party. At the height of the party, a storm breaks and Simon arrives to tell them that there is no beast. In a frenzy, they kill Simon. Later, Ralph, Piggy, Sam, and Eric are alone on the beach. All the boys agree that they left the dance early and that they did not see anything. The four boys try to keep the fire going, but they cannot. Jack's hunters attack the boys and steal Piggy's glasses so that they have the power of fire. Enraged, Ralph and Piggy go to retrieve the glasses. There is a fight, and Roger, the most vicious of the hunters, launches a rock at Piggy, knocking the conch from his hands, and sending him some forty feet to the rocks in the sea below.

The Rescue: Chapter 12

The scene shifts to Ralph, alone, hiding from the rest of the boys who are hunting him. The language used to describe the boys has shifted: they are now "savages," and "the tribe." Ralph is utterly alone, trying to plan his own survival. He finds the Lord of the Flies, and hits the skull off the stick.

From the film Lord of the Flies, *1963.*

Ralph sees Sam and Eric serving as lookouts for the tribe and approaches them carefully. They warn him off, saying that they've been forced to participate with the hunters. When Ralph asks what the tribe plans on doing when they capture him, the twins will only talk about Roger's ferocity. They state obliquely, "Roger sharpened a stick at both ends."

Ralph tells the twins where he will hide; but soon the twins are forced to reveal this location and Ralph is cornered. However, the tribe has once again set the island on fire, and Ralph is able to creep away under the cover of smoke. Back on the beach, Ralph finds himself once again pursued. At the moment that the savages are about to capture him, an adult naval officer appears. Suddenly, with rescue at hand, the savages once again become little boys and they begin to cry. The officer cannot seem to understand what has happened on the island. "Fun and games," he says, unconsciously echoing Ralph's words from the opening chapter. Ralph breaks down and sobs, mourning Simon and mourning Piggy. In the final line of the book, Golding reminds the reader that although adults have arrived, the rescue is a faulty one. The officer looks out to sea at his "trim cruiser in the distance." The world, after all, is still at war.

Characters

Bill

Like Maurice, Bill is initially confused by the clash of values among the boys. At first he seems seduced by Jack's painted face into joining the hunters in their anonymity; yet he then turns fearful and runs away. Eventually, however, Bill imagines group hunting and "being savages" as "jolly good fun" and thus a way of banishing these fears. He tries to convince Ralph's group to accept Jack's invitation to the feast, thinking that Jack is less fearful than Ralph about going into the jungle to hunt. Soon he has defected to Jack's group and is seen painted like a savage and stalking Ralph.

Eric

See Samneric

Henry

Henry is the biggest littlun and a relative of the littlun with the mulberry-marked face who disappears after the first big fire. Henry is the object of Roger's seemingly innocent game of throwing stones. Later, Henry defects to Jack's camp and is part of the raiding party that steals fire from Ralph and Piggy.

Johnny

Along with Percival, Johnny is the smallest of the littluns. He is described as "well built, with fair hair and a natural belligerence," which he soon shows by throwing sand in Percival's face. Later, Johnny is shown crying when he thinks Eric may be bleeding from his encounter with Jack's fire-stealers.

The littlun with the mulberry-marked face

Otherwise unidentified except as a distant relative of Henry, this littlun was noticed immediately after the boys came on the island; he is the first boy to mention seeing a "snake-thing," a "beastie [who] came in the dark." He is not seen after the fire got out of control. He is therefore the focus of much anxiety, especially among Ralph's group, which had tried to make a special point of looking after the littluns.

Percival Wemys Madison

Percival Wemys Madison, of the Vicarage, Harcourt St. Anthony, Hants, as he has been taught to introduce himself, is "mouse-colored and had not been very attractive even to his mother." Along with Johnny, Percival is the smallest littlun. When Ralph and Piggy are trying to seek a rational explanation for Phil's dream of having seen and fought with "twisty things in the trees," they call on Percival as someone who was supposed to have been up that night and who might have been mistaken for the fearful thing that has so terrorized the littluns. But Percival's mere recitation of his name and address is enough to set off sad memories of his former life. His wails, along with his speculation that the beast comes from the sea, soon set off the other littluns on similar crying jags.

Maurice

One of the "biguns," he is next in size to Jack among the choir boys. Like most of the boys, he is a mixture of potentially good and bad traits. Which traits are developed depends on how strong the call of society and law is over the powers of darkness and savagery. In the beginning Maurice is helpful by suggesting that the boys use green branches on the fire to make smoke. He also makes the "littluns" forget their sorrow by pretending to fall off the twister log and making them laugh. Like Piggy, Maurice wants to believe that the world is a scientific place where human fears can be explained and needs can be met. Yet Maurice, who "of all the boys … was the most at home" on the island, is still fearful that "we don't know [about the beast], do we? Not certainly, I mean…." Giving in to his fears, Maurice joins Roger in asserting his power by kicking over the littluns' sand castles. He also suggests adding a drum to the mock pig-killing ritual. Maurice's capitulation to his repressive leanings is complete when he defects to Jack and helps him steal fire from Piggy and Ralph.

Jack Merridew

Jack would have preferred to be called Merridew, his last name, rather than a "kid name." This attitude may suggest the "simple arrogance" that causes Jack to propose himself for chief. After all, he exclaims, "I'm chapter chorister and head boy." (The rough American equivalents of these positions might be president of the glee club and head of the student council.) It's true that Jack has the advantage of being tall; his direction of the choir is another sign of an "obvious leader." As a political animal, however, Jack recognizes that choir conducting won't get him far on a deserted island. His decision to turn the choir into a group of hunters with himself as leader shows that he can be a wily strategist. In other ways, however, Jack is careless and destructive, as when he accidentally steps on

L o r d   o f   t h e   F l i e s

Piggy's glasses and breaks a lens. Similarly, Jack becomes so fixated with hunting that he neglects the fire, which goes out before the boys can signal a passing ship. Nevertheless, Jack is successful in daring Ralph to come with him to hunt the mysterious beast when darkness is falling. On that hunt Jack and Ralph, joined by Roger, perceive through the falling darkness the dim, shrouded figure of the dead parachutist—an image of the adult world that suggests the destruction of the rational society envisioned by Ralph and Piggy.

As Ralph's civilized world disintegrates, Jack's savage society becomes more distinct and powerful. Jack separates his group from Ralph's when the group fails to dethrone Ralph and recognize Jack as leader. Then Jack sets about wooing away the other boys to his group. One way is by inviting everyone to a pig roast. Another is by painting his hunters' bodies and masking their faces, thus turning them into an anonymous mob of fighters who can wound and kill without fear of being singled out as guilty. Significantly, it is Jack who is the first of the older boys to see the possibility of the beast's existence, and ultimately the ways to use the fear of the beast to his advantage: as a motivation for hunting, and as a means of keeping the littluns under his control. When Simon seeks to expose the beast as just a "dead man on a hill," he is killed by Jack's group.

With Jack's successful theft of Piggy's last glass lens, the hunters' raid on Ralph and Piggy's fire, the capture and defection of Sam and Eric, and finally Piggy's death, as engineered by Jack and Roger, the "savages'" power is almost absolute. Only the intervention of adult society, represented by the British captain, is able to save Ralph from being killed and to reduce Jack to embarrassed silence at his failure to harness the powers of evil.

Phil

One of the more self-confident littluns, Phil straightforwardly describes his dream of the "twisty things" when requested by Piggy.

Piggy

Piggy is an intelligent and rational boy whose excess weight and asthma often make him the butt of the others' jokes. Yet because of his scientific approach to problems, Piggy is a voice of reason without whom Ralph's leadership would have been undermined far sooner. It is Piggy who not only recognizes the significance of the conch but whose spectacles enable Ralph to start the fire, whose smoke is their only chance of being saved. It is

Media Adaptations

- *Lord of the Flies* enjoys the unusual status of being one of the few serious contemporary novels to have been made into a movie twice. The first, directed by Peter Brook in 1963 with an all-English cast, as has been described as "compelling," but was only moderately successful at the box office. Available from Home Vision Cinema and Fusion Video.

- The remake in 1990 featured an American cast and was directed by Harry Hook. While well-photographed and "visceral," with R-rated content, it is generally regarded as inferior to Brooks's version. Available from Columbia Tristar Home Video, The Video Catalog, and New Line Home Video.

- An 89-minute sound recording on cassette (JRH 109), book, and study guide, produced in 1984 and featuring excerpts from the novel, are available from the Listening Library, Old Greenwich, CT.

Piggy who realizes that building the shelters is at least as important for their long-term survival as keeping the fire going. It is Piggy whose understanding of the depths of Jack's hatred for Ralph forces Ralph to confront his despair at their prospects for getting along. And it is Piggy who makes the brilliant, however simple, suggestion that the fire be moved down to the beach away from the "beast from air."

For all his intellectual powers, however, Piggy is basically ineffectual without Ralph. Piggy is a man of thought, not of action, and he is physically weak because of his asthma. Without his spectacles, he is blind and helpless. After Jack has broken one lens from his glasses and stolen the other, Piggy is doomed in a society where irrational fears and physical strength are more respected than science, law, and dialogue. It is significant that Piggy and the conch are both destroyed at the same time by a huge rock rolled down a cliff by Roger, who

1 7 9

has been freed by Jack from the "taboo of the old life … the protection of parents and school and policemen and the law" to unleash his savage instincts. Of all the children, Piggy is the most adult in his appearance, behavior, and beliefs. His thinning hair, which never seems to grow, and his frequent appeals to "what grownups would do" suggest his maturity and wisdom. In the closing lines of the book, Ralph weeps not only for "the end of innocence, the darkness of man's heart," but for "the fall through the air of the true, wise friend called Piggy."

Ralph

The fair-haired, tall, handsome Ralph is an obvious choice to lead the band of children stranded on the island. He has a "directness" in his manner that the narrator calls a sign of "genuine leadership." As E. M. Forster describes Ralph in an introduction to one of novel's editions, he is "sunny and decent, sensible and considerate." He seems to be genuinely interested in the welfare of the entire group and can get along with all kinds of people. Perhaps he gets his sense of natural authority from his father, a commander in the Navy. He also has above-average powers of observation. He is the first to see the conch shell buried in the sand, though it is significant that it is Piggy who points out how it can be used as a signaling device.

In fact, Ralph is far from the ideal leader, and certainly far from the idealized Ralph in *The Coral Island,* R. M. Ballantyne's romantic children's story for which Golding intended his book to be a reality check. Ralph lacks the charisma and strategic skills to get the other boys to recognize what the conch represents—order, authority, dialogue, democracy. These are the qualities that are necessary if the group is to keep its signal fire going long enough to attract a passing ship. Golding often notes the "shutter" or cloud that sometimes comes over Ralph's mind when he is addressing the group and that prevents him from finding the right word to get their attention or galvanize them to action. This cloud of imperfection makes Ralph a kind of everyman with whom we can each identify, but it contributes to the gradual descent of the boys into a savagery to which Ralph himself succumbs by the end of the story.

Robert

Like Simon and Maurice, Robert is one of the medium-sized boys on the lower end of the biguns' spectrum. In the stripped-down world of the island where the physical assumes more weight, Robert finds his niche guarding Castle Rock. Robert is more comfortable taking orders than giving them. The one time he takes any initiative, pretending to be the pig in a ritual game, he is quickly reduced to a sniveling child. He also serves with Jack and Maurice on the committee that welcomes Ralph's group to Jack's feast.

Roger

Just as Piggy represents Ralph's best quality, his attempts to act mature, so Roger stands for Jack's worst characteristic, his lust for power over living things. Roger is first introduced as one of the biguns who "kept to himself with an inner intensity of avoidance and secrecy." While Piggy thinks about ways to be rescued, Roger is "gloomily" pessimistic about the group's chances. Acting on his darker impulses, at first in small ways, he knocks over Percival and Johnny's sand castles. Then he throws stones at Henry, only missing because his arm "was conditioned by a civilization that knew nothing of him and was in ruins." Once he sees how Jack's "dazzle paint" created a mask that "liberated him from shame and self-consciousness," however, it is only a matter of time before Roger comes under Jack's power. First we see him, along with Ralph and the rest, participate in the mock pig kill in celebration of the successful hunt. Then, not long after Jack secedes from the group, Roger follows him and is soon hunting pigs and offering to help Jack steal fire from Ralph's group. Though part of Roger still questions the irresponsibility of some of Jack's actions, like beating Wilfred, he nevertheless goes along with them. It is Roger who, "with a sense of delirious abandonment," finally releases the boulder from Castle Rock that kills Piggy and destroys the conch. And it is Roger who, "wielding a nameless authority," moves to detain Sam and Eric.

Sam

See Samneric

Samneric

As twins, the two always act together and indeed are often called Samneric as one unit. In the beginning Sam and Eric are especially helpful to Ralph, rekindling the fire on top of the mountain after it almost goes out. Even after being scared by the "beast from air," the twins do not desert Ralph, as Maurice and Roger do; instead the twins go with Piggy to gather fruit for their own feast. After attending Jack's pig roast, Sam and Eric return to Ralph and Piggy's shelters, the last "biguns" to remain loyal, though none will admit to the other that they were in any way involved in Simon's death. Finally Sam and Eric are captured by Jack's group while accompanying Piggy and Ralph to demand that Jack return Piggy's glasses. In the ensuing confrontation, Ralph attacks Jack and runs into the jungle, where his presence is then betrayed by the twins, who fear for their lives.

Simon

Perhaps the most symbolic character in the story, Simon represents the religious prophet or seer who is sensitive and inarticulate yet who, of all the boys, perhaps sees reality most clearly. Simon's special powers are signaled early in the story when, even though he is not one of the bigger boys, he is chosen by Ralph to join him and Jack to explore the island. Among all the boys, it is Simon whose behavior is perhaps the most exemplary during the first part of the story. He is Ralph's faithful helper in building the shelters. Simon alone recognizes that "maybe [the beast is] only us" or just a "pig's head on a stick." Simon, for all his sensitivity and fears, knows that the only way to deal with fear is to face it. When no one else wants to climb back up the mountain after seeing the "beast from air," it is Simon who proposes just such a climb. "What else is there to do?" he reasons. And even after Simon imagines the beast telling him, with the "infinite cynicism of adult life," that "everything was a bad business," he answers, "I know that." Ralph's vision of how things are is all-too-human and clouded compared to Simon's, though Simon must periodically retreat to the candle-budded trees in the forest to restore and maintain this clearsightedness.

Yet even Simon faints with weakness and disgust after seeing the beast and imagining it saying, "You knew, didn't you? I'm part of you? ... I'm the reason why it's no go? Why things are what they are?" When confronted with the realization that he is isolated and cut off from the others in his special knowledge, and just as afraid to die as any of them, Simon begins to lose the vision that had made him a potential savior of the group.

What began as a ritual and make-believe killing of the pig as a way of celebrating a good hunt now becomes a real ritual murder. Simon, in an attempt to tell the others about his discovery of the "man on the hill," accidentally stumbles into a ring of littluns and is killed in the confusion. The shame that Ralph, Piggy, Sam, and Eric all feel the day after Simon's death, despite their attempts to ignore it, show that civilized values still have some

hold on them. Yet the incident marks an important turning point in the story, for it is the first time that the boys have deliberately killed one of their own.

Themes

Good and Evil

During their abandonment on the island, Ralph, Piggy, Simon, and many of the other boys show elements of good in their characters. Ralph's calm "stillness," and his attentiveness to others' needs, make him a potentially good person. Good may be defined here as something just, virtuous, or kind that conforms to the moral order of the universe. Piggy's knowledge and belief in the power of science and rational thought to help people understand and thus control the physical world for their mutual benefit are also obviously a force for good. Simon, always ready to help out, sensitive to the power of evil but not afraid to stand up to it, is perhaps the strongest representative of the forces of good in the story.

Yet all of these characters ultimately fall victim to the forces of evil, as represented by the cruelties of the hunters, especially Jack and Roger. Piggy loses his glasses, and thus the power to make fire. This power, when controlled by the forces of reason, is a powerful tool for good: it warms the boys, cooks their food, and provides smoke for the rescue signals that are their only hope for survival. But in the hands of those with less skill and knowledge, the fire becomes an agent of destruction—first unintentionally in the hands of those who are ignorant of its powers, then purposefully when Jack and the hunters use it to smoke out and destroy their opponents. It is Simon's bad luck to stumble upon the feasting group of boys with his news about the "man on the hill" just as the group's ritual pig hunt is reaching its climax. Simon's ritual killing, to which Piggy and Ralph are unwitting yet complicit witnesses, is perhaps the decisive blow in the battle between the forces of good and evil. Later Piggy loses his life at the hand of the almost totally evil Roger, who has loosed the boulder from Castle Rock. Now, without Piggy's glasses and wise counsel and Simon's steadfastness, Ralph is greatly weakened, and to survive he must ultimately be rescued by adult society, represented by the British captain. It is important, however, to note that Jack, too, is defeated because he cannot control the forces of evil. It is Jack's order to use fire to destroy Ralph's hiding place that virtually destroys the is-

Topics for Further Study

- Compare and contrast the attitudes of Piggy, Ralph, Jack, and Simon toward the environment, as shown in the novel. Argue whether there is or is not any hope for environmental conservation as illustrated in the story.

- Research the weather, plant and animal life, and ocean life of a tropical island in the Pacific Ocean. Imagine you have been abandoned on the island and write a week-long journal detailing how you would survive there.

- Research actual instances of groups of adults or children being abandoned in the wilderness. Compare the outcomes of these cases to the events that occur in *Lord of the Flies*.

- Read one of the inspirations for *Lord of the Flies,* R. M. Ballantyne's *The Coral Island.* Compare the characters and events of the two books, and argue which book you think portrays a more realistic outcome. Use examples from the text to support your argument.

land, although, ironically, it is the smoke from that fire that finally attracts the British ship and leads to the boys' rescue.

Appearances and Reality

At several points in the story, Golding is at pains to stress the complexity of human life. During the novel, neither a firm grasp of reality (represented by Piggy's scientific bent and the island's ocean side) nor the comfort of illusions (seen in Ralph's daydreaming, Simon's silent communion with nature among the candlebud trees, and symbolized by the sleepy lagoon side of the island) is enough to save the boys from the forces of evil. The sun, which should represent life and the power of reason, can also be blinding. Yet darkness is no better, as can be seen when the littluns' fantasies and fears are only further distorted by nighttime shadows. This sense of complexity is perhaps best summed up by Ralph, speculating on how shadows

at different times of day change the appearance of things: "If faces were different when lit from above or below—what was a face? What was anything?" This comment can also relate to the power of the painted faces of Jack's hunters to remove the hunters from a sense of individual responsibility for their masked deeds.

Reason and Emotion

Because of Golding's great interest in Greek and Roman mythology, this theme is sometimes summarized by critics as the conflict between the Apollonian and the Dionysian aspects of life. This refers to the Greek gods Apollo, the god of reason, and Dionysus, the god of wine and emotion. Most characters in the story show elements of both reason and emotion. Piggy, with his interest in science and fact, may seem to represent the life of reason, while Jack and the hunters may seem to represent the emotional side of life. To Golding, however, matters are not that simple. Just as in Greek mythology the grave of Dionysus is found within the temple of Apollo at Delphi, so in the story reason and emotion may battle with each other within the same character. Thus when Roger first throws rocks, his arm is conditioned by rational society to avoid hitting the littlun Henry. Later his emotions will overcome his reason and he will loose the boulder that kills Piggy. Sometimes Golding shows the struggle between reason and emotion using two characters, as when Ralph the daydreamer struggles to remember the rational ideas Piggy told him about rescue. In the end, reason, in the form of the British captain, seems to triumph over the runaway emotion that has led to the destruction of the island and at least two of its temporary inhabitants. But the reflective reader will remember that the world to which the captain will presumably be trying to return has, in fact, been destroyed by an atom bomb. This suggests that in the end the grand achievements of science, compounded with the irrational emotions of warring powers, may have spelled the doom of humanity.

Morals and Morality

Golding himself has said that the writing of *Lord of the Files* was "an attempt to trace the defects of society back to the defects of human nature." Golding sets a group of children, who should supposedly be closest to a state of innocence, alone on an island without supervision. In this fashion, he can test whether the defects of society lie in the form of society or in the individuals who create it. Ralph tries to maintain order and convince the boys to work for the common good, but he can't overcome the selfishness of Jack and his hunters. By the time Piggy makes his plea for the return of his glasses—"not as a favor ... but because what's right's right"—Jack and his gang can no longer recognize a moral code where law and cooperation is best and killing is wrong. As the author once commented, "the moral is that the shape of a society must depend on the ethical nature of the individual and not on any political system."

Style

Point of View

All novels use at least one perspective, or point of view, from which to tell the story. This may consist of a point of view of no single character (the omniscient, or "all-knowing" point of view), a single character, multiple characters in turn, and combinations or variations on these. Golding uses the omniscient point of view, which enables him to stand outside and above the story itself, making no reference to the inner life of any of the individual characters. From this lofty point he comments on the action from the point of view of a removed, but observant, bystander. Golding has commented in interviews that the strongest emotion he personally feels about the story is grief. Nevertheless, as the narrator he makes a conscious decision, like the British captain at the end of the story, to "turn away" from the shaking and sobbing boys and remain detached. The narrator lets the actions, as translated through the artist's techniques of symbolism, structure, and so on, speak for themselves. Even so dramatic and emotional an event as Piggy's death is described almost clinically: "Piggy fell forty feet and landed on his back across that square red rock in the sea. His head opened and stuff came out and turned red."

Symbolism

A symbol can be defined as a person, place, or thing that represents something more than its literal meaning. The conch shell, to take an obvious example in the story, stands for a society of laws in which, for example, people take their turn in speaking. The pig's head is a more complex example of a symbol. To Simon, and to many readers, it can have more than one meaning. On a rational level, Simon knows the pig's head is just that: a "pig's head on a stick." But on a more emotional level, Simon realizes that the pig's head represents an evil so strong that it has the power to make him

faint. When he thinks of the head as "The Lord of the Flies," the symbol becomes even more powerful, as this title is a translation of "Beelzebub," another name for the Devil. Similarly, the fire set by using Piggy's glasses, when controlled, could be said to represent science and technology at their best, serving humans with light and heat. When uncontrolled, however, fire represents science and technology run amok, killing living things and destroying the island. Simon himself can be said to symbolize Christ, the selfless servant who is always helping others but who dies because his message—that the scary beast on the hill is only a dead parachutist—is misunderstood. Throughout the story, the noises of the surf, the crackling fire, the boulders rolling down hills, and trees exploding from the fire's heat are often compared to the boom of cannons and drum rolls. In this way, Golding reminds us that the whole story is intended to repeat and symbolize the atomic war which preceded it.

Setting

In the setting for *Lord of the Flies,* Golding has created his own "Coral Island"—an allusion, or literary reference, to a book of that name by R. M. Ballantyne. Using the same scenario of boys being abandoned on a tropical island, *The Coral Island* (1857) is a classic boys' romantic adventure story, like Johann Wyss's *The Swiss Family Robinson,* in which everyone has a great time and nobody dies or ends up unhappy. Golding, however, has quite different ideas, and he has used the setting in his story to reinforce those concepts. Yes, the island can be a wonderful place, as the littluns discover by day when they are bathing in the lagoon pool or eating fruit from the trees. But at night the same beach can be the setting for nightmares, as some boys fancy that they see "snake-things" in the trees.

Golding builds a similar contrast between the generally rocky side of the island that faces the sea, and the softer side that faces the lagoon. On the ocean side of the island, "the filmy enchantments of mirage could not endure the cold ocean water.... On the other side of the island, swathed at midday with mirage, defended by the shield of the quiet lagoon, one might dream of rescue; but here, faced by the brute obtuseness of the ocean ... one was helpless." Thus the setting reinforces Golding's view of human nature as a struggle of good intentions and positive concepts like love and faith against the harshness of nature and human failings like anger.

A bus overturned by a bomb in World War II London, 1940.

Historical Context

Golding and World War II

"When I was young, before the war, I did have some airy-fairy views about man.... But I went through the war and that changed me. The war taught me different and a lot of others like me," Golding told Douglas A. Davis in the *New Republic*. Golding was referring to his experiences as captain of a British rocket-launching craft in the North Atlantic, where he was present at the sinking of the *Bismarck*, crown ship of the German navy, and participated in the D-Day invasion of German-

occupied France. He was also directly affected by the devastation of England by the German air force, which severely damaged the nation's infrastructure and marked the beginning of a serious decline in the British economy. Wartime rationing continued well into the postwar period. Items like meat, bread, sugar, gasoline, and tobacco were all in short supply and considered luxuries. To turn their country around, the government experimented with nationaliz. tion of key industries like coal, electric power, and gas companies as well as the transportation industry. Socialized medicine and government-sponsored insurance were also introduced. Such

Compare & Contrast

- **1950s:** Economically, Great Britain was devastated by World War II. Homes, factories, railroads, docks, and other facilities had been destroyed by the German air force. Rationing of bread, meat, sugar, and gasoline continued well into the postwar period. Formerly a creditor, or lending nation, Great Britain for the first time in its history became a debtor nation.

  Today: Great Britain has regained economic stability, though not the economic power it had enjoyed before World War II. The discovery of oil in the North Sea and membership in the European Union (despite occasional disagreements) have enhanced Great Britain's economic strength.

- **1950s:** Politically, Great Britain was ruled in the immediate post-World War II period by the Labor Party, under which basic industries like coal, electric power, gas, and transportation were nationalized, social security was expanded, and universal health care was made available. With the coming of the Cold War, Great Britain sided with its World War II ally the United States against Russian expansionism, although a strong strain of antinuclear activism arose, centered around the placement of American nuclear missiles on British bases.

  Today: Great Britain remains politically strong, though a separatist movement in Northern Ireland continues to cause unrest. With the fall of the Berlin Wall and the end of the Cold War, Great Britain has been able to focus its energies more on domestic problems and regional cooperation.

- **1950s:** Biologically oriented psychologists like Arnold Gesell believe that a child's intellectual development is only marginally affected by environment, while other scientists argue that it plays a dominant role.

  Today: Scientific studies using brain scans have shown physical differences between the brains of healthy children and abused children, suggesting experiences can actually change the circuity of the brain.

---

changes, and the difficult conditions that produced them, suggest the climate of the postwar years in which Golding wrote *Lord of the Flies.*

The Geography of a Tropical Island

Although highly romanticized in both Western fiction and nonfiction, life on a typical tropical island is not all that easy. The weather is usually very hot and humid, and there is no breeze once one enters the jungle. While fish abound in the surrounding waters and the scent of tropical flowers wafts through the air, one must still watch out for sharks, and one cannot live on a diet of fruit and flowers. James Fahey, a naval seaman who served in the Pacific islands during the war, concluded: "We do not care too much for this place, the climate takes the life right out of you."

The Political Climate of the 1950s

The rise of the Cold War between the Soviet Union (U.S.S.R.) and the western powers after the end of World War II signaled a new phase in world geopolitics. Actual wars during the 1950s were confined to relatively small-scale conflicts, as in Korea (involving the United States) and Vietnam (involving the French). The nonviolent yet still threatening sabre-rattling between the USSR and the United States, however, reached a peak with the first successful hydrogen bomb test by the United States on November 1, 1952, at Eniwetok Atoll in the Pacific. A second device, hundreds of times more powerful than the atomic bombs dropped over Japan, was successfully detonated on March 1, 1954, at Bikini Atoll. In the United States, public fallout shelters were designated for large cities, allegedly to protect citizens from the rain of radioactive materials produced by such nuclear explosions. Schoolchildren practiced taking cover under their desks during regular air raid drills. Also in 1954, Canada and the United States agreed to build a "DEW" line (Distant Early Warning Line) of radar stations across the Arctic to warn of approaching aircraft or missiles over the Arctic. In short, the atmosphere of the first half of the 1950s was one of suspicion, distrust, and threats among the big powers. An atomic war on the scale that *Lord of Flies* suggested did not seem out of the realm of possibility during the early 1950s.

Critical Overview

Lord of the Flies has attracted an immense amount of both favorable and unfavorable criticism. Most vehement among the latter critics are Kenneth Rexroth, whose essay in the *Atlantic Monthly* castigated the author for having written a typical "rigged" "thesis novel" whose characters "never come alive as real boys." In the same camp is Martin Green (1960), who criticizes Golding's early works, including *Lord of the Flies,* as "not importantly original in thought or feeling." Otherwise admiring critics like James R. Baker have claimed that the popularity of the book peaked by the end of the 1960s because of that decade's naive view of humanity and rejection of original sin.

Among critics who admire *Lord of the Flies,* there is remarkable disagreement about the book's influences, genre, significant characters, and theme, not to mention the general philosophy of the author. Frank Kermode's early essay, excerpts of which appear in Baker & Ziegler's casebook edition of the novel, examines R. M. Ballantyne's Victorian boys' adventure story *The Coral Island* as Golding's primary influence. He interprets Golding's book as a powerful story, capable of many interpretations, precisely because of the author's "mythopoeic power to transcend" his own allegorical "programme." Bernard F. Dick, while acknowledging *The Coral Island's* influence, builds on Kermode's observation that the book's strength is grounded in its mythic level by tracing the influence of the Greek dramatists, especially Euripides, whose play *The Bacchae* Golding himself acknowledged as an important source of his thinking. Dick notes that *The Bacchae* and *Lord of the Flies* both "portray a bipolar society in which the Apollonian [represented by Ralph] refuses or is unable

to assimilate the Dionysian [represented by the hunters]." Dick finds fault with the author's having profound thoughts come out of the mouths of children, especially Simon. The critic recognizes, however, that this flaw grew out of Golding's decision to model his characters on the children in *Coral Island.* Nevertheless Dick is an overall admirer of Golding's craft in producing a work whose "foundation … is mythic" yet which is perhaps most accurately called a "serious parody."

Using a psychoanalytic approach to the novel, Claire Rosenfield (1961) finds yet another source for Golding's ideas in psychoanalyst Sigmund Freud's *Totem and Taboo.* Golding claimed in an interview that he had read "absolutely no Freud." Even so, Rosenfield's close reading argues that Golding must have been influenced, directly or indirectly, by Freudian ideas. Rosenfield reminds us that according to Freud, gods and devils are basically human processes projected into the outer world. Specifically, "Ralph is a projection of man's good impulses from which we derive the authority figures—whether god, king, or father…. Jack becomes an externalization of the evil instinctual forces of the unconscious." Piggy, whose knowledge of science, thinning hair, and respect for adults make him the most adultlike child on the island, is both a father figure and a symbol of the progressive degeneration of the boys from adults to animalistic savages.

The abundance of possible critical stances on *Lord of the Flies* is summarized by Patrick Reilly in his chapter "The Strife of Critics" from his study *"Lord of the Flies": Fathers and Sons.* Reilly notes that the book "has been read as a moral fable of personal disintegration, as a social fable of social regression, as a religious fable of the fall of man." One critic is sure that civilization is victorious in the book, while another scoffs at the very idea that the book ends happily.

Reilly himself puts Golding's work squarely in the tradition of the "dark epiphany" as used in Jonathan Swift's *Gulliver's Travels.* Both authors work under the notion that man is so thoroughly corrupted that his redemption as a species is hopeless, however gallant and inspirational individual attempts may be. Thus the reader of Golding at the end of book is left wondering how, if the world has been destroyed by atomic war, the captain and his ship will be rescued after he has rescued the boys. Reilly, however, does find hope in the figure of Simon, whose slow death ennobles him as a "hero, saint, martyr," in contrast to Piggy's quick dispatch and equally sudden disappearance. Thus the darkness within man as a whole in the story is balanced by the "brightness within" individual hearts, and Reilly concludes that "if we cannot be certain of salvation, perhaps it is enough to sustain us if we know that the darkness need not prevail."

Criticism

Diane Andrews Henningfeld

Henningfeld is a professor at Adrian College. In the following essay, she explores how Golding's novel can be interpreted in a variety of different ways—including as political, psychological, and religious allegory.

Lord of the Flies, William Golding's first novel, was published in London in 1954 and in New York in 1955. Golding was forty-three years old when he wrote the novel, having served in the Royal Navy during the Second World War. According to Bernard Oldsey, "The war appears to have been an important influence on him."

Lord of the Flies is deliberately modeled after R. M. Ballantyne's 1857 novel *The Coral Island.* In this story, a group of English boys are shipwrecked on a tropical island. They work hard together to save themselves. The only evil in the book is external and is personified by a tribe of cannibals that live on the island. The book offers a Victorian view of the world: through hard work and earnestness, one can overcome any hardship.

By giving his characters the same names as those in Ballantyne's book and by making direct reference to *The Coral Island* in the text of *Lord of the Flies,* Golding clearly wants readers to see his book as a response to the Victorian world view. Golding's view is a much bleaker one: the evil on the island is internal, not external. At the end of the book, the adult naval officer who invokes *The Coral Island* almost serves as Ballantyne's voice: "I should have thought that a pack of British boys—you're all British, aren't you?—would have been able to put up a better show than that." Golding's understanding of the world, colored by his own experiences in World War II, is better represented by Ralph's weeping "for the end of innocence, the darkness of man's heart, and the fall through the air of the true, wise friend called Piggy."

Initially, critics commented less on the novel as a work of art than on its political, religious, and psychological symbolism. For example, James Stern in a 1955 review for *The New York Times*

What Do I Read Next?

- Euripides's ancient Greek tragedy *The Bacchae,* (405 BC), whose influence on *Lord of the Flies* is widely acknowledged, dramatizes the influence of the worship of Dionysus on the city of Thebes. In the play, King Pentheus tries to stop the Bacchantes' Dionysian ceremony and as a result is taken for a wild animal and killed by his mother.

- Just as *Lord of the Flies* is a post-World War II response to R. M. Ballantyne's *The Coral Island,* so Golding's next novel, *The Inheritors* (1955), is a realistic response to H. G. Wells's optimistic theory of history as propounded in his *Outline of History.*

- *Animal Farm* by George Orwell (1945), like *Lord of the Flies,* is an allegory influenced by its author's war experiences, and one that probes the nature of man and his attempts to form a just society.

- The view of man and society in J. D. Salinger's *Catcher in the Rye* (1951), in which a psychologically convalescing young man looks back on his experiences, has often been contrasted with the perspective of Golding's novel, and both books have been campus favorites at different times.

- Praised for its style of its prose, Marianne Wiggin's 1989 novel *John Dollar* has been described as a "girl's version" of *Lord of the Flies.* Set in the 1910s, the novel follows a group of girls and their blinded schoolmistress who are stranded on an island near Burma after a storm.

Book Review wrote "*Lord of the Flies* is an allegory on human society today, the novel's primary implication being that what we have come to call civilization is at best no more than skin deep."

Indeed, many critics have argued that *Lord of the Flies* is an allegory. An allegory is a story in which characters, setting, objects, and plot stand for a meaning outside of the story itself. Frequently, the writers of allegory illustrate an abstract meaning by the use of concrete images. For example, George Orwell, in *Animal Farm,* uses animals and the barnyard as concrete representations of the Russian Revolution. Often, characters in allegories personify some abstract quality. In the medieval drama *Everyman,* for instance, the concrete character Everyman stands for all of humanity.

While it is possible to read *Lord of the Flies* as allegory, the work is so complex that it can be read as allegorizing the political state of the world in the postwar period; as a Freudian psychological understanding of human kind; or as the Christian understanding of the fall of humankind, among others.

As a political allegory, each character in *Lord of the Flies* represents some abstract idea of government. Ralph, for example, stands for the good-hearted but not entirely effective leader of a democratic state, a ruler who wants to rule by law derived from the common consent. Piggy is his adviser, someone who is unable to rule because of his own social and physical shortcomings, but who is able to offer sound advice to the democratic leader. Jack, on the other hand, represents a totalitarian dictator, a ruler who appeals to the emotional responses of his followers. He rules by charisma and hysteria. Roger, the boy who takes the most joy in the slaughter of the pigs and who hurls the rock that kills Piggy, represents the henchman necessary for such a totalitarian ruler to stay in power.

Such a reading takes into account the state of the world at the end of the World War II. For many years, leaders such as British Prime Minister Winston Churchill and U.S. President Franklin D. Roosevelt led democratic countries against totalitarian demigods such as Germany's Adolf Hitler and Italy's Benito Mussolini. Further, in the early 1950s, the world appeared to be divided into two camps: the so-called Free World of Western Europe and the United States, and the so-called Iron Curtain world of communist eastern Europe and the Soviet Union. At the time of the writing of *Lord of the Flies,* the world appeared to be teetering on the brink of total nuclear annihilation. Thus, by taking into account the historical context of *Lord of the Flies,* it is possible to understand the work as political and historical allegory, even as a cautionary tale for the leaders of the world.

Freudian psychological critics, on the other hand, are able to read *Lord of the Flies* as an allegory of the human psychology. In such a reading,

each of the characters personifies a different aspect of the human psyche: the id, the super ego, and the ego. According to Freud, the id (located in the unconscious mind) works always to gratify its own impulses. These impulses, often sexual, seek to provide pleasure without regard to the cost. Jack's impulse to hunt and kill reaches its peak with the killing of the sow pig, a killing rife with sexual overtones. Jack never considers anything but his own pleasure; thus he can be considered an allegorical representation of the id. The superego is the part of the mind that seeks to control the impulsive behavior of the id. It acts as an internal censor. In *Lord of the Flies,* Piggy serves this role. He constantly reminds Ralph of their need to keep the fire burning and to take proper responsibility for the litluns. By so doing, he urges Ralph to control Jack. Piggy understands that Jack hates him, because he stands between Jack and his achievement of pleasure. Further, just as the superego must employ the ego to control the id, Piggy cannot control Jack on his own; he must rely on Ralph to do so. Finally, the ego is the conscious mind whose role it is to mediate between the id's demand for pleasure and the social pressures brought to bear by the superego. Freud calls this mediation process the reality principal; that is, the notion that immediate pleasure must be denied in order to avoid painful or deadly consequences. Ralph clearly fills this role. He attempts to control Jack and engage his energy for the tending of the fire. To do so requires him to put off the pleasure of the hunt in order to secure rescue. In a Freudian reading of *The Lord of the Flies,* Golding seems to be saying that without the reinforcement of social norms, the id will control the psyche.

Finally, it is possible to read *Lord of the Flies* as a religious allegory. In such a reading, the tropical island, filled with fruit and everything needed for sustenance, becomes a symbol of the Garden of Eden. The initial identification of the beastie as a snake also brings to mind the story of the Fall of Man. Indeed, it is possible to read the fall of the parachutist as the event which leads to the ouster from Eden of the boys. Further, Jack's identification with hunting and Ralph's identification with shelter as well as their natural antagonism appear to be allegorization of the Cain and Abel story. Indeed, it is only the intercession of the adult who comes looking for them which saves Ralph from murder. Many critics have attempted to read Simon as a Christ figure; he is the one boy who has the true knowledge which can save them. Like Christ, he is martyred. Unlike Christ, however, his death seems to have no significance for the boys; his knowledge dies with him.

More recently, critics have recognized the technical and artistic skill exhibited by Golding in *Lord of the Flies*. Especially notable is the way in which Golding fuses allegorical structure with strong, realistic descriptions, well-developed characterizations, and a coherent, fast moving plot. The description of the death of Piggy, for example, demonstrates Golding's skill with realistic, graphic prose:

> The rock struck Piggy a glancing blow from chin to knee; the conch exploded into a thousand white fragments and ceased to exist. Piggy, saying nothing, with no time for even a grunt, traveled through the air sideways from the rock, turning over as he went. The rock bounded twice and was lost in the forest. Piggy fell forty feet and landed on his back across the square red rock in the sea. His head opened and stuff came out and turned red. Piggy's arms and legs twitched a bit, like a pig's after it has been killed. Then the sea breathed again in a long, slow sigh, the water boiled white and pink over the rock; and when it went, sucking back again, the body of Piggy was gone.

Golding also provides strong characterizations. While it is possible to see each boy fulfilling an allegorical role, none of the characters (with the possible exception of Simon) functions solely as part of the allegory. This can perhaps best be seen in the development of Jack. During the first trip into the jungle, he is unable to kill the pig with his knife; by the end of the book he is hunting human quarry. Jack's growth from choirboy to murderer is accomplished with great skill.

Finally, Golding writes a fast-moving, suspenseful adventure story. The book moves quickly from the first days on the beach to the final hunt scene, reaching a feverish pitch that is broken abruptly by the appearance of the naval officer, just as it appears that Ralph will be killed. While the appearance of the adult, however, closes the action, it does not provide us with a happy ending. Indeed, at the moment of the climax of the adventure story, Golding suddenly reminds us of the allegorical nature of the book: the naval officer's cruiser is a weapon of war. Although we feel relief over Ralph's rescue, we suddenly understand that the adult world is little different from the world of the island, a place where men hunt and kill each other indiscriminately, a place where men can blow up the entire planet, our island in the sea of the universe.

Source: Diane Andrews Henningfeld, in an essay for Novels for Students, Gale, 1997.

Paul Slayton

In the following excerpt, Slayton finds Lord of the Flies *to be a parable about modern civilization and human morality, and describes Golding's literary techniques.*

Lord of the Flies is William Golding's parable of life in the latter half of the twentieth century, the nuclear age, when society seems to have reached technological maturity while human morality is still prepubescent. Whether or not one agrees with the pessimistic philosophy, the idiocentric psychology or the fundamentalist theology espoused by Golding in the novel, if one is to use literature as a "window on the world," this work is one of the panes through which one should look.

The setting for *Lord of the Flies* is in the literary tradition of Daniel Defoe's *Robinson Crusoe* and Johann Wyss's *The Swiss Family Robinson,* and like these earlier works provides the necessary ingredients for an idyllic utopian interlude. A plane loaded with English school boys, aged five through twelve, is being evacuated to a safe haven in, perhaps, Australia to escape the "Reds," with whom the English are engaged in an atomic war. Somewhere in the tropics the plane is forced to crash land during a violent storm. All the adults on board are lost when the forward section of the plane is carried out to sea by tidal waves. The passenger compartment, fortuitously, skids to a halt on the island, and the young passengers escape uninjured.

The boys find themselves in a tropical paradise: bananas, coconuts and other fruits are profusely available. The sea proffers crabs and occasional fish in tidal pools, all for the taking. The climate is benign. Thus, the stage is set for an idyllic interlude during which British fortitude will enable the boys to master any possible adversity. In fact, Golding relates that just such a nineteenth century novel, R. M. Ballantyne's *Coral Island,* was the inspiration for *Lord of the Flies.* In that utopian story the boy castaways overcame every obstacle they encountered with the ready explanation, "We are British, you know!"

Golding's tropical sojourners, however, do not "live happily ever after." Although they attempt to organize themselves for survival and rescue, conflicts arise as the boys first neglect, then refuse, their assigned tasks. As their "society" fails to build shelters or to keep the signal fire going, fears emanating from within—for their environment is totally non-threatening—take on a larger than life reality. Vines hanging from trees become "snake things" in the imaginings of the "little 'uns." A nightmare amidst fretful sleep, causing one of the boys to cry out in the night, conjures up fearful "beasties" for the others. Their fears become more real than existence on the tropical paradise itself when the twins, Sam 'n Eric, report their enervating experience with the wind-tossed body of the dead parachutist. Despite Simon's declaration that "there is no beast, it's only us," and Piggy's disavowal of "ghosts and things," the fear of the unknown overcomes their British reserve and under Jack's all-too-willing chieftainship the boys' retreat from civilization begins.

In the initial encounter with a pig, Jack is unable to overcome his trained aversion to violence to even strike a blow at the animal. Soon, however, he and his choirboys-turned-hunters make their first kill. They rationalize that they must kill the animals for meat. The next step back from civilization occurs and the meat pretext is dropped; the real objective is to work their will on other living things.

Then, killing begins to take on an even more sinister aspect. The first fire the boys build to attract rescuers roars out of control and one of the younger boys is accidentally burned to death. The next death, that of Simon, is not an accident. He is beaten to death when he rushes into the midst of the ritual dance of the young savages. Ironically, he has come to tell the boys that he has discovered that the beast they fear is not real. Then Piggy, the last intellectual link with civilization, is killed on impulse by the sadistic Roger. Last, all semblance of civilized restraint is cast-off as the now-savage tribe of boys organizes itself to hunt down and kill their erstwhile leader, Ralph, who had tried desperately to prepare them to carry on in the fashion expected of upper middle-class British youth.

That Golding intended *Lord of the Flies* as a paradigm for modern civilization is concretely evident at the conclusion of the work. During the final confrontation at the rock fort between Ralph and Piggy and Jack and his tribe, the reader readily forgets that these individuals in conflict are not adults. The manhunt for Ralph, too, seems relative only to the world of adults. The reader is so inclined to lose sight of the age of his characters that Golding must remind that these participants are pre-adolescents: The naval officer who interrupts the deadly manhunt sees "A semicircle of little boys, their bodies streaked with colored clay, sharp sticks in hand...." Unlike that officer, the reader knows that it was not "fun and games" of the boys that the naval officer interrupted. The officer does

not realize—as the reader knows—that he has just saved Ralph from a sacrificial death and the other boys from becoming premeditated murderers. Neither is the irony of the situation very subtle: The boys have been "rescued" by an officer from a British man-of-war, which will very shortly resume its official activities as either hunter or hunted in the deadly adult game of war.

Golding, then, in *Lord of the Flies* is asking the question which continues as the major question haunting the world today: How shall denizens of the earth be rescued from our fears and our own pursuers—ourselves? While Golding offers no ready solutions to our dilemma, an understanding of his parable yields other questions which may enable readers to become seekers in the quest for a moral world. Even if one disagrees with Golding's judgment of the nature of human beings and of human society, one profits from his analysis of the problems confronting people today....

Golding is a master at his trade and *Lord of the Flies* has achieved critical acclaim as the best of his works. Indeed, a dictionary of literary terminology might well be illustrated with specific examples from this piece of prose. The development of the several focal characters in this work is brilliantly and concretely done. In addition, the omniscient narrative technique, plotting, relating story to setting and the use of irony, foreshadowing, and certainly, symbolism are so carefully and concretely accomplished that the work can serve as an invaluable teaching aid to prepare students to read other literature with a degree of understanding far beyond a simplistic knowledge of the surface events of the story. Golding's characterizations will be used in this rationale to illustrate these technical qualities of the novel.

A strength of *Lord of the Flies* lies in techniques of characterization. There are five major characters who are developed as wholly-rounded individuals whose actions and intensity show complex human motivation: Ralph, Jack, Roger, Simon and Piggy. A study of these characterizations shows the wide range of techniques for developing persona utilized by Golding and by other authors:

Ralph, the protagonist, is a rather befuddled everyman. He is chosen for leadership by the group for all the wrong reasons. Ralph does not seek the leadership role; he is elected because he is older (12 plus), somewhat larger, is attractive in personal appearance and, most strikingly, he possesses the conch shell which reminds the boys of the megaphone with which their late adult supervisors directed and instructed them. In the unsought leadership role Ralph demonstrates courage, intelligence and some diplomatic skill. On the negative side he quickly becomes disillusioned with the democratic process and without Piggy's constant urgings would have cast aside the chief's role even before Jack's *coup d'etat*. Ralph also demonstrates other weaknesses as he unthinkingly gives away Piggy's hated nickname and, more significantly, he gets caught up in the mob psychology of the savage dance and takes part in the ritualistic murder of Simon. Thus, by relating causes and effects, Golding reveals Ralph's change from a proper British lad to group leader to his disenchantment and finally to his becoming the object of the murderous hunt by the boys who once chose him as their leader.

Jack, the antagonist, is developed as the forceful villain. Outgoing, cocky and confident, Jack marches his choir boys in military formation up the beach to answer the call of the conch. Jack is a natural leader who, except for his exploitative nature, might have been a congealing force for good. Instead, his lust for power precipitates the conflict with Ralph and Piggy's long-range planning for rescue. To attain leadership, Jack caters to boyish desires for ready delights and after he is assured that his choir boys will follow in this new direction, he resorts to intimidation to increase his following. In Jack, Golding has developed a prototype of the charismatic leader who gains adherents by highlighting the fears and fulfilling the ephemeral needs and desires of followers.

Roger, "the hangman's horror," is a stereotyped character who does not change. He readily sheds a thin veneer of civilization which has been imposed upon him by the authority of the policeman and the law. So easily his arm loses the restraints which had once prohibited him from hitting the littl'uns with tossed rocks to a point where he can kill Piggy on impulse. It is but one more small step for him to proclaim the ritual dance must end in killing and to premeditate the murder of Ralph.

Simon is the quintessential Christ-figure. A thin, frail little boy, subject to fainting spells, he alone has the mental acumen and the courage to go onto the mountain and disprove the existence of the "beast." He is martyred for his efforts by the group which no longer wishes to hear his "good news."

Piggy, the pragmatic intellectual, is of necessity the most steadfast in motivation. He is tied to civilization by his physical weaknesses. Over-

weight, asthmatic, and completely dependent for sight upon his spectacles, the life of the happy savage has no allure for him. Without the aids of civilization, such as eye glasses and allergy shots, he cannot long survive. Consequently, he must reject the ephemeral allures offered by Jack and steadfastly hold, and seek to hold Ralph, to maintaining the smoke signal, his only hope for the aid and succor of rescue. His steadfastness in this aim enables him to call up the uncharacteristic courage to make the last appeal to Jack and his tribe before the rock fort because "right is right." His plea is to no avail; the sadistic Roger releases the boulder which throws Piggy from the cliff to his death.

Another minor character, Percival Weems Botts, is developed as a stereotype to demonstrate the fragility of rote learning. This "little'un" who can only recite his name and address as a response soon forgets even that as all trappings of civilization are lost by the boys.

Thus, Golding's techniques of characterization afford superior examples of the writer's craft and apt material to use to help students learn to interpret authorial voice and to respond to a piece of literature as a level beyond the denotative.

Lord of the Flies has earned for itself and its author great critical acclaim. It has also been extolled by teachers for the excitement it can engender in readers and as a work in which the motivation of characters is readily understood by adolescent readers. Despite these accolades for the novel as a work of literary art and as a teaching tool, *Lord of the Flies* has on occasion aroused the ire of would-be censors.

Some have opposed the use of the novel in the classroom because of the use of "vulgar" language. Certain words, notably "sucks," "ass," and the British slang word "bloody," are used. It is patently obvious that there is no prurient motivation behind the author's choice of these words. Not one of these words is ever used outside of a context in which the word appears to be quite naturally the word the character would use. The choir boys may well sing like "angels," as is stated; nevertheless, these are perfectly normal pre-adolescent boys. Given the proclivities of such youth the world over, verisimilitude would be lost had they, amongst themselves, always spoken like angels.

The sexual symbolism of the killing of the sow has also raised some puritanical brows. This violent scene is described in terms which might well be used to describe a rape. Such symbolism is fully justified, however, if the author is to be allowed to make his point that the motivation of the boys, casting away the cloak of civilization, is no longer merely securing food. Rather, they have moved from serving practical needs to an insane lust for working their will upon other creatures. The next step is the slaughter of their own kind.

Objection, too, has come upon that very point: children killing children. One must remind those who object to this violence that this piece of literature is a parable. Children are specifically used to show that even the innocence of childhood can be corrupted by fears from within. Those who would deny Golding this mode of establishing his theme would deny to all authors the right to make their point in an explicit fashion.

The most vociferous denunciation of *Lord of the Flies* has been vocalized by those who have misread the book to the point that they believe it deals with Satanism. The symbolism of the title, which is the English translation of the Greek word "Beelzebub," is surely being misinterpreted by such folk. In fact, theologian Davis Anderson states unequivocally that "Golding is a Christian writer." Anderson defines the central theme of *Lord of the Flies* as a statement of what it is like to experience the fall from innocence into sin and to experience damnation. Thus, a theologian sees the novel as one dealing with the Christian doctrine of original sin and of the rupture of man's relationship with God! Consequently, one who would attack this novel as an exercise in Satanism assuredly holds an indefensible premise.

Source: Paul Slayton, "Teaching Rationale for William Golding's *Lord of the Flies,*" in *Censored Books: Critical Viewpoints,* Nicholas J. Karolides, Lee Burress, John M. Kean, eds., The Scarecrow Press, Inc., 1993, pp. 351–57.

Carl Niemeyer

In the following excerpt, Niemeyer compares Lord of the Flies *to an earlier, utopian British children's novel,* The Coral Island.

One interested in finding about Golding for oneself should probably begin with *Lord of the Flies....* The story is simple. In a way not clearly explained, a group of children, all boys, presumably evacuees in a future war, are dropped from a plane just before it is destroyed, on to an uninhabited tropical island. The stage is thus set for a reworking of a favorite subject in children's literature: castaway children assuming adult responsibilities without adult supervision. Golding expects his readers to recall the classic example of such a book, R. M. Ballantyne's *The Coral Island*

(1857), where the boys rise to the occasion and behave as admirably as would adults. But in *Lord of the Flies* everything goes wrong from the beginning. A few boys representing sanity and common sense, led by Ralph and Piggy, see the necessity for maintaining a signal fire to attract a rescue. But they are thwarted by the hunters, led by red-haired Jack, whose lust for blood is finally not to be satisfied by killing merely wild pigs. Only the timely arrival of a British cruiser saves us from an ending almost literally too horrible to think about. Since Golding is using a naive literary form to express sophisticated reflections on the nature of man and society, and since he refers obliquely to Ballantyne many times throughout the book, a glance at *The Coral Island* is appropriate.

Ballantyne shipwrecks his three boys—Jack, eighteen; Ralph, the narrator, aged fifteen; and Peterkin Gay, a comic sort of boy, aged thirteen—somewhere in the South Seas on an uninhabited coral island. Jack is a natural leader, but both Ralph and Peterkin have abilities valuable for survival. Jack has the most common sense and foresight, but Peterkin turns out to be a skillful killer of pigs, and Ralph when later in the book he is temporarily separated from his friends and alone on a schooner, coolly navigates it back to Coral Island by dead reckoning, a feat sufficiently impressive, if not quite equal to Captain Bligh's. The boys' life on the island is idyllic; and they are themselves without malice or wickedness, though there are a few curious episodes in which Ballantyne seems to hint at something he himself understands as little as do his characters. One is Peterkin's wanton killing of an old sow, useless as food, which the boy rationalizes by saying he needs leather for shoes. This and one or two other passages suggest that Ballantyne was aware of some darker aspects of boyish nature, but for the most part he emphasizes the paradisiacal life of the happy castaways. Like Golding's, however, Ballantyne's story raises the problem of evil, but whereas Golding finds evil in the boys' own natures, it comes to Ballantyne's boys not from within themselves but from the outside world. Tropical nature, to be sure, is kind, but the men of this non-Christian world are bad. For example, the island is visited by savage cannibals, one canoeful pursuing another, who fight a cruel and bloody battle, observed by the horrified boys, and then go away. A little later the island is again visited, this time by pirates (i.e., white men who have renounced or scorned their Christian heritage), who succeed in capturing Ralph. In due time the pirates are deservedly destroyed, and in the final episode of the book the natives undergo an unmotivated conversion to Christianity, which effects a total change in their nature just in time to rescue the boys from their clutches.

Thus Ballantyne's view of man is seen to be optimistic, like his view of English boys' pluck and resourcefulness, which subdues tropical islands as triumphantly as England imposes empire and religion on lawless breeds of men. Golding's naval officer, the *deus ex machina* of *Lord of the Flies,* is only echoing Ballantyne when, perceiving dimly that all has not gone well on the island, he says: "I should have thought that a pack of British boys—you're all British aren't you?—would have been able to put up a better show than that—I mean—"

This is not the only echo of the older book. Golding boldly calls his two chief characters Jack and Ralph. He reproduces the comic Peterkin in the person of Piggy. He has a wanton killing of a wild pig, accomplished, as E. L. Epstein points out, "in terms of sexual intercourse." He uses a storm to avert a quarrel between Jack and Ralph, as Ballantyne used a hurricane to rescue his boys from death at the hands of cannibals. He emphasizes physical cruelty but integrates it into his story, and by making it a real if deplorable part of human, or at least boyish, nature improves on Ballantyne, whose descriptions of brutality—never of course performed by the boys—are usually introduced merely for their sensational effect. Finally, on the last page Golding's officer calls Ralph mildly to task for not having organized things better.

"It was like that at first," said Ralph, "before things—"

He stopped.

"We were together then—"

The officer nodded helpfully.

"I know. Jolly good show. Like the Coral Island."

Golding invokes Ballantyne, so that the kind but uncomprehending adult, the instrument of salvation, may recall to the child who has just gone through hell, the naiveté of the child's own early innocence, now forever lost; but he suggests at the same time the inadequacy of Ballantyne's picture of human nature in primitive surroundings.

Golding, then, regards Ballantyne's book as a badly falsified map of reality, yet the only map of this particular reality that many of us have. Ralph has it and, through harrowing experiences, replaces it with a more accurate one. The naval officer, though he should know better, since he is on the scene and should not have to rely on memories of his boyhood reading, has it, and it seems unlikely

that he is ever going to alter it, for his last recorded action is to turn away from the boys and look at his "trim" cruiser, in other words to turn away from a revelation of the untidy human heart to look at something manufactured, manageable, and solidly useful.

Golding, who being a grammar-school teacher should know boys well, gives a corrective of Ballantyne's optimism. As he has explained, the book is "an attempt to trace the defects of society back to the defects of human nature." These defects turn out, on close examination, to result from the evil of inadequacy and mistakenness. Evil is not the positive and readily identifiable force it appears to be when embodied in Ballantyne's savages and pirates. Golding's Ralph, for example, has real abilities, most conspicuous among them the gift of leadership and a sense of responsibility toward the "littluns." Yet both are incomplete. "By now," writes Golding, "Ralph had no self-consciousness in public thinking but would treat the day's decisions as though he were playing chess." Such detachment is obviously an important and valuable quality in a leader, but significantly the next sentence reads: "The only trouble was that he would never be a very good chess player." Piggy on the other hand no doubt would have been a good chess player, for with a sense of responsibility still more acute than Ralph's he combines brains and common sense. Physically, however, he is ludicrous—fat, asthmatic, and almost blind without his specs. He is forever being betrayed by his body. At his first appearance he is suffering from diarrhoea; his last gesture is a literally brainless twitch of the limbs, "like a pig's after it has been killed." His further defect is that he is powerless, except as he works through Ralph. Though Piggy is the first to recognize the value of the conch and even shows Ralph how to blow it to summon the first assembly, he cannot sound it himself. And he lacks imagination. Scientifically minded as he is, he scorns what is intangible and he dismisses the possibility of ghosts or an imaginary beast. "'Cos things wouldn't make sense. Houses an' streets, an'—TV—they wouldn't work." Of course he is quite right, save that he forgets he is now on an island where the artifacts of the civilization he has always known are meaningless.

It is another important character, Simon, who understands that there may indeed be a beast, even if not a palpable one—"maybe it's only us." The scientist Piggy has recognized it is possible to be frightened of people, but he finds this remark of Simon's dangerous nonsense. Still Simon is right, as we see from his interview with the sow's head on a stake, which is the lord of the flies. He is right that the beast is in the boys themselves, and he alone discovers that what has caused their terror is in reality a dead parachutist ironically stifled in the elaborate clothing worn to guarantee survival. But Simon's failure is the inevitable failure of the mystic—what he knows is beyond words; he cannot impart his insights to others. Having an early glimpse of the truth, he cannot tell it.

> Simon became inarticulate in his effort to express mankind's essential illness. Inspiration came to him.
>
> "What's the dirtiest thing there is?"
>
> As an answer Jack dropped into the uncomprehending silence that followed it the one crude expressive syllable. Release was like an orgasm. Those littluns who had climbed back on the twister fell off again and did not mind. The hunters were screaming with delight.
>
> Simon's effort fell about him in ruins; the laughter beat him cruelly and he shrank away defenseless to his seat.

Mockery also greets Simon later when he speaks to the lord of the flies, though this time it is sophisticated, adult mockery:

> "Fancy thinking the Beast was something you could hunt and kill!" said the head. For a moment or two the forest and all the other dimly appreciated places echoed with the parody of laughter.

Tragically, when Simon at length achieves a vision so clear that is is readily communicable he is killed by the pig hunters in their insane belief that he is the very evil which he alone has not only understood but actually exorcised. Like the martyr, he is killed for being precisely what he is not.

The inadequacy of Jack is the most serious of all, and here perhaps if anywhere in the novel we have a personification of absolute evil. Though he is the most mature of the boys (he alone of all the characters is given a last name), and though as head of the choir he is the only one with any experience of leadership, he is arrogant and lacking in Ralph's charm and warmth. Obsessed with the idea of hunting, he organizes his choir members into a band of killers. Ostensibly they are to kill pigs, but pigs alone do not satisfy them, and pigs are in any event not needed for food. The blood lust once aroused demands nothing less than human blood. If Ralph represents purely civil authority, backed only by his own good will, Piggy's wisdom, and the crowd's easy willingness to be ruled, Jack stands for naked ruthless power, the police force or the military force acting without restraint and gradually absorbing the whole state into itself and anni-

hilating what it cannot absorb. Yet even Jack is inadequate. He is only a little boy after all, as we are sharply reminded in a brilliant scene at the end of the book, when we suddenly see him through the eyes of the officer instead of through Ralph's, and he is, like all sheer power, anarchic. When Ralph identifies himself to the officer as "boss," Jack, who has just all but murdered him, makes a move in dispute, but overawed at last by superior power, the power of civilization and the British Navy, implicit in the officer's mere presence, he says nothing. He is a villain (are his red hair and ugliness intended to suggest that he is a devil?), but in our world of inadequacies and imperfections even villainy does not fulfill itself completely. If not rescued, the hunters would have destroyed Ralph and made him, like the sow, an offering to the beast; but the inexorable logic of Ulysses makes us understand that they would have proceeded thence to self-destruction.

> Then everything includes itself in power,
> Power into will, will into appetite;
> And appetite, an universal wolf,
> So doubly seconded with will and power,
> Must make perforce an universal prey,
> And last eat up himself.

The distance we have travelled from Ballantyne's cheerful unrealities is both artistic and moral. Golding is admittedly symbolic; Ballantyne professed to be telling a true story. Yet it is the symbolic tale that, at least for our times, carries conviction. Golding's boys, who choose to remember nothing of their past before the plane accident; who, as soon as Jack commands the choir to take off the robes marked with the cross of Christianity, have no trace of religion; who demand to be ruled and are incapable of being ruled properly; who though many of them were once choir boy's (Jack could sing C sharp) never sing a note on the island; in whose minds the great tradition of Western culture has left the titles of a few books for children, a knowledge of the use of matches (but no matches), and hazy memories of planes and TV sets—these boys are more plausible than Ballantyne's. His was a world of blacks and whites: bad hurricanes, good islands; good pigs obligingly allowing themselves to be taken for human food, bad sharks disobligingly taking human beings for shark food; good Christians, bad natives; bad pirates, good boys. Of the beast within, which demands blood sacrifice, first a sow's head, then a boy's, Ballantyne has some vague notion, but he cannot take it seriously. Not only does Golding see the beast; he sees that to keep it at bay we have civilization; but when by some magic or accident civilization is abolished and the human animal is left on his own, dependent upon his mere humanity, then being human is not enough. The beast appears, though not necessarily spontaneously or inevitably, for it never rages in Ralph or Piggy or Simon as it does in Roger or Jack; but it is latent in all of them, in the significantly named Piggy, in Ralph, who sometimes envies the abandon of the hunters and who shares the desire to "get a handful" of Robert's "brown, vulnerable flesh," and even in Simon burrowing into his private hiding place. After Simon's death Jack attracts all the boys but Ralph and the loyal Piggy into his army. Then when Piggy is killed and Ralph is alone, only civilization can save him. The timely arrival of the British Navy is less theatrical than logically necessary to make Golding's point. For civilization defeats the beast. It slinks back into the jungle as the boys creep out to be rescued; but the beast is real. It is there, and it may return.

Source: Carl Niemeyer, "The Coral Island Revisited," in *College English,* Vol. 22, No. 4, January, 1961, pp. 241–45.

Sources

James R. Baker, "The Decline of *Lord of the Flies,*" *South Atlantic Quarterly,* Vol. 69, Autumn, 1970, pp. 446-60.

Douglas A. Davis, "A Conversation with Golding," *New Republic,* May 4, 1963, pp. 28-30.

Bernard F. Dick, *William Golding,* revised edition, Twayne, 1987.

James J. Fahey, *Pacific War Diary: 1942-1945,* Houghton Mifflin, 1963.

Martin Green, "Distaste for the Contemporary," *Nation,* Vol. 190, May 21, 1960, pp. 451-54.

Frank Kermode, "The Novels of William Golding." In *International Literary Annual,* Vol. III, 1961, pp. 11-29. Also appears in shorter form in Baker & Ziegler (1964), pp. 203-6.

Patrick Reilly, *'Lord of the Flies': Fathers and Sons,* Twayne's Masterwork Studies No. 106, 1992.

Kenneth Rexroth, *Atlantic Monthly,* May, 1965.

Claire Rosenfield, "'Men of Smaller Growth': A Psychological Analysis of William Golding's *Lord of the Flies,*" in *William Golding's "Lord of the Flies," A Casebook Edition,*

edited by James R. Baker and Arthur P. Ziegler, Jr., Putnam, 1964, pp. 261-76. Also appears in Leonard and Eleanor Manheim, editors, *Hidden Patterns: Studies in Psychoanalytic Literary Criticism,* Macmillan, 1966.

For Further Study

James R. Baker and Arthur P. Ziegler, Jr., editors, *William Golding's 'Lord of the Flies,' A Casebook Edition: Text, Notes, and Criticism,* Putnam, 1964, esp. pp. ix-xxiv, 189-291.
> Includes the text of the novel, early critical articles pro and con, two interviews with Golding, and a checklist of other criticism.

C. B. Cox, review of *Lord of the Flies,* in *Critical Quarterly,* Vol. 2, no. 2, Summer, 1960, pp. 112–17.
> A contemporary review calling *Lord of the Flies* one of the most important novels to be published in the 1950s.

James Gindin, *William Golding,* St. Martin's, 1988.
> Gindin provides a good discussion of Golding's prose techniques and the way he suggests abstract ideas through his use of concrete detail.

G. C. Herndl, "Golding and Salinger: A Clear Choice," *Wiseman Review,* No. 502, Winter, 1964-65, pp. 309-22.
> Herndl sees Golding coming out of a classical and Christian tradition that implicitly honors social institutions and refutes individualism.

John Peter, "The Fables of William Golding," *Kenyon Review,* Vol. 19, Autumn, 1957, pp. 577-92. A section of this essay appears in Baker & Ziegler, pp. 229-34.
> Peter finds this article "important and influential in attempting to define critical terms for an understanding of Golding's work." Bernard F. Dick notes that Golding himself especially liked this essay.

David Spitz, "Power and Authority: An Interpretation of Golding's 'Lord of the Flies,'" in *Antioch Review,* Vol. 30, no. 1, Spring, 1970, pp. 21–33.
> A careful study of characterization in Golding's novel.

James Stern, "English Schoolboys in the Jungle," in *New York Times Review of Books,* October 23, 1995, p. 38.
> Stern interprets the novel as social commentary.

Virginia Tiger, *William Golding: The Dark Fields of Discovery,* Calder & Boyars, 1974.
> Tiger summarizes religious, political, psychological, and anthropological interpretations while arguing that the story's structure "portrays its thematic meaning."

Time, June 22, 1962, p. 64.
> An article tracing the growing popularity in America of Golding's novel.

My Ántonia

Willa Cather

1918

Willa Cather's *My Ántonia* (1918) is the story of both Ántonia Shimerda, a Bohemian immigrant to the state of Nebraska in the 1880s, and the novel's American-born narrator, Jim Burden. The story is told as Jim relates his own image of Ántonia in a nostalgic re-creation of his childhood and youth. Their wildly differing places in the social hierarchy account for their respective fortunes. Ántonia survives her father's suicide, hires herself out as household help, is abandoned at the altar, gives birth out of wedlock, but achieves fulfillment in her marriage to a Czech farmer, her loving children, and their flourishing farm. Jim, a successful well-traveled and cultured East-coast lawyer, remains romantic, nostalgic, and unfulfilled in life. This portrait of Ántonia is widely acknowledged as one of the most memorable characters in twentieth-century literature. Through her, Cather celebrates the vitality and fruitfulness of the pioneering era as a type of lost paradise. *My Ántonia* is widely considered the best of the author's "Nebraska" novels which reflect her childhood experiences growing up on the plains. Since its appearance, Cather's carefully crafted fiction has gathered a steady following. Her reputation has continued to grow since her death in 1947. Although contemporary reviewers sometimes faulted the author's work as overly nostalgic and obsessed with the past, today critics see Cather's Nebraska novels, and *My Ántonia* in particular, as well-crafted, sympathetic portrayals of the uniquely American experience of immigrant pioneers.

Author Biography

Born in Virginia in 1873, Willa Cather spent the first decade of her life on her family's farm in Back Creek Valley. In 1884, her family moved to join her father's relatives among the ethnically diverse settlers of the Great Plains. This area would serve as the inspiration for several of her novels, including *My Ántonia* (1918). Her father tried farming but soon settled the family in Red Cloud, Nebraska, a town of approximately 2,500 people. Cather remembered vividly both the trauma of leaving a hill farm for a flat, empty land and the subsequent excitement of growing up in the new country. She took intense pleasure in riding her pony to neighboring farms and listening to the stories of the immigrant farm women she met there. Cather accompanied a local doctor on house calls and by her thirteenth birthday had adopted the outward appearance and manner of a male. She signed her name "William Cather, Jr." or "William Cather, M.D." Eventually returning to more conventional modes of dress, she later dismissed the episode as juvenile posturing.

At sixteen, she left home to prepare to enroll at the University of Nebraska in Lincoln, which she entered in 1891. Her freshman English instructor gave her essay on Thomas Carlyle to a Lincoln newspaper for publication and by her junior year, she was supporting herself as a journalist. From Lincoln, she moved to Pittsburgh as a magazine editor and newspaper writer. She then became a high school teacher, using summer vacations to concentrate on fiction. In 1905, she published her first collection of short stories, *The Troll Garden.*

In 1906, Cather was hired to edit *McClure's,* a leading muckraking magazine, and moved to New York City. Her older literary friend Sarah Orne Jewett advised her to "find your own quiet centre of life, and write from that to the world." Nevertheless she found it difficult to give up a position as a highly successful woman editor during a time when journalism was almost wholly dominated by men, and did not quit her position for three years. In 1912, on a visit to her family in Red Cloud, she stood on the edge of a wheat field and watched her first harvest in years. By then, she was emotionally ready to use her youthful memories of Nebraska. From this experience evolved *O Pioneers!,* the novel she preferred to think of as her first. It is this long perspective that gives Cather's work about Nebraska a rich aura of nostalgia, a poignancy also found in her next Nebraska novel, 1918's *My Ántonia.*

Willa Cather

Although Cather's 1922 novel about World War I, *One of Ours,* was received with mixed critical reviews, it was a best-seller and won Cather the Pulitzer Prize. She continued to write until physical infirmities prevented her from doing so. In 1945, she wrote that she had gotten much of what she wanted from life and had avoided the things she most violently had not wanted—too much money, noisy publicity, and the bother of meeting too many people. Willa Cather died from a massive cerebral hemorrhage on April 24, 1947.

Plot Summary

Introduction

Willa Cather's *My Ántonia* begins in the voice of an unnamed narrator who "introduces" not only the novel but also Jim Burden, whose first-person narration begins with chapter one. When these two "old friends" meet on a train crossing the plains of Iowa, they reminisce together about growing up in a small town on the Nebraska prairie, "buried in wheat and corn, under stimulating extremes of climate." Both have long since moved away from the prairie to New York, but their recollections of childhood remain sharp, especially their memories of one "central figure," the "Bohemian girl" named Ántonia. "To speak her name," the narrator writes, "was to call up pictures of people and places, to set a quiet drama going in one's brain." The narrator challenges Jim to write down all that he can remember of Ántonia, and the manuscript that he creates he calls, "My Ántonia."

Book I: The Shimerdas

Jim Burden's story begins with a journey, after the death of his parents, to the home of his grandparents in Black Hawk, Nebraska. Jim learns from the train conductor that a family in the "immigrant car" are traveling to the same town. In the station he hears, for the first time, the sounds of "a foreign tongue." At the station Jim and his traveling companion, Jake Marpole, are picked up by his grandfather's hired man, Otto Fuchs. Riding in the back of a wagon through the broad prairie land, a land that seems to be "outside man's jurisdiction," Jim feels "erased, blotted out," separated from even the spirits of his deceased parents.

Jim is soon comfortably settled in his grandparents' home and he begins to explore the strange environment of waving red grass that surrounds him there. After the family meets their "new Bohemian neighbors," the Shimerdas, Jim quickly becomes Ántonia Shimerda's friend and language tutor. But he is less comfortable with the other Shimerdas, especially Ántonia's angry and arrogant brother, Ambrosch, and her jealous, deceitful mother. In spite of frequent tensions between the Burdens and the Shimerdas, Jim and Ántonia become close companions while exploring the countryside together. Ántonia's respect for the younger Jim grows after he kills an enormous rattlesnake; Jim's understanding of what Ántonia left behind in Bohemia deepens when they revive a dying cricket that reminds her of her Bohemian childhood.

Memories of life in the "old country" also afflict the Russians, Pavel and Peter, as well as Mr. Shimerda. Pavel and Peter are haunted by the actions of their past: Pavel dies soon after he unburdens his mind to Mr. Shimerda about throwing a bride and groom from their wedding sleigh to a pack of wolves. For Mr. Shimerda, leaving his former life in Bohemia takes the spirit out of him; when Jim first sees him, he thinks his face looks "like ashes—like something from which all the warmth and light had died out." Although Mr. Shimerda pleads with Jim to teach Ántonia English, so that she might adjust to life in a new place, he never finds happiness or contentment in America and finally kills himself. After his death, Jim

imagines Mr. Shimerda's spirit traveling across the prairie once more, all the way to Baltimore, then over "the great wintry ocean" and back to his homeland.

After the local Norwegian church refuses to allow the burial of Mr. Shimerda in their graveyard, a grave is dug, at the demand of Mrs. Shimerda, directly on the corner of their property. She believes the spot will be a crossroads some day. Her insistence on this Bohemian custom is granted, but Mr. Burden remarks, "If she thinks she will live to see the people of this country ride over that old man's head, she is mistaken." The strongly Protestant Mr. Burden disapproves of the Catholic rituals of the Shimerdas and of a new Bohemian homesteader, Anton Jelinek. Nevertheless, he respects the strength of their faith, and he offers a moving prayer at Mr. Shimerda's graveside. Jim begins attending the country school and asks Ántonia to do so with him, but she refuses because of her increased responsibilities on the farm. Although she admired her father's learning, she also takes pride in her strength and ability on the farm and in helping to "make this land one good farm." Finally, when Jim asks her why she is working so hard and emulating her brother Ambrosch, Ántonia responds, "Things will be easy for you. But they will be hard for us."

Book II: The Hired Girls

Three years after Jim's arrival, his grandfather moves the family from the farm into Black Hawk, and they quickly come to feel "like town people." Jim's grandmother convinces the family next door, the Harlings, to hire Ántonia as a live-in cook. In town, Ántonia renews her friendship with Jim and begins to socialize with the other "hired girls," especially Lena Lingard and Tiny Soderball. To Jim and to the girls, town life offers more interesting diversions than farm life. This includes a visit by a negro piano player, Blind d'Arnault, and the dance pavilion set up by traveling dance instructors. Ántonia's enthusiasm for dancing leads Mr. Harling to accuse her of earning "a reputation for being free and easy." He demands that she stop attending dances or find new employment. Ántonia refuses to yield to his demand and leaves the Harlings to work for Wick Cutter, a disreputable money-lender who was "notoriously dissolute with women." When Jim's grandmother suspects that Cutter will assault Ántonia, Jim takes her place for one night and is savagely attacked by Cutter. Jim grows increasingly restless in Black Hawk, becoming contemptuous of the narrow, small-minded ways of the townsfolk. After graduating from high school and exhausting the limited possibilities for diversion in the town, Jim resolves to study through the summer so that he can leave for college as soon as possible.

Book III: Lena Lingard

At the university, Jim is introduced to "the world of ideas" by his professor and advisor, Gaston Cleric. Lena Lingard, who has set up a dressmaking shop in Lincoln, visits Jim one night and the two quickly renew their friendship. Jim's attraction to Lena grows as they attend the theater and spend more time together. But at the urging of Gaston Cleric he resolves to leave Lincoln for Harvard to continue his education. Before he informs Lena of his decision, she tells him that she never wishes to marry, stating that she has experienced enough of the trials of "family life" to last her a lifetime.

Book IV: The Pioneer Woman's Story

Returning to Black Hawk for a summer before entering law school, Jim seeks out information about Ántonia, who has returned to her family after being deserted, with child, by her fiance, Larry Donovan. Jim reflects on the unexpected success of the other "hired girls," Lena and Tiny Soderball, and he feels "bitterly disappointed" in Ántonia for "becoming an object of pity." Jim visits the Widow Steavens, who lives on the Burden's old farm, and she recounts Ántonia's sad story. Finally, Jim visits Ántonia herself, who is working in the fields once again. They express their deep feelings of attachment to each other, and Jim leaves with a promise to return.

Book V: Cuzak's Boys

Jim fulfills his promise after twenty years, finally returning to visit Ántonia in spite of his fears of finding her "aged and broken." He finds her aged but not broken, instead glowing with the "fire of life," delighted with her husband and happy children, and proud of their productive farm. Jim takes pleasure in watching Ántonia interact with her children, "conscious of a kind of physical harmony" around her, and he recognizes the powerful place that Ántonia holds in his own mind.

> Ántonia had always been one to leave images in the mind that did not fade—that grew stronger with time. In my memory there was a succession of such pictures, fixed there like the old woodcuts of one's first primer: Ántonia kicking her bare legs against the sides of my pony when we came home in triumph with our snake; Ántonia in her black shawl and fur

cap, as she stood by her father's grave in the snowstorm; Ántonia coming in with her work-team along the evening sky-line. She lent herself to immemorial human attitudes which we recognize by instinct as universal and true.... [S]he still had that something which fires the imagination, could still stop one's breath for a moment by a look or gesture that somehow revealed the meaning in common things. She had only to stand in the orchard, to put her hand on a little crab tree and look up at the apples, to make you feel the goodness of planting and tending and harvesting at last....

> It was no wonder that her sons stood tall and straight. She was a rich mine of life, like the founders of early races.

After leaving Ántonia and her family with a promise that he will return, Jim stands on the "old road" outside of Black Hawk that he and Ántonia had traveled as children, now confident that this "road of Destiny ... was to bring us together again."

Characters

Mrs. Emmaline Burden

Jim's sturdy grandmother runs an orderly, proper household, a counterpoint to the Shimerda's animal-like cave. Awareness of differences makes her generally tolerant and concerned. The narrow attitudes of the Norwegians who won't let Mr. Shimerda be buried in their cemetery offend her: "If these foreigners are so clannish, Mr. Bushy, we'll have to have an American graveyard that will be more liberal-minded." But she has her own biases. She is contemptuous of Mrs. Shimerda's gift of dried mushrooms, declaring "I shouldn't want to eat anything that had been shut up for months with old clothes and goose pillows." And she is conventional too. She worries that people will say she hasn't brought Jim up correctly because he dances with the country girls. And when he is at school, she informs him only of those friends she approves of. She does not let him know that Lena Lingard is in Lincoln.

Grandmother Burden

See Mrs. Emmaline Burden

Grandfather Burden

See Mr. Burden

Jim Burden

As narrator, Jim Burden is Cather's persona—that is, he serves as a stand-in for the author. He

Media Adaptations

- *My Ántonia* was adapted for television in 1994 by Victoria Riskin and David W. Finteis, Fast Track Films, Inc., Wilshire Productions, and is distributed by Paramount Home Video. It stars Neil Patrick Harris, as Jim Burden, Jason Robards Jr. and Eva Marie Saint as Jim's grandparents, and Elina Lowensohn as Ántonia. The film was directed by Joseph Sargent.

- Charles Jones adapted *My Ántonia* for the stage. The work was published by Samuel French in 1994.

- Sound recordings of *My Ántonia* are available from Bookcassette Sales, Brilliance Corp., and Blackstone Audio Books.

comes to Nebraska at about the same age and time that Cather moved west with her family; he lives on a farm for a time with his grandparents just as Cather did; and Jim's neighbors, the Shimerdas, may have been inspired by the Cathers' Bohemian neighbors, the Sadileks. As an adult, Jim Burden returns to Nebraska just as Cather returned to Red Cloud and visited her friend Annie Sadilek, who was then surrounded by a large brood of children and happily married to a Czech farmer (Cuzak in the novel).

Jim is not merely Cather's voice. He is a full-bodied character with a nature and point of view of his own. Although sensitive, dreamy, and somewhat alienated, he is also conventional, a product of his own social class and family aspirations. But it is not simply class attitudes that keep a wedge between him and Ántonia. He is at turns intrigued by Ántonia's will-power and vitality and disgusted by her strongheadedness and outspoken nature. People talk about him, that there is something strange about his lack of interest in girls of his own age and class and his lively relationships with the hired girls, the daughters of immigrants. Yet, once scolded by his grandmother, he stops socializing with them at the dances. While attending college

in Lincoln, he starts a relationship with Lena Lingard. Yet he accepts her declaration that she will never marry and he eventually marries someone else. Returning to Black Hawk, he learns of Ántonia's betrayal by Larry Donovan. Bothered that she apparently threw herself away so cheaply, he is also aware how much she means to him. Again, he goes away. This time he does not see her for another twenty years. By then, seeing Ántonia in the midst of her large family, Jim realizes the sterility of his own life and marriage and the vitality that is symbolized by Ántonia. However, despite his admiration for and familiarity with Ántonia, he cannot come any closer to her than as a sympathetic observer.

Mr. Burden

Grandfather Burden is reserved, dignified, but occasionally outspoken. Religious and broadminded, he accepts that "The prayers of all good people are good." Grandfather does not join the feud between his hired men and the Shimerdas and continues to help Ambrosch and Ántonia with advice and materials.

Gaston Cleric

Jim's Latin teacher in Lincoln awakens his mind and makes the classics come alive for him. Jim believes that Cleric "narrowly missed being a great poet," but spends all his creative energy in his lectures. It is on his account that Jim goes to Harvard.

Curly Peter

See Peter

Wick Cutter

The Black Hawk money lender fleeces Russian Peter and many others. He talks of his religious nature and contributions to Protestant churches, yet is known as a gambler and womanizer. His crafty plot to assault Ántonia, who comes to work for him and his wife, is thwarted by Mrs. Burden and Jim.

Wycliffe Cutter

See Wick Cutter

Anton Cuzak

Ántonia's husband had made several bad decisions in his youth in Vienna and in America. He finally comes to Black Hawk to visit his cousin, Anton Jelinek. When he meets Ántonia, he finds exactly the kind of girl he had always wanted. Lena thinks he is the perfect partner for Ántonia: "He isn't a hustler, but a rough man would never have suited Tony." Anton also loves his children and has an artistic sense; he is very fond of music, just as Ántonia's father was.

Ántonia Cuzak

See Ántonia Shimerda

Blind Samson d'Arnault

Blind d'Arnault, a Negro musician, comes to Black Hawk. He was born in the South, "where the spirit if not the fact of slavery persisted," but was given encouragement by his white mistress after his incredible musical talent was discovered. His music brings excitement to Jim's life and contrasts to the dull Nebraska winter. Jim thinks when d'Arnault plays he looks like an "African god of pleasure."

Otto Fuchs

Otto, the Burden's hired hand, is an Austrian immigrant who has been a cowboy, a stage-driver, a bartender, and a miner. He impresses Jim with his Jesse James-look and regales him with stories of outlaws and desperadoes. Like Jake, he is a hard worker with nothing to show for it. When the Burdens move to town, Otto goes out West in search of his fortune and, except for one letter, is not heard from again.

Mrs. Molly Gardener

Owner of Black Hawk's hotel, Mrs. Gardener is the best-dressed woman in town but "seemed indifferent to her possessions," as Jim says. Nevertheless, she is cold and rare is the guest who is given the privilege of speaking with her. She runs the business while her mild-mannered husband greets guests. It is while she is out of town that there is an impromptu dance at the hotel with Blind d'Arnault playing.

Charley Harling

The only Harling son, older than Jim by two years, Charley is indulged and is a favorite of Ántonia, a fact that makes Jim jealous. He goes to Annapolis and serves on a battleship.

Mr. Christian Harling

A grain merchant and cattle-buyer who lives next door to the Burdens in Black Hawk, Mr. Harling is autocratic and imperial. His reputation as the town's leading businessman helps persuade Ambrosch to allow Ántonia to work for the family. When he catches a boy trying to kiss Ántonia, he

has Mrs. Harling issue an ultimatum that she must quit the dances or leave the Harling's house.

Frances Harling

The oldest Harling daughter, Frances helps her father in his business, is familiar with all the farm people, and has a keen eye for both business and people. As Jim's friend she tells him, "I expect I know the country girls better than you do. You always put a kind of glamour over them. The trouble with you, Jim, is that you're a romantic."

Mrs. Harling

The town neighbor of the Burdens, Mrs. Harling is encouraged to hire Ántonia. Jim describes a basic harmony between the two; despite their different backgrounds, they are both strong-willed, loving, down-to-earth women. Ántonia flourishes at the Burdens and learns how to run a household and to be a good mother. Mrs. Harling is very hurt when Ántonia chooses to leave the Harling family in order to keep attending the Saturday night dances. However, she does not try to change the mind of either her husband or Ántonia, and eventually forgives her. As Jim Burden describes her, she is "quick to anger, quick to laughter, and jolly from the depths of her soul."

Anton Jelinek

A young Bohemian settler, Jelinek comes to help his fellow countrymen after Mr. Shimerda's death. "Everything about him was warm and spontaneous," Jim says, and he impresses the Burdens with a tale of religious faith from his youth. It is his cousin, Anton Cusak, who comes to Black Hawk and marries the disgraced Ántonia.

Peter Krajiek

The first Bohemian settler in Black Hawk, Krajiek provides land and supplies for the Shimerdas' homestead—at a grossly inflated price. Krajiek takes advantage of the family in every way he can, even though he is distantly related to Mrs. Shimerda. After Mr. Shimerda's suicide, Krajiek "behaved like a guilty man," and Jim believes he may feel some remorse in addition to his fear.

Lena Lingard

Norwegian-born Lena is one of the "hired girls," immigrant daughters who work in Black Hawk to earn money for their farm families. Outgoing and pretty, she is both a friend and rival of Ántonia's. While working in Lincoln as a dressmaker, she diverts Jim from his college studies. Although his relationship with her matures him, he returns East to attend Harvard. Never married, Lena is a flirt who gives her heart away but keeps her head for business. Her experiences helping her mother run the household as a child have decided her against marriage: "I've seen a good deal of married life, and I don't care for it." She becomes a successful dressmaker and even as an older woman remains stylish. It is Lena who persuades Jim to visit Ántonia after twenty years.

Sylvester Lovett

Sylvester, a cashier at his father's bank, also prefers the Saturday night dances with the hired girls. He was especially crazy about Lena. Jim says, "In my ingenuousness I hoped that Sylvester would marry Lena, and thus give all the country girls a better position in town." When he marries a respectable widow instead, Jim is contemptuous of him.

Jake Marpole

Jake is the farmhand who accompanies Jim on his train ride from Virginia to Nebraska. An illiterate and provincial "mountain boy," he thinks foreigners spread diseases. Lured by Otto's tales of western wealth, Jake thinks a silver mine is waiting for him in Colorado. When the Burdens move to town, he follows his dream there. Otto's letter from the Yankee Girl Mine tells that Jake has recuperated from mountain fever, but when Jim writes back, the letter is returned unclaimed.

Pavel

Sickly and sad, Pavel's "generally excited and rebellious manner" supports rumors that he was once an anarchist. On his death bed, Pavel tells Mr. Shimerda about a crime he committed in his youth. In Russia, he had saved his own life by throwing his friends, a new bride and groom, from a sleigh to hungry wolves that chased them. This led him and Peter to come to America. Shortly after this confession, Pavel dies from a strain brought on by hard labor.

Peter

One of the two Russian men whose farm Mr. Shimerda visits. Short, curly-haired, bow-legged, and as "fat as butter," he is friendly and shares his milk and garden produce with the Shimerdas. He loves his new country, where anyone who can care for a cow can own one—not just rich men. He is deeply in debt to Wick Cutter, and shortly after his friend Pavel's death, must sell his farm to pay his

mortgage. Peter ends up leaving America to work as a railway cook.

Rooshian Peter

See Peter

Russian Peter

See Peter

Ambrosch Shimerda

The oldest of the four Shimerda children, Ambrosch is ambitious and hardworking. He works Ántonia hard and sometimes rents her out to other farmers. When she goes to work for the Harlings, Ambrosch tries to get her entire salary sent to him. Although he is not a generous man, he is deeply concerned for his father and spends money on masses for him. One of Ántonia's sons is named after her brother Ambrosch.

Ántonia Shimerda

Ántonia is fourteen when she first meets Jim and gives him a ring. Her warmth and impulsiveness are immediately evident, the very characteristics that both intrigue and frighten Jim. She is both a realist and a loyalist, who makes excuses for her mother's behavior but does not complain about her. Her father wants to develop her loftier side: "Te-e-ach, te-e-ach my An-tonia!" he tells Mrs. Burden. But his suicide puts an end to such refined aspirations. Ántonia's hardy side is developed instead. She works in the fields, proud to be competing with men. Her physicality makes her great; she belongs to the earth. At the end of Book One, Ántonia corrects Jim's blindness to their difference in circumstance: "If I live here, like you, that is different. Things will be easy for you. But they will be hard for us."

Hired out to the Harlings, she learns how things are done in a well-ordered American home, things her own overwhelmed and disappointed mother could not have taught her. A basic harmony exists between Ántonia and Mrs. Harling: they have strong, independent natures, and they know what they like. They both love children, animals, and music, as well as rough play and digging in the earth. As Jim says "Deep down in each of them there was a kind of hearty joviality, a relish of life, not over-delicate, but very invigorating." But Ántonia is young, high-tempered, and stubborn. When she has to choose between her work at the Harlings and dancing, she chooses dancing. "A girl like me has got to take her good times when she can. Maybe there won't be any tent next year. I guess I want to have my fling, like the other girls."

Pregnant, Ántonia is abandoned at the altar by the worthless Larry Donovan. Decades later, when Jim returns for a visit, he finds her the mother of a large, loving, demonstrative family. Falling asleep in the barn, he thinks, "Ántonia had always been one to leave images in the mind that did not fade.... She lent herself to immemorial human attitudes which we recognize by instinct as universal and true.... She was a battered woman now, not a lovely girl; but she still had that something which fires the imagination.... All the strong things of her heart came out in her body.... She was a rich mine of life, like the founders of early races."

Mr. Shimerda

Mr. Shimerda, with his iron-grey hair, well-shaped hands, and silk neck cloth, has a genteel, dignified bearing, a shadow from a different world. He was a musician, older and of higher social rank than his wife, whom he married honorably. Mr. Shimerda would have preferred to remain in Bohemia, where he made a good living and was well-respected, but his wife insisted the family move to America, where opportunity is greater. After Mr. Shimerda dies, Jim imagines his spirit travelling back to his much-loved homeland. While Mrs. Shimerda favors Ambrosch, Mr. Shimerda feels closest to Ántonia. Considerate and well-groomed even in his suicide, Mr. Shimerda's memory is cherished by both Ántonia and Jim throughout their lives.

Mrs. Shimerda

When we first meet Ántonia's mother, she is hugging her trunk "as if it were a baby." Possessions are dear to her and she bears the deprivations of immigrant life poorly. "A conceited, boastful old thing," as Jim calls her, is not even humbled by misfortune; nevertheless she is capable of gratitude. She gives Mrs. Burden mushrooms, a hoarded treasure brought from Bohemia; but poignantly, what she values has no worth at all to Americans. Typically, when Mrs. Shimerda almost washes Ántonia's baby with harsh soap, we don't know whether to attribute her action to ignorance, to disregard, or even to hostility. It is as Mrs. Burden says, "A body never knows what traits poverty might bring out in 'em."

Tony Shimerda

See Ántonia Shimerda

Tiny Soderball

Another hired girl, Tiny works at the Boys' Home Hotel in Black Hawk. She starts a lodging-house in Seattle and later helps found Dawson City during the gold rush in Alaska. After a Swede whom she had befriended died and left his claim to her, she returned a rich woman to San Francisco. But by then, Tiny had lost the ability to be interested in anything.

Mrs. Vanni

Along with her husband, Mrs. Vanni brings the trends and style of the world to Black Hawk. The excitement generated in their dance pavilion affects all the groups in town: the town ladies send their daughters to Mrs. Vanni's dancing classes, while the country girls and boys and working men enjoy the nightly dances. The Progressive Euchre Club arranges exclusive use of the tent on Tuesday and Friday nights but Jim prefers Saturday nights, when the country boys and girls joined the hired girls.

Themes

Change and Transformation

Willa Cather's straightforward story of Ántonia Shimerda, a Bohemian immigrant to Nebraska, parallels the change in the lives of the two principal characters with the transformation of the Great Plains. Ántonia is fourteen when we first see her; Jim Burden ten. Both have been wrenched from their origins, Ántonia from her native Bohemia, Jim from his parents' home in Virginia. She is an immigrant. He is an orphan. It is no surprise we encounter them first in motion on a train. They are carried through an empty land. "There seemed to be nothing to see; no fences, no creeks or trees, no hills or fields.... There was nothing but land: not a country at all, but the material out of which countries are made." That first ride is in sharp contrast with Jim's train crossing as an adult, when the "train flashed through never-ending miles of ripe wheat, by country towns and bright-flowered pastures and oak groves wilting in the sun." Ántonia has become the mother of a large family, and Jim is a successful Eastern lawyer, childless and unhappily married. Jim takes a long walk out of Black Hawk: "I had the good luck to stumble upon a bit of the first road.... Everywhere else it had been ploughed under when the highways were surveyed; this half-mile or so within the pasture fence was all

Topics for Further Study

- Explore the religious, social, and national background of the various waves of European immigration to the Great Plains and how these factors affected their assimilation into "American" society.

- Track the correlation between changing economic conditions and the changing American attitude toward immigration.

- Consider how much of Mrs. Shimerda's greed and false pride is a product of her own psychological nature or of the circumstances we find her in.

- Consider reasons why Willa Cather chose a male narrator and why women dominate the novel.

- Compare Willa Cather's writing style to that of Herman Melville, that of Ernest Hemingway, or that of Virginia Woolf.

- Create two differing interpretations of *My Ántonia*, one depending on Jim Burden as its center and one with Ántonia Shimerda at its center.

---

that was left of that old road which used to run like a wild thing across the open prairie…. This was the road which Ántonia and I came on that night when we got off the train at Black Hawk and were bedded down in the straw, wondering children, being taken we knew not whither."

American Dream

The novel is populated predominantly by immigrants and the successes and failures of the American Dream are manifest. What drove people to make the long haul across oceans and then across the continent? Some came because they were ambitious. Mrs. Shimerda uprooted her family against her husband's wishes. She said, "America big country, much money, much land for my boys, much husband for my girls." Anton Cuzak seems to have drifted to Nebraska to keep away from the bad luck and trouble he seemed to have attracted

in the past. Pavel and Peter were fugitives. The burgeoning country and economy provided many opportunities. The immigrant farmers hire out their daughters to the townspeople. Anton Jelinek rented his homestead and ran a saloon in town. Tiny Soderball follows the frontier to Seattle and then, during the gold rush, to Alaska. The Vannis take their musical talents and dancing tent on the road. And, as always, swindlers and loan sharks, like Wick Cutter, preyed on the weak. The immigrants pay an enormous price for these opportunities. The differences in language, occupation, and geography created hardships. "'It must have been a trial for our mothers,' said Lena, 'coming out here and having to do everything different. My mother always lived in town. She says she started behind in farmwork, and never has caught up.'" There is loss of social status. Even Jim, who prefers the hired girls, is aware they are not of his own set. Marriage to Lena or Ántonia is not even a consideration. And for many, there is homesickness. Ántonia says "I ain't never forgot my own country." For some the price seems materially worth it. Lena is a successful dressmaker in San Francisco. Tiny owns a house there and is wealthy, although soured. Ántonia and her husband flourish. For all the successes, the novel is riddled with disappointments and failures. Otto and Jake go west, and except for one postcard, they are never heard of again. "Rooshian" Peter, who proudly told Ántonia that "in his country only rich people had cows, but here any man could have one who would take care of her," loses his brother and bankruptcy forces him to sell his possessions. When Jim tells Ántonia that Coronado, who searched the American west for the Seven Golden Cities, died in the wilderness of a broken heart, she sighs, "More than him has done that." The American Dream had also broken her father.

Difference

It is through the eyes of Jim Burden, an orphan and thus something of an outsider himself, that Willa Cather considers differences of class, nationality, and gender. Even before young Jim arrives in Nebraska, he is met with prejudice against foreigners. Jake thinks that foreigners spread diseases. But Cather makes it clear that prejudice was not invented in America. Otto tells Mrs. Burden, "Bohemians has a natural distrust of Austrians." And Norwegian Lena feels fated by the Lapp blood of her paternal grandmother. "I guess that's what's the matter with me; they say Lapp blood will out." Throughout the novel, Jim himself is a perpetrator of pervading prejudices and conventions. As a boy, he is indignant that Ántonia, a girl, should have a superior attitude toward him. After his success in killing a snake wins her admiration, he cannot help insulting her, "What did you jabber Bohunk for?" *My Ántonia* is not simply a study in human difference but in the destiny that binds us into the human condition. Stargazing with Ántonia, Jim muses, "Though we had come from such different parts of the world, in both of us there was some dusky superstition that those shining groups have their influences upon what is and what is not to be."

Coming of Age

My Ántonia is a *bildungsroman,* or coming-of-age story, that traces Jim Burden's development from the age of ten. It begins when he is orphaned and newly transplanted to his grandparents' farm in Nebraska, where he first feels erased and blotted out. His escape into romanticism first takes the form of a young boy's fascination with outlaws, such as Jesse James, and lost adventurers, such as the Swiss Family Robinson. As an adolescent, he remains estranged although conventional. Bored by the sameness of his small, pioneer town, he is intrigued by the romantic foreignness of the hired girls, girls he will never marry, and he keeps away from girls that would be suitable for him. As an adult, he remains virtually without a real home. His marriage is childless; he and his wife live almost separate lives, his being a life of travel on the railway through the land that he loves.

Memory and Reminiscence

The novel has a rich aura of nostalgia and evokes a departed grandeur of a vast land that had once been a sea of red grass in motion. There is a sense of longing and homesickness that accompanies the characters as they move on in their lives. Ántonia misses the flowers and the woodland pathways of her homeland. Life-hardened Otto carries Christmas-tree ornaments from Austria in his trunk. The age-old prejudices that have been brought from Europe are familiar relics and, being so, are hard to relinquish. Ántonia's big box of pictures seems to be a container of this past, a past she has managed to pass on to her children. "Ántonia herself had always been one to leave images in the mind that did not fade—that grew stronger with time." Jim has his own stores of pictures in his mind's memory. And he consoles himself by saying, "Whatever we had missed, we possessed together the precious, the incommunicable past."

Style

Point of View

My Ántonia is at once the story of Ántonia Shimerda, a Bohemian immigrant to the Great Plains in the 1880s, and the story of Jim Burden, the narrator who creates his own image of Ántonia. As Jim's memoirs, the novel is the re-creation of a middle-aged lawyer whose failed marriage leaves him unloved and alone. His childhood in Nebraska becomes, in retrospect, the happiest time of his life, the period of potential and expectancy before the disappointments of adulthood. The rose-color cast and purple rhapsodies are products of this sentimental and romantic look backward. Ironically, despite the revisionist representation, it is clear that even as a child Jim is already alienated, different, orphaned. This use of a male narrator is typical in Cather's writing and has attracted much critical attention. It may account for Jim's inability to make Ántonia his girlfriend or wife, even though he clearly loves her. *My Ántonia* is also Willa Cather's story of children discovering the beauties and terrors of a vast new country and of themselves. While Ántonia emerges as an equally strong character, she is observed only from the outside. As Cather told a friend, she wanted her heroine to be "like a rare object in the middle of a table, which one may examine from all sides ... because she is the story."

Setting

Deeply rooted in a sense of time and place, Cather evokes the shaggy virgin prairie around Red Cloud, Nebraska. During the late nineteenth century, immigrants helped populate this new land. The novel has been said to be a tapestry in the colors of the land that Cather describes for us. Time is measured by the seasons that appear in distinct colors; the sunflower-border roads to the pale-yellow cornfields of summer or the slimy green of frozen asparagus, the frail green of the half-frozen insect, and the rosy haystacks of autumn. In a sense. Cather's work is a metaphor for the American pioneer experience and the prairie, the land itself, is a force as important to the novel as its characters.

Structure

My Ántonia is not a tightly plotted novel. Instead, it is told in a loose but focused episodic fashion. Like a painting with a small, almost incidental window that reveals an open landscape or a distant city, this collection of memories is inter-

Illustration by W. T. Benda, from My Ántonia.

rupted at rare moments with stories from another time, from another life. The wretched past of Peter and Pavel and the humble and miraculous past of Blind d'Arnault are two such windows that open up this painting of the American Great Plains during the period of immigration. For those critics who believe that Ántonia is the center of the novel, these interruptions in the story are problematic—as is the long section about Jim's life in Lincoln and his affair with Lena Lingard.

Style

Cather's superb prose style is disarmingly clear and simple, relying on a straightforward narration of facts. Yet it is also subtle, using carefully selected images to create a rich portrayal of the prairie environment. She worked consciously to achieve this effect through the selection of which details to include and which to leave out. She also heaped up incidents to achieve a realistic portrayal of life, known as verisimilitude. Cather described this prose style as "unfurnished" in an essay entitled "The Novel Demeuble." She compared it to throwing all the furniture out of a room and leaving it as bare as the stage of a Greek theater. To accomplish this, she eliminated many adverbs, used strong verbs, and many figures of speech.

Imagery

Cather's sparse but allusive style relies on the quality and depth of her images. She consciously used the land, its colors, seasons, and changes to suggest emotions and moods. Summer stands for life (Ántonia can't imagine who would want to die during the summer) and winter for death (Mr. Shimerda commits suicide during the winter). Animals are used as symbols of the struggle for survival experienced by the Shimerdas during their first winter. The essential grotesque image of the cost of this struggle is that of Mr. Shimerda's corpse frozen in his blood, his coat and neckcloth and boots removed and carefully laid by for the survivors. At the end of the novel, Cather uses animalistic images as symbols of fertility and abundance. Ántonia's children come up out of the well-stocked larder like "a veritable explosion of life out of the dark cave into the sunlight." One image has become almost emblematic of the novel. A plough, magnified through the distance, "heroic in size, a picture writing on the sun," freezes the moment when Jim picnics for the last time with his childhood friends. The vision disappears, the sun sets, and "that forgotten plough had sunk back to its own littleness somewhere on the prairie."

Realism

Jim Burden gives voice to a romanticism, or overly sentimental or positive outlook, that Cather was not quite distant from. The homesteading German, Danish, Bohemian, and Scandinavian settlers were the embodiment of a cultural tradition she cherished. However, the novel is saved from sentimentality by the evocative depiction of the harsh realities of pioneer and immigrant life and the complexity of the characters, who are rarely, if ever, only sympathetic or only despicable.

Historical Context

Immigration

Up until 1825, less than 10,000 new immigrants came to the United States each year. By the late 1840s, revolutions in Europe and the devastating potato famine in Ireland sent people to this country by the hundreds of thousands. Immigration increased steadily during the 1850s, and by 1860, one-eighth of America's 32 million people were foreign born. While many of these immigrants settled around the mill towns of the east as well as in the larger urban centers, the promotional activities

Compare & Contrast

- **1880s:** The "new immigrants" who came from eastern and southern Europe in the 1880s are considered a potential threat to the "American" character. For the first time, in 1882, Congress acts to restrict immigration on a selective basis, although standards are not very stringent. The Chinese Exclusion Act of 1882 puts an end to the importation of cheap Chinese labor which had caused some ugly racial riots in the West.

  Post World War I: Congress passes the Immigration Act of 1924; it institutes a quota system based on the U.S. population in 1920 and was an overt attempt to keep the country's ethnic "composition" what it had been—that is, predominantly Northern European.

  Today: The Immigration Reform and Control Act of 1986 gave legal status to millions of illegal aliens living in the U.S. since January 1982 and established penalties for anyone found hiring illegal aliens. Immigration preferences are extended due to family relationships and needed skills, not country of origin. In the 1990s, states like California attempt to pass legislation restricting government services to legal immigrants.

- **1880s:** After the Civil War, the Fifteenth Amendment extended the right to vote to include black males. Women of all races remained unable to vote. An active woman's movement in the 1880s consolidated in 1890 into the National American Woman Suffrage Association.

  Post World War I: In August, 1920, the Nineteenth Amendment was added to the Constitution and stated that the "right of citizens of the United States to vote shall not be denied by the United States or any State on account of sex."

  Today: In 1963, Betty Friedan's book *The Feminine Mystique* jumpstarted a stalled women's rights movement. Issues such as the right for equal pay, the need for child-care services, and the problem of gender stereotyping became the critical concerns on the agenda of the current feminist movement.

- **1880s:** The Monroe Doctrine, articulated in 1823 by U.S. President James Monroe, held sway throughout the century. It represented a mood of isolation from the political turbulence of Europe as well as an increased awareness of the opportunities for expansion on the American continent.

of the railroads brought many immigrants straight past them to the prairies. The railroad companies even sent scouts abroad to encourage people to come and settle the plains and prairies. It has been claimed that the transcontinental railroad could not have been built without immigrant labor. The railroad was not just crucial to economic success of the town and countryside: it was a powerful monopoly charging what it wished to ship grain to the market. Another flood of immigrants came in the 1860s and 1870s, just after the Homestead Act of 1862. This legislation granted, for a small fee, 160 acres of Western public land to citizens or prospective citizens who would stay and settle it for five years. These settlers were predominantly from western and northern Europe. They became the "old immigrants" when the numbers of "new immigrants" from eastern and southern Europe swelled in the 1880s and 1890s.

In Willa Cather's Nebraska, the population quadrupled between the Civil War and 1880, and then doubled again during the 1880s. Low prices for farm products in the late 1880s and early 1890s compounded by drought in the mid-1890s made success elusive for many on the Great Plains until almost the turn of the century. By the time Cather was writing *My Ántonia,* immigration to the Great Plains had slowed. Urban immigration, however, continued to cause miserable situations in the cities. As a journalist in Pittsburgh and New York City and as a newspaperwoman and editor for a radical magazine, *McClure's,* Cather was exposed to the conditions in which numerous urban immigrants lived. She also saw the mounting fear that the arrival of cheap foreign labor was not only undesirable competition but a contribution to the widening and hardening gap between rich and poor. During World War I, German-Americans were definitely suspect and stories of their victimization can be found in almost any midwestern state histories. Even the Czechs, who were eager to help free their homeland from the domination of Austria-Hungary, suffered during the war years. The country's anxiety over the role immigrants were to play in our society did not ease, even though the "tide" of immigration was stemmed briefly by World War I.

Theories of Americanization

By the time Willa Cather was writing *My Ántonia,* reaction to the massive European immigration of the nineteenth century had fostered two opposing theories of Americanization. These models have come to be called the "melting pot" theory and the "salad bowl" theory and still define the debate on difference even today, almost a century later. In the 1890s Frederick Jackson Turner popularized the image of the American West as a crucible where European immigrants would be "Americanized, liberated, and fused into a mixed race." One can read *My Ántonia* as a tribute to this view and appreciate Ántonia herself as "the rich mine of life, like the founders of early races" that produces the American people from the raw material that has been gathered on its shores. At its best, this view can serve as a model of assimilation. At its worst, it argues for a nativism, or favoring of native-born citizens, which is vulnerable to a fear or hatred of foreigners. Indeed, the American Nativists of the 1910s and 1920s fiercely opposed the waves of immigration. An alternative view of Americanization was articulated by philosopher Horace M. Kallen in an article in the *Nation,* circulated three years before *My Ántonia* was published. Each nationality should express its "emotional and voluntary life in its own language, in its own inevitable aesthetic and intellectual form," according to Kallen. This idea has since been termed cultural pluralism. Carl Degler coined the expression "salad bowl."

Critical Overview

Cather's fourth novel, and her third to be set in the West, *My Ántonia* drew attention as the work of an already established writer. In *The Borzoi 1920,*

H. L. Mencken enthusiastically called Cather extraordinary. "I know of no novel that makes the remote fold of the western farmlands more real than *My Ántonia* and I know of none that makes them seem better worth knowing." The nucleus of subsequent discussions over who is the protagonist can be detected in early reviews. The *Nation* critic declared the novel the "portrait of a woman," as did other observers; however, some reviewers thought Ántonia no more important than the physical background of the story. Perhaps the best all-around contemporary estimate of *My Ántonia* is Randolph Bourne's, who recognized in it the realist's command of material, knowledge of the countryside, and understanding of its people. He praised the "gold charm" of its style. In his *Dial* review, he defined Jim's vision as "romantic" and Ántonia as the "imaginative center" of *his* memoir. Within this book, he claimed, Cather "has taken herself out of the rank of provincial writers" and given readers a modern, universal interpretation of the spirit of youth. The feeling that Cather had arrived with *My Ántonia* was shared by Carl Van Doren, who, three years after the novel came out, distinguished her work from that of local colorist Sarah Orne Jewett, whose *The Country of the Pointed Firs* had been a major influence on Cather. However, troubled by the novel's structural irregularities, or what he felt to be the "largely superfluous" introduction, he admonished her in a *Nation* article "to find the precise form for the representation of a memorable character." He added that it is not enough merely to free oneself "from the bondage of 'plot.'" One critic compared Cather to English novelist Thomas Hardy in making setting epic in scope and integral to story.

My Ántonia remained a benchmark for Cather but earned her very little money. The World War I novel that followed, however, *One of Ours* (1922) was not only a best-seller, but also earned Cather the Pulitzer Prize. Ironically, the critics were not impressed, and some were outright derisive. During the 1920s and 1930s, Cather was often criticized for retreating from the present to the romanticized past. In a 1933 *English Journal* article, Marxist critic Granville Hicks continued to praise *My Ántonia* as a "faithful re-creation" of the "bleakness and cruelty" of prairie monotony and small-town narrowness, but condemned Cather for turning to a remote world in *Death Comes for the Archbishop* (1927). Alfred Kazin gave faint praise in his 1942 study *On Native Ground,* saying Cather could "secede with dignity" from modern America by using nostalgia to create values.

The explosion of criticism that followed Cather's death in 1947 was more focused on textual problems in *My Ántonia* and, again, the issue has been raised as to who is the real protagonist. Maxwell Geismar detected a split between the "ostensible heroine, Ántonia" and Lena Lingard, "who almost runs away with the show." For those who saw Ántonia as the main character, the structure of the book became a problem. British critic David Daiches, in his 1951 book-length study of Cather, is typical in this regard. He faults the author for occasionally losing sight of her theme, which he conceives to be the "development and self-discovery of the heroine." E. K. Brown notes in his 1953 critical biography that Cather's strategy of having a male narrator fascinated with Ántonia but remaining detached results in an emptiness at the novel's center. Richard Giannone's 1968 study *Music in Willa Cather's Fiction* suggests a different center. Because Ántonia's *joie de vivre* cannot be conveyed in words, it is "more a rhythm than a reason" and is expressed through music. Giannone puts the d'Arnault episode at the "pulsating center," prepared for by musical references in the first book and then in the scenes at the Harlings', and followed by the "infamous" dances and the playing of Mr. Shimerda's violin at the end. John Randall claimed in his 1960 book *The Landscape and the Looking Glass* that Cather balances two protagonists; he sees the novel as a system of contrasts: head (Jim) and heart (Ántonia), past (Jim) and future (Ántonia), contemplative life (Jim) and active life (Ántonia), town life (Jim) and country life (Ántonia); also, there are contrasts between life and death, warmth and cold, and order and chaos. Randall also notes Jim's significant crisis in moving from his original family in Virginia to his second one. Similarly psychological in approach, Terence Martin views the novel in his *PMLA* article in terms of Jim's conflicting impulses toward Lena and Ántonia, between forgetfulness and remembering. He sees Jim as defining both theme and structure, and the novel as presenting his story, not Ántonia's. It is a drama of memory, of "how he has come to see Ántonia as the epitome of all he has valued." The tendency among recent critics of *My Ántonia* is to dislodge it from its niche as a work of country-life optimism by exploring undercurrents of death, violence, and sex. In a 1967 *Western American Literature* article, Charles linked Jim to Mr. Shimerda as a Thanatos (Death) character, arguing that they provide a dark frame for the vibrant story of Ántonia's Eros (Love) nature. However, Susan J. Rosowski, in her 1986 book-length study of Cather, sees *My Ántonia* as defying analysis, as "a continuously changing work" in the Wordsworthian tradition, a successful balancing of the world of ideas and the world of experience through imaginative fusion. In this interpretation Jim becomes a reacting mind and Ántonia is the object.

Criticism

Anthony M. Dykema-VanderArk

In the following essay, Dykema-VanderArk, a doctoral candidate at Michigan State University, looks at how the stories of Jim Burden and Ántonia intertwine throughout Cather's novel to address themes of childhood, friendship, permanence, and the quest to find meaning in life.

"I first heard of Ántonia on what seemed to me an interminable journey across the great midland plain of North America." So begins Jim Burden's story of "his" Ántonia, and it is no accident that Jim's recollections are rooted in a journey. Willa Cather's *My Ántonia* was inspired by her own travels back to her childhood home of Red Cloud, Nebraska, and the novel is full of change, transition, and travel. Many of its characters are immigrants, classified by their very movement, and the divergent journeys through life of Jim and Ántonia are its central focus. Jim's narration of his story is, itself, a journey of sorts, a journey *back* through his life to recapture his relationship with Ántonia and all that she represents to him. And, finally, the reader of *My Ántonia* in a sense travels along with Jim as he returns to the country of his childhood, seeking something permanent and enduring beneath the unsettled surface of his life.

The Introduction of *My Ántonia,* narrated by an unnamed woman, provides some important clues to the motives and the manner of Jim Burden's story. This narrator, a childhood friend of both Jim and Ántonia, in some sense verifies Jim's impassioned view of Ántonia: "More than any other person we remembered," the narrator remarks, "this girl seemed to mean to us the country, the conditions, the whole adventure of our childhood. To speak her name was to call up pictures of people and places, to set a quiet drama going in one's brain." The narrator's comment also suggests the motives that inspire Jim to write his "manuscript" about "My Ántonia." By translating into writing the "pictures" and the "quiet drama" that Ántonia's name recalls, Jim hopes to revisit

What Do I Read Next?

- In *The American* (1877), Henry James presents a clash between an aristocratic old French family and a wealthy, self-made American. This novel is the first of his studies of the contrast between the simple, innocent American and the sophisticated, corrupt European.

- In Franz Kafka's unfinished novel *Amerika* (1927, translated 1938), he deals with the adventures and ordeals of a young European in an unreal, expressionistically depicted America.

- Sarah Orne Jewett's *The Country of Pointed Firs* (1896) is a book of tales and sketches thinly bound together by a faint thread of plot which portrays a Maine seaport town from the point of view of a summer resident.

- *Giants in the Earth: A Saga of the Prairie* (1924-25 in Norwegian; 1927 in English) is a stark and realistic work by the Norwegian-American novelist Ole E. Rolvaag describing the hardships, both mental and physical, of a small group of Norwegian farmers who set out from Minnesota with their families in 1873 to settle in the then unopened Dakota Territory. It is the first in a trilogy that also contains *Peder Victorious* and *Their Father's God*.

- Sinclair Lewis' *Main Street* (1920) is both a satire and an affectionate portrait of Gopher Prairie, a typical American town, which was undoubtedly suggested by Sauk Centre, Minnesota, where Lewis was born.

- In Nathaniel Hawthorne's *The Scarlet Letter* (1850), Hester Prynne evolves through the shame of her punishment, to wear an embroidered scarlet letter A on her breast as a symbol of her adultery.

- *O Pioneers!* (1913) is Willa Cather's second novel and the first to be set in Nebraska. Alexandra Bergson, deeply devoted to the land, takes over the care of her family on the death of her father and establishes a prosperous farm.

- *Death Comes for the Archbishop* (1927) is one of Cather's Southwest novels and describes the missionary efforts of the French bishop Jean Latour and his vicar to establish a diocese in the territory of New Mexico.

- The angriest piece of fiction that Willa Cather ever wrote is *My Mortal Enemy* (1926). Myra Henshawe feels cheated by life and dies of cancer, alone and embittered.

---

the "whole adventure" of his early life and recapture its emotional significance. The narrator of the Introduction also gives the reader fair warning that the subject of Jim's story is out of the ordinary, unknown to most people, even, perhaps, unknowable: "We agreed that no one who had not grown up in a little prairie town could know anything about it. It was a kind of freemasonry, we said." Paradoxically, this comment suggests that Jim's story will not succeed in explaining "the country" and "the conditions" of his childhood to anyone but his friend and a select group of readers, those with first hand knowledge of small-town prairie life. But Cather's introduction also gives away, in a sense, the secret password needed to understand the story

that follows, the "name" that, once spoken, might recall the past and set it moving with life: Ántonia.

On one level, Cather uses Ántonia's simple story to bring to life the "country" and the "conditions" encountered and endured by many of the immigrants who settled the American frontier in the late nineteenth century. By telling this one "Pioneer Woman's Story," Cather portrays the immense hardships faced by figures like Ántonia Shimerda and her family, not only the hardships of poverty, landscape, and climate, but also the social barriers erected against immigrants of particular ethnic and religious backgrounds. Cather also uses Ántonia's story to celebrate the virtues of the immigrant pioneers, virtues unnoted or ignored by many of her contemporaries who, like the people of Black Hawk, viewed all "foreigners" as "ignorant people who couldn't speak English." As a poor immigrant from Bohemia, Ántonia first appears an unlikely American heroine, but Cather celebrates Ántonia for her strength of character, her resilience, and her tenacity in the face of social ostracism. She appears at the end of *My Ántonia* as a figure who has triumphed over the hardships of her life through stalwart struggle, producing a fruitful farm from the difficult land, upholding a large and joyful family, and ensuring an easier future for her children.

Ántonia also provides the key to Jim Burden's story, in part because it is Jim who tells her story and reflects on its significance. In writing down all that he remembers of Ántonia, Jim discovers the extent to which his own identity is rooted in his relationship to her. As a ten-year-old orphan at the start of his story, Jim remembers seeing the Shimerdas "huddled together on the platform" of the train station, and the sound of their "foreign tongue" is as new and strange to him as the land that surrounds him. In the years that follow his first encounter with the Shimerdas, Jim's relationship with Ántonia provides him with several roles to play, acting as a language tutor, a companion, a helpmate, a suitor, and, in his "mock adventure" with the rattlesnake, a savior of sorts. As a young man, Jim distinguishes himself from what he sees as the narrow-mindedness of his immediate community by identifying with Ántonia and the other "hired girls" who were "considered a menace to the social order." He expresses his "contempt" for the veneer of "respect for respectability" that defines the townsfolk. In Ántonia's refusal to deny her desires, he sees an antidote to the town's "evasions and negations," its repression of "every individual taste, every natural appetite." Although Jim does not face the same restrictions as Ántonia and the other "country girls," he identifies with their experience of town life and, in a sense, this identification inspires his moving away from Black Hawk.

Jim also finds a key to his own life in Ántonia's ability to hold onto her past—both its joys and its sorrows—through memory and through storytelling. When Jim returns from college and meets Ántonia working in the fields, they "instinctively" walk to Mr. Shimerda's graveside as "the fittest place to talk to each other," a place symbolizing the connection they shared as children. But as they talk there, Ántonia does not dwell on the painful loss of her father as a young girl; instead, she tells Jim that her father "never goes out of my life.... The older I grow, the better I know him and the

more I understand him." Ántonia does not try to escape or ignore her past but embraces it, carrying it with her in the present. Jim sees in Ántonia's example a way to ground his life in something strong and permanent in spite of the continual movement that seems to define him. In the same conversation, Ántonia also looks to the future, telling Jim how eager she is to pass on her memories of childhood to her daughter: "I can't wait till my little girl's old enough to tell her about all the things we used to do." When Jim returns to visit Ántonia twenty years later, he finds her doing just that: Ántonia's box of photographs and her stories about each picture draw all of her children to her side, bonding the family together in "a kind of physical harmony." Jim sees that Ántonia uses her stories of the past not only to entertain but also to educate her children, to root their lives in the "people and places" of her childhood just as they are rooted in the language and customs of the "old country" despite being products of the new. In his own narration, Jim follows the example of Ántonia's storytelling, learning from her how to recapture the emotional significance of his childhood experiences and to create stories that keep the past alive in the present.

As many critics have noted, however, the stories that Jim tells in *My Ántonia* do not always provide a complete or entirely reliable portrait of Ántonia's life or of his own. The narrator of the Introduction, for example, calls attention to Jim's "naturally romantic and ardent disposition," and Frances Harling suggests to Jim that his "romantic" temperament influences his view of the country girls: "You always put a kind of glamour over them." Jim himself notes that the "places and people" of his past stand out "strengthened and simplified" in his memory. Although Jim identifies himself with Ántonia throughout his story, he also frequently reveals the limitations of his understanding of her life. Early in their friendship, for example, Jim repeatedly finds himself confused and frustrated by the particular customs and religious rituals of the Bohemians. Even the simple, well-intended gift of dried mushrooms from the "old country" fails to connect the two families: In spite of Ántonia's testimony to their usefulness and flavor, Jim's grandmother cannot identify the strange chips and throws the gift into the fire. A similar inability to understand fully all that the Shimerdas "had brought so far and treasured so jealously" continues throughout Jim's story. Even after Jim travels around the world and visits Bohemia, the "old country" of Ántonia's youth, he remains isolated from her and her family life by their language, the same "foreign tongue" that he heard for the first time as a ten-year-old boy at the train station in Black Hawk.

But this sense of distance between Jim and Ántonia, even at the end of *My Ántonia,* only adds poignancy to Jim's story and interest to Cather's novel. Perhaps the deep and lasting appeal of Cather's novel reflects the sense of mystery that she weaves into its many stories, the unanswered questions that Jim's narration evokes. How, for example, might the narrator of the Introduction, who only "watched her come and go," tell Ántonia's story? How might Mr. Shimerda and the Widow Steavens, each of whom also calls her "My Ántonia," tell her story? And, perhaps most intriguing of all, how does Ántonia tell and retell her gathered children about "the country, the conditions, the whole adventure" of her life in Bohemia and America? While these questions remain, at the close of Jim's story, part of the "incommunicable past," the broader themes of Cather's novel—the child's sense of undistilled happiness, the dream of being "dissolved into something complete and great," the mystery of genuine friendship, the quest for permanence and meaning in one's life—become real in the present for each new reader of *My Ántonia.*

Source: Anthony M. Dykema-VanderArk, in an essay for *Novels for Students,* Gale, 1997.

James E. Miller, Jr.

In the following excerpt, Miller explains how Cather's book is about the failure to find happiness by pursuing materialistic dreams.

[*My Ántonia*] does not portray, in any meaningful sense, the fulfillment of the American dream. By and large, the dreams of the pioneers lie shattered, their lives broken by the hardness of wilderness life. Even those who achieve, after long struggle, some kind of secure life are diminished in the genuine stuff of life. For example, in one of his accounts that reach into the future beyond the present action, Jim Burden tells us of the eventual fate of the vivacious Tiny Soderball, one of the few to achieve "solid worldly success." She had a series of exciting adventures in Alaska, ending up with a large fortune. But later, when Jim encountered her in Salt Lake City, she was a "thin, hard-faced woman.... She was satisfied with her success, but not elated. She was like someone in whom the faculty of becoming interested is worn out."

One of the major material successes of the book is Jim Burden, and in many ways the novel traces his rise in position and wealth. As most of the characters of the book travel west, his is a journey east, and, in the process, the acquisition of education, wealth, social position. In short, Jim has all the appearances of one who has lived the American dream and achieved fulfillment. But the material fulfillment has not brought the happiness promised. The entire novel is suffused with his melancholy at the loss of something precious— something that existed back in the hard times, now lost amidst comfort and wealth. The whole promise of the dream has somehow slipped through his fingers right at the moment it appeared within his grasp. Why? The question brings us around to a central problem in the novel: Why has Jim, so appreciative of the vitality and freedom represented by the hired girls, ended up in a marriage so empty of meaning?

Perhaps Jim's melancholy itself tells us the reason. The book in a way represents his confession, a confession of unaware betrayal of the dream. In looking back from his vantage point in time, Jim can come to the full realization of what the hired girls (especially such as Ántonia Shimerda and Lena Lingard) represented and what they have come to symbolize: simply all that is best, all that survives of worth, of the faded dream. Some critics have seen in Jim's obtuseness in his male-female relationship with Ántonia and Lena a defect in the book's construction. On the contrary, this theme is very much a part of the book's intention. Jim looking back from the wisdom of his later years and the unhappiness of his meaningless marriage can come to a much sharper awareness of precisely what he missed in his ambitious movement eastward and upward.

In Book II, "The Hired Girls," we are in a way witness to the dream turning sour: "The daughters of Black Hawk merchants had a confident, unenquiring belief that they were 'refined,' and that the country girls, who 'worked out,' were not." "The country girls were considered a menace to the social order. Their beauty shone out too boldly against a conventional background. But anxious mothers need have felt no alarm. They mistook the mettle of their sons. The respect for respectability was stronger than any desire in Black Hawk youth." Jim Burden remembered his roaming the streets of Black Hawk at night, looking at the "sleeping houses": "for all their frailness, how much jealousy and envy and unhappiness some of them managed to contain! The life that went on in them seemed to me made up of evasions and negations; shills to save cooking, to save washing and cleaning, devices to propitiate the tongue of gossip. This guarded mode of existence was like living under a tyranny. People's speech, their voices, their very glances, became furtive and repressed. Every individual taste, every natural appetite, was bridled by caution."

"Respect for respectability" is, perhaps, the cancer battening at the heart of the dream (a theme that William Faulkner was to emphasize later in his Snopes trilogy), and the reader may wonder to what extent Jim Burden himself had been infected, especially in view of the brittle wife he had acquired at some stage in his rise to the top. Moreover, Jim was strongly attracted to the vitality of the hired girls, consciously and unconsciously, as revealed in a recurring dream he had: "One dream I dreamed a great many times, and it was always the same. I was in a harvest-field full of shocks, and I was lying against one of them. Lena Lingard came across the stubble barefoot, in a short skirt, with a curved reaping-hook in her hand, and she was flushed like the dawn, with a kind of luminous rosiness all about her. She sat down beside me, turned to me with a soft sigh and said, 'Now they are all gone, and I can kiss you as much as I like.'" After this remarkable sexual revelation, Jim adds: "I used to wish I could have this flattering dream about Ántonia, but I never did." Sister-like Ántonia cannot be transfigured, even in dream, to sexual figure. Her role in the book, and in Jim's psyche, is destined to be more idealized, more mythic.

But Lena Lingard is the subject of an entire book of *My Ántonia.* And that book works out metaphorically the meaning of the novel's epigraph from Virgil as well as the specific personal relation of Jim and Lena, this latter through symbolic use of a play they both attend, Dumas's *Camille.* The epigraph for *My Ántonia* is drawn from Virgil's *Georgics,* and reads: *"Optima dies … prima fugit."* This phrase comes into the novel in Book III, after Jim has entered the University of Nebraska and begun his study of Latin, translating the phrase "the best days are the first to flee." As Lena Lingard, now with a dressmaking shop in Lincoln, brings to mind for Jim all the vitality of the hired girls of Black Hawk, he makes the connection between them and the haunting phrase from Virgil: "It came over me, as it had never done before, the relation between girls like those and the poetry of Virgil. If there were no girls like them in the world, there would be no poetry. I understand that clearly, for the first time. This revelation seemed to me inestimably precious. I clung to it as if it might suddenly vanish."

But if Lena (along with Ántonia and the others) is equated with poetry, she is also a breathing physical reality to Jim, and Book III brings Jim as close physically to one of the hired girls as the novel permits. A large part of the Book is taken up with a description of Jim's and Lena's attendance at a performance of *Camille,* the sentimental but highly effective drama by Dumas *fils.* As Jim remarks: "A couple of jack-rabbits, run in off the prairie, could not have been more innocent of what awaited them than were Lena and I." Although some critics see the long account of theatre-going as a kind of inserted story or intrusion, in fact it provides a kind of sophisticated mirror image in literature for the thematic dilemma posed in the novel itself—and particularly the dilemma Jim faces in his attraction to Lena. Only a few pages before this episode, he has come to the insight equating the hired girls, in all their vitality and freedom, with poetry. Now he is confronted with the physical presence of one for whom he feels a strong attraction.

The hired girls are not, of course, Camilles, but they have some of the same kind of magic, poetry, freedom, love of life that attracted Armand to Camille—and that attract Jim to Lena. As Jim and Lena find themselves drawn closer and closer together in Lincoln, their conversation turns more and more to marriage—but only obliquely do they hint of anything deeper than friendship between themselves. Lena, pressed by Jim about her future, says she will never marry, that she prefers to be "lonesome," that the experience of marriage as she has witnessed it is even repellent. Jim answers, "'But it's not all like that.'" Lena replies: "'Near enough. It's all being under somebody's thumb. What's on your mind, Jim? Are you afraid I'll want you to marry me some day?'" Jim's immediate remark after this, to the reader, is: "Then I told her I was going away." The moment has passed, the future for Jim has been, in a sense, determined. Lena will go on her successful, "lonesome" way; Jim will go on to his considerable achievement and position—and his disastrous marriage.

What happened to the dream—to Jim's dream of Lena, to the larger dream of personal fulfillment? Was his failure in not seeing some connection between the dreams? Was Jim's destiny in some obscure sense a self-betrayal? And is this America's destiny, a self-betrayal of the possibilities of the dream? …

This road is not, of course, simply Jim's and Ántonia's road. It is America's road, leading not into the future, but into the past, fast fading from the landscape, fast fading from memory.... It is Jim's and Ántonia's—and perhaps America's—"road of Destiny":

> This was the road over which Ántonia and I came on that night when we got off the train at Black Hawk and were bedded down in the straw, wondering children, being taken we knew not whither. I had only to close my eyes to hear the rumbling of the wagons in the dark, and to be again overcome by that obliterating strangeness. The feelings of that night were so near that I could reach out and touch them with my hand. I had the sense of coming home to myself, and of having found out what a little circle man's experience is. For Ántonia and for me, this had been the road of Destiny; had taken us to those early accidents of fortune which predetermined for us all that we can ever be. Now I understood that the same road was to bring us together again. Whatever we had missed, we possessed together the precious, the incommunicable past.

As Americans who have dreamed the dream, we might say with Jim: "Whatever we have missed, we possess together the precious, the incommunicable past." In some dark sense, Jim's experience is the American experience, his melancholy sense of loss also his country's, his longing for something missed in the past a national longing.

The lost promise, the misplaced vision, is America's loss—our loss—and it haunts us all, still.

Source: James E. Miller, Jr., "*My Ántonia* and the American Dream," in *Prairie Schooner,* Vol. XLVIII, No. 2, Summer, 1974, pp. 112–23.

Robert E. Scholes

In the following excerpt, Scholes compares the characters of Jim Burden and Ántonia Shimerda.

The two central figures in *My Ántonia* are, in different senses, Innocents. Jim Burden, bereft of both his parents within a year, is removed from the warm and comfortable Virginia of his early days and thrust into the strange and frightening world of Nebraska. As he bumps along on the wagon ride to his new home, he feels that he has left even the spirits of his dead parents behind him:

> The wagon jolted on, carrying me I know not whither. I don't think I was homesick. If we never arrived anywhere, it did not matter. Between that earth and that sky I felt erased, blotted out. I did not say my prayers that night: here, I felt, what would be would be.

Ántonia Shimerda, though also a young, innocent creature in a raw country, is not bereft of the past as Jim Burden is. Ántonia's Bohemian ancestry is a part of her and exerts a decided influence on her present and future. We are reminded of this past constantly: by the Bohemian customs and culinary practices of the Shimerdas; by the observations of Otto Fuchs on the relationship of Austrians and Bohemians in the old country; and especially by the Catholic religion of the Bohemians, which is their strongest link with the past, and which serves to bind them together and to separate them from the Protestant society of their adopted land. But, most important, Ántonia herself cherishes her connection with the past. When Jim asks if she remembers the little town of her birth, she replies,

> "Jim … if I was put down there in the middle of the night, I could find my way all over that little town; and along the river where my grandmother lived. My feet remember all the little paths through the woods, and where the big roots stick out to trip you. I ain't never forgot my own country."

But despite the importance of the past for Ántonia, she and the other hired girls are figures of heroic and vital innocence, associated with nature and the soil. Like Lena Lingard, they all "waked fresh with the world every day." They are unused to the ways of society, and Ántonia, especially, is too trusting. Lena tells Jim that Ántonia "won't hear a word against [Larry Donovan]. She's so sort of innocent." The struggle of the "hired girls" with society is one of the important themes of the novel. Jim Burden remarks that

> the country girls were considered a menace to the social order. Their beauty shone out too boldly against a conventional background. But anxious mothers need have felt no alarm. They mistook the mettle of their sons. The respect for respectability was stronger than any desire in Black Hawk youth.

This struggle of the country girls with the city is a very perplexing one, in which apparent victory and apparent defeat are both apt to prove evanescent in time. Lena Lingard and Tiny Soderball become successful, triumphing even in the metropolis of San Francisco, while Ántonia becomes the foolish victim of her love for a conniving railroad conductor. But Lena and Tiny succeed only in becoming more like the society from which they had been ostracized, while Ántonia, and the other country girls who stay on the land, ultimately change the structure of society itself. Jim Burden remarks,

> I always knew I should live long enough to see my country girls come into their own, and I have. Today the best that a harassed Black Hawk merchant can hope for is to sell provisions and farm machinery and automobiles to the rich farms where that first crop of stalwart Bohemian and Scandinavian girls are now the mistresses.

Jim Burden, like Lena and Tiny, has made his success in the city and on the city's terms. From the narrator of the introductory chapter we learn that Jim's personal life, his marriage, has not been a success though his legal work flourishes. Jim's failure to find happiness or satisfaction in his career and in the city, constitutes for him the "fall" into self-knowledge which is characteristic of the Adamic hero. It is Jim's recognition of his own fall that makes him superior to Lena and Tiny, and enables him to live vicariously through Ántonia and her children.

Ántonia's seduction is a more clear-cut "fall" than Jim's unhappiness, and her subsequent self-knowledge is more strikingly evidenced. When Jim meets Ántonia after she has had her illegitimate child, he notices "a new kind of strength in the gravity of her face." At this meeting she asks Jim whether he has learned to like big cities, adding that she would die of lonesomeness in such a place. "I like to be where I know every stack and tree, and where all the ground is friendly," she says; and after they part Jim feels "the old pull of the earth, the solemn magic that comes out of those fields at night-fall," and he wishes he could be a little boy again, and that his way would end there.

When Jim revisits Ántonia and her thriving family, she has in some ways relapsed toward the past. " 'I've forgot my English so.' " She says, " 'I don't often talk it any more. I tell the children I used to speak it real well.' She said they all spoke Bohemian at home. The little ones could not speak English at all—didn't learn it until they went to school." But her children, her involvement in life, makes her concerned for the future. She has lived "much and hard," reflects Jim as they meet, but "she was there, in the full vigor of her personality, battered but not diminished, looking at me, speaking to me in the husky, breathy voice I remembered so well." Jim, however, is not recognized by Ántonia at first, even though he has "kept so young." He is less battered, perhaps, but he is more diminished.

So it is that Ántonia, who is always conscious of the past, is nevertheless free of it, and capable of concern for the future. And her past is not merely that of a generation or so. Jim observes, "She lent herself to immemorial human attitudes which we recognize by instinct as universal and true.... It was no wonder that her sons stood tall and straight. She was a rich mine of life, like the founders of early races." Whereas Jim, who has no such connection with the past, who came to Nebraska without a family and rode on a wagon into a new life which he felt was beyond even the attention of God, is still bound by the recent past, by what has happened to him in his own youth, and he lives in both the present and the future only vicariously through the plans and lives of others. He reflects, "In the course of twenty crowded years one parts with many illusions. I did not wish to lose the early ones. Some memories are realities, and are better than anything that can happen to one again." Jim is haunted by the past, by the sense that, in the phrase of Virgil which is the novel's epigraph, *Optima dies ... prima fugit*. When he contemplates in the closing lines of his narrative the road on which he had entered his new life as a boy, he reconsiders his whole existence:

> I had the sense of coming home to myself, and of having found out what a little circle man's experience is. For Ántonia and for me, this had been the road of Destiny; had taken us to those early accidents of fortune which predetermined for us all that we can ever be. Now I understood that the same road was to bring us together again. Whatever we had missed, we possessed together the precious, the incommunicable past.

Ántonia's life is not tragic. She is neither defeated nor destroyed by life, not even diminished. Yet the distinguishing characteristic of this novel is its elegiac tone; the eternal note of sadness pervades especially the closing passages of the book. The direct cause of this element of sadness is the nostalgia of Jim Burden, through which the story of Ántonia filters down to the reader. But behind Jim Burden's nostalgia, and merged with it, is the nostalgia of Willa Cather herself.

There is a suggestion in this novel and in the earlier *O Pioneers!* that the younger brothers and the sisters of this splendid generation of pioneer women will not be their equals. Emil Bergson—the youth in *O Pioneers!* for whom his older sister Alexandra labors and plans—attends the university, escapes from the plough, only to ruin several lives through his adulterous love. And in *My Ántonia* there is the suggestion that the coming generations will be less heroic and more ordinary than the present breed. Jim Burden at one point muses on this problem, thinking of the hired girls in Black Hawk:

> Those girls had grown up in the first bitter-hard times, and had got little schooling themselves. But the younger brothers and sisters, for whom they made such sacrifices and who have had "advantages," never seem to me, when I meet them now, half as interesting or as well educated. The older girls, who helped to break up the wild sod, learned so much

from life, from poverty, from their mothers and grandmothers; they had all, like Ántonia, been early awakened and made observant by coming at a tender age from an old country to a new.

The circumstances which formed Ántonia will not be repeated; the future will be in the hands of a diminished race. It is the feeling which haunts Willa Cather's novel. Ántonia looks to the future of her children, but Jim Burden knows that the future will be at best a poor imitation of the past. Ántonia's life is a triumph of innocence and vitality over hardship and evil. But Willa Cather does not celebrate this triumph; rather, she intones an elegy over the dying myth of the heroic Innocent, over the days that are no more.

Source: Robert E. Scholes, "Hope and Memory in *My Ántonia*," in *Shenandoah*, Vol. XIV, No. 1, Autumn, 1962, pp. 24–29.

Sources

Randolph Bourne, "Morals and Art from the West," in *The Dial*, Vol. LXV, No. 779, December 14, 1981, pp. 556–57.

E. K. Brown, *Willa Cather: A Critical Biography*, Knopf, 1953.

Sister Peter Damian Charles, "*My Ántonia*: A Dark Dimension," in *Western American Literature*, Vol. II, No. 2, Summer, 1967, pp. 91–108.

David Daiches, *Willa Cather: A Critical Introduction*, Cornell University Press, 1951

Maxwell Geismar, *The Last of the Provincials: The American Novel, 1915–1925*, Houghton, 1947.

Richard Giannone, *Music in Willa Cather's Fiction*, University of Nebraska Press, 1968.

Granville Hicks, "The Case against Willa Cather," in *English Journal*, Vol. XXII, No. 9, November, 1933, pp. 703–10.

Alfred Kazin, *On Native Grounds: An Interpretation of Modern American Prose Literature*, Reynal and Hitchcock, 1942.

Terence Martin, "The Drama of Memory in *My Ántonia*," in *PMLA*, Vol. 84, No. 2, March, 1969, pp. 304-10.

H. L. Mencken, "Willa Cather," *The Borzoi 1920*, edited by Alfred A. Knopf, 1920, pp. 28–31.

Review of *My Ántonia*, in *The Nation* Vol. 107, No. 2783, Nov. 2, 1918, pp. 522-23.

John H. Randall, III, *The Landscape and the Looking Glass: Willa Cather's Search for Meaning*, Houghton, 1960.

Susan J. Rosowski, *The Voyage Perilous: Willa Cather's Romanticism*, University of Nebraska Press, 1986.

Carl Van Doren, *Nation*, July 27, 1921, reprinted in his *Contemporary American Novelists: 1900-1920*, Macmillan, 1922.

For Further Study

Joan Acocella, "Cather and the Academy," in *New Yorker*, November 27, 1995, pp. 56-71.
An insightful essay examining the varying responses of the "literary establishment" to Cather's fiction during this century.

Mildred R. Bennett, *The World of Willa Cather*, Dodd, Mead, 1951; University of Nebraska Press, 1961.
This book is of primary value in understanding the influence of Cather's childhood on her fiction.

Edward Bloom and Lillian Bloom, *Willa Cather's Gift of Sympathy*, Southern Illinois University Press, 1962.
A book-length appraisal of Cather's place in American literature, with comparisons to Cooper, Hawthorne, Melville, and James, especially valuable for its contribution in exploring Cather's literary theories and practices.

Harold Bloom editor, *Willa Cather's "My Ántonia,"* Chelsea House, 1987.
A useful collection of essays on Cather's novel representing a range of critical perspectives.

Brent L. Bohlke editor, *Willa Cather in Person: Interviews, Speeches, and Letters*, University of Nebraska Press, 1986.
This selection of Cather's written and spoken words offers insight into her fictional writing.

Willa Cather, *The World and the Parish*, University of Nebraska Press, 1970.
A two-volume set of Cather's early articles and reviews, published in periodicals between 1893 and 1902.

Robert W. Cherney, "Willa Cather's Nebraska" in *Approaches to Teaching Cather's "My Ántonia,"* edited by Susan J. Rosowski, Modern Language Association of America, New York, 1989, pp. 31-36.
An essay that focuses specifically on the socio-economic and demographic climate in Willa Cather's Nebraska at the end of the 19th century.

Judith Fryer, *Felicitous Space: The Imaginative Structures of Edith Wharton and Willa Cather*, University of North Carolina Press, 1986.
Attending to the painted quality of Cather's landscape, this book focuses on the influence Millet and the Barbizon painters had on Cather.

Blanche H. Gelfant, "The Forgotten Reaping-hook: Sex in *My Ántonia*," *American Literature*, Vol. 43, 1971, pp. 60-82.
Gelfant questions the reliability of Jim's narration and argues that "Jim Burden belongs to a remarkable gallery of characters for whom Cather consistently invalidates sex."

Philip Gerber, *Willa Cather*, Twayne, 1995.
A recently revised critical overview of Cather's life and work, including a brief character study of Ántonia.

Sally Allen McNall, "Immigrant Backgrounds to *My Ántonia*: A Curious Social Situation in Black Hawk" in *Approaches to Teaching Cather's 'My Ántonia,'* edited by Susan J. Rosowski, Modern Language Association of America, 1989. pp. 22-30.

A fact-filled essay on the social conditions that provided the background for Cather's *My Ántonia* and the questions that arise from the novel.

John J. Murphy, *'My Ántonia': The Road Home,* Twayne's Masterwork Studies, Twayne Publishers, 1989.

A comprehensive book including textual analysis, critical summary, chronology, and historical context.

Paul A. Olsen, "The Epic and Great Plains Literature: Rolvaag, Cather and Neihardt," *Prairie Schooner,* Vol. 55, 1981, pp. 263-85.

This article attempts to show that when a redefined epic tradition is applied to *My Ántonia,* Ántonia becomes the heroic creator of the new civilization and Jim the hymner singing her accomplishments.

Susan J. Rosowski editor, *Approaches to Teaching Cather's 'My Ántonia,'* Modern Language Association, 1989.

Though intended primarily for teachers, this collection of brief essays also offers the first-time reader several productive avenues into Cather's novel.

David Stouck, *Willa Cather's Imagination,* Lincoln: University of Nebraska Press, 1975.

A book-length study using the pastoral mode as key to understanding Jim's compulsion to return to the past.

William J. Stuckey, "My Ántonia: A Rose for Miss Cather," *Studies in the Novel,* Vol. 4, 1972, pp. 473-83.

In this article, Cather, is compared to Fitzgerald and is faulted for not making a clear distinction between realistic skepticism and romantic vision.

James Woodress, *Willa Cather: A Literary Life,* University of Nebraska Press, 1987.

A recent biography in which the author praises *My Ántonia* for its breadth of appeal and its depth of intellectual and emotional content.

James Woodress, "Willa Cather," in *Concise Dictionary of American Literary Biography: Realism, Nationalism and Local Color, 1986-1917,* Gale, 1988, pp. 36-51.

A comprehensive essay of both Cather's life and work by Cather's biographer with a special focus on her novels.

One Flew Over the Cuckoo's Nest

Ken Kesey
1962

Ken Kesey's tragicomic novel, *One Flew Over the Cuckoo's Nest,* takes place in a mental hospital during the late 1950s. The book can be read on two levels; if one looks on the surface, there is the story of how a highly individualistic, near-superman named McMurphy becomes a patient and for a time overturns the senseless and dehumanizing routines of the ward. If one looks deeper, however, there is a commentary on U.S. society, which the Beat generation of the late 1950s viewed as so hopelessly conformist as to stifle individuality and creativity.

First published in 1962, Kesey's book bridges the transition from the Beatniks of the late 1950s, who used poetry, music, and fashion to express their dissatisfaction with conformist society, to the hippies of the 1960s, whose counterculture rebellion included free love and drug use. Because *Cuckoo's Nest* was both timely and provocative, it became an instant hit with critics and with a college generation that was ready to take on the establishment full-tilt. Over the years, the book has enjoyed many reprintings in paperback form. It started receiving scholarly attention in the 1970s, particularly after it was made into an Academy Award-winning movie of the same title starring Jack Nicholson, who gave a brilliant performance as the irrepressible McMurphy. Although the novel has sometimes been faulted as sexist and racist, it still endures as an example of the individual's battle not to succumb to the forces of a dehumanizing, demoralizing society.

Author Biography

Ken Kesey was born in 1935 in LaJunta, Colorado. The family moved to Springfield, Oregon, where he attended public school before attending and graduating from the University of Oregon. While in college, he pursued drama and athletics. A champion wrestler, he nearly won a place on the U.S. Olympic team. After graduating, he worked for a year, thought about becoming a movie actor, and wrote an unpublished novel about college athletics entitled "End of Autumn." Kesey married his high-school sweetheart, Faye Haxy, in 1956, and the couple became the parents of three children. In 1958, Kesey began graduate work in creative writing at Stanford University in California, where he studied with several noted writers, including novelist Wallace Stegner. He wrote a second unpublished novel, "Zoo," before beginning *One Flew Over the Cuckoo's Nest* in the summer of 1960. Around this time, he became a paid volunteer in government-sponsored drug experiments at the Veteran's Hospital in Menlo Park, California. There he was introduced to psychoactive drugs such as mescaline and LSD, and became a frequent user of them. He was under the influence of these drugs during some of the time he wrote this, his first published novel.

Cuckoo's Nest enjoyed considerable critical and popular success after its 1962 publication, becoming especially popular on college campuses. Kesey himself gained additional notoriety with a group of friends who titled themselves the "Merry Pranksters" and travelled the country promoting the new "counterculture" of social protest and psychedelic drugs. The experiences of Kesey and his friends were chronicled in Tom Wolfe's noted 1968 work *The Electric Kool-Aid Acid Test*. This trip was not without cost, however, for Kesey was arrested in 1965 for drug possession and eventually spent about five months in jail and in the San Mateo County Sheriff's Honor Camp. Released in 1967, he moved back to Oregon in 1968, taking up residence on a farm in Pleasant Hills. He gave up writing for a period of time before returning to his former art. He also kicked his drug habit successfully, and has since disavowed experimental drug use, saying "There are dues." None of his subsequent works have received the same attention as *Cuckoo's Nest,* which is seen as both a predecessor to and representative of the counterculture movement of the 1960s.

Ken Kesey

Plot Summary

Part 1

One Flew Over the Cuckoo's Nest is the story of a few remarkable weeks in an Oregon insane asylum and the events that lead to the narrator's escape. A tall and broad Indian, Chief Bromden is a long-term inmate who tells the story. His insanity appears to stem from a paranoid belief in the existence of a machine, "The Combine," which controls people's behavior. He feigns deafness and dumbness in order to fight this control. In looking back on his time in the ward, he finds that he must recount the horrible experiences suffered by him and his fellow inmates. In particular he tells of the conflict between Randle McMurphy and Big Nurse Ratched.

Bromden's story begins with the day McMurphy is first admitted to the ward. McMurphy is loud and disruptive, and introduces himself as a gambling man who has only pretended to be crazy in order to get out of a work camp. He introduces himself to the "Chronics" (permanent residents), including Bromden himself, and the "Acutes" (who may still recover). McMurphy immediately attempts to take charge of the bunch by instigating a who-is-crazier-than-whom debate with Harding, an Acute who is president of the Patients Council.

Nurse Ratched knows that McMurphy represents a disruptive force on the ward, and Bromden explains her reaction to disruptive forces:

> The big nurse tends to get real put out if something keeps her outfit from running like a smooth, accurate, precision-made machine. The slightest thing messy or out of kilter or in the way ties her into a little white knot of tight-smiled fury. She walks around with that same doll smile crimped between her chin and her nose and that same calm whir coming from her eyes, but down inside of her she's tense as steel. I know, I can feel it. And she don't relax a hair till she gets the nuisance attended to—what she calls "adjusted to surroundings."

McMurphy questions the others, particularly Harding, about why they accept her power over them. He bets the entire ward that within a week he can force Nurse Ratched to lose control without her gaining any over him.

Interspersed with his own hallucinations, Bromden recounts how McMurphy persistently taunts the Nurse and her attendants. Some ward-members gain access to an old hydrotherapy room—the "tub room"— to escape the very loud music in the day room. In an effort to motivate the Acutes into fighting Big Nurse, McMurphy purposefully loses a wager that he can heave an old concrete console through a tub room window and escape. One week after the original bet, he succeeds in turning the entire ward against Ratched in a vote over television privileges during the World Series. Bromden's is the decisive vote, and McMurphy gains the majority he needs to win. The nurse refuses to turn the television on, but the entire ward ignores her orders and sits patiently in front of the blank set while she screams hysterically.

Part 2

In response to her failure, Nurse Ratched decides to wait until McMurphy realizes his fate is ultimately in her hands. At the same time, Bromden grows stronger from McMurphy's tireless example, hallucinating less and avoiding his medication. The other patients follow suit, growing more unruly and argumentative.

One day while swimming at the hospital pool, a lifeguard/inmate explains to McMurphy the danger of being permanently committed. As a result, McMurphy's unruliness seems to end. The other patients are not surprised by his change in attitude and recognize that he wants to avoid being com-

mitted. Bromden's mechanistic hallucinations return, however, and although Cheswick claims to understand McMurphy's attitude, he kills himself at the bottom of the swimming pool.

In the days following this last incident, McMurphy learns more about the contradictions of medication and other forms of treatment at the hospital. He sees the dilemma faced by epileptics regarding their medication. Harding and Billy Bibbit explain not only the horrors of shock treatment and lobotomy, but also reveal that they are voluntary detainees of the mental hospital. McMurphy is angry and confused at these revelations. When Big Nurse takes away the ward's tub room privileges in an attempt to cement her victory, McMurphy responds by smashing the window that separates the Nurse's Station from the day room.

Part 3

In the days that follow, McMurphy continues to harass the nurse by organizing a deep-sea fishing expedition for the ward. Bromden's hallucinations recede once more, and he begins to think about joining the salmon-fishing list. He worries again about disclosing his ability to hear and talk, but eventually speaks to McMurphy almost without realizing it. McMurphy helps to build the Chief's confidence by signing his name to the fishing list, and by convincing him that he can once again feel tall and strong—strong enough, in fact, to lift the cement console in the tub room.

McMurphy surpasses several hurdles while the appointed fishing-day approaches. When one of the prostitutes hired to take them to the boat doesn't show up, McMurphy even convinces the hospital's Doctor Spivey to drive half of them to the boat and join them fishing. Along the way, they encounter unfriendly outsiders and the group awaits McMurphy's leadership to turn their morale around.

As they set sail in the fishing boat with the obsessive-compulsive George Sorensen at the helm, McMurphy reveals that the boat owner, Captain Block, has been duped, and that they will be renting the boat without his permission. After a spectacular day, Captain Block and the police await them at the docks. Doctor Spivey discourages legal action by disputing local jurisdiction and the safety of the boat. The catcallers who insulted the group upon their first arrival are humbled by the success of the fishing expedition. During the drive back to the hospital, Billy Bibbit and Candy sit together, and McMurphy encourages a clandestine late-night "date" between the innocent Billy and the prostitute at the hospital. Thus inspired, they pause in front of the house in which McMurphy was raised while he brags about his first sexual experience.

Part 4

Nurse Ratched's response to McMurphy's success is to try to turn the men on the ward against him by demonstrating how much money he has taken from them since his arrival. As the Chief's confidence grows and, with McMurphy's help, he begins to recognize his own physical size and strength, and the bet regarding the cement console in the tub room is revived. McMurphy makes a bet that it is possible for a man to lift the console, and Bromden lifts it. McMurphy attempts to compensate the Chief with a piece of the winnings, but Bromden becomes upset, saying of McMurphy's activities on the ward, "we thought it wasn't to be *winning* things!"

When Big Nurse orders that the men be cleaned with a special liquid because of vermin they may have encountered on their fishing trip, a fight breaks out. Sorensen is compulsively clean and cannot bear the thought of having the strong smelling disinfectant on (or in) his body. The attendants persist and McMurphy picks a fight with one of them. When the other attendants join in, Bromden enters the fray and settles it decisively in favor of the ward. They thus provide Nurse Ratched with the excuse she needs, and she sends both of the men to the "Disturbed" ward, where they face electroshock therapy. McMurphy refuses to concede victory to Ratched by admitting his fault and undergoes several shock treatments.

Eventually, the day for Billy and Candy's late-night date arrives. The ward prepares by bribing Turkle, the night orderly, and Candy arrives with her friend Sandy in tow. A great party ensues, and although McMurphy's plan is to escape with girls before morning, the entire ward drunkenly falls asleep until discovered the next morning. Billy Bibbit and Candy are found naked together in the Seclusion Room, and Nurse Ratched taunts Billy with the prospect of revealing his activities to his mother. Unable to bear this possibility, Billy kills himself while waiting in Doctor Spivey's office. McMurphy, enraged but calm, smashes into the Nurses' Station and attempts to strangle Ratched. The Nurse is badly shaken in the days that follow, and orders McMurphy's lobotomy. He is wheeled, comatose, to the ward for all to see. Late that night, Bromden suffocates McMurphy, then heaves the cement console through the window and escapes.

From the film One Flew Over the Cuckoo's Nest, *starring Jack Nicholson, Josip Elic, and Will Sampson.*

Characters

Pete Bancini

A self-pitying patient who suffered brain damage at birth and says he's been dead for all of his fifty-five years. Constantly complaining of being tired, at times he is forcibly removed from group therapy session and put to bed. As the book unfolds, however, Bancini begins to escape the imprisonment of his fixation on the past and take a more active role in the ward.

Billy Bibbit

A weak mama's boy who is totally under Big Nurse's thumb. She has extra control over him because she has befriended his mother, who works for the hospital. Billy's most notable feature is his severe stutter, which he says he's had since he said his first word: "M-m-m-m-mamma." His mother still treats him as a child, even though he is over thirty years old, and he has problems dealing with women. He eventually begins to assert some limited independence, and loses his virginity with one of McMurphy's girls. But in the end, he becomes victim to Nurse Ratched's manipulation and commits suicide.

Media Adaptations

- A play version of *One Flew Over the Cuckoo's Nest* was written by Dale Wasserman and appeared on Broadway with Kirk Douglas as McMurphy in 1963; the play was revived in 1971. Published by Samuel French, 1970.

- An acclaimed film version of *Cuckoo's Nest* appeared in 1975, starring Jack Nicholson as McMurphy and Louise Fletcher as Nurse Ratched. Named best film of the year at the Academy Awards, the film also won Oscars for the two leads, as well as director Milos Forman and screenwriter Bo Goldman. It is available from Republic Pictures Home Video.

Big Nurse
See Nurse Ratched

The Three Black Boys

How Chief refers to the black men who come in early, clean the ward, and herd the patients around according to Nurse Ratched's orders. They hate the nurse, who manipulates them, and take their frustration out on the inmates, often taunting them and otherwise taking advantage of them. McMurphy finally comes to blows with them after they torture Rub-a-Dub George with threats of dirt and bugs. The one-dimensional depiction of these characters has been faulted as racist and stereotypical by several critics.

Chief Bromden

Chief Bromden is the schizophrenic narrator of story, and has been in the mental institution since leaving the Army shortly after World War II. Harding says he's heard that Chief has received over two hundred shock treatments. The son of an American Indian father and a Caucasian mother, he attributes his shrewdness to his Native American heritage. Chief has a paranoid belief in something he calls the "Combine," a collaboration of governmental and industrial groups he believes are trying to control people by way of machines. For many years, Chief has isolated himself from the bizarre environment of the Chronic and Acute ward by pretending to be deaf and dumb. This way, he finds out everything he wants to know and yet is able to keep his own counsel and stay out of trouble.

Chief pushes a broom all day, sweeping the same territory over and over again. He's classified as a Chronic: "Not in the hospital, these, to get fixed, but just to keep them from walking about the street giving the product a bad name," muses Chief. "Chronic are in for good ... divided into Walkers like me, can still walk around if you keep fed, and Wheelers and Vegetables." Chief harbors a deep hatred of the Big Nurse, Miss Ratched, and like all the other ward residents fears her power. Chief holds an almost equal anger at the three black assistants who do Miss Ratched's icy bidding—and worse. (In fact, some consider the book racist because of the negative way in which author—and his narrator storyteller—portray these black characters.)

Chief imagines that every day the staff creates a fog that hangs over the ward. Sometimes the fog is smoke because he believes that walls are wired and filled with humming mechanisms. But he snaps to awareness when a new admission, the irrepressible, irreverent McMurphy, arrives and immediately tries to take over as boss of the ward. At first, Chief is able to hide behind his feigned deafness and just watch McMurphy's antics. But McMurphy soon tricks him into revealing to him that he can both hear and speak—a secret guarded from everyone else. Gradually, under McMurphy's influence, Chief begins to withdraw from his hallucinatory world and begins to join the other residents in activities, even joining them on a fishing expedition.

At one point, he thinks to himself: "I noticed vaguely that I was getting so's I could see some good in the life around me. McMurphy was teaching me. I was feeling better than I'd remembered feeling since I was a kid, when everything was good and land still singing kids' poetry to me." Finally he reveals the source of the book's title, a singsong chant his grandmother used to say as they played a finger game: "one flew east, one flew west, one flew over the cuckoo's nest ... O-U-T spells out ... goose swoops down and plucks *you* out." Although McMurphy's power over Nurse Ratched eventually ends, his sacrifice serves as an inspiration for Chief. Chief takes pity on McMurphy after he is left a vegetable from a lobotomy, smothering him with a pillow, and then leaves the institution to take control of his own destiny.

Chief Broom

See Chief Bromden

Charles Cheswick

Supposedly tough and aggressive, Cheswick is actually afraid to take any definitive actions. Faced with a challenge, he makes noise as if he will attack, but he always backs down. But he likes to cheer others on from the sidelines, and soon becomes an enthusiastic supporter of McMurphy's ideas. Soon after making a fuss when McMurphy won't protest against Nurse Ratched's cigarette rationing, Cheswick drowns in the swimming pool, something Big Nurse blames on McMurphy.

Ellis

A Chronic who was an Acute before undergoing shock treatment, Ellis is "nailed" to the wall in a position that recalls Christ's crucifixion.

Mr. Fredrickson

Sefelt's friend and protector, he worries about having epileptic fits and secretly takes Sefelt's medicine for him. After McMurphy is sent from the ward, he and Sefelt sign out of the hospital together.

Mr. Dale Harding

Mr. Harding is president of the Patient's Council. Intelligent, college-educated, he speaks to his fellow-patients like a professor. McMurphy takes him on verbally right away, saying he wants to displace him as the "bull goose loony" who runs things. Harding pretends to compete, but gives McMurphy his position as king of the card games. Harding, while articulate and assertive, is basically like a frightened child, and waves his overly pretty hands when he gets upset. His psychological problems include the inferiority and insecurity he feels because of his young, sexy wife, who continually casts doubts on his manhood. He submits to Big Nurse's verbal humiliations during the group therapy sessions unprotestingly. McMurphy tells Harding these sessions are like pecking parties, in which a flock of chickens rip one of their own to shreds, but Harding refuses to believe that Big Nurse does not intend to help him with these sessions. Under McMurphy's influence, Harding gradually begins to see the truth—that the Big Nurse is slowly emasculating the patients. When the Nurse lies to him about McMurphy's return, he checks himself out of the hospital.

Mrs. Vera Harding

Dale Harding's attractive wife, who has been the subject of many of Big Nurse's group-therapy meetings because Harding thinks Vera may be cheating on him. She makes a brief appearance on a cursory visit to her husband in the hospital, during which she flirts with many of the staff and inmates and casts doubts on her husband's manhood. Later, Harding returns home to her.

Martini

One the patients who often seems to be suffering hallucinations, a fact McMurphy uses to cheat against him in Monopoly.

Colonel Matterson

The oldest Chronic on the ward, a World War I veteran who lectures the other inmates by reading from his palm.

Randle Patrick McMurphy

McMurphy bursts on the well-ordered, claustrophobic scene of the psychiatric ward like a psychological bombshell. Streetwise, smart, aggressive, vigorous, he challenges the status quo—the "way things are"—from day one. He introduces himself to everyone in the ward, shaking hands and filling the silence with loud laughter. Is this man mentally ill? Probably not. He has elected to be sent to the psychiatric hospital because he did not like to work on the prison farm, where he had six months to go before his release. His crime: statutory rape of a willing fifteen year old. The attraction of the psychiatric hospital for him was the idea of enjoying better meals and an easier lifestyle. This is not exactly what he finds.

McMurphy immediately engages in a long, hopeless, and endless battle with Big Nurse, a classic control freak. What McMurphy has brought to the ward is a touch of normalcy. What Nurse Ratched wants is a group of docile and quiet men who do not upset or question how she has ordered things. It is their incarceration, voluntary or otherwise, upon which her job and role in life depends. Therefore McMurphy is the ultimate threat—a nonconformist who stirs the residents into a desire for action. He wakes them up out of the dullness and quiet in which they have been dwelling. In fact, he provides them with the beginning of a cure to their problems.

The more successful McMurphy is at upsetting the status quo, the more intense the battle becomes between him and Nurse Ratched. He takes over as boss of the endless poker game played by some of the Acutes. He also demands in group therapy meetings that democracy reign and that Nurse Ratched loosen up some of the ties that bind the residents to a senseless, rigid schedule that only serves to dehumanize them.

McMurphy is a very funny character. But the humor ends when he discovers that Big Nurse has total control over his fate—over what treatment he receives and when he is discharged—because he is one of the two residents who have been committed. The other is Chief, McMurphy's best friend. What starts as a rollicking rebellion against authority becomes a tragedy. McMurphy is repeatedly subjected to electric shock therapy. He manages to joke about it and to gather the strength to organize a fishing expedition for some of the men. His final challenge is a party at night in the ward that turns into a fiasco. The drunken orgy, complete with prostitutes, is McMurphy's demise. Big Nurse finally pulls the plug and sends him for psychosurgery. He returns, lobotomized, as a human vegetable. All the lights in this bright mind and brave personality have been extinguished. His energizing influence on the residents lives on, however. Several leave to go home after McMurphy's demise as their leader, and Chief Bromden escapes from the ward and heads for the country. Despite his final degradation to a vegetative state, he wins the fight for freedom that he has fought so bravely. But the rewards are not his. They belong to his fellow patients.

Old Pete

See Pete Bancini

Miss Pilbow

One of Nurse Ratched's timid assistants, Miss Pilbow has a highly noticeable blood-colored birthmark. Because of Big Nurse's warnings, she is frightened of McMurphy even when he speaks kindly to her.

Public Relation

An obnoxiously jolly public relations man who shows local society matrons around the ward, pointing out how great everything is. He is more concerned with the appearance of the ward than with the quality of life there.

Nurse Ratched

A sexless, rigid caricature of a nurse, Nurse Ratched imposes discipline on her ward with all the fervor of an Army nurse, which she had been. Large, with huge breasts only partially disguised by her ultra-starched white uniform, she nevertheless has a pretty, delicate face that belies her cruelty.

Manipulative to the core, the only thing that really matters to Ratched is her desire to control everything around her—the environment, the staff, the patients. She has rendered the staff doctor who is in charge of the ward helpless and ineffectual. Her methods are subtle: She speaks with the calm voice of reason, dealing with patients as though they are children. Her group therapy sessions are intentionally humiliating to patients. Her agenda clearly is to turn the group members against one another. That protects her from any unified action against her rules and her dominating role. As long as everyone stays in line, she retreats to her safe place—a glassed-in office overlooking the ward.

Chief sums her up mentally as follows: "So after the nurse gets her staff, efficiency locks the ward like a watchman's clock. Everything the guys think and say and do is all worked out months in advance, based on the little notes the nurse makes during the day. This is typed and fed into the machine I hear humming behind the steel door in the rear of the Nurses' Station."

Small wonder that McMurphy becomes the ultimate threat to her tight, close little domain. He demands that the patients be given rights. She believes they have only the rights she decides to give them. Cruel in the extreme, she plays repetitious loud music over the ward's speaker system, successfully drowning out normal conversation. As her battle with McMurphy intensifies, his hatred of her leads him to aggressive actions against her. Finally, he can stand no more. In his last battle against reasonless authority, he tries to strangle her. That may be the end of both of them, not just McMurphy, for his example inspires several of the inmates to check themselves out of the ward and out of her power.

Nurse Ratched's character has been the subject of much critical discussion and even controversy, for several observers consider her a sexist stereotype of the controlling female.

Rub-a-Dub George

See George Sorenson

Ruckly

A Chronic who is considered one of the ward's "failures." Aggressive and violent before undergoing a lobotomy, now all Ruckly can say is "Ffff-fuck da wife!"

Sandy

Candy's prostitute friend, who does not make it to the fishing trip, but joins her at the clandestine ward party.

Mr. Scanlon

A stubborn patient preoccupied with explosives who depends on seeing the six o'clock news every day to make sure the country has not been bombed. He is one of the few Acutes who has been committed. He encourages Chief Bromden to leave after the Chief smothers McMurphy.

Mr. Bruce Sefelt

An epileptic, Sefelt is constantly suspicious that his anticonvulsant medication is causing severe medical problems, so he gives his drugs to Fredrickson, who worries about having fits. After McMurphy is sent away for an operation, Sefelt and Fredrickson sign out of the hospital together.

George Sorenson

A "big, toothless knotty old Swede" who has a fetish about cleanliness. When the group goes on a fishing trip organized by McMurphy, George is the captain. It turns out that he skippered a PT boat during World War II and was a fisherman for twenty-five years. After McMurphy's lobotomy, he transfers to another ward.

Dr. Spivey

Dr. Spivey is generally spineless when dealing with Nurse Ratched, because his job depends on the hospital's administrator, a woman who is an ex-Army friend of Nurse Ratched's. Dr. Spivey finds McMurphy as amusing as the patients do, and discovers that he and McMurphy attended the same high school. He begins to assert his authority as a doctor, sticking up for the patients when they want to continue their basketball games and joining them on the hilarious fishing trip set up by McMurphy.

Candy Starr

McMurphy's prostitute friend who joins the patients and the doctor on the fishing trip and later at McMurphy's final jaunt, the party. She has sex with Billy Bibbit, which leads to tragedy. Her stereotypical portrayal as a "hooker with a heart of gold" has led some critics to call the book sexist.

Maxwell Wilson Taber

A patient who is forcibly given a shot of medicine after he questions what is in it. Chief Bromden pictures him as a success story—a "Dismissal" who returns to the community, readjusted from his stay at the hospital.

Mr. Turkle

An older black man who is an orderly on the night shift. He treats the patients kindly, even though he fears if he is discovered he might be fired. He cooperates with McMurphy's plans to have a party on the ward, but resigns the next day after things get out of hand.

Mr. Warren

See The Three Black Boys

Mr. Washington

See The Three Black Boys

Mr. Williams

See The Three Black Boys

Themes

Individual vs. Society

The main action of *One Flew Over the Cuckoo's Nest* consists of McMurphy's struggles against the strict rules of Big Nurse Ratched. Her ward at the hospital is a society in itself, for it has its own laws and punishments, both for the inmates and for the orderlies and nurses who watch over them. McMurphy challenges the rules from the time he arrives, from upsetting the supposedly "democratic" procedure of group therapy to brushing his teeth before the appointed time. By having McMurphy question and ridicule Nurse Ratched's ludicrous, controlling rules, Kesey portrays the individual's struggle against a conformist society as a noble, meaningful task. McMurphy's fight within the small world of the hospital can also be extended to the outside world. During the time Kesey was writing the novel, society emphasized conformity as a means of upholding law and order. Through the portrayal of one individual's meaningful fight against a small society, Kesey brought into question the standards of his own society at large.

Sanity and Insanity

One of society's standards provides the most pervasive theme in the book: What is sane—and

Topics for Further Study

- Write a short essay or story on what would happen if McMurphy took a job in a large corporation with a formal culture and a hierarchical structure. Be imaginative. Create characters who represent a variety of corporate types (the boss, the flatterer, the slacker, the busybody). Do not change McMurphy's personality, character, or behavior.

- Research the definitions of various mental illnesses, such as schizophrenia. Was McMurphy mentally ill or just a maverick who didn't fit into structured society? Defend your point of view with facts and illustrations.

- If you consider McMurphy to be a hero, how would you categorize Chief Bromden? Defend your points with facts and illustrations from the book, and compare him to other characters in the book.

- Research current laws concerning mental illness and criminal prosecution. Explain how a person might be classified as "mentally ill" and prosecuted under current law, and explain whether or not McMurphy would have received the same sentencing today.

what is insane? Is sanity conformance with society and its norms? Or is sanity a sense of self as separate from society? These are questions that psychiatrists have wrestled with for over a century. Is it their job to reprogram a person to fit better into what may be an unsatisfactory life or a flawed society? Or is it their responsibility to guide a person toward self-realization, no matter how that differs from the norm of the patient's environment?

In portraying McMurphy's struggles on the Acute/Chronic Ward, Kesey questions his society's definitions of sanity, which seem to ask all people to conform to the same standards of behavior. When McMurphy discovers that many of the Acutes are at the hospital voluntarily, he wants to know why: "You, you're not exactly the everyday man on the street, but you're not *nuts*." Billy Bibbit replies that they don't have the "guts" to get along in outside society, but ironically, Nurse Ratched's methods are designed to undermine the men's confidence, not encourage it. In this way, Kesey portrays his society's definition of "madness" as something used by an authoritarian culture to dehumanize the individual and replace it with an automaton that dwells in a safe, blind conformity. His hero, McMurphy, is the person who sees through this sham. By showing his fellow patients how to create their own standards of sanity, McMurphy leads a bunch of institutionalized robots back towards their humanity. In the process, he suffers greatly and in fact lays down his life.

Sacrifice

McMurphy's struggle against Nurse Ratched, although eventually lost, is shown to be a sacrifice which liberates his fellow inmates. As Scanlon encourages Chief Bromden to escape at the end of the novel, he says that McMurphy "showed you how one time, if you think back." Reinforcing this theme of sacrifice are the recurring images of crucifixion that appear throughout the book. Consider the pathetic character of the mind-destroyed Chronic Ellis, "nailed" in Chief's eyes to the wall behind which sinister wires and machinery hum. Or the cross-shaped table on which the victims of electroshock therapy lie. The image of the cross is repeated in Chief's description of the position in which Sefelt lies after he suffers an epileptic episode: "His hands are nailed out to each side with the palms up and the fingers jerking open and shut, just the way I've watched men jerk at the Shock Shop strapped to the crossed table, smoke curling up out of the palms from the current."

Style

Point of View

Kesey seems to follow a fairly straightforward course in unfolding the plot of *One Flew Over the Cuckoo's Nest*. Except for a few flashbacks and digressions, the story is essentially told from beginning to end. The first-person ("I") narrator Chief Bromden, however, is a schizophrenic—a person prone to hallucinations and delusions. As a result, the reader is sometimes unsure whether some of the events he describes really happened or not. After all, Chief believes he sees small mechanical items inside the capsules of medicine he receives and believes that a machine is responsible for creating the "fog" that enfolds his perceptions. Having Chief as a narrator also adds to the development of the story, however, for told through his eyes, the story unfolds in part through Chief's changing emotional and intellectual state. After McMurphy leads the revolt over the World Series, for example, Chief notes that "there's no more fog any place," implying that McMurphy is actually helping to bring sanity to the ward.

Setting

The setting plays a pivotal role in the novel, especially because it rarely changes. By keeping the action in one place—the Chronic/Acute Ward of a mental institution—Kesey is able to create a whole society in miniature. As the novel opens, this society is an ordered holding pen for men who have various degrees of mental illness. When the outsider McMurphy arrives, he brings the monotonous, repetitive qualities of this setting into focus. Only on one occasion does the action take place outside of the hospital, when the men go on the fishing party. With the vivid descriptions of this trip, the pace picks up as the men come alive. This provides further contrast to life on the ward, which is increasingly seen as cruel and dehumanizing. The author further enriches the setting with language that is strong, concrete, direct, and vivid. It brings the reader right into the midst of the action.

Characterization

The portrayal of the inmates of the institution, for the most part, are real and believable. Some are modeled on patients Kesey observed while doing night supervisory duty on a mental ward. For instance, the behavior of George Sorenson, known as "Rub-a-Dub," who is so concerned about cleanliness he won't touch anyone, is an example of obsessive-compulsive disorder. Especially moving is Chief's slow awakening to a validation of himself as a person, after experiencing years of racial slurs and physical degradation. The novel's portrayal of female and African American characters, however, is more problematic. Women are either control freaks who emasculate the men around them, such as Nurse Ratched, Vera Harding, and Billy Bibbit's mother, or objects for sexual gratification, such as the two hookers Candy and Sandy. The "black boys" Chief describes are alternately servile to their boss, Nurse Ratched, and cruel to the patients, showing no emotion but hatred. While Mr. Turkle's character is more sympathetic, he too is portrayed as fearful of authority and responsibil-

ity. While broad stereotypes such as these serve a purpose in creating a satire such as *Cuckoo's Nest*, they have still led to accusations of sexism and racism.

Historical Context

The 1950s: Conformity and Change

The late 1950s, the time period in which the book was written and set, saw the end of a decade in which people outside the mainstream were often viewed with suspicion. The United States was engaged in a "cold war" with the Soviet Union, in which relations were tense and hostile even though no open warfare was declared. Americans feared the possibility of a nuclear conflict, and people identified as communist sympathizers—"reds"—were frequently ostracized and even persecuted for their supposed beliefs by government committees such as that headed by Senator Joseph McCarthy. But toward the end of the decade, a national rebellion against civil injustice and cultural mediocrity was in the making. Young people in particular began questioning the values and beliefs of those in power. One such group of people were the Beat Generation, who expressed their dissatisfaction with society through art, dress, and nonviolent action. Poetry readings were a common forum beatniks used to communicate their ideas, and Allen Ginsberg's 1955 poem "Howl" articulated what many people saw as the moral and social problems of the time.

Groups such as the Beat generation became part of a larger movement known as the counterculture. What began as a band of political protesters eventually gave rise in the 1960s to the hippies, a group dedicated to peace, love, and the quest to expand one's inner horizons through the use of mind-altering drugs such as LSD. Kesey's experiences bridged the two groups, for he was a subject in a scientific experiment on the effects of LSD—lysergic acid diethylamide-25, one of the most potent mind-altering chemicals known. The drug had been discovered in 1938 by the Swiss chemist Dr. Albert Hofmann, and scientists determined that when carefully regulated, LSD was nonfatal and could even be used in the treatment of such psychological disorders as schizophrenia. In treating these disorders, however, successful results were often marred by the sometimes dramatic and unpleasant reactions—usually manifested in visual and/or audible hallucinations—that would accompany them. To the rising counterculture of the

Compare & Contrast

- **Early 1960s:** In 1962, the Cold War reaches its most fevered pitch during the Cuban Missile Crisis. U.S. President John F. Kennedy imposes a naval blockade on Cuba after discovering evidence of Soviet missile construction on the island, and the U.S.S.R. goes on special military alert.

  Today: The Soviet Union no longer exists, and Russia, the largest country left from the Soviet breakup, has a democratically elected president. The Russian government's biggest problems are paying their military, funding the government, and rising organized crime.

- **Early 1960s:** After the government shuts down official studies of LSD in the late 1950s, research into the effects of the hallucinogenic drug is carried on at a few universities. The drug, still legal, becomes popular with young people, particularly members of the "counterculture."

  Today: A controlled substance since 1966, LSD is illegal throughout the United States. Although its popularity has largely been replaced by drugs like cocaine and heroin, its use has increased over the last decade.

- **Early 1960s:** New thinking on the nature of mental illness—that it might not be medically related to the brain—leads to a decrease in the number of institutionalized patients. Where in 1955 half of all hospital beds were occupied by the mentally ill, over the next two decades there is a 65% reduction in the number of mental patients, many of whom end up on the street.

  Today: Many forms of mental illness, such as schizophrenia, have been traced to malfunctions in specific areas of the brain. Researchers have even located the genes which, if defective, can lead to certain types of mental illness. In 1997, the National Coalition for the Homeless estimated that 20–25% of all homeless people have some form of mental illness.

1960s, LSD served as a way to help explore their own minds and expand their horizons. However, the hallucinations could induce aggressive, even dangerous, behavior in users, who also were prone to uncontrollable "flashback" episodes. LSD has been a controlled substance—illegal to make, distribute, sell, or possess—since 1966, and Kesey himself has since disavowed the use of drugs, saying that the costs far exceed the benefits.

Mental Illness and Its Treatment

For many years in the United States, mental illness was often ignored or misinterpreted; treatment often consisted of nothing more than chaining or caging the sufferer. During the mid-1800s, attitudes regarding the mentally ill slowly began to change. Thanks to the efforts of humanitarian reformers such as Dorothea Dix, millions of dollars were raised to establish state mental institutions capable of caring for large numbers of patients. After World War II, when more soldiers were medically discharged because of neuropsychiatric disorders than for any other reason, the medical community began to more closely evaluate the conditions that existed in the mental health care system.

In the 1950s, advances in pharmaceuticals led to more methods of treatment for mental patients; in 1956, more patients were being discharged from U.S. mental institutions than admitted for the first time in over a century, many aided by prescribed drugs to manage irrational behavior. In addition to medication, the use of electroshock therapy and psychosurgery were common treatments for psychiatric disorders. Electroshock therapy, or ECT, was discovered in 1937 by two Italian psychiatrists who thought to apply an electrical charge directly to the brain. Despite the harsh stigma that has been unfairly associated with this type of treatment—in Kesey's novel it is seen as a means of punishment rather than a cure—the use of electroshock therapy has proven immensely successful in cases involving moderate to severe bouts of depression. Others

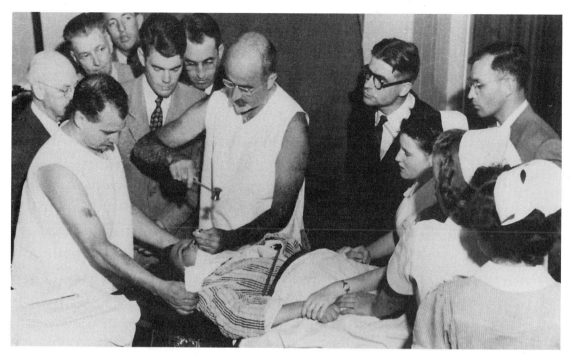

A patient undergoing a lobotomy, Dr. Freeman's psychosurgical invention, 1949.

argue that its side effects make it one of the more barbaric forms of legal medical procedures in the modern age.

A third mode of treatment, and by far the most controversial, is the destruction of certain cells or fibers in the brain through surgical measures. At the onset, this technique was labeled a "lobotomy" because it required the removal of the frontal lobe of the brain. Later, with modern, more precise means of locating desired tissues, it is more commonly referred to as psychosurgery. The first lobotomy on record was performed in the United States in 1936 by Dr. Walter Freeman. Although original results proved successful in calming down patients with highly energetic or exceedingly violent personalities, soon physicians began noticing undesirable effects on the patient's mental and physical health. These effects are epitomized by Kesey's character McMurphy after his experience in undergoing such surgery.

Critical Overview

When *One Flew Over the Cuckoo's Nest* was published in 1962, it was well received by the critics and swiftly gained popularity among college-age readers. Critic Malcolm Cowley, one of Kesey's teachers at Standard, commented in a letter to Kesey that the book (which he read in rough draft) contained "some of the most brilliant scenes I have ever read" and "passion like I've not seen in young writers before." R. A. Jelliffe, writing in the *Chicago Sunday Tribune Magazine of Books,* praised the novel for its brilliant mixture of realism and myth, noting "this is an allegory with a difference." *Time* magazine praised Kesey for both his power and humor, describing the book as "a strong, warm story about the nature of human good and evil, despite the macabre setting." While some initial reviews faulted the novel as rambling, the majority agreed with *New York Times Book Review* contributor Martin Levin that *Cuckoo's Nest* was "a work of genuine literary merit."

It wasn't long after the novel appeared, however, that criticism arose over its negative portrayal of female characters. Julian Moynahan, for instance, argued in a 1964 *New York Review of Books* article that *Cuckoo's Nest* was "a very beautiful and inventive book violated by a fifth-rate idea which made Woman, in alliance with modern technology, the destroyer of masculinity and sensuous enjoyment." Similarly, Marcia L. Falk criticized the popular acceptance of the work and its Broadway adaptation in a 1971 letter to the *New York Times.* She noted that people "never even noticed, or cared to question, the psychic disease out of which the book's vision was born." Other critics have defended the work by noting, for instance, that the negative female stereotypes are there to support the novel's satire or that these negative characters are not truly representatives of women, but rather representatives of evil. Either way, the novel has inspired many articles analyzing how it portrays gender conflict and defines masculinity and humanity in general. As Richard D. Maxwell wrote in *Twenty-Seven to One:* "It is apparent that Kesey is not putting the entire blame [on women for men's loss of power].... It is the male who is allowing the female and the corporation to chip away at his masculinity."

Another debated aspect of the novel has been its portrayal of racial groups, specifically the black orderlies who work on the ward. Chief expresses hatred for these men, who are little more than stupid and cruel stereotypes, and he and McMurphy often express their anger with racial slurs. Several critics have pointed out, however, that these men are seen through the mind of the Chief, who himself has been the victim of prejudice as well as the "Combine" that dehumanizes people of all races. In this fashion Chief's racial observations create an ironic commentary on the nature of racism, as Janet R. Sutherland remarked in *English Journal:* "Just as the reader has to look beyond the typically racist language of the inmate to find in the book as a whole a document of witness against the dehumanizing, sick effects of racism in our society, so Bromden has to look beyond the perception of the world which limits his concept of self."

A large number of articles have examined how the novel defines the role of the hero in a society which stifles individuality, and who exactly is the hero of the novel. While some observers have argued that McMurphy, who through his example and sacrifice shows the men how to escape, is the hero, many others suggest that it is Chief Bromden who is ultimately the hero of the work. While McMurphy leads his "disciple" Bromden to a new understanding, Barry H. Leeds noted in *Connecticut Review,* "it is not until the very end of the novel ... that it becomes clear that Bromden has surpassed his teacher in the capacity to survive in American society." Ronald Wallace likewise argued in his *The Last Laugh* that Bromden rejects the "extreme" of total freedom and chaos that McMurphy represents and "has recreated himself in his own best image: strong, independent, sensitive, sympathetic, and loving, with a comic perspective on his human

limitations." In the *Rocky Mountain Review of Language and Literature,* Thomas H. Fick placed Bromden's triumph as the hero in the tradition of the mythology of the American West, where a Native American guides a white man to greater understanding. Kesey has turned this myth on its side, noted Fick, creating "the first [instance], surely, that the Indian partner in such a pair has outlived his White brother." The result, concluded the critic, is "a powerful novel which effectively translates into contemporary terms the enduring American concern with a freedom found only in—or in between—irreconcilable oppositions."

Criticism

Ian Currie

Currie is a freelance writer based in British Columbia who has taught at Dalhousie University. In the following essay he looks at the cultural climate that inspired the writing of One Flew over the Cuckoo's Nest *and discusses how a reader may interpret the book by keeping its origins in mind.*

One Flew Over the Cuckoo's Nest has sold over eight million copies since its publication in 1962. Imagine a first novel so relevant to popular audiences and universities alike that it has spawned an Academy Award-winning film as well as hundreds, if not thousands, of academic articles, essays, and dissertations. Ken Kesey's first novel was certainly a blockbuster in every sense of the word, but what does this mean to readers thirty-five years and more after the fact? *Cuckoo's Nest* captured the fear and uncertainty of a postwar generation who came of age with the still-new and very real possibility of total nuclear destruction. Dissatisfied with the easy answers and assurances of their parents' generation, people began to explore for themselves new ways of coping with a rapidly changing world. The result was a culture of rebellion in the form of social protest, usually aided and abetted by the use of hallucinogenic drugs. Kesey's novel, like many others written between the mid-1950s and the mid-1970s, is a chronicle of that exploration of new possibilities. In the years since the publication of *Cuckoo's Nest,* new readers of the novel are not only further away in time from that era, they are also shaped by modern sensibilities about culture (especially music and literature) that were born in the 1960s. *One Flew Over The Cuckoo's Nest* has endured because under these influences and through the passage of time, reading the novel has become a much more complicated task.

Perhaps the biggest of these ongoing influences is Kesey himself. Although his celebrity status has considerably diminished, he was for years as well known as anyone in popular culture. Tom Wolfe, a novelist and frequent contributor to *Rolling Stone* and *Esquire* magazines, wrote a novel (*The Electric Kool-Aid Acid Test*) about Kesey and his group of friends, the Merry Pranksters. The group, including authors Larry McMurtry and Ken Babbs, met at Stanford University in 1959, and many volunteered for government experiments with LSD and related pharmaceuticals. Their most famous stunt was a cross-country bus trip made with movie cameras in hand so that the trip could be made into "The Movie." In 1961, Kesey volunteered on the mental ward of a veteran's hospital, whose patients inspired the characters in *Cuckoo's Nest.*

The novel's narrator is Chief "Broom" Bromden, a man whose madness stems from a long process of isolation from his community of Native Americans in Oregon. This ultimately leads to confinement in the asylum and an attempted withdrawal from all of his surroundings as he feigns deafness and dumbness. Similarly, he clings to the drug-induced "fog" that he perceives around him because "you can slip back in it and feel safe." He needs to feel safe from "The Combine," that evil mechanical power whose stronghold is the mental hospital, and whose chief instrument is Big Nurse Ratched

Bromden's situation paints a tiny picture of society as many saw it in the 1960s. Individual needs and desires were becoming less individual; government and corporate powers seemed to be either marginalizing these needs or making them conform to arbitrary moral standards about everything from race to sex to drugs and alcohol (Kesey himself was in and out of court and jail for over a year on the basis of a marijuana possession charge). Bromden's reaction is to withdraw from a society that wants control over him. He retains some sense of himself by pretending to be overcome by Nurse Ratched; this allows him to see and hear things that others do not. For example, he is permitted to clean the staff room during meetings because he is assumed to be deaf.

Into this world marches Randle P. McMurphy. A confessed con-man and brawler, he is determined to manipulate the system rather than allow it to manipulate him. While serving a sentence in a work

What Do I Read Next?

- In the 1986 collection *Demon Box,* Kesey reflects on his experiences as a member of the counterculture in the 1960s and 1970s.

- J. D. Salinger's classic of adolescent rebellion, *The Catcher in the Rye* (1951) tells of how sixteen-year-old Holden Caulfield rebels against all that he perceives as phony in upper-middle-class 1940s society.

- The semiautobiographical novel *The Bell Jar* (1963), by poet Sylvia Plath, traces protagonist Esther Greenwood's battles with depression as she struggles to find her place in a society which limits women's roles to that of wife and mother.

- *Nobody Nowhere* (1992) is Donna Williams's powerful autobiography about growing up autistic—unable to process emotions normally—and discovering how to relate to the outside world.

- Mary Jane Ward's classic 1946 novel *The Snake Pit* tells of a young woman's year of treatment in a mental hospital. The book inspired a 1948 movie of the same title, starring Olivia de Havilland, which in turn prompted legislation on treatment for the mentally ill in several states.

camp, he gains access to the comparatively easy life of the mental hospital by playing at insanity as a fighting madman. Once admitted to Big Nurse's ward, he begins to subvert her systematic control by using it against her: his first big victory about television privileges during the World Series is gained through authorized patient voting, and he turns Doctor Spivey, the ward psychiatrist, to his side on issues like the basketball team and the fishing expedition. In the process, other patients are urged to do the same. Cheswick becomes more argumentative; voluntary inmates like Harding and the innocent Billy Bibbit begin to think about leaving, and Bromden defeats his fear of the system by choosing to speak again, and eventually escapes from the hospital.

Of course, the system is not defeated so easily. Cheswick kills himself out of despair when McMurphy temporarily gives up the fight for fear of being permanently committed; Billy Bibbit kills himself rather than face his mother with the shame of having slept with a prostitute; and McMurphy is lobotomized into a comatose state by Nurse Ratched when he is finally pushed too far and tries to kill her. If the mental ward is a miniature version, a microcosm, of the world as seen by a generation of young people in the 1960s, then these losses are symbolic of a warning. In the fight between the individual and those who would disempower him or her, there will be losses, and a clear winner may not emerge. McMurphy loses his life, certainly, but in the process, Chief Bromden regains his, as do Sefelt, Frederickson and three other voluntary patients who choose the dangers of freedom over the safety of a controlled environment.

These distinctions make for grey areas in any modern reading of the novel. Big Nurse Ratched and the system with which she controls the hospital are clearly evil, and McMurphy's ultimate sacrifice on behalf of his friends on the ward is clearly good. But do readers still see all of society reflected in Big Nurse's hospital? Do we, like Kesey and like so many novelists of his generation, see the same need to fight or escape from a tyrannical society?

One Flew Over the Cuckoo's Nest fits into a series of works that set a protagonist in search of freedom against a society determined to restrict that freedom. In 1953, Ralph Ellison published *The Invisible Man.* In it, Ellison chillingly portrays a black man bouncing off the walls of a white world where he had no voice and no power. Jack Kerouac's 1957 novel *On the Road* is a much less gloomy novel that focuses on freedom rather than constraint. Its protagonist is Dean Moriarty, an unstoppable vagabond who pursues women, jazz music, and marijuana on coast-to-coast rides across the country in borrowed cars. Other members of Kerouac's "Beat Generation" included Lawrence Ferlinghetti, William Burroughs, and Allen Ginsberg, whose long poem "Howl" (1956) is just that: a long and bitter complaint that "the best minds of [his] generation" have been destroyed by a brutally cold society. In 1961, Joseph Heller published *Catch-22,* in which the members of a World War II bomber squadron find themselves in absurd and unfair conflict with their superior officers and the rules and regulations they control. This trend continues in the more obscure works of John Barth and Thomas

Pynchon. Pynchon's 1973 novel *Gravity's Rainbow* depicts a World War II U.S. Army soldier whose entire life is a sinister experiment by world governments and international corporations.

Like these novels, *Cuckoo's Nest* raises serious issues about the individual's relationship with an often unfair society. Perhaps because these issues have become less central to contemporary readers, literary critics have over the years chosen very different paths in discussing Kesey's novel. Early interviews with Kesey reveal a standard interpretation of the novel. One, in *The Whole Earth Catalog,* has the interviewer asking questions like, "Do you think policemen and Richard Nixon and the rich people who run the country can relate to that?" Some years later, Leslie Fiedler and Carol Pearson argued that the novel owes more to ancient myths than social turmoil. Fiedler sees in the novel a pattern that dates back to ancient English verse, in which "the white outcast" (McMurphy) and the "noble Red Man" (Bromden) join forces against "home and mother" (Big Nurse). Pearson finds another myth wherein the buffoon (McMurphy) and the quiet hero (Bromden) defeat an evil king (Big Nurse) who has laid waste to the kingdom in pursuit of ultimate power.

Fiedler and other critics also see the novel as an updated version of the western. McMurphy ("He's got iron on his heels and he rings it on the floor like horseshoes") is the cowboy come to a corrupt town to set it right. Still another interpretation, popularized by Joseph Waldmeir, is that *Cuckoo's Nest* is a "Novel of the Absurd," a novel that presents an unreasonable, impossible world with usually comic results. Another critical catchphrase is "the Carnivalesque": some critics believe that the novel fits into an ancient tradition of stories whose meaning derives from the pleasures and perils of wild carnivals. These critics usually point to the disorganized fun McMurphy brings to the ward with basketball, gambling, and fishing, despite Big Nurse's efforts to spoil the party. These different critical points of view all bring something to a modern reader's understanding of the novel.

Any interpretation of *One Flew Over the Cuckoo's Nest,* however, must address basic story elements like character and narrative voice. As critical views multiply, this task becomes more difficult. For example, if this is truly a "Novel of the Absurd" that portrays an impossible, unrealistic world, what can we say about characters like McMurphy and Bromden? If they are not supposed to represent real people with real emotions and motivations, they are flat characters stripped of much of what Kesey has given them. Yes, McMurphy's behavior is sometimes inhuman. It seems doubtful that anyone could remain untouched by the multitude of shock treatments he undergoes, and his emotional reactions are not consistent: he barely notices Cheswick's suicide, while Billy Bibbitt's sends him over the edge. But Kesey does make the effort to round out McMurphy's character: "I'd see him do things ... like painting a picture at OT with real paints on a blank paper ... or like writing letters to somebody in a beautiful flowing hand." And once, he even looks "upset and worried."

We must also remember that all these observations are Chief Broom's. Bromden is both a character and the narrator who tells the story, and he is certainly insane. Perhaps the novel only seems absurd because its narrator believes that most everyone around him is built of metal, springs, and cogs. This type of narration makes it difficult to distinguish between the observations of the storyteller, Bromden, and the insights of the novelist, Kesey. For example, when McMurphy moves to kill Nurse Ratched, Bromden sees "slow, mechanical gestures" and hears "iron in his bare heels ring sparks out of the tile." At this point, we either hear Bromden telling us that McMurphy in nothing but boxer shorts is still the cowboy hero, or we hear Kesey telling us that McMurphy has lost and become one with his enemy, as mechanical and metallic as "The Combine" itself.

The greatest challenge presented by *One Flew Over the Cuckoo's Nest,* and by any novel of its stature in American literature, is to find the right balance of critical insight and personal opinion. Ken Kesey has gone on to write ten works of fiction and nonfiction, and the criticism and reviews of these books are ongoing. Kesey's second published novel, *Sometimes a Great Notion* explores many of the same themes we see in *Cuckoo's Nest,* as its hero Hank Stamper struggles for freedom and independence within his Oregon home town. If *Cuckoo's Nest* is the first in Kesey's line of works to explore the theme of individual freedom, then it is the modern reader's enviable task to read it with a sort of double vision: one eye on the social history that inspired Kesey and his generation, and one eye on the contemporary critical views that continue to expand our understanding of it.

Source: Ian Currie, in an essay for *Novels for Students,* Gale, 1997.

Laura Quinn

In the following excerpt, Quinn argues that despite its language, sexual content, and graphic portrayal of psychological treatments, One Flew over the Cuckoo's Nest *can be a valuable subject for high-school discussion if issues of sexism and racism are addressed.*

One Flew Over the Cuckoo's Nest, Ken Kesey's 1962 novel of life in a hospital for the mentally ill, is a document of the sixties. Its anti-institutionalism, its celebration of boisterous rebellion against a seemingly rational (but actually unnecessarily repressive) establishment spoke to a generation of long-haired beaded and bearded anti-war activists. That the novel records something important to that era is not enough (perhaps) to justify its inclusion in a public school curriculum; we generally seek a universal and timeless quality in the works we teach to students. *One Flew Over the Cuckoo's Nest* possesses this broader vision, however, and transcends its own timeliness by addressing a social problem that is both ever and omnipresent— that of the relationship between institutional authority and individual and/or subjected group desire for autonomy and self-determination. Kesey's novel raises crucial questions about power and control, about how groups establish and maintain the particular kind of order that they deem necessary to their survival, about ways in which the "controlled" resist that order. This book belongs in the high school curriculum for the following reasons:

a) It "opens" the issue of social control in the truest sense. The novel offers no simple answers to the question of what to do with the "dysfunctional"—with those whose behavior disrupts the social order. While some of the ward's inmates are there for socio-cultural reasons (Chief Bromden, the narrator, most notably), others are "voluntary," that is, self-committed and clearly hiding from a threatening and hostile outside world; still others are Chronics, the radically dysfunctional psychically and physically, in need of total institutional care—though the question is repeatedly raised in the novel of whether the institution itself is not the agent of much of the dysfunction of its wards.

b) It treats a problem that is particularly relevant to teenaged readers, whose chafing under institutional rules and constraints and whose ambivalence toward authority is often acute.

c) It is a readable book, dramatic, immediate, accessible to young readers.

d) It is a work of substantial literary merit that features an interesting narrative situation—Chief Bromden, the towering Indian who has posed as a deaf-mute on the ward for many years, narrates the novel, creating a complex, ironic, and privileged perspective on events and personalities in the hospital, privileged by virtue of his deaf-mute disguise which tricks authority figures into speaking freely in his presence.

e) Finally, it is a work that is seriously problematic in its treatment of gender and race. While this might seem a spurious asset in our age of multicultural and gender-balanced curricular imperatives, I believe that the particular nature of its race and gender problems as a text makes these issues accessible at the high school level in illuminating ways. Far from justifying any censorship in the interests of political correctness, the novel's lapses afford teaching opportunities (to be elaborated later in this chapter).

The novel's structure is that of a contest between Nurse Ratched and Randle McMurphy, the new guy on the block/ward. The contest is waged and staged in the mind of Chief Bromden, whose narrative goes back in time (when prompted to do so by disturbing events on the ward) to recall his father's degradation at the hands of white government agents who coerced him into selling the tribal lands. In shame his father descended into drunken oblivion while the young son lapsed into silence as a means of self-protection and as a reaction to the discovery that he was a voiceless nonentity anyway in the white community. In addition to his silenced persona, the Chief (his ward nickname) has developed the theory of the "Combine," his reification of the ubiquitous social control machine which subdues all autonomous human behavior by means of wires, fogs, implants, recording devices, and robotics; only, he muses, moving targets like McMurphy, those who stay outside of and on the edges of institutions, can evade the Combine, and their evasions are precarious. The notion of the Combine is important, because it connects the abuses of authority within the hospital to the larger society outside; as one patient, Harding, says, (referring to the submissiveness of the ward's population) "we are—the *rabbits,* one might say, of the rabbit world!" Clearly the inmates/rabbits have been waiting for a savior, for a newcomer with "a very wolfy roar" to model resistance to the form that the Combine takes on the hospital ward, to the "Big Nurse."…

Since it achieved popularity in the sixties, *One Flew Over the Cuckoo's Nest* has been subject to censorship in the public school system in the United States.… All of these charges are, from a surface standpoint, understandable; the novel contains four-letter words in abundance, and McMurphy expresses his sexuality blatantly, constantly, and in a sexist manner. Moreover, the four-letter words and the sexual language are uttered by characters with whom we sympathize and identify, often in reaction to characters with far more propriety and institutional legitimacy whom we, as readers, loathe. The book, thus, seems to advocate or at least sanction profanity and male sexual braggadocio. Further, it seems to encourage and support disruptive, anti-authoritarian behavior. The reader experiences exhilaration when McMurphy puts his fist through the nurses' station window to grab a forbidden pack of cigarettes; we applaud the weekend furlough fishing expedition in which the group from the ward, led by Mac, steals a fishing boat. Disregard for rules, property, and the fights of others on the part of protagonist/heroes may (somewhat understandably) not be what parents and teachers beset with disciplinary problems want their children to celebrate in their reading.

Those who don't find raw language, sexual remarks or mutinous behavior necessarily offensive in reading material for young people may still take issue with *One Flew Over the Cuckoo's Nest* for two other reasons: first, it contains disturbing material that some may find too distressing for young readers. Kesey depicts electro-shock therapy and lobotomy graphically. The patients who die in the text die gruesomely—Cheswick, Mac's first disciple, drowns in the therapeutic swimming pool when his fingers get stuck in the grate at the bottom; Billy Bibbit, the over-aged, underdeveloped stutterer, cuts his own throat when Big Nurse threatens to tell his overpowering mother of his sexual escapade with a prostitute, sneaked onto the ward by McMurphy; the lobotomized Irish hero himself is smothered, flailing in his bed, by the Chief.…

This is a difficult moment for a reader. The resistance of McMurphy's body to death is consistent with his character, the euthanasia decision taken by the Chief may be controversial, the homoerotic overtones of the passage are unmistakable. Even though the novel ends on a positive note with the empowering and the escape of the Chief, much of what facilitates his liberation is brutal.

The second "liberal" objection to the novel as a high school text is to its stereotyped treatment of blacks and women. Big Nurse's hatchet men are three black orderlies who are despised and feared by patients, are referred to as boys, coons, and niggers at various moments in the text, and who are presented as being lazy and sneaky. The Chief first presents the trio to us in this way:

> They're out there. Black boys in white suits up before me to commit sex acts in the hall and get mopped up before I can catch them.

The black orderlies are "them," the enemy, or, at least, agents of the enemy Big Nurse. They are sneaky, perverted, and sadistic (in the eyes of the inmate/narrator), but they are also powerless, like the patients, in the face of Big Nurse's authority and powerful manipulative skills. She is herself, of course, a stereotyped castrating female of mythic proportions. Chief Bromden alludes to her size and sees her grow larger at times—this from a man who is 6'8'' whom Mac calls the biggest Indian he's ever seen. Big Nurse is also known as Mother Ratched by the male patients. The Chief gives us McMurphy assessing her power in these terms:

> There's something strange about a place where the men won't let themselves loose and laugh, something strange about the way they all knuckle under to that smiling flour-faced old mother there with the too red lipstick and the too big boobs.

That "something strange" is what Mac, newcomer on the ward, is so incredulous about—the fact that grown men tremble in the formidable woman's presence. She fuels the Chief's imagination in a variety of interesting ways; he, whose white mother tricked his Indian father into selling tribal land, whose father took the white mother's name upon their marriage, believes that a gust of cold follows Big Nurse as she walks through the ward, believes that, as she gets angry, "she blows up bigger and bigger, big as a tractor, so big I can smell the machinery inside the way you smell a motor pulling too big a load." Images of cold steel, machinery, wires, porcelain, hard glitter, and whiteness are what he repeatedly associates with her. She is the nexus of all of his fears, and the main reason the Chief grows to love and admire McMurphy is that the latter refuses to fear her.

Authority, then, in the novel is female—a large-breasted mother figure, "a bitch and a buzzard and a ballcutter." Strong women are evil and emasculating. The women viewed positively in the novel are the kind-hearted whores whom Mac introduces to the men and the sympathetic—and very tiny—Japanese nurse who works on the Disturbed ward. Once authority is constituted in this gendered manner—and once the clichéd mother/whore di-

chotomy is established in the novel—the form that resistance "naturally" takes is that of machismo, of the restoration and re-emergence of phallic power. The intellectual and articulate patient, Harding, explains to McMurphy that "we are victims of a matriarchy here, my friend," and a bit later refers to big Nurse as being "impregnable." All of the challenges that McMurphy organizes against institutional authority are reassertions of maleness—poker games, fishing trips, watching the World Series on television, smuggling in prostitutes, drinking, locker-room jokes, insistently asking Big Nurse if she wears C or D cups. A teacher or parent may well hesitate to recommend or teach a text in which the center of authority is a large, white mother figure, the subordinate authority figures are black males, and the endorsed protagonists are all subjugated white males (with the exception of Chief Bromden, whose treatment as a Native American figure in the text also partakes of cliché and stereotype, even if he is given the subject position of narrator) who are exuberantly acting out adolescent male fantasies of competition and sexual aggression. *One Flew Over the Cuckoo's Nest* is a text which violates a whole spectrum of contemporary versions of "political correctness."

I wish to argue that it is the proliferation of "problems" with the book that combines with its anti-authoritarian appeal to render this novel a profitably teachable text for high school students. Indeed, each of the objections presented above (and there may well be more I've missed)—to the book's language, its sexuality, its anti-institutionalism, its particularly disturbing violence, its racism, sexism, celebration of machismo—can open stimulating, illuminating, and, indeed, vital classroom discussions....

[For instance,] any teacher of this text must address the problems of racial and sexual stereotypes directly. At one point early in the novel Chief chronicles the history of black "boys" who have come and gone as ward workers:

> The first one she gets five years after I been on the ward, a twisted sinewy dwarf the color of cold asphalt. His mother was raped in Georgia while his papa stood by tied to the hot iron stove with plow-traces, blood streaming into his shoes. The boy watched from a closet, five years old and squinting his eyes to peep out the crack between the door and the jamb, and he never grew an inch after.

The Chief has contempt for this black dwarf as he has for all of the orderlies, but he does supply us with this mitigating narrative, one that calls attention to and makes connection with the experience of people of color in the United States. The Chief also lets us know that Big Nurse treats her black orderlies (wonderful job title in this institutional context) in a degrading, dehumanizing manner; they, in turn, "kick ass below," by mistreating the patients. The fact that their jobs are demeaning, low-level, no doubt poorly paid, dangerous, and unlikely to lead anywhere needs to be brought to light in a discussion of the treatment of race in the novel. When Chief Bromden awakes one night (he is tied to his bed) to discover one of the orderlies scraping his carefully hoarded and rechewed gum from the underside of his bunk, we see all the pathos and degradation of the orderlies' work life, of the Chief's poverty (he is a ward indigent) and of the antagonism that this institution generates in two characters who may have a connection to one another as men of color in white America. Discussions of race and racism in the novel must attend to such narrative moments, to the position of the black orderlies within the institution, and to the class and ethnic background that helps to account for McMurphy's bantering racist remarks.

It is not, alas, so easy to mitigate the castrating female stereotype that Big Nurse embodies nor the way in which institutional power and authority are so aggressively gendered in the novel. Here, it is crucial to bring students to an understanding of the limitations of first person narrative. Big Nurse is far more a creation of the Chief's and other residents' imaginations than she is a representative reality. Deep archetypal male fear of a dominant mother figure finds expression in her narrative treatment. The Chief's own experience of his traitorous white mother is projected onto Big Nurse. Student readers must learn to step back from the narrative perspective to see that the Chief's unreliability—to a degree—lies in his overblown sense of this woman—a distortion in which all of the residents participate. Because so much of the Chief's experience is perceived metaphorically—the wires, gadgets, buttons, fog machine, that he sees Big Nurse manipulating are metaphors for her manipulative skills, institutional power, and pharmaceutical regime—her representation in his narrative can, by extension, be seen as metaphoric; indeed, the way in which she grows larger and then reverts to size for him, regularly, places her in the metaphoric field. Careful readerly attention to those moments in which she expands in the Chief's eyes will help students to see her as an allegorized force rather than a realistic character in the novel. Still, we must eventually confront the distressing artistic choice that Kesey made when he chose to pre-sent his conflict in gendered terms. I find myself resisting angrily the *unfairness* of such a portrait of power, of locating what is vile and repressive in the novel in a female figure that is granted no mitigating story of her own, no redemptive moments, no context that will at least reveal her power to be exceptional, unusual, un-nurse-like. Nonetheless, I would teach this book to high school students. In teaching it, as a feminist teacher, I would engage in the following interventions:

a) I would acknowledge to students—at an advanced rather than an early stage of the discussion, so as not to establish mine as the "original" position on gender in the novel—my resistance to the use to which Big Nurse is put in the text.

b) I would encourage full discussion of gender and power, of male fears of emasculation, or the mother as a site of power, of the way in which Big Nurse's body—her breasts in particular—becomes the target of male anger.

c) I would pair *One Flew Over the Cuckoo's Nest* with a parallel text that represents institutional power as male; Charlotte Perkins Gilman's "The Yellow Wallpaper" or Margaret Atwood's *The Handmaid's Tale* could each engage Kesey's novel in a dialectic that would preclude reductive reader acceptance of Big Nurse as quintessential female power principle.

Finally, the novel opens one way out of the gendered deadlock that it creates, and that is the particular form that male bonding ultimately takes in the narrative; there is identifiable tenderness in this bond that transcends the locker room talk, the poker games, the fishing trip, the "rape" of Big Nurse as projected solution to the ward's problems. The group develops a solidarity, sensitivity, and protectiveness that permits McMurphy to subside for a while as their leader/savior when he begins to realize the price he will pay for assuming that role. When he does pay this price—the lobotomy—for having resumed leadership to avenge the death of Billy Bibbit, the love which prompts Chief to murder him is much like that which moves George to shoot Lenny in *Of Mice and Men*. After Chief breaks his silence and he and Mac have their first conversation from their neighboring bunks, the Indian experiences a strong urge to touch McMurphy. He fears for his masculinity at first, then realizes that he just wants to touch him because of who he is and what he means to all of the men on the ward. McMurphy's gift to him includes more than the power to speak, more than the restoration of his mammoth strength— it includes the power to love and, thereby, goes some distance toward subverting the machismo that provides so much of the text's momentum.

One Flew Over the Cuckoo's Nest is rich in teaching possibilities; it stimulates literary, cultural, historical, and psychological questions. It is alas, for many of us, a problematic text. Because the classroom is a space in which teachers and students can and should grapple with difficult problems, this book should be taught.

Source: Laura Quinn, "Moby Dick vs. Big Nurse: A Feminist Defense of a Misogynist Text: *One Flew Over the Cuckoo's Nest,*" in *Censored Books: Critical Viewpoints,* edited by Nicholas J. Karolides, Lee Burress, and John M. Kean, Scarecrow Press, 1993, pp. 398–413.

Elizabeth McMahan

In the following essay, McMahan argues that despite the sexist portrayal of Nurse Ratched's character, One Flew Over the Cuckoo's Nest *can be a valuable book for classroom study when issues of sexism are addressed.*

Ken Kesey's *One Flew Over the Cuckoo's Nest* is a good novel—a really teachable novel. Students get caught up in it and are eager to talk about the characters and to explore the ramifications of the partial allegory. But despite these positive qualities, *Cuckoo's Nest* is a sexist novel. Certainly I don't want to discourage anyone from teaching it, but I do urge that colleagues should present the novel in a way that will disclose its concealed sexist bias. In order to get at the invidious aspect of *Cuckoo's Nest,* let me review the way Kesey structures his microcosm.

The novel offers a compelling presentation of the way society manipulates individuals in order to keep the bureaucracy running smoothly. The mental hospital is "a little world Inside that is a made to scale prototype of the big world Outside," with both worlds being operated by the Combine, Chief Broom's appropriate name for the Establishment. A combine is a group united to pursue commercial or political interests and is also a machine that cuts off and chews up and spits out a product. Kesey has fused both meanings in his image, with the byproduct being us—the members of society.

Boss of that "factor for the Combine" is the Big Nurse, the embodiment of the castrating female. If you're old enough to remember Philip Wylie's *Generation of Vipers,* you have met the Big Nurse before: she is Mom. Wylie described her this way:

She is a middle-aged puffin with an eye like a hawk that has just seen a rabbit twitch far below. She is about twenty-five pounds overweight … with sharp heels and a hard backhand which she does not regard as a foul but a womanly defense. In a thousand of her there is not sex appeal enough to budge a hermit ten paces off a rock ledge.

You remember good old Mom. Kesey calls her Miss Ratched and thus acknowledges her role as a tool of the Combine. A ratchet is a mechanism that engages the teeth of a wheel permitting motion in one direction only. Kesey's metaphor is perfect. The ward is littered with casualties of "momism": Billy Bibbit's stuttering began with his first word, M-m-m-m-mama; Ruckley's only utterance throughout the novel is "Ffffuck da wife"; Harding's neurosis stems from inferiority feelings agitated by his wife's "ample bosom"; Chief Broom's self-concept shrank in sympathy with his once-powerful father after, he says, "my mother made him too little to fight any more and he gave up." McMurphy, on the other hand, has escaped the controls of the Combine because he has "no wife wanting new linoleum."

Kesey's eye is accurate in his depiction of this microcosm. The ward hums along on beams of fear and hate. The black boys are clearly serving the Combine in order to wreak vengeance on their white oppressors. The best hater of the bunch, "a dwarf the color of cold asphalt," peered from a closet at age five to watch his mother's rape, "while his papa stood by tied to the hot iron stove with plow traces, blood streaming into his shoes." Kesey makes his point melodramatically clear: the blacks are portrayed as villains because society has victimized them. They are merely retaliating.

But why is the Big Nurse so eager to emasculate the men in her charge? Why does *she* serve as a dedicated tool of the Combine? This is a question Kesey never answers; he apparently never thinks to ask it. He understands and castigates the injustice of prejudice against Indians. Remember how Chief Broom developed his habit of feigning deaf and dumbness: it was his response to people, he says, "that first started acting like I was too dumb to hear or see or say anything at all." You recall how the Indians are conned out of their homes and their way of life by the sneering, deprecating white people from town. Kesey shows himself sympathetic to oppressed minorities in our society. But what about our oppressed majority?

It never seems to occur to Kesey that possibly the Big Nurse relishes her job as "ball cutter" for precisely the same reason that the black boys take pleasure in their work. But anyone who has read Germain Greer's *The Female Eunuch* can see in the novel the fulfillment of the biblical injunction: an eye for an eye, a tooth for a tooth, a castration for a castration. Philip Wylie thirty years ago observed that "the mealy look of men today is the result of momism and so is the pinched and baffled fury in the eyes of womankind." True, perhaps. But Wylie thought the solution to the problem was to force woman back into her proper subservient place where she would become content again—like those happy slaves on the plantation, I suppose. And you remember Kesey's solution: Harding suggests that "man has only *one* truly effective weapon against the juggernaut of modern matriarchy." But even our virile hero McMurphy confesses that there's no way he could "get a bone up over that old buzzard." "There you are," says Harding. "She's won."

Women, you notice, keep winning these sexual battles—according to the men who manufacture them. Truth is, *nobody* wins—certainly not women. Consider how women are portrayed in Kesey's novel. We've already noted examples of the castrating bitch—Nurse Ratched, Mrs. Bibbit, Mrs. Harding, and Mrs. Bromden. Then we have the little nurse who hates the patients because her weak mind has been so warped by the Church that she thinks her birthmark a stain visited upon her because of her association with the depraved inmates. And there is the townswoman with the eyes that "spring up like the numbers in a cash register," who dupes the Indians by negotiating with *Mrs.* Bromden, rather than dealing with the Chief.

You may ask, are there no *good* women in Kesey's estimation? Well, yes. There is the nurse on the Disturbed Ward, an angel of mercy by virtue of ethnic origin—the little Japanese nurse. She accepts woman's time-honored role as nurturer of men and agrees with McMurphy that sexual starvation prompts Miss Ratched's perversity. "I sometimes think," she says, "all single nurses should be fired after they reach thirty-five." A sympathetic woman—to men, at least.

And there is also Candy, the whore with a heart of gold, and her friend, Sandy, who is equally charitable with her body. These women ask nothing of the men—not even money for their sexual performances. Kesey fantasizes that they come willingly to this insane asylum to service the inmates for the sheer joy of it. In his euphoric state, Chief Broom marvels:

> Drunk and running and laughing and carrying on with women square in the center of the Combine's most

powerful stronghold! ... I had to remind myself that it had *truly* happened, that we had made it happen. We had just unlocked a window and let it in like you let in the fresh air. Maybe the Combine wasn't so all-powerful.

What came in through the window "like fresh air"? The two prostitutes. Kesey implies that if all women would just behave generously like Candy and Sandy, the Combine might then become vulnerable.

Kesey, I think, is wrong about the way to loosen the stranglehold of the emasculating female and break up the Combine. He is simply visionary to suggest that women should emulate the attitude of the happy hookers. The truth is that women are not likely at this point to give up bossing their men around when this remains their only means of achieving a semblance of importance in society. Yet I agree with Ann Nietzke [who writes in *Human Behavior*] that

> contrary to popular belief, women do not want to castrate men; it's just that we are tired of being eunuchs ourselves. This does not mean that women want penises but that we want the powers, freedoms, and dignities that are automatically granted to the people who happen to have them.

If the Combine could be subverted to the extent of giving up its ratchet—of allowing women genuine equality—then women could stop emasculating men and turn their energies to more self-fulfilling pursuits. Given the opportunity to run that ward in her own right, instead of having to manipulate the rabbity doctor, perhaps Miss Ratched might have run it more humanely. Forcing people into deviousness can hardly be expected to improve their character. And inequality is almost guaranteed to generate malice.

Thus we need to help students see that Nurse Ratched is no more to blame for her malice than the black boys are for theirs. The Big Nurse happens also to be the Big Victim when viewed with an awareness of the social and economic exploitation of women. Kesey didn't have exactly this in mind, I grant, but we can still derive this insight from his novel and correct the damaging impression that the book leaves—that women, through some innate perversity, are the cause of all of society's failings.

Source: Elizabeth McMahan, "The Big Nurse as Ratchet: Sexism in Kesey's Cuckoo's Nest," in *CEA Critic*, Vol. 37, 1975, reprinted in *A Casebook on Ken Kesey's "One Flew Over the Cuckoo's Nest,"* edited by George J. Searles, University of New Mexico Press, 1992, pp. 145–49.

Sources

Marcia L. Falk, in a letter to the *New York Times,* December 5, 1971, reprinted in *One Flew Over the Cuckoo's Nest: Text and Criticism by Ken Kesey,* edited by John Clark Pratt, Viking, 1973, pp. 450–53.

Thomas H. Fick, "The Hipster, the Hero, and the Psychic Frontier in 'One Flew Over the Cuckoo's Nest," in *Rocky Mountain Review of Language and Literature,* Vol. 43, Nos. 1–2, 1989, pp. 19–32.

R. A. Jelliffe, review of *One Flew over the Cuckoo's Nest,* in *Chicago Sunday Tribune,* February 4, 1962, p. 3.

Barry H. Leeds, "Theme and Technique in *One Flew Over the Cuckoo's Nest,*" in *Connecticut Review*Vol. 7, No. 2, April, 1974, pp. 35–50.

Martin Levin, review of *One Flew over the Cuckoo's Nest,* in *New York Times Book Review,* February 4, 1962, p. 32.

Richard D. Maxwell, "The Abdication of Masculinity in *One Flew Over the Cuckoo's Nest,''* in *Twenty-Seven to One,* edited by Bradford C. Broughton, Ryan Press, 1970, pp. 203–11.

Julian Moynahan, "Only in America," in *New York Review of Books,* Vol. III, No. 2, September 10, 1964, pp. 14–15.

A review of *One Flew over the Cuckoo's Nest,* in *Time,* Vol. 79, February 16, 1962, p. 90.

Janet Sutherland, "A Defense of Ken Kesey's 'One Flew Over the Cuckoo's Nest,'" in *English Journal,* Vol. 61, No. 1, January, 1972, pp. 28–31.

Ronald Wallace, "What Laughter Can Do: Ken Kesey's 'One Flew Over the Cuckoo's Nest,'" in his *The Last Laugh: Form and Affirmation in the Contemporary American Comic Novel,* University of Missouri Press, 1979, pp. 90–114.

For Further Study

John A. Barsness, "Ken Kesey: The Hero in Modern Dress," in *Bulletin of the Rocky Mountain Modern Language Association,* Vol. 23, No. 1, March, pp. 27-33.

Argues that the novel is an updated version of the Western and its cowboy hero.

Annette Benert, "The Forces of Fear: Kesey's Anatomy of Insanity," in *Lex et Scientia* Vol. 13, Nos. 1-2, January-June, 1977, pp. 22-26.

Analyzes the novel's connections to fear of woman, fear of the machine, and glorification of the hero.

Robert Boyers, "Porno-Politics," in *The Annals of the American Academy of Political and Social Sciences,* No. 376, March, 1968, pp. 36-52.

Examines the novel's attitudes towards sex and the linkages between sexuality and laughter.

Leslie A. Fiedler, in his *The Return of the Vanishing American,* Stein & Day, 1968.

Fiedler's views on the mythic relationships in *Cuckoo's Nest* are almost as well-known as the novel itself.

Benjamin Goluboff, "The Carnival Artist in The Cuckoo's Nest," in *Northwest Review,* Vol. 29, No. 3, 1991, pp. 109-122.

A contemporary reading of the novel employing the Russian critic Mikhail Bakhtin's ideas of the carnivalesque.

Leslie Horst, "Bitches, Twitches, and Eunuchs: Sex-Role Failure and Caricature," in *Lex et Scientia* Vol. 13, Nos. 1-2, January-June, 1977, pp. 14-17.

This essay frankly confronts the novel's narrow portrayals of sex roles, both masculine and feminine.

Ken Kesey, *Kesey's Garage Sale,* Viking, 1973.

Contains stories and interviews, as well as a screenplay.

Ken Kesey, *One Flew Over the Cuckoo's Nest: Text and Criticism by Ken Kesey,* edited by John Clark Pratt, Viking, 1973, pp. 450–53.

An edition of the novel that includes reprints of important early critical essays on the novel.

Irving Malin, "Ken Kesey: 'One Flew Over The Cuckoo's Nest,'" in *Critique,* Vol. 5, No. 2, 1962, pp. 81-84.

Irving's essay situates the novel in the mode of the New American Gothic, which "gives us violent juxtapositions, distorted vision, even prophecy."

Carol Pearson, "The Cowboy Saint and the Indian Poet: The Comic Hero in Ken Kesey's 'One Flew Over the Cuckoo's Nest,'" in *Studies in American Humor,* Vol. 1, No. 2, October, 1974, pp. 91-98.

Employs the myth of the king, the hero, and fool to an understanding of the novel.

M. Gilbert Porter, *One Flew Over the Cuckoo's Nest: Rising to Heroism,* Twayne Masterwork Studies No. 22, Twayne, 1989.

A book-length study of Kesey's novel which explores the concept of heroism in the novel.

Terry G. Sherwood, "'One Flew Over the Cuckoo's Nest' and the Comic Strip," in *Critique,* Vol. 13, No. 1, 1971, pp. 96-109.

A clever analysis of the role of comic books and comic book figures in the novel.

Joseph J. Waldmeir, "Two Novels of the Absurd: Heller and Kesey," in *Wisconsin Studies in Contemporary Literature,* Vol. 5, No. 3, 1964, pp. 192-204.

This essay argues that Kesey's novel is in fact a better example of the absurd than Heller's *Catch-22.*

Tom Wolfe, *The Electric Kool-Aid Acid Test,* Farrar, Strauss, 1968.

Wolfe's "New Journalism" novel about Kesey and the Merry Pranksters.

A Separate Peace

John Knowles

1959

Since it was first published in 1959, John Knowles's novel *A Separate Peace* has gradually acquired the status of a minor classic. Set in the summer of 1942 at a boys' boarding school in New Hampshire, the novel focuses on the relationship between two roommates and best friends, Gene Forrester and Phineas. Both approaching their last year of high school and anticipating their involvement in World War II, Gene and Phineas have very different dispositions. Gene, from whose point of view *A Separate Peace* is told, is a somewhat athletic, shy intellectual; Phineas is a reckless non-intellectual and the best athlete at the school. As an adult looking back fifteen years, Gene recalls and comes to terms with an act he committed that left his friend physically incapacitated and ultimately contributed to his death. While daring each other to jump from a tree in a cold river, Gene jounces the limb Phineas is standing on. The latter lands on the bank of river, shattering several bones and terminating his athletic career.

A Separate Peace, which evolved from Knowles's short story "Phineas," brought its author both critical and commercial success. First published in England, it received excellent reviews there. Many critics praised the novel for its rich characterizations, artful symbolism, and effective narrative. Despite its success in England, eleven publishers in the United States turned it down before Macmillan decided to publish the American edition. As in England, the novel received excellent notices in the U.S. press. Many critics noted

that the novel could be read as an allegory about the causes of war. Although *A Separate Peace* did not become an instant best-seller—only selling seven thousand copies in its first American printing—it has gradually become a commercial success, selling more than nine million copies to date.

Author Biography

John Knowles was born on 16 September 1926, in the coal mining town of Fairmont, West Virginia. He was the third child of James Myron and Mary Beatrice Shea Knowles. At the age of fifteen, Knowles attended New Hampshire's prestigious Phillips Exeter Academy. The Devon School, where most of the action of *A Separate Peace* takes place, is based on Phillips Exeter, and many of Knowles' friends and acquaintances at Phillips Exeter were incorporated into the novel. In a *New York Times* interview, Knowles confirmed that the novel's "Super Suicide Society," in which members jumped from a tree into the river, really did exist at Exeter. Although not rendered permanently physically handicapped like Phineas, Knowles, after an unfortunate leap, spent most of the summer of 1943 on crutches.

After graduation from Exeter, Knowles entered Yale University for the 1944 fall term before going into the U.S. Army Air Force. Following his discharge from the service in November 1945, he reentered Yale. As a college student, Knowles submitted stories to the *Yale Record,* the college humor magazine. In 1949, he graduated with a B.A. in English; from 1950 to 1952, he worked as a drama critic and reporter for the *Hartford Courant* in Hartford, Connecticut. In the early 1950s, his novel *Descent to Proselito* was accepted for publication, but Knowles withdrew it on the advice of his mentor, the famous writer Thornton Wilder. In 1953, *Story Magazine* published his first story, "A Turn in the Sun." In 1956, *Cosmopolitan* published Knowles's short story "Phineas," which was later expanded into *A Separate Peace.*

By the middle 1950s, Knowles had become a member of the editorial staff of *Holiday* and was living in Philadelphia. He was also starting work on the novel that would become his most famous work: *A Separate Peace.*

In an *Esquire* article from 1985 entitled "My Separate Peace," Knowles recalled that writing the manuscript for *A Separate Peace* came quickly and

John Knowles

easily for him. Working on a regular schedule, Knowles usually went to bed at midnight, awoke at seven, wrote for an hour, turning out five to six hundred words, then went to his job at *Holiday.* He believed "No book can have been easier to get down on paper," adding, "… *A Separate Peace* wrote itself." Getting the book published, however, did not come easily at all. Turning the manuscript over to a literary agent, Knowles saw his book rejected by eleven publishers. Knowles recalled the most common reaction was "Who's going to want to read about a bunch of prep boys and what happened to them long ago in the past?" Finally, in 1959, the London publisher Secker and Warburg agreed to put out the British edition of the novel. After the book opened to almost unanimous praise from English reviewers, Macmillan brought out the American edition in 1960. *A Separate Peace* did equally well in the United States with the American critics. With the stunning success of the novel, Knowles quit his job at *Holiday* and was able to devote himself to writing fiction—a luxury that very few American writers had then or have today.

Following *A Separate Peace,* Knowles went on to publish several other novels, including *Morning in Antibes* (1962), *Indian Summer* (1966), *The Paragon* (1971), *Spreading Fires,* and *A Vein of Riches* (1974). In 1981, he published *Peace Breaks*

Out—the sequel to *A Separate Peace*—which retained the Devon School setting but had a different cast of characters. While *Peace Breaks Out* did not receive as favorable reviews as *A Separate Peace,* some critics commended the sequel for solid characterization and tight plotting.

Plot Summary

In John Knowles's *A Separate Peace,* Gene Forrester returns to visit New Hampshire's Devon School after a fifteen-year absence. He recalls his complex relationship with his roommate and best friend Phineas. His narrative begins during the summer of 1942, when Phineas goads him into jumping off a tree into the Devon River. Phineas—nicknamed Finny—is the best athlete in school, with a charismatic personality that wins over both teachers and students. He lives a life ruled by inspiration and anarchy, following his own set of rules and appearing tireless. Gene has mixed feelings about Phineas: despite his admiration and gratitude for their friendship, he envies Finny's apparent ease and the charm which allows him to break school rules without reproof. Nevertheless, when Phineas suggests they form a secret society, whose membership requires jumping from the tree into the river, Gene agrees.

When Gene fails a test after a clandestine trip to the beach with Phineas, he decides that Finny is trying to jeopardize his studies. One night before another exam, Phineas asks Gene to come to the tree to witness Leper Lepellier make the jump. Gene declines, saying that he needs to study. When Phineas accepts his excuse, Gene realizes his suspicions were unfounded. This makes him feel inferior to Phineas. He stops studying, visits the tree, and agrees to Finny's suggestion of jumping from the tree together. When they're both balanced on its branch, Gene jiggles it and Phineas falls to the ground.

Phineas's leg is shattered, and he recovers in the infirmary and later at home in Boston. He doesn't mention Gene's part in the accident, nor does anyone else. During his absence, Gene tries on Finny's clothes and feels like him, which gives him confidence. Dr. Stanpole tells Gene that Phineas will recover, but will never participate in sports again. Gene visits Finny on his way back to school after his vacation, and is shocked to see him looking like an invalid. He decides to tell Phineas the accident was his fault.

My blood could start to pound if it wanted to; let it. I was going ahead. "I was thinking about you most of the trip up."

"Oh, yeah?" He glanced briefly into my eyes.

"I was thinking about you ... and the accident."

"There's loyalty for you. To think about me when you were on a vacation."

"I was thinking about it ... about you because—I was thinking about you and the accident because I caused it."

Finny looked steadily at me, his face very handsome and expressionless. "What do you mean, you caused it?" his voice was as steady as his eyes.

My own voice sounded quiet and foreign. "I jounced the limb. I caused it." One more sentence. "I deliberately jounced the limb so you would fall off."

He looked older than I had ever seen him. "Of course you didn't."

"Yes I did. I did!"

"Of course you didn't do it. You damn fool. Sit down, you damn fool."

"Of course I did!"

"I'm going to hit you if you don't sit down."

"*Hit* me!" I looked at him. "*Hit* me!" You can't even get up! You can't even come near me!"

Phineas ends their discussion by telling Gene he's tired and Gene leaves, deciding to make things up to Finny once he's back at school.

Phineas telephones Gene at school. Upon learning that Gene doesn't have another roommate, he's reassured that Gene didn't mean what he said about the accident. He refuses to accept Gene's decision to become Assistant Senior Crew manager, commenting: "Listen, pal, if *I* can't play sports, *you're* going to play them for me." His words help Gene realize that one of his purposes was to become a part of Phineas. When Brinker Hadley, the head student, heckles Gene about the accident, Gene ignores the teasing although he feels terribly guilty. One afternoon, Brinker and Gene meet Leper, whose nonsensical comments drive Brinker to decide to enlist in the army. Gene is tempted to do the same. He regards enlisting as a way of escaping the past and entering adulthood. Feeling that he owes nothing to anyone, except himself, he returns to his room to find Phineas, who has returned to school.

The next morning, Brinker asks Gene about enlisting with him. Gene realizes that Phineas needs him and changes his mind. Phineas announces his intention to groom Gene for the 1944 Olympics, in which he had intended to participate before the accident. Gene begins tutoring Finny in academics and Finny tutors Gene in athletics. When a teacher declares that the purpose of exercise is to prepare for war, Phineas reminds Gene of his theory that the war is really a conspiracy amongst the world's leaders. He states his theory so convincingly that Gene momentarily believes him. Nevertheless, when Leper enlists after seeing a propaganda film, Gene joins the others in creating an heroic fantasy life for Leper. Brinker drops his enlistment plan after Gene decides not to join him and becomes a quiet rebel, quitting most of the school activities in which he's been involved.

Phineas suggests holding a winter carnival. Once the games begin, he performs a dance of joy on the prize table. Gene becomes the star of Phineas's gala and surpasses himself, feeling liberated during "this afternoon of momentary, illusory, special and separate peace." The festivities end when a cryptic telegram from Leper arrives, saying that he's escaped and needs help. Gene travels to Leper's home in Vermont, where he discovers that Leper has deserted and is suffering mental problems. Leper calls Gene a savage underneath, taunting him for having knocked Phineas out of the tree. Gene returns to school, desperate to see Phineas, and finds him in the middle of a snowball fight. Gene joins in and enjoys the fight's vitality and energy, though he wonders what will happen when they all get drafted. When Brinker asks Gene about Leper, he admits that Leper has cracked up. Brinker observes that two of their classmates—Leper and Phineas—have already been sidelined from the war. Brinker confronts Gene, insisting that they have to stop pitying Phineas so that life can go on. Phineas tells Gene he's changed his mind about the war, because he saw Leper outside the school and believes that the war caused his breakdown.

That night, Brinker takes Gene and Phineas to the Assembly Room for a mock inquiry about Finny's accident. Phineas remembers climbing the tree and falling out, and asks Gene whether he noticed the tree shaking. Gene says he doesn't recall anything like that. Phineas then remembers his suggestion they make a double jump, and that they started to climb. Someone else says Leper was there, and he's brought in. Leper admits that he saw Gene and Phineas on the tree limb, adding that they moved up and down like a piston. When Brinker insists upon getting all the facts, Phineas loses control, rushes from the Assembly Room, and falls down the marble stairs, breaking his leg again.

Dr. Stanpole comments that this break is much simpler. Gene sneaks into Finny's infirmary room, and Phineas accuses him of wanting to break something else in him. Gene flees, but returns to visit Phineas the next day. They talk about Finny's unsuccessful attempts to enlist. Gene observes that Phineas would have been lousy in the war: once bored, he would make friends with the enemy and get things "so scrambled up nobody would know who to fight any more." Finally they confront what happened in the tree. Gene agrees with Finny's analysis that "It was just some kind of blind impulse you had…. It wasn't anything you really felt against me, it wasn't some kind of hate you've felt all along. It wasn't anything personal." When Gene arrives at the infirmary the next day, he's told Phineas is dead: during the operation, some bone marrow escaped into his blood stream and stopped his heart. Dr. Stanpole likens the operating room to the war, where the risks "are just more formal than in other places."

Gene enlists in the Navy, but feels no sense of patriotism. He disagrees with Brinker's notion that the older generation is responsible for the war and with Finny's idea that the war is just a huge practical joke. Instead, he believes war is the result of "something ignorant in the human heart." He can't talk about Phineas because he can't accept the loss of his vitality, and he continues to feel guilty about his death. Gene realizes that he's ready for the war because he no longer feels any hatred. His war "ended before I ever put on a uniform; I was on active duty all my time at school; I killed my enemy there." He believes the real enemy is something he and the others have created out of their own fear.

Characters

Chet Douglass

Gene Forrester's rival for the position of class valedictorian. Unlike Gene, Chet has a genuine interest in learning and does not thrive simply on competition.

Finny

See Phineas

Gene Forrester

The narrator of *A Separate Peace,* Gene as an adult recalls himself at sixteen: a lonely intellectual with the tendency of analyzing his and every-

Movie still from A Separate Peace.

one else's motives. At various times in the novel, he is highly competitive, selfish, insecure, and combative. On other occasions, he is courageous, mature, and dependable.

Throughout the novel, Gene compares and contrasts himself with his best friend, Finny, and often falls short in his own estimation. Although Gene is obviously the more scholarly of the two (Gene is academically near the top of his high school class, while Finny seldom achieves more than a "C" in his courses), Finny is the better athlete and more self-confident than his friend. Also troubling to Gene is that Finny openly flouts conventions but never gets punished for his acts. For example, on an occasion when Finny and Gene miss the mandatory school dinner, Finny cheerfully rambles a bizarre explanation to Mr. Prud'homme, the summer substitute teacher. Mr. Prud'homme, more amused than angry, decides not to punish the boys.

Gene observes many other occasions when Finny breaks the rules but never gets his comeuppance, because he has so much charm and self-confidence. He becomes increasingly jealous of Finny, and for a while he assumes Finny reciprocates those feelings. That Gene works systematically and diligently for his academic and athletic success

and Finny's athletic achievements seem to come effortlessly to him fuels Gene's rivalry. Worse still for Gene, Finny doesn't even want acknowledgment for his accomplishments. For example, when Finny breaks the school swimming record with virtually no preparation, he insists that Gene—the only witness to the event—not tell anyone. For a while, it seems logical to Gene that Finny, as the school's best athlete, envies Gene his academic success. Ultimately, Finny proves Gene's theory wrong, when he genuinely encourages Gene to pursue his studies rather than join the "Super Suicide Society" one evening. Now Gene realizes that Finny never did envy him and finds this knowledge intolerable. In light of all the above, Gene impulsively jounces the limb Finny is standing on during a Super Suicide Society ritual, causing Finny his crippling accident.

As Ronald Weber writes in an article from *Studies in Short Fiction*, "It is Phineas's innocence that Gene cannot endure. As long as he can believe Phineas shares his enmity, he can find relief, but with this assurance gone, he stands condemned before himself and must strike out against his tormentor."

Ultimately, Gene matures through his introspection, coming to understand his terrible action against his friend. Shortly before Finny's death, he and Gene fully explore the dynamics of their relationship and the circumstances that caused Finny's accident. When Gene explains "it was just some ignorance inside me, some crazy thing inside me, something blind"—not a personal hatred of Finny or a premeditated action—Finny accepts the apology. As Ronald Weber has written, "Gene Forrester comes to learn that his war, the essential war, is fought on the battlefield within. Peace comes only when he faces up to the fact. The only escape, the price of peace, is self-awareness." James Ellis, in an *English Journal* article, puts it in similar terms: "Gene has discovered that his private evil, which caused him to hurt Phineas, is the same evil—only magnified—that results in war."

Mr. Hadley

Brinker Hadley's father, a World War I veteran whose patriotism offends both Brinker and Gene.

Brinker Hadley

Described as "the big name on campus," Brinker Hadley's characterization was actually based on the novelist Gore Vidal. In an interview with the *Exonion,* Knowles remembers Vidal as an "unusual and thriving" person, although he did not know him very well. In his realization of Hadley's slick temperament, Gene appreciates his own maturity. At one time, Gene would have ingratiated himself with someone like Hadley, but after Finny's fall Gene comes to prefer the sincerity of someone like Leper. Brinker Hadley also serves the function of being the character that arranges the mock tribunal to determine whether Gene is innocent or guilty in regard to Finny's fall.

Phil Latham

One of the less impressive authority figures at the Devon School, Phil Latham is the wrestling coach. His advice, "Give it the old college try," seems to pertain to all situations, whether they be sexual, psychological, or academic. He is not really an unsympathetic character, so much as a man without much intelligence or creativity.

Elwin Lepellier

A gentle, nonconformist student at Devon School, "Leper," as he is nicknamed, prefers snails and science projects to sports and competition. Ironically, he is the first student in the novel to enlist in the Army, because a deceptive recruiting film convinced Leper that Army life is a clean, pure experience. Soon after his induction into the Army,

Media Adaptations

- *A Separate Peace* was adapted as a film directed by Larry Peerce, starring John Heyl and Parker Stevenson, Paramount Pictures, 1972, available from Paramount Home Video, Home Vision Cinema. Although generally faithful to the novel, the film of the same name received mostly poor reviews. Typical was movie critic Leonard Maltin's opinion that the "story is morbid, acting incredibly amateurish, and direction has no feeling at all for the period."

Leper realizes that he cannot adapt to the Spartan environment, and goes AWOL (absent without leave) in order to avoid being discharged as psychologically unfit for service. When Gene Forrester visits Leper in his Vermont home, the latter has been badly shaken by his Army experiences. Leper, aware of Gene's contempt for him, strikes back, calling him "a savage underneath." Leper also reveals that he knows Gene knocked Finny out of the tree earlier in the summer. Gene, realizing some truth to the "savage underneath" remark, physically strikes the frail Leper but does not hurt him badly.

While generally a pitiable character, Leper has a streak of pride. For example, at the tribunal scene, in which several Devon School students attempt to discover whether Gene really did cause Finny's traumatic fall, Leper will not reveal the extent of what he knows. Up until this point, most Devon School students have either ignored or ridiculed him, so he announces, "Why should I tell! Just because it happens to suit you!"

Leper

See Elwin Lepellier

Mr. Ludsbery

One of the permanent teachers at the Devon School, Mr. Ludsbery represents the worst stereotype of a schoolmaster: phony, a stickler for rules, and given to fatuous remarks such as "Has it been raining in your part of town?" When he reproaches Gene for "[slipping] in any number of ways since last year," Gene is reminded of his friend Finny and does not care about anything else the teacher says.

Mr. Patch-Withers

A stern history teacher at the Devon School, he and his wife give a tea party for the students. There, he shows a gentler side by not punishing Finny for flagrantly violating the dress code.

Mrs. Patch-Withers

The wife of the history teacher at the Devon School, she is appalled to see Finny wear his official school tie as a belt to her party.

Phineas

One of the two central characters in the novel. Phineas, also known as Finny, is Devon School's best athlete and a handsome, self-confident teenager. Despite or because of these qualities, he is also arguably the most innocent of all the characters in *A Separate Peace.* For example, just before he and Gene fall asleep on the beach one night, Finny honestly declares that Gene is his "best pal." Somewhat taken aback, Gene cannot return the compliment and reflects "It was a courageous thing to say. Exposing a sincere emotion nakedly like that at the Devon School was the next thing to suicide." Finny is naive in other ways as well. When Gene complains about not having enough time to study, Finny is genuinely puzzled. "I didn't know you needed to study," he said simply. "I didn't think you ever did. I thought it came to you." Since Finny excels at sports with a minimum of effort—Gene witnesses his breaking the school swimming record with no preparation—he does not understand that Gene works diligently to be at the top of his class scholastically.

In Hallman Bell Bryant's *A Separate Peace: The War Within,* the author compares Finny to many literary or historical figures. For example, he brings to mind Mark Twain's Huckleberry Finn; just as Huck could not accept the Old Testament story of Moses because he did not have any "stock" in dead folks, Finny doubts the authenticity of the Latin language because it is a "dead language." Many critics have compared Finny to J. D. Salinger's Holden Caulfield in *Catcher in the Rye* for both characters' unpretentiousness, honesty, and anti-establishment attitudes. However, other critics dissent; for example, Granville Hicks wrote in a *Saturday Review* article that Finny's spontaneity and unconventionality were not, like Holden's, a form of protest against authority; they

were an inherent part of his nature. At one point in *A Separate Peace,* Gene compares the sleeping Finny to Lazarus.

After Gene causes Finny his crippling fall, Finny loses some of his innocence. Ironically, however, because of his physical disability, he becomes increasingly dependent on Gene; in fact, he even comes to see Gene as an "extension of himself," while always suspecting that Gene caused his accident. Dr. Stanpole medically explains Finny's unexpected death in these terms: "As I was moving the bone some of the marrow must have … gone directly to his heart and stopped it." Symbolically, of course, Finny's death can be interpreted otherwise; although he forgave Gene on some level, Finny's heartbreak still lingered.

Given the distance of time and the impact of maturity, the adult Gene realizes Finny's principal virtue is his lack of malice. As James Ellis puts it, "Because of his ability to admit only as much of the ugliness of life as he could assimilate, Phineas was unique."

Mr. Prud'homme

A substitute teacher at the Devon School for the summer. Given that he is not entirely familiar with the rules, he is not so strict in enforcing them.

Cliff Quackenbush

The opposite of Finny in nearly every respect, he is also Gene's nemesis. The crew manager at the Devon School, Quackenbush is a colorless, humorless character, someone who never seems to have been a child emotionally. Openly scornful of Gene for becoming assistant crew manager, Quackenbush calls him to his face "a maimed son-of-a-bitch," and a fight between them ensues. Although Quackenbush never realizes it, the insult heightens Gene's guilt and confusion over causing Finny's accident. He also touches a nerve when he sarcastically asks Gene "Who the hell are you anyway?" because introverted Gene often seems uncertain as to why he acts as he does.

Dr. Stanpole

One of the more sympathetic adults in the novel, Dr. Stanpole is a well-meaning character who speaks with a vocabulary too sophisticated for the students at Devon School. To what extent his skill as a doctor is responsible for Finny's death remains uncertain.

Themes

Guilt and Innocence

In John Knowles's novel that chronicles the coming of age of two prep-school friends, one character—Finny—loses much of his trustfulness and innocence, while the other—Gene—progresses toward self-knowledge and maturity. That *A Separate Peace* takes place in the first half of the 1940s explains so many references to war. In this novel, however, the real struggle is fought in the hearts of the characters, not on the battlefield. After Gene causes Finny's crippling fall, everything that follows, as Knowles has written, is "one long abject confession, a *mea culpa,* a tale of crime—if a crime has been committed—and of no punishment. It is a story of growth through tragedy." While Gene does eventually reconcile to his transgression against Finny, the process takes many years. Gene obtains some peace of mind through his final encounter with Finny, in which he shows both humility and understanding of Finny's pacifist nature. But it is only as a thirty-something adult revisiting his former school that Gene has accumulated the wisdom and maturity to fully understand the significance of what happened in his adolescence. In reconciling with his guilty conscience, Gene does more than understand the dark side of human nature. He also absorbs the best of Finny's code of behavior, "a way of sizing up the world with erratic and entirely personal reservations." While Gene will never again possess the innocence he recalls from the summer of 1942, as James M. Mellard writes in *Studies in Short Fiction,* "if he and the others fall short of Finny's standard, as they must, they will still gain from having reached for it."

Finny's development in the latter half of the novel can be seen in terms of loss of innocence. Since he is now physically incapacitated, unlikely to ever regain his athletic powers, his carefree ways are also gone. Although he superficially denies the existence of World War II, he secretly goes to great lengths to enlist. However, since no army will accept him due to his accident, Finny loses much of his self-confidence. He increasingly lives vicariously through Gene, coming to perceive Gene as "an extension of himself," but he always knows on some level that Gene deliberately caused his accident. Although Dr. Stanpole gives a medical explanation for Finny's death, the event can also be seen symbolically. As Douglas Alley in an *English Journal* article writes of Finny, "For him, there

Topics for Further Study

- Explore the reasons for the American involvement in World War II. Compare the American degree of popular support to that of such other wars as World War I, the Vietnam War, and the Korean War.

- Compare and contrast three significant fictional works about World War II. Some possibilities include James Jones's novel *From Here to Eternity,* Norman Mailer's novel *The Naked and the Dead,* and Arthur Miller's play *All My Sons.*

- Discuss the economic impact of World War II on the United States and on Europe.

could be no growing up. A loss of innocence could only result in death."

War

On one level, *A Separate Peace* can be read as a war novel. Its title is taken from Ernest Hemingway's novel *A Farewell to Arms,* in which the book's protagonist, Lt. Frederic Henry, declares his own private armistice during World War I. However, unlike Hemingway's novel, Knowles's book does not concern soldiers on the battlefield; rather, it focuses on the impact of war on the lives of male adolescents, none of whom have yet engaged in combat. Despite their lack of direct involvement in World War II, boys who were not quite of draft age were often preoccupied by the American war effort. The idea of avoiding military service in World War II was unthinkable to most young men; the questions were when they would be called to serve and which branch of the military would accept them. As Gene Forrester in the late 1950s reflects on the impact of World War II for him, "The war was and is reality for me. I still instinctively live and think in its atmosphere."

As Gene recalls, the American war effort had enormous domestic implications on his generation. For example, since nearly all of the Devon School's younger faculty were away serving in the military or in war-related jobs, substitute teachers—usually men between the ages of fifty and seventy—were brought into the school. Given the great age differences between the students and their new teachers, the former did not usually see the latter as accessible role models. Hence, the bonds between the students intensified. Yet, the new faculty members were not unkind; as Gene recalls, "I think we reminded them of what peace was like, we boys of sixteen. We registered with no draft board, we had taken no physical examinations…. We were carefree and wild, and I suppose we could be thought of as a sign of the life the war was being fought to preserve. Anyway, they were more indulgent toward us than at any other time."

The American war effort impacted everyday life in more general ways. For example, as Gene recalls, "Nylon, meat, gasoline, and steel are rare. There are too many jobs and not enough workers. Money is very easy to earn but rather hard to spend, because there isn't very much to buy."

Style

Point of View

Told in first person ("I") by Gene Forrester, a man in his thirties recalling his adolescence, *A Separate Peace* begins with Gene's visit to the Devon School. The first pages of the novel mainly describe the physical landscape of the institution; the rest tells Gene's story, a tale in which he serves as both an observer and a participant at the center of the action. As Ronald Weber notes, "Generally, first-person narration gives the reader a heightened sense of immediacy, a sense of close involvement with the life of the novel…. With Knowles's novel, however, this is not the case … throughout it he remains somewhat outside the action and detached from the narrator, observing the life of the novel rather than submerged in it." This is not intended as a criticism, however. As Weber explains, Knowles's choice of narration is "a highly-calculated effect…. It indicates a sharply different thematic intention, and one that is rooted in a skillful alteration of the conventional method of first-person telling."

It is important to remember that Gene, through the distance of time—specifically fifteen years—has arrived at a level of self-knowledge that few teenagers could achieve. Had Knowles limited the perspective to the highly introspective, but still adolescent Gene, *A Separate Peace* would have been told in a very different tone. As Ronald Weber writes, "Gene's voice … is dispassionate, reflective, and controlled; it is, in his own words, a voice from which fury is gone, dried up at its source long before the telling begins."

Setting

Most of the action of the novel is confined to the Devon School, the prep school based on Phillips Exeter. An exception is found in Chapter 10, in which Gene visits his friend Leper in his family's Vermont home. When Gene revisits the Devon School, he is particularly interested in confronting two fearful places on campus. The first is the First Academy Building, a Georgian-style red-brick structure, in which a group of Devon students brought Gene to accuse him of causing the accident that crippled Finny's life. On the stairs of the First Academy Building, another misfortune occurred which ultimately ended Finny's life. The second place of significance is the tree from which Gene and Finny leaped in their "Super Suicide Society" escapades. While the adult Gene recalls the tree as an enormous, forbidding structure, when he actually rediscovers it, the tree appears much smaller and similar to all the other trees in the vicinity.

In terms of time, *A Separate Peace* skips back and forth between the early 1940s and the late 1950s. Again, this time difference creates a retrospective which allows the narrator Gene to relate the events with more depth and analysis.

Symbolism

A Separate Peace is a book full of symbolism. One pair of symbols can be found in two rivers that flow through the school: the Devon and the Naguamsett. Gene remembers the freshwater Devon River fondly, for this was the body of water that he and Finny had leaped into many times from the tree. Ironically, after Finny's accident, Gene does not remember the Devon River with fear or disgust; the river to him symbolizes the carefree summer days, a peaceful time. On the other hand, the Naguamsett River ("governed by imaginable factors like the Gulf Stream, the Polar Ice Cap, and the moon") is an ugly, marshy, saline river into which Gene falls after a fight with quarrelsome Cliff Quackenbush. If the Devon River represents serenity, Gene associates the Naguamsett with war and winter.

Another obvious pair of symbols is in the contrast between the war being fought abroad and the relative tranquility of the Devon School, particularly in its summer session. To Gene "the war was

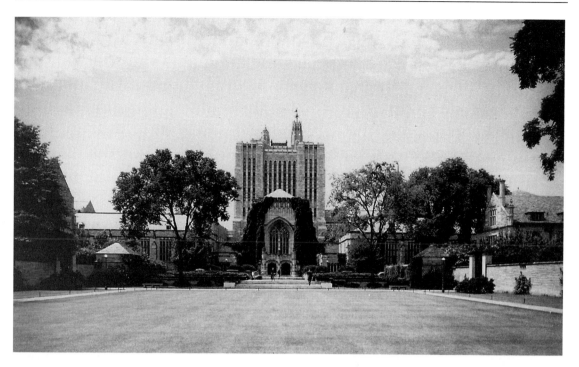

Sterling Memorial Library at Yale University, the private Ivy League where Knowles attended college along with many other prep school graduates.

and is reality," yet by completing his final year at the Devon School he is literally avoiding military service. Still, he and his classmates realize it is only a matter of time before they enlist or are drafted. So, if the war represents a harsh reality that schoolboys like Gene must eventually confront, then Gene and Finny's "gypsy" summer spent at the Devon School denotes illusion. In the only summer session in the school's long history, the students defy many rules, still maintain the faculty's goodwill, create new games such as "Blitzball," and begin unheard-of clubs such as the "Super Suicide Society of the Summer Session." The summer is a period of escape for Devon School's students. As Gene observes, "Bombs in Central Europe were completely unreal to us here, not because we couldn't imagine it … but because our place here was too fair for us to accept something like that." Still, Gene realizes that the "gypsy" summer spirit will not last indefinitely; "official class leaders and politicians" will replace the "idiosyncratic, leaderless band" of the summer. To recapture the carefree summer spirit, Gene and Finny have a "Winter Carnival" in which "there was going to be no government," and "on this day even the schoolboy egotism of Devon was conjured away."

Epiphany

An epiphany is a sudden flash of perception into the nature of a thing or event. In his most provocative insight into human nature, Gene realizes toward the conclusion of *A Separate Peace* "that wars were not made by generations and their special stupidities, but that wars were made instead by something ignorant in the human heart." As James Ellis writes, "Gene has discovered that his private evil, which caused him to hurt Phineas, is the same evil—only magnified—that results in war."

Historical Context

American Feelings about War

Although first published in 1959 in England, *A Separate Peace* is about an earlier period, specifically the early 1940s when United States had declared its involvement in World War II. It must be remembered that World War II brought out enormous patriotism in most Americans, whether they were actually working in war-related jobs, engaged in combat, or neither. While intelligent adolescents such as Gene Forrester and Hadley Brinker in *A*

Compare
&
Contrast

- **1940s:** In the middle of World War II, the United States had compulsory draft registration for young men, most of whom expected to eventually enlist in the military.

  Early 1960s: While the United States still had compulsory draft registration for young men, only a few were being called up for military duty in Vietnam.

  Today: Reinstated in the early 1980s after a brief dismissal in the 1970s, draft registration is still required for young men in America, although there is little chance of being called up into a military that is currently all-volunteer.

- **1940s:** America declared its involvement in World War II, and had troops in Europe and the Pacific.

  Early 1960s: Although America had sent some troops to Vietnam, their commitment to the war

effort was insignificant at the time compared to the escalation after 1965.

Today: The United States of America is not involved in any major war effort, and relies on all-volunteer armed forces.

- **1940s:** The path to success for young men from upper-class white families often led from the best prep school to an Ivy League university.

  Early 1960s: University enrollment soared as the baby boom generation reached college age. Many government programs existed to help more young people from middle-class and impoverished backgrounds attain a college education.

  Today: College graduates still have higher average salaries than people with less education. With government financing for higher education on the decline, universities find themselves competing for the enrollment dollars of a decreasing college-age population.

Separate Peace might have mixed feelings about being drafted or enlisting in the war, shirking responsibility (in other words, draft dodging) was virtually unthinkable. Elwin "Leper" Lepellier, a major character in Knowles's novel, enlists in the war and does go AWOL (absent without leave). However, although he is often a sincere, sympathetic character, he does not ultimately emerge a hero.

It is also worth remembering that when *A Separate Peace* was first published in the United States in 1960, the Korean War had been over for about seven years, and American involvement in the War in Vietnam had not yet escalated to horrific proportions. There was little protest over compulsory enrollment in the military—the draft—or the U.S.'s role in Vietnam in the early 1960s. As U.S. involvement and troop movement escalated after 1965, however, public support for the war diminished and many young antiwar protesters responded by burning their draft notices. Thus, while numerous critics submitted scholarly articles on

Knowles's novel throughout the 1960s, by the end of the decade, the book was being considered in light of the devastation that the Vietnam War had wrought. Interestingly, left-wing and conservative critics praised *A Separate Peace* in different ways. The former found its antiwar sentiments appropriate and timely, particularly in light of what they perceived as the threat of atomic warfare. Yet right-wing reviewers also liked the book, often commending its treatment of original sin and redemption.

Education and Adolescence in the 1960s

Many of the young people of the 1960s grew up in a different atmosphere from the youth of the 1990s. After the Soviet launch of the Sputnik satellite in 1957, education was beginning to be emphasized as important not only to individual success but to the success of the nation. Not only were new teaching methods and standards being put into place, but the federal government began taking a greater role in funding and setting policy for education. College enrollment soared, as young people saw higher education as providing a chance to get ahead in life. Nevertheless, there were many problems with the educational system. Segregation persisted in many areas and opportunities were limited for women. The all-white, male prep school of *A Separate Peace* was still thriving in 1960. It was seen as a student's best chance to get into the best private universities, so pressure to succeed could be great.

The culture of the young also came of age in the 1960s. When the first American edition of the novel appeared in 1960, the United States had its youngest elected president, John F. Kennedy, who at the age of forty-three had defeated Vice President Richard M. Nixon by a margin of only 113,000 votes out of more than 69 million cast. The children of the "Baby Boom"—the large population surge that began after World War II—were adolescents. As the decade progressed and the Baby Boomers reached college, they became an increasingly vocal part of American politics and culture. Brought up in prosperity and peace, these children questioned the morality and authority of their parents' generation and pursued individual fulfillment. Their search for meaning and identity is reflected in Gene's narrative of his own adolescent years.

Critical Overview

John Knowles's *A Separate Peace,* a critical success from its first printing, has evolved into one of the most frequently read novels in American high schools today. In fact, in the words of its author, it has captured a "destiny apart" from his own. Although Knowles has published many other novels, essays, and works of nonfiction, none has received the critical attention or praise of *A Separate Peace.* While that novel no longer commands the massive scholarly attention that it did throughout the 1960s, according to Hallman Bell Bryant, it has gone through at least seventy printings and earns Knowles somewhere between $30,000 and $40,000 a year in royalties.

Right from the start, *A Separate Peace* received extremely favorable notices. Since it was first published by Secker and Warburg in London, England, the British reviewers were the first to write what they liked about the book. The most significant of these pieces appeared in the *Times Literary Supplement* section on 1 May 1959. This review con-

gratulated Knowles for having written a "novel of altogether exceptional power and distinction." Other English critics praised *A Separate Peace,* many of them saying it was the best American novel since J. D. Salinger's *Catcher in the Rye,* which had been published in 1953. In her *Manchester Guardian* review, Ann Duchene enjoyed the "tenderness and restraint" that Knowles expressed for his two major characters, Gene and Finny.

After the favorable English reception, the publishing firm of Macmillan bought the rights to the novel and issued the first American edition in February, 1960. Among the earliest reviews, Edmund Fuller wrote in the *New York Times* that Knowles was a writer "already skilled in craft and discerning in his perceptions." He went on to say the World War II background was more central to the action of the novel than the Devon School setting, which he realized was based on Exeter. Although Fuller found several incidents in the book to be unconvincing, he thought the novel's "major truths" more than compensated for this shortcoming. Among the few negative reviews of *A Separate Peace,* a *Commonweal* critic shrugged it off as "one more foray into the territory of guilt earned in adolescence." While most other American critics found the book a compelling achievement, several reserved criticism for the trial scene in which several Devon students attempt to ascertain the extent of Gene Forrester's involvement in Finny's accident. Fifteen years later, after *A Separate Peace* had been made into a movie of the same name, Linda Heinz of *Literature Film Quarterly* wrote that she found the mock tribunal in both the book and the movie unconvincing.

Despite *A Separate Peace*'s immediate critical acclaim, it did not become a best-seller, nor did any book clubs immediately select it for inclusion. However, its sales picked up considerably after it won the William Faulkner Foundation Award, as well as the Richard and Hinda Rosenthal Foundation Award. John K. Crabbe, writing for the *English Journal* in 1963, recommended high school teachers of American literature consider Knowles's novel as an alternative to J. D. Salinger's popular *Catcher in the Rye.* Many teachers were relieved to do so, having had some apprehensions about the profanity in *Catcher.* James Ellis, also writing for the *English Journal,* called William Golding's *Lord of the Flies* and *A Separate Peace* major finds for the high school classroom. By the middle 1960s, many English teachers had made *A Separate Peace* a part of their curriculum.

What Do I Read Next?

- *Catcher in the Rye,* J. D. Salinger's famous novel about Holden Caulfield's troubled adolescence and the phoniness he detects in adults, is in many ways as relevant today as when it was published in 1953.

- F. Scott Fitzgerald's 1920 novel *This Side of Paradise* is the story of how wealthy, young Amory Blaine struggles for self-knowledge in his provincial world.

- John Knowles's novel *Peace Breaks Out* is the sequel to *A Separate Peace.* Published in 1981, *Peace Breaks Out* features the same setting as *A Separate Peace* but includes a different cast of characters.

- Mary Gordon's 1991 collection *Good Boys and Dead Girls* contains twenty-eight of her essays on such writers as Virginia Woolf, Mary McCarthy, David Plante, and Edith Wharton.

- *The Portable Malcolm Cowley,* edited by Donald W. Faulkner. Published in 1990, the volume contains many of Malcolm Cowley's perceptive reflections on American writers and writing.

By the early 1970s, the barrage of articles analyzing the novel had subsided. However, even in the late 1970s—almost twenty years after the book had been published—some critique and analysis persisted. For example, in George-Michael Sarotte's book *Like a Brother, Like a Lover,* published in 1978, the author speculates that Gene may have homoerotic feelings for Finny. As late as 1992, the *English Journal* was still extolling the virtues of *A Separate Peace* in the article "Still Good Reading: Adolescent Novels Written Before 1967."

Criticism

Anne Hiebert Alton

Alton is a member of an honorary research association at the University of Sydney, Australia. In the following essay, she places A Separate Peace *within three distinct literary traditions and examines the novel's strengths and weaknesses.*

John Knowles based his first novel, *A Separate Peace* (1959), on two short stories, entitled "Phineas" and "A Turn in the Sun." An immediate success, it won the William Faulkner Foundation Award, the Rosenthal Award of the National Institute of Arts and Letters, and an award from the Independent School Education Board. Adapted into both a stage play and a film, the novel has been praised for its "clear craftsmanship and careful handling of form" by Jay Halio in *Studies in Short Fiction.* It has also been hailed for its exceptional power and distinction. In addition to exploring the pathos of a complicated friendship, the novel provides insights into the human psyche and the heart of man.

A Separate Peace emulates three major literary traditions. First, it focuses on the fall of man, something central in such works as the Bible's Book of Genesis, *Paradise Lost,* and *Lord of the Flies.* The novel can be read as Gene's movement from innocence to experience, as he progresses from his ignorance of humanity's tendency towards thoughtless yet harmful actions to recognizing his own potential for such acts. More significantly, the novel chronicles Phineas' progression from his initial belief in the world's benevolence and in his own integrity—defined by a rigid set of rules such as winning at sports, never lying about one's height, saying prayers just in case God exists, and never blaming a friend without cause—to his final realization of Gene's role in the accident.

Second, the novel is a *bildungsroman,* a German term meaning "novel of formation." This tradition includes such literary masterpieces as *The Adventures of Huckleberry Finn, David Copperfield,* and *Little Women.* The *bildungsroman* focuses on the development of the protagonist's mind and character from childhood to adulthood, charting the crises which lead to maturation and recognition of one's identity and place in the world. *A Separate Peace* follows Gene Forrester's progress through the formative years of his adolescence, and specifically his relationship with Phineas. Gene—short for Eugene—is Greek for "well-born." While Gene is from a Southern family affluent enough to send him to prep school, his identity isn't as secure as his name suggests: before the accident, he implies the posters on his wall of a large Southern estate represent his home. Initially Gene emulates Phineas: he joins him in climbing the tree and jumping into the river, being late for dinner, and taking a forbidden trip to the beach. Later, he wants to become Phineas, as when he tries on his clothes and feels confident "that I would never stumble through the confusions of my own character again." Phineas, too, feels their connection: after the accident, he informs Gene that he must become an athlete in Finny's stead. Later, Gene realizes that his "aid alone had never seemed to him in the category of help .... Phineas had thought of me as an extension of himself." However, as Gene matures he starts to develop his own identity. He recognizes his attraction to deadly things and, more significantly, he writes a narrative about his relationship with Phineas revealing the flaws in his own character which led to Phineas's death.

Third, *A Separate Peace* is a boys' school story, a tradition which includes such books as *Tom Brown's Schooldays, Stalky and Co, Goodbye Mr. Chips,* and even *Dead Poets Society.* It is set in what John Rowe Townsend in *Written for Children* refers to as the "hothouse environment" of boarding school, a self-contained world with an aura of privilege based on class and money. Typically, such a school is a place for education and growth. Here it also represents the last place of freedom and safety for the boys, guarding their last days of childhood and standing as "the tame fringe of the last and greatest wilderness," adulthood. Moreover, it functions as a microcosm of the real world, dealing with issues of leadership, discipline, rivalry, and friendship. The novel diverges from this tradition in one respect: while pre-World War I school stories focused on what Townsend maintains were "'Games to play out, whether earnest or fun'—it was magnificent but it was not war; it had nothing to do with life and death in the trenches," *A Separate Peace* has everything to do with it. Gene fights his private war at school, and his actions and their effects echo the world's large-scale war. When he leaves Devon School, he feels ready to enter this war, for he no longer has any enmity to contribute. Indeed, Gene comments that he never killed anyone, nor did he develop an intense hatred for the enemy, "Because my war ended before I ever put on a uniform; I was on active duty all my time at school; I killed my enemy there." In the end, Gene realizes that his real enemy is himself and his impulse towards mindless destruction—and he believes he overcame this enemy only after causing Phineas's death.

One of the novel's strengths lies in its structure, and particularly its treatment of time. The narrative is designed as a story within a story, with the outer layer occurring on a dark November day. In contrast, the inner layer follows a progression through the seasons, beginning and ending in June. This cycle implies the notion of life going on despite everything, while the seasons' passing, along with the bleak winter's day at the beginning, suggest time's inevitable passage. The narrative is exceptionally good where time becomes broken into pieces on the day of Phineas' operation and death: Gene's movements at 10:10, 11:00, 11:10, 12:00, 2:30, and 4:45 are like heartbeats, which stop with Phineas's heart.

Another of the novel's strengths is Knowles' remarkable economy of language. The key to many of the minor characters appears in a single phrase: Elwin 'Leper' Lepellier is "the person who was most often and most emphatically taken by surprise," while Brinker Hadley cannot, "for all his self-sufficiency … do much without company." Significant events occur almost as briefly, such as when Gene reads Leper's cryptic telegram and faces "in advance whatever the destruction was. That was what I learned to do that winter." Leper's description of Gene and Phineas on the tree limb is meticulous and evocative: "'The one holding on to the trunk sank for a second, up and down like a piston, and then the other one sank and fell.'" The last sentence of the novel, where Gene acknowledges the truth of humanity's inherent evil, is just as precise: "this enemy they thought they saw across the frontier, this enemy who never attacked that way—if he ever attacked at all; if he was indeed the enemy."

Knowles is a master of characterization, which we see best in his creation of Phineas who, as the epitome of careless grace, resembles the figurehead of a ship. Like Beowulf, Tarzan, and Hercules, Phineas has no last name; he is only Phineas. The name, which means "oracle" in Hebrew, has threefold Biblical significance. Phinehas, son of Aaron, was a judge and priest: Phineas constantly judges Gene, but always with complete integrity, and in the end offers him forgiveness. Phinehas, son of Eli, was a rebellious youth who redeemed himself by protecting the Ark: while Phineas too is rebellious, he redeems himself by embodying the essence of boyhood before the war, in his love of sport for its own sake—he breaks the swimming record simply for the challenge—and in his indefatigability, always displaying "a steady and formidable flow of usable energy." Finally, Phineas the angel was the youngest of the seventy-two angels of the Lord: like these traditional bearers of peace, Phineas is unfit for war because of his fundamental idealism. As Gene comments, once Phineas became bored with the war he'd be making friends with the enemy, chatting, and generally getting things "'so scrambled up nobody would know who to fight any more.'" His major role is as catalyst for Gene's developing personality. By presenting Gene with his utter uniqueness, Phineas forces him to grapple with questions of identity and to confront the unrealized depths of his own character.

Despite its many strengths, *A Separate Peace* contains a few flaws. Its detailed descriptions of setting are rarely well-integrated into the narrative. In addition, many of the minor characters (with the exception of Leper and Brinker) are poorly developed: Mr. Prud'homme appears as a foolish cipher, and the few women in the novel—such as the faculty wives, Leper's mother, or Hazel Brewster, the town belle—are mere stock characters. Furthermore, Knowles' symbolism falls short of its potential. While Gene implies that the tree holds great significance for him as something which is no longer intimidating or unique but to which he is still drawn, he goes no further with his speculations. However, this lack of development was intentional: as Knowles comments in his "The Young Writer's Real Friends," "If anything appeared which looked suspiciously like a symbol, I left it on its own …. I know that if I began with symbols, I would end with nothing; if I began with certain individuals I might end up by creating symbols." Finally, Gene's vantage point from fifteen years later is problematic, for it raises questions about the unreliability of his narrative and creates a disquieting sense of vagueness. We see Phineas only as Gene remembers him, thus Phineas is a construction of Gene's memory. In addition, Gene's refusal to pursue the question of whether or not he's truly changed is disturbing: while he insists he's improved since his days at school, noting his achievements of security and peace after having survived the war and gained worldly success, his tone suggests a lack of conviction. Moreover, though he implies that he's imbued some of Phineas' vitality, this doesn't appear in his narrative, and we're left to wonder whether he's really grown.

Nevertheless, Gene's narrative provides us with one valuable insight into the effects of humanity's unthinking tendencies. After the second accident, Phineas comments to Gene: "'It was just some kind of blind impulse you had in the tree there …. It wasn't anything you really felt against me, it wasn't some kind of hate you've felt all along. It wasn't anything personal.'" Here,

Knowles makes the point that it's exactly this sort of impulsive and impersonal action which causes war, death, and conflict in the world—and it happens constantly and repeatedly. Gene supports this notion, realizing that "wars were not made by generations and their special stupidities, but that wars were made instead by something ignorant in the human heart." This is what happened between him and Phineas, and what he believes happened to bring the world to war.

The real meaning of *A Separate Peace* lies in its title. Phineas' imaginary worlds create a peace separate from the world at war, and he invites others—and especially Gene—into this peaceful sphere. As the champion of Phineas' world, Gene delights in "this liberation we had torn from the gray encroachments of 1943, the escape we had concocted, this afternoon of momentary, illusory, special and separate peace." In the end, however, Gene arrives at his real peace—if he indeed does—apart from Phineas. Though he says that Finny's life and death taught him a way of living—"an atmosphere in which I continued now to live, a way of sizing up the world with erratic and entirely personal reservations"—he reaches this atmosphere only after separating himself from Phineas and finding his own identity. This process is ongoing, and entails Gene's acknowledgement that the real enemy is within himself and, indeed, within each of us: we're all liable to corruption from within by our own envy, anger, and fear. In the end, inner peace is achieved only after fighting one's own, private war of growing up. In this sense, the war is symbolic also of the inner struggle from adolescence to maturity.

Source: Anne Hiebert Alton, in an essay for *Novels for Students*, Gale, 1997.

David G. Holborn

In the following excerpt, Holborn describes A Separate Peace *as a novel about war, especially within the human heart.*

It is hard to imagine a book that has more to say to youth about to enter the conflict-ridden adult world than John Knowles' *A Separate Peace*. *Huck Finn* and *The Catcher in the Rye* come immediately to mind as forbears of this novel of maturation, and if Knowles lacks the range and dramatic intensity of Twain, he at least provides more answers than Salinger to the vexing problems of adolescence.

The novel is set at Devon, a small New England prep school, during the Second World War.

The details and atmosphere of such a school are re-alistically rendered in the dormitories and playing fields, the lawn parties and the truancies. Accuracy of fact and mood makes this an interesting and grip-ping story. But it is more than just a good story be-cause it has at least two other dimensions. From beginning to end little Devon is impinged upon by the world at war, so much so that the ordinary round of prep school activities takes on a militaristic fla-voring. Along with the outward pressures exerted by the war are the internal pressures, particularly in the narrator Gene, which lead to self-discovery and an acceptance of human ideals and human frail-ties. It is the integration of these three focuses that makes this such an effective and satisfying novel.

The novel opens with the narrator's return to Devon fifteen years after the action of the story he is about to tell. He presents two realistic scenes that later become associated with important events in the story: the First Academy Building, with its un-usually hard marble floors that cause the second break in Phineas's leg; and the tree, that real and symbolic tree which is the place of Finny's initial accident and the presentation of lost innocence. These detailed places occasion the narrator's med-itation, and suddenly through flashback we are transported to the idyllic summer of 1942. This framework narrative and flashback technique is im-portant because it sets up a vehicle for conveying judgments to the reader about character and action from two perspectives: sometimes we are getting Gene's reaction at the moment and other times we are receiving the retrospective judgment of the ma-ture man.

I mention this narrative technique not merely as a matter of literary style but as an indication of the serious, thoughtful quality of the novel. The au-thor wishes us to see the growth of Gene and at the same time experience an exciting story, not a philo-sophical or psychological tract. This is deftly ac-complished by means of the dual perspective. The following comment on the important motif of fear illustrates the mature man reflecting on the entire experience at Devon:

> Preserved along with it, like stale air in an unopened room, was the well-known fear which had surrounded and filled those days, so much of it that I hadn't even known it was there. Because, unfamiliar with the ab-sence of fear and what that was like, I had not been able to identify its presence.

> Looking back now across fifteen years, I could see with great clarity the fear I had lived in, which must mean that in the interval I had succeeded in a very

important undertaking: I must have made my escape from it.

This statement is more philosophical and judgmental than most later reflective statements, since at this point the story proper has not even be-gun. But the mature man is heard at intervals throughout the novel, as in this analogy of war to a wave:

> So the war swept over like a wave at the seashore, gathering power and size as it bore on us.... I did not stop to think that one wave is inevitably followed by another even larger and more powerful, when the tide is coming in.

Comments such as these encourage the reader to pause in the story and reflect on the significance of events, certainly an important thing to do with any novel but particularly with a novel of matura-tion.

The story proper begins in the summer of 1942. It is the calm before the storm, the storm of course being the world at war. For these boys—primarily Gene, Finny, and Leper—the war is still a year away. Even the faculty at Devon treat the reduced summer school class with a bemused tolerance. This summertime Devon is like Eden: the sun al-ways seems to shine, the days endlessly filled with games on the playing fields. This Eden also has its tree and, like the original, this is the tree of the knowledge of good and evil. At first, however, it is just a tree, something to jump from into the clear cool waters of the Devon River. As idyllic as this summer and this particular game of jumping from the tree are, hints of the impending war keep creep-ing in. Jumping from the tree becomes a test of courage, a kind of boot camp obstacle. So, taking a cue from war literature, the boys call their jump-ing group the Super Suicide Society of the Sum-mer Session. Always the consummate athlete, Finny jumps first with fluid grace and without ap-parent fear. Gene is reluctant, but cannot refuse the challenge. The two close buddies cement their friendship in this test. Leper, at least on this first occasion, does not jump. This foreshadows his later inability to cope with the pressures of the war. Al-ready the superficial harmony of the summer is dis-rupted by this competition which separates the boys according to those who possess the particular skills and temperament necessary in the world of war and those who don't. The scene is a preparation for the key event of the book where Finny breaks his leg, and an early reminder that Eden cannot really ex-ist in this world.

Certainly not all generations have had to face impending world war, but this fact does not lessen the relevance of this book for young readers today. Until recently, the nuclear threat was very much on the minds of our youth. While that threat has been greatly reduced, instant communications have made regional conflicts a part of the average family's daily viewing. Though this vicarious experience is not the same as Gene's and Finny's virtual certainty of going to war, most of today's young readers fear war and have a similar sense of a demon lurking in the woods beyond the playing fields, threatening at any moment to swallow them in their innocent play.

In *A Separate Peace,* however, Knowles plumbs more deeply than the war on the surface. We get hint after hint, culminating in Gene's and Finny's awareness of what really happened in the tree, that the war is also within, its battles waged in the individual breast and then subsequently between bosom buddies.

Gene and Finny have a special relationship but it is not immune—at least on Gene's part—from the petty jealousies that infect most relationships. In Gene's own words, Finny is "too good to be true." He plays games, like the blitzball he invented, for the sheer joy of exhibiting his remarkable athletic skills. He is a natural. One day he breaks the school swimming record in the hundred yard freestyle, with Gene as the only witness, but has no desire to repeat it in an official meet. The idea of having done it is enough. And because of his affability, he can talk his way out of almost any jam, as he did the day he was caught at the headmaster's lawn party wearing the school tie for a belt. One side of Gene admires Finny for these feats, while another, darker side envies him for his ability to glide through life unscathed. As Gene says about Finny after the party at the headmaster's:

> He had gotten away with everything. I felt a sudden stab of disappointment. That was because I just wanted to see some more excitement; that must have been it.

The last statement is a rationalization, and a weak one at that. Knowles lets the rationalization stand without a direct statement of truth from the older man's perspective, but the irony leaves no doubt as to Gene's true feelings. Surely any reader, and particularly the youthful one, can identify with this ambivalent reaction to a friend's success. In the end Gene comes to understand and accept these feelings, and the book as a whole makes the statement that only by becoming conscious of these feelings, and coming to terms with them, can a person

grow toward maturity. Refusing to face up to jealousies leads only to tragedies such as the one that occurs in this book.

Gene's envy of Finny comes to a head when he concludes wrongly that Finny is keeping him occupied with games so that his grades will suffer. Gene is the best student in the class and Finny the best athlete, but Gene thinks Finny wants him to jeopardize his supremacy in academics so Finny can shine more brightly. It is at this juncture in the book that the boys go off to the tree for what turns out to be the last meeting of the Super Suicide Society of the Summer Session.

The basic facts concerning Finny's fall from the tree that results in his broken leg are revealed in the first narration of the event, but the reader has to wait for the corroborating evidence presented by Leper months later at a mock trial, along with his peculiar emotional and artistic perception of the event. The facts as presented by Gene are that his knees bent and he "jounced the limb." It is impossible to know how much, if any, forethought was involved in the disastrous movement itself. What is clear from the juxtaposition of this event and the commentary that precedes it is that Gene reacts in some recess of his being, not, as we might have expected, to get back at Finny for hampering him in his studies, but out of a sudden awareness that Finny was not jealous of him, was not competing. It goes back to the statement that Finny is too good to be true. This is a particularly keen insight into the human heart; namely, that we often strike out at others not because of the harm they have done us but because their goodness sheds light on our own mistrustfulness.

In the case of Finny, his goodness is of a peculiar kind. He is not good from the faculty's point of view since he does not study very hard and breaks as many of the rules as he can. His is a kind of natural goodness, a harmoniousness with the sun, the earth and its seasons, and his fellow man— so long as his fellow man preserves his imagination and participates in Finny's rituals of celebration. It has justly been said that Finny is not a realistic character, yet he is an interesting one, and something more than a foil for Gene. Most readers have probably had childhood friends with some of the characteristics of Finny; it is in the sum of his part that he deviates from reality.

Finny is a character fated to die, not because of anything he does, or anything anyone does to him—though Gene's action against him is significant—but because of what he is and what the world is. If the idyllic summer could have lasted forever, then Finny could have lived a full life. If winter Olympic games could have taken the place of fighting troops on skis, then Finny's leg might have been made whole again. But the world is at war and the first casualties—Leper and Finny—are those whose beings are antithetical to the disruption that is war. Finny's harmoniousness cannot coexist with the dislocation of war. Gene humorously acknowledges this when he says:

> "They'd get you some place at the front and there'd be a lull in the fighting, and the next thing anyone knew you'd be over with the Germans or the Japs, asking if they'd like to field a baseball team against our side. You'd be sitting in one of their command posts, teaching them English. Yes, you'd get confused and borrow one of their uniforms, and you'd lend them one of yours. Sure, that's what would happen. You'd get things so scrambled up nobody would know who to fight anymore. You'd make a mess, a terrible mess, Finny, out of the war."

To Finny, the war was like blitzball, a free-flowing, individualistic game, with no allies and no enemies. To Gene, though he doesn't like to admit it, the war was all too real before he even got to it, so much so that his best friend became his enemy.

Leper, the character third in importance in the book, is the one most directly affected by the war and the one whose testimony at the mock trial seals the truth of the tree incident. Leper returns to Devon after having a nervous breakdown in boot camp. He is the most sensitive of all the boys, a loner and a lover of nature. His testimony not only confirms what actually happened in the tree, but also, through descriptive imagery, places the event in the context of the war. Leper's distracted mind remembers all the concrete details of the scene. Finny and Gene were in the tree and Leper was looking up, with the sun in his eyes, "and the rays of the sun were shooting past them, millions of rays shooting past them like—like golden machine-gun fire." And when the two in the tree moved, "they moved like an engine. The one holding on to the trunk sank for a second, up and down like a piston, and then the other one sank and fell." Leper, who previously saw the world in terms of snails and beaver dams, sees the action in the tree in terms of engines and machine-guns. This is because of what the war has done to him, and more subtly, it is a commentary on how a game in a tree has become a wartime battle. All three boys are pummelled by the machine of war, because, as the book seems to tell us, war is a condition of the human heart and soul.

The ultimate meaning of this book, and its universal message, is in this idea about war being something that is within us. Of the three characters discussed here, the war within is really only dramatized in Gene, but Gene is the representative boy; Leper and especially Finny are exceptions. Gene is our narrator and it is he with whom we identify. The war may flare out at various times and take on form in France or Germany, Korea or Vietnam, but when we look for the causes we should look first within. This concept ties together all the strands of the novel.

But as much as this is a book about war—within and without—it is also a book about peace. The human heart stripped naked to reveal its pride and jealousy, is a cause for sober reflection. But the title, *A Separate Peace,* encourages the reader to pass with Gene through the sufferings of war to achieve a peace. This peace is based upon understanding and the growth that follows such understanding. Finny achieves one kind of separate peace, the peace of death; it is left to Gene to achieve a separate peace that will allow him to live with himself and others in the adult world, chastened and strengthened by his mistake. His words at the end show us that he has succeeded:

> I never killed anybody and I never developed an intense level of hatred for the enemy. Because my war ended before I ever put on a uniform; I was on active duty all my time at school; I killed my enemy there.

This growth in awareness that leads Gene to his separate peace makes the ending of this book an optimistic one. Some readers seem to feel this book is another *Lord of the Flies,* a novel that depicts human nature when stripped of social institutions as reverting to a frighteningly depraved state. This is not the case in *A Separate Peace.* Once recognized and accepted the war within is tamed.

Furthermore, Knowles does not describe the weakness within as evil, but rather as a form of ignorance. After the mock trial, Gene tries to tell Finny what it was that caused him to jounce the limb: "It was just some ignorance inside me, some crazy thing inside me, something blind, that's all it was." One chapter later war is described in the same terms by the narrator: "Because it seemed clear that wars were not made by generations and their special stupidities, but that wars were made by something ignorant in the human heart." Most ignorance is not invincible; Gene proves this.

A Separate Peace is a novel that should be read by adolescents and adults alike, and it should be discussed openly. Jealousy, misunderstanding, and fear do indeed breed violence when they are kept within. Or they can be liberated, not once and for all perhaps, but over and over again if they are seen for what they are in the light of day. This is all we know of peace in this world.

Source: David G. Holborn, "A Rationale for Reading John Knowles' *A Separate Peace*," in *Censored Books: Critical Viewpoints*, Nicholas J. Karolides, Lee Burress, John M. Kean, eds., The Scarecrow Press, Inc., 1993, pp. 456–63.

Marvin E. Mengeling

In the following excerpt, Mengeling examines allusions to classical myth, particularly Greek mythology, in A Separate Peace.

There is an obvious pattern of Greek allusions in *A Separate Peace*. At one important point Phineas is described as "Greek inspired and Olympian." He is athletic and beautiful, blazing with "sunburned health." He walks before Gene in a "continuous flowing balance" that acknowledges an "unemphatic unity of strength." Though Gene, as any boy his age, is often given to imaginative hyperbole (as we all are when our Gods are involved), there is no doubt that to him and the other boys Phineas is "unique." Behind his "controlled ease" there rests the "strength of five people." And even if he cannot carry a tune as well as he carries other people, Phineas loves all music, for in it, as in the sea and all nature, he seems to sense the basic beat of life, health, and regeneration. His voice carries a musical undertone. It is as naked and sincere as his emotions. Only Phineas has what to Gene is a "shocking self-acceptance." Only Phineas never really lies.

At the beginning of the book Phineas sets the stage for his own special function. On forcing Gene out of the tree for the first time, he says, "I'm good for you that way. You tend to back away otherwise." Phineas knows that Gene must jump from the tree, because in some cryptic fashion which only he seems to understand, they are "getting ready for the war." Among the Devon boys only Phineas knows that they must be conforming in every possible way to what is happening and what is going to happen in the general warfare of life. The first necessary step toward successful confrontation of what is going to happen rests in self-knowledge.

One cold winter morning, after Finny's "accident," Gene is running a large circle around Phineas, being trained, as Phineas puts it, for the 1944 Olympic Games. With his broken leg Phineas

knows that the Games are closed to himself; he will have to participate through Gene, who was always as disinterested in sports as Phineas seemed to be in his studies. Gene is huffing, his body and lungs wracked with tiring pains that hit like knife thrusts. "Then," he says, "for no reason at all, I felt magnificent. It was as though my body until that instant had simply been lazy, as though the aches and exhaustion were all imagined, created from nothing in order to keep me from truly exerting myself. Now my body seemed at last, to say, 'Well, if you must have it, here!' and an accession of strength came flooding through me. Buoyed up, I forgot my usual feeling of routine self-pity when working out, I lost myself, oppressed mind along with aching body; all entanglements were shed, I broke into the clear." After finishing the grueling run Gene and his Olympian coach have the following significant and two-leveled conversation:

Phineas: You found your rhythm, didn't you, that third time around. Just as you came into that straight part there.

Gene: Yes, right there.

Phineas: You've been pretty lazy all along, haven't you?

Gene: Yes, I guess I have been.

Phineas: You didn't even know anything about yourself.

Gene: I don't guess I did, in a way.

At one point Gene decides that Phineas' seemingly irrepressible mind (he ignored many of the small rules of behavior at Devon) was not completely unleashed, that he did abide by certain rules of conduct "cast in the form of Commandments." One rule is that you should not lie. Another is that one should always pray because there just might be a God. And there is the idea that is the key to the entire Phineas outlook: that "You always win at sport." To Phineas, sports were the absolute good, the measure of the balanced life. The significance that eludes Gene at this point, as it eludes most people everywhere today, is that everyone *can* and *should* win at sports, because in the Greek view of Phineas sports are not so much a competition against others—a matter of pride and winning at any cost—but a competition against oneself, a healthy struggle in which one measures his capacities without ego, fear, or *hubris*. We easily identify with Gene's total disbelief when Phineas privately shatters a school swimming record but wishes no public recognition. He says, "I just wanted to see if I could do it. Now I know." This is the Olympic Games spirit as it should be and as it perhaps once was. Phineas adds, "when they discovered the circle they created sports." And when they discovered the circle they also created the universal symbol for the whole man.

Using classical myth as a tool for understanding the present is hardly new to literature. James Joyce, for one, demonstrated with genius its relevance to modern life and art. In *A Separate Peace,* myth is molded and altered when necessary to fit Knowles' dramatic purposes. The episode concerning the Devon Winter Carnival, that special artistic creation of Phineas, not only provides excellent examples of Knowles' mythological method, but is thematically very important as marking the symbolic point of passage for the Olympic spirit—its flame of life—from Phineas to Gene. It is during the carnival scene that Phineas, leg in cast, dances a rapturous and wild bacchanal, his special, and last, "choreography of peace." For the briefest of moments in a drab world's drabbest season Phineas creates a world of Dionysian celebration that infuses Gene with divine enthusiasm. At this point, Knowles chooses to blend the figure of the young Phoebus Apollo (Phineas before the fall) with that of the resurrected Dionysus (Phineas after his fall; who has finally discovered what "suffering" is).

In ancient Greece the Dionysian festival began in the spring of the year with Greek women travelling into the hills to be "reborn" again through mystical union with the God of Wine. They danced, they drank, they leaped in wild frenzy as all restraint melted away. At the center of the ceremony they seized a goat, perhaps a bull, sometimes a man (all believed to be incarnations of Dionysus), and tore the live victim to shreds. A ceremony of pagan communion followed in which the victim's blood was quaffed and the flesh eaten, whereby the communicants thought their souls would be entered and possessed by their resurrected god. Knowles surely bore in mind the festival of Dionysus when erecting his superb carnival scene. In a sense, this invention of Phineas marks his resurrection, for it is the first project in which he has exhibited personal interest since his fall. At last, though briefly, the "old" Phineas seems to have returned somewhat in body and spirit. Amid a scene of mayhem, in which "there was going to be no government, even by whim," the boys circle around Brinker Hadley, throw themselves upon him, and forcibly take his jealously guarded cache of hard cider. They drink, they dance, they throw off the fear and "violence latent in the day," losing themselves completely in the festival of Phineas. Then, with the burning of

Homer's book of war, *The Iliad,* a specialized version of the Olympic Games begins, a somewhat nicer type of "warfare." Soon, from the monarch's chair of black walnut—whose regal legs and arms end in the paws and heads of lions—Phineas rises to full height on the prize table, and at the "hub" of the proceedings begins his wild bacchanal. Gene says that "Under the influence not I know of the hardest cider but of his own inner joy at life for a moment as it should be, as it was meant to be in his nature, Phineas recaptured that magic gift for existing primarily in space, one foot conceding briefly to gravity its rights before spinning him off again into the air. It was his wildest demonstration of himself, of himself in the kind of world he loved; it was his choreography of peace."

Prior to the Carnival, Gene says he had acted simply as a "Chorus" to Phineas, but now the beautiful boy-god, sitting amid the tabled prizes, makes a request of Gene: on a physical level, to qualify for their Olympic Games; on a spiritual level, to qualify for salvation. During the past weeks Gene has made the Phineas outlook and spirit more and more a part of his own, and so infused, he now reacts to the request in the only way possible: "...it wasn't cider which made me in this moment champion of everything he ordered, to run as though I were the abstraction of speed, to walk the half-circle of statues on my hands, to balance on my head on top of the icebox on top of the Prize Table, to jump if he had asked it across the Naguamsett and land crashing in the middle of Quackenbush's boat house, to accept at the end of it amid a clatter of applause—for this day even the schoolboy egotism of Devon was conjured away—a wreath made from the evergreen trees which Phineas placed on my head."

Somehow, Gene has mystically been passed the saving spirit and Code of Phineas. His new growth and knowledge are immediately tested. The Carnival ends prematurely when Gene receives an ominous telegram from Leper Lepellier asking Gene to come to his winter-bound home in Vermont. Gene suspects that the fruits of such an isolated meeting will not be pleasant ones, but he also knows that he must sometimes face certain harsh realities alone, even if only a little at a time. Also, he realizes that he has a chance to endure now, for the influence of Phineas, god of sun, light, and truth, is always with him. As he finally approaches Leper's house he thinks that, like Phineas, "The sun was the blessing of the morning, the one celebrating element, an aesthete with no purpose except to shed radiance. Everything else was sharp and hard, but this *Grecian sun* (my italics) evoked joy from every angularity and blurred with brightness the stiff face of the countryside. As I walked briskly out the road the wind knifed at my face, but this sun caressed the back of my neck."

Now Gene does not immediately dash away when learning the grim tale of Leper's Section-Eight. The summer before Gene would have run quickly from such unpleasantness back to the maternal and more secure confines of old Devon, but now he needs "too much to know the facts," and though he finally does run away in the "failing sunshine" from the horrible details of Leper's casualty, he has shown strong signs of significant progress. "I had had many new experiences," Gene says, "and I was growing up."

Physically, Phineas dies. The reasons are twofold. All gods must die physically; it is in their nature to be spiritual, and in the case of many, sacrificial. Phineas dies that Gene might live. Second, Phineas must be crushed physically to emphasize that the present world is really no place for the full-blown powers and principles which he represents in his symbolic guise of Phoebus Apollo. Changes in man's psychological makeup do not erupt like some overnight volcano of the sea. Such transition is always painfully slow, necessarily too slow. But perhaps now, in a ruptured world that is heaped with war's unromantic statistics and computerized cruelties, humanity will choose to reemerge from its emotional rubble. Gene always had the brilliance, the IQ, the "brains," but they were untempered by a proper emotional stance. He had envy and he had great fear. He had no balance. Phineas disappears in a physical sense, but his spiritual influence, a portion of his code, will endure in Gene—a tiny spark in the darkness searching for human tinder. The spirit of Apollo has possessed its prophet and will now speak through his mouth. Gene's self has become "Phineas-filled," and to Gene, Phineas was "present in every moment of every day" since he died. First Gene and then perhaps a few others will relearn the road to Greece. "I was ready for the war," Gene says, "now that I no longer had any hatred to contribute to it. My fury was gone, I felt it gone, dried up at the source, withered and lifeless. Phineas had absorbed it and taken it with him, and I was rid of it forever." Even fifteen years later when Gene returns to Devon he approaches the school down a street lined with houses to him reminiscent of "Greek Revival tempes." The cause of wars within and without the individual, that "something ignorant in the human heart," has now been exorcised.

The purgated emotions of negative content had been fear, jealousy, and hate, emotions which result in wars both personal and global. The positive emotions which then must replace them are friendship, loyalty, and love toward all mankind and nature, emotions which result in peace and an appreciation of life and its beauty. Even though Phineas had broken every minor and stuffy Devon regulation, never had a student seemed to love the school more "truly and deeply." Edith Hamilton writes in *The Greek Way* that "To rejoice in life, to find the world beautiful and delightful to live in, was a mark of the Greek spirit which distinguished it from all that had gone before. It is a vital distinction." So although the world is not yet ready for the apotheosis of some golden Greek Apollo, perhaps it is prepared, after its most recent blood gluts and promises of human extinction, for the first faltering step toward a world full of the Phineas-filled, a step which must necessarily begin with the conquering of a small part of the forest of self—a step toward the far frontiers of ancient Greece.

Source: Marvin E. Mengeling, " *A Separate Peace:* Meaning and Myth," in *English Journal,* Vol. 58, No. 9, December, 1969, pp. 1322–29.

Sources

Douglas Alley, "Teaching Emerson Through 'A Separate Peace,'" in *English Journal,* January, 1981, pp. 19-23.

Hallman Bell Bryant, *"A Separate Peace": The War Within,* Twayne, 1990.

John K. Crabbe, "On the Playing Fields of Devon," in *English Journal,* Vol. 58, 1969, pp. 519-20.

Anne Duchene, in a review of *A Separate Peace* in *Manchester Guardian,* May 1, 1959.

James Ellis, "'A Separate Peace': A Fall From Innocence," in *English Journal,* May, 1964, pp. 313-18.

Edmund Fuller, "Shadow of Mars," in *New York Times Book Review,* February 7, 1960.

Linda Heinz, "'A Separate Peace': Filming the War Within," in *Literature Film Quarterly,* No. 3, 1975, p. 168.

John Knowles, "The Young Writer's Real Friends," *The Writer,* Vol. 75, July, 1962, pp. 12-14.

John Knowles, "My Separate Peace," in *Esquire,* March, 1985, pp. 106–09.

James M. Mellard, "Counterpoint and 'Double Vision' in 'A Separate Peace'," in *Studies in Short Fiction,* No. 4, 1966, pp. 127-35.

J. Noffsinger, A. M. Rice, et al. "Still Good Reading: Adolescent Novels Written Before 1967," *English Journal,* April, 1992, p. 7.

A review of *A Separate Peace,* in *Commonweal,* December 9, 1960.

A review of *A Separate Peace,* in *Times Literary Supplement,* May 1, 1959.

Ronald Weber, "Narrative Method in 'A Separate Peace'," in *Studies in Short Fiction 3,* 1965, pp. 63-72.

For Further Study

Hallman Bell Bryant, "Symbolic Names in Knowles's *A Separate Peace,*" in *Names,* Vol. 34, No. 1, March, 1986, pp. 83-8.

An analysis of some of the character's names in the novel.

Concise Dictionary of Literary Biography Broadening Views, 1968-1988, Gale, 1989, pp. 120-35.

Biographical information on John Knowles and his work. Includes revised typescript from one of Knowles's works.

Jay L. Halio, "John Knowles's Short Novels," *Studies in Short Fiction* Vol. I, Winter, 1964, pp. 107-09.

A survey of several of Knowles's shorter novels.

Granville Hicks, "The Good Have a Quiet Heroism," in *Saturday Review,* March 5, 1960, p. 15.

Early review which praises *A Separate Peace,* and analyzes Finny's character, concluding he is not really a hero.

Isabel Quigly, *The Heirs of Tom Brown: The English School Story,* Oxford University Press, 1984.

This book-length study looks at the genre of the "school story" and is useful in an analysis of Knowles's novel as it fits into this genre.

Michael-George Sarotte, *Like a Brother, Like a Lover,* Doubleday, 1978.

In this book-length study of male homosexuality in literature, Sarotte argues that Gene's suppressed homoerotic emotions for Finny are integral to his character.

Things Fall Apart

Chinua Achebe

1958

The story of Chinua Achebe's novel *Things Fall Apart* takes place in the Nigerian village of Umuofia in the late 1880s, before missionaries and other outsiders have arrived. The Ibo clan practices common tribal traditions—worship of gods, sacrifice, communal living, war, and magic. Leadership is based on a man's personal worth and his contribution to the good of the tribe. Okonkwo stands out as a great leader of the Ibo tribe. Tribesmen respect Okonkwo for his many achievements.

Even though the tribe reveres Okonkwo, he must be punished for his accidental shooting of a young tribesman. The Ibo ban Okonkwo from the clan for seven years. Upon his return to the village, Okonkwo finds a tribe divided by the influence of missionaries and English bureaucrats who have interrupted the routine of tradition. Only when Okonkwo commits the ultimate sin against the tribe does the tribe come back together to honor custom.

Critics appreciate Achebe's development of the conflict that arises when tradition clashes with change. He uses his characters and their unique language to portray the double tragedies that occur in the story. Readers identify not only with Okonkwo and his personal hardships but also with the Ibo culture and its disintegration. Chinua Achebe wrote *Things Fall Apart* not for his fellow Nigerians, but for people beyond his native country. He wanted to explain the truth about the effects of losing one's culture. Published in 1958, the book was not widely read by Nigerians or by Africans in general. When Nigeria became independent in 1960, however,

Africans appreciated the novel for its important contribution to Nigerian history.

Author Biography

Chinua Achebe is a world-renowned scholar recognized for his ability to write simply, yet eloquently, about life's universal qualities. His writing weaves together history and fiction to produce a literary broadcloth that offers visions of people enduring real life. Critics appreciate his just and realistic treatment of his topics.

Achebe writes primarily about his native Africa, where he was born Albert Chinualumogu Achebe in 1930. He grew up in Ogidi, Nigeria, one of the first centers of Anglican missionary work in Eastern Nigeria. His father and mother, Isaiah and Janet Achebe, were missionary teachers. Achebe's life as a Christian and member of the Ibo tribe enables him to create realistic depictions of both contemporary and pre-colonized Africa. He blends his knowledge of Western political ideologies and Christian doctrine with folklore, proverbs, and idioms from his native tribe to produce stories of African culture that are intimate and authentic.

Achebe left the village of Ogidi to attend Government College in Umuahia, and later, University College in Ibadan. He received his Bachelor of Arts degree from University College in 1953. He worked first for the Nigerian Broadcasting Corporation as a writer and continued radio work in various capacities until 1966, when he resigned from his post as Director of External Broadcasting. Dissatisfied with the political climate that would later prompt the Biafran War, he began traveling abroad and lectured as the appointed Senior Research Fellow for the University of Nigeria, Nsukka.

Continuing his teaching career, Achebe accepted a position with the University of Massachusetts, Amherst, in 1972. He was a visiting Professor of English at that institution until 1976 and again in 1987-1988. He also spent a year as a visiting professor at the University of Connecticut. In the intervening years, Achebe returned to his native country to teach at the University of Nigeria, Nsukka.

Achebe has written extensively throughout his adult life. His numerous articles, novels, short stories, essays, and children's books have earned prestigious awards. For example, his book of poetry *Christmas in Biafra* was a winner of the first Commonwealth Poetry Prize. His novels *Arrow of God* and *Anthills of the Savannah* won, respectively, the

Chinua Achebe

New Statesman-Jock Campbell Award and finalist for the 1987 Booker Prize in England.

Achebe continues to write and participate in scholarly activities throughout the world, while making his home in Annandale, New York, with his wife, Christie. They have four children and teach at Bard College.

Plot Summary

Part I—Okonkwo's Rise to Fame

Achebe's *Things Fall Apart* describes the tragic demise of an Ibo man named Okonkwo. Initially, Okonkwo rises from humble origins to become a powerful leader in Umuofia, a rural village in southeastern Nigeria. As Okonkwo climbs the ladder to success, however, it becomes apparent that his strengths are also his weaknesses: his self-confidence becomes pride, his manliness develops into authoritarianism, and his physical strength eventually turns into uncontrolled rage. In a broader sense, Achebe sets this story about Okonkwo at the end of the nineteenth century, when Europeans first began colonizing this region of Nigeria on a large scale. By so doing, Achebe establishes a parallel between Okonkwo's personal tragedy and colonialism's tragic destruction of native African cultures.

The first section of the novel describes Okonkwo's rise to a position of power. Determined to overcome the unmanly and unsuccessful example of his father, Unoka, Okonkwo develops a strength and determination unmatched among his peers. These attributes enable him to become a great wrestler, strong warrior, wealthy farmer, and prestigious member of his community. As the Umuofians notice his extraordinary talents, they reward him with numerous titles and honors. For example, they make him the guardian of Ikemefuna, a young boy awarded to Umuofia as compensation for wrongs committed by a neighboring village. Similarly, when Okonkwo starts a farm, he receives a generous loan of 800 yams from Nwakibie, a wealthy farmer. Nwakibie is willing to loan these yams to Okonkwo because he knows that Okonkwo will succeed. Okonkwo proves his ability to succeed by surviving even after a terrible drought destroys his crops. Undaunted by either his humble origins or the forces of nature, Okonkwo soon becomes one of the most successful and well respected men in Umuofia.

Okonkwo's success, however, quickly begins to lead toward his ultimate downfall. Because he is so successful, he has little patience with unsuccessful and "unmanly" men like his father. In fact, he publicly insults Osugo, a less successful man, by calling him a woman during a kindred meeting. Not only does Okonkwo's success lead to conflicts with other members of the village, but it also drastically disrupts his ability to rule his own family. Because of his autocratic style of ruling and impulsive anger, his own family fears him. In fact, his own son, Nwoye, eventually rejects him, much like Okonkwo had rejected his own father earlier—only Nwoye rejects Okonkwo for being excessively masculine, whereas Okonkwo rejected Unoka for not being manly enough. Even more significantly, Okonkwo's hasty temper provokes him to beat his third wife, Ojiugo, during the sacred Week of Peace, a festival time during which Ibo custom strictly forbids any form of violence. Okonkwo commits his worst crime, however, when he participates in the sacrifice of Ikemefuna. After Okonkwo had raised Ikemefuna as his own son for several years, an Oracle required that the Umuofians sacrifice Ikemefuna. Because Okonkwo had been like a father to Ikemefuna, Okonkwo's friend Ezeudu warns him not to participate in the sacrifice. When the rest of the men begin sacrificing Ikemefuna, however, Okonkwo disregards Ezeudu's advice and participates in the sacrifice because he fears that the others might consider him

unmanly. When Nwoye eventually finds out about Ikemefuna's death, he has a serious crisis that causes him to question not only his father's example but also the customs and beliefs of his people.

Despite Okonkwo's numerous violations of custom and violent behavior, he ultimately loses his prestigious position in Umuofia not because of his misdeeds but because of an accident. During Ezeudu's funeral ceremony, his gun misfires and accidentally kills a boy. Ironically, it is for this accident rather than for his numerous misdeeds that the Umuofians burn down Okonkwo's home and exile him for a period of seven years.

Part II—Okonkwo's Exile to Mbanta

After being exiled from Umuofia, Okonkwo seeks refuge among his mother's kinsmen in Mbanta, a neighboring village. During this time, the British begin colonizing the surrounding areas, and this begins a vicious cycle of mutual confrontation as the two cultures clash. For example, the inhabitants of Abame kill the first white man who arrives in their city because they fear him and cannot communicate with him, and the British destroy Abame in retaliation for this murder. Christian missionaries also begin arriving in Umuofia and Mbanta, and they hold debates to gain converts. Most of the people are not interested in the missionaries' religion, but a few people, including Okonkwo's son Nwoye, convert. When Okonkwo finds out about Nwoye's conversion, he becomes enraged and disowns Nwoye. Toward the end of Okonkwo's exile, the tensions between the village and the missionaries escalate when the Christian converts kill a sacred python and the tribe retaliates by ostracizing the Christians. After Okonkwo's period of exile ends, he holds a great feast to thank his relatives, and he begins making preparations for his return to Umuofia.

Part III—Okonkwo's Return to Umuofia

In the final section, Okonkwo returns from exile with hopes of reclaiming a position of power in Umuofia, but Umuofia has changed drastically since the arrival of the Europeans. The first missionary in Umuofia, Mr. Brown, won the people's admiration because he respected their customs and developed personal relationships with them. When Mr. Brown has to leave for health reasons, however, he is replaced by the Reverend James Smith, an ethnocentric zealot who stirs up deep antagonism between the new Christian converts and the rest of the town. These tensions finally explode when Enoch, an overzealous new convert, eats a sacred python and publicly unmasks an egwugwu spirit. The Umuofians avenge Enoch's blasphemies by burning down the Christian church, and the British retaliate in turn by arresting the leaders of Umuofia and fining them 200 bags of cowries.

The Umuofians pay the fine, but the leaders are angered by the duplicitous and unjust manner in which the District Commissioner treated them. Consequently, they hold a meeting to decide how to respond. The village is divided as to whether they should ignore this injustice or retaliate with violence, but Okonkwo has made up his mind that he will oppose British colonization even if nobody else will join him. When a messenger from the government arrives to stop their meeting, Okonkwo kills the messenger, and the meeting ends in chaos.

The next day the District Commissioner himself comes to arrest Okonkwo, but Okonkwo has already committed suicide. The people of Umuofia ask the commissioner to bury Okonkwo because it is against their custom to bury a man who has committed suicide. The commissioner orders his men to take down Okonkwo's body because he has an interest in African customs, but he refuses to help personally because he fears that cutting down a dead body might give the natives a poor opinion of him. Achebe's bitterly ironic conclusion to the novel describes the District Commissioner's callous response to Okonkwo's tragedy.

> In the many years that he had toiled to bring civilization to different parts of Africa he had learnt a number of things. One of them was that a District Commissioner must never attend to such undignified details as cutting down a hanged man from the trees. Such attention would give the natives a poor opinion of him. In the book which he planned to write he would stress that point. As he walked back to the court he thought about that book. Every day brought him some new material. The story of this man who had killed a messenger and hanged himself would make interesting reading. One could almost write a whole chapter on him. Perhaps not a whole chapter but a reasonable paragraph, at any rate. There was so much else to include, and one must be firm in cutting out the details. He had already chosen the title of the book, after much thought: *The Pacification of the Primitive Tribes of the Lower Niger.*

Ironically, the District Commissioner thinks that he has helped pacify the "primitive" tribes of the Lower Niger, but he is blind to his complicity in destroying these tribes and provoking the chain of events leading to Okonkwo's suicide. The District Commissioner's thoughts are doubly ironic because he claims to understand Africa enough to write a history of it, but he remains thoroughly ig- norant of the people he intends to write about. Okonkwo's tragic demise, like the tragic destruction of indigenous African people and their traditions, is a long and complex history. Unfortunately, the District Commissioner only sees it as a mere paragraph. For far too long, Europeans like the District Commissioner have ignored and misrepresented the history of Africa, but Achebe's *Things Fall Apart* begins to correct the historical record by retelling the conquest of Africa from Okonkwo's African perspective rather than the District Commissioner's European one.

Characters

Mr. Brown

The first white missionary to come to Umuofia, Mr. Brown gains the clan's respect through his calm nature and patience. He neither attacks the tribe's customs nor badgers them to join him. He restrains his overzealous members from harsh tactics. He simply offers education to the Umuofians and their children. The mission is flourishing when Mr. Brown has to leave for health reasons.

The District Commissioner

The District Commissioner arrives in Umuofia at the same time as the missionaries. He and his court messengers—called "Ashy-Buttocks" for the ash-colored shorts they wear—try clansmen for breaking the white man's law. These white men are greatly hated for their arrogance and disrespect for tribal customs.

Ekwefi

Ekwefi, forty-five years old, is Okonkwo's second wife. Although she fell in love with Okonkwo when he won the famous wrestling match, she did not move in with him until she left her husband three years after the contest. Ekwefi had been lovely in her youth, referred to as "Crystal of Beauty." The years have been hard on her. She has become a courageous and strong-willed woman, overcoming disappointment and bitterness in her life. She has borne ten children, only one of whom has lived. She stands up to Okonkwo and lives for her daughter, Ezinma.

Enoch

Enoch is an overzealous member of Mr. Brown's mission. While Mr. Brown restrains Enoch from taking his faith to extremes, Mr. Smith does not. Mr. Smith not only condones Enoch's ex-

Ibo children dancing, 1970.

cessive actions, he encourages them. Enoch instigates the battle between Umuofia and the church by unmasking an egwugwu, or ancestor spirit, during a public ceremony. This is one of the greatest crimes a man could commit.

Ogbuefi Ezeudu

A noble warrior and the oldest man in all the village, Ogbuefi Ezeudu has achieved a rare three titles. He is the one to tell Okonkwo that the tribe has decided to kill Ikemefuna. Ezeudu warns Okonkwo not to be a part of Ikemefuna's death.

At Ezeudu's death, the clan gathers to bid a final sacred tribute to a man who has nearly attained the highest tribal honor—lord of the land. When Okonkwo accidentally kills Ezeudu's son during the ceremony, the clan is horrified. Okonkwo can think only of Ezeudu's warning.

Ezinma

Ekwefi lives for Ezinma, her only living child, her pride and joy. Okonkwo favors his daughter, who is not only as beautiful as her mother once was, but who grows to understand her father and his moods as no one else does. Father and daughter form a special bond. Okonkwo and Ekwefi treat Ezinma like she is their equal rather than their child. They permit her privileges that other family and tribal children are not granted. Okonkwo's only regret towards Ezinma is that she is not a boy.

Ikemefuna

Ikemefuna comes to live with Okonkwo's family as a peace offering from Ikemefuna's home tribe to the Ibo for the killing of a Umuofian daughter. From the beginning, Ikemefuna fills the void in Okonkwo's life that Okonkwo's own son cannot.

Ikemefuna adjusts quickly to his new family and tribe and energetically participates in activities. He earns everyone's love and respect because he is so lively and talented. Only two years older than Nwoye, Ikemefuna already knows much about the world and can do almost anything. He can identify birds, trap rodents, and make flutes. He knows which trees make the best bows and tells delightful folk stories. Okonkwo appreciates Ikemefuna for the example he sets for Nwoye.

Ikemefuna lives with Okonkwo for three years. The tribe then agrees to kill Ikemefuna because the Oracle of the Hills and the Caves has requested it. Ikemefuna's death brings far-reaching consequences.

Nwoye

Okonkwo's son, Nwoye, disappoints him. Nwoye shows all the signs of his grandfather's sensitivity and laziness, and Okonkwo fears that Nwoye will shame the reputable name Okonkwo has worked so hard to achieve. Nwoye knows that he should enjoy the masculine rites of his fellow tribesmen, but he prefers his mother's company and the stories she tells. He questions and is disturbed by many of the tribe's customs. Okonkwo beats and nags Nwoye, making Nwoye more unhappy and further distancing him from the ways of the clan.

When Ikemefuna comes to live with Okonkwo's family, Nwoye grows to admire his knowledge and to love him like a real brother. Out of his respect for Ikemefuna, Nwoye begins to associate more with the men of the family and tribe, and to act more like the man that his father wants him to become.

After Ikemefuna's death, Nwoye feels an emptiness that cannot be filled by the clan's traditions. He is plagued by old questions for which the clan has no answers.

Nwoye's mother

Okonkwo's first wife, Nwoye's mother is wise to the ways of the tribe. While she knows that her sons will never be able to display such emotions, she tells her children wonderful stories that describe feelings like pity and forgiveness. She attempts to keep peace in the family by lying to Okonkwo at times to help the other wives avoid punishment. She tries to adhere to sacred tribal customs. She shows compassion at the message that Ikemefuna is to return to his family. In her own way, Nwoye's mother displays the courage of a tribesman.

Obierika

Obierika is Okonkwo's best friend. Unlike Okonkwo, he is a thinking man. He questions the circumstances that are sending his friend into exile, even while trying to console Okonkwo and taking care of Okonkwo's preparation for departure. Obierika is the one who visits Okonkwo while Okonkwo is exiled. He brings him the first news of the missionaries' arrival, knowing that Okonkwo's son has joined them. At the end of the seven-year exile, Obierika builds Okonkwo two huts and sends for him. Finally, a sad and weary Obierika bids a last tribute to his friend when he leads the diminishing clansmen through the rituals required to cleanse the land Okonkwo has desecrated.

Ojiugo

Ojiugo is Okonkwo's third and youngest wife. She evokes Okonkwo's anger through thoughtless acts and prompts him to break the sacred Week of Peace. As a result, the priest of the earth goddess punishes Okonkwo.

Okonkwo

Out of awe and respect, the Ibo tribe refers to Okonkwo as "Roaring Flame." Fiery of temper with a blazing appearance, Okonkwo strikes fear in the hearts of his clan members as well as his own family unit. Okonkwo's huge build, topped by bushy eyebrows and a very broad nose, give him the look of a tornado on the warpath. His whole demeanor reeks of controlled fury; he even breathes heavily, like a dragon ready to explode. He always appears to be wound for fierce action.

While Okonkwo's appearance portrays a man people fear, it belies the terror Okonkwo hides within himself. For his entire life, Okonkwo has had to deal with having a father who is considered weak and lazy—"agabala" in the tribe's terms. The tribe detests weak, effeminate men. Okonkwo is terrified to think that the tribe will liken him to his father. He is even more afraid of recognizing in himself some semblance of weakness that he sees in his father. Thus, he despises gentleness, idleness, and demonstrations of sensitivity. He will not allow himself to show love, to enjoy the fruits of hard work, or to demonstrate concern for others, nor can he tolerate these in other men. He rules his family unit with an iron fist and expects everyone to act on his commands. He speaks curtly to those he considers less successful than himself and dismisses them as unimportant. An extremely proud man, Okonkwo continually pushes to overcome the image his heredity might have given him.

The tribe sees Okonkwo as powerful. They respect him for his many achievements. Not only has he overcome his father's weaknesses, but also he has accomplished more than the average tribesman. As a young man, he wrestles and beats one of the fiercest fighters in the land. Next, Okonkwo goes on to amass three wives and two barns full of yams. Then, he acquires two titles and is considered the greatest warrior alive.

Mr. Smith

See Reverend James Smith

Reverend James Smith

Mr. Smith replaces Mr. Brown when Mr. Brown has to leave the mission. The Reverend Smith leads the overzealous with a passion. Where Mr. Brown was mild-mannered and quiet, Mr. Smith is angry and flamboyant. He denounces the tribe's customs and bans from his church clan members who must be, according to him, filled with the devil's spirit to want to continue tribal tradition.

Ogbuefi Ugonna

A worthy tribesman of two titles, Ogbuefi Ugonna is one of the first of the village men to receive the sacrament of Holy Communion offered by the Christian missionaries.

Unoka

Unoka is Okonkwo's father, the root of Okonkwo's fear and problems. Unoka represents all that the Ibo abhor—gentleness, lack of ambition, and sensitivity to people and nature. He is a gifted musician who loves fellowship, the change of the seasons, and children. Although Unoka is tall, his stooped posture bears the weight of the tribe's scorn.

Unoka is happy only when he is playing his flute and drinking palm wine. Tribal customs frighten, sicken, and bore him. He hates war and is nauseated by the sight of blood. He would rather make music than grow crops. As a result, his family is more often hungry than not, and he borrows constantly from fellow tribesmen to maintain his household. He dies in disgrace, owing everyone and holding no titles.

Themes

Custom and Tradition

Okonkwo's struggle to live up to what he perceives as "traditional" standards of masculinity, and his failure adapt to a changing world, help point out the importance of custom and tradition in the novel. The Ibo tribe defines itself through the age-old traditions it practices in *Things Fall Apart*. While some habits mold tribe members' daily lives, other customs are reserved for special ceremonies. For example, the head of a household honors any male guest by praying over and sharing a kola nut with him, offering the guest the privilege of breaking the nut. They drink palm-wine together, with the oldest person taking the first drink after the provider has tasted it.

Ceremonial customs are more elaborate. The Feast of the New Yam provides an illustration. This Feast gives the tribe an opportunity to thank Ani, the earth goddess and source of all fertility. Preparations for the Feast include thorough hut-cleaning and decorating, cooking, body painting, and head shaving. Relatives come from great distances to partake in the feast and to drink palm-wine. Then, on the second day of the celebration, the great wrestling match is held. The entire village meets in the village playground, or ilo, for the drumming, dancing, and wrestling. The festival continues through the night until the final round is won. Because the tribe views winning a match as a great achievement, the winner earns the tribe's ongoing respect.

Tribal custom dictates every aspect of members' lives. The tribe determines a man's worth by the number of titles he holds, the number of wives he acquires, and the number of yams he grows. The tribe acknowledges a man's very being by the gods' approval of him. Without custom and tradition, the tribe does not exist.

Choices and Consequences

In *Things Fall Apart,* Okonkwo makes a choice early in life to overcome his father's legacy. As a result, Okonkwo gains the tribe's respect through his constant hard work. The tribe rewards him by recognizing his achievements and honoring him as a great warrior. The tribe believes that

Topics For Further Study

- How does the displacement from one's culture affect a person psychologically? Explain possible reactions a person might have and the steps someone might take to help him or her adjust.

- School integration is being attempted across America. How successful has it been? Cite specific examples, such as court cases, to support your answer.

- Integration is being attempted in a high school in Capetown, South Africa. At the beginning of each school day, white students and students from one of the black societies are required to attend a formal assembly. Students are also required to wear school uniforms. What might the students infer from these requirements? Support your answer by discussing the purpose of assemblies and uniforms in our society and researching cultural aspects of one of the black societies in Capetown.

- Compare and contrast American and African colonization by discussing the events and their effects.

- Investigate women's roles in tribal society. Find and discuss specific examples from *Things Fall Apart.*

- Women in tribal societies were often forced to undergo female circumcision. Investigate the purpose of this ritual. What are the medical implications of this procedure?

- Language is an important means of communication as well as a prominent culture marker. What does a person's language tell us about him or her? What effects could loss of one's language—through physical disability or societal disallowance—have on a person?

- Missionaries went to Umuofia to convert the Ibo to Christianity. Should anyone try to change another's religious beliefs? Take a stand from either a Christian's point of view or from an opposite point of view. Prepare a logical argument for presentation in a debate.

- What is the purpose of multicultural education in our country? Describe some of the efforts that are being undertaken by schools around the country. What have been your own experiences? Discuss the methods being used to implement these programs and their success.

Okonkwo's personal god, or chi, is good (fate has blessed him). Nevertheless, they realize that Okonkwo has worked hard to achieve all that he has (if a man says yes, his chi says yes). When he breaks the Week of Peace, however, the tribe believes that Okonkwo has begun to feel too self-important and has challenged his chi. They fear the consequences his actions may bring.

The tribe decides to kill Ikemefuna. Even though Ezeudu warns Okonkwo not to be a part of the plan, Okonkwo himself kills Ikemefuna. Okonkwo chooses to kill the boy rather than to appear weak.

When Okonkwo is in exile, he ponders the tribe's view of his chi. He thinks that maybe they have been wrong—that his chi was not made for great things. Okonkwo blames his exile on his chi. He refuses to accept that his actions have led him to this point. He sees no connections among his breaking the Week of Peace, his killing Ikemefuna, and his shooting Ezeudu's son. In Okonkwo's eyes, his troubles result from ill fate and chance.

Alienation and Loneliness

Okonkwo's exile isolates him from all he has ever known in *Things Fall Apart.* The good name he had built for himself with his tribesmen is a thing of the past. He must start anew. The thought overwhelms him, and Okonkwo feels nothing but despair. Visits from his good friend, Obierika, do little to cheer Okonkwo. News of the white man's intrusion and the tribe's reactions to it disturb him.

His distance from the village, and his lack of connection to it, give him a sense of helplessness. Even worse, Okonkwo's son, Nwoye, joins the white man's mission efforts.

Okonkwo's return to the village does nothing to lessen his feelings of alienation and loneliness. The tribe he rejoins is not the same tribe he left. While he does not expect to be received as the respected warrior he once was, he does think that his arrival will prompt an occasion to be remembered. When the clan takes no special notice of his return, Okonkwo realizes that the white man has been too successful in his efforts to change the tribe's ways. Okonkwo grieves the loss of his tribe and the life he once knew. He is not able to overcome his sense of complete alienation.

Betrayal

In *Things Fall Apart,* Okonkwo feels betrayed by his personal god, or chi, which has allowed him to produce a son who is effeminate. Nwoye continually disappoints Okonkwo. As a child, Nwoye prefers his mother's stories to masculine pursuits. As an adult, Nwoye joins the white missionaries.

Okonkwo also feels betrayed by his clan. He does not understand why his fellow tribesmen have not stood up against the white intruders. When Okonkwo returns from exile, his clan has all but disintegrated. Many of the tribe's leaders have joined the missionaries' efforts; tribal beliefs and customs are being ignored. Okonkwo mourns the death of the strong tribe he once knew and despises the "woman-like" tribe that has taken its place.

Change and Transformation

The tribe to which Okonkwo returns has undergone a complete transformation during his absence in *Things Fall Apart.* The warlike Ibo once looked to its elders for guidance, made sacrifices to gods for deliverance, and solved conflicts though confrontation. Now the Ibo are "woman-like"; they discuss matters among themselves and pray to a god they can not see. Rather than immediately declare war on the Christians when Enoch unmasks the egwugwu, or ancestral spirit, the Ibo only destroy Enoch's compound. Okonkwo realizes how completely the Christians have changed his tribe when the tribesmen allow the remaining court messengers to escape after Okonkwo beheads one of them.

Good and Evil

Many of the tribesmen view the white man as evil in *Things Fall Apart.* Tribesmen did not turn their backs on one another before the white man came. Tribesmen would never have thought to kill their own brothers before the white man came. The arrival of the white man has forced the clan to act in ways that its ancestors deplore. Such evil has never before invaded the clan.

Culture Clash

The arrival of the white man and his culture heralds the death of the Ibo culture in *Things Fall Apart.* The white man does not honor the tribe's customs and strives to convince tribesmen that the white man's ways are better. Achieving some success, the white man encourages the tribesmen who join him, increasing the white man's ranks. As a result, the tribe is split, pitting brother against brother and father against son. Tribal practices diminish as the bond that ties tribesmen deteriorates. Death eventually comes to the weaker of the clashing cultures.

Style

Tragedy

Things Fall Apart chronicles the double tragedies of the deaths of Okonkwo, a revered warrior, and the Ibo, the tribe to which Okonkwo belongs. In literature, tragedy often describes the downfall of a great individual which is caused by a flaw in the person's character. Okonkwo's personal flaw is his unreasonable anger, and his tragedy occurs when the tribe bans him for accidentally killing a young tribesman, and he returns to find a tribe that has changed beyond recognition. The Ibo's public demise results from the destruction of one culture by another, but their tragedy is caused by their turning away from their tribal gods.

Setting

Things Fall Apart is set in Umuofia, a tribal village in the country of Nigeria, in Africa. It is the late 1800s, when English bureaucrats and missionaries are first arriving in the area. There is a long history of conflict between European colonists and the Africans they try to convert and subjegate. But by placing the novel at the beginning of this period Achebe can accentuate the clash of cultures that are just coming into contact. It also sets up a greater contrast between the time Okonkwo leaves the tribe and the time he returns, when his village is almost unrecognizable to him because of the changes brought by the English.

Conflict

In *Things Fall Apart,* the Ibo thrive in Umuofia, practicing ancient rituals and customs.

When the white man arrives, however, he ignores the Ibo's values and tries to enforce his own beliefs, laws, and religious practices. Some of the weaker tribesmen join the white man's ranks, leaving gaps in the clan's united front. First, the deserters are impressed with the wealth the white man brings into Umuofia. Second, they find in the white man's religion an acceptance and brotherhood that has never been afforded them due to their lower status in the tribe. As men leave the tribe to become members of the white man's mission, the rift in the tribe widens. Social and psychological conflict abounds as brothers turn their backs on one another, and fathers and sons become strangers.

Narration

Achebe develops *Things Fall Apart* through a third-person narrative—using "he" and "she" for exposition—rather than having the characters tell it themselves. Often speaking in the past tense, he also narrates the story with little use of character dialogue. The resulting story reads like an oral tale that has been passed down through generations of storytellers.

Imagery

While the characters in *Things Fall Apart* have little dialogue, the reader still has a clear image of them and is able to understand their motives. Achebe accomplishes this through his combination of the English language with Ibo vocabulary and proverbs. When the characters do talk, they share the rich proverbs that are "the palm-oil with which words are eaten." Achebe uses the proverbs not only to illustrate his characters but also to paint pictures of the society he is depicting, to reveal themes, and to develop conflict. Vivid images result, giving the reader a clear representation of people and events.

Point of View

Critics praise Achebe for his adept shifts in point of view in *Things Fall Apart*. Achebe begins the story from Okonkwo's point of view. Okonkwo's story helps the reader understand the Ibo's daily customs and rituals as well as celebrations for the main events in life: birth, marriage, and death. As the story progresses, however, it becomes more the clan's story than Okonkwo's personal story. The reader follows the clan's life, gradual disintegration, and death. The novel becomes one of situation rather than character; the reader begins to feel a certain sympathy for the tribe instead of the individual. The final shift occurs when

Achebe ends the story from the District Commissioner's viewpoint. While some critics feel that Achebe's ending lectures, others believe that it strengthens the conclusion for the reader. Some even view it as a form of functionalism, an African tradition of cultural instruction.

Plot and Structure

Divided into three parts, *Things Fall Apart* comprises many substories. Yet Achebe holds the various stories together through his use of proverbs, traditional oral tales, and *leitmotif,* or recurring images or phrases. Ibo proverbs occur throughout the book, providing a unity to the surface progression of the story. For example, "when a man says yes, his chi says yes" is the proverb the tribe applies to Okonkwo's success, on the one hand, but is also the proverb Okonkwo, himself, applies to his failure. Traditional oral tales always contain a tale within the tale. Nwoye's mother is an expert at telling these tales—morals embedded in stories. The stories Achebe tells throughout *Things Fall Apart* are themselves tales within the tale. Leitmotif is the association of a repeated theme with a particular idea. Achebe connects masculinity with land, yams, titles, and wives. He repeatedly associates this view of masculinity with a certain stagnancy in Umuofia. While a traditional Western plot may not be evident in *Things Fall Apart,* a definite structure with an African flavor lends itself to the overall unity of the story.

Foil

Achebe uses foil—a type of contrast—to strengthen his primary characters in *Things Fall Apart,* illuminating their differences. The following pairs of characters serve as foils for each other: Okonkwo and Obierika, Ikemefuna and Nwoye, and Mr. Brown and the Reverend Smith. Okonkwo rarely thinks; he is a man of action. He follows the tribe's customs almost blindly and values its opinion of him over his own good sense. Obierika, on the other hand, ponders the things that happen to Okonkwo and his tribe. Obierika often makes his own decisions and wonders about the tribe's wisdom in some of its actions. Ikemefuna exemplifies the rising young tribesman. A masculine youth, full of energy and personality, Ikemefuna participates in the manly activities expected of him. In contrast, Nwoye appears lazy and effeminate. He prefers listening to his mother's stories over making plans for war. He detests the sight of blood and abhors violence of any kind. Mr. Brown speaks gently and restrains the overzealous members of his mission from overwhelming the clan. He seeks to win the people over by offering education and sincere faith. The Reverend Smith is the fire-and-brimstone preacher who replaces Mr. Brown. He sees the world in black and white; either something is evil, or it is good. He thrives on his converts' zeal and encourages them to do whatever it takes to gain supporters for his cause.

Historical Context

Tribal Society

Things Fall Apart was published in 1958 just prior to Nigerian independence, but it depicts pre-colonial Africa. Achebe felt it was important to portray Nigerians as they really were—not just provide a shallow description of them as other authors had. The story takes place in the typical tribal village of Umuofia, where the inhabitants (whom Achebe calls the Ibo, but who are also known as the Igbo) practice rituals common to their native traditions.

The Ibo worshipped gods who protect, advise, and chastise them and who are represented by priests and priestesses within the clan. For example, the Oracle of the Hills and the Caves grants knowledge and wisdom to those who are brave enough to consult him. No one has ever seen the Oracle except his priestess, who is an Ibo woman who has special powers of her own. Not only did the gods advise the Ibo on community matters, but also they guided individuals. Each person had a personal god, or chi, that directed his or her actions. A strong chi meant a strong person; people with weak chis were pitied. Each man kept a separate hut, or shrine, where he stored the symbols of his personal god and his ancestral spirits.

A hunting and gathering society, the Ibo existed on vegetables, with yams as the primary crop. Yams were so important to them that the Ibo celebrated each new year with the Feast of the New Yam. This festival thanked Ani, the earth goddess and source of all fertility. The Ibo prepared for days for the festival, and the celebration itself lasted for two days. Yams also played a part in determining a man's status in the tribe—the more yams a man has, the higher his status. Trade with other villages was facilitated by small seashells called cowries which were used as a form of currency.

Within the village, people were grouped according to families, with the eldest man in the family having the most power. On matters affecting the whole village, an assembly of adult men debated courses of action, and men could influence these assemblies by purchasing "titles" from the tribal elders. This system encouraged hard work and the spread of wealth. People who transgressed against the laws and customs of the village had to confront the egwugwu, an assembly of tribesmen masked as spirits, who would settle disputes and hand out punishment. Individual villages also attained various degrees of political status. In the novel, other tribes respect and fear Umuofia. They believe that Umuofia's magic is powerful and that the village's war-medicine, or agadi-nwayi, is particularly potent. Neighboring clans always try to settle disputes peacefully with Umuofia to avoid having to war with them.

Christianity and Colonization

While Christianity spread across North and South Africa as early as the late fifteenth century, Christianity took its strongest hold when the majority of the missionaries arrived in the late 1800s. After centuries of taking slaves out of Africa, Britain had outlawed the slave trade and now saw the continent as ripe for colonization. Missionaries sent to convert the local population were often the first settlers. They believed they could atone for the horrors of slavery by saving the souls of Africans.

At first, Africans were mistrustful of European Christians, and took advantage of the education the missionaries provided without converting. Individuals who had no power under the current tribal order, however, soon converted; in the novel, the missionaries who come to Umuofia convert only the weaker tribesmen, or efulefu. Missionaries would convince these tribesmen that their tribe worshipped false gods and that its false gods did not have the ability to punish them if they chose to join the mission. When the mission and its converts accepted even the outcasts of the clan, the missionaries' ranks grew. Eventually, some of the more important tribesmen would convert. As the mission expanded, the clan divided, discontent simmered, and conflicts arose.

English Bureaucrats and Colonization

After the arrival of the British, when conflicts came up between villages the white government would intervene instead of allowing villagers to settle them themselves. In the novel, a white District Commissioner brings with him court messengers whose duty it is to bring in people who break the white man's law. The messengers, called "Ashy-Buttocks" for the ash-colored shorts they wear, are hated for their high-handed attitudes. These mes-

Compare & Contrast

- **1800s:** Prior to colonization, common language and geography differentiated African societies. Six types of societies existed: hunting and gathering societies, cattle-herding societies, forest dwellers, fishermen, grain-raising societies, and city (urban) societies. The geographic area in which people lived determined their lifestyle.

  Colonial Africa: Africa was divided into more than fifty nation-states, with no regard for maintaining groups sharing common language and livelihood.

  Today: Societies are no longer as clear-cut. People have more opportunities for education, better jobs, and improved means of communication and transportation. They marry individuals from other societies. As a result, the societies have become mixed, but ethnic conflicts still lead to violence.

- **1800s:** While religion varied from society to society, most Africans shared some common beliefs and practices. They believed in a supreme creator god or spirit. Other lesser gods revealed

themselves as, and worked through, community ancestors.

Colonial Africa: Missionaries arrived and introduced Christianity. Many tribesmen converted to the new religion.

Today: While more than an estimated 25% of Africa is Christian, traditional African religion is still practiced, as is Islam. Islam is a monotheistic religion related to the Jewish and Christian traditions.

- **1800s:** Prior to colonization, Africans had their own identities and cultures and were not concerned with participating in the modern world.

  Colonial Africa: After colonization, African children were taught European history and literature so that they might compete in the modern world, while their own heritage was ignored.

  Today: Africans continue to seek the independence they began to achieve in the 1950s and 1960s. There is, however, a renewed interest in cultural heritage, and traditional customs are being taught to African children.

---

sengers and interpreters were often African Christian converts who looked down on tribesmen who still followed traditional customs. If violence involved any white missionaries or bureaucrats, British soldiers would often slaughter whole villages instead of seeking and punishing guilty individuals. The British passed an ordinance in 1912 that legalized this practice, and during an uprising in 1915, British troops killed more than forty natives in retaliation for one dead and one wounded British soldier.

One of the most important results of Europe's colonization of Africa was the division of Africa into at least fifty nation-states. Rather than being a part of a society determined by common language and livelihood, Africans lived according to political boundaries. The divisions often split ethnic groups, leading to tension and sometimes violence. The cohesiveness of the traditional society was gone.

Nigerian Independence

British colonial rule in Nigeria lasted only fifty-seven years, from 1903 to 1960. Although Nigerians had long called for self-rule, it was not until the end of World War II that England began heeding these calls. The Richards Constitution of 1946 was the first attempt to grant some native rule by bringing the diverse peoples of Nigeria under one representative government. The three regions (northern, southern and western) were brought under the administration of one legislative council composed of twenty-eight Nigerians and seventeen British officers. Regional councils, however, guaranteed some independence from the national council and forged a link between local authorities, such as tribal chiefs, and the national government. There were three major tribes (the Hausa, the Yoruba and the Igbo) and more than eight smaller ones living in Nigeria. This diversity complicated the creation of a unified Nige-

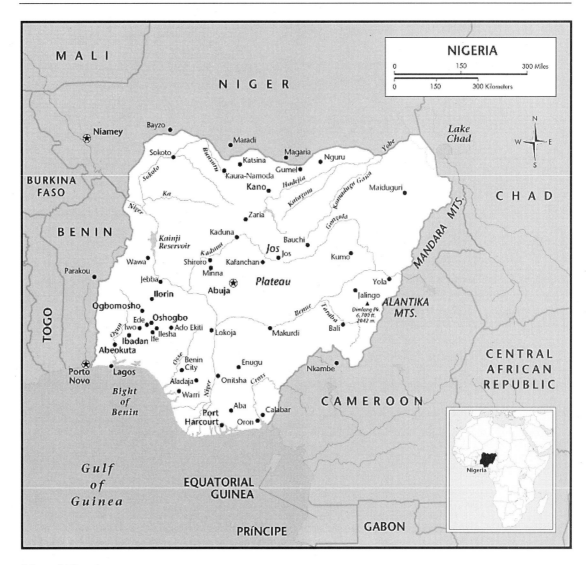

Map of Nigeria.

ria. Between 1946 and 1960 the country went through several different constitutions, each one attempting to balance power between the regional and the national bodies of government.

On October 1, 1960, Nigeria attained full status as a sovereign state and a member of the British Commonwealth. But under the Constitution of 1960 the Queen of England was still the head of state. She remained the commander-in-chief of Nigeria's armed forces, and the Nigerian navy operated as part of Britain's Royal Navy. Nigerians felt frustrated by the implication that they were the subjects of a monarch living over 4,000 miles away. In 1963, five years after the publication of Achebe's novel, a new constitution would replace the British monarch with a Nigerian president as head of state in Nigeria.

Literary Traditions

Achebe wrote *Things Fall Apart* just before Nigeria received its independence. He intended the book for audiences outside Africa; he wanted to paint a true picture of precolonial Africa for those people who had no direct knowledge of traditional African societies. As a result of the Nigerians' acquisition of independence, the Nigerian educational system sought to encourage a national pride through the study of Nigerian heritage. The educational system required Achebe's book in high schools throughout the English-speaking countries in Africa. The book was well received. Chinua Achebe has been recognized as "the most original African novelist writing in English," according to Charles Larson in *The Emergence of African Fiction*. Critics throughout the world have praised

Things Fall Apart as the first African English-language classic.

Critical Overview

Things Fall Apart has experienced a huge success. Since it was published in 1958, the book has sold more than two million copies in over thirty languages. Critics attribute its success not only to the book's message, but also to Achebe's talents as a writer. Achebe believes that stories should serve a purpose; they should deliver a meaningful message to the people who hear or read them. When Achebe wrote *Things Fall Apart,* his intent was to explain the beginnings of the turmoil Africans have been experiencing over the past century. He wanted to describe the integrity of precolonial Nigeria, detail the effects of colonialism on tribal societies, and reveal the kinds of immoral treatment that people in modern society are often made to suffer. Critics agree that he accomplished all of these purposes. They feel that he writes honestly about tribal life and the colonial legacy. They also believe that Achebe delivers another important message: man will always face change, and he who can accommodate change will survive.

While some readers will view Okonkwo's deterioration and demise as a tragic result of his going against the will of the gods, others see the new "world order" as inevitable. Okonkwo's acts do not bring the tribe to an end; it is the tribe's lack of adaptability that destroys it. These opposing interpretations strengthen the impact of the book. In *The Growth of the African Novel,* Eustace Palmer states that "while deploring the imperialists' brutality and condescension, [Achebe] seems to suggest that change is inevitable and wise men ... reconcile themselves to accommodating change. It is the diehards ... who resist and are destroyed in the process."

Achebe successfully communicates his message through skillful writing. From the time critics first read his book, they have concurred that Achebe's craftsmanship earns him a place among the best writers in the world. An example of his craftsmanship is Achebe's ability to convey the essence of traditional Nigeria while borrowing from the conventions of the European novel. He was the first Nigerian writer to adapt African oral tradition to novel form. In doing so, "he created a new novel that possesses its own autonomy and transcends the limits set by both his African and European teachers," as Kofi Awoonor observes in

The Breast of the Earth. The borrowed European elements Achebe contrasts are communal life over the individual character and the beauty and detail of traditional tribal life over brief references to background. His descriptions of day-to-day life and special ceremonial customs provide a "powerful presentation of the beauty, strength, and validity of traditional life and values," as Palmer observes.

Literary experts also point out Achebe's ability to combine language forms, maintain thematic unity, and shape conflict in *Things Fall Apart.* His use of Ibo proverbs in conjunction with the English language places the reader in Africa with the Ibo tribe. Adrian A. Roscoe explains in his book *Mother Is Gold: A Study of West African Literature,* "Proverbs are cherished by Achebe's people as tribal heirlooms, the treasure boxes of their cultural heritage." In addition, the combination of languages helps reiterate the theme of tradition versus change. Roscoe goes on to say, "Through [proverbs] traditions are received and handed on; and when they disappear or fall into disuse ... it is a sign that a particular tradition, or indeed a whole way of life, is passing away."

The death of the language then, a powerful cultural tradition, signifies the ultimate discord in the novel—the fall of one culture to another. G. D. Killam observes in *The Novels of Chinua Achebe* that "the conflict in the novel, vested in Okonkwo, derives from the series of crushing blows which are levelled at traditional values by an alien and more powerful culture causing, in the end, the traditional society to fall apart." Achebe's mastery of content and his talent as a writer contribute to his worldwide success with this novel as well as his other novels, articles, poems, and essays. As Killam concludes, his writing conveys that "the spirit of man and the belief in the possibility of triumph endures."

Criticism

Robert Bennett

In the following essay, Bennett, a doctoral candidate at the University of California—Santa Barbara, examines how issues of history, culture, and gender have affected Achebe's Things Fall Apart, *and how the novel is valuable both as a literary work and an introduction to African literature.*

As the most widely read work of African fiction, *Things Fall Apart* has played an instrumental role in introducing African literature to readers throughout the world. In particular, Achebe's fic-

What Do I Read Next?

- One of Chinua Achebe's more recent novels, *Anthills of the Savannah,* was published in 1988 by Anchor Books. It tells the story of three childhood friends who become leaders in their West African country and who are destroyed by their ambition.

- *Hopes and Impediments: Selected Essays* is a nonfiction work by Achebe also published in 1988. The collection of political essays and speeches shows the depth of Achebe's thoughts about his homeland and its problems.

- After reading *Things Fall Apart,* a person feels compelled to read Achebe's sequel, *No Longer at Ease,* which first came out in 1960. The story of Okonkwo's family continues with Okonkwo's grandson, Obi, as the main character. Obi has been raised a Christian and has been educated at a university in England.

- Ben Okri's *The Famished Road* won England's prestigious Booker Prize in 1991. The novel is set in a West African ghetto during British colonial rule and tells of the spirit-child Azaro, who has broken a pact with the spirit world.

- In 1990, Barbara K. Walker collected eleven tales from folklore in *The Dancing Palm Tree and Other Nigerian Folktales.*

- *Migrations of the Heart* (1983) is Marita Golden's autobiography that relates her marriage to a Nigerian native. It recounts how she felt as an African American woman making her first trip to Africa and her troubles fitting into the traditional role of a Nigerian wife.

---

tion has contributed to world literature by retelling African history, as well as the history of European colonization, from an Afro-centric perspective rather than a Euro-centric one. By shifting the narrative focus from the perspective of the colonizer to the perspective of the colonized, Achebe's novels reveal and correct many of the biased assumptions found in previous historical and literary descriptions of Africa. Specifically, they reaffirm the value of African cultures by representing their rich and complex cultural traditions instead of stereotyping them as irrational and primitive. As Achebe explains in his frequently quoted essay, "The Novelist as Teacher," his novels seek to teach Africans that "their past—with all its imperfections—was not one night of savagery from which the first Europeans acting on God's behalf delivered them." To say that Achebe affirms African culture and history, however, is not to imply that he simply inverts European ethnocentrism by romanticizing African culture as perfect or vilifying European cultures as entirely corrupt. Instead, Achebe presents a remarkably balanced view of how all cultures encompass both good and bad dimensions.

In addition to re-interpreting African culture and history from an African perspective, *Things Fall Apart* is also significant because of its mastery of literary conventions. In fact, many critics argue that it is the best African novel ever written, and they specifically praise its sophisticated development of character, tragedy, and irony. Okonkwo, in particular, is a complex character, and consequently there are many ways to interpret his role in the novel. On one level, he can be interpreted psychologically in terms of the oedipal struggle that he has with his father and the very different oedipal struggle that his son, Nwoye, has with him. As each son rejects the example of his father, these three generations form a reactionary cycle that ironically repeats itself: when Nwoye rejects Okonkwo's masculinity, he ironically returns to the more feminine disposition that Okonkwo originally rejected in his father. Many of the major events of the novel, including both Okonkwo's tragic drive to succeed and Nwoye's eventual conversion to Christianity, largely result from the inter-generational struggle created when each son rejects his father.

Another way to analyze the psychological dimensions of Okonkwo's character is to examine how he constructs his sense of gender by asserting a strong sense of masculinity and repressing any sense of femininity. Just as there is an external psychological conflict between Okonkwo and his father, there is also an internal psychological conflict between the masculine and feminine sides within Okonkwo. While Okonkwo's hyper-masculinity initially enables him to achieve success as a great wrestler and warrior, his refusal to balance this masculine side with feminine virtues eventually contributes to his later destruction. At virtually every turn in the novel, his excessive masculinity nudges him toward new troubles. Because of his contempt for unmanliness, he rudely insults Osugo, destroys his relationship with his own son Nwoye, and lets himself be pressured into sacrificing Ikemefuna in spite of Ezeudu's warning. Moreover, Okonkwo's lack of respect for women is equally pervasive and problematic. He ignores the wisdom found in women's stories, he frequently intimidates and beats his wives, and he can only relate to his daughter Ezinma because he thinks of her as a boy. Consequently, Okonkwo is a man out of balance who has only developed one half of his full self because he only accepts the masculine side of his culture.

In addition to noting how gender influences Okonkwo's behavior within the story, many critics also note that gender influences Achebe as an author. Feminist critics, in particular, have criticized *Things Fall Apart* both for suggesting that men are representative of all Africans and for focusing too exclusively on masculine activities and male characters. Though it is perhaps inevitable that Achebe would write his novel from a male perspective, these critics raise interesting questions about how Achebe's male perspective might ignore and misrepresent the experiences of African women. Nevertheless, despite Achebe's male bias, there are moments in the novel when Achebe emphasizes female characters and valorizes their perspectives. It is the women who pass on many of the cultural traditions through stories, and it is Okonkwo's daughter, Ezinma, not his son, Nwoye, who understands Okonkwo in the end. Moreover, Okonkwo's wife, Ekwefi, shows more courage and parental love in defending the life of her daughter, Ezinma, than Okonkwo does in participating in the sacrifice of Ikemefuna. Consequently, even though Achebe might emphasize male characters and perspectives, he does not simply represent men as superior to women. In fact, there are many ways in which Achebe critiques Okonkwo's inflated sense of masculinity.

Another way to interpret Okonkwo's character is to focus less on his internal personality and look instead at how this personality is shaped by the various social and historical contexts in which he lives. From such a perspective, *Things Fall Apart* does not explore oedipal conflicts or gender identity as much as it explores the tension between pursuing individual desires and conforming to the community's values and customs. In many ways, Okonkwo's tragic death results directly from his inability to balance these competing demands of individuality and community. At first, Okonkwo seems an ideal representative of his community's

values. He earns honor and respect from his people by developing the physical strength, manly courage, and disciplined will valued by his Igbo culture. As the novel progresses, however, Okonkwo's success gradually develops into a dangerous sense of individualism that flagrantly disregards the community's rules and decisions. For example, he beats his wife during the sacred Week of Peace, and he attempts to single-handedly attack the British instead of waiting for and accepting the community's collective decision. In fact, many critics have argued that this individualistic disregard for the community is Okonkwo's primary tragic flaw, though it is perhaps difficult to separate this individualism from Okonkwo's other character flaws such as inflexibility, hyper-masculinity, and an obsessive reaction against his father.

In an even broader context, Achebe adds yet another dimension to Okonkwo's tragedy by situating it within the historical context of British colonial expansion. As the novel progresses, the initial focus on Okonkwo's psychological struggles enlarges to include Okonkwo's political struggle against British colonialism. By situating the personal tragedy of Okonkwo's suicide within this larger historical tragedy of colonial domination, *Things Fall Apart* develops a double-tragedy. Moreover, this double-tragedy further complicates the interpretation of Okonkwo's character because the external tragedy of colonial domination largely provokes Okonkwo's internal aggression. Although both Okonkwo and his society are responsible for their own destruction to some degree, there is also another sense in which they are destroyed by forces beyond their control. While the reader might condemn Okonkwo's rash outburst of violence, the reader also sympathizes with and perhaps even justifies the rage that Okonkwo feels while watching foreign invaders unjustly accuse and dominate his people. Even though Okonkwo's final act of resistance is ineffective and perhaps even misguided, it exemplifies how Africans and other colonized peoples have courageously resisted colonialism instead of passively accepting it. Consequently, Okonkwo's character is both tragically flawed and tragically heroic, and instead of separating the intermixed heroism and destructiveness that defines Okonkwo throughout the novel, Achebe's conclusion only emphasizes how Okonkwo's strengths and weaknesses are interrelated. Thus, Achebe's conclusion brings together a masterful sense of character, tragedy, and irony.

In addition, *Things Fall Apart* is also important stylistically because it develops a hybrid aesthetic form that creatively fuses European and African cultural forms. At the simplest level, Achebe does this through his use of language. By introducing numerous African terms throughout the novel, he develops a hybrid language that mixes Igbo and English words. While some of these words may be confusing at first, by the end of the novel the reader learns to recognize many basic Igbo words like *chi* (fate), *obi* (hut), and *osu* (outcast). At a more complex level, however, Achebe also integrates African cultural traditions into the structure of the novel through his use of proverbs and folktales. Many of the insights developed in the novel are presented either through proverbs or through stories drawn from the rich oral traditions of Igbo culture. These stories, like the story about Mosquito's marriage proposal to Ear and the story about Tortoise's attempt to trick the birds out of their feast, function as stories-within-the-story, and they add additional layers of meaning to the main plot of the novel.

In addition to its literary and political value, *Things Fall Apart* is also a novel rich in anthropological detail. In many ways, it can be read as an anthropological description of the daily life and customs of the Igbo people because Achebe blends his description of Okonkwo's tragedy with a richly detailed description of Igbo culture before European colonization. Throughout the novel, Achebe describes numerous aspects of daily life in a traditional Igbo community ranging from methods of farming and forms of entertainment to dietary practices, clan titles, kinship structures, and marriage customs. In addition, he also describes a wide variety of Igbo religious beliefs and ceremonies such as the Week of Peace, the Feast of the New Yam, the Ozo dance, *ogbanje* spirit-children who keep dying and being reborn, the Evil Forest, and various gods and goddesses. This comprehensive, detailed description of African customs not only helps the reader understand the daily activities and religious beliefs of the Igbo people, but it also helps the reader begin to understand an Igbo world view. Consequently, it represents not only how Igbo people live but also what they believe and how they think and feel.

Finally, Achebe adds yet another dimension to *Things Fall Apart* by concluding the novel with a strong critique of how western colonial histories have been written from biased, ethnocentric perspectives. While this historical dimension of the novel may not be readily apparent at first, Achebe makes it unmistakably clear in the concluding paragraph, which describes the District Commissioner's callous response to Okonkwo's suicide. In addition to being generally apathetic to Okonkwo's death, the District Commissioner seems even more inhuman because he takes interest in Okonkwo's suicide only because it will give him "new material" for his book. After the reader has read Achebe's detailed and moving description of Okonkwo's life, the District Commissioner dismisses this story as only worth a "reasonable paragraph" because there is "so much else to include, and one must be firm in cutting out the details." At this point, Achebe begins to turn the reader's attention from the District Commissioner's lack of compassion to his historical ignorance, which grossly underestimates the long and complex history leading up to Okonkwo's tragic death. Moreover, the District Commissioner's decision to title his book *The Pacification of the Primitive Tribes of the Lower Niger,* demonstrates both his inability to think of African people as anything other than primitive and his inability to recognize how he has brought violence instead of peace to the Lower Niger. By ending the novel with the District Commissioner's complete misinterpretation and miswriting of the scene of colonial conflict, Achebe suggests that his novel is not simply about the colonial encounter between two cultures. At a deeper level, it is also about how the story of that encounter is told. It is a story about the telling of history itself. By drawing attention to the District Commissioner's erroneous sense of history, Achebe reminds the reader that western descriptions of Africa have largely been written by men like the District Commissioner. Consequently, *Things Fall Apart* seeks to correct such erroneous historical records by retelling African history from an African perspective that intimately understands Okonkwo's pain and outrage, even if it does not completely condone Okonkwo's violent actions.

Source: Robert Bennett, in an essay for *Novels for Students,* Gale, 1997.

Diana Akers Rhoads

In the following excerpt, Rhoads contrasts African and British culture in Things Fall Apart, *as well as related shortcomings in criticism of the work.*

That Achebe sees the best of Igbo village life as offering something of the ideal is suggested by an interview in 1988 with Raoul Granqvist [in *Travelling: Chinua Achebe in Scandinavia. Swedish Writers in Africa,* Umea University, 1990]. Achebe, talking of the importance of ideals, refers to the example of village life based on a kind of equality. "This," he says, is what the Igbo people chose, the small village entity that was completely self-governing.... The reason why they chose it [this system] was because they wanted to be in control of their lives. So if the community says that we will have a meeting in the market place tomorrow, everybody should go there, or could go there. And everybody could speak.

Since Achebe is not the first to write of Africa, he must dispel old images in order to create a true sense of his people's dignity. Works such as Joseph Conrad's *Heart of Darkness* see Africans as primitives representing Europeans at an earlier stage of civilization, or imaging all humanity's primal urges which civilization hides. Firsthand European accounts of the colonial period, such as the district commissioner's *Pacification of the Primitive Tribes of the Lower Niger* in *Things Fall Apart*, reduce the African experience to an anthropological study told from the white man's point of view. Achebe reveals that the Europeans' ideas of Africa are mistaken. Perhaps the most important mistake of the British is their belief that all civilization progresses, as theirs has, from the tribal stage through monarchy to parliamentary government....

The Igbos, on the other hand, have developed a democratic system of government. For great decisions the *ndichie*, or elders, gather together all of Umuofia. The clan rules all, and the collective will of the clan can be established only by the group. Further, as is appropriate in a democracy, each man is judged on his own merits, "according to his worth," not those of his father, as would be appropriate in an aristocracy or an oligarchy.

Within this system the Igbos as a whole reveal themselves more tolerant of other cultures than the Europeans, who merely see the Igbos as uncivilized. In other words, the Igbo are in some ways superior to those who come to convert them. Uchendu, for example, is able to see that "what is good among one people is an abomination with others," but the white men tell the Igbos that Igbo customs are bad and that their gods are not true gods at all. Unlike the Europeans, the Igbos believe that it "is good that a man should worship the gods and spirits of his fathers" even if these gods are not the Igbos' gods. While the European tradition allows men to fight their brothers over religion, the Igbo tradition forbids them to kill each other: it is an abomination to kill a member of the clan. Further, the long history of Crusades and holy wars and of religious persecution in Europe occurs because men can fight for gods, but it is not the Igbo "custom to fight for [their] gods." Rather, heresy is a matter only between the man and the god.

The Christian missionary in Mbanta objects to the Igbo gods on the belief that they tell the Igbos to kill each other, and, in fact, the gods are invoked in the fighting of wars against another village—though not indiscriminately, only when the war is just. At times the oracle forbids the Umuofians to go to war. The Europeans in *Things Fall Apart*, however, kill far more in the name of religion than the Igbos: the British, for example, wipe out the whole village of Abame in retaliation for the killing of one white man.

The Igbos do not fight each other because they are primitive. Achebe implies the existence of the conditions in Nigeria which historically led to the need for war as a matter of survival. The land, consisting of rock underlying an almost nonexistent topsoil, was very poor and thus would not support large numbers of people. Planting soon depleted the soil, and so villagers were forced to move further and further afield to find land which would yield a crop to support them. Okonkwo's father, the lazy Unoka, has little success planting yams because he sows on "exhausted farms that take no labor to clear." Meanwhile, his neighbors, crossing "seven rivers to make their farms," plant the "virgin forests." As the population of Nigeria increased, land and food were insufficient to provide for everyone. The novel seems to make the turning point in the alteration from plenty to scarcity some time between the generation of Okonkwo's Uncle Uchendu and that of Okonkwo, for Uchendu speaks of "the good days when a man had friends in distant clans." Although the state of constant warfare was hardly desirable, at least it provided a means for survival....

The Christian missionary, then, is mistaken about the perversity of the Igbo religion: some wars are inevitable if the clan is to survive, but war is not indiscriminate. Religion is a factor both in limiting war and in supporting it when it is just. In the latter case war might be seen as a deterrent to future crimes against Umuofia. Neighboring clans try to avoid war with Umuofia because it is "feared" as a village "powerful in war," and when someone in Mbaino kills a Umuofian woman, "[e]ven the enemy clan know that" the threatened war is "just."

In fact, the Igbo have a highly developed system of religion which works as effectively as Christianity. The Igbo religion and the Christian religion are equally irrational, but both operate along similar lines to support morality. To the Christians it seems crazy to worship wooden idols, but to the Igbos it seems crazy to say that God has a son when he has no wife. Both systems of religion look to only one supreme god, Chukwu for the Umuofians.

Both supreme gods have messengers on earth, Christ for the British and the wooden idols for the Igbos. Both religions support humility; the Igbos speak to Chukwu through messengers because they do not want to worry the master, but they deal with Chukwu directly if all else fails. Both gods are vengeful only when disregarded. If a person disobeys Chukwu, the god is to be feared, but Chukwu "need not be feared by those who do his will."

In addition to revealing that the original Igbo religion is not inferior to Christianity, Achebe makes it clear that the demoralizing current state of political affairs in Africa is the result of European interference rather than simply the natural outgrowth of the native culture. The Igbos have a well-established and effective system of justice which the British replace with the system of district commissioners and court messengers. Disputes in the tribe which cannot be resolved in other ways come before the *egwugwu,* the greatest masked spirits of the clan, played by titled villagers. Hearing witnesses on both sides, for example, the tribunal comes to a decision in the case of Uzowoli, who beat his wife, and his indignant in-laws, who took his wife and children away. In this dispute the *egwugwu* try to assuage each side. They warn Uzowoli that it "is not bravery when a man fights a woman" and tell him to take a pot of wine to his in-laws; they tell Odukwe to return Uzowoli's wife if he comes with wine. The system helps to dispel hard feelings by refusing "to blame this man or to praise that"; rather the *egwugwu*'s duty is simply "to settle the dispute."

Although the conditions in Nigeria require warlike men for the survival of the village, the Igbos have realized the danger of such men to their own society. Warriors must be fierce to their enemies and gentle to their own people, yet spirited men can bring discord to their own societies. The tribe has institutions to control the anger of its own men. For instance, there is a Week of Peace sacred to the earth goddess. Moreover, as indicated earlier, killing members of one's own clan is forbidden, and even inadvertent death such as Okonkwo's killing of Ezeudu's son must be expiated. Recognizing the need for Okonkwo to distinguish between friends and enemies, Ogbuefi Ezeudu calls on Okonkwo to tell him to have nothing to do with the killing of Ikemefuna because the boy is too much like a family member: "He calls you his father."...

In addition to supplying a workable system of government and institutions supporting moderation and morality, the Igbos have an economic system which redistributes wealth in a manner preventing any one tribesman from becoming supreme. As Robert Wren asserts [in *Achebe's World,* 1981] *ozo* requires that every ambitious man of wealth periodically distribute his excess. In order to take any of the titles of the clan, a man has to give up a portion of his wealth to the clan. Okoye, in *Things Fall Apart,* is gathering all his resources in preparation for the "very expensive" ceremony required to take the Idemili title, the third highest in the land. As Achebe explains in *Arrow of God,* long ago there had been a fifth title among the Igbos of Umuaro—the title of king:

> But the conditions for its attainment had been so severe that no man had ever taken it, one of the conditions being that the man aspiring to be king must first pay the debts of every man and every woman in Umuaro.

Along with the representation of the viability of Igbo institutions in a world without Europeans, Achebe gives a sense of the beauty of Igbo art, poetry and music by showing how it is interwoven with the most important institutions of the clan and by creating a sense of the Igbo language through his own use of English. The decorating of walls and bodies or the shaving of hair in "beautiful patterns" recurs in various ceremonies. Music and dancing are a part of Igbo rituals which call for talent such as that of Obiozo Ezikolo, king of all the drums. Stories become the means of inciting men to strength, of teaching about the gods, and of generally passing on the culture....

In addition to portraying the dignity of Igbo village life, Achebe makes it clear that the Igbos did not need the white man to carry them into the modern world. Within the Igbo system change and progress were possible. When old customs were ineffective, they were gradually discarded. Formerly the punishment for breaking the Week of Peace was not so mild as that meted out to Okonkwo, an offering to Ani. In the past "a man who broke the peace was dragged on the ground through the village until he died. But after a while this custom was stopped because it spoiled the peace which it was meant to preserve." Such changes were likely to be brought about by men who, like Obierika, "thought about things," such as why a man should suffer for an inadvertent offense or why twins should be thrown away.

Although Achebe has the Igbo culture meet certain standards, he does not idealize the past. Probably the most troubling aspect of Igbo culture for modern democrats is the law that requires the killing of Ikemefuna for the sins of his clan. Achebe's description of Ikemefuna makes him a sympathetic character, and it is difficult not to side with Nwoye in rebelling against this act. Nevertheless, Igbo history does not seem so different from that of the British who think they are civilizing the natives. A form of the principle of an eye for an eye is involved in Mbaino's giving Mbanta a young virgin and a young man to replace the "daughter of Mbanta" killed in Mbaino. It is the Old Testament principle cast in a more flexible and gentler mold, for the killing of Ikemefuna is dependent on the Oracle and thus is not, like the Old Testament law, inevitable. Further, the sacrifices of the virgin to replace the lost wife and of the young boy become a way to "avoid war and bloodshed" while still protecting one's tribe from injustices against it. Achebe, then, seems to depict this episode in terms which relate it to the development of the British, while also sympathizing with the impulses to change in Obierika and with the revulsion of Nwoye against the sacrifice which to him is so like the abandonment of twins in the Evil Forest. The sacrifice of the virgin, of course, is also a reminder of the sacrifices of young virgins in the classical literature which is so basic a part of the British heritage....

Although Achebe depicts the treachery and ignorance and intolerance of the British, he does not represent the Europeans as wholly evil. Both the Igbo and the British cultures are for Achebe a mixture of types of human beings. Okonkwo and Mr. Smith are warrior types who will not compromise when their own cultures are threatened. Okonkwo favors fighting the Christians when in Abame one of them kills the sacred python, and he favors war with the Christians in Umuofia. In the end he cuts down the court messengers who come to disband the meeting in Umuofia. Likewise, the Reverend James Smith is against compromise: "He saw the world as a battlefield in which the children of light were locked in mortal conflict with the sons of darkness."

Mr. Brown, on the other hand, is more like Akunna or Obierika. He and Akunna are willing to learn about the other's beliefs even if they are not converted to them. He and Obierika are thoughtful defenders of their own cultures. Mr. Brown recognizes the difficulty with a frontal attack on the Igbos' religion, and so he favors compromise and accommodation. Obierika realizes that if Umuofia kills the Christians, the soldiers from Umuru will annihilate the village.

Achebe's novel, then, depicts for both Africans and Americans the actual and potential sources of modern Nigerian dignity. *Things Fall Apart* suggests that the perpetual human types recur in all cultures and that all effective civilizations must

learn to deal with those types. Revealing the Igbo ability in precolonial times to incorporate the variety of humans in a well-functioning culture, Achebe refers his Igbo society to a series of standards which both Africans and Americans can seek as goals—a degree of redistribution of wealth, a combining of male and female principles, compelling art and poetry and music, tolerance, democracy, morality, a sound system of justice and, perhaps most important, the capacity for meaningful change. Lending veracity to his depiction of Igbo history by remaining clearsighted about cultural weaknesses which need correction, Achebe depicts a worthy precursor of a healthy and just modern civilization.

Source: Diana Akers Rhoads, "Culture in Chinua Achebe's *Things Fall Apart,*" in *The African Studies Review,* Vol. 26, No. 2, September, 1993, pp. 61–72.

Ndiawar Sarr

In the following excerpt, Sarr explores Achebe's novel Things Fall Apart *from a cultural perspective.*

Written about the past of Africa by a novelist who sees himself as a "teacher," *Things Fall Apart* encompasses several worlds, several experiences, sometimes complex, all altered or mixed. Achebe is never a mere reporter of public events. Talking of *Things Fall Apart,* he said: "I now know that my first book was an act of atonement with my past, the ritual return and homage of a prodigal son" [Achebe in *Morning Yet on Creation Day,* Heinemann, 1975]. The past that Chinua Achebe describes so beautifully in *Things Fall Apart* is a past that Achebe himself had to rediscover. It is a past that was largely lost as a result of twentieth-century Europeanization. This rediscovery of the suppressed past is an act of faith and religious revival. Achebe, like the majority of African writers today, wants his writings to be functional, to serve as oral literature did in traditional Africa, reflecting the totality of actual experience. As David Cook tells us:

> Close study of a passage from *Things Fall Apart* out of context is particularly likely to lead to pedantic fault-finding and to have little relation to the full impact the novel makes upon us since ... the achievement of this work is essentially an epic achievement in which the whole is greater than the parts and in which the parts cannot be appreciated properly when separated from the whole. [*African Literature: A Critical View,* by David Cook, Longman, 1977.]

John Mbiti similarly sees the holistic and communal nature of African culture in his statement: "I am because we are and since we are therefore I am" [in *African Religions and Philosophy,* by John Mbiti, Anchor Books Doubleday, 1970]. This communal sense makes it necessary to see Okonkwo as something other than just a tragic hero in the usual Western sense—a lonely figure who passes moral judgment the group.

The "we" of Achebe's story is the Ibo society of Umuofia, which has no centralized authority or king. The tribal setup is very different from most tribal societies in Africa, because of its respect for individualism and its rejection of any inherited or hierarchical system of authority. The Ibo people's highly individualistic society may have developed partly because of geography, for they lived in forest areas which were difficult to penetrate, and each village lived separated from the next. These natural obstacles are described by another Ibo writer, Elechi Amadi, in his novel *The Concubine* [Heinemann, 1982]:

> Only the braves could go as far as Alyi. It was a whole day's journey from Omokachi. The path went through forests and swamps and there is no knowing when and where headhunters would strike. When there was any message to be relayed to Alyi two strong men ran the errand.

In spite of its isolation, Umuofia society is proud, dignified, and stable. It is governed by a complicated system of customs, traditions, and rituals extending from birth through marriage to death. It has its own legal, educational, and religious system and conventions governing relations between men and women, adults and children, and the various generations. The first part of the book allows us to see the customs, rituals, and traditions of Umuofia (e.g., consultation of oracles, the Week of Peace, the New Yam Festival) and to see the myths operating in the clan (e.g., Ogbanje, or a child that repeatedly dies and returns to the mother to be reborn, the exposure of twins, and taboos about shedding the blood of one's clansmen).

In addition, we are shown a society that is competitive and materialistic. A man's prestige is in direct proportion to the size of his barns and his compounds, to the number of titles he has taken. As *Things Fall Apart* shows the first impact of European invasion upon the old Ibo society, Achebe presents, in a very fair and objective way, the strengths and weaknesses of this society. Contrary to the views of the District Commissioner who plans to write a book, *The Pacification of the Primitive Tribes of the Lower Niger,* Achebe presents an Ibo culture which is neither "primitive" nor "barbaric." Even though his ambition to prove that "African peoples did not hear of culture for the first time

from Europeans" might seem to cast doubt on his objectivity, he does not romanticize the Ibo society, but reveals instead the bad side as well as the good. He acts as the conscientious teacher he wants to be. Nothing is left aside.

To his credit, Achebe does not merely describe these traditions, values, and customs; he brings the ceremonial to life, presenting events and conversations dramatically. In so doing, he presents convincingly a rich Ibo culture which is not static, but clearly in a state of transition. Outwardly, Umuofia is a world of serenity, harmony, and communal activity, but inwardly it is torn by the individual's personal doubts and fears. At times, the reader is faced with contradictions. For example, although the child is valued more than any material thing in Umuofian society, an innocent child named Ikemefuna is denied life by traditional laws and customs which demand his life in return for that of a Umuofian who was killed by his people. But Ibo society is full of contradictions. It is a world in which the spiritual dimension is a part of daily life, but also a world in which a man's success is measured by his material goods. It is a world which is at once communal and individualistic, a world in which human relations are paramount, but in which old people and twins are left in the forest to die. It is a male-dominated society, in which the chief goddess is female and in which proverbial wisdom maintains "Mother is supreme." This sustained view of the duality of the traditional Ibo society intensifies the wider tragedy and reveals the dilemma that shapes and destroys the life of Okonkwo....

In providing a context for interpreting Okonkwo's relationship with his society, the novel's use of proverbs plays an important role. They reveal the clan's dependence upon traditional wisdom and help to present the whole way of life. Many critics have demonstrated the power of proverbs in the work of Achebe in general and in *Things Fall Apart* in particular. Bernth Lindfors sums up the role of the proverbs in Achebe's fictions when he declares:

> Proverbs can serve as keys to an understanding of his novels because he uses them not merely to add a touch of local color but to sound and reiterate themes, to sharpen characterization, to clarify conflict, and to focus on the values of the society he is portraying. [*Folklore in Nigerian Literature,* by Bernth Lindfors, Africana Publishing, 1973.]

Such an understanding of the subtleties of language by the reader is possible only through personal effort linked with open-mindedness. It is, unfortunately, those elements which are lacking among many of the characters in the novel and which have led also to cultural misunderstanding among its readers. Achebe is using English, a worldwide language, to translate African experience. In other words, English, a tool in the hands of all those who have learnt to master it, can be submitted to different kinds of use. Critics of African literature must keep this fact in mind and try to grasp all the riches of the Ibo language and rhetoric that Achebe, as a son of the tribe, has tried to translate. With such an attitude, the critic will contribute to consolidating and widening our experience, the human experience. Hasn't the reader grown into accepting, for instance, that the natural world is penetrated by the supernatural, thanks to Achebe's ability to make us live (with the characters) the various stages of their cultural life?

Things Fall Apart, the title of which is an allusion to W. B. Yeats's poem "The Second Coming," is a novel in which Achebe is interested in analyzing the way things happen and in giving language to the Ibo experience. He offers a larger view of history and of individual life:

> No civilization can either remain static or evolve forever towards a more inclusive perfection. It must both collapse from within and be overwhelmed from without, and what replaces it will appear most opposite to itself, being built from all that it overlooked or undervalued. [In *Critical Perspectives on Achebe,* edited by C. L. Innes and Bernth Lindfors, Three Continents Press, 1978.]

The novel, therefore, celebrates stability in human affairs despite its apparent "anarchy" (to use a word from Yeats's poem). Ibo culture, even while changing, is very much alive. Despite the tragic loss of Okonkwo, the society of the Ibos, because of its flexibility, survives. Despite the loss, "the center holds."

Source: Ndiawar Sarr, "The Center Holds: The Resilience of Ibo Culture in *Things Fall Apart,*" in *Global Perspectives on Teaching Literature: Shared Visions and Distinctive Visions,* Sandra Ward Lott, Maureen S. G. Hawkins, Norman McMillan, eds., National Council of Teachers of English, 1993, pp. 347–55.

Sources

Kofi Awoonor, *The Breast of the Earth,* Doubleday, 1975.

G. D. Killam, *The Novels of Chinua Achebe,* Africana Publishing, 1969.

Charles Larson, "Chinua Achebe's 'Things Fall Apart': The Archetypal African Novel" and "Characters and Modes of Characterization: Chinua Achebe, James Ngugi, and Peter Abrahams," in *The Emergence of African Fiction,* revised edition, Indiana University Press, 1972, pp. 27-65, 147-66.

Eustace Palmer, *The Growth of the African Novel,* Heinemann, 1979.

Adrian A. Roscoe, *Mother Is Gold: A Study of West African Literature,* Cambridge University Press, 1971.

For Further Study

Chinua Achebe, "The Novelist as Teacher," in *Hope and Impediments: Selected Essays,* Anchor Books, 1988, pp. 40-46.
     Achebe's own explanation of the social significance of his fiction.

Edna Aizenberg, "The Third World Novel as Counterhistory: *Things Fall Apart* and Asturias's *Men of Maize,*" in *Approaches to Teaching Achebe's "Things Fall Apart,"* edited by Bernth Lindfors, Modern Language Association of America, 1991, pp. 85-90.
     An analysis of how *Things Fall Apart* revises biased colonial histories.

Ernest N. Emenyonu, "Chinua Achebe's *Things Fall Apart:* A Classic Study in Colonial Diplomatic Tactlessness," in *Chinua Achebe: A Celebration,* edited by Kirsten Holst Petersen and Anna Rutherford, Heinemann, 1990, pp. 83-88.
     An analysis of the political significance of *Things Fall Apart* as a critique of colonialism.

Abiola Irele, "The Tragic Conflict in the Novels of Chinua Achebe," in *Critical Perspectives on Chinua Achebe,* edited by C. L. Innes and Bernth Lindfors, Three Continents Press, 1978, pp. 10-21.
     An analysis of Achebe's use of tragedy.

Solomon O. Iyasere, "Narrative Techniques in *Things Fall Apart,*" in *Critical Perspectives on Chinua Achebe,* edited by C. L. Innes and Bernth Lindfors, Three Continents Press, 1978, pp. 92-110.
     A general introduction to the themes and narrative structure of *Things Fall Apart.*

Abdul JanMohamed, "Sophisticated Primitivism: The Syncretism of Oral and Literate Modes in Achebe's *Things Fall Apart,*" *Ariel: A Review of International English Literature,* Vol. 15, No. 4, 1984, pp. 19-39.
     An analysis of how Achebe synthesizes African oral cultural traditions with English literary conventions.

Biodun Jeyifo, "Okonkwo and His Mother: *Things Fall Apart* and Issues of Gender in the Constitution of African Postcolonial Discourse," in *Callaloo: A Journal of African-American and African Arts and Letters,* Vol. 16, No. 4, 1993, pp. 847-58.
     An analysis of the role of gender in *Things Fall Apart.*

Bernth Lindfors, "The Palm-Oil with Which Achebe's Words are Eaten," in *African Literature Today,* Vol. 1, 1968, pp. 3-18.
     An analysis of Achebe's use of traditional proverbs in *Things Fall Apart.*

Alastair Niven, "Chinua Achebe and the Possibility of Modern Tragedy," in *Chinua Achebe: A Celebration,* edited by Kirsten Holst Petersen and Anna Rutherford, Heinemann, 1990, pp. 41-50.
     An analysis of Achebe's use of tragedy.

Emmanuel Obiechina, "Narrative Proverbs in the African Novel," *Research in African Literatures,* Vol. 24, No. 4, 1993, pp. 123-40.

An analysis of Achebe's use of African oral cultural traditions such as proverbs and storytelling.

Ato Quayson, "Realism, Criticism, and the Disguises of Both: A Reading of Chinua Achebe's *Things Fall Apart* with an Evaluation of the Criticism Relating to It," in *Research in African Literatures,* Vol. 25, No. 4, 1994, pp. 117-36.

Argues that most critics have emphasized the realistic dimensions of *Things Fall Apart* without adequately discussing how the novel has its own biased perspective.

Joseph Swann, "From *Things Fall Apart* to *Anthills of the Savannah:* The Changing Face of History in Chinua Achebe's Novels," in *Crisis and Creativity in the New Literatures in English,* edited by Geoffrey V. Davis and Hena Maes-Jelinek, Rodopi, 1990, pp. 191-203.

An analysis of how Achebe's approach to history changes in each of his novels.

To Kill a Mockingbird

Harper Lee
1960

When *To Kill a Mockingbird* was published in 1960, it brought its young first-time author, Harper Lee, a startling amount of attention and notoriety. The novel replays three key years in the life of Scout Finch, the young daughter of an Alabama town's principled lawyer. The work was an instant sensation, becoming a best-seller and winning the Pulitzer Prize for fiction. Scout's narrative relates how she and her elder brother Jem learn about fighting prejudice and upholding human dignity through the example of their father. Atticus Finch has taken on the legal defense of a black man who has been falsely charged with raping a white woman. Lee's story of the events surrounding the trial has been admired for its portrayal of Southern life during the 1930s, not only for its piercing examination of the causes and effects of racism, but because it created a model of tolerance and courage in the character of Atticus Finch. Some early reviewers found Scout's narration unconvincing, its style and language too sophisticated for a young girl. Since then, however, critics have hailed Lee's rendering of a child's perspective—as told by an experienced adult—as one of the most technically proficient in modern fiction. A regional novel dealing with universal themes of tolerance, courage, compassion, and justice, *To Kill a Mockingbird* combined popular appeal with literary excellence to ensure itself an enduring place in modern American literature.

Author Biography

Although Harper Lee has long maintained that *To Kill a Mockingbird* is not autobiographical, critics have often remarked upon the striking similarities between the author's own childhood and that of her youthful heroine, Scout Finch. Nelle Harper Lee was born in 1926, the youngest of three children of Amasa Coleman Lee, a lawyer who practiced in the small town of Monroeville, Alabama. Like Scout, who could be bullied into submission with the remark that she was "gettin' more like a girl," Lee was "a rough 'n' tough tomboy," according to childhood friends. Summers in Monroeville were brightened by the visits of young Truman Capote, who stayed with the Lees' next-door neighbors and who later became a famous writer himself. The games young Nelle and her brother played with Capote were likely the inspiration for the adventures Scout and Jem had with Dill, their own "summer" friend.

After graduating from the public schools of Monroeville, Lee attended a small college in nearby Montgomery before attending the University of Alabama for four years. She left school six months short of earning a law degree, however, in order to pursue a writing career. In the early 1950s, the author worked as an airline reservations clerk in New York City, writing essays and short stories in her spare time. After her literary agent suggested that one of her stories might be expanded into a novel, Lee quit her airline job. With the financial support of some friends, she spent several years revising the manuscript of *To Kill a Mockingbird* before submitting it to publishers. Several more months of revision followed the feedback of her editors, who found the original version more like a string of short stories than a cohesive novel. The final draft was finally completed in 1959 and published in 1960. The novel was a dramatic success, earning generally positive reviews and achieving bestseller status. Lee herself attained considerable celebrity as the novel won the Pulitzer Prize for fiction in 1961 and was made into an Oscar-winning film in 1962. Since then, aside from a few magazine pieces in the early 1960s, the reclusive author has published nothing, although she has been reported to have been working on a second novel. Despite the lack of a follow-up work, Lee's literary reputation remains secure and even has grown since the debut of her remarkable first novel.

Harper Lee

Plot Summary

Part One

Harper Lee's *To Kill a Mockingbird* depicts the life of its young narrator, Jean Louise "Scout" Finch, in the small town of Maycomb, Alabama, in the mid-1930s. Scout opens the novel as a grown woman reflecting back on key events in her childhood. The novel covers a two-year period, beginning when Scout is six and ending when she is eight. She lives with her father, Atticus, a widowed lawyer, and her older brother, Jem (short for Jeremy). Their black housekeeper, Calpurnia, tends to the children. Scout and Jem's summer playmate, Dill Harris, shares the Finch children's adventures and adds imagination and intrigue to their game playing. In the novel, we see Scout grow in awareness and come to new understandings about her town, her family, and herself.

During the summer before Scout enters school, the children become fascinated with Arthur "Boo" Radley, a reclusive neighbor. Radley's father, a religious fanatic, confined Boo to the house because he was arrested for youthful pranks as a teenager. Some years later, Boo casually stabbed his father in the leg with a pair of scissors, confirming people's worst fears about him. The children are naturally afraid of and intrigued by such a "malevolent phantom," as Scout calls him. Yet they only approach the house once, when Jem runs and touches the porch on a dare.

Scout enters first grade the following September and must confront new challenges and learn new ways to deal with people. She cannot understand, for instance, her young teacher's lack of familiarity with the town families and their peculiarities, such as the Cunningham children's poverty and pride. Later, Atticus explains to Scout that she must put herself in others' places before judging them, one of the many lessons she learns by making mistakes.

With summer's return, Dill arrives and the children's absorption with Boo Radley begins again in earnest. Ultimately, they attempt to look in the house to see Boo, but a shotgun blast from Nathan Radley, Boo's brother, drives them off. In their panic, Jem catches his overalls in the Radley fence and must abandon them. Later that night, he returns to retrieve them and finds them neatly folded on the fence with the ripped fabric poorly resewn.

Their contact with Boo Radley continues into the school year. Before the previous summer, Scout and Jem had discovered gum and Indian head pennies in a knot-holed tree by the Radley house. Now more objects begin to appear in the knothole, including replicas of Scout and Jem carved in soap. They decide to leave a note for whoever is leaving the objects, but before they can, Nathan Radley fills the hole with cement, upsetting Jem.

Scout soon encounters trouble at school when a schoolmate condemns Atticus for "defending niggers." Atticus confirms that he is defending a black man named Tom Robinson, who is accused of raping a white woman, and that his conscience compels him to do no less. He warns her that she will encounter more accusations of this kind and to remember that despite their views, the people who cast slurs at them are still their friends. Atticus later tells his brother Jack that he hopes he can guide his children through this time without them becoming bitter and "without catching Maycomb's usual disease" of racism.

That Christmas, Atticus gives the children air-rifles and admonishes them to shoot no mockingbirds. Miss Maudie Atkinson, their neighbor, explains Atticus's reasons when she says that "Mockingbirds don't do one thing but make music for us to enjoy." Hence, it is a sin to kill them. At this time, the children feel disappointed in Atticus because he is old (almost fifty) and does nothing of interest. They soon learn, however, about one of their father's unique talents when he shoots a rabid dog that threatens the neighborhood, killing the beast with one shot. The neighbors tell them that Atticus is the best shot in the county, he just chooses not to shoot a gun unless he must. Scout admires Atticus for his shooting talent, but Jem admires him for his gentlemanly restraint.

Part Two

The family's involvement in Tom Robinson's trial dominates Part Two of the novel. One personal inconvenience of the trial is the arrival of Aunt Alexandra, Atticus's sister, who comes to tend to the family. Scout finds her presence unwelcome because Aunt Alexandra disapproves of her tomboyish dress and activities and tries to make Scout wear dresses and attend women's socials.

The time for the trial arrives, and Atticus guards the jail door the night Tom Robinson is brought to Maycomb. The children, including Dill, sneak out to watch over him and soon become involved in a standoff. Carloads of men drive up and demand that Atticus let them have Tom Robinson, and he gently refuses. Scout recognizes a schoolmate's father, Mr. Cunningham, and asks him polite questions about his legal debt to Atticus, who did work for him, and about his son. Scout's innocent questioning of Mr. Cunningham shames him, and he convinces the men to leave.

The children also sneak to the courthouse to attend the trial. They sit in the balcony with the black townspeople because no seats are available on the ground floor. Atticus's questioning of Bob Ewell and Mayella Ewell, both of whom claim Tom Robinson beat and raped Mayella, reveals their lies. Mayella was beaten primarily on the right side of her body by a left-handed man. By having Bob Ewell sign his name, Atticus shows him to be left-handed. Tom Robinson's left arm, however, is crippled from a boyhood accident. Tom's story rings truer. He contends that Mayella invited him into the house and tried to seduce him, a story made credible by Mayella's and Tom's descriptions of her lonely life. Tom resisted her advances, but before he could leave Bob Ewell discovered them. Tom ran and Ewell beat Mayella. To avoid social disgrace, the Ewells claimed Tom had raped her.

Despite the evidence, Tom is convicted. Atticus has expected this verdict and believes he can win on appeal. Jem has difficulty accepting the injustice of the verdict. Others, however, remain angry over Atticus's sincere defense of Robinson, particularly Bob Ewell. Ewell confronts Atticus, threatens him, and spits on him. Soon after, Tom Robinson's story ends in tragedy as he is shot trying to escape from prison. He ran because he believed he could find no justice in a white-dominated legal system.

The following October, Scout dresses as a ham for the school Halloween pageant. On the way home from the pageant, she and Jem are followed, then attacked. Scout cannot see their assailant because of her costume, but she hears Jem grappling with him and hears Jem being injured. After the confused struggle, she feels a man lying on the ground and sees another man carrying Jem. She follows them home. The doctor arrives and assures her that Jem is alive and has suffered only a broken arm. The man who carried him home is standing in Jem's room. To Scout's tearful amazement, she realizes that he is Boo Radley. Sheriff Heck Tate informs them that Bob Ewell attacked them and that only Scout's costume saved her. Ewell himself now lies dead, stabbed in the ribs. Atticus believes Jem killed Ewell in self-defense, but Tate makes him realize that Boo Radley actually stabbed Ewell and saved both children's lives. The men agree to claim that Ewell fell on his knife in order to save Boo the spectacle of a trial. Scout walks Boo home:

> He had to stoop a little to accommodate me, but if Miss Stephanie Crawford was watching from her upstairs window, she would see Arthur Radley escorting me down the sidewalk, as any gentleman would do.

> We came to the street light on the corner, and I wondered how many times Dill had stood there hugging the fat pole, watching, waiting, hoping. I wondered how many times Jem and I had made this journey, but I entered the Radley front gate for the second time in my life. Boo and I walked up the steps to the porch. His fingers found the front doorknob. He gently released my hand, opened the door, went inside, and shut the door behind him. I never saw him again.

> Neighbors bring food with death and flowers with sickness and little things in between. Boo was our neighbor. He gave us two soap dolls, a broken watch and chain, a pair of good-luck pennies, and our lives. But neighbors give in return. We never put back into the tree what we took out of it; we had given him nothing, and it made me sad.

She returns home to Atticus, who stays up all night waiting for Jem to awake.

Characters

Aunt Alexandra
See Alexandra Finch Hancock

Miss Maudie Atkinson

Maudie Atkinson is a strong, supportive woman who lives across the street from the Finches. A forthright speaker, she never condescends to Jem and Scout, but speaks to them as equals. It is Miss Maudie who affirms that it is a sin to kill a mockingbird, since "they don't do one thing but sing their hearts out for us." A respected community member who often teasingly reproaches the children, Miss Maudie nevertheless has a impish streak: she likes to quote scripture back to conservative religious folk who frown on her brightly colored garden. Miss Maudie provides another example of bravery to the children when her home burns down. Instead of lamenting her fate, she tells Jem she looks forward to rebuilding a smaller house which will have more room for her flowers.

Mr. Avery

A good-natured if somewhat coarse neighbor of the Finches who helps fight the fire at Miss Maudie's house at risk to his own life.

Calpurnia

One of several strong female figures in the lives of the Finch children, Calpurnia is the family's black housekeeper. She has helped to raise Jem and Scout since their mother's death four years ago. Like Atticus, Calpurnia is a strict but loving teacher, particularly in regard to Scout, whose enthusiasm sometimes makes her thoughtless. On Scout's first day of school, for example, Calpurnia scolds Scout for criticizing the table manners of Walter Cunningham Jr., whom the children have brought home as a lunch guest. That day after school, however, Calpurnia prepares Scout's favorite food, crackling bread, as a special treat. Calpurnia also gives Scout her first awareness of the contrast between the worlds of black and white. During a visit to Calpurnia's church, her use of black dialect with her friends makes Scout realize that Calpurnia has a wider life outside the Finch household. Calpurnia also helps Scout understand how people can serve as a bridge between these differing worlds. Although the majority of parishioners welcome them during their church visit, one woman challenges the white children. Calpurnia responds by calling them her guests and saying "it's the same God, ain't it?"

Stephanie Crawford

The "neighborhood scold" who is always ready to gossip about anything or anyone.

From the film To Kill a Mockingbird, *starring Gregory Peck, Mary Badham, Phillip Alford, and John Megna, 1962.*

Walter Cunningham Jr.

A poor but proud classmate of Scout's.

Walter Cunningham Sr.

Walter Cunningham, Sr., is a member of a poor family who "never took anything they couldn't pay back." A former client of Atticus's, he paid for legal service with goods such as firewood and hickory nuts. After Scout recognizes him in the potential lynch mob and speaks to him of his son, he leads the crowd away from violence.

Link Deas

A local farmer who hires a lot of black help and once employed Tom Robinson.

Mrs. Henry Lafayette Dubose

According to Scout, Mrs. Henry Lafayette Dubose is "the meanest old woman who ever lived." She regularly insults and harasses the children as they walk by. When Jem wrecks her garden in retaliation for a nasty remark about his father, Atticus punishes him by forcing him to spend many hours reading to her. She dies later that year, and Jem learns that his reading helped her to courageously defeat an addiction to morphine.

Bob Ewell

The head of family who's been "the disgrace of Maycomb for three generations," Bob Ewell is despised by Maycomb society as a shiftless drunkard. He is unable to keep a job, spends all his relief money on alcohol, and traps animals outside of hunting season. He provides little support to his large, motherless family, and is reputed to beat his children (and perhaps sexually abuse them too, as Mayella's testimony hints). Angered and shamed by his exposure on the witness stand, Ewell makes threats to Atticus and others involved in the trial, but never risks direct confrontation. This cowardice reaches its peak in his violent attack on Scout and Jem, during which he is killed by Boo Radley.

Mayella Ewell

The eldest daughter of Bob Ewell, Mayella Ewell lives a lonely life keeping house for her father and seven siblings without assistance. Although she can only afford small gestures such as a potted plant, Mayella tries to brighten her situation and the lives of her siblings. During the trial it is revealed that Tom Robinson's occasional stops to help her with heavy chores were her only contact with a sympathetic soul. When Bob Ewell discovers Mayella's attempt to seduce the unwilling

Media Adaptations

- To Kill a Mockingbird was adapted as a film by Horton Foote, starring Gregory Peck and Mary Badham, Universal, 1962; available from MCA/ Universal Home Video.

- It was also adapted as a full-length stage play by Christopher Sergel, and was published as *Harper Lee's To Kill a Mockingbird: A Full-length Play,* Dramatic Publishing Co., 1970.

Tom, his violent outburst leads her to accuse Tom of rape. Despite her situation, she loses the reader's sympathy when she repays Tom's kindness with open contempt and a lie that costs him his life. The fact that the jury accepts her word over his, even when it is demonstrated to be false, further illustrates the malicious power of racist thinking.

Mrs. Gertrude Farrow

One of the hypocritical members of Aunt Alexandra's missionary circle.

Atticus Finch

Atticus Finch, Scout's widowed father, is a member of one of Maycomb County's oldest and most prominent families. Nevertheless, he refuses to use his background as an excuse to hold himself above others and instead is a model of tolerance and understanding. Atticus is a lawyer and also a member of the state legislature, elected by townspeople who respect his honesty even if they don't always approve of his actions. For example, when Atticus is appointed the defense attorney for Tom Robinson, a black man accused of raping a white woman, the town disapproves because he aims to do the best job he can. As a father Atticus is affectionate with Jem and Scout, ready with a hug when they need comfort and available to spend time reading to them. Although he allows his children freedom to play and explore, he is also a firm disciplinarian, always teaching his children to think of how their actions affect others and devising punishments to teach his children valuable lessons. When Jem damages the camellia bushes of Mrs.

Henry Lafayette Dubose, a neighbor who scolds and insults the children, Atticus sentences him to read to her each day. As Jem reads, he and Scout witness the dying woman's battle against her morphine addiction and learn the true meaning of courage: "it's when you know you're licked before you begin but you see it through no matter what," Atticus tells them. Atticus's own actions in arguing the Robinson case demonstrate this kind of courage, and his behavior throughout embodies values of dignity, integrity, determination, and tolerance. Although Atticus's character is somewhat idealized, critic William T. Going calls Lee's creation "the most memorable portrait in recent fiction of the just and equitable Southern liberal."

Jack Finch

See John Hale Finch

Jean Louise Finch

The narrator of the novel, Jean Louise "Scout" Finch is almost six years old at the time her story begins. A tomboy most frequently clad in overalls, Scout spends much of her time with her older brother Jem and is constantly trying to prove herself his equal. Throughout the book Scout maintains an innocence and an innate sense of right and wrong that makes her the ideal observer of events, even if she doesn't always fully understand them. She naturally questions the injustices she sees instead of accepting them as "the way things are." For instance, she doesn't understand why her aunt makes social distinctions based on "background" when Scout thinks "there's just one kind of folks: Folks." Her independence and outspokenness often get Scout into trouble, however; she is quick to respond to insults with her fists and frequently opens her mouth at inappropriate moments, as when she rudely remarks on the table manners of a guest. By the end of the novel, however, eight-year-old Scout has learned a measure of restraint, primarily through the influence and example of her father Atticus.

Jem Finch

See Jeremy Finch

Jeremy Finch

Four years older than his sister Scout, Jeremy "Jem" Finch seems to have a deeper understanding of the events during the three years of the novel, for his emotional reactions to them are stronger. As the story begins, Jem is a quick-witted but fun-loving ten year old who spends a lot of time in creative play with Scout and Dill Harris, a summer visitor to the neighborhood. Jem is frequently exasperated by his sister, and requires her to keep her distance during school hours. Nevertheless, for the most part Jem is an understanding and encouraging older brother, allowing Scout to join in his games and even dignifying her with an occasional fistfight. He is anxious to please his father, and hates to disappoint him. When Jem loses his pants in the "raid" on the Radley house, he insists on returning for them during the middle of the night—not so much to avoid the pain of punishment, but because "Atticus ain't ever whipped me since I can remember. I wanta keep it that way." As he approaches adolescence, however, Jem becomes quieter and more easily agitated: he reacts angrily when Mrs. Dubose leaves him a small peace offering after her death. Although more socially aware than Scout, he is genuinely surprised at Tom Robinson's guilty verdict. The trial leaves Jem a little more withdrawn and less self-confident, and he spends much of the following fall concerned for his father's safety. He demonstrates his own courage, however, when he protects his sister from the attack of Bob Ewell without regard for his own safety.

John Hale Finch

Atticus's younger brother, a doctor who left Maycomb to study in Boston.

Scout Finch

See Jean Louise Finch

Miss Caroline Fisher

Scout's first-grade teacher who is a newcomer to Maycomb. She misunderstands the social order of Maycomb and punishes Scout for trying to explain it. She also comes into conflict with Scout because of the girl's reading ability.

Miss Gates

Scout's hypocritical third-grade teacher who condemns Hitler's persecution of the Jews even as she discriminates against her own students and complains about blacks "getting above themselves."

Mr. Gilmer

The circuit prosecutor from Abbottsville who leads the case against Tom Robinson.

Alexandra Finch Hancock

Atticus's sister, Alexandra Finch Hancock, is a conservative woman concerned with social and class distinctions and bound to the traditions of the South. She tries to counteract her brother's liberal influence on his children by reminding them of their family's eminence and by trying to make Scout behave in a more ladylike manner. When she moves in with Atticus's family, her efforts to reform Scout include requiring her attendance at regular meetings of a "missionary circle," whose discussions focus on improving the lives of "heathens" in distant Africa rather than on the needy in their own town. Aunt Alexandra is not completely unsympathetic, however; she also shows—in private—some anger towards the hypocrites in her missionary circle. Although she disapproves of Atticus's role in the Robinson case, she becomes upset upon hearing news of Robinson's death during one of her parties. Her ability to continue on leads Scout to state that "if Auntie could be a lady at a time like this, so could I."

Francis Hancock

Scout and Jem's cousin and Alexandra's grandson.

Charles Baker Harris

Small and devilish, Charles Baker "Dill" Harris is Scout and Jem's summer friend. He instigates much of the children's mischief by daring Jem to perform acts such as approaching the Radley house. He seems to have a limitless imagination, and his appeal is only enhanced by his firsthand knowledge of movies such as *Dracula.* Seemingly ignored (but not neglected) by his parents, Dill enjoys his yearly visits to his aunt, Rachel Haverford, who lives next door to the Finches—he even runs away from home one summer to come to Maycomb. A year older than Scout, Dill has declared he will one day marry her, a statement she seems to accept matter-of-factly.

Dill Harris

See Charles Baker Harris

Rachel Haverford

Dill Harris's sympathetic aunt, who lives next door to the Finches.

Grace Merriweather

A member of Alexandra's missionary circle who has a reputation as the "most devout lady in Maycomb" even though she is a hypocritical bigot.

Arthur Radley

Arthur "Boo" Radley has a strong presence in the novel even though he isn't seen until its last pages. A local legend for several years, Boo is rumored to wander the neighborhood at night and dine on raw squirrels and cats. He has spent the last fifteen years secluded in his own house. An adolescent prank led his late father to place him under house arrest. His sinister reputation stems from a later incident, when it was rumored that he stabbed his father in the leg with a pair of scissors. Boo becomes a central figure in the imaginations of Scout, Jem, and their neighbor Dill Harris, for their summers are occupied with dramatic re-creations of his life and plans to lure "the monster" out of his house. Despite his history of being abused by his father, Boo is revealed to be a gentle soul through his unseen acts: the gifts he leaves in the tree; his mending of Jem's torn pants; the blanket he puts around Scout the night of the fire; and finally, his rescue of the children from Bob Ewell's murderous attack. The children's fear of Boo Radley, based on ignorance rather than knowledge, subtly reflects the prejudice of the town against Tom Robinson—a connection mirrored in the use of mockingbird imagery for both men.

Boo Radley
See Arthur Radley

Nathan Radley
Boo's hardhearted older brother who spoils Boo's secret game with the children by filling the empty treehole with cement.

Dolphus Raymond
A local man from a good white family with property who has a black mistress and children. He fosters a reputation as a drunk to give townspeople a reason to excuse his flaunting of social taboos.

Tom Robinson
Tom Robinson is a mild-mannered, conscientious black man whose kind acts earn him only trouble when Mayella Ewell accuses him of rape. Because he saw she was left alone to maintain the household without any help from her family, he often performed small chores for her. During his testimony, he relates that he felt sorry for the girl. This remark affronts the white men in the jury, who see it as evidence that he is overreaching his social station. Although he is clearly proven innocent, the all-white jury convicts him of rape, a crime punishable by death. Unconvinced that he can find justice on appeal, Robinson attempts to escape from his prison camp and is shot dead.

Reverend Sykes
The minister of Maycomb's black church.

Heck Tate
The sheriff of Maycomb who is sympathetic towards Atticus and who insists on keeping Boo Radley's role in the death of Bob Ewell a secret.

Judge John Taylor
The deceivingly sleepy but fair judge whose sympathy for Tom Robinson can be seen in the fact that he appointed Atticus, whom he knew would do his best, as Robinson's public defender.

Uncle Jack
See John Hale Finch

B. B. Underwood
See Braxton Bragg Underwood

Braxton Bragg Underwood
The owner and editor of the local newspaper who was ready to defend Atticus and Tom Robinson from the lynch mob with a shotgun even though he is known to "despise" black people.

Themes

Prejudice and Tolerance
Comprising the main portion of the book's examination of racism and its effects are the underlying themes of prejudice vs. tolerance: how people feel about and respond to differences in others. At one end of the spectrum are people who fear and hate, such as the members of the jury who convict an innocent man of rape because of his race. Atticus and Calpurnia, on the other hand, show understanding and sympathy towards those who might be different or less fortunate. When Scout brings a poor classmate home for dinner and then belittles his table manners, for instance, Calpurnia scolds her for remarking upon them and tells her she is bound to treat all guests with respect no matter what their social station. Atticus similarly bases his opinions of people on their behavior and not their background. Unlike Alexandra, who calls poor people like the Cunninghams "trash" because of their social station, Atticus tells his children that any white man who takes advantage of a black man's ignorance is "trash."

Guilt and Innocence
Closely linked to these themes of prejudice are issues of guilt and innocence, for the same ignorance that creates racist beliefs underlies assump-

tions of guilt. The most obvious instance is the case of Tom Robinson: the jury's willingness to believe what Atticus calls "the evil assumption ... that *all* Negroes are basically immoral beings" leads them to convict an innocent man. Boo Radley, unknown by a community who has not seen or heard from him in fifteen years, is similarly presumed to be a monster by the court of public opinion. Scout underscores this point when she tells her Uncle Jack he has been unfair in assigning all the blame to her after her fight with Cousin Francis. If he had stopped to learn both sides of the situation he might have judged her differently—which he eventually does. The novel's conclusion also reinforces the theme of guilt and innocence, as Atticus reads Scout a book about a boy falsely accused of vandalism. As Scout summarizes: "When they finally saw him, why he hadn't done any of those things. Atticus, he was real nice." To which Atticus responds, "Most people are, once you see them."

Knowledge and Ignorance

Because a lack of understanding leads to prejudice and false assumptions of guilt, themes of ignorance and knowledge also play a large role in the novel. Lee seems to suggest that children have a natural instinct for tolerance and understanding; only as they grow older do they learn to react to differences with fear and disdain. For example, Scout is confused when one of Dolphus Raymond's mixed-race children is pointed out to her. The child looks "all Negro" to Scout, who wonders why it matters that "you just hafta know who [the mixed-race children] are." That same day Dill is made sick during the trial by the way in which Mr. Gilmer, the prosecuting attorney, sneeringly cross-examines Tom Robinson. As Dolphus Raymond tells Scout, "Things haven't caught up with that one's instinct yet. Let him get a little older and he won't get sick and cry." Lee seems to imply that children learn important lessons about life through the examples of others, not through school. In an ironic commentary on the nature of knowledge, formal education—as Scout experiences it—fails to teach or even contradicts these important lessons. Scout's first-grade teacher, Miss Caroline Fisher, is more concerned with making her students follow a system than in teaching them as individuals. This is why she forbids Scout to continue reading with her father, whose "unqualified" instruction would "interfere" with her education. Whatever the method, however, the most important factor in gaining knowledge is an individual's motivation. As Calpurnia tells Scout, people "got to want to

learn themselves, and when they don't want to learn there's nothing you can do but keep your mouth shut or learn their language."

Courage and Cowardice

Another important theme appearing throughout the novel is that of cowardice and heroism, for Scout observes several different kinds of courage during her childhood. The most common definition of bravery is being strong in the face of physical danger. Atticus demonstrates this when he stops in the path of a rabid dog and drops it with one rifle shot. Other kinds of courage, however, rely more on moral fortitude. For instance, Atticus talks pleasantly to Mrs. Henry Lafayette Dubose, even though she regularly heaps verbal abuse on him and his children. At times like these, Scout says, she thought "my father, who hated guns and had never been to any wars, was the bravest man who ever lived." Mrs. Dubose teaches the children another lesson in courage when Jem is sentenced to spend two hours a day reading to her as repayment for the flowers he damaged. Scout tags along as Jem visits after school to read Sir Walter Scott's *Ivanhoe,* a tale of chivalry and heroism. Mrs. Dubose's behavior seems strange; she often drifts off during the readings and begins to drool and have seizures.

Topics for Further Study

- Research the 1930s trials of the Scottsboro Boys and compare how the justice system worked in this case to the trial of Tom Robinson.

- Explore the government programs of President Franklin D. Roosevelt's "New Deal" and explain how some of the characters in *To Kill a Mockingbird* could have been helped by them.

- Investigate the various groups involved in the Civil Rights Movement of the 1950s and 1960s and compare their programs to the community supports found in Lee's imaginary town of Maycomb.

After her death some months later, the children discover that she was trying to overcome an addiction to morphine, a painkiller. Jem's reading served as a distraction that helped her die free from addiction. Atticus tells his children that despite her faults, Mrs. Dubose was the bravest person he ever knew, for real courage is "when you know you're licked before you begin but you begin anyway and you see it through no matter what." Atticus shows the same type of bravery in fighting the Robinson case; although he knows it would be nearly impossible for a white jury to return a verdict of "not guilty," he nonetheless argues the case to the best of his ability. In contrast to Atticus's bravery stands the cowardly behavior of Bob Ewell, who never directly faces those whom he thinks have wronged him. He vandalizes Judge Taylor's home when he thinks no one is there; he throws rocks and harasses Helen Robinson, Tom's widow, from a distance; and assaults Atticus's children as they walk alone on a deserted street at night.

Style

Point of View

The most outstanding aspect of *To Kill a Mockingbird*'s construction lies in its distinctive narrative point of view. Scout Finch, who narrates in the first person ("I"), is nearly six years old when the novel opens. The story, however, is recalled by the adult Scout; this allows her first-person narrative to contain adult language and adult insights yet still maintain the innocent outlook of a child. The adult perspective also adds a measure of hindsight to the tale, allowing for a deeper examination of events. The narrative proceeds in a straightforward and linear fashion, only jumping in time when relating past events as background to some present occurrence. Scout's account is broken into two parts: the two years before the trial, and the summer of the trial and the autumn that follows. Some critics have proposed that Part II itself should have been broken into two parts, the trial and the Halloween pageant; William T. Going suggests that this arrangement would keep the latter section from "seeming altogether an anticlimax to the trial of Tom."

Setting

The setting of *To Kill a Mockingbird* is another big factor in the story, for the action never leaves the town of Maycomb, Alabama. Maycomb is described variously as "an old town," "an an-

cient town," and "a tired old town," suggesting a conservative place that is steeped in tradition and convention. Scout's description of the local courthouse reinforces this impression. The building combines large Greek-style pillars—the only remnants from the original building that burned years ago—with the early Victorian design of its replacement. The result is an architectural oddity that indicates "a people determined to preserve every physical scrap of the past." The time of the novel is also significant, for the years 1933 to 1935 were in the midst of the Great Depression. These economic hard times affected the entire town, for if farmers and other laborers made barely enough money to survive, they had no extra money with which they could pay professionals like doctors and lawyers. When Atticus renders a legal service for Walter Cunningham Sr., a farmer whose property rights are in question because of an entailment, he is repaid with goods such as firewood and nuts instead of cash. This history between the two men influences events during the novel; when a lynch mob appears at the local jail, Scout recognizes Cunningham as her father's former client. The conversation she strikes up with him recalls him to his senses, and he sheepishly leads the mob away.

Symbolism

As the title of the novel implies, the mockingbird serves as an important symbol throughout the narrative. When the children receive guns for Christmas, Atticus tells them it's all right to shoot at blue jays, but "it's a sin to kill a mockingbird." As Miss Maudie Atkinson explains, it would be thoughtlessly cruel to kill innocent creatures that "don't do one thing but make music for us to enjoy." The mockingbirds are silent as Atticus takes to the street to shoot the rabid dog, and Scout describes a similar silence in the courtroom just prior to the jury pronouncing Tom Robinson guilty. The innocent but suffering mockingbird is recalled in an editorial B. B. Underwood writes about Robinson's death, and again when Scout tells her father that revealing Boo Radley's role in Bob Ewell's death would be "like shootin' a mockingbird." Another powerful symbol is contained in the snowman Scout and Jem build after Maycomb's rare snowfall. Because there is very little snow, Jem makes the base of the figure from mud; they then change their "morphodite" from black to white with a coating of snow. When Miss Maudie's house catches fire that night, the snow melts and the figure becomes black once again. Its transfor-

Sharecropper's house, Memphis, Tennessee, 1937.

mation suggests that skin color is a limited distinction that reveals little about an individual's true worth.

Humor

One element of the novel's construction that shouldn't be overlooked is Lee's use of humor. The serious issues the novel grapples with are lightened by episodes that use irony and slapstick humor, among other techniques. Just prior to Bob Ewell's attack on the children, for instance, is a scene where Scout misses her cue during the Halloween pageant, only to make her entrance as a ham during Mrs. Merriweather's sober grand finale. Scout's matter-of-fact, childish recollections also provide entertainment; she recalls that when Dill ignored her, his "fiancee," in favor of Jem, "I beat him up twice but it did no good." Other characters are full of wit as well, Miss Maudie Atkinson in particular. When exasperated by Stephanie Crawford's tales of Boo Radley peeking in her windows at night, she replies, "What did you do, Stephanie, move over in the bed and make room for him?" Including such humorous portrayals of human faults enlivens a serious plot, adds depth to the characterizations, and creates a sense of familiarity and universality, all factors that have contributed to the success and popularity of the work.

Historical Context

Civil Rights in the 1950s

Despite the end of slavery almost a century before *To Kill a Mockingbird* was published in 1960 (President Abraham Lincoln issued the Emancipation Proclamation in 1863), African Americans were still denied many of their basic rights. Although Lee sets her novel in the South of the 1930s, conditions were little improved by the early 1960s in America. The Civil Rights movement was just taking shape in the 1950s, and its principles were beginning to find a voice in American courtrooms and the law. The famous 1954 U.S. Supreme Court trial of *Brown v. the Board of Education of Topeka, Kansas* declared the long-held practice of segregation in public schools unconstitutional and quickly led to desegregation of other public institutions. However, there was still considerable resistance to these changes, and many states, especially those in the South, took years before they fully integrated their schools.

Other ways blacks were demeaned by society included the segregation of public rest rooms and drinking fountains, as well as the practice of forcing blacks to ride in the back of buses. This injustice was challenged by a mild-mannered department store seamstress named Rosa Parks. After she

Compare & Contrast

- **1930s:** During the Great Depression, unemployment rose as high as 25%; the New Deal program of government-sponsored relief leads to a deficit in the federal budget.

  1960: After a decade of record-high American production and exports, unemployment dips to less than 5 percent, while the federal government runs a small surplus.

  Today: Unemployment runs between 5 and 6 percent, while the federal government works to reduce a multi-billion dollar deficit amidst an increasingly competitive global economy.

- **1930s:** Schools are racially segregated; emphasis in the classroom was on rote learning of the basics.

  1960: Although backed up by force at times, school integration laws were being enforced; the 1959 launch of the Soviet satellite *Sputnik* leads to math and science gaining increased importance.

  Today: School populations are as racially diverse as their communities; classes include a focus on combining subjects and problem-solving skills.

- **1930s:** Only property owners who were white and male could serve on juries.

  1960: Women and minorities could now serve on juries; while the Supreme Court ruled that eliminating jurors from duty on the basis of race is unconstitutional, many trials still exclude blacks and Hispanics.

  Today: All registered voters are eligible to serve on juries, although in many cases prosecution and defense teams aim to create a jury with a racial balance favorable to their side.

- **1930s:** A big trial serves as a entertainment event for the whole town and a child who has been to the movies is unusual.

  1960: Television was becoming the dominant form of popular entertainment, while families might see films together at drive-in movie theaters.

  Today: Although television and film are still large presences, computers and computer games swiftly gain a share in the entertainment market. Trials still provide public entertainment and are featured on their own cable channel.

---

was arrested for failing to yield her seat to a white passenger, civil rights leaders began a successful boycott of the bus system in Montgomery, Alabama, on December 5, 1955. The principal leader of the boycott was the Reverend Martin Luther King, Jr. Along with other black pastors, such as Charles K. Steele and Fred Shuttlesworth, King organized the Southern Christian Leadership Conference in January, 1957, one of the leading organizations that helped end legal segregation by the mid-1960s. The same year that Lee won a contract for the unfinished manuscript of *To Kill a Mockingbird,* Congress passed the Civil Rights Act of 1957, which provided penalties for the violation of voting rights and created the Civil Rights Commission. African Americans would not see protec-

tion and enforcement of all of their rights, however, until well into the next decade, when the Civil Rights Act of 1964, the Voting Rights Act of 1965, and the Civil Rights Bill of 1968 were passed. These laws banned racial discrimination from public places, workplaces, polling places, and housing.

The justice system was similarly discriminatory in the 1950s, as blacks were excluded from juries and could be arrested, tried, and even convicted with little cause. One notable case occurred in 1955, when two white men were charged with the murder of Emmett Till, a fourteen-year-old African American youth who had allegedly harassed a white woman. Like the jury in Tom Robinson's trial, the jury for the Till case was all white and all male; the trial was also held in a segregated courtroom. Although the defense's case rested on the unlikely claims that the corpse could not be specifically identified as Till and that the defendants had been framed, the jury took only one hour to acquit the men of all charges. The men later admitted their crimes to a journalist in great detail, but were never punished for the murder.

The Great Depression and Race Relations

The events surrounding race relations in the 1950s and 1960s have a strong correspondence with those in *To Kill a Mockingbird,* which is set nearly thirty years earlier. The South, which was still steeped in its agricultural traditions, was hit hard by the Great Depression. Small farmers like Lee's Walter Cunningham Sr. often could not earn enough cash from their crops to cover their mortgages, let alone living expenses. Lee's novel captures the romanticism many white people associated with the Southern way of life, which many felt was being threatened by industrialization. Part of this tradition, however, protected such practices as sharecropping, in which tenant farmers would find themselves virtually enslaved to landowners who provided them with acreage, food, and farming supplies. The desperation sharecroppers felt was brilliantly depicted in Erskine Caldwell's 1932 novel, *Tobacco Road.* The racism of the South—many blacks were sharecroppers—is also portrayed in Richard Wright's novel *Uncle Tom's Children* (1938).

There was little opportunity for African Americans to advance themselves in the South. Schools were segregated between whites and blacks, who were not allowed to attend white high schools. Blacks were therefore effectively denied an education, since, in the early 1930s, there was not a single high school built for black students in the South. The result was that nearly half of all blacks in the South did not have an education past the fifth grade; in *To Kill a Mockingbird,* Calpurnia tells the children she is only one of four members of her church who can read. Ironically, the Depression helped to change that when northern school boards began integrating schools to save the costs of running separate facilities. President Franklin Delano Roosevelt's New Deal also led to the creation of the National Youth Administration (founded in 1935) and its Division of Negro Affairs, which helped teach black students to read and write. The Depression was particularly painful to blacks, who, in the 1920s, were already grossly underemployed. With worsening economic times, however, they found that even the menial jobs they once had—

like picking cotton—had been taken by whites. The New Deal helped here, too, with the creation of the Federal Housing Administration, the Works Progress Administration, and other agencies that assisted poor blacks in obtaining jobs and housing.

Yet the oppressive society in the South often prevented blacks from taking advantage of this government assistance. Racist groups like the Ku Klux Klan and the Black Shirts terrorized blacks out of their jobs. The vigilante practice of lynching was still common in the South in the early 1930s. Only North Carolina, South Carolina, Kentucky, and Alabama had laws specifically outlawing lynching as an illegal activity. (Surprisingly, only two northern states had similar laws.) By 1935, however, public outrage had reached a point where lynchings were no longer generally tolerated, even by whites. In Lee's novel, for instance, the local sheriff tries to warn Atticus Finch of a possible lynch mob while a concerned citizen, B. B. Underwood, is prepared to turn them away from the jail with his shotgun.

Critical Overview

Although *To Kill a Mockingbird* was a resounding popular success when it first appeared in 1960, initial critical response to Lee's novel was mixed. Some reviewers faulted the novel's climax as melodramatic, while others found the narrative point of view unbelievable. For instance, *Atlantic Monthly* contributor Phoebe Adams found Scout's narration "frankly and completely impossible, being told in the first person by a six-year-old girl with the prose style of a well-educated adult." Granville Hicks likewise observed in *Saturday Review* that "Miss Lee's problem has been to tell the story she wants to tell and yet stay within the consciousness of a child, and she hasn't consistently solved it." In contrast, Nick Aaron Ford asserted in *PHYLON* that Scout's narration "gives the most vivid, realistic, and delightful experiences of child's world ever presented by an American novelist, with the possible exception of Mark Twain's *Tom Sawyer* and *Huckleberry Finn.*"

Other early reviews of the novel focused on Lee's treatment of racial themes. Several observers remarked that while the plot of *To Kill a Mockingbird* was not particularly original, it was well executed; *New Statesman* contributor Keith Waterhouse, for instance, noted that Lee "gives freshness to a stock situation." In contrast, Harding LeMay asserted in the *New York Herald Tribune Book Review* that the author's "valiant attempt" to combine Scout's amusing recollections of her eccentric neighborhood with the serious events surrounding Tom Robinson's trial "fails to produce a novel of stature, or even of original insight," although "it does provide an exercise in easy, graceful writing." Richard Sullivan, on the other hand, claimed in the *Chicago Sunday Tribune* that *To Kill a Mockingbird* "is a novel of strong contemporary national significance. And it deserves serious consideration. But first of all it is a story so admirably done that it must be called both honorable and engrossing." The Pulitzer Prize committee agreed with this last opinion, awarding the novel its 1961 prize for fiction.

Later appraisals of the novel have also supported these favorable assessments, emphasizing the technical excellence of Lee's narration and characterizations. In a 1975 article, William T. Going called Scout's point of view "the structural *forte*" of the novel, adding that it was "misunderstood or misinterpreted" by most early critics. "Maycomb and the South, then," the critic explained, "are all seen through the eyes of Jean Louise, who speaks from the mature and witty vantage of an older woman recalling her father as well as her brother and their childhood days." Critic Fred Erisman interpreted the novel as presenting a vision for a "New South" that can retain its regional outlook and yet treat all its citizens fairly. He praised Atticus Finch as a Southern representation of the ideal man envisioned by nineteenth-century American philosopher Ralph Waldo Emerson: "the individual who vibrates to his own iron string, the one man in the town that the community trusts 'to do right,' even as they deplore his peculiarities." R. A. Dave similarly found the novel a success in its exploration of Southern history and justice. He claimed that in *To Kill a Mockingbird* "there is a complete cohesion of art and morality. And therein lies the novelist's success. She is a remarkable storyteller. The reader just glides through the novel abounding in humor and pathos, hopes and fears, love and hatred, humanity and brutality—all affording him a memorable human experience of journeying through sunshine and rain at once.... The tale of heroic struggle lingers in our memory as an unforgettable experience."

Criticism

Darren Felty

Felty is a visiting instructor at the College of Charleston. In the following essay, he explores how the narrative structure of To Kill a Mockingbird *supports a reading of the novel as a protest against prejudice and racism.*

Most critics characterize Harper Lee's *To Kill a Mockingbird* as a novel of initiation and an indictment of racism. The novel's point of view, in particular, lends credence to these readings. As an older woman, Jean Louise "Scout" Finch, the narrator, reflects on three crucial summers in her childhood. During this time, she, her brother Jem, and their friend Dill encounter two figures who change their views of themselves and their community. The first of these people, Boo Radley, the Finches' reclusive neighbor, develops from a "malevolent phantom" who dominates the children's imaginations to a misunderstood man who saves Scout's and Jem's lives. Tom Robinson, the second and more tragic figure, loses his life because of racial prejudice, teaching the children about the more malicious characteristics of their society and fellow citizens. Guided by the ethical example of their father, Atticus, the children attempt to understand the lives of these two men. Gradually, through their exposure to Boo Radley's life and Tom Robinson's death, they learn about the grave ramifications of the social and racial prejudice that permeate their environment. Their honest and often confused reactions reflect their development as people and also help the reader to gauge the moral consequences of the novel's events.

Boo Radley is a compelling enigma and source of adventure for the children, but he also represents Scout's most personal lesson in judging others based upon surface appearance. In their attempts to see and communicate with Boo, the children enact in miniature their overall objective in the novel: to try to comprehend a world that defies easy, rational explanation. At first, Boo represents the mysterious, the unfathomable, which to the children is necessarily malevolent. They cannot understand why he would remain shut away, so he must be terrifying and evil. They ascribe nightmarish qualities to him that both scare them and stimulate their imaginations. In Jem's "reasonable" description of him, Boo is "six-and-a-half feet tall," dines on raw squirrels and cats, bears a "long jagged scar" on his face, has "yellow and rotten" teeth and "popped" eyes, and drools. He is, in essence, a monster who has lost all traces of his former humanity. And by never appearing to them, Boo always plays the part the children assign him: the silent, lurking antagonist.

Yet even their imaginations cannot keep the children from recognizing incongruities between their conceptions of Boo and evidence about his real character. The items they discover in the tree knothole, for instance, tell them a different story about Boo than the ones they hear around town. The gifts of the gum, Indian head pennies, spelling contest medal, soap-carving dolls, and broken watch and knife all reveal Boo's hesitant, awkward attempts to communicate with them, to tell them about himself. The reader recognizes Boo's commitment to the children in these items, as do Jem and Scout after a time. The children, we see, are as fascinating to him as he to them, only for opposite reasons. They cannot see him and must construct a fantasy in order to bring him into their world; he watches them constantly and offers them small pieces of himself so he can become a part of their lives. The fact that Nathan Radley, Boo's brother, ends this communication by filling the hole with cement underscores the hopeless imprisonment that Boo endures, engendering sympathy both in the reader and the children.

After Boo saves the children's lives, Scout can direct her sympathy toward a real person, not a spectral presence. Because of this last encounter with Boo, she learns firsthand about sacrifice and mercy, as well as the more general lesson that Atticus has been trying to teach her: "You never understand a person until you consider things from his point of view … until you climb into his skin and walk around in it." Boo left the safe environment of his home to risk his life for hers, and she knows that his essential goodness and vulnerability need protecting. Hence, he is a like a mockingbird, and to assail him with public notice would be comparable to destroying a defenseless songbird who gives only pleasure to others. As she stands on his porch, she reflects on her former behavior and feels shame: "Boo was our neighbor. He gave us two soap dolls, a broken watch and chain, a pair of good-luck pennies, and our lives. But neighbors give in return. We never put back into the tree what we took out of it; we had given him nothing, and it made me sad." Scout feels remorse over the children's isolation of Boo because of their fear and the prejudices they had accepted at face value. As a result of her experiences with Boo, she can never be comfortable with such behavior again.

While Scout's encounter with Boo Radley makes Atticus's lessons about tolerance tangible and personal, Tom Robinson's trial teaches her about intolerance on a social level. But Lee does not treat this trial solely as a means to develop Scout's character. Instead, the Tom Robinson story becomes the vehicle for Lee's overt social criticism

What Do I Read Next?

- In *A Gathering of Old Men,* Ernest Gaines's 1983 novel, a white Cajun work boss is found shot in a black man's yard. Nineteen elderly black men and a young white woman all claim responsibility for the murder in order to thwart the expected lynch mob.

- Nobel Prize-winner Toni Morrison's *Song of Solomon* (1977) is the story of Milkman Dead's quest for identity and how he discovers his own courage, endurance, and capacity for love and joy when he discovers his connection with his ancestors.

- Mark Twain's 1884 popular and sometimes controversial classic *The Adventures of Huckleberry Finn* follows the satirical adventures and moral development of Huck Finn, a young white boy, as he accompanies Jim, an escaped slave, down the Mississippi River in a quest for freedom.

- *Uncle Tom's Children,* a 1938 collection of stories by Richard Wright, relates how African Americans struggle for survival in a racist world and explores themes of fear, violence, flight, courage, and freedom.

- Taylor Branch's social history *Parting the Waters: American in the King Years, 1954–63,* which won the 1988 National Book Critics Circle Award for nonfiction, looks at the state of the American civil rights movement between World War II and the 1960s. While focusing on the life of Martin Luther King, Jr., the work also includes profiles of other important leaders and traces key historical events.

in the novel. We see the town of Maycomb in its worst light, willing to execute an innocent man for a crime he did not commit rather than question their belief in black inferiority and their social taboos about interracial relationships. Lee wants to make explicit the consequences of racism and to guide the reader's judgment of this episode in the novel. She accomplishes these goals, in part, by employing Tom Robinson's trial to allude to the famous "Scottsboro Boys" trials of the 1930s. These trials featured nine black defendants accused of rape by two white women. Despite a lack of evidence and the questionable credibility of the witnesses, the men were sentenced to death by an all-white jury. Unlike Tom Robinson, however, all of these men escaped death after a long series of new trials, in some of which the defendants were still convicted in spite of the evidence. These trials, like Tom Robinson's, revealed the deep-seated racial divisions of the South and the tenacious efforts to maintain these divisions. With the "Scottsboro Boys" trials as historical echoes, Lee points to fundamental American ideals of equality and equal protection under the law (as expressed by and portrayed in Atticus) to criticize the people's failure to meet those ideals. Through Lee's treatment, the white citizens of Maycomb become hypocrites, blind to the contradictions in their own beliefs. Hence, these people are judged, however benignly, by their own standards, standards which the reader shares.

Many of the lessons Tom Robinson's story dramatizes escape Scout's comprehension, but the reader still recognizes them, as does the older Jean Louise. The town of Maycomb is a sustaining force in Scout's life, and she views it uncritically as a child and even shares its prejudices. During the trial, for instance, she answers Dill's distress over the prosecuting attorney's sneering treatment of Robinson with "Well, Dill, after all he's just a Negro." She does not experience Dill's visceral repulsion at the trial's racist manipulations, but instead accepts the premise that blacks are treated as inferiors, even to the point of their utter humiliation. But this attitude stems mostly from her immaturity and inability to comprehend the ramifications of racism. Ultimately, Tom Robinson's trial and death initiate Scout's early questioning of racist precepts and behavior. She sees the effects of racism on her teachers and neighbors, and even feels the sting of it herself. Because of Atticus's involvement with Tom Robinson, for the first time the children must face the social rejection caused by racial bias. They become victims of exclusion and insult, which they would never have expected.

Lee poses a limitation on her social critique in the novel, however, by directing it almost completely through the Finch family rather than through Tom Robinson and his family. This focus makes sense given the point of view of the novel, but it still keeps the Robinson family at a distance from the reader. Calpurnia acts as a partial bridge

to the black community, as does the children's sitting with the black townspeople at the trial, but we still must discern the tragedy of Robinson's unjust conviction and murder predominantly through the reactions of white, not black, characters, a fact many might consider a flaw in the novel. Like the children, the reader must rely on Atticus's responses and moral rectitude to steer through the moral complications of Robinson's story. His is a tolerant approach, warning the reader against over-harsh judgment. He teaches the children that their white neighbors, no matter their attitudes, are still their friends and that Maycomb is their home. Yet he also asserts that the family must maintain its resolve because "The one thing that doesn't abide by majority rule is a person's conscience." We see the results of Atticus's words and behavior in the older Jean Louise, who becomes a compassionate yet not uncritical member of her community, both local and national. Finally, through the Finch family's resolve and sympathy, Lee lyrically communicates the need to cherish and protect those who, like mockingbirds, do no harm but are especially vulnerable to the violent injustices of our society.

Source: Darren Felty, in an essay for *Novels for Students,* Gale, 1997.

Claudia Durst Johnson

In the following excerpt, Johnson explores the role of stories, art, and other forms of communication in Lee's novel.

The subject of *To Kill a Mockingbird* is also song, that is, expression: reading and literacy; both overt and covert attempts at articulation; and communicative art forms, including the novel itself. The particulars of setting in the novel are children's books, grade school texts, many different local newspapers and national news magazines, law books, a hymnal, and the reading aloud of Sir Walter Scott's *Ivanhoe*. Much of the novel's action is actually reading, for as the locals and the children believe, that is Atticus Finch's only activity. These expressions are not only attempts to have the self broadcast and realized; more significantly, they are attempts to establish connections beyond or through boundaries.

Contrary to the notion that language and art are cold (for example, the Dracula theme frequently expresses the cold tendency of artists to sacrifice everything, even their own humanity, for their art), in *TKM,* language and art are usually borne of love and linked to expressions of charity and affection. The Gothic degeneracy of *TKM* derives from love's opposite—imprisonment and insularity, producing, in the extreme, incest and insanity, a gazing in or a gazing back. Its opposite is the social self, which is civilized in its high and positive sense, and reaches out in the love that overcomes ego in language and art.

Language and other modes of communication are usually not only civilizing in a very positive way, but are avenues of benevolence, and even charity and love. In the novel, we remember Scout reading in Atticus's lap, Atticus reading as he keeps vigil beside Jem's bed, Atticus armed only with a book as he plans to protect Tom Robinson from a lynch mob. The society that imprisons Tom Robinson is the same one that imprisons Scout in the "Dewey Decimal System," Jem's garbled version of the pedagogical theories of the University of Chicago's father of progressive education, John Dewey, which are being faddishly inflicted on the children of Maycomb. The practical result of Dewey's system on Scout is to diminish or hinder her reading and writing, and along with it, her individuality. Each child is herded into a general category that determines whether he or she is "ready" to read or print or write ("We don't write in the first grade, we print"). The life of the mind and reading in particular is replaced in this progressive educational world with Group Dynamics, Good Citizenship, Units, Projects, and all manner of clichés. As Scout says, "I could not help receiving the impression that I was being cheated out of something. Out of what I knew not, yet I did not believe that twelve years of unrelieved boredom was exactly what the state had in mind for me."

As it is in a black man's account of slavery (*Narrative of the Life of Frederick Douglass*), reading and writing are major themes in *TKM*. Reading is first introduced with Dill's announcement that he can read, and Jem's counterboast that his sister, Scout, has been reading for years:

"I'm Charles Baker Harris," he said. "I can read."

"So what?" I said.

"I just thought you'd like to know I can read. You got anything needs readin' I can do it...."

The theme continues with Scout's difficulty with her first grade teacher, who resents that Scout is already able to read when she enters school. The heartfelt importance of reading to the child is considered as she contemplates its being denied to her. One notes in the following passage that reading is inextricably connected with her father and with the civilizing, everyday business of this world, that it is somehow as natural as breathing, and that she has learned that it is a crime in the view of her teacher, possibly because reading and writing (the latter taught to her by Calpurnia) are means of empowerment that place her beyond the control of her teacher:

I mumbled that I was sorry and retired meditating upon my crime. I never deliberately learned to read, but somehow I had been wallowing illicitly in the daily papers. In the long hours of church—was it then I learned? I could not remember not being able to read hymns. Now that I was compelled to think about it, reading was something that just came to me, as learning to fasten the seat of my union suit without looking around, or achieving two bows from a snarl of shoelaces. I could not remember when the lines above Atticus's moving finger separated into words, but I had stared at them all the evenings in my memory, listening to the news of the day, Bills To Be Enacted into Laws, the diaries of Lorenzo Dow—anything Atticus happened to be reading when I crawled into his lap every night. Until I feared I would lose it, I never loved to read. One does not love breathing.

Atticus's civilizing power comes from his reading, a power he has taken on in place of the power of the gun. It is his sole pastime. The narrator reports, "He did not do the things our schoolmates' fathers did: he never went hunting, he did not play poker or fish or drink or smoke. He sat in the living room and read." Atticus is reading under the light outside the jail, with only a book and without a gun for protection, when the mob from Old Sarum arrives to harm his client, Tom Robinson. The novel closes with Atticus reading a book in Jem's room as he watches over his son. Members of The Idler's Club, the old men whose chief activity is attending court sessions together, know him as a lawyer whose skill arises from his being "'a deep reader, a mighty deep reader.'" They disparage his reluctance to depart from the civilizing force of the law by saying, "'He reads all right, that's all he does.'" The love of reading is also true of Jem, for "no tutorial system devised by man could have stopped him from getting at books."

The theme of reading and writing as emblems for civilization are shown further in Jem's and Scout's discussion of what determines a "good" or "quality" or "old" family, and Scout's recognition of the importance of literacy: "'I think its how long your family's been readin' and writin'. Scout, I've studied this real hard and that's the only reason I can think of. Somewhere along when the Finches were in Egypt one of 'em must have learned a hieroglyphic or two and he taught his boy.'" To this Scout replies: "'Well, I'm glad he could, or who'da taught Atticus and them, and if Atticus couldn't read, you and me'd be in a fix.'"

By contrast, the more powerless Old Sarum residents and black citizens of Maycomb County are rarely literate; they are generally able only to sign their names. Calpurnia is one of the few black people in the area who can read. She shocks the children with the information that only four members of her church can read, and one, whom she has taught to read, "lines" the hymns from the hymnbook for all the others to follow. And finally, in contemplating the meaning of "Old Families," Scout realizes that literacy has little to do with intelligence. What she doesn't realize is that it has a great deal to do with power of an intellectual sort.

While reading threads the narrative as surely as the subject of the law does, its meaning is less consistent and more elusive. Despite Scout's reservation about Jem's speculation that reading is connected to "Old Families," it is apparent that, in that it is connected to Atticus, reading denotes a pinnacle of civilized progress. The most civilized, the most humane, the wisest character is the one who reads obsessively.

The continuing powerlessness of the black and poor white people of Maycomb County is incidental to their inability to read, and their children, in contrast to Scout, are taken out of school, and thus denied their only access to power. A related idea is the control that Mrs. Dubose has over narcotics through forcing Jem to read to her. On the other hand, Zeebo, who leads the singing in the black church, is an example of one who imbues his reading with spirit and offers it as a gift to his people. Like Calpurnia, he has learned to read from Blackstone's *Commentaries,* but he uses the language he has been given from the cold letter of the law and imbues it with the warmth and life of the spirit, as he alone is able to lead his church congregation in singing hymns like "On Jordan's Stormy Banks." For the three children, reading, as we have seen, is a way of sharpening the imagination and gaining knowledge of the Other.

The children obsessively make attempts to communicate verbally with Arthur Radley, first by leaving a message for him in the tree, and then, in a blundering fashion, by sticking a note to his window.

Like other dispossessed people in the novel, Boo is doomed to communicate without language, though we suspect him to be literate, for he gives the children a spelling bee medal and is rumored to have stabbed his father in the leg while clipping articles from the newspaper. This begs the question of whether his assault on his father is provoked while he is reading the newspaper because it reminds him of his forced prohibition from establishing an intercourse with the world. So Boo attempts to reach out to the world through other means, and he is thwarted again. A real tragedy of Jem's boyhood, and most likely of Boo's life, is the severing of their channel of communication, the hole in the oak tree, which Boo's older brother cements up. The presents that he leaves in the tree appear to be Boo's last attempt to reach outside his prison. And each present, which is a means of communication, has significance. The chewing gum seems to be a way of proving that he isn't poisonous. The penny, an ancient medium of exchange, is something from the past. The spelling medal is also connected with literacy and communication. The carvings are works of art, communication, and love. The aborted mail profoundly affects Jem, who has played the part of Boo in the childhood dramas with conviction. Right after Jem's discovery of the cemented hole in the tree, Scout observes that "when we went in the house I saw he had been crying." For in shutting off Boo's avenue of expression, Mr. Radley, his brother, has thwarted Jem's as well, and has, more importantly, committed what would be a mortal sin in this novel—he has attempted to silence love.

Art forms other than literary ones occur in the novel, sometimes inadvertently communicating messages that the children don't intend. There is the Radley drama, performed for their own edification, which the neighbors and Atticus finally see. And there is the snow sculpture of Mr. Avery, which the neighbors also recognize. Perhaps because these are self-serving art works, created without a sense of audience, as if art's communicative essence could be ignored, the effects of the play and the snow sculpture are not entirely charitable. On the other hand, Boo's art—the soap sculptures—are lovingly executed as a means of extending himself to the children.

Then there is the story the narrator tells, which, again, unites art with love, somehow making up for the novel's missed and indecipherable messages, like those so frequently found in the Gothic. The novel is a love story about, a love song to, Jem and Atticus, and to Dill, the unloved child, and Boo Radley, whose love was silenced.

The reader of the Gothic, according to William Patrick Day [in *In the Circles of Fear and Desire*] is "essentially voyeuristic." He further states, "Just as when we daydream and construct idle fantasies for ourselves, the encounter with the Gothic [as readers] is a moment in which the self defines its internal existence through the act of observing its fantasies." Not only are characters in the Gothic enthralled, but the reader of the Gothic is as well. In the case of *TKM,* readers learn of the enthrallments of Jem, Dill, and Scout. But the reader of their story is also enthralled, not by the horror of racial mixing or the Dracularian Boo, but by the reminders of a lost innocence, of a time past, as unreal, in its way, as Transylvania. We, as readers, encounter the ghosts of ourselves, the children we once were, the simplicity of our lives in an earlier world. While the children's voyeurism is Gothic, our own as readers is romantic. In either case, the encounter is with the unreal. The children's encounter is in that underworld beneath reality, and ours is in a transcendent world above reality, which nostalgia and memory have altered. It is a world where children play in tree houses and swings and sip lemonade on hot summer days, and in the evenings, sit in their fathers' laps to read. Reality and illusion about the past is blurred. Within the novel's Gothicism and Romanticism, we as readers are enthralled with the past, and, like the responses elicited by the Gothic, we react with pain and pleasure to an involvement with our past world and our past selves.

Source: Claudia Durst Johnson, "The Mockingbird's Song," in *To Kill a Mockingbird: Threatening Boundaries,* Twayne Publishers, 1994, pp. 107–14.

Jill May

In the following excerpt, May looks at the history of censorship attempts on To Kill a Mockingbird, *which came in two onslaughts—the first from conservatives, the second from liberals.*

The critical career of *To Kill a Mockingbird* is a late-twentieth-century case study of censorship. When Harper Lee's novel about a small southern town and its prejudices was published in 1960, the book received favorable reviews in professional journals and the popular press. Typical of that opinion, *Booklist*'s reviewer called the book "melodramatic" and noted "traces of sermonizing," but the book was recommended for library purchase, commending its "rare blend of wit and compassion." Reviewers did not suggest that the book was young adult literature, or that it belonged in adolescent collections; perhaps that is why no one mentioned the book's language or violence. In any event, reviewers seemed inclined to agree that *To Kill a Mockingbird* was a worthwhile interpretation of the South's existing social structures during the 1930s.

In 1961 the book won the Pulitzer Prize Award, the Alabama Library Association Book Award, and the Brotherhood Award of the National Conference of Christians and Jews. It seemed that Harper Lee's blend of family history, local custom, and restrained sermonizing was important reading, and with a young girl between the ages of six and nine as the main character, *To Kill a Mockingbird* moved rapidly into junior and senior high school libraries and curriculum. The book was not destined to be studied by college students. Southern literature's critics rarely mentioned it; few university professors found it noteworthy enough to "teach" as an exemplary southern novel.

By the mid-sixties *To Kill a Mockingbird* had a solid place in junior and senior high American literature studies. Once discovered by southern parents, the book's solid place became shaky indeed. Sporadic lawsuits arose. In most cases the complaint against the book was by conservatives who disliked the portrayal of whites. Typically, the Hanover County School Board in Virginia first ruled the book "immoral," then withdrew their criticism and declared that the ruckus "was all a mistake" (*Newsletter* [*on Intellectual Freedom*] 1966). By 1968 the National Education Association listed the book among those which drew the most criticism from private groups. Ironically it was rated directly behind *Little Black Sambo* (*Newsletter* 1968). And then the seventies arrived.

Things had changed in the South during the sixties. Two national leaders who had supported integration and had espoused the ideals of racial equality were assassinated in southern regions. When John F. Kennedy was killed in Texas on November 22, 1963, many southerners were shocked. Populist attitudes of racism were declining, and in the aftermath of the tragedy southern politics began to change. Lyndon Johnson gained the presidency; blacks began to seek and win political offices. Black leader Martin Luther King had stressed the importance of racial equality, always using Mahatma Gandhi's strategy of nonviolent action and civil disobedience. A brilliant orator, King grew up in the South; the leader of the [Southern Christian Leadership Conference], he lived in Atlanta, Georgia. In 1968, while working on a garbage strike in Memphis, King was killed. The death of this 1965 Nobel Peace Prize winner was further embarrassment for white southerners. Whites began to look at public values anew, and gradually southern blacks found experiences in the South more tolerable. In 1971 one Atlanta businessman observed [in *Ebony*], "The liberation thinking is here. Blacks are more together. With the doors opening wider, this area is the mecca...." Southern arguments against *To Kill a Mockingbird* subsided. *The Newsletter on Intellectual Freedom* contained no record of southern court cases during the seventies or eighties. The book had sustained itself during the first period of sharp criticism; it had survived regional protests from the area it depicted.

The second onslaught of attack came from new groups of censors, and it came during the late seventies and early eighties. Private sectors in the Midwest and suburban East began to demand the book's removal from school libraries. Groups, such as the Eden Valley School Committee in Minnesota, claimed that the book was too laden with profanity (*Newsletter* 1978). In Vernon, New York, Reverend Carl Hadley threatened to establish a private Christian school because public school libraries contained such "filthy, trashy sex novels" as *A Separate Peace* and *To Kill a Mockingbird* (*Newsletter* 1980). And finally, blacks began to censor the book. In Warren, Indiana, three black parents resigned from the township Human Relations Advisory Council when the Warren County school administration refused to remove the book from Warren junior high school classes. They contended that the book "does psychological damage to the positive integration process and represents institutionalized racism" (*Newsletter* 1982). Thus, censorship of *To Kill a Mockingbird* swung from the conservative right to the liberal left. Factions representing racists, religious sects, concerned parents, and minority groups vocally demanded the book's removal from public schools. With this kind of offense, what makes *To Kill a Mockingbird* worth defending and keeping?

When Harper Lee first introduces Scout in *To Kill a Mockingbird,* she is almost six years old. By the end of the book Scout is in the third grade. Throughout the book events are described by the adult Scout who looks back upon life in the constricted society of a small southern town. Since it is the grown-up Scout's story, the young Scout Finch becomes a memory more than a reality. The book is not a vivid recollection of youth gone by so much as a recounting of days gone by. Yet, Scout Finch's presence as the events' main observer establishes two codes of honor, that of the child and of the adult. The code of adult behavior shows the frailty of adult sympathy for humanity and emphasizes its subsequent effect upon overt societal attitudes. Throughout the book Scout sees adults accepting society's rules rather than confronting them. When Scout finds school troublesome, Atti-

cus tells Scout that they will continue reading together at night, then adds, "you'd better not say anything at school about our agreement." He explains away the Maycomb Ku Klux Klan, saying, "it was a political organization more than anything. Besides, they couldn't find anybody to scare." And when he discusses the case of a black man's word against a white man's with his brother, Atticus says, "The jury couldn't possibly be expected to take Tom Robinson's word against the Ewells' ... Why reasonable people go stark raving mad when anything involving a Negro comes up, is something I don't pretend to understand." The author tells us that Atticus knew Scout was listening in on this conversation and purposely explained that he had been court appointed, adding, "I'd hoped to get through life without a case of this kind...." And when the jury does see fit to try and condemn Tom Robinson, Scout's older brother Jem and good friend Dill see the white southern world for what it is: a world of hypocrisy, a world burdened with old racist attitudes which have nothing to do with humanity. Jem says, "I always thought Maycomb folks were the best folks in the world, least that's what they seemed like." Dill decides he will be a new kind of clown. "I'm gonna stand in the middle of the ring and laugh at the folks.... Every one of 'em oughta be ridin' broomsticks."

The majority of white adults in Maycomb are content to keep blacks, women and children in their place. Atticus's only sister comes to live with the family and constantly tells Scout she must learn how to act, that she has a place in society: womanhood with its stifling position of prim behavior and wagging tongues is the essence of southern decorum. Even Atticus, the liberal minded hero, says that perhaps it's best to keep women off the juries of Alabama because, "I doubt if we'd ever get a complete case tried—the ladies'd be interrupting to ask questions." By the end of the book Scout has accepted the rules of southern society. The once hated aunt who insisted upon Scout's transformation into a proper young lady becomes an idol for her ability to maintain proper deportment during a crisis. Scout follows suit, reasoning "if Aunty could be a lady at a time like this, so could I."

The courtroom trial is a real example of Southern justice and Southern local color storytelling. Merrill Skaggs has analyzed the local color folklore of southern trials in his book *The Folk of Southern Fiction*. Skaggs comments that there is a formula for court hearings, and he suggests that local color stories show that justice in the courtroom is, in fact, less fair than justice in the streets. He discusses justice in terms of the black defendant, saying, "Implicit in these stories ... is an admission that Negroes are not usually granted equal treatment before the law, that a Negro is acquitted only when he has a white champion." During the trial in *To Kill a Mockingbird* Tom Robinson says he ran because he feared southern justice. He ran, he says, because he was "scared I'd hafta face up to what I didn't do." Dill is one of Lee's young protagonists. He is angered by the southern court system. The neglected son of an itinerant mother, Dill is a stereotype of southern misfits. Lee doesn't concentrate upon Dill's background; she concentrates upon his humanity. The courtroom scene is more than local humor to him. It is appalling. When he flees the trial, Scout follows. She cannot understand why Dill is upset, but the notorious rich "drunk" with "mixed children" can. He sees Dill and says, "it just makes you sick, doesn't it?" No one, save Jem and his youthful converts, expects Atticus to win. The black minister who has befriended the children warns, "I ain't ever seen any jury decide in favor of a colored man over a white man." In the end Atticus says, "They've done it before and they did it tonight and they'll do it again and when they do it—seems that only children weep." And Miss Maudie tells the children, "as I waited I thought, Atticus Finch won't win, he can't win, but he's the only man in these parts who can keep a jury out so long in a case like that." Then she adds, "we're making a step—it's just a baby-step, but it's a step."

In his book, Skaggs points out that obtaining justice through the law is not as important as the courtroom play in southern trials and that because the courtroom drama seldom brings real justice, people condone "violence within the community." Atticus realizes that "justice" is often resolved outside of the court, and so he is not surprised when the sheriff and the town leaders arrive at his house one night. The men warn Atticus that something might happen to Tom Robinson if he is left in the local jail; the sheriff suggests that he can't be responsible for any violence which might occur. One of the men says, "—don't see why you touched it [the case] in the first place.... You've got everything to lose from this, Atticus. I mean everything." Because Atticus wants courtroom justice to resolve this conflict, he tries to protect his client. On the night before the trial Atticus moves to the front of the jail, armed only with his newspaper. While there, the local lynching society arrives, ready to take justice into its own hands. Scout, Jem, and Dill have been watching in their own dark corner, but the crowd bothers Scout and so she bursts from her hiding spot. As she runs by, Scout smells "stale whiskey and pigpen," and she realizes that these are not the same men who came to the house earlier. It is Scout's innocence, her misinterpretation of the seriousness of the scene, her ability to recognize one of the farmers and to talk with guileless ease to that man about his own son which saves Tom Robinson from being lynched. The next morning Jem suggests that the men would have killed Atticus if Scout hadn't come along. Atticus who is more familiar with adult southern violence, says "might have hurt me a little, but son, you'll understand folks a little better when you're older. A mob's always made up of people, no matter what.... Every little mob in every little southern town is always made up of people you know—doesn't say much for them does it?" Lynching is a part of regional lore in the South. In his study of discrimination, Wallace Mendelson pointed out that the frequency of lynchings as settlement for black/white problems is less potent than the terrorizing aspect of hearing about them. In this case, the terrorizing aspect of mob rule had been viewed by the children. Its impact would remain.

After the trial Bob Ewell is subjected to a new kind of Southern justice, a polite justice. Atticus explains, "He thought he'd be a hero, but all he got for his pain was ... was, okay, we'll convict this Negro but get back to your dump." Ewell spits on Atticus, cuts a hole in the judge's screen, and harasses Tom's wife. Atticus ignores his insults and figures, "He'll settle down when the weather changes." Scout and Jem never doubt that Ewell is serious, and they are afraid. Their early childhood experiences with the violence and hypocrisy in southern white society have taught them not to trust Atticus's reasoning but they resolve to hide their fear from the adults around them. When Ewell does strike for revenge, he strikes at children. The sheriff understands this kind of violence. It is similar to lynching violence. It strikes at a minority who cannot strike back, and it creates a terror in law-abiding citizens more potent than courtroom justice. It shows that southern honor has been consistently dealt with outside of the courtroom.

Harper Lee's book concerns the behavior of Southerners in their claim for "honor," and Boo Radley's presence in the story reinforces that claim. When Boo was young and got into trouble, his father claimed the right to protect his family name. He took his son home and kept him at the house. When Boo attacked him, Mr. Radley again asked for family privilege; Boo was returned to his home, this time never to surface on the porch or in the yard during the daylight hours. The children are fascinated with the Boo Radley legend. They act it out, and they work hard to make Boo come out. And always, they wonder what keeps him inside. After the trial, however, Jem says, "I think I'm beginning to understand something. I think I'm beginning to understand why Boo Radley's stayed shut up in the house ... it's because he *wants* to stay inside."

Throughout the book Boo is talked about and wondered over, but he does not appear in Scout's existence until the end when he is needed by the children. When no one is near to protect them from death, Boo comes out of hiding. In an act of violence he kills Bob Ewell, and with that act he becomes a part of southern honor. He might have been a hero. Had a jury heard the case, his trial would have entertained the entire region. The community was unsettled from the rape trial, and this avenged death in the name of southern justice would have set well in Maycomb, Alabama. Boo Radley has been outside of southern honor, however, and he is a shy man. Lee has the sheriff explain the pitfalls of southern justice when he says, "Know what'd happen then? All the ladies in Maycomb includin' my wife'd be knocking on his door bringing angel food cakes. To my way of thinkin' ... that's a sin.... If it was any other man it'd be different." The reader discovers that southern justice through the courts is not a blessing. It is a carnival.

When Harper Lee was five years old the Scottsboro trial began. In one of the most celebrated southern trials, nine blacks were accused of raping two white girls. The first trial took place in Jackson County, Alabama. All nine were convicted. Monroeville, Lee's hometown, knew about the case. Retrials continued for six years, and with each new trial it became more obvious that southern justice for blacks was different from southern justice for whites. Harper Lee's father was a lawyer during that time. Her mother's maiden name was Finch. Harper Lee attended law school, a career possibility suggested to Scout by well-meaning adults in the novel. *To Kill a Mockingbird* is set in 1935, midpoint for the Scottsboro case.

Scout Finch faces the realities of southern society within the same age span that Harper Lee faced Scottsboro. The timeline is also the same. Although Lee's father was not the Scottsboro lawyer who handled that trial, he was a southern man of honor related to the famous gentleman soldier, Robert E. Lee. It is likely that Harper Lee's father was the author's model for Atticus Finch and that the things Atticus told Scout were the kinds of things Ama Lee told his daughter. The attitudes depicted are ones Harper Lee grew up with, both in terms of family pride and small town prejudices.

The censors' reactions to *To Kill a Mockingbird* were reactions to issues of race and justice. Their moves to ban the book derive from their own perspectives of the book's theme. Their "reader's response" criticism, usually based on one reading of the book, was personal and political. They needed to ban the book because it told them something about American society that they did not want to hear. That is precisely the problem facing any author of realistic fiction. Once the story becomes real, it can become grim. An author will use first-person flashback in story in order to let the reader live in another time, another place. Usually the storyteller is returning for a second view of the scene. The teller has experienced the events before and the story is being retold because the scene has left the storyteller uneasy. As the storyteller recalls the past both the listener and the teller see events in a new light. Both are working through troubled times in search of meaning. In the case of *To Kill a Mockingbird* the first-person retelling is not pleasant, but the underlying significance is with the narrative. The youthful personalities who are recalled are hopeful. Scout tells us of a time past when white people would lynch or convict a man because of the color of his skin. She also shows us three children who refuse to believe that the system is right, and she leaves us with the thought that most people will be nice if seen for what they are: humans with frailties. When discussing literary criticism, Theo D'Haen suggested [in *Text to Reader*] that the good literary work should have a life within the world and be "part of the ongoing activities of that world." *To Kill a Mockingbird* continues to have life within the world; its ongoing activities in the realm of censorship show that it is a book which deals with regional moralism. The children in the story seem very human; they worry about their own identification, they defy parental rules, and they cry over injustices. They mature in Harper Lee's novel, and they lose their innocence. So does the reader. If the readers are young, they may believe Scout when she says, "nothin's real scary except in books." If the readers are older they will have learned that life is as scary, and they will be prepared to meet some of its realities.

Source: Jill May, "In Defense of *To Kill a Mockingbird*," in *Censored Books: Critical Viewpoints,* edited by Nicholas J. Karolides, Lee Burress, John M. Kean, The Scarecrow Press, Inc., 1993, pp. 476–84.

Sources

Phoebe Adams, review in *Atlantic Monthly,* Vol. 206, August 26, 1960, pp. 98-99.

R. A. Dave, *"To Kill a Mockingbird:* Harper Lee's Tragic Vision," in *Indian Studies in American Fiction,* edited by M. K. Naik, S. K. Desai, Punekar S. Mokashi, and M. Jayalakshammanni. Karnatak University Press, 1974, pp. 311-23.

Fred Erisman, "The Romantic Regionalism of Harper Lee," in *The Alabama Review,* Vol. 26, No. 2, April, 1973, pp. 122-36.

Nick Aaron Ford, review in *PHYLON,* Vol. XXII, Second Quarter (June), 1961, p. 122.

William T. Going, "Store and Mockingbird: Two Pulitzer Novels about Alabama," in his *Essays on Alabama Literature,* The University of Alabama Press, 1975, pp. 9-31.

Granville Hicks, "Three at the Outset," in *Saturday Review,* Vol. XLIII, No. 30, July 23, 1960, pp. 15-16.

Harding LeMay, "Children Play: Adults Betray," in *New York Herald Tribune Book Review,* July 10, 1960, p. 5.

Richard Sullivan, "Engrossing First Novel of Rare Excellence," *Chicago Sunday Tribune,* July 17, 1960, p. 1.

Keith Waterhouse, review in *New Statesman,* October 15, 1960, p. 580.

For Further Study

Edwin Bruell, "Keen Scalpel on Racial Ills." *The English Journal,* Vol. 53, December, 1964, pp. 658-61.
  An article that touches on Lee's "warm" portrayal of Scout and the ironic tone in Lee's treatment of the bigoted.

Claudia Durst Johnson, *Understanding 'To Kill a Mockingbird': A Student Casebook to Issues, Sources, and Historic Documents,* Greenwood Press, 1994.
  Johnson's book is the most thorough analysis of the novel to date. She discusses the literary and historical context of the book, then analyzes its form, its connections to Gothic tradition, its treatment of prejudicial and legal boundaries, and its focus on communication. Johnson provides a large collection of sources relating to the novel, including documents about the "Scottsboro Boys" trials, the Civil Rights Movement, issues of stereotyping, the debates over Atticus in legal circles, and the censorship of the novel.

Frank H. Lyell, "One-Taxi Town," in *The New York Book Review,* July 10, 1960, pp. 5, 18.
  Lyell praises Lee for her characterization and provides some limited criticism of her style.

Edgar H. Schuster, "Discovering Theme and Structure in the Novel," in *The English Journal,* Vol. 52, 1963, pp. 506-11.
  Schuster presents a practical classroom approach to the novel and an analysis of its themes and structure.

Wuthering Heights

Emily Brontë

1847

First published in 1847, Emily Brontë's *Wuthering Heights* ranks high on the list of major works of English literature. A brooding tale of passion and revenge set in the Yorkshire moors, the novel has inspired no fewer than four film versions in modern times. Early critics did not like the work, citing its excess of passion and its coarseness. A second edition was published in 1850, two years after the author's death. Sympathetically prefaced by her sister Charlotte, it met with greater success, and the novel has continued to grow in stature ever since. In the novel a pair of narrators, Mr. Lockwood and Nelly Dean, relate the story of the foundling Heathcliff's arrival at Wuthering Heights, and the close-knit bond he forms with his benefactor's daughter, Catherine Earnshaw. One in spirit, they are nonetheless social unequals, and the saga of frustrated yearning and destruction that follows Catherine's refusal to marry Heathcliff is unique in the English canon. The novel is admired not least for the power of its imagery, its complex structure, and its ambiguity, the very elements that confounded its first critics. Emily Brontë spent her short life mostly at home, and apart from her own fertile imagination, she drew her inspiration from the local landscape— the surrounding moorlands and the regional architecture of the Yorkshire area—as well as her personal experience of religion, of folklore, and of illness and death. Dealing with themes of nature, cruelty, social position, and indestructibility of the spirit, *Wuthering Heights* has surpassed the more successful Charlotte Brontë's *Jane Eyre* in academic and popular circles.

Author Biography

Emily Jane Brontë was born on July 30, 1818, to Maria Branwell and the Reverend Patrick Brontë, in Thornton, Yorkshire, England. She was the fifth of six children, and the fourth daughter. The family moved to a parsonage in Haworth in 1820, and following the death of Maria Brontë in 1821, the children's maternal aunt came to care for them. In 1825 Emily was sent to join her sisters Maria, Elizabeth, and Charlotte at school, but after an epidemic at the school claimed the lives of Maria and Elizabeth, Emily and Charlotte returned home. Emily would remain at home for the next ten years. In 1826 Patrick Brontë gave his children a set of toy soldiers, and the children began to make up stories about them. A realm in Africa, called Angria, was largely the inspiration of Charlotte and brother Branwell, but soon Emily and Anne had invented the Pacific Island of Gondal, which would figure in poems and stories they wrote throughout their lives. Emily was uncomfortable with outsiders and made only brief, intermittent attempts to construct a life for herself away from the parsonage. An unsuccessful experiment as Charlotte's pupil in East Yorkshire that began in 1835 ended after a year. She was similarly ill-suited for a position as assistant teacher at Law Hill School near Halifax. In 1842, Charlotte and Emily traveled to Brussels, Belgium, intending to study languages, but returned home later that year because of the death of their aunt, who had left them what money she had.

In 1845 Charlotte discovered a private notebook of Emily's poems and persuaded her to publish a selection of them. Emily reluctantly agreed, and a volume of poetry that included "Remembrance," "The Prisoner," "The Philosopher," and "Stars" appeared in 1846. It sold only two copies, but one critic was flattering. *Wuthering Heights* appeared in 1847 under the pseudonym Ellis Bell and was panned by contemporary critics, who objected to its coarseness and brutality. In contrast, Charlotte's novel *Jane Eyre,* published the same year, was a runaway success. Emily produced one further poem in 1846; *Wuthering Heights* was her only novel. In 1848 Branwell Brontë died, in part owing to his dissolute ways, which were a source of constant concern to his sisters. Emily caught cold at his funeral and developed tuberculosis. Refusing to seek medical treatment, she died on December 19, 1848.

The lack of biographical material about Emily Brontë makes her an enigmatic figure and her work difficult to evaluate. The poems, in particular, suf-

Emily Bronte

fer from a lack of context, and ambiguous punctuation. Although the poems are often clumsy, they show flashes of the same originality that makes *Wuthering Heights* so compelling. Emily Brontë did not know success during her lifetime, but despite the initial failure of *Wuthering Heights,* she has proved a giant among writers.

Plot Summary

Part I—Childhood

Set on the Yorkshire moors of England, *Wuthering Heights* opens with the comments of Mr. Lockwood, the newly arrived tenant of Thrushcross Grange. He tells of his visit to Wuthering Heights, where he encounters his landlord and neighbor, Mr. Heathcliff; Joseph, Heathcliff's pious and surly old servant; Hareton Earnshaw, an ignorant and impoverished young man; and the beautiful Catherine Heathcliff, widow of Heathcliff's dead son. Rough weather forces Lockwood to spend the night. He finds several old books, the margins of which had been used as a childhood diary by Catherine Earnshaw, mother to the current Catherine. Perusing these pages, Lockwood learns about the childhood adventures of Heathcliff and the first

Catherine, and of their oppression by Catherine's brother, Hindley. Lockwood falls into a restless sleep, punctuated by nightmares in which the first Catherine Earnshaw comes to the bedroom window and begs to be let in. He awakes screaming, and in so doing he wakes Heathcliff, who opens the window and begs Catherine to come again. At sunrise Heathcliff escorts Lockwood back to Thrushcross Grange.

The next day, Lockwood, finding himself sick, persuades the servant, Nelly Dean, to sit and talk with him. She relates how she grew up at Wuthering Heights, and she tells how one night Mr. Earnshaw brought home the mysterious boy, Heathcliff, whom he had found starving in Liverpool. Mr. Earnshaw favors Heathcliff, causing his son Hindley to hate the interloper, but Heathcliff and the first Catherine become fast friends. Hindley is sent off to college, but after Mr. Earnshaw's death he returns with a wife and becomes master of Wuthering Heights. Under Hindley's tyranny, Catherine and Heathcliff grow closer and more mischievous, their favorite pastime being to wander the moors. On one such excursion they are caught looking in the windows of Thrushcross Grange, and Catherine is bitten by a bulldog and has to stay at the Grange for five weeks. Hindley, meanwhile, forbids Heathcliff to have further contact with Catherine.

Catherine returns much changed. She now dresses and acts like a lady, and she has befriended Edgar and Isabella Linton, the siblings who live at the Grange. Heathcliff feels her neglect sharply, and Catherine feels torn between loyalty to her old friend and attraction to her new companions. Hindley's new wife, Frances, gives birth to a son, Hareton, and dies of consumption, and Hindley starts drinking and becomes even more tyrannical. Heathcliff is deprived of all education and is forced to labor as one of the servants of the Heights. When Edgar proposes to Catherine, she accepts, but tells Nelly that she would never have done so if her brother had not turned Heathcliff into someone it would disgrace her to marry. Heathcliff overhears this comment and flees Wuthering Heights before she goes on to explain to Nelly the depth of her feelings for Heathcliff:

> "I cannot express it; but surely you and everybody have a notion that there is, or should be an existence of yours beyond you. What were the use of my creation if I were entirely contained here? My great miseries in this world have been Heathcliff's miseries, and I watched and felt each from the beginning; my great thought in living is himself. If all else perished, and *he* remained, I should still continue to be; and, if all else remained, and he were annihilated, the Uni-

verse would turn to a mighty stranger. I should not seem a part of it. My love for Linton is like the foliage in the woods. Time will change it, I am well aware, as winter changes the trees—my love for Heathcliff resembles the eternal rocks beneath—a source of little visible delight, but necessary. Nelly, I *am* Heathcliff—he is always, always in my mind—not as a pleasure, any more than I am always a pleasure to myself—but as my own being—so, do not talk of our separation again."

Part II—Marriage and Death

Catherine and Edgar are married and seem happy, until Heathcliff returns, mysteriously wealthy and educated. He takes up residence at Wuthering Heights, where he gambles Hindley out of all his possessions. Heathcliff quickly resumes his acquaintance with Catherine, to her delight and Edgar's annoyance. Isabella, Edgar's sister, begins to love Heathcliff, in spite of repeated warnings about his character. Heathcliff, desiring Isabella's inheritance, begins to encourage the attraction, and when Nelly informs Edgar of this courtship he becomes enraged. A fight ensues between Edgar and Heathcliff, and Heathcliff is banished from the Grange. Catherine, to punish Edgar, refuses to eat for three days and drives herself into a feverish delirium. While Edgar is nursing her back to a fragile state of health, Isabella and Heathcliff elope. Isabella soon regrets her marriage to the cruel Heathcliff. She writes to Nelly, telling her of her miserable life at Wuthering Heights and begging her to visit. Heathcliff takes advantage of Nelly's visit to request a meeting with Catherine, who is pregnant. Nelly reluctantly agrees, and a few days later, while Edgar is at church, Heathcliff enters the Grange and sees Catherine for the last time. Edgar enters and finds Heathcliff embracing Catherine, who has fainted. Catherine dies without ever fully regaining her senses, although two hours before her death, she gives birth to a daughter. Edgar and Heathcliff are both distraught at Catherine's death, and Heathcliff begs her ghost to haunt him.

Days after Catherine's death, Isabella appears at the Grange, having fled the Heights. She swears she will not return, but she refuses to stay at the Grange because she fears Heathcliff will find her there. She moves to the South of England and gives birth to a sickly boy she names Linton.

Part III—The Second Generation

Shortly after Isabella's escape, the doctor, Kenneth, brings news of Hindley's death. Nelly wants Edgar to take in Hindley's son Hareton, but Heathcliff vows that if they take Hareton from him he will take his child from Isabella. He asserts that he wants to see if the same mistreatment will affect Hindley's child as Hindley's abuse affected Heathcliff.

Twelve years later, Isabella, near death, writes to her brother and asks him to care for her son after her death. Edgar brings Linton home, but Heathcliff immediately demands custody of his son. He reveals to Nelly his plan to see his child ruling over both Thrushcross Grange and Wuthering Heights.

Young Catherine, daughter of Catherine and Edgar, is not told that her cousin is so close by, but one day on a walk on the moor, she meets Heathcliff and Hareton and is reacquainted with Linton. Heathcliff tells Nelly that he hopes Linton and young Catherine will fall in love and marry. He boasts about how he has turned Hareton, a naturally intelligent boy, into an ignorant brute, while raising his own weak and selfish son up as Hareton's master. When Edgar hears of his daughter's visit, he does his best to impress on her the evil nature of Heathcliff and the importance of avoiding the Heights. Catherine nevertheless commences a secret correspondence with Linton, which only ends when Nelly discovers the love letters and threatens to tell Catherine's father. Heathcliff, however, convinces Catherine that Linton is dying of grief because of their broken correspondence, and Nelly reluctantly agrees to accompany Catherine on a visit to the Heights. That visit leads to a series of clandestine visits by young Catherine to the Heights. Edgar puts a stop to the visits, but finally agrees to let Catherine and Linton meet for weekly strolls on the moor. During the second of these excursions, Heathcliff, knowing that Edgar is near death, tricks Catherine and Nelly into entering Wuthering Heights, where he imprisons them and forces Catherine to marry Linton. Catherine convinces Linton to help her escape, and she arrives at the Grange just in time to see her dying father. During her absence from the Heights, Heathcliff forces Linton to make Heathcliff the inheritor of all of his and Catherine's property. After her father's death, young Catherine is forced to return to the Heights and tend to her dying husband. He dies shortly after her arrival, and Catherine, impoverished and alone, is forced to stay on at the Heights.

The day after hearing this story, Lockwood visits the Heights and gives notice that he will be leaving for London. Returning months later to settle some business, he finds Thrushcross Grange deserted and matters much changed at the Heights. Hareton and Catherine, previously sworn enemies, have fallen in love, and Catherine is aiding Hare-

ton in his attempts to educate himself. Nelly is now employed at the Heights, and while the lovers enjoy a walk on the moor, Nelly informs Lockwood of Heathcliff's death, which followed four days of starvation during which he was haunted by the vision of his beloved Catherine. He was buried, as requested, next to Catherine, with the adjoining sides of the two coffins removed so that their ashes could mingle, and the country folks claim that a person walking on the moors will sometimes see the ghosts of Heathcliff and Catherine wandering their old playground.

Characters

Ellen Dean

One of the novel's two narrators, Nelly is loyal but conventional, and reads very little into events. In his introduction to *Wuthering Heights,* David Daiches remarks on the contrast between the tone of the narrative and the high drama of the goings-on of the story: "It is to what might be called the sublime deadpan of the telling that the extraordinary force of the novel can largely be attributed.... At no point does Nelly throw up her hands and exclaim: 'For God's sake, what is going on here? What kind of people *are* they?'" For instance, after Heathcliff has spent the night in the Linton's garden bashing his head against a tree trunk, Nelly notices "several splashes of blood about the bark of the tree, and his hands and forehead were both stained; probably the scene I witnessed was a repetition of others acted during the night. It hardly moved my compassion—it appalled me; still I felt reluctant to quit him so." Nelly's familiarity with the actors is an important element of the narration, and a hazard of her station is that she must repeatedly be the bearer of news that will move the action in a fateful direction. On the eve of Heathcliff's return, for example, Edgar and the first Catherine look "wonderfully peaceful," and Nelly shrinks from having to announce Heathcliff, though duty compels her to, just as she shrinks later from having to tell Heathcliff of the first Catherine's death, but does. Nelly has a mind of her own, and she does not hesitate to query the first Catherine about her reasons for marrying Edgar, or to suggest to Heathcliff at the end of the novel that he might want to make his confession before dying. Nevertheless, the kind of passion that exists between Heathcliff and the first Catherine is far beyond her imagination.

Still from the film Wuthering Heights, *starring Merle Oberon and Laurence Olivier, 1939.*

Nelly Dean

See Ellen Dean

Catherine Earnshaw

Cathy Earnshaw is six when her father brings back with him from Liverpool not the whip she asked for but the seven-year-old foundling Heathcliff, who is soon her constant companion. Cathy is a "wild, wick slip," beautiful, and "much too fond of Heathcliff." Though capable of sweetness, she likes "to act the little mistress," and it is the awareness of the social differences between her and Heathcliff that lead her, despite her love for him, to marry Edgar Linton, whom she finds "handsome, and pleasant to be with." When Nelly implies that her reasons are superficial, Cathy tells of her plan to use Edgar's money to help Heathcliff to rise. "It would degrade me to marry Heathcliff, now," she tells Nelly, "so he shall never know how I love him"; yet "he's more myself than I am…. Nelly, I *am* Heathcliff." Five months after Cathy's marriage to Linton, during which time Nelly observes that the couple seem to be increasingly happy, Heathcliff returns, transformed. Their "mutual joy" at seeing each other again is undeniable, and from that point on Cathy lives with a painfully divided heart. She refuses to respond to Edgar's request that she choose between the two men. Although Heathcliff

has the looks and manners of a gentleman, the revenge he plans is diabolical, and though she loves him, Cathy is not fooled. "He's a fierce, pitiless, wolfish man…: and he'd crush you, like a sparrow's egg," she tells an infatuated Isabella. When Cathy and Heathcliff meet for the last time, she tells him, "You and Edgar have broken my heart, Heathcliff! … I shall not be at peace." She dies two hours after midnight, having given birth to a "puny, seven months' child."

Cathy Earnshaw

See Catherine Earnshaw

Frances Earnshaw

Wife of Hindley. Dies after giving birth to Hareton.

Hareton Earnshaw

The son of Frances and Hindley Earnshaw, Hareton, too, is initially targeted by Heathcliff as an object of revenge, and is degraded by him. But Heathcliff develops a grudging affection for the boy, favoring him over his own weakling son, Linton, and when Heathcliff dies, Hareton weeps over his body. Nelly sees him as "owning better qualities than his father ever possessed. Good things lost among a wilderness of weeds." Hareton is, however, transformed by his love for Catherine, who teaches him to read.

Hindley Earnshaw

Hindley Earnshaw, the first Catherine's brother, is fourteen when Heathcliff is brought to Wuthering Heights. Hindley hates and envies him because Mr. Earnshaw clearly favors the new boy. Hindley continually degrades Heathcliff, a habit that intensifies after the death of Mr. Earnshaw. After the death of his beloved wife Frances, Hindley resorts to drinking and gambling, and neglects both his sister Catherine and his son Hareton. Upon Heathcliff's return to Wuthering Heights after a three-year absence, five months after Edgar Linton and the first Catherine have married, Hindley befriends Heathcliff in the hopes of winning money from him. Blaming Hindley for the loss of the first Catherine, Heathcliff ruthlessly encourages Hindley to drink and eventually wins Wuthering Heights from him. After Hindley dies, Heathcliff brutalizes Hareton, though he eventually abandons the attempt after the second Catherine Linton and Hareton fall in love.

Mr. Earnshaw

Father of Hindley and the first Catherine. He brings Heathcliff home into the family. He was strict with his children.

Mrs. Earnshaw

Mother of Hindley and the first Catherine. She didn't protest the mistreatment of Heathcliff and died two years after he joined the Earnshaw household.

Heathcliff

On his return from a business trip to Liverpool, Mr. Earnshaw brings with him "a dirty, ragged, black-haired" orphan from a Liverpool slum. The boy, seven-year-old Heathcliff, and the first Catherine Earnshaw are almost immediately inseparable. Hindley Earnshaw, however, is jealous of Mr. Earnshaw's obvious preference for Heathcliff, and he abuses him. Heathcliff returns the hatred. "From the very beginning he bred bad feeling in the house," says Nelly Dean, one of the two narrators of *Wuthering Heights,* about the force that has entered their lives. Heathcliff knows only two loyalties, to the first Cathy and to Mr. Earnshaw, and at Earnshaw's death he and Cathy "both set up a heart-breaking cry." He tries to control his jealousy over Cathy's growing friendship with Edgar Linton for her sake—"Nelly, make me decent, I'm go-

Media Adaptations

- *Wuthering Heights* continues to inspire filmmakers: adaptations include those by William Wyler, starring Laurence Olivier and Merle Oberon, 1939, available from HBO Home Video and Home Vision Cinema; by Robert Fuest, starring Timothy Dalton and Anna Calder-Marshall, 1970, available from Congress Entertainment, Karol Video, The Video Catalog; a reworking under the title "Abismos de pasion", by Luis Buñuel, starring Jorge Mistral and Irasema Dilian, 1953, available from Xenon, Media Home Entertainment, Applause Productions; and by Peter Kosminsky, starring Ralph Fiennes and Juliette Binoche, 1992 (not released in the U.S., but later broadcast on Turner Network Television).

- Sound recordings have been published by Listen for Pleasure, 1981; Recorded Books, 1981, and Bantam Doubleday Dell Audio, 1995. The novel was read by Michael Page and Laurel Merlington for an audio version, Brilliance Corporation, 1992, entitled *Wuthering Heights Readalong,* Lake Publishing Co., 1994.

- The novel has been adapted as a four-act opera by Bernard Herrman, libretto by Lucille Fletcher, 1950. An adaptation by Carlisle Floyd, who also wrote the libretto, in three acts was first performed in 1958. The novel was also adapted for the stage by Charles Vance and published by Samuel French, 1990.

ing to be good." But later, overhearing a conversation in which Cathy says it would degrade her to marry him, he steals away and does not return to Wuthering Heights until five months after Cathy has married Edgar Linton.

Heathcliff is transformed on his return—"tall, athletic, well-formed"—but he is hell-bent on avenging the loss of Cathy, and he sets about destroying the inhabitants of both Wuthering Heights and Thrushcross Grange with a fury. His assertion of what David Daiches, in his introduction to *Wuthering Heights,* calls Heathcliff's "natural claims" to Cathy "over the artificial claim of her husband" is welcomed by Cathy, though the strain eventually kills her. Heathcliff cruelly exploits Hindley, Isabella, Hareton, the second Catherine, and Linton, his own son. "I have no pity," he tells Nelly. Yet when the first Catherine dies, he is inconsolable, bashing his head repeatedly against a tree trunk: "I *cannot* live without my life! I *cannot* live without my soul!" And he has an obvious affection for Hareton, despite his determination to degrade the boy. Heathcliff is largely incomprehensible to those around him, seemingly human and inhuman, a walking contradiction. "Is Mr. Heathcliff a man?" Isabella writes to Nelly, following her marriage to him, "If so, is he mad? And if not, is he a devil?" Toward the end of the novel Heathcliff confesses to Nelly that he no longer cares for revenge: "I have lost the faculty of enjoying their destruction." As determined to join his "immortal love" as he once was to ruin his enemies, he tells Nelly that he feels "a strange change coming," and, forgetting to eat, starves himself. Even death, however, does not compose his features, and Joseph remarks that he looks as though the devil has carried him off.

Catherine Heathcliff

See Catherine Linton

Isabella Heathcliff

See Isabella Linton

Linton Heathcliff

Linton Heathcliff is the spoiled, weakling son of Isabella and Heathcliff. He is forced by Heathcliff to marry the second Catherine Linton to secure for Heathcliff, at Linton's death, Thrushcross Grange. Nobody except the second Catherine Linton likes Linton very much; the housekeeper at the Heights complains to Nelly that he is "a fainthearted creature" who can't bear to have the window open at night. His character serves the dual purpose of providing a mechanism whereby Heathcliff can acquire Thrushcross Grange and re-create the Edgar-Cathy-Heathcliff triangle of the previous generation. Linton dies soon after his marriage to the second Catherine.

Joseph

Joseph is the curmudgeonly, judgmental long-time servant at Wuthering Heights. He believes in eternal damnation and the likelihood of everyone he knows being bound for it, and he scolds constantly in a sometimes difficult-to-follow Yorkshire accent. As in the case of the narrators of the novel, Joseph's authenticity anchors the wilder elements of the story. Winifred Gerin observes in *Reference Guide to English Literature* that "in creating such a character as Joseph, Emily Brontë showed that, undoubted visionary as she was, she also had her feet firmly planted on earth."

Catherine Linton

Catherine Linton is the daughter of Cathy and Edgar, beautiful, like her mother, but cooler. "Her anger was never furious, her love never fierce," Nelly remarks about her. Although forced by Heathcliff to marry Linton Heathcliff, she genuinely seems to care for her cousin. She is obviously less a force than her mother, but spirited nonetheless, and refuses to be cowed by Heathcliff: "You *are* miserable, are you not? Lonely, like the devil, and envious like him? *Nobody* loves you— *nobody* will cry for you, when you die! I wouldn't be you!" Although Catherine is at first put off by Hareton's loutishness, the sheer bleakness of their existence propels them toward each other, and she teaches him to read. They fall in love, and the understanding at the end of the novel is that they will marry and go to live at Thrushcross Grange.

Catherine Earnshaw Linton

See Catherine Earnshaw

Cathy Linton

See Catherine Linton

Edgar Linton

Edgar Linton is all the things Heathcliff is not: handsome, refined, kind, and patient, although the first Cathy later describes Edgar and his sister Isabella as "spoiled children, [who] fancy the world was made for their accommodation." When Heathcliff says he wishes he had Edgar's looks and breeding, Nelly retorts: "And cried for Mamma at every turn, and trembled if a country lad heaved his fist against you, and sat at home all day for a shower of rain." On the other hand, Nelly observes that the first Cathy's spells of bad humor are "respected with sympathizing silence by her husband," and that Edgar has a "deep-rooted fear of ruffling her humor." Linton loves his wife genuinely, but he is ineffectual. Unable to get her to choose between himself and Heathcliff, he retreats to his library, oblivious to her distress until alerted to it by

Nelly. After his wife dies, Edgar sits all night beside her body. Taking the measure of both Edgar and Hindley, Nelly remarks that Linton "displayed the true courage of a loyal and faithful soul: he trusted God; and God comforted him." Hindley, with the stronger head, proved the worse and weaker man.

Isabella Linton

Like her brother Edgar, Isabella is perceived by the inhabitants of Wuthering Heights as spoiled. Having glimpsed them through a window quarreling amid the splendor of Thrushcross Grange, Heathcliff tells Nelly, "We laughed outright at the petted things, we did despise them!" Nelly observes that Isabella is "infantile in manners, though possessed of keen wit, keen feelings, and a keen temper, too, if irritated." On Heathcliff's return to Wuthering Heights after the first Cathy's marriage to Edgar, Isabella becomes infatuated with him, despite Cathy's warning that he "couldn't love a Linton." At first indifferent, Heathcliff responds when he realizes he might gain control of her property through marriage. Once she is committed to him, he cruelly mistreats her. Despite the abuse, Isabella refuses to help Hindley in his attempt to murder Heathcliff, though she has enough of a sense of self-preservation to escape back to Thrushcross Grange, where she crushes her wedding ring with a poker. "I can recollect yet how I loved him," she tells Nelly, "and can dimly imagine that I could still be loving him, if—." Pregnant, Isabella flees to London, where she bears Linton. She dies when Linton is twelve, after which the boy comes to live with Heathcliff at the Heights.

Mr. Linton

Father of Edgar and Isabella. He is the owner of Thrushcross Grange.

Mrs. Linton

Mother of Edgar and Isabella. She takes the first Catherine in for a short while and exposed her to fine clothes and social behavior.

Mr. Lockwood

The other narrator of *Wuthering Heights,* Mr. Lockwood is, like Nelly Dean, conventional. But he lacks Nelly's perception, and appears even a little foolish. At first he judges Heathcliff to be a "capital fellow," and later he fantasizes a liaison with the second Catherine Linton. Several critics have remarked on his name as hinting at a "locked or closed mind." In his introduction to *Wuthering Heights,*

David Daiches describes his general timidity: "he had aroused the love of 'a fascinating creature,' but retreated in panic when he realized it." Mr. Lockwood foreshadows the theme of cruelty that pervades the novel, rubbing the wrist of the ghost of the first Catherine Linton across a broken pane of glass in an attempt to loosen her grasp of his hand. Mr. Lockwood serves to vary the narrative perspective of the novel; his view of events in the present contrasts with Nelly's retrospective view.

Zillah

A servant at Wuthering Heights.

Themes

Love and Passion

Passion, particularly unnatural passion, is a predominant theme of Wuthering Heights. The first Catherine's devotion to Heathcliff is immediate and absolute, though she will not marry him, because to do so would degrade her. "Whatever our souls are made of, his and mine are the same, and Linton's is as different as a moonbeam from lightning, or frost from fire." Although there has been at least one Freudian interpretation of the text, the nature of the passion between Catherine and Heathcliff does not appear to be based on sex. David Daiches writes, "Ultimate passion is for her rather a kind of recognition of one's self—one's true and absolute self—in the object of passion." Catherine's passion is contrasted to the coolness of Linton, whose "cold blood cannot be worked into a fever." When he retreats into his library, she explodes, "What in the name of all that feels, has he to do with *books,* when I am dying?"

Revenge

Heathcliff's devotion to Catherine, on the other hand, is ferocious, and when frustrated, he conceives a plan of revenge of enormous proportions. Catherine's brother Hindley shares her passionate nature, though he devotes most of his energies to degrading Heathcliff. In some respects the passion that Catherine and Heathcliff share is so pure that it approaches a kind of spirituality. "I cannot express it," says Catherine, "but surely you and everybody have a notion that there is, or should be an existence of yours beyond you." In the characters of Heathcliff and Hindley, who both feel slighted in love, Brontë draws a parallel between the need for love and the strength of revenge.

Topics for Further Study

- What achievements of modern medicine have reduced the high rates of maternal deaths in childbirth that were commonplace during the period of the novel? How have social factors compromised advances in the treatment of tuberculosis?

- What were the milestones in women's rights that have reduced the vulnerability of women like the second Catherine Linton to loss of property?

- Explore how people grieve their dead in various cultures around the world, and how these customs compare with Edgar's request in *Wuthering Heights* that Nelly "get mourning" for the second Catherine after Isabella's death.

Violence and Cruelty

Closely tied to the theme of revenge, but sometimes independent of it, are themes of cruelty and sadism, which are a recurring motif throughout the novel. Cruelty can be manifested emotionally, as in Mr. Earnshaw's disdain for his natural-born son, or in the first Catherine's apparent rejection of Heathcliff in favor of Edgar. The characters are given to physical cruelty as well. "Terror made me cruel," says Lockwood at the outset of the story, and proceeds to rub the wrists of the ghost Catherine against a broken windowpane in an effort to free himself from her grasp. Hindley torments Heathcliff, as Heathcliff will later torment Hareton. And although he has no affection for her, Heathcliff marries Isabella and then treats her so badly that she asks Nelly whether he is a devil. Sadism is also a recurring thematic element. Heathcliff tries to strangle Isabella's dog, and Hareton hangs a litter of puppies from the back of a chair. The first Catherine's early refusal of Heathcliff has elements of masochism (self-abuse) in it, as does her letting him back into her life, since her divided heart will eventually kill her.

Class Conflict

To the characters of Wuthering Heights, property ownership and social standing are inextricable.

The Earnshaws and the Lintons both own estates, whereas Heathcliff is a foundling and has nothing. The first Catherine plans to marry Linton to use her husband's money to raise Heathcliff's social standing, thus freeing him from Hindley's domination. Her plan is foiled when Heathcliff disappears after hearing Catherine say that to marry him would degrade her. When he returns, he exerts great efforts to do people out of their property: first Hindley, then Isabella, then the second Catherine Linton. He takes revenge on Hareton by ensuring that the boy is raised in ignorance, with loutish manners, so that he will never escape his station. The story comes full cycle when Catherine Linton teaches Hareton to read, thus winning his love. The understanding at the end of the novel is that the couple will move to Thrushcross Grange.

Nature

"Wuthering" is a Yorkshire term for roaring of the wind, and themes of nature, both human and nonhuman, are closely associated with violence throughout the story. The local landscape is as storm-tossed as are the hearts of the inhabitants of Wuthering Heights; cycles of births and deaths occur as relentlessly as the cycles of the seasons. The characters feel themselves so intrinsically a part of their environment that the first Catherine compares her love for Edgar to "foliage in the woods," and that for Heathcliff to "the eternal rocks beneath." In detailing his plan to debase Hareton, Heathcliff says, "We will see if one tree will not grow as crooked as another, with the same wind to twist it!" The novel opens with a snowstorm, and ends with the flowering of spring, mirroring the passions that fuel the drama and the peace that follows its resolution.

Supernatural

There are many references in the novel to the supernatural, and even when the references seem fairly literal, the characters do not seem to think them odd. When Lockwood first arrives, he encounters the ghost of the first Catherine Linton, and his telling of the event to Heathcliff arouses not disbelief but a strange passion. The bond between the first Catherine and Heathcliff is itself superhuman, and after she dies, Heathcliff implores her spirit, "I pray one prayer—I repeat it till my tongue stiffens—Catherine Earnshaw, may you not rest, as long as I am living! You said I killed you—haunt me then!" At Edgar Linton's death, Heathcliff persuades the gravedigger to open Catherine's coffin, and later confesses to Nelly that he has been haunted by Catherine's spirit for eighteen years. At the end of the novel, after Heathcliff's death, Nelly reports to Lockwood a child's claim that he has seen Heathcliff and a woman walking on the moors.

Style

Narration

The power of *Wuthering Heights* owes much to its complex narrative structure and to the ingenious device of having two conventional people relate a very unconventional tale. The story is organized as a narrative within a narrative, or what some critics call "Chinese boxes." Lockwood is used to open and end the novel in the present tense, first person ("I"). When he returns to Thrushcross Grange from his visit to Wuthering Heights sick and curious, Nelly cheerfully agrees to tell him about his neighbors. She picks up the narrative and continues it, also in the first person, almost until the end, with only brief interruptions by Lockwood. The critic David Daiches notes in his introduction of *Wuthering Heights* the "fascinating counterpoint" of "end retrospect and present impression," and that the strength of the story relies on Nelly's familiarity with the main characters.

Setting

The novel is set in the Yorkshire moors of England, even now a bleakly beautiful, sparsely populated area of high rolling grassy hills, few trees, and scattered rocky outcroppings or patches of heather. The lowlands between the hills are marshy. The weather is changeable and, because the area is so open, sometimes wild. The exposed location of Wuthering Heights high on the moors is contrasted with the sheltered calm of Thrushcross Grange, which is nestled in a soft valley. Both seats reflect the characters of those who inhabit them. The descriptions of both houses also reflect the influence of the local architecture at the time of Brontë's writing, which often incorporated a material called grit stone.

Images and Symbolism

Emily Brontë's poetic vision is evident in the imagery used throughout Wuthering Heights. Metaphors of nature and the animal kingdom are pervasive. For example, the first Catherine describes Heathcliff to Isabella as "an arid wilderness of furze and whinstone," and as Catherine lies dying, Heathcliff foams "like a mad dog." References to weather are everywhere. A violent storm blows up the night Mr. Earnshaw dies; rain pours down the night Heathcliff runs off to London and again the night of his death. There are many scenes of raw violence, such as the bulldog attacking Catherine and Isabella crushing her wedding ring with a poker. The supernatural is evoked in the many references to Heathcliff as diabolical (literally, "like the devil") and the descriptions of the ghost of the first Catherine Linton. David Daiches points out in his introduction to *Wuthering Heights* that the references to food and fire, and to what he calls domestic routine, help "to steady" the story and to give credibility to the passion.

Structure

One of the major strengths of Wuthering Heights is its formal organization. The design of the time structure has significance both for its use of two narrators and because it allows the significant events in the novel to be dated precisely, though dates are almost never given explicitly. The triangular relationship that existed between Heathcliff, Catherine, and Edgar is repeated in Heathcliff's efforts to force young Catherine to marry Linton, though its resolution is ultimately different. On his arrival at Wuthering Heights, Lockwood sees the names "Catherine Earnshaw, Catherine Linton, Catherine Heathcliff" scratched into the windowsill. In marrying Hareton, young Catherine Heathcliff will in turn become Catherine Earnshaw, thus completing the circle.

Historical Context

The Victorian Age (1837-1901)

England under the reign of Queen Victoria was in a prolonged phase of expansion. The Industrial Revolution saw the transformation of a predominately agricultural economy to a factory economy. Millions would eventually flock to London in search of the new jobs, but Emily Brontë grew up in the last days of rural England. The tenor of the times was conservative, and sensitive to society's unwillingness to accept women as authors, Emily, Charlotte, and Anne Brontë all published under male pseudonyms.

The tempestuous climate of northern England in Haworth, Yorkshire, left its mark on the Brontë children, whose fascination with the expanse and storms of the moors is emphasized in the novel. For Emily, who was never happy far from home, the

Compare
&
Contrast

- **Late 1700s:** World economies are predominately agrarian.

  1847: England is in the midst of an Industrial Revolution whose effects will be felt worldwide. Workers flock to cities from the countryside.

  Today: World economies are increasingly linked in a "global community." Intercultural communication and cultural diversity in the so-called service economy are a direct result of advances in transportation and communications.

- **Late 1700s:** Life expectancy is short, owing to harsh living and working conditions. Death in childbirth is common.

  1847: Medical advances and improved public health and sanitation decrease maternal and infant mortality.

  Today: Though high-technology medicine offers solutions to many medical problems, heart disease and cancer remain major killers, there is no cure for AIDS, and many countries grapple with increasing costs of health care for aging populations.

- **Late 1700s:** Inheritance in England passes from the father to the first-born male. A procedure called "strict settlement" must be invoked to bypass inheritance laws.

  1847: Full legal and economic equality for women is first championed in the United States by Elizabeth Cady Stanton.

  Today: Women worldwide have the right to vote, except in a few Muslim countries. In the United States, while the Equal Rights Amendment failed to obtain ratification, women increasingly bring successful sexual discrimination and sexual harassment suits against employers.

---

local moorland and valleys, and the grit stone architecture typical of the age were the basis for the setting of *Wuthering Heights*.

Another influence on Brontë's writing was the folklore of the Yorkshire community. Tabitha Ackroyd, a maid in the Brontë household, was a rich source of stories about fairies and ghosts. References to folk beliefs and rituals are scattered throughout *Wuthering Heights*, particularly with reference to the deathwatch traditional in Yorkshire, as when Edgar sits the entire night with Catherine's body after her death, or to rituals surrounding funerals such as "bidding," an invitation to accompany a body to the grave. Extending or withholding such an invitation gave some indication of the state of family relationships.

Illness, Death, and Funeral Customs

Owing to the unforgiving climate and poor heating, illness and death were common occurrences in Yorkshire at the time the novel was created. Ill partly as a result of his stay at Wuthering Heights, Lockwood laments, "Oh, these bleak winds, and bitter, northern skies, and impassable roads, and dilatory country surgeons!" Emily Brontë's older sisters Maria and Elizabeth died of tuberculosis before they were fifteen, and in *Wuthering Heights*, Edgar and Linton also die of wasting diseases. Maria Branwell's death when Emily was only three may be the inspiration for the many motherless children in *Wuthering Heights*.

A period of mourning was formally observed after the death of a family member. The appropriate period of mourning depended on whether the deceased was a close or distant relative. For example, a year's mourning was usually observed for a husband or wife, and a week for the death of a second cousin. In *Wuthering Heights* Nelly is "bid to get mourning"—that is, to lay out dark clothes—for Catherine, whose aunt Isabella has died.

As the children of a minister, the Brontës felt the influence of religion both at home and at school. A fire-and-brimstone instructor may have been Emily Brontë's inspiration for Joseph, who can barely speak a word that does not invoke hellfire. Critics also suspect that this influence is at the root of Lockwood's dream at the beginning of *Wuthering Heights,* in which he is forced to listen to the Reverend Jabes Branderham preach a sermon divided into 490 parts.

Literary Traditions and Romanticism

Whereas Charlotte Brontë's *Jane Eyre* won immediate acclaim, the wild passion and coarseness of *Wuthering Heights* baffled its readers. In an essay in *Reference Guide to English Literature,* Winifred Gerin attributes the failure of the novel to its theme of indestructibility of the spirit, which was a "subject … far removed from the general run of Victorian fiction—it belonged, if anywhere, to the gothic tradition, still being followed by Mary Shelley with her *Valperga* (1823) in Emily Brontë's childhood."

The time in which the action of *Wuthering Heights* takes place, and its themes of nature and the individual, coincides with the Romantic Movement in Europe, a turning away from reason and intellect in favor of free and more mystical ideas, inspired in part by the French Revolutionary War of 1789.

Inheritance and Social Position

Social position and respectability in this period were directly tied to possession of property. A country house owned by landed gentry like the Earnshaws and the Lintons was known as a "seat," a broad term that included both the tangible assets (for instance, the house and land) and intangible assets (for instance, the family name and any hereditary titles) of the family that owned it. In *Wuthering Heights,* the first Catherine tells Nelly that she is marrying Edgar Linton because to marry Heathcliff would degrade her (they would be beggars) and because she plans to use Linton's money to help Heathcliff to rise.

Seats passed from father to first-born male or to the next closest male relative if there were no sons in a family. The only way around this process was to invoke a device called "strict settlement," in force between 1650 and 1880, which allowed a father to dispose of his holdings as he liked through a trustee. Because Edgar Linton dies before ensuring that his daughter Catherine will inherit Thrushcross Grange, the land passes first to her husband, Linton, and after Linton's death to his father, Heathcliff.

In contrast to earlier times when incest was forbidden by law, in eighteenth-century England marriage between first cousins was looked upon favorably as a way of preserving position and prop-

"Top Withens," the farm which served as a model for the one in Wuthering Heights.

erty. A typical union was one of a woman who married her father's brother's son, which kept the seat of the bride's family under their control. In *Wuthering Heights,* in a perverse twist, the second Catherine Linton marries her father's sister's son, and in the absence of a strict settlement ends up losing her family's seat.

Landholding families typically maintained a large staff of servants who fulfilled the functions (for a man) of steward, valet, butler, and gardener, or (for a woman) of lady's maid, housekeeper, cook, and nurse. In a household the size of Wuthering Heights, whose inhabitants did not entertain, combining functions made economic sense. In the novel Joseph serves as both valet and steward, and Ellen as housekeeper, though her duties are fairly broadly defined.

Critical Overview

Initial reception to the publication of *Wuthering Heights* in 1847 was overwhelmingly negative. Published in a volume that also included her sister Anne Brontë's first novel, *Agnes Grey,* Emily's brooding tale managed to find favor only with Sydney Dobell and Algernon Charles Swinburne. "I have just read over *Wuthering Heights,*" wrote Charlotte Brontë in her preface to the 1850 edition of her sister's book, "and, for the first time, have obtained a clear glimpse of what are termed (and, perhaps, really are) its faults.... *Wuthering Heights* must appear a rude and strange production ... in a great measure unintelligible, and—where intelligible—repulsive." The preface was intended as a defense of the writer and the work and must have achieved its aim, for the second edition of the novel was received more favorably. Algernon Charles Swinburne, writing in *The Athenaeum* in 1883, admitted to the awkward construction and clumsy method of narration "which no reader ... can undertake to deny," although these were minor faults. He was more troubled by "the savage note or the sickly symptom of a morbid ferocity," but was overall so impressed by the "special and distinctive character of its passion" that "it is certain that those who do like it will like nothing very much better in the whole world of poetry or prose."

A monograph by Charles Percy Sanger published in 1926 marked a major turning point in critical appreciation of the sophistication and complexity of the writing in *Wuthering Heights,* and today the novel is indisputably considered a work of genius. That critics cannot agree whether the book falls more neatly into the Gothic or Romantic literary tradition is accepted as further evidence of the work's uniqueness. In his introduction to the novel, David Daiches argues that the central question of *Wuthering Heights* is "Who and what is Heathcliff?", a question Daiches argues can be answered only by looking at the effect Heathcliff has on those around him. While Daiches agrees with the conventional view that the relationship between Heathcliff and the first Catherine is "curiously" sexless, he does find persuasive Thomas Moser's (1962) case for recurring sexual symbolism in the novel. Daiches echoes other critics in praising the book's narrative structure and other elements of its organization. He places special emphasis on the details of everyday living, and descriptions of food and hearth, that help to anchor the story and to make it believable. "One of Emily Brontë's most extraordinary achievements in this novel is the domiciling of the monstrous in the ordinary rhythms of life and work, thereby making it at the same time less monstrous and more disturbing." Tom Winnifrith, in the *Dictionary of Literary Biography,* picks up on the idea of Heathcliff as a force of na-

ture and attributes his attraction in part to his association with the landscape and to his honesty, however brutal. This last idea highlights one of many ambiguities of the novel, a strength often commented on by scholars and critics. "Brontë's defiance of rigid categories and her refusal to divide people into saints and sinners," says Winnifrith, "is very un-Victorian.... Heathcliff's cruelty and Cathy's selfishness do not prevent them from being attractive. The Lintons are spoiled and weak, but Isabella's and her son's sufferings and Edgar's devotion to his wife win them sympathy." Winnifrith dismisses the oft-cited effort to fit the novel into an overall framework of storm and calm—that is, storm and calm opposed in the persons of Catherine and Heathcliff, but fused in the union of Catherine and Hareton—proposed by Lord David Cecil in *Early Victorian Novelists* (1934) as too schematic. He argues that some modern sociological interpretations ignore the book's enigmatic ending. Other modern critical articles on the novel, he says, "tend to be eccentric or to deal with only a very small section of the book." In an essay in *Reference Guide to English Literature,* Winifred Gerin describes the message of "the indissoluble nature of earthly love" as "profoundly metaphysical," its original failure easily explained by its gothic atmosphere, no longer in fashion at the time of publication. Gerin attributes the novel's "curious and lasting appeal" to the "unflagging excitement of the plot; the wild moorland setting; [and] ... the originality of the characters." She calls Heathcliff's self-induced death by starvation "one of the most powerful and daring climaxes in English fiction."

"Whether it is right or advisable to create things like Heathcliff, I do not know," wrote Charlotte Brontë at the end of the preface to the 1850 edition. "I scarcely think it is. But this I know; the writer who possesses the creative gift owns something of which he is not always master—something that at times strangely wills and works for itself." It is English literature's gain that Emily lost herself in her creation.

Criticism

Donna C. Woodford

In the following essay, Woodford, a doctoral candidate at Washington University, explores how an examination of the patterns that recur through-

out Wuthering Heights *provide a useful way of reading and interpreting the novel.*

Wuthering Heights was the only novel Emily Brontë ever published, and both it and the book of poetry she published with her sisters were printed under the pen name, Ellis Bell, a name which Emily chose because she was afraid works published under a woman's name would not be taken seriously. Emily Brontë died shortly after her book was published and just prior to her thirtieth birthday, but her single novel remains one of the classics of English literature. *Wuthering Heights* is a complex novel, and critics have approached it from many different standpoints. Feminist critics have examined the strong female characters and their oppression by and resistance to violent men. Marxist critics have pointed to the class differences that set in motion the primary conflicts of *Wuthering Heights,* and psychoanalytic critics have analyzed the dreams that fill the book. While all of these approaches are useful and valid, *Wuthering Heights* is, above all, a book of repeating cycles and recurring patterns, and perhaps the simplest way to begin an examination of this book is by tracing the course and resolution of some of these patterns.

When Lockwood spends the night at the Heights, he finds the window ledge covered with "a name repeated in all kinds of characters, large and small—*Catherine Earnshaw,* here and there varied to *Catherine Heathcliff,* and then again to *Catherine Linton.*" Indeed, the repetition and variation of these four names, Catherine, Earnshaw, Heathcliff, and Linton, fills the book just as the writing fills the window ledge. The original Catherine begins life as Catherine Earnshaw. In what Terry Eagleton in *Case Studies In Contemporary Criticism: Wuthering Heights* calls "a crucial act of self-betrayal and bad faith," she rejects the opportunity to become Catherine Heathcliff and instead becomes Catherine Linton. She then gives birth to another Catherine Linton, who enters the world only hours before her mother leaves it, and this second Catherine first marries Linton Heathcliff, becoming Catherine Heathcliff, and finally, at the end of the book, becomes engaged to Hareton Earnshaw. The cycle of names thus comes full circle as this final marriage will give the second Catherine the original name of the first.

At the same time, Catherine's marriage with Hareton completes another cycle—the union of souls for which the reader has longed. The second Catherine is in many ways a reincarnation of her

What Do I Read Next?

- *The Complete Poems of Emily Jane Brontë* (1910) is a collection of Brontë's metaphysical poetry.

- The memorable heroine of Charlotte Brontë's *Jane Eyre* (1847) finds love with her moody employer, Mr. Rochester, but manages not to give up her independence.

- George Eliot's *Middlemarch: A Study of Provincial Life* (1871-72) is a portrait of life in a small rural town. George Eliot was the pseudonym of Mary Ann Evans.

- *Frankenstein* (1818) is Mary Wollstonecraft Shelley's gothic tale of destructive pride. Dr. Victor Frankenstein makes a living monster out of inanimate matter and is ultimately destroyed by his creation.

mother. Though she is softened by the characteristics which she has inherited from her father, she has "the Earnshaw's handsome, dark eyes" and, as Nelly states, she has the same "capacity for intense attachments" as her mother. Similarly, Hareton is a gentler version of his oppressor and foster father, Heathcliff. Though Heathcliff does his best to make Hareton a tool of his revenge against the first Catherine's brother Hindley Earnshaw, he succeeds instead in creating a reproduction of himself. He reveals his own knowledge of this strange turn of events when he tells Nelly, "Hareton [seems] a personification of my youth .... the ghost of my immortal love, of my wild endeavours to hold my right, my degradation, my pride, my happiness, and my anguish." Thus, even more than the reunion of Catherine's and Heathcliff's ghosts, the union of their spiritual descendants gives the reader the impression that a great wrong has finally been set right.

In addition to being later versions of Heathcliff and the first Catherine, Hareton and the second Catherine are the last in a long line of orphans and outcasts. In an article in *American Imago* Philip K. Wion has observed that the absence of mothers in *Wuthering Heights* has a profound effect on the identities of the orphaned children, and certainly the book is full of orphaned and abandoned characters seeking fulfillment through union with others. Heathcliff, of course, is a foundling taken in by Mr. Earnshaw, and after the old man's death Hindley makes him an outcast. The first Catherine, also orphaned by Earnshaw's death, becomes still more isolated after Heathcliff's departure. Heathcliff has been her one true companion, so much a part of herself that she tells Nelly, "if all else perished, and *he* remained, I should still continue to be; and, if all else remained, and he were annihilated, the Universe would turn to a mighty stranger." The loss of her soul mate thus leaves her alone in the world, and her death, likewise, orphans him for a second time, leaving him "lonely, like the devil, and envious like him." The next generation fares no better. Linton Heathcliff loses his mother and is raised by a father who despises him; Hareton's mother dies shortly after his birth, and the death of his alcoholic and abusive father leaves him penniless and at the mercy of Heathcliff. Likewise, the second Catherine is born only hours before her mother's death, and the death of her father leaves her "destitute of cash and friends." Once again, it is the marriage of Hareton and Catherine that will bring this cycle of orphanhood to a close. The housekeeper, Nelly, proudly tells the tenant Lockwood that they are both "in a measure, [her] children," and the union of her two charges finally ends the progression of lonely, isolated, orphaned individuals.

Heathcliff's death and the second Catherine's gaining control of the property also bring to an end the series of tyrannical men who rule the Heights with violence and curses. The first Mr. Earnshaw is easily vexed, and "suspected slights of his authority nearly [throw] him into fits." Hindley, Mr. Earnshaw's successor, is still worse. He threatens to "demolish the first who puts [him] out of temper," and his abuse of Heathcliff is "enough to make a fiend of a saint." Heathcliff, in his turn, does turn out to be a fiend, and deserves the term "Devil daddy" with which young Hareton christens him. He takes pleasure in inflicting on Hindley's son the same abuse which Hindley had given Heathcliff because he wants to see "if one tree won't grow as crooked as another, with the same wind to twist it," and he values his own son only because he wants "the triumph of seeing [his] descendent fairly lord of their estates; [his] child hiring their children, to till their father's lands for wages." Thus, even Heathcliff's plot to reverse past

patterns by making his child lord of the Earnshaws and Lintons, only results in the reestablishment of an old pattern. Heathcliff, the former victim of tyranny, becomes yet another tyrannical man ruling Wuthering Heights. This cycle is only broken when, after Heathcliff's death, the property is granted to the second Catherine, the first woman in the book to own her own property. Her marriage to Hareton will, of course, make her property his, but it seems unlikely that his "honest, warm, intelligent nature" will allow him to become a tyrant like his predecessors. The pattern of violent men ruling the Heights, like so many other patterns in the book, ends with the death of Heathcliff and the marriage of the second Catherine and Hareton.

Source: Donna C. Woodford, in an essay for *Novels for Students,* Gale, 1997.

Annette R. Federico

In the following essay, Federico maintains that Wuthering Heights *is a bildungsroman—a novel which outlines the initiation of a young character into adulthood—focusing on the development of young Cathy Linton rather than that of her mother.*

In their study of nineteenth-century women writers, *The Madwoman in the Attic,* Sandra M. Gilbert and Susan Gubar argue persuasively that because the story of *Wuthering Heights* is built around a central fall—generally understood to be Catherine and Heathcliff's anti-Miltonic fall *from* hell *to* heaven—"a description of the novel as in part a *Bildungsroman* about a girl's passage from 'innocence' to 'experience' (leaving aside the precise meaning of these terms) would probably be widely accepted."

This is an interesting interpretation, and brilliantly demonstrated. But like other views of *Wuthering Heights* as a feminine *Bildungsroman,* the focus of development is Catherine, and by association her male doppelganger Heathcliff. The emphasis upon the first generation of the Heights is, of course, important, and certainly Catherine and Heathcliff suffer their own peculiar rites of passage in their search for identity and wholeness. And yet it is curious that the tortured first generation of Wuthering Heights fail to develop a mature understanding of themselves and others—in fact, Catherine and Heathcliff actually shrink from full participation in adult life, regressing into the adolescent preoccupation with self and the desperate need to feel loved. Catherine, especially, is not so much struggling to grow up as she is struggling *not* to: it is significant that it is the "waif" not the woman who appears in Lockwood's terrifying dream.

So the critical view of Catherine and Heathcliff as *Bildungsroman* protagonists neglects these characters' inability to interpret experience realistically and face the limitations of adulthood. In fact, in terms of the first generation, *Wuthering Heights* is not a *Bildungsroman* at all, but an *Entwickslungroman,* a novel of mere physical passage without psychological development. Catherine and her male soul-mate remain stubbornly adolescent from beginning to end; granted, they are triumphant, rebellious, passionate characters, and Emily Brontë is obviously celebrating the untamed and undisciplined spirit of adolescent love. But in view of this first generation, *Wuthering Heights* is less a novel of development than a novel of arrested childhood. It is actually with Catherine's death in childbirth that Brontë's *Bildungsroman* begins. In fact, the second half of *Wuthering Heights* and the concern with young Cathy is a fascinating variation of the prototypic novel of female education in the nineteenth century, a dramatization of the struggle to relinquish childhood for the duties of womanhood in the most traditional, romantic capacity: marriage with the man of one's choice. Cathy emerges from a relatively happy childhood and a lonely adolescence as an assertive, sharing, and contented adult who is prepared to accept the responsibilities and limitations of marriage.

Cathy's marriage to Hareton is in a sense a revision of her mother's unsuccessful marriage to Edgar Linton, and a significant role reversal of the traditional feminine *Bildungsroman* in which a woman can achieve intellectual and social advancement only through marriage. For example, the elder Catherine looks at marriage as a means of achieving outward sophistication, as well as an escape from mental and emotional stagnation: Edgar is the man who will define her, who will shape her identity and give her status—"He will be rich, and I shall be the greatest woman of the neighborhood, and I shall be proud to have such a husband," she tells Nelly Dean. Catherine's selfish and shortsighted attitude toward marriage is not only indicative of her childish sensibilities, but underscores the traditional theme of the feminine *Bildungsroman*—that is, the woman must seek knowledge by attaching herself to a knowledgeable male. Brontë varies this theme in her description of young Cathy's courtship with Hareton; instead of marrying to be advanced, Brontë's true female *Bildungsroman* protagonist marries in order to advance the intellectual and moral status of the male.

In young Cathy, Brontë gives us a woman whose acquired humility, patience, and affection yield what promises to be a satisfying marriage and a mutual broadening of experience. More than her mother, Cathy represents a successful passage through the difficult rites of adolescence: the search for self, and the sharing of self with others.

If one looks closely at the novel, it becomes clear that Cathy and Hareton are not merely watered down versions of Catherine and Heathcliff, as Richard Chase suggests. Although the strange, transcendental love of the first generation of the Heights is more stirring, more piquant than the settled affections of Cathy and Hareton, it is only because their type of frenzied passion is so rare—and so typical of adolescence. It is well to ask why Catherine marries Edgar at all, considering her feelings for Heathcliff; her naive belief that she can have *both* Edgar—who represents culture and security—*and* Heathcliff, who is the embodiment of sexual and natural energy, proves her complete inability to understand reality outside of her own narrow perspective. When Nelly Dean suggests that by marrying Edgar, Catherine will lose Heathcliff, she is incredulous: "Oh, that's not what I intend—that's not what I mean! I shouldn't be Mrs. Linton were such a price demanded! He'll be as much to me as he has been all his lifetime. Edgar must shake off his antipathy and tolerate him, at least. He will when he learns my true feelings...." It is obvious that Catherine is entering marriage with the stubborn adolescent sensibility that she can have her cake and eat it, too. Of course, this has been her spoiled way of looking at life all along; many times in the novel Brontë portrays Catherine as a selfish, demanding, manipulative child. "I demand it!" is, in fact, Catherine's favorite expression, and completely consistent with the adolescent determination to have everything.

By contrast, young Cathy gradually develops a sensitivity towards the feelings and needs of others. This is most explicit in her devotion to her father, Edgar Linton—and a complete contrast to Catherine's "naughty delight" in provoking Mr. Earnshaw. The young Cathy tells Nelly, "I fret about nothing on earth except papa's illness.... And I'll never—never—oh, never, while I have my senses, do anything to vex him. I love him better than myself...." Cathy's comparatively happy childhood has certainly influenced her idealized view of Edgar Linton, and she is naturally submissive to patriarchal authority. But Cathy is not without spirit; she exhibits the typical adolescent preoccupation with love intrigues, and shares her mother's rebelliousness and scorn for those who interfere with her plans. The important difference between the two generations is in the nature of the rebellion; Catherine's disregard for others— *all* others, except her other-self, Heathcliff—has a cruel, manipulative quality that takes pleasure in deceitfulness and in "punishing" others for their lack of devotion to her. Her many melodramatic "scenes" illustrate Catherine's acting talent in the service of narcissism: as a child, after an argument with Edgar Linton, she says to him, "…get away! And now I'll cry—I'll cry myself sick!" and she proceeds to deliver a perfect fit of weeping which softens poor Edgar's heart. Catherine never outgrows these willful displays of mad emotion, and by feigning a fit to arouse her husband's concern, she ultimately brings about her own death. She begs Nelly to tell Edgar she is "in danger of being seriously ill…. I want to frighten him…. Will you do so, my good Nelly? You are aware that I am in no way blameable in this matter." Catherine often uses Nelly Dean as an instrument for her guile: "… and remind Edgar of my passionate temper verging, when kindled, on frenzy." Certainly Catherine's last performance is magnificent, if unsuccessful, for even Nelly is startled by "the aspect of death" her mistress is able to assume. This undisciplined and domineering child—the little girl who wanted her father to bring her a whip from Liverpool—fails to mature at all because she never learns to control her perverse egotism. That in her last breath Catherine looks to Nelly "like a child reviving" aptly suggests the adolescent spirit of the woman's rebellion, a fatal result of Catherine's last scene of "mad resolution."

Unlike her mother's obsessiveness, young Cathy's rebellion is actually a healthy curiosity about her relatives at Wuthering Heights. Certainly it is not surprising that a young and intelligent girl who has not been beyond the range of the park before the age of thirteen, whose only companion is her nurse, and whose only amusements are rambling on the moors and reading, should be eager to make new acquaintances. And of course Cathy passes through certain predictable stages of adolescence; but unlike her mother, she does *pass* through, and restlessness, romantic love, and rebellion are only stages of her development. For example, Cathy and Linton Heathcliff's "love affair" is typical of the adolescent absorption with romantic notions, and the fact that the relationship is somehow taboo makes it all the more alluring. Cathy exaggerates the importance of her love letters, weeping and pleading to Nelly "to spare one or two." Nelly Dean's common sense reply to the

mere suggestion of Cathy loving Linton is, "Loving! Pretty loving indeed, and both times together you have seen Linton hardly four hours in your life!" That Cathy is able to open her mind to this objective, adult point of view is a credit to her maturity, and something the older Catherine never learned to do.

In her relationship to Linton, Cathy begins to learn that her desires are complex and that her experience of reality must be reconciled to actual reality—in other words, *her* view of Linton Heathcliff as "a pretty little darling" must be reconciled to Nelly's less generous description: "The worst-tempered bit of a sickly slip that ever struggled into its teens!" In learning to distinguish between what she *thinks* she wants (Linton) and what she *really* wants (an energetic and empathetic companion), Cathy begins to achieve the disciplined growth and broad perspective which is the undertaking of the *Bildungsroman* protagonist. Simply the way she handles Heathcliff and her captivity at Wuthering Heights demonstrates an intelligent, unselfish, and practical kind of defiance which Catherine never displayed, because Catherine acknowledged only her own needs and desires. When Linton says, "You *must* obey my father, you *must*," Cathy replies, "I must obey my own," reflecting her growing sense of responsibility. After her forced marriage, she is prepared to accept the consequences of her situation by loving Linton in spite of Heathcliff—"You cannot make us hate each other!" Cathy remains dignified and controlled, and speaks "with a kind of dreary triumph: she seemed to have made up her mind to enter into the spirit of her future family, and draw pleasure from the griefs of her enemies."

If Nelly's narrative makes Cathy's behavior sound reminiscent of the older Catherine's vengeful fits, it should be pointed out that Cathy's "enemies" are *real,* not fancied, conspirators. Heathcliff at this point has kidnapped her, kept her from her dying father, abused her physically, and forced her to marry his sickly, peevish son. Cathy's situation is wretched, almost hopeless; when Linton dies shortly after their degenerate union, she is left at Wuthering Heights with only Hareton and Heathcliff. And here her *bildung* or education needs to be emphasized. Part of education and development is arriving at an understanding of one's value; this, I would argue, is the major undertaking of adolescence. The older Catherine never sees herself realistically. She has notions of superiority and self importance that can be justified only in terms of her exceptionally passionate nature and her extraordinary bond to Heathcliff. Catherine's immature and narrow vision cannot imagine that she is not the central concern in everyone else's life. It is almost an epiphany when she says to Nelly, "How strange! I thought, though everybody hated and despised each other, they could not avoid loving me." Despite Heathcliff's furious devotion and her husband's genuine affection, Catherine always feels unloved and undervalued. Even as she is dying, she cries, "*That* is how I am loved!" like a self-pitying child. Nor does Catherine value the love of others: "I have such faith in Linton's love," she says, "that I believe I might kill him, and he wouldn't wish to retaliate." Rarely if ever is Catherine described as a loving person, one who is willing to give the self freely to another; even her professed love for Heathcliff is strangely qualified by her claim, "I *am* Heathcliff!" He seems to be only a kind of narcissistic double.

Young Cathy of course wants to be loved, but unlike her mother she is willing to take the risks and suffer the consequences of loving another. When she kisses Hareton in an effort to make peace, she is conquering her pride and scorn—and her loneliness—in a way that truly suggests maturity. She is beginning to see herself in relation to others, beginning to develop a realistic adult perspective. For example, Cathy knows she has been unfair and cruel to Hareton, and sincerely tries to improve their relationship in the best—the most straightforward—way she knows how. "When I call you stupid, I don't mean anything—I don't mean that I despise you," she explains, and by articulating her meaning she arrives at a closer understanding of the way she affects others. By humbling herself, Cathy learns to master herself, and by offering her friendship to Hareton, she is on the verge of a new, perhaps more traditional, kind of education: marriage. But the marriage of Cathy and Hareton is not the traditional union of the male teacher/master and the female learner/servant. By reversing the roles and making Cathy the educator, *Wuthering Heights* takes on the aspects of a new feminine *Bildungsroman* in which a woman emerging from childhood and adolescence approaches marriage not merely as a means of social advancement, or knowledge, or security, but as a mutual broadening of experience in which love balances power, with "both their minds tending to the same point."

So it is with the second generation of the Heights that Brontë begins her feminine *Bildungsroman*. If Catherine and Heathcliff have a more tumultuous and exciting story, it may be be-

cause theirs is the tale of arrested childhood, a furious protest against the necessity of growing up. Perhaps Cathy's struggle is less stormy and her future too settled and neat to satisfy our lingering adolescent admiration for rebellion, stubborn self satisfaction, and emotional intensity. But in the world of *Wuthering Heights,* as in our own, the passage from innocence to experience is an awkward limbo, a thin papery wall, between two selves—between the waif outside the window, and the woman within.

Source: Annette R. Federico, "The Waif at the Window: Emily Brontë's Feminine 'Bildungsroman'," in *The Victorian Newsletter,* No. 68, Fall, 1985, pp. 26–28.

Vereen M. Bell

In the following essay, Bell comments on moral themes in Wuthering Heights, *focusing in particular on the Biblical allusions in narrator Lockwood's first dream.*

The two dreams Lockwood experiences early in *Wuthering Heights*—the first of a visit to Gimmerton Kirk, and the second of a visit from the ghost-child Catherine—have recently received critical attention from Ruth M. Adams and Edgar Shannon. Of the two interpretations Shannon's ["Lockwood's Dreams and the Exegesis of *Wuthering Heights, Nineteenth-Century Fiction,* September, 1959] seems the most convincing in that it offers the only plausible source for the Biblical allusion in the first dream; but in discussing the relationship of the dream sermon and its title to the tragedy of Heathcliff and Catherine, Shannon ignores significant aspects of the dream itself, and consequently the value of his interpretation seems impaired somewhat, like Miss Adams's, by its own ingenuity.

The preacher that Lockwood hears in the first dream is Jabes Branderham, and the sermon is entitled "Seventy Times Seven and the First of the Seventy-first." Shannon identifies the sermon's text as Matt. 18: 21-22. In this passage Peter asks Jesus, "Lord, how oft shall my brother sin against me, and I forgive him? Till seven times?" and Jesus answers, "I say not unto thee Until seven times: but, Until seventy times seven." "The First of the Seventy-first," then, Shannon asserts, "advances the idea of an unpardonable sin beyond the ordinary scale of human wrongs." The subsequent nightmare, he continues, connects this idea with Catherine, who appears as an outcast, and we are asked to believe that it is she who has committed the unforgivable sin by marrying Edgar and denying the "natural and elemental affinity" inherent in her love for Heathcliff. "Adhered to, [love] is at once the source of joy and harmony; rejected or subverted, it becomes the fountainhead of enmity and strife."

One cannot challenge Shannon's assertion that thematically *Wuthering Heights* displays the "destructive consequences of thwarted love"; but it seems both unfair and inexact to imply that the guilt devolves upon Catherine exclusively. Moreover such an interpretation does not seem to be substantiated by a close reading of the literal and symbolic action of Lockwood's first dream. Shannon implies that the nature of the unpardonable sin is merely hinted at rather than defined, and that the reader is left to infer its nature from the second dream and from the the action that follows. In fact, however, through a curious kind of logical paradox, the unpardonable sin is defined within the action of the dream itself. Not long after Branderham's sermon opens Lockwood begins to fidget, laboring under the four hundred and ninety heads of discourse—each in itself the length of a separate sermon. Finally, when Branderham reaches the "First of the Seventy-first" Lockwood can bear it no longer; he rises and denounces Branderham as

> the sinner of the sin that no Christian need pardon [emphasis supplied]. Seventy times seven times have I plucked up my hat and been about to depart—Seventy times seven times have you preposterously forced me to resume my seat. The four hundred and ninety-first is too much. Fellow-martyrs, have at him!

Branderham's reply is equally significant as he turns the congregation back upon Lockwood.

> "*Thous art the Man!*" cried Jabes.… "Seventy times seven times didst thou gapingly contort thy visage—seventy times seven times did I take counsel with my soul—Lo, this is human weakness; this also may be absolved! *The First of the Seventy-first is come* [emphasis supplied]. Brethren, execute upon him the judgment written.…"

Lockwood himself, in other words, commits (in the dream at least) the unforgivable sin in accusing Branderham of that sin no Christian need pardon. That is, the unforgivable sin is to accuse another of committing the unforgivable sin—or, more simply put, the absence of forgiveness, of forbearance, of mercy. Each man forgives the other four hundred and ninety times, as Jesus enjoins, but neither has the charity to forbear the four hundred and ninety-first offense; each then denounces the other, and chaos erupts—"Every man's hand was against his neighbour."

Moreover, it is manifestly forgiveness, and not, as Shannon suggests, sin that Jesus is talking about; Peter in using the verb *sin* refers to a personal offense, not to mortal transgression; and of course what Jesus is urging is perpetual forgiveness, perpetual charity, only he phrases it in finite terms.

The relation of the dream and its Biblical source to the tragedy that follows would seem obvious. It is the want of forgiveness—or phrased positively, it is vengeance—that disrupts the moral and social order of Wuthering Heights. Hindley cannot forgive Heathcliff for usurping the love of his father; so once he is master of the Heights, he sees that Heathcliff is methodically humiliated and degraded. Heathcliff's degradation in turn enforces a physical and psychological separation from Catherine which preordains marriage to Edgar Linton. When Heathcliff acquires his fortune, he uses the power it affords to avenge himself against Hindley, whom he easily corrupts and destroys; against Hareton and Catherine, the children, who of course are innocent; against Isabella, who is equally blameless; and through all of these, against Edgar Linton, whom he hates not just as a rival but as an embodiment of everything effete and conventional that erodes Catherine's spirit and finally destroys her. Father is turned against son, brother against sister, servant against master, husband against wife, lover against lover—"Every man's hand was against his neighbour."

Catherine is really less a perpetrator than a victim of this turmoil. She shares the guilt of course because her union with Edgar is the act which hastens the tragedy. But hers is an error in judgment rather than a mortal transgression; she marries Edgar in faith, naïvely assuming that she can preserve her intense sibling affinity with Heathcliff and perhaps redeem him (and herself) as well. But neither man can forgive her for loving the other and what he represents. In his last interview with Catherine, Heathcliff tells her, "It is hard to forgive, and to look at those eyes, and feel those wasted hands.… I forgive what you have done to me. I love *my* murderer—but *yours!* How can I?" Torn between the two men, who inspire contrary impulses within her, she grows weak—almost as an act of will—and ultimately dies. When she appears to Lockwood as a ghost and an outcast, his cruelty to her is merely a vivid physical image of the emotional torment she has been made to suffer during her mortal existence.

Among those whom Catherine loves there is no one who can forgive her human error; there is love abundant for her, but it is always conditional love that demands and punishes. Young Catherine and Hareton, we are led to believe, eventually come to love with patience and understanding, but only after Heathcliff's influence is removed. And Heathcliff's rancor merely epitomizes the chief moral defect of all of the characters concerned. That defect would seem to be not so much the denial of love that Shannon suggests as love's failure to attain charity, to achieve moral fulfillments as well as emotional intensity.

Source: Vereen M. Bell, "Wuthering Heights and the Unforgivable Sin," in *Nineteenth-Century Fiction,* Vol. 17, No. 2, September, 1962, pp. 188–91.

Sources

Charlotte Brontë, "Editor's Preface to the New [1850] Edition of Wuthering Heights," in *Wuthering Heights,* edited by David Daiches, Penguin, 1965, pp. 37-41.

David Daiches, editor, in the introduction to *Wuthering Heights,* Penguin, 1965, pp. 7-29.

Winifred Gerin, "Emily Brontë," in *Reference Guide to English Literature,* edited by D. L. Kirkpatrick, St. James Press, 1991, pp. 300-02.

Algernon Charles Swinburne, "Emily Brontë," in *The Athenaeum,* No. 2903, June 16, 1883, pp. 762-63.

Tom Winnifrith, "Emily Brontë," in *Dictionary of Literary Biography, Volume 21: Victorian Novelists before 1885,* edited by Ira B. Nadel and William E. Fredeman, Gale Research, 1983, pp. 55-67.

For Further Study

Miriam Allot, *The Brontës: The Critical Heritage,* Routledge, 1974.
A collection of criticism on the works of the Brontë sisters, including reprints of early reviews of *Wuthering Heights* and *Poems by Currer, Ellis and Acton Bell* and Charlotte Brontë's observations on her sister's novel.

Terry Eagleton, "Myths of Power: A Marxist Study on *Wuthering Heights*" in *Case Studies In Contemporary Criticism: Wuthering Heights,* St. Martin's, 1992, pp. 399-414.
Eagleton analyzes the novel in terms of class differences in nineteenth-century England.

Winifred Gerin, *Emily Brontë: A Biography,* Clarendon, 1971.
Gerin discusses Emily Brontë's life and the effect of her environment on her work.

Philip K. Wion, "The Absent Mother in *Wuthering Heights*" in *American Imago,* Vol. 42, No. 2, 1985.
Wion suggests that the early death of Emily Brontë's mother accounts for Brontë's portrayal of orphaned characters in search of mother figures.

Glossary of Literary Terms

A

Abstract: As an adjective applied to writing or literary works, abstract refers to words or phrases that name things not knowable through the five senses.

Aestheticism: A literary and artistic movement of the nineteenth century. Followers of the movement believed that art should not be mixed with social, political, or moral teaching. The statement "art for art's sake" is a good summary of aestheticism. The movement had its roots in France, but it gained widespread importance in England in the last half of the nineteenth century, where it helped change the Victorian practice of including moral lessons in literature.

Allegory: A narrative technique in which characters representing things or abstract ideas are used to convey a message or teach a lesson. Allegory is typically used to teach moral, ethical, or religious lessons but is sometimes used for satiric or political purposes.

Allusion: A reference to a familiar literary or historical person or event, used to make an idea more easily understood.

Analogy: A comparison of two things made to explain something unfamiliar through its similarities to something familiar, or to prove one point based on the acceptedness of another. Similes and metaphors are types of analogies.

Antagonist: The major character in a narrative or drama who works against the hero or protagonist.

Anthropomorphism: The presentation of animals or objects in human shape or with human characteristics. The term is derived from the Greek word for "human form."

Antihero: A central character in a work of literature who lacks traditional heroic qualities such as courage, physical prowess, and fortitude. Antiheroes typically distrust conventional values and are unable to commit themselves to any ideals. They generally feel helpless in a world over which they have no control. Antiheroes usually accept, and often celebrate, their positions as social outcasts.

Apprenticeship Novel: See *Bildungsroman*

Archetype: The word archetype is commonly used to describe an original pattern or model from which all other things of the same kind are made. This term was introduced to literary criticism from the psychology of Carl Jung. It expresses Jung's theory that behind every person's "unconscious," or repressed memories of the past, lies the "collective unconscious" of the human race: memories of the countless typical experiences of our ancestors. These memories are said to prompt illogical associations that trigger powerful emotions in the reader. Often, the emotional process is primitive, even primordial. Archetypes are the literary images that grow out of the "collective unconscious." They appear in literature as incidents and plots that repeat basic patterns of life. They may also appear as stereotyped characters.

***Avant-garde*:** French term meaning "vanguard." It is used in literary criticism to describe new writing that rejects traditional approaches to literature in favor of innovations in style or content.

B

Beat Movement: A period featuring a group of American poets and novelists of the 1950s and 1960s—including Jack Kerouac, Allen Ginsberg, Gregory Corso, William S. Burroughs, and Lawrence Ferlinghetti—who rejected established social and literary values. Using such techniques as stream of consciousness writing and jazz-influenced free verse and focusing on unusual or abnormal states of mind—generated by religious ecstasy or the use of drugs—the Beat writers aimed to create works that were unconventional in both form and subject matter.

***Bildungsroman*:** A German word meaning "novel of development." The *bildungsroman* is a study of the maturation of a youthful character, typically brought about through a series of social or sexual encounters that lead to self-awareness. *Bildungsroman* is used interchangeably with *erziehungsroman,* a novel of initiation and education. When a *bildungsroman* is concerned with the development of an artist (as in James Joyce's *A Portrait of the Artist as a Young Man*), it is often termed a *kunstlerroman.* Also known as Apprenticeship Novel, Coming of Age Novel, *Erziehungsroman,* or *Kunstlerroman.*

Black Aesthetic Movement: A period of artistic and literary development among African Americans in the 1960s and early 1970s. This was the first major African-American artistic movement since the Harlem Renaissance and was closely paralleled by the civil rights and black power movements. The black aesthetic writers attempted to produce works of art that would be meaningful to the black masses. Key figures in black aesthetics included one of its founders, poet and playwright Amiri Baraka, formerly known as LeRoi Jones; poet and essayist Haki R. Madhubuti, formerly Don L. Lee; poet and playwright Sonia Sanchez; and dramatist Ed Bullins. Also known as Black Arts Movement.

Black Humor: Writing that places grotesque elements side by side with humorous ones in an attempt to shock the reader, forcing him or her to laugh at the horrifying reality of a disordered world. Also known as Black Comedy.

Burlesque: Any literary work that uses exaggeration to make its subject appear ridiculous, either by treating a trivial subject with profound seriousness or by treating a dignified subject frivolously. The word "burlesque" may also be used as an adjective, as in "burlesque show," to mean "striptease act."

C

Character: Broadly speaking, a person in a literary work. The actions of characters are what constitute the plot of a story, novel, or poem. There are numerous types of characters, ranging from simple, stereotypical figures to intricate, multifaceted ones. In the techniques of anthropomorphism and personification, animals—and even places or things—can assume aspects of character. "Characterization" is the process by which an author creates vivid, believable characters in a work of art. This may be done in a variety of ways, including (1) direct description of the character by the narrator; (2) the direct presentation of the speech, thoughts, or actions of the character; and (3) the responses of other characters to the character. The term "character" also refers to a form originated by the ancient Greek writer Theophrastus that later became popular in the seventeenth and eighteenth centuries. It is a short essay or sketch of a person who prominently displays a specific attribute or quality, such as miserliness or ambition.

Climax: The turning point in a narrative, the moment when the conflict is at its most intense. Typically, the structure of stories, novels, and plays is one of rising action, in which tension builds to the climax, followed by falling action, in which tension lessens as the story moves to its conclusion.

Colloquialism: A word, phrase, or form of pronunciation that is acceptable in casual conversation but not in formal, written communication. It is considered more acceptable than slang.

Coming of Age Novel: See *Bildungsroman*

Concrete: Concrete is the opposite of abstract, and refers to a thing that actually exists or a description that allows the reader to experience an object or concept with the senses.

Connotation: The impression that a word gives beyond its defined meaning. Connotations may be universally understood or may be significant only to a certain group.

Convention: Any widely accepted literary device, style, or form.

D

Denotation: The definition of a word, apart from the impressions or feelings it creates (connotations) in the reader.

Denouement: A French word meaning "the unknotting." In literary criticism, it denotes the resolution of conflict in fiction or drama. The *denouement* follows the climax and provides an outcome to the primary plot situation as well as an explanation of secondary plot complications. The *denouement* often involves a character's recognition of his or her state of mind or moral condition. Also known as Falling Action.

Description: Descriptive writing is intended to allow a reader to picture the scene or setting in which the action of a story takes place. The form this description takes often evokes an intended emotional response—a dark, spooky graveyard will evoke fear, and a peaceful, sunny meadow will evoke calmness.

Dialogue: In its widest sense, dialogue is simply conversation between people in a literary work; in its most restricted sense, it refers specifically to the speech of characters in a drama. As a specific literary genre, a "dialogue" is a composition in which characters debate an issue or idea.

Diction: The selection and arrangement of words in a literary work. Either or both may vary depending on the desired effect. There are four general types of diction: "formal," used in scholarly or lofty writing; "informal," used in relaxed but educated conversation; "colloquial," used in everyday speech; and "slang," containing newly coined words and other terms not accepted in formal usage.

Didactic: A term used to describe works of literature that aim to teach some moral, religious, political, or practical lesson. Although didactic elements are often found in artistically pleasing works, the term "didactic" usually refers to literature in which the message is more important than the form. The term may also be used to criticize a work that the critic finds "overly didactic," that is, heavy-handed in its delivery of a lesson.

Doppelganger: A literary technique by which a character is duplicated (usually in the form of an alter ego, though sometimes as a ghostly counterpart) or divided into two distinct, usually opposite personalities. The use of this character device is widespread in nineteenth- and twentieth-century literature, and indicates a growing awareness among authors that the "self" is really a composite of many "selves." Also known as The Double.

Double Entendre: A corruption of a French phrase meaning "double meaning." The term is used to indicate a word or phrase that is deliberately ambiguous, especially when one of the meanings is risqué or improper.

Dramatic Irony: Occurs when the audience of a play or the reader of a work of literature knows something that a character in the work itself does not know. The irony is in the contrast between the intended meaning of the statements or actions of a character and the additional information understood by the audience.

Dystopia: An imaginary place in a work of fiction where the characters lead dehumanized, fearful lives.

E

Edwardian: Describes cultural conventions identified with the period of the reign of Edward VII of England (1901-1910). Writers of the Edwardian Age typically displayed a strong reaction against the propriety and conservatism of the Victorian Age. Their work often exhibits distrust of authority in religion, politics, and art and expresses strong doubts about the soundness of conventional values.

Empathy: A sense of shared experience, including emotional and physical feelings, with someone or something other than oneself. Empathy is often used to describe the response of a reader to a literary character.

Enlightenment, The: An eighteenth-century philosophical movement. It began in France but had a wide impact throughout Europe and America. Thinkers of the Enlightenment valued reason and believed that both the individual and society could achieve a state of perfection. Corresponding to this essentially humanist vision was a resistance to religious authority.

Epigram: A saying that makes the speaker's point quickly and concisely. Often used to preface a novel.

Epilogue: A concluding statement or section of a literary work. In dramas, particularly those of the seventeenth and eighteenth centuries, the epilogue is a closing speech, often in verse, delivered by an actor at the end of a play and spoken directly to the audience.

Epiphany: A sudden revelation of truth inspired by a seemingly trivial incident.

Episode: An incident that forms part of a story and is significantly related to it. Episodes may be either self-contained narratives or events that depend on a larger context for their sense and importance.

Epistolary Novel: A novel in the form of letters. The form was particularly popular in the eighteenth century.

Epithet: A word or phrase, often disparaging or abusive, that expresses a character trait of someone or something.

Existentialism: A predominantly twentieth-century philosophy concerned with the nature and perception of human existence. There are two major strains of existentialist thought: atheistic and Christian. Followers of atheistic existentialism believe that the individual is alone in a godless universe and that the basic human condition is one of suffering and loneliness. Nevertheless, because there are no fixed values, individuals can create their own characters—indeed, they can shape themselves—through the exercise of free will. The atheistic strain culminates in and is popularly associated with the works of Jean-Paul Sartre. The Christian existentialists, on the other hand, believe that only in God may people find freedom from life's anguish. The two strains hold certain beliefs in common: that existence cannot be fully understood or described through empirical effort; that anguish is a universal element of life; that individuals must bear responsibility for their actions; and that there is no common standard of behavior or perception for religious and ethical matters.

Expatriates: See *Expatriatism*

Expatriatism: The practice of leaving one's country to live for an extended period in another country.

Exposition: Writing intended to explain the nature of an idea, thing, or theme. Expository writing is often combined with description, narration, or argument. In dramatic writing, the exposition is the introductory material which presents the characters, setting, and tone of the play.

Expressionism: An indistinct literary term, originally used to describe an early twentieth-century school of German painting. The term applies to almost any mode of unconventional, highly subjective writing that distorts reality in some way.

F

Fable: A prose or verse narrative intended to convey a moral. Animals or inanimate objects with human characteristics often serve as characters in fables.

Falling Action: See *Denouement*

Fantasy: A literary form related to mythology and folklore. Fantasy literature is typically set in non-existent realms and features supernatural beings.

Farce: A type of comedy characterized by broad humor, outlandish incidents, and often vulgar subject matter.

Femme fatale: A French phrase with the literal translation "fatal woman." A *femme fatale* is a sensuous, alluring woman who often leads men into danger or trouble.

Fiction: Any story that is the product of imagination rather than a documentation of fact. Characters and events in such narratives may be based in real life but their ultimate form and configuration is a creation of the author.

Figurative Language: A technique in writing in which the author temporarily interrupts the order, construction, or meaning of the writing for a particular effect. This interruption takes the form of one or more figures of speech such as hyperbole, irony, or simile. Figurative language is the opposite of literal language, in which every word is truthful, accurate, and free of exaggeration or embellishment.

Figures of Speech: Writing that differs from customary conventions for construction, meaning, order, or significance for the purpose of a special meaning or effect. There are two major types of figures of speech: rhetorical figures, which do not make changes in the meaning of the words, and tropes, which do.

Fin de siecle: A French term meaning "end of the century." The term is used to denote the last decade of the nineteenth century, a transition period when writers and other artists abandoned old conventions and looked for new techniques and objectives.

First Person: See *Point of View*

Flashback: A device used in literature to present action that occurred before the beginning of the story. Flashbacks are often introduced as the dreams or recollections of one or more characters.

Foil: A character in a work of literature whose physical or psychological qualities contrast strongly with, and therefore highlight, the corresponding qualities of another character.

Folklore: Traditions and myths preserved in a culture or group of people. Typically, these are passed on by word of mouth in various forms—such as legends, songs, and proverbs—or preserved in customs and ceremonies. This term was first used by W. J. Thoms in 1846.

Folktale: A story originating in oral tradition. Folktales fall into a variety of categories, including legends, ghost stories, fairy tales, fables, and anecdotes based on historical figures and events.

Foreshadowing: A device used in literature to create expectation or to set up an explanation of later developments.

Form: The pattern or construction of a work which identifies its genre and distinguishes it from other genres.

G

Genre: A category of literary work. In critical theory, genre may refer to both the content of a given work—tragedy, comedy, pastoral—and to its form, such as poetry, novel, or drama.

Gilded Age: A period in American history during the 1870s characterized by political corruption and materialism. A number of important novels of social and political criticism were written during this time.

Gothicism: In literary criticism, works characterized by a taste for the medieval or morbidly attractive. A gothic novel prominently features elements of horror, the supernatural, gloom, and violence: clanking chains, terror, charnel houses, ghosts, medieval castles, and mysteriously slamming doors. The term "gothic novel" is also applied to novels that lack elements of the traditional Gothic setting but that create a similar atmosphere of terror or dread.

Grotesque: In literary criticism, the subject matter of a work or a style of expression characterized by exaggeration, deformity, freakishness, and disorder. The grotesque often includes an element of comic absurdity.

H

Harlem Renaissance: The Harlem Renaissance of the 1920s is generally considered the first significant movement of black writers and artists in the United States. During this period, new and established black writers published more fiction and poetry than ever before, the first influential black literary journals were established, and black authors and artists received their first widespread recognition and serious critical appraisal. Among the major writers associated with this period are Claude McKay, Jean Toomer, Countee Cullen, Langston Hughes, Arna Bontemps, Nella Larsen, and Zora Neale Hurston. Also known as Negro Renaissance and New Negro Movement.

Hero/Heroine: The principal sympathetic character (male or female) in a literary work. Heroes and heroines typically exhibit admirable traits: idealism, courage, and integrity, for example.

Holocaust Literature: Literature influenced by or written about the Holocaust of World War II. Such literature includes true stories of survival in concentration camps, escape, and life after the war, as well as fictional works and poetry.

Humanism: A philosophy that places faith in the dignity of humankind and rejects the medieval perception of the individual as a weak, fallen creature. "Humanists" typically believe in the perfectibility of human nature and view reason and education as the means to that end.

Hyperbole: In literary criticism, deliberate exaggeration used to achieve an effect.

I

Idiom: A word construction or verbal expression closely associated with a given language.

Image: A concrete representation of an object or sensory experience. Typically, such a representation helps evoke the feelings associated with the object or experience itself. Images are either "literal" or "figurative." Literal images are especially concrete and involve little or no extension of the obvious meaning of the words used to express them. Figurative images do not follow the literal meaning of the words exactly. Images in literature are usually visual, but the term "image" can also refer to the representation of any sensory experience.

Imagery: The array of images in a literary work. Also, figurative language.

In medias res: A Latin term meaning "in the middle of things." It refers to the technique of beginning a story at its midpoint and then using various flashback devices to reveal previous action.

Interior Monologue: A narrative technique in which characters' thoughts are revealed in a way that appears to be uncontrolled by the author. The interior monologue typically aims to reveal the inner self of a character. It portrays emotional experiences as they occur at both a conscious and unconscious level. Images are often used to represent sensations or emotions.

Irony: In literary criticism, the effect of language in which the intended meaning is the opposite of what is stated.

J

Jargon: Language that is used or understood only by a select group of people. Jargon may refer to terminology used in a certain profession, such as computer jargon, or it may refer to any nonsensical language that is not understood by most people.

L

Leitmotiv: See *Motif*

Literal Language: An author uses literal language when he or she writes without exaggerating or embellishing the subject matter and without any tools of figurative language.

Lost Generation: A term first used by Gertrude Stein to describe the post-World War I generation of American writers: men and women haunted by a sense of betrayal and emptiness brought about by the destructiveness of the war.

M

Mannerism: Exaggerated, artificial adherence to a literary manner or style. Also, a popular style of the visual arts of late sixteenth-century Europe that was marked by elongation of the human form and by intentional spatial distortion. Literary works that are self-consciously high-toned and artistic are often said to be "mannered."

Metaphor: A figure of speech that expresses an idea through the image of another object. Metaphors suggest the essence of the first object by identifying it with certain qualities of the second object.

Modernism: Modern literary practices. Also, the principles of a literary school that lasted from roughly the beginning of the twentieth century until the end of World War II. Modernism is defined by its rejection of the literary conventions of the nineteenth century and by its opposition to conventional morality, taste, traditions, and economic values.

Mood: The prevailing emotions of a work or of the author in his or her creation of the work. The mood of a work is not always what might be expected based on its subject matter.

Motif: A theme, character type, image, metaphor, or other verbal element that recurs throughout a single work of literature or occurs in a number of different works over a period of time. Also known as *Motiv* or *Leitmotiv*.

Myth: An anonymous tale emerging from the traditional beliefs of a culture or social unit. Myths use supernatural explanations for natural phenomena. They may also explain cosmic issues like creation and death. Collections of myths, known as mythologies, are common to all cultures and nations, but the best-known myths belong to the Norse, Roman, and Greek mythologies.

N

Narration: The telling of a series of events, real or invented. A narration may be either a simple narrative, in which the events are recounted chronologically, or a narrative with a plot, in which the account is given in a style reflecting the author's artistic concept of the story. Narration is sometimes used as a synonym for "storyline."

Narrative: A verse or prose accounting of an event or sequence of events, real or invented. The term is also used as an adjective in the sense "method of narration." For example, in literary criticism, the expression "narrative technique" usually refers to the way the author structures and presents his or her story.

Narrator: The teller of a story. The narrator may be the author or a character in the story through whom the author speaks.

Naturalism: A literary movement of the late nineteenth and early twentieth centuries. The movement's major theorist, French novelist Emile Zola, envisioned a type of fiction that would examine human life with the objectivity of scientific inquiry. The Naturalists typically viewed human beings as either the products of "biological determinism," ruled by hereditary instincts and engaged in an endless struggle for survival, or as the products of "socioeconomic determinism," ruled by social and economic forces beyond their control. In their works, the Naturalists generally ignored the highest levels of society and focused on degradation: poverty, alcoholism, prostitution, insanity, and disease.

Noble Savage: The idea that primitive man is noble and good but becomes evil and corrupted as he becomes civilized. The concept of the noble savage originated in the Renaissance period but is more closely identified with such later writers as

Jean-Jacques Rousseau and Aphra Behn. See also Primitivism.

Novel of Ideas: A novel in which the examination of intellectual issues and concepts takes precedence over characterization or a traditional storyline.

Novel of Manners: A novel that examines the customs and mores of a cultural group.

Novel: A long fictional narrative written in prose, which developed from the novella and other early forms of narrative. A novel is usually organized under a plot or theme with a focus on character development and action.

Novella: An Italian term meaning "story." This term has been especially used to describe fourteenth-century Italian tales, but it also refers to modern short novels.

O

Objective Correlative: An outward set of objects, a situation, or a chain of events corresponding to an inward experience and evoking this experience in the reader. The term frequently appears in modern criticism in discussions of authors' intended effects on the emotional responses of readers.

Objectivity: A quality in writing characterized by the absence of the author's opinion or feeling about the subject matter. Objectivity is an important factor in criticism.

Oedipus Complex: A son's amorous obsession with his mother. The phrase is derived from the story of the ancient Theban hero Oedipus, who unknowingly killed his father and married his mother.

Omniscience: See *Point of View*

Onomatopoeia: The use of words whose sounds express or suggest their meaning. In its simplest sense, onomatopoeia may be represented by words that mimic the sounds they denote such as "hiss" or "meow." At a more subtle level, the pattern and rhythm of sounds and rhymes of a line or poem may be onomatopoeic.

Oxymoron: A phrase combining two contradictory terms. Oxymorons may be intentional or unintentional.

P

Parable: A story intended to teach a moral lesson or answer an ethical question.

Paradox: A statement that appears illogical or contradictory at first, but may actually point to an underlying truth.

Parallelism: A method of comparison of two ideas in which each is developed in the same grammatical structure.

Parody: In literary criticism, this term refers to an imitation of a serious literary work or the signature style of a particular author in a ridiculous manner. A typical parody adopts the style of the original and applies it to an inappropriate subject for humorous effect. Parody is a form of satire and could be considered the literary equivalent of a caricature or cartoon.

Pastoral: A term derived from the Latin word "pastor," meaning shepherd. A pastoral is a literary composition on a rural theme. The conventions of the pastoral were originated by the third-century Greek poet Theocritus, who wrote about the experiences, love affairs, and pastimes of Sicilian shepherds. In a pastoral, characters and language of a courtly nature are often placed in a simple setting. The term pastoral is also used to classify dramas, elegies, and lyrics that exhibit the use of country settings and shepherd characters.

Pen Name: See *Pseudonym*

Persona: A Latin term meaning "mask." *Personae* are the characters in a fictional work of literature. The *persona* generally functions as a mask through which the author tells a story in a voice other than his or her own. A *persona* is usually either a character in a story who acts as a narrator or an "implied author," a voice created by the author to act as the narrator for himself or herself.

Personification: A figure of speech that gives human qualities to abstract ideas, animals, and inanimate objects. Also known as *Prosopopoeia*.

Picaresque Novel: Episodic fiction depicting the adventures of a roguish central character ("picaro" is Spanish for "rogue"). The picaresque hero is commonly a low-born but clever individual who wanders into and out of various affairs of love, danger, and farcical intrigue. These involvements may take place at all social levels and typically present a humorous and wide-ranging satire of a given society.

Plagiarism: Claiming another person's written material as one's own. Plagiarism can take the form of direct, word-for-word copying or the theft of the substance or idea of the work.

Plot: In literary criticism, this term refers to the pattern of events in a narrative or drama. In its simplest sense, the plot guides the author in composing the work and helps the reader follow the work. Typically, plots exhibit causality and unity and have a beginning, a middle, and an end. Sometimes, however, a plot may consist of a series of disconnected events, in which case it is known as an "episodic plot."

Poetic Justice: An outcome in a literary work, not necessarily a poem, in which the good are rewarded and the evil are punished, especially in ways that particularly fit their virtues or crimes.

Poetic License: Distortions of fact and literary convention made by a writer—not always a poet—for the sake of the effect gained. Poetic license is closely related to the concept of "artistic freedom."

Poetics: This term has two closely related meanings. It denotes (1) an aesthetic theory in literary criticism about the essence of poetry or (2) rules prescribing the proper methods, content, style, or diction of poetry. The term poetics may also refer to theories about literature in general, not just poetry.

Point of View: The narrative perspective from which a literary work is presented to the reader. There are four traditional points of view. The "third person omniscient" gives the reader a "godlike" perspective, unrestricted by time or place, from which to see actions and look into the minds of characters. This allows the author to comment openly on characters and events in the work. The "third person" point of view presents the events of the story from outside of any single character's perception, much like the omniscient point of view, but the reader must understand the action as it takes place and without any special insight into characters' minds or motivations. The "first person" or "personal" point of view relates events as they are perceived by a single character. The main character "tells" the story and may offer opinions about the action and characters which differ from those of the author. Much less common than omniscient, third person, and first person is the "second person" point of view, wherein the author tells the story as if it is happening to the reader.

Polemic: A work in which the author takes a stand on a controversial subject, such as abortion or religion. Such works are often extremely argumentative or provocative.

Pornography: Writing intended to provoke feelings of lust in the reader. Such works are often condemned by critics and teachers, but those which can be shown to have literary value are viewed less harshly.

Post-Aesthetic Movement: An artistic response made by African Americans to the black aesthetic movement of the 1960s and early '70s. Writers since that time have adopted a somewhat different tone in their work, with less emphasis placed on the disparity between black and white in the United States. In the words of post-aesthetic authors such as Toni Morrison, John Edgar Wideman, and Kristin Hunter, African Americans are portrayed as looking inward for answers to their own questions, rather than always looking to the outside world.

Postmodernism: Writing from the 1960s forward characterized by experimentation and continuing to apply some of the fundamentals of modernism, which included existentialism and alienation. Postmodernists have gone a step further in the rejection of tradition begun with the modernists by also rejecting traditional forms, preferring the anti-novel over the novel and the antihero over the hero.

Primitivism: The belief that primitive peoples were nobler and less flawed than civilized peoples because they had not been subjected to the tainting influence of society. See also Noble Savage.

Prologue: An introductory section of a literary work. It often contains information establishing the situation of the characters or presents information about the setting, time period, or action. In drama, the prologue is spoken by a chorus or by one of the principal characters.

Prose: A literary medium that attempts to mirror the language of everyday speech. It is distinguished from poetry by its use of unmetered, unrhymed language consisting of logically related sentences. Prose is usually grouped into paragraphs that form a cohesive whole such as an essay or a novel.

Prosopopoeia: See *Personification*

Protagonist: The central character of a story who serves as a focus for its themes and incidents and as the principal rationale for its development. The protagonist is sometimes referred to in discussions of modern literature as the hero or antihero.

Protest Fiction: Protest fiction has as its primary purpose the protesting of some social injustice, such as racism or discrimination.

Proverb: A brief, sage saying that expresses a truth about life in a striking manner.

Pseudonym: A name assumed by a writer, most often intended to prevent his or her identification as the author of a work. Two or more authors may work together under one pseudonym, or an author may use a different name for each genre he or she publishes in. Some publishing companies maintain "house pseudonyms," under which any number of authors may write installations in a series. Some authors also choose a pseudonym over their real names the way an actor may use a stage name.

Pun: A play on words that have similar sounds but different meanings.

R

Realism: A nineteenth-century European literary movement that sought to portray familiar characters, situations, and settings in a realistic manner. This was done primarily by using an objective narrative point of view and through the buildup of accurate detail. The standard for success of any realistic work depends on how faithfully it transfers common experience into fictional forms. The realistic method may be altered or extended, as in stream of consciousness writing, to record highly subjective experience.

Repartee: Conversation featuring snappy retorts and witticisms.

Resolution: The portion of a story following the climax, in which the conflict is resolved. See also *Denouement.*

Rhetoric: In literary criticism, this term denotes the art of ethical persuasion. In its strictest sense, rhetoric adheres to various principles developed since classical times for arranging facts and ideas in a clear, persuasive, appealing manner. The term is also used to refer to effective prose in general and theories of or methods for composing effective prose.

Rhetorical Question: A question intended to provoke thought, but not an expressed answer, in the reader. It is most commonly used in oratory and other persuasive genres.

Rising Action: The part of a drama where the plot becomes increasingly complicated. Rising action leads up to the climax, or turning point, of a drama.

Roman a clef: A French phrase meaning "novel with a key." It refers to a narrative in which real persons are portrayed under fictitious names.

Romance: A broad term, usually denoting a narrative with exotic, exaggerated, often idealized characters, scenes, and themes.

Romanticism: This term has two widely accepted meanings. In historical criticism, it refers to a European intellectual and artistic movement of the late eighteenth and early nineteenth centuries that sought greater freedom of personal expression than that allowed by the strict rules of literary form and logic of the eighteenth-century neoclassicists. The Romantics preferred emotional and imaginative ex-

pression to rational analysis. They considered the individual to be at the center of all experience and so placed him or her at the center of their art. The Romantics believed that the creative imagination reveals nobler truths—unique feelings and attitudes—than those that could be discovered by logic or by scientific examination. Both the natural world and the state of childhood were important sources for revelations of "eternal truths." "Romanticism" is also used as a general term to refer to a type of sensibility found in all periods of literary history and usually considered to be in opposition to the principles of classicism. In this sense, Romanticism signifies any work or philosophy in which the exotic or dreamlike figure strongly, or that is devoted to individualistic expression, self-analysis, or a pursuit of a higher realm of knowledge than can be discovered by human reason.

Romantics: See *Romanticism*

S

Satire: A work that uses ridicule, humor, and wit to criticize and provoke change in human nature and institutions. There are two major types of satire: "formal" or "direct" satire speaks directly to the reader or to a character in the work; "indirect" satire relies upon the ridiculous behavior of its characters to make its point. Formal satire is further divided into two manners: the "Horatian," which ridicules gently, and the "Juvenalian," which derides its subjects harshly and bitterly.

Science Fiction: A type of narrative about or based upon real or imagined scientific theories and technology. Science fiction is often peopled with alien creatures and set on other planets or in different dimensions.

Second Person: See *Point of View*

Setting: The time, place, and culture in which the action of a narrative takes place. The elements of setting may include geographic location, characters' physical and mental environments, prevailing cultural attitudes, or the historical time in which the action takes place.

Simile: A comparison, usually using "like" or "as", of two essentially dissimilar things, as in "coffee as cold as ice" or "He sounded like a broken record."

Slang: A type of informal verbal communication that is generally unacceptable for formal writing. Slang words and phrases are often colorful exaggerations used to emphasize the speaker's point; they may also be shortened versions of an often-used word or phrase.

Slave Narrative: Autobiographical accounts of American slave life as told by escaped slaves. These works first appeared during the abolition movement of the 1830s through the 1850s.

Socialist Realism: The Socialist Realism school of literary theory was proposed by Maxim Gorky and established as a dogma by the first Soviet Congress of Writers. It demanded adherence to a communist worldview in works of literature. Its doctrines required an objective viewpoint comprehensible to the working classes and themes of social struggle featuring strong proletarian heroes. Also known as Social Realism.

Stereotype: A stereotype was originally the name for a duplication made during the printing process; this led to its modern definition as a person or thing that is (or is assumed to be) the same as all others of its type.

Stream of Consciousness: A narrative technique for rendering the inward experience of a character. This technique is designed to give the impression of an ever-changing series of thoughts, emotions, images, and memories in the spontaneous and seemingly illogical order that they occur in life.

Structure: The form taken by a piece of literature. The structure may be made obvious for ease of understanding, as in nonfiction works, or may be obscured for artistic purposes, as in some poetry or seemingly "unstructured" prose.

***Sturm und Drang*:** A German term meaning "storm and stress." It refers to a German literary movement of the 1770s and 1780s that reacted against the order and rationalism of the enlightenment, focusing instead on the intense experience of extraordinary individuals.

Style: A writer's distinctive manner of arranging words to suit his or her ideas and purpose in writing. The unique imprint of the author's personality upon his or her writing, style is the product of an author's way of arranging ideas and his or her use of diction, different sentence structures, rhythm, figures of speech, rhetorical principles, and other elements of composition.

Subjectivity: Writing that expresses the author's personal feelings about his subject, and which may or may not include factual information about the subject.

Subplot: A secondary story in a narrative. A subplot may serve as a motivating or complicating force for the main plot of the work, or it may provide emphasis for, or relief from, the main plot.

Surrealism: A term introduced to criticism by Guillaume Apollinaire and later adopted by Andre Breton. It refers to a French literary and artistic movement founded in the 1920s. The Surrealists sought to express unconscious thoughts and feelings in their works. The best-known technique used for achieving this aim was automatic writing—transcriptions of spontaneous outpourings from the unconscious. The Surrealists proposed to unify the contrary levels of conscious and unconscious, dream and reality, objectivity and subjectivity into a new level of "super-realism."

Suspense: A literary device in which the author maintains the audience's attention through the buildup of events, the outcome of which will soon be revealed.

Symbol: Something that suggests or stands for something else without losing its original identity. In literature, symbols combine their literal meaning with the suggestion of an abstract concept. Literary symbols are of two types: those that carry complex associations of meaning no matter what their contexts, and those that derive their suggestive meaning from their functions in specific literary works.

Symbolism: This term has two widely accepted meanings. In historical criticism, it denotes an early modernist literary movement initiated in France during the nineteenth century that reacted against the prevailing standards of realism. Writers in this movement aimed to evoke, indirectly and symbolically, an order of being beyond the material world of the five senses. Poetic expression of personal emotion figured strongly in the movement, typically by means of a private set of symbols uniquely identifiable with the individual poet. The principal aim of the Symbolists was to express in words the highly complex feelings that grew out of everyday contact with the world. In a broader sense, the term "symbolism" refers to the use of one object to represent another.

T

Tall Tale: A humorous tale told in a straightforward, credible tone but relating absolutely impossible events or feats of the characters. Such tales were commonly told of frontier adventures during the settlement of the west in the United States.

Theme: The main point of a work of literature. The term is used interchangeably with thesis.

Thesis: A thesis is both an essay and the point argued in the essay. Thesis novels and thesis plays share the quality of containing a thesis which is supported through the action of the story.

Third Person: See *Point of View*

Tone: The author's attitude toward his or her audience may be deduced from the tone of the work. A formal tone may create distance or convey politeness, while an informal tone may encourage a friendly, intimate, or intrusive feeling in the reader. The author's attitude toward his or her subject matter may also be deduced from the tone of the words he or she uses in discussing it.

Transcendentalism: An American philosophical and religious movement, based in New England from around 1835 until the Civil War. Transcendentalism was a form of American romanticism that had its roots abroad in the works of Thomas Carlyle, Samuel Coleridge, and Johann Wolfgang von Goethe. The Transcendentalists stressed the importance of intuition and subjective experience in communication with God. They rejected religious dogma and texts in favor of mysticism and scientific naturalism. They pursued truths that lie beyond the "colorless" realms perceived by reason and the senses and were active social reformers in public education, women's rights, and the abolition of slavery.

U

Urban Realism: A branch of realist writing that attempts to accurately reflect the often harsh facts of modern urban existence.

Utopia: A fictional perfect place, such as "paradise" or "heaven."

V

Verisimilitude: Literally, the appearance of truth. In literary criticism, the term refers to aspects of a work of literature that seem true to the reader.

Victorian: Refers broadly to the reign of Queen Victoria of England (1837-1901) and to anything with qualities typical of that era. For example, the qualities of smug narrowmindedness, bourgeois materialism, faith in social progress, and priggish morality are often considered Victorian. This stereotype is contradicted by such dramatic intellectual developments as the theories of Charles Darwin, Karl Marx, and Sigmund Freud (which stirred strong debates in England) and the critical attitudes of serious Victorian writers like Charles Dickens and George Eliot. In literature, the Victorian Period was the great age of the English novel, and the latter part of the era saw the rise of movements such as decadence and symbolism. Also known as Victorian Age and Victorian Period.

W

Weltanschauung: A German term referring to a person's worldview or philosophy.

Weltschmerz: A German term meaning "world pain." It describes a sense of anguish about the nature of existence, usually associated with a melancholy, pessimistic attitude.

Z

Zeitgeist: A German term meaning "spirit of the time." It refers to the moral and intellectual trends of a given era.

Cumulative Author/Title Index

Cumulative
Nationality/Ethnicity Index

Subject/Theme Index